SEX, MORALITY, AND THE LAW

SEX, MORALITY, AND THE LAW

EDITED BY

LORI GRUEN and
GEORGE E. PANICHAS

ROUTLEDGE • NEW YORK AND LONDON

Published in 1997 by
Routledge
29 West 35th Street
New York, NY 10001

Published in Great Britain by
Routledge
11 New Fetter Lane
London EC4P 4EE

Library of Congress Cataloging-in-Publication Data
    Sex, morality, and the law / edited by Lori Gruen and George E.
Panichas.
        p.   cm.
    Includes bibliographical references and index.
    ISBN 0-415-91635-6 (hb).—ISBN 0-415-91636-4 (pb)
    1. Sex and law—United States. 2. Sexual ethics—United States.
    I. Gruen, Lori. II. Panichas, George E., 1948–
    KF9325.S49   1996
    306.7'0973—dc20   96-41606
                                                   CIP

PREFACE

Sex saturates our society. From sex clubs to sex manuals, from salacious advertisements to mainstream cinema, sex surrounds us. Ironically though, while sex permeates our culture, very few people speak comfortably about sex with their friends or family members, or even with their sex partners. Small wonder, then, that the public discourse on sex is so contentious, contradictory, and confusing. But, given the central role sex plays in most of our lives, it is baffling that clear, rational, and factual discussions about sex and sexuality are so rare, and that appeals to superstition, shame, and sin continue to contaminate what little public discussion occurs.

In this volume, we attempt to provide an antidote to this defective state of affairs by presenting some of the most carefully reasoned and theoretically provocative works on the topic of sex currently available. One of our goals in this anthology is to bring into focus the various ways that irrational prejudices and unfounded beliefs about sex and sexuality impede the creation and implementation of rational social and legal policies. Our strategy is to initiate the discussion on each topic by presenting recent or influential court decisions that frequently contain both popular attitudes about sex and sexuality and views that are more reflective and thoughtful. These cases serve, in some ways, as embodiments of the tension between conventional and often anxious views about sex, and calmer, more careful assessments of matters of intimate concern.

One might wonder, however, why these issues are before the courts in the first place. What role, if any, should the state have with respect to intimate matters? What power, if any, should governments have and exercise to interfere in the sexual and reproductive lives of citizens? As a subject of great theoretical interest, this fundamental question of moral and political philosophy has been debated since the earliest days of the discipline. But even as philosophy has become significantly more sophisticated on these issues, this fundamental question continues to be debated. Part of the reason an enduring resolution eludes us is that two compelling yet contrary traditions dominate the debates. The first tradition on the morally and legally appropriate role of the state in matters of intimate concern—the tradition usually identified as the classical liberal position—received its first systematic expression in John Stuart Mill's "On Liberty." Mill argued that a necessary condition of justifiable interference in the free choice and conduct of relatively well informed and mature adults was harm to others. Thus, the state can exercise its power in interfering with the choices and conduct of such persons only where there is harm to other identifiable individuals. So long as their conduct affects only themselves, persons ought be immune from interference. By contrast, the second tradition advocates what has been called a classical conservative view. Here the state can be justified in interfering with the choices and conduct of citizens for additional reasons, included among which are: maintaining a certain social climate and moral tone, preserving historical and cultural traditions, protecting and promoting public opinion and values, and causing harm to oneself. Now, given the incompatible implications of these positions, and the fact that both traditions endure, it should not be surprising that the issue of how the state can and should act in limiting the liberty of its citizens remains contentious. And nowhere is this contentiousness more palpable than in cases dealing with sex.

Rational discussions about such cases are complicated, however, by the ambiguity in the notion of sex itself. To what does "sex" refer? Does it name an activity, a sequence of behaviors, an identity, a choice, physical body parts, a set of desires? We take "sex" to refer to a constellation of phenomena and concerns, including same-sex activity, commercial sexual encounters, reproductive decisions, and sexual self-determination.

Discussions about sex and social policy have taken on a new complexity in light of recent advances in feminist theory and politics. An awareness of the role sex and sexuality play in the subordination of women has permanently transformed the way we understand these issues. As a result, any acceptable answer to the core question of the role of the state in the lives of individuals must incorporate an analysis of gender inequality. Thus, for example, whereas the debate over prostitution was cast traditionally in terms of an individual's choice to buy sexual services and the social and health hazards of prostitution, currently the topic cannot be addressed adequately unless viewed against the backdrop of the role and the consequences of prostitution with respect to the history and culture of patriarchy. Sex can no longer be seen as an isolated event outside the context of gender oppression.

In every chapter that follows, various feminist perspectives as well as the classical liberal and conservative positions are included. The essays contained within the chapters provide interrelated analyses which consider, develop, and rigorously debate a set of common issues and themes, including privacy, freedom of association and choice, equality, and consent. While each chapter is self-contained, the sequence of the chapters is not arbitrary, and thus we believe there is great value in reading the chapters in sequence. We begin with a chapter on the issue of lesbian and gay sex, in which, so long as consent between informed adults is clear and harm is absent, legal intervention is most suspicious. In subsequent chapters, as consent and its weight against other morally relevant considerations such as harm to others become less clear, arguments for social and legal intervention become more plausible. The book ends with a chapter on rape. Here consent is absent and harm is clear; thus legal intervention seems required. Yet determining the appropriate standards of consent is complex and constitutes the focal point of the essays.

The essays appearing in this volume have been edited, in some cases extensively. We urge those interested in pursuing these topics (or the views of the various authors on these topics) to consult the original essays. Further, many footnotes and citations have been omitted. However, we have attempted to retain those notes in which substantive points or arguments are made, or where important works are cited. We have suggested additional readings for each chapter, and these combined with the works cited in footnotes provide the reader a rich basis for further study.

In addition to those whose works are included in this volume, many others gave of their time and energy in making this book possible. Numerous colleagues provided advice and assistance. We would especially like to thank Yvonne Osman, Tom Regan, Deb Markowitz, Maureen MacGrogan, Alison Shonkwiler, Laska Jimsen, and several anonymous reviewers. A special debt of gratitude is owed to Michiko Okaya for her help on this project and her continuing support. And to Dooley, he of remarkable patience, who waits as we work.

Table of Contents

CHAPTER 4   ABORTION

CHAPTER 5   SEXUAL HARASSMENT

CHAPTER 6   RAPE

CHAPTER 1

Lesbian and Gay Sex

INTRODUCTION

A detached account of lesbian and gay sex would simply describe sexual conduct between persons of the same sex. And, so long as these persons are consenting adults, this conduct seems morally noncontroversial. How is it, then, that more than any other issue involving consensual sexual conduct, lesbian and gay sex elicits remarkably passionate and paradoxical reactions from even the most level-headed people? As is apparent from the heated public debates of the last decade concerning, for example, whether gay sex should be outlawed, whether lesbian couples should be parents, whether gays and lesbians should openly serve in the military, there is obviously much more at stake than any detached account indicates.

Disputes over gay sex force different but deeply held convictions into incompatibility. On the one hand, there is the tradition of moral, legal, and religious condemnation of gay, lesbian, and bisexual conduct. On the other hand, there is a tradition of liberty and tolerance regarding intimate personal choices. This incompatibility was prominent in the well-known debate between Lord Patrick Devlin and Professor H.L.A. Hart concerning, among other things, the legalization of homosexual conduct. Devlin took the conservative position that the state was justified in upholding popular opinion about sexual morality in order to preserve and protect the foundations and character of society. Hart, in contrast, argued for a liberal position which holds that the purpose of the law is not to enforce public morality but rather, to prevent harm to individuals. He believed that consensual sexual activity between adults is generally harmless, and that liberty of choice and action should be protected against state interference.

As Anne B. Goldstein argues, this debate in political philosophy anticipates the disagreement between the majority and the minority opinions in *Bowers v. Hardwick*. In this 1986 U.S. Supreme Court decision, the majority, making selective reference to the history and tradition of religious and legal condemnation of homosexual sex, held that there is no constitutional right to engage in homosexual sodomy. They found the tradition of liberty and tolerance which grounded rights to privacy in matters of sexual and otherwise intimate contact among heterosexuals (particularly married heterosexuals in matters of reproductive choice; see *Griswold v. Connecti-*

cut in Chapter 4) to be inadequate to establish a right to engage in homosexual sodomy. Thus, in those states where homosexual sodomy is illegal, homosexuals can be arrested and prosecuted for having consensual sex behind closed doors. This is precisely what happened to Michael Hardwick when a police officer went to Hardwick's home, found him engaged in oral sex with his male lover, and arrested him.

The Court's majority found the Georgia law under which Hardwick was arrested constitutional, and did so by appealing to the history of public morality. But is this appeal legitimate? The minority argued that it is not. Historical attitudes and religious doctrines are not sufficient, on their view, for determining the rights of individuals. The minority denied that a history of legal proscription and religious condemnation of homosexuality justifies denying individuals the right to "be left alone" in matters of intimate association. Arguments from "history and tradition" could, after all, justify the reintroduction of slavery or the disenfranchisement of women. Furthermore, as Goldstein argues, the historical record concerning sodomy laws in the United States and "Western Civilization" generally is not unambiguous—the facts of the matter are in dispute—so the majority's appeals to early American law and to the "ancient roots" of moral censure of homosexuality are unconvincing.

If appeals to history and public morality are inadequate in morally justifying state interference in the private sexual conduct of individuals, then what sorts of considerations are adequate? Some claim that the state can legitimately interfere with the private sexual acts of individuals because such acts are "unnatural." Homosexual sex, it is argued, is unnatural and therefore should be legally and morally prohibited. As Burton M. Leiser demonstrates, however, one cannot move from the assertion that an action or event is unnatural (assuming there is a nonambiguous meaning of "natural") to any moral judgment about the act or event. Just as the use of a condom can be considered "unnatural" because it is artificial and prevents conception, it does not follow that its use is immoral. Indeed, given the alarming rates of unwanted pregnancies and the spread of sexually transmitted diseases, some may argue that the use of condoms is morally obligatory, but not on grounds that have anything to do with what is "natural."

Neither appeals to history and public morality nor to what is natural morally justify the Court's decision in *Bowers*. As Richard D. Mohr argues, sound moral reasoning reveals that sodomy laws themselves are immoral. He claims that, even though they are seldom enforced, and many people, including gay men and lesbians, are unaware of their existence, sodomy laws should be abolished. Such laws not only lead to bad consequences in that they cause psychological harm to individuals, but they can be employed to harm gay men and lesbians socially, for example, by denying them certain parental rights; economically, by denying them employment and job benefits; and physically, by contributing to an atmosphere where gay-bashing is tolerated. But there is a another kind of moral reason for eliminating these laws. Mohr argues that the existence of sodomy laws amounts to a direct affront to the dignity of gays and lesbians. Emphasizing the Kantian notion of respect for persons, Mohr says these laws attempt to manipulate "the conditions in which a person makes choices" and thus are insulting and disrespectful to persons as moral agents.

Furthermore, the existence of laws that criminalize homosexual sex has serious implications regarding the civil rights and civil liberties of gays, lesbians, and bisexuals. Given that in many states simply being intimate with a same-sex partner makes one a criminal, some, like Anthony Scalia in his dissent in *Romer v. Evans*, argue that it is permissible for a state to deny gays, lesbians, and bisexuals certain claims to equal protection of the law. This civil rights issue came before the Supreme Court after a challenge to the 1992 amendment ("Amendment 2") to the Colorado constitution. Amendment 2 would invalidate existing anti-discrimination policies and prevent any others from being enacted. The Supreme Court's majority found Amendment 2 to be unconstitutional as it made "a class of persons a stranger to its laws."

The dispute between the majority and the minority in *Romer v. Evans*, like that in *Bowers*, exemplifies how judicial opinions frequently presuppose questionable moral attitudes. This is one reason why gays and lesbians have argued for both recognition and protection of their basic liberties in matters of sexual association. Arguments for and against civil rights protection for gays, lesbians, and bisexuals are presented by Vincent J. Samar. After rejecting a number of the most common arguments against protecting gay men and lesbians from discrimination in respect to employment, housing and public accomodations, Samar shows how the two leading moral theories, rights theory and utilitarian theory, clearly demonstrate what is wrong with discriminatory practices.

Currently, many Americans are working for policies and laws which protect gays, lesbians and bisexuals from discrimination in the workplace, in housing, and in other public arenas. They do so in the face of powerful and obdurate opposition. Now, in light of the *Romer* decision, those seeking a full complement of civil rights for lesbians, gays, and bisexuals are provided long-awaited encouragement.

SUGGESTED READINGS

Henry Abelove, Michel Aina Barale, and David M. Halperin, *The Lesbian and Gay Studies Reader* (New York: Routledge, 1993).

Mark Blasius, *Gay and Lesbian Politics: Sexuality and the Emergence of a New Ethic* (Philadelphia: Temple University Press, 1994).

Claudia Card, *Lesbian Choices* (New York: Columbia University Press, 1995).

John D'Emilio and Estelle Freedman, *Intimate Matters: A History of Sexuality in America* (New York: Harper & Row, 1988).

Eric Marcus, *Making History: The Struggle for Gay and Lesbian Equal Rights, 1945–1990* (New York: Harper Collins, 1992).

BOWERS v. HARDWICK

478 U.S. 186 (1986)

Argued March 31, 1986, Decided June 30, 1986

Justice Byron White for the majority.

In August 1982, respondent Hardwick (hereafter respondent) was charged with violating the Georgia statute criminalizing sodomy[1] by committing that act with another adult male in the bedroom of respondent's home. After a preliminary hearing, the District Attorney decided not to present the matter to the grand jury unless further evidence developed.

Respondent then brought suit in the Federal District Court, challenging the constitutionality of the statute insofar as it criminalized consensual sodomy.[2] He asserted that he was a practicing homosexual, that the Georgia sodomy statute, as administered by the defendants, placed him in imminent danger of arrest, and that the statute for several reasons violates the Federal Constitution. The District Court granted the defendants' motion to dismiss for failure to state a claim, relying on *Doe v. Commonwealth's Attorney for the City of Richmond*, 403 F. Supp. 1199 (E.D. Va. 1975), which this Court summarily affirmed, (1976)....

This case does not require a judgment on whether the laws against sodomy between consenting adults in general, or between homosexuals in particular, are wise or desirable. It raises no question about the right or propriety of state legislative decisions to repeal their laws that criminalize homosexual sodomy, or of state-court decisions invalidating those laws on state constitutional grounds. The issue presented is whether the Federal Constitution confers a fundamental right upon homosexuals to engage in sodomy and hence invalidates the laws of the many States that still make such conduct illegal and have done so for a very long time. The case also calls for some judgment about the limits of the Court's role in carrying out its constitutional mandate.

We first register our disagreement with the Court of Appeals and with respondent that the Court's prior cases have construed the Constitution to confer a right of privacy that extends to homosexual sodomy and for all intents and purposes have decided this case. The reach of this line of cases was sketched in *Carey v. Population Services International*, 431 U.S. 678, 685 (1977). *Pierce v. Society of Sisters*, 268 U.S. 510 (1925) and *Meyer v. Nebraska*, 262 U.S. 390 (1923), were described as dealing with child rearing and education; *Prince v. Massachusetts*, 321 U.S. 158 (1944), with family relationships; *Skinner v. Oklahoma ex rel. Williamson*, 316 U.S. 535 (1942), with procreation; *Loving v. Virginia*, 388 U.S. 1 (1967), with marriage; *Griswold v. Connecticut*, 381 U.S. 479 (1965) and *Eisenstadt v. Baird*, 405 U.S. 438 (1972) with contraception; and *Roe v. Wade*, 410 U.S. 113 (1973) with abortion. The latter three cases were interpreted as construing the Due Process Clause of the Fourteenth Amendment to confer a fundamental individual right to decide whether or not to beget or bear a child. . . .

Accepting the decisions in these cases and the above description of them, we think it evident that none of the rights announced in those cases bears any resemblance to the claimed constitutional right of homosexuals to engage in acts of sodomy that is asserted in this case. No connection between family, marriage, or procreation on the one hand and homosexual activity on the other has been demonstrated. . . . Moreover, any claim that these cases nevertheless stand for the proposition that any kind of private sexual conduct between consenting adults is constitutionally insulated from state proscription is unsupportable. Indeed, the Court's opinion in *Carey* twice asserted that the privacy right, which the *Griswold* line of cases found to be one of the protections provided by the Due Process Clause, did not reach so far.

Precedent aside, however, respondent would have us announce, as the Court of Appeals did, a fundamental right to engage in homosexual sodomy. This we are quite unwilling to do. It is true that despite the language of the Due Process Clauses of the Fifth and Fourteenth Amendments, which appears to focus only on the processes by which life, liberty, or property is taken, the cases are legion in which those Clauses have been interpreted to have substantive content, subsuming rights that to a great extent are immune from federal or state regulation or proscription. Among such cases are those recognizing rights that have little or no textual support in the constitutional language. *Meyer*, *Prince*, and *Pierce* fall in this category, as do the privacy cases from *Griswold* to *Carey*.

Striving to assure itself and the public that announcing rights not readily identifiable in the Constitution's text involves much more than the imposition of the Justices' own choice of values on the States and the Federal Government, the Court has sought to identify the nature of the rights qualifying for heightened judicial protection. In *Palko v. Connecticut*, 302 U.S. 319, 325, 326 (1937), it was said that this category includes those fundamental liberties that are "implicit in the concept of ordered liberty," such that "neither liberty nor justice would exist if [they] were sacrificed." A different description of fundamental liberties appeared in *Moore v. East Cleveland*, 431 U.S. 494, 503 (1977) (opinion of Powell, J.), where they are characterized as those liberties that are "deeply rooted in this Nation's history and tradition." See also *Griswold v. Connecticut*.

It is obvious to us that neither of these formulations would extend a fundamental right to homosexuals to engage in acts of consensual sodomy. Proscriptions against that conduct have ancient roots.... Sodomy was a criminal offense at common law and was forbidden by the laws of the original 13 States when they ratified the Bill of Rights. In 1868, when the Fourteenth Amendment was ratified, all but 5 of the 37 States in the Union had criminal sodomy laws. In fact, until 1961, all 50 States outlawed sodomy, and today, 25 States and the District of Columbia continue to provide criminal penalties for sodomy performed in private and between consenting adults. Against this background, to claim that a right to engage in such conduct is "deeply rooted in this Nation's history and tradition," or "implicit in the concept of ordered liberty" is, at best, facetious.

Nor are we inclined to take a more expansive view of our authority to discover new fundamental rights imbedded in the Due Process Clause. The Court is most vulnerable and comes nearest to illegitimacy when it deals with judge-made constitutional law having little or no cognizable roots in the language or design of the Constitution. That this is so was painfully demonstrated by the face-off between the Executive and the Court in the 1930s, which resulted in the repudiation of much of the substantive gloss that the Court had placed on the Due Process Clause of the Fifth and Fourteenth Amendments. There should be, therefore, great resistance to expand the substantive reach of those Clauses, particularly if it requires redefining the category of rights deemed to be fundamental. Otherwise, the Judiciary necessarily takes to itself further authority to govern the country without express constitutional authority. The claimed right pressed on us today falls far short of overcoming this resistance.

Respondent, however, asserts that the result should be different where the homosexual conduct occurs in the privacy of the home. He relies on *Stanley v. Georgia*, 394 U.S. 557 (1969), where the Court held that the First Amendment prevents conviction for possessing and reading obscene material in the privacy of one's home: "If the First Amendment means anything it means that a State has no business telling a man, sitting alone in his house, what books he may read or what films he may watch." *Id.* at 565.

Stanley did protect conduct that would not have been protected outside the home, and it partially prevented the enforcement of state obscenity laws; but the decision was firmly grounded in the First Amendment. The right pressed upon us here has no similar support in the text of the Constitution, and it does not qualify for recognition under the prevailing principles for construing the Fourteenth Amendment. Its limits are also difficult to discern. Plainly enough, otherwise illegal conduct is not always immunized whenever it occurs in the home. Victimless crimes, such as the possession and use of illegal drugs, do not escape the law where they are committed at home. *Stanley* itself recognized that its holding offered no protection for the possession in the home of drugs, firearms, or stolen goods. And if respondent's submission is limited to the voluntary sexual conduct between consenting adults, it would be difficult, except by fiat, to limit the claimed right to homosexual conduct while leaving exposed to prosecution adultery, incest, and other sexual crimes even though they are committed in the home. We are unwilling to start down that road.

Even if the conduct at issue here is not a fundamental right, respondent asserts that there must be a rational basis for the law and that there is none in this case other than the presumed belief of a majority of the electorate in Georgia that homosexual sodomy is immoral and unacceptable. This is said to be an inadequate rationale to support the law. The law, however, is constantly based on notions of morality, and if all laws representing essentially moral choices are to be invalidated under the Due Process Clause, the courts will be very busy indeed. Even respondent makes no such claim, but insists that majority sentiments about the morality of homosexuality should be declared inadequate. We do not agree, and are unpersuaded that the sodomy laws of some 25 States should be invalidated on this basis.

Accordingly, the judgment of the Court of Appeals is reversed.

Separate Opinion

Chief Justice Warren Burger, concurring.

I join the Court's opinion, but I write separately to underscore my view that in constitutional terms there is no such thing as a fundamental right to commit homosexual sodomy.

As the Court notes, the proscriptions against sodomy have very "ancient roots." Decisions of individuals relating to homosexual conduct have been subject to state intervention throughout the history of Western Civilization. Condemnation of those practices is firmly rooted in Judeo-Christian moral and ethical standards. Homosexual sodomy was a capital crime under Roman law. See Code Theod. 9.7.6; Code Just. 9.9.31. See also

D. Bailey, *Homosexuality and the Western Christian Tradition* 70–81 (1975). During the English Reformation, when powers of the ecclesiastical courts were transferred to the King's Courts, the first English statute criminalizing sodomy was passed. 25 Hen. VIII, ch 6. Blackstone described "the infamous crime against nature" as an offense of "deeper malignity" than rape, a heinous act "the very mention of which is a disgrace to human nature," and "a crime not fit to be named." 4 W. Blackstone, *Commentaries* *215. The common law of England, including its prohibition of sodomy, became the received law of Georgia and the other Colonies. In 1816 the Georgia Legislature passed the statute at issue here, and that statute has been continuously in force in one form or another since that time. To hold that the act of homosexual sodomy is somehow protected as a fundamental right would be to cast aside millennia of moral teaching.

This is essentially not a question of personal "preferences" but rather of the legislative authority of the State. I find nothing in the Constitution depriving a State of the power to enact the statute challenged here....

Justice Blackmun, with whom Justice Brennan, Justice Marshall, and Justice Stevens join, dissenting.

This case is no more about "a fundamental right to engage in homosexual sodomy," as the Court purports to declare...than *Stanley v. Georgia* was about a fundamental right to watch obscene movies.... Rather, this case is about "the most comprehensive of rights and the right most valued by civilized men," namely, "the right to be let alone." *Olmstead v. United States*, 277 U.S. 438, 478 (1928).

The statute at issue, Ga. Code Ann. §16–6–2 (1984), denies individuals the right to decide for themselves whether to engage in particular forms of private, consensual sexual activity. The Court concludes that §16–6–2 is valid essentially because "the laws of...many States...still make such conduct illegal and have done so for a very long time."... But the fact that the moral judgments expressed by statutes like §16–6–2 may be "'natural and familiar...ought not to conclude our judgment upon the question whether statutes embodying them conflict with the Constitution of the United States.'" *Roe v. Wade*.... Like Justice Holmes, I believe that "[i]t is revolting to have no better reason for a rule of law than that so it was laid down in the time of Henry IV. It is still more revolting if the grounds upon which it was laid down have vanished long since, and the rule simply persists from blind imitation of the past." Holmes, "The Path of the Law," 10 *Harv. L. Rev.* 457, 469 (1897). I believe we must analyze respondent Hardwick's claim in the light of the values that underlie the constitutional right to privacy. If that right means anything, it means that, before Georgia can prosecute its citizens for making choices about the most intimate aspects of their lives, it must do more than assert that the choice they have made is an "'abominable crime not fit to be named among Christians.'"

I

In its haste to reverse the Court of Appeals and hold that the Constitution does not "confe[r] a fundamental right upon homosexuals to engage in sodomy,"…the Court relegates the actual statute being challenged to a footnote and ignores the procedural posture of the case before it. A fair reading of the statute and of the complaint clearly reveals that the majority has distorted the question this case presents.

First, the Court's almost obsessive focus on homosexual activity is particularly hard to justify in light of the broad language Georgia has used. Unlike the Court, the Georgia Legislature has not proceeded on the assumption that homosexuals are so different from other citizens that their lives may be controlled in a way that would not be tolerated if it limited the choices of those other citizens.… Rather, Georgia has provided that "[a] person commits the offense of sodomy when he performs or submits to any sexual act involving the sex organs of one person and the mouth or anus of another." Ga. Code Ann. §16–6–2(a) (1984). The sex or status of the persons who engage in the act is irrelevant as a matter of state law. In fact, to the extent I can discern a legislative purpose for Georgia's 1968 enactment of §16–6–2, that purpose seems to have been to broaden the coverage of the law to reach heterosexual as well as homosexual activity. I therefore see no basis for the Court's decision to treat this case as an "as applied" challenge to §16–6–2…or for Georgia's attempt, both in its brief and at oral argument, to defend §16–6–2 solely on the grounds that it prohibits homosexual activity. Michael Hardwick's standing may rest in significant part on Georgia's apparent willingness to enforce against homosexuals a law it seems not to have any desire to enforce against heterosexuals.… But his claim that §16–6–2 involves an unconstitutional intrusion into his privacy and his right of intimate association does not depend in any way on his sexual orientation.

Second, I disagree with the Court's refusal to consider whether §16–6–2 runs afoul of the Eighth or Ninth Amendments or the Equal Protection Clause of the Fourteenth Amendment.… Respondent's complaint expressly invoked the Ninth Amendment, see App. 6. and he relied heavily before this Court on *Griswold v. Connecticut*, which identifies that Amendment as one of the specific constitutional provisions giving "life and substance" to our understanding of privacy.… I need not reach either the Eighth Amendment or the Equal Protection Clause issues because I believe that Hardwick has stated a cognizable claim that §16–6–2 interferes with constitutionally protected interests in privacy and freedom of intimate association. But neither the Eighth Amendment nor the Equal Protection Clause is so clearly irrelevant that a claim resting on either provision should be peremptorily dismissed. The Court's cramped reading of the issue before it makes for a short opinion, but it does little to make for a persuasive one.

II

"Our cases long have recognized that the Constitution embodies a promise that a certain private sphere of individual liberty will be kept largely beyond the reach of government." *Thornburgh v. American College of Obstetricians and Gynecologists*, 476 U.S. 747 (1986). In construing the right to privacy, the Court has proceeded along two somewhat distinct, albeit complementary, lines. First, it has recognized a privacy interest with reference to certain decisions that are properly for the individual to make, e.g., *Roe v. Wade*,... Second, it has recognized a privacy interest with reference to certain *places* without regard for the particular activities in which the individuals who occupy them are engaged.... The case before us implicates both the decisional and the spatial aspects of the right to privacy.

A

The Court concludes today that none of our prior cases dealing with various decisions that individuals are entitled to make free of governmental interference "bears any resemblance to the claimed constitutional right of homosexuals to engage in acts of sodomy that is asserted in this case."... While it is true that these cases may be characterized by their connection to protection of the family, see *Roberts v. United States Jaycees*, 468 U.S. 609 (1984), the Court's conclusion that they extend no further than this boundary ignores the warning in *Moore v. East Cleveland* (1977) against "clos[ing] our eyes to the basic reasons why certain rights associated with the family have been accorded shelter under the Fourteenth Amendment's Due Process Clause." We protect those rights not because they contribute, in some direct and material way, to the general public welfare, but because they form so central a part of an individual's life. "[T]he concept of privacy embodies the 'moral fact that a person belongs to himself and not others nor to society as a whole.'" *Thornburgh v. American College of Obstetricians & Gynecologists* (1986). And so we protect the decision whether to marry precisely because marriage "is an association that promotes a way of life, not causes; a harmony in living, not political faiths; a bilateral loyalty, not commercial or social projects." *Griswold v. Connecticut.* We protect the decision whether to have a child because parenthood alters so dramatically an individual's self-definition, not because of demographic considerations or the Bible's command to be fruitful and multiply.... And we protect the family because it contributes so powerfully to the happiness of individuals, not because of a preference for stereotypical households.... The Court recognized in *Roberts* that the "ability independently to define one's identity that is central to any concept of liberty" cannot truly be exercised in a vacuum; we all depend on the "emotional enrichment from close ties with others."

Only the most willful blindness could obscure the fact that sexual intimacy is "a sensitive, key relationship of human existence central to family life, community welfare, and the development of human personality," *Paris Adult Theatre I v. Slaton*, 413 U.S. 49 (1973).... The fact that individuals define themselves in a significant way through their intimate sexual relationships with others suggests, in a Nation as diverse as ours, that there may be many "right" ways of conducting those relationships, and that much of the richness of a relationship will come from the freedom an individual has to choose the form and nature of these intensely personal bonds....

In a variety of circumstances we have recognized that a necessary corollary of giving individuals freedom to choose how to conduct their lives is acceptance of the fact that different individuals will make different choices. For example, in holding that the clearly important state interest in public education should give way to a competing claim by the Amish to the effect that extended formal schooling threatened their way of life, the court declared: "There can be no assumption that today's majority is 'right' and the Amish and others like them are 'wrong.' A way of life that is odd or even erratic but interferes with no rights or interests of others is not to be condemned because it is different." *Wisconsin v. Yoder*, 406 U.S. 205 (1972). The Court claims that its decision today merely refuses to recognize a fundamental right to engage in homosexual sodomy; what the Court really has refused to recognize is the fundamental interest all individuals have in controlling the nature of their intimate associations with others.

B

The behavior for which Hardwick faces prosecution occurred in his own home, a place to which the Fourth Amendment attaches special significance. The Court's treatment of this aspect of the case is symptomatic of its overall refusal to consider the broad principles that have informed our treatment of privacy in specific cases. Just as the right to privacy is more than the mere aggregation of a number of entitlements to engage in specific behavior, so too, protecting the physical integrity of the home is more than merely a means of protecting specific activities that often take place there. Even when our understanding of the contours of the right to privacy depends on "reference to a 'place,'" *Katz v. United States*, 389 U.S. at 661, "the essence of a Fourth Amendment violation is 'not the breaking of [a person's] doors, and the rummaging of his drawers,' but rather is 'the invasion of his indefeasible right of personal security, personal liberty and private property.'" *California v. Ciraolo*, 476 U.S. 207 (1986).

The Court's interpretation of the pivotal case of *Stanley v. Georgia* is entirely unconvincing. *Stanley* held that Georgia's undoubted power to punish the public distribution of constitutionally unprotected, obscene material did not permit the State to punish the private possession of such material. According to the majority here, *Stanley* relied entirely on the First Amendment, and thus, it is claimed, sheds no light on cases not involving printed materials. But that is not what *Stanley* said. Rather, the *Stanley* Court anchored its holding in the Fourth Amendment's special protection for the individual in his home:

> The makers of our Constitution undertook to secure conditions favorable to the pursuit of happiness. They recognized the significance of man's spiritual nature, of his feelings and of his intellect. They knew that only a part of the pain, pleasure and satisfactions of life are to be found in material things. They sought to protect Americans in their beliefs, their thoughts, their emotions and their sensations....

III

The Court's failure to comprehend the magnitude of the liberty interests at stake in this case leads it to slight the question whether petitioner, on behalf of the State, has justified Georgia's infringement on these interests....

The core of the petitioner's defense of §16–6–2, however, is that respondent and others who engage in the conduct prohibited by §16–6–2 interfere with Georgia's exercise of the "'right of the Nation and of the States to maintain a decent society,'" *Paris Adult Theater I v. Slaton* (1964). Essentially, petitioner argues, and the Court agrees, that the fact that the acts described in §16–6–2 "for hundreds of years, if not thousands, have been uniformly condemned as immoral" is sufficient reason to permit a State to ban them today....

I cannot agree that either the length of time a majority has held its convictions or the passions with which it defends them can withdraw legislation from this Court's scrutiny.... As Justice Jackson wrote so eloquently for the Court of *West Virginia Board of Education v. Barnette*, 319 U.S. 624, 641–642 (1943), "we apply the limitations of the Constitution with no fear that freedom to be intellectually and spiritually diverse or even contrary will disintegrate the social organization...[F]reedom to differ is not limited to things that do not matter much. That would be a mere shadow of freedom. The test of its substance is the right to differ as to things that touch the heart of the existing order."... It is precisely because the issue raised by this case touches the heart of what makes individuals what they are that we should be especially sensitive to the rights of those whose choices upset the majority.

The assertion that "traditional Judeo-Christian values proscribe" the conduct involved, Brief for Petitioner 20, cannot provide an adequate justification for §16–6–2. That certain, but by no means all, religious groups condemn the behavior at issue gives the State no license to impose their judgments on the entire citizenry. The legitimacy of secular legislation depends instead on whether the State can advance some justification for its law beyond its conformity to religious doctrine.... Thus, far from buttressing his case, petitioner's invocation of Leviticus, Romans, St. Thomas Aquinas, and sodomy's heretical status during the Middle Ages undermines his suggestion that §16–6–2 represents a legitimate use of secular coercive power. A State can no more punish private behavior because of religious intolerance than it can punish such behavior because of racial animus. "The Constitution cannot control such prejudices, but neither can it tolerate them. Private biases may be outside the reach of the law, but the law cannot, directly or indirectly, give them effect." *Palmore v. Sidoti*, 466 U.S. 429, 433 (1984). No matter how uncomfortable a certain group may make the majority of this Court, we have held that "[m]ere public intolerance or animosity cannot constitutionally justify the deprivation of a person's physical liberty." *O'Connor v. Donaldson*, 422 U.S. 563, 575 (1975)....

Nor can §16–6–2 be justified as a "morally neutral" exercise of Georgia's power to "protect the public environment," *Paris Adult Theatre*.... Certainly, some private behavior can affect the fabric of society as a whole. Reasonable people may differ about whether particular sexual acts are moral or immoral, but "we have ample evidence for believing that people will not abandon morality, will not think any better of murder, cruelty and dishonesty, merely because some private sexual practice which they abominate is not punished by the law." H.L.A. Hart, "Immorality and Treason," reprinted in *The Law as Literature*, 220, 225 (L. Blom-Cooper ed. 1961). Petitioner and the Court fail to see the difference between laws that protect public sensibilities and those that enforce private morality. Statutes banning public sexual activity are entirely consistent with protecting the individual's liberty interest in decisions concerning sexual relations: the same recognition that those decisions are intensely private which justifies protecting them from governmental interference can justify protecting individuals from unwilling exposure to the sexual activities of others. But the mere fact that intimate behavior may be punished when it takes place in public cannot dictate how States can regulate intimate behavior that occurs in intimate places. See *Paris Adult Theatre I*, 413 U.S., at 66 ("marital intercourse on a street corner or a theater stage" can be forbidden despite the constitutional protections identified in *Griswold v. Connecticut*. ...

This case involves no real interference with the rights of others, for the mere knowledge that other individuals do not adhere to one's value system cannot be a legally cognizable interest ... let alone an interest that can justify invading the houses, hearts, and minds of citizens who choose to live their lives differently. ...

NOTES

[1]Georgia Code Ann. §16–6–2 (1984) provides, in pertinent part, as follows:

(a) A person commits the offense of sodomy when he performs or submits to any sexual act involving the sex organs of one person and the mouth or anus of another. ...

(b) A person convicted of the offense of sodomy shall be punished by imprisonment for not less than one nor more than 20 years. ...

[2]John and Mary Doe were also plaintiffs in the action. They alleged that they wished to engage in sexual activity proscribed by §16–6–2 in the privacy of their home, App. 3, and that they had been "chilled and deterred" from engaging in such activity by both the existence of the statute and Hardwick's arrest. Id., at 5. The District Court held, however, that because they had neither sustained, nor were in immediate danger of sustaining, any direct injury from the enforcement of the statute, they did not have proper standing to maintain the action. Id., at 18. The Court of Appeals affirmed the District Court's judgment dismissing the Does' claim for lack of standing, 760 F.2d 1202, 1206–1207 (C.A. 11 1985), and the Does do not challenge that holding in this Court. ...

ROMER v. EVANS

116 S.C.T. 1620 (1996)

Argued October 10, 1995, Decided May 20, 1996

Justice Kennedy delivered the opinion of the Court.

One century ago, the first Justice Harlan admonished this Court that the Constitution "neither knows nor tolerates classes among citizens." *Plessy v. Ferguson*, 163 U.S. 537, 559 (1896) (dissenting opinion). Unheeded then, those words now are understood to state a commitment to the law's neutrality where the rights of persons are at stake. The Equal Protection Clause enforces this principle and today requires us to hold invalid a provision of Colorado's Constitution.

I

The enactment challenged in this case is an amendment to the Constitution of the State of Colorado, adopted in a 1992 statewide referendum. The parties and the state courts refer to it as "Amendment 2," its designation when submitted to the voters. The impetus for the amendment and the contentious campaign that preceded its adoption came in large part from ordinances that had been passed in various Colorado municipalities. For example, the cities of Aspen and Boulder and the City and County of Denver each had enacted ordinances which banned discrimination in many transactions and activities, including housing, employment, education, public accommodations, and health and welfare services.... What gave rise to the statewide controversy was the protection the ordinances afforded to persons discriminated against by reason of their sexual orientation.... Amendment 2 repeals these ordinances to the extent they prohibit discrimination on the basis of homosexual, lesbian or bisexual orientation, conduct, practices or relationships.

Yet Amendment 2, in explicit terms, does more than repeal or rescind these provisions. It prohibits all legislative, executive or judicial action at any level of state or local government designed to protect the named class, a class we shall refer to as homosexual persons or gays and lesbians. The amendment reads:

> No Protected Status Based on Homosexual, Lesbian, or Bisexual Orientation. Neither the State of Colorado, through any of its branches or departments, nor any of its agencies, political subdivisions, municipalities or school districts, shall enact, adopt or enforce any statute, regulation, ordinance or policy whereby homosexual, lesbian or bisexual orientation, conduct, practices or relationships shall constitute or otherwise be the basis of or entitle any person or class of persons to have or claim any minority status, quota preferences, protected status or claim of discrimination. This Section of the Constitution shall be in all respects self-executing.

Soon after Amendment 2 was adopted, this litigation to declare its invalidity and enjoin its enforcement was commenced in the District Court for the City and County of Denver. Among the plaintiffs (respondents here) were homosexual persons, some of them government employees. They alleged that enforcement of Amendment 2 would subject them to immediate and substantial risk of discrimination on the basis of their sexual orientation. Other plaintiffs (also respondents here) included the three municipalities whose ordinances we have cited and certain other governmental entities which had acted earlier to protect homosexuals from discrimination but would be prevented by Amendment 2 from continuing to do so. Although Governor Romer had been on record opposing the adoption of Amendment 2, he was named in his official capacity as a defendant, together with the Colorado Attorney General and the State of Colorado.

The trial court granted a preliminary injunction to stay enforcement of Amendment 2, and on appeal was taken to the Supreme Court of Colorado. Sustaining the interim injunction and remanding the case for further proceedings, the State Supreme Court held that Amendment 2 was subject to strict scrutiny under the Fourteenth Amendment because it infringed the fundamental right of gays and lesbians to participate in the political process. *Evans v. Romer*, 854 P. 2d 1270 (Colo. 1993) (Evans I). To reach this conclusion, the state court relied on our voting rights cases, e.g., *Reynolds v. Sims*, 377 U.S. 533 (1964); *Carrington v. Rash*, 380 U.S. 89 (1965);

Harper v. Virginia Bd. of Elections, 383 U.S. 663 (1966); *Williams v. Rhodes*, 393 U.S. 23 (1968), and on our precedents involving discriminatory restructuring of governmental decision making, see, e.g., *Hunter v. Erickson*, 393 U.S. 385 (1969); *Reitman v. Mulkey*, 387 U.S. 369 (1967); *Washington v. Seattle School Dist. No.1*, 458 U.S. 457 (1982); *Gordon v. Lance*, 403 U.S. 1 (1971). On remand, the State advanced various arguments in an effort to show that Amendment 2 was narrowly tailored to serve compelling interests, but the trial court found none sufficient. It enjoined enforcement of Amendment 2, and the Supreme Court of Colorado, in a second opinion, affirmed the ruling…. We granted certiorari and now affirm the judgment, but on a rationale different from that adopted by the State Supreme Court.

II

The State's principal argument in defense of Amendment 2 is that it puts gays and lesbians in the same position as all other persons. So, the State says, the measure does no more than deny homosexuals special rights. This reading of the amendment's language is implausible. We rely not upon our own interpretation of the amendment but upon the authoritative construction of Colorado's Supreme Court. The state court, deeming it unnecessary to determine the full extent of the amendment's reach, found it invalid even on a modest reading of its implications. The critical discussion of the amendment, set out in Evans I, is as follows:

> The immediate objective of Amendment 2 is, at a minimum, to repeal existing statutes, regulations, ordinances, and policies of state and local entities that barred discrimination based on sexual orientation…. and various provisions prohibiting discrimination based on sexual orientation at state colleges…. The "ultimate effect" of Amendment 2 is to prohibit any governmental entity from adopting similar, or more protective statutes, regulations, ordinances, or policies in the future unless the state constitution is first amended to permit such measures….

Sweeping and comprehensive is the change in legal status effected by this law. So much is evident from the ordinances that the Colorado Supreme Court declared would be void by operation of Amendment 2. Homosexuals, by state decree, are put in a solitary class with respect to transactions and relations in both the private and governmental spheres. The amendment withdraws from homosexuals, but no others, specific legal protection from the injuries caused by discrimination, and it forbids reinstatement of these laws and policies.

The change that Amendment 2 works in the legal status of gays and lesbians in the private sphere is far-reaching, both on its own terms and when considered in light of the structure and operation of modern antidiscrimination laws. That structure is well illustrated by contemporary statutes and ordinances prohibiting discrimination by providers of public accommodations. "At common law, innkeepers, smiths, and others who 'made profession of a public employment,' were prohibited from refusing, without good reason, to serve a customer." *Hurley v. Irish-American Gay, Lesbian and Bisexual Group of Boston, Inc.*, 115 U.S. 2338 (1995). The duty was a general one and did not specify protection for particular groups. The common law rules, however, proved insufficient in many instances, and it was settled early that the Fourteenth Amendment did not give Congress a general power to prohibit discrimination in public accommodations, Civil Rights Cases, 109 U.S. 3, 25 (1883). In consequence, most States have chosen to counter discrimination by enacting detailed statutory schemes....

Colorado's state and municipal laws typify this emerging tradition of statutory protection and follow a consistent pattern. The laws first enumerate the persons or entities subject to a duty not to discriminate. The list goes well beyond the entities covered by the common law. The Boulder ordinance, for example, has a comprehensive definition of entities deemed places of "public accommodation." They include "any place of business engaged in any sales to the general public and any place that offers services, facilities, privileges, or advantages to the general public or that receives financial support through solicitation of the general public or through governmental subsidy of any kind." Boulder Rev. Code 12–1–1(j) (1987). The Denver ordinance is of similar breadth, applying, for example, to hotels, restaurants, hospitals, dental clinics, theaters, banks, common-carriers, travel and insurance agencies, and "shops and stores dealing with goods or services of any kind," Denver Rev. Municipal Code, Art. IV, 28–92.

These statutes and ordinances also depart from the common law by enumerating the groups or persons within their ambit of protection. Enumeration is the essential device used to make the duty not to discriminate concrete and to provide guidance for those who must comply. In following this approach, Colorado's state and local governments have not limited antidiscrimination laws to groups that have so far been given the protection of heightened equal protection scrutiny under our cases.... Rather, they set forth an extensive catalogue of traits which cannot be the basis for discrimination, including age, military status, marital status, pregnancy, parenthood, custody of a minor child, political affiliation, physical or mental disability of an individual or of his or her associates— and, in recent times, sexual orientation....

Amendment 2 bars homosexuals from securing protection against the injuries that these public-accommodations laws address. That in itself is a severe consequence, but there is more. Amendment 2, in addition, nullifies specific legal protections for this targeted class in all transactions in housing, sale of real estate, insurance, health and welfare services, private education, and employment....

Not confined to the private sphere, Amendment 2 also operates to repeal and forbid all laws or policies providing specific protection for gays or lesbians from discrimination by every level of Colorado government. The State Supreme Court cited two examples of protections in the governmental sphere that are now rescinded and may not be reintroduced. The first is Colorado Executive Order D0035 (1990), which forbids employment discrimination against "all state employees, 'classified and exempt' on the basis of sexual orientation." 854 P. 2d, at 1284. Also repealed, and now forbidden, are "various provisions prohibiting discrimination based on sexual orientation at state colleges." Id., at 1284, 1285. The repeal of these measures and the prohibition against their future reenactment demonstrates that Amendment 2 has the same force and effect in Colorado's governmental sector as it does elsewhere and that it applies to policies as well as ordinary legislation.

Amendment 2's reach may not be limited to specific laws passed for the benefit of gays and lesbians. It is a fair, if not necessary, inference from the broad language of the amendment that it deprives gays and lesbians even of the protection of general laws and policies that prohibit arbitrary discrimination in governmental and private settings.... At some point in the systematic administration of these laws, an official must determine whether homosexuality is an arbitrary and thus forbidden basis for decision. Yet a decision to that effect would itself amount to a policy prohibiting discrimination on the basis of homosexuality, and so would appear to be no more valid under Amendment 2 than the specific prohibitions against discrimination the state court held invalid.

If this consequence follows from Amendment 2, as its broad language suggests, it would compound the constitutional difficulties the law creates. The state court did not decide whether the amendment has this effect, however, and neither need we. In the course of rejecting the argument that Amendment 2 is intended to conserve resources to fight discrimination against suspect classes, the Colorado Supreme Court made the limited observation that the amendment is not intended to affect many anti-discrimination laws protecting non-suspect classes.... In our view that does not resolve the issue. In any event, even if, as we doubt, homosexuals could find some safe harbor in laws of general application, we cannot accept the view that Amendment 2's prohibition on specific legal protections does no more than deprive homosexuals of special rights. To the contrary, the amendment imposes a special disability upon those persons alone. Homosexuals are forbidden the safeguards that others enjoy or may seek without constraint. They can obtain specific protection against discrimination only by enlisting the citizenry of Colorado to amend the state constitution or perhaps, on the State's view, by trying to pass helpful laws of general applicability. This is so no matter how local or discrete the harm, no matter how public and widespread the injury. We find nothing special in the protections Amendment 2 withholds. These are protections taken for granted by most people either because they already have them or do not need them; these are protections against exclusion from an almost limitless number of transactions and endeavors that constitute ordinary civic life in a free society.

III

The Fourteenth Amendment's promise that no person shall be denied the equal protection of the laws must co-exist with the practical necessity that most legislation classifies for one purpose or another, with resulting disadvantage to various groups or persons. *Personnel Administrator of Mass. v. Feeney*, 442 U.S. 256, 271–272 (1979); *F.S. Royster Guano Co. v. Virginia*, 253 U.S. 412, 415 (1920). We have attempted to reconcile the principle with the reality by stating that, if a law neither burdens a fundamental right nor targets a suspect class, we will uphold the legislative classification so long as it bears a rational relation to some legitimate end....

Amendment 2 fails, indeed defies, even this conventional inquiry. First, the amendment has the peculiar property of imposing a broad and undifferentiated disability on a single named group, an exceptional and, as we shall explain, invalid form of legislation. Second, its sheer breadth is so discontinuous with the reasons offered for it that the amendment seems inexplicable by anything but animus toward the class that it affects; it lacks a rational relationship to legitimate state interests.

Taking the first point, even in the ordinary equal protection case calling for the most deferential of standards, we insist on knowing the relation between the classification adopted and the object to be attained. The search for the link between classification and objective gives substance to the Equal Protection Clause; it provides guidance and discipline for the legislature, which is entitled to know what sorts of laws it can pass; and it marks the limits of our own authority. In the ordinary case, a law will be sustained if it can be said to advance a legitimate government interest, even if the law seems unwise or works to the disadvantage of a particular group, or if the rationale for it seems tenuous. See *New Orleans v. Dukes*, 427 U.S. 297 (1976) (tourism benefits justified classification favoring pushcart vendors of certain longevity); *Williamson v. Lee Optical of Okla., Inc.*, 348 U.S. 483 (1955) (assumed health concerns justified law favoring optometrists over opticians).... The laws challenged in the cases just cited were narrow enough in scope and grounded in a sufficient factual context for us to ascertain that there existed some relation between the classification and the purpose it served. By requiring that the classification bear a rational relationship to an independent and legitimate legislative end, we ensure that classifications are not drawn for the purpose of disadvantaging the group burdened by the law. See *United States Railroad Retirement Bd. v. Fritz*, 449 U.S. 166, 181 (1980) (Stevens, J., concurring). ("If the adverse impact on the disfavored class is an apparent aim of the legislature, its impartiality would be suspect.")

Amendment 2 confounds this normal process of judicial review. It is at once too narrow and too broad. It identifies persons by a single trait and then denies them protection across the board. The resulting disqualification of a class of persons from the right to seek specific protection from the law is unprecedented in our jurisprudence....

It is not within our constitutional tradition to enact laws of this sort. Central both to the idea of the rule of law and to our own Constitution's guarantee of equal protection is the principle that government and each of its parts remain open on impartial terms to all who seek its assistance. "Equal protection of the laws is not achieved through indiscriminate imposition of inequalities." *Sweatt v. Painter*, 339 U.S. 629, 635 (1950) (quoting *Shelley v. Kraemer*, 334 U.S. 1, 22 [1948]). Respect for this principle explains why laws singling out a certain class of citizens for disfavored legal status or general hardships are rare. A law declaring that in general it shall be more difficult for one group of citizens than for all others to seek aid from the government is itself a denial of equal protection of the laws in the most literal sense....

...[L]aws of the kind now before us raise the inevitable inference that the disadvantage imposed is born of animosity toward the class of persons affected. "[I]f the constitutional conception of 'equal protection of the laws' means anything, it must at the very least mean that a bare...desire to harm a politically unpopular group cannot constitute a legitimate governmental interest." *Department of Agriculture v. Moreno*, 413 U.S. 528, 534 (1973). Even laws enacted for broad and ambitious purposes often can be explained by reference to legitimate public policies which justify the incidental disadvantages they impose on certain persons. Amendment 2, however, in making a general announcement that gays and lesbians shall not have any particular protections from the law, inflicts on them immediate, continuing, and real injuries that outrun and belie any legitimate justifications that maybe claimed for it. We conclude that, in addition to the far-reaching deficiencies of Amendment 2 that we have noted, the principles it offends, in another sense, are conventional and venerable; a law must bear a rational relationship to a legitimate governmental purpose, *Kadrmas v. Dickinson Public Schools*, 487 U.S. 450, 462 (1988), and Amendment 2 does not.

The primary rationale the State offers for Amendment 2 is respect for other citizens' freedom of association, and in particular the liberties of landlords or employers who have personal or religious objections to homosexuality. Colorado also cites its interest in conserving resources to fight discrimination against other groups. The breadth of the Amendment is so far removed from these particular justifications that we find it impossible to credit them. We cannot say that Amendment 2 is directed to any identifiable legitimate purpose or discrete objective. It is a status-based enactment divorced from any factual context from which we could discern a relationship to legitimate state interests; it is a classification of persons undertaken for its own sake, something the Equal Protection Clause does not permit....

We must conclude that Amendment 2 classifies homosexuals not to further a proper legislative end but to make them unequal to everyone else. This Colorado cannot do. A State cannot so deem a class of persons a stranger to its laws. Amendment 2 violates the Equal Protection Clause, and the judgment of the Supreme Court of Colorado is affirmed. It is so ordered.

Justice Scalia, with whom The Chief Justice and Justice Thomas join, dissenting.

The Court has mistaken a Kulturkampf for a fit of spite. The constitutional amendment before us here is not the manifestation of a "bare...desire to harm" homosexuals, but is rather a modest attempt by seemingly tolerant Coloradans to preserve traditional sexual mores against the efforts of a politically powerful minority to revise those mores through use of the laws. That objective, and the means chosen to achieve it, are not only unimpeachable under any constitutional doctrine hitherto pronounced (hence the opinion's heavy reliance upon principles of righteousness rather than judicial holdings); they have been specifically approved by the Congress of the United States and by this Court.

In holding that homosexuality cannot be singled out for disfavorable treatment, the Court contradicts a decision, unchallenged here, pronounced only 10 years ago, see *Bowers v. Hardwick*, 478 U.S. 186 (1986), and places the prestige of this institution behind the proposition that opposition to homosexuality is as reprehensible as racial or religious bias. Whether it is or not is precisely the cultural debate that gave rise to the Colorado constitutional amendment (and to the preferential laws against which the amendment was directed). Since the Constitution of the United States says nothing about this subject, it is left to be resolved by normal democratic means, including the democratic adoption of provisions in state constitutions. This Court has no business imposing upon all Americans the resolution favored by the elite class from which the Members of this institution are selected, pronouncing that "animosity" toward homosexuality, is evil. I vigorously dissent.

I

Let me first discuss Part II of the Court's opinion, its longest section, which is devoted to rejecting the State's arguments that Amendment 2 "puts gays and lesbians in the same position as all other persons," and "does no more than deny homosexuals special rights." The Court concludes that this reading of Amendment 2's language is "implausible."

In reaching this conclusion, the Court considers it unnecessary to decide the validity of the State's argument that Amendment 2 does not deprive homosexuals of the "protection [afforded by] general laws and policies that prohibit arbitrary discrimination in governmental and private settings." ... I agree that we need not resolve that dispute, because the Supreme Court of Colorado has resolved it for us. In *Evans v. Romer*, 882P. 2d 1335 (1994), the Colorado court stated: "[I]t is significant to note that Colorado law currently proscribes discrimination against persons who are not suspect classes, including discrimination based on age,...marital or family status,...veterans' status,... and for any legal, off-duty conduct such as smoking tobacco,..." Of course Amendment 2 is not intended to have any effect on this legislation, but seeks only to prevent the adoption of anti-discrimination laws intended to protect gays, lesbians, and bisexuals.... The clear import of the Colorado court's conclusion that it is not affected is that "general laws and policies that prohibit arbitrary discrimination" would continue to prohibit discrimination on the basis of homosexual conduct as well. This analysis, which is fully in accord with (indeed, follows inescapably from) the text of the constitutional provision, lays to rest such horribles, raised in the course of oral argument, as the prospect that assaults upon homosexuals could not be prosecuted. The amendment prohibits special treatment of homosexuals, and nothing more. It would not affect, for example, a requirement of state law that pensions be paid to all retiring state employees with a certain length of service; homosexual employees, as well as others, would be entitled to that benefit. But it would prevent the State or any municipality from making death-benefit payments to the "life partner" of a homosexual when it does not make such payments to the long-time roommate of a nonhomosexual employee....

Despite all of its hand-wringing about the potential effect of Amendment 2 on general anti-discrimination laws, the Court's opinion ultimately does not dispute all this, but assumes it to be true.... The only denial of equal treatment it contends homosexuals have suffered is this: They may not obtain preferential treatment without amending the state constitution. That is to say, the principle underlying the Court's opinion is that one who is accorded equal treatment under the laws, but cannot as readily as others obtain preferential treatment under the laws, has been denied equal protection of the laws. If merely stating this alleged "equal protection" violation does not suffice to refute it, our constitutional jurisprudence has achieved terminal silliness.

The central thesis of the Court's reasoning is that any group is denied equal protection when, to obtain advantage (or, presumably, to avoid disadvantage), it must have recourse to a more general and hence more difficult level of political decision making than others. The world has never heard of such a principle, which is why the Court's opinion is so long on emotive utterance and so short on relevant legal citation. And it seems to me most unlikely that any multilevel democracy can function under such a principle. For whenever a disadvantage is imposed, or conferral of a benefit is prohibited, at one of the higher levels of democratic decision making (i.e., by the state legislature rather than local government, or by the people at large in the state constitution rather than the legislature), the affected group has (under this theory) been denied equal protection. To take the simplest of examples, consider a state law prohibiting the award of municipal contracts to relatives of mayors or city councilmen. Once such a law is passed, the group composed of such relatives must, in order to get the benefit of city contracts, persuade the state legislature—unlike all other citizens, who need only persuade the municipality. It is ridiculous to consider this a denial of equal protection, which is why the Court's theory is unheard of.

The Court might reply that the example I have given is not a denial of equal protection only because the same "rational basis" (avoidance of corruption) which renders constitutional the substantive discrimination against relatives (i.e., the fact that they alone cannot obtain city contracts) also automatically suffices to sustain what might be called the electoral-procedural discrimination against them (i.e., the fact that they must go to the state level to get this changed). This is of course a perfectly reasonable response, and would explain why "electoral-procedural discrimination" has not hitherto been heard of: a law that is valid in its substance is automatically valid in its level of enactment. But the Court cannot afford to make this argument, for as I shall discuss next, there is no doubt of a rational basis for the substance of the prohibition at issue here. The Court's entire novel theory rests upon the proposition that there is something special—something that cannot be justified by normal "rational basis" analysis—in making a disadvantaged group (or a nonpreferred group) resort to a higher decision making level. That proposition finds no support in law or logic.

II

I turn next to whether there was a legitimate rational basis for the substance of the constitutional amendment—for the prohibition of special protection for homosexuals. It is unsurprising that the Court avoids discussion of this question, since the answer is so obviously yes. The case most relevant to the issue before us today is not even mentioned in the Court's opinion: In *Bowers v. Hardwick*, 478 U.S. 186 (1986), we held that the Constitution does not prohibit what virtually all States had done from the founding of the Republic until very recent years—making homosexual conduct a crime. That holding is unassailable, except by those who think that the Constitution changes to suit current fashions. But in any event it is a given in the present case: Respondents' briefs did not urge overruling *Bowers*, and at oral argument respondents' counsel expressly disavowed any intent to seek such overruling. If it is constitutionally permissible for a State to make homosexual conduct criminal, surely it is constitutionally permissible for a State to enact other laws merely disfavoring homosexual conduct. (As the Court of Appeals for the District of Columbia Circuit has aptly put it: "If the Court [in *Bowers*] was unwilling to object to state laws that criminalize the behavior that defines the class, it is hardly open…to conclude that state sponsored discrimination against the class is invidious. After all, there can hardly be more palpable discrimination against a class than making the conduct that defines the class criminal." *Padula v. Webster*, 822F. 2d 97, 103 [1987].) And a fortiori it is constitutionally permissible for a State to adopt a provision not even disfavoring homosexual conduct, but merely prohibiting all levels of state government from bestowing special protections upon homosexual conduct. Respondents (who, unlike the Court, cannot afford the luxury of ignoring inconvenient precedent) counter *Bowers* with the argument that a greater-includes-the-lesser rationale cannot justify Amendment 2's application to individuals who do not engage in homosexual acts, but are merely of homosexual "orientation." Some courts of appeals have concluded that, with respect to laws of this sort at least, that is a distinction without a difference. See *Equality Foundation of Greater Cincinnati, Inc. v. Cincinnati*, 54F. 3d 261, 267 (CA6 1995) ("[F]or purposes of these proceedings, it is virtually impossible to distinguish or separate individuals of a particular orientation which predisposes them toward a particular sexual conduct from those who actually engage in that particular type of sexual conduct"); *Steffan v. Perry*, 41 F. 3d 677, 689–690 (CADC 1994). The Supreme Court of Colorado itself appears to be of this view. See 882 P. 2d, at 1349–1350 ("Amendment 2 targets this class of persons based on four characteristics: sexual orientation; conduct; practices; and relationships. Each characteristic provides a potentially different way of identifying that class of persons who are gay, lesbian, or bisexual. These four characteristics are not truly severable from one another because each provides nothing more than a different way of identifying the same class of persons").

But assuming that, in Amendment 2, a person of homosexual "orientation" is someone who does not engage in homosexual conduct but merely has a tendency or desire to do so, *Bowers* still suffices to establish a rational basis for the provision. If it is rational to criminalize the conduct, surely it is rational to deny special favor and protection to those with a self-avowed tendency or desire to engage in the conduct. Indeed, where criminal sanctions are not involved, homosexual "orientation" is an acceptable stand-in for homosexual conduct. A State "does not violate the Equal Protection Clause merely because the classifications made by its laws are imperfect," *Dandridge v. Williams*, 397 U.S. 471, 485 (1970). Just as a policy barring the hiring of methadone users as transit employees does not violate equal protection simply because some methadone users pose no threat to passenger safety, see *New York City Transit Authority v. Beazer*, 440 U.S. 568 (1979), and just as a mandatory retirement age of 50 for police officers does not violate equal protection even though it prematurely ends the careers of many policemen over 50 who still have the capacity to do the job, see *Massachusetts Bd. of Retirement v. Murgia*, 427 U.S. 307 (1976) (per curiam), Amendment 2 is not constitutionally invalid simply because it could have been drawn more precisely so as to withdraw special antidiscrimination protections only from those of homosexual "orientation" who actually engage in homosexual conduct. As Justice Kennedy wrote, when he was on the Court of Appeals, in a case involving discharge of homosexuals from the Navy: "Nearly any statute which classifies people may be irrational as applied in particular cases. Discharge of the particular plaintiffs before us would be rational, under minimal scrutiny, not because their particular cases present the dangers which justify Navy policy, but instead because the general policy of discharging all homosexuals is rational." *Beller v. Middendorf*, 632F. 2d 788, 808–809, n. 20 (CA9 1980) (citation omitted)....

Moreover, even if the provision regarding homosexual "orientation" were invalid, respondents' challenge to Amendment 2—which is a facial challenge—must fail. "A facial challenge to a legislative Act is, of course, the most difficult challenge to mount successfully, since the challenger must establish that no set of circumstances exists under which the Act would be valid." *United States v. Salerno*, 481 U.S. 739, 745 (1987). It would not be enough for respondents to establish (if they could) that Amendment 2 is unconstitutional as applied to those of homosexual "orientation"; since, under *Bowers*, Amendment 2 is unquestionably constitutional as applied to those who engage in homosexual conduct, the facial challenge cannot succeed. Some individuals of homosexual orientation who do not engage in homosexual acts might successfully bring an as-applied challenge to Amendment 2, but so far as the record indicates, none of the respondents is such a person....

III

The foregoing suffices to establish what the Court's failure to cite any case remotely in point would lead one to suspect: No principle set forth in the Constitution, nor even any imagined by this Court in the past 200 years, prohibits what Colorado has done here. But the case for Colorado is much stronger than that. What it has done is not only unprohibited, but eminently reasonable, with close, congressionally approved precedent in earlier constitutional practice.

First, as to its eminent reasonableness. The Court's opinion contains grim, disapproving hints that Coloradans have been guilty of animus or animosity toward homosexuality, as though that has been established as Unamerican. Of course it is our moral heritage that one should not hate any human being or class of human beings. But I had thought that one could consider certain conduct reprehensible—murder, for example, or polygamy, or cruelty to animals—and could exhibit even animus toward such conduct. Surely that is the only sort of animus at issue here: moral disapproval of homosexual conduct, the same sort of moral disapproval that produced the centuries-old criminal laws that we held constitutional in *Bowers*. The Colorado amendment does not, to speak entirely precisely, prohibit giving favored status to people who are homosexuals; they can be favored for many reasons—for example, because they are senior citizens or members of racial minorities. But it prohibits giving them favored status because of their homosexual conduct—that is, it prohibits favored status for homosexuality.

But though Coloradans are, as I say, entitled to be hostile toward homosexual conduct, the fact is that the degree of hostility reflected by Amendment 2 is the smallest conceivable. The Court's portrayal of Coloradans as a society fallen victim to pointless, hate-filled-gay-bashing is so false as to be comical. Colorado not only is one of the 25 States that have repealed their antisodomy laws, but was among the first to do so.... But the society that eliminates criminal punishment for homosexual acts does not necessarily abandon the view that homosexuality is morally wrong and socially harmful; often, abolition simply reflects the view that enforcement of such criminal laws involves unseemly intrusion into the intimate lives of citizens....

There is a problem, however, which arises when criminal sanction of homosexuality is eliminated but moral and social disapprobation of homosexuality is meant to be retained. The Court cannot be unaware of that problem; it is evident in many cities of the country, and occasionally bubbles to the surface of the news, in heated political disputes over such matters as the introduction into local schools of books teaching that homosexuality is an optional and fully acceptable alternate lifestyle. The problem (a problem, that is, for those who wish to retain social disapprobation of homosexuality) is that, because those who engage in homosexual conduct tend to reside in disproportionate numbers in certain communities,... have high disposable income,... and of course care about homosexual rights issues much more ardently than the public at large, they possess political power much greater than their numbers, both locally and statewide. Quite understandably, they devote this political power to achieving not merely a grudging social toleration, but full social acceptance, of homosexuality.... By the time Coloradans were asked to vote on Amendment 2, their exposure to homosexuals' quest for social endorsement was not limited to newspaper accounts of happenings in places such as New York, Los Angeles, San Francisco, and Key West. Three Colorado cities—Aspen, Boulder, and Denver—had enacted ordinances that listed sexual orientation as an impermissible ground for discrimination, equating the moral disapproval of homosexual conduct with racial and religious bigotry. The phenomenon had even appeared statewide: the Governor of Colorado had signed an executive order pronouncing that "in the State of Colorado we recognize the diversity in our pluralistic society and strive to bring an end to discrimination in any form," and directing state agency-heads to ensure non-discrimination in hiring and promotion based on, among other things, sexual orientation. Executive Order No. D0035 (Dec. 10, 1990). I do not mean to be critical of these legislative successes; homosexuals are as entitled to use the legal system for reinforcement of their moral sentiments as are the rest of society. But they are subject to being countered by lawful, democratic countermeasures as well.

That is where Amendment 2 came in. It sought to counter both the geographic concentration and the disproportionate political power of homosexuals by (1) resolving the controversy at the statewide level, and (2) making the election a single-issue contest for both sides. It put directly, to all the citizens of the State, the question: Should homosexuality be given special protection? They answered no. The Court today asserts that this most democratic of procedures is unconstitutional. Lacking any cases to establish that facially absurd proposition, it simply asserts that it must be unconstitutional, because it has never happened before. [Amendment 2] identifies persons by a single trait and then denies them protection across the board. The resulting disqualification of a class of persons from the right to seek specific protection from the law is unprecedented in our jurisprudence. The absence of precedent for Amendment 2 is itself instructive....

"It is not within our constitutional tradition to enact laws of this sort. Central both to the idea of the rule of law and to our own Constitution's guarantee of equal protection is the principle that government and each of its parts remain open on impartial terms to all who seek its assistance." (ante) As I have noted above, this is proved false every time a state law prohibiting or disfavoring certain conduct is passed, because such a law prevents the adversely affected group—whether drug addicts, or smokers, or gun owners, or motorcyclists—from changing the policy thus established in each of [the] parts of the State. What the Court says is even demonstrably false at the constitutional level. The Eighteenth Amendment to the Federal Constitution, for example, deprived those who drank alcohol not only of the power to alter the policy of prohibition locally or through state legislation, but even of the power to alter it through state constitutional amendment or federal legislation. The Establishment Clause of the First Amendment prevents theocrats from having their way by converting their fellow citizens at the local, state, or federal statutory level; as does the Republican Form of Government Clause prevent monarchists.

But there is a much closer analogy, one that involves precisely the effort by the majority of citizens to preserve its view of sexual morality statewide, against the efforts of a geographically concentrated and politically powerful minority to undermine it. The constitutions of the States of Arizona, Idaho, New Mexico, Oklahoma, and Utah to this day contain provisions stating that polygamy is forever prohibited.... Polygamists, and those who have a polygamous "orientation," have been singled out by these provisions for much more severe treatment than merely denial of favored status; and that treatment can only be changed by achieving amendment of the state constitutions. The Court's disposition today suggests that these provisions are unconstitutional, and that polygamy must be permitted in these States on a state-legislated, or perhaps even local-option, basis—unless, of course, polygamists for some reason have fewer constitutional rights than homosexuals.

The United States Congress, by the way, required the inclusion of these antipolygamy provisions in the constitutions of Arizona, New Mexico, Oklahoma, and Utah, as a condition of their admission to statehood.... Idaho adopted the constitutional provision on its own, but the 51st Congress, which admitted Idaho into the Union, found its constitution to be "republican in form and...in conformity with the Constitution of the United States." Act of Admission of Idaho, 26 Stat. 215. Thus, this "singling out" of the sexual practices of a single group for statewide, democratic vote so utterly alien to our constitutional system, the Court would have us believe—has not only happened, but has received the explicit approval of the United States Congress....

This Court cited Beason with approval as recently as 1993, in an opinion authored by the same Justice who writes for the Court today. That opinion said: "[A]dverse impact will not always lead to a finding of impermissible targeting. For example, a social harm may have been a legitimate concern of government for reasons quite apart from discrimination.... See, e.g.,... *Davis v. Beason*, 133 U.S. 333 (1890)." *Church of Lukumi Babalu Aye, Inc. v. Hialeah*, 508 U.S. 520, 535 (1993). It remains to be explained how 501 of the

Idaho Revised Statutes was not an impermissible targeting of polygamists, but (the much more mild) Amendment 2 is an impermissible targeting of homosexuals. Has the Court concluded that the perceived social
harm of polygamy is a legitimate concern of government, and the perceived social harm of homosexuality is not?

IV

I strongly suspect that the answer to the last question is yes, which
leads me to the last point I wish to make: The Court today, announcing
that Amendment 2 "defies...conventional [constitutional] inquiry," and
"confounds [the] normal process of judicial review," *ante*, employs a constitutional theory heretofore unknown to frustrate Colorado's reasonable
effort to preserve traditional American moral values. The Court's stern
disapproval of "animosity" towards homosexuality might be compared
with what an earlier Court (including the revered Justices Harlan and
Bradley) said in *Murphy v. Ramsey*, 114 U.S. 15 (1885), rejecting a constitutional challenge to a United States statute that denied the franchise in federal territories to those who engaged in polygamous cohabitation:

> [C]ertainly no legislation can be supposed more wholesome and nec-
> essary in the founding of a free, self-governing commonwealth, fit to
> take rank as one of the co-ordinate States of the Union, than that which
> seeks to establish it on the basis of the idea of the family, as consisting in
> and springing from the union for life of one man and one woman in the
> holy estate of matrimony; the sure foundation of all that is stable and
> noble in our civilization; the best guaranty of that reverent morality
> which is the source of all beneficent progress in social and political
> improvement. *Id.,* at 45.

I would not myself indulge in such official praise for heterosexual
monogamy, because I think it no business of the courts (as opposed to the
political branches) to take sides in this culture war.

But the Court today has done so, not only by inventing a novel and
extravagant constitutional doctrine to take the victory away from traditional forces, but even by verbally disparaging as bigotry adherence to
traditional attitudes. To suggest, for example, that this constitutional
amendment springs from nothing more than "a bare...desire to harm a
politically unpopular group,"...is nothing short of insulting. (It is also
nothing short of preposterous to call "politically unpopular" a group
which enjoys enormous influence in American media and politics, and
which, as the trial court here noted, though composing no more than 4%
of the population had the support of 46% of the voters on Amendment 2,
see App. to Pet. for Cert. C-18.)

When the Court takes sides in the culture wars, it tends to be with the knights rather than the villeins—and more specifically with the Templars, reflecting the views and values of the lawyer class from which the Court's Members are drawn. How that class feels about homosexuality will be evident to anyone who wishes to interview job applicants at virtually any of the Nation's law schools. The interviewer may refuse to offer a job because the applicant is a Republican; because he is an adulterer; because he went to the wrong prep school or belongs to the wrong country club; because he eats snails; because he is a womanizer; because she wears real-animal fur; or even because he hates the Chicago Cubs. But if the interviewer should wish not to be an associate or partner of an applicant because he disapproves of the applicant's homosexuality, then he will have violated the pledge which the Association of American Law Schools requires all its member-schools to exact from job interviewers: "assurance of the employer's willingness" to hire homosexuals. By laws of the Association of American Law Schools, Inc. 6–4(b); Executive Committee Regulations of the Association of American Law Schools 6.19, in 1995 Handbook, Association of American Law Schools. This law-school view of what prejudices must be stamped out may be contrasted with the more plebeian attitudes that apparently still prevail in the United States Congress, which has been unresponsive to repeated attempts to extend to homosexuals the protections of federal civil rights laws, see, e.g., Employment Non-Discrimination Act of 1994, S. 2238,103d Cong., 2d Sess. (1994); Civil Rights Amendments of 1975, H.R. 5452, 94th Cong., 1st Sess. (1975), and which took the pains to exclude them specifically from the Americans With Disabilities Act of 1990, see 42 U.S.C. 12211(a) (1988 ed., Supp. V).

* * *

Today's opinion has no foundation in American constitutional law, and barely pretends to. The people of Colorado have adopted an entirely reasonable provision which does not even disfavor homosexuals in any substantive sense, but merely denies them preferential treatment. Amendment 2 is designed to prevent piecemeal deterioration of the sexual morality favored by a majority of Coloradans, and is not only an appropriate means to that legitimate end, but a means that Americans have employed before. Striking it down is an act, not of judicial judgment, but of political will. I dissent.

HISTORY, HOMOSEXUALITY, AND POLITICAL VALUES: SEARCHING FOR THE HIDDEN DETERMINANTS OF *BOWERS v. HARDWICK*

Anne B. Goldstein

On August 3, 1982, Michael Hardwick was arrested in his own bedroom for making love with another consenting adult, and charged with sodomy.[1] Hardwick and his male lover spent ten humiliating hours in jail, but the district attorney decided not to prosecute them.[2] In response to this experience with Georgia's criminal justice system, Hardwick filed a federal civil rights challenge to the statute that made his private lovemaking a crime, alleging that it violated his "fundamental right of privacy." In considering this case, the various courts analyzed the issues he raised under the modern cases establishing a constitutional right of privacy. Writing for a majority of five, Justice White concluded that the constitutional right of privacy described by the Court's prior cases did not extend to "homosexual sodomy." Writing for the four dissenters, Justice Black-

---

mun argued that Hardwick's lovemaking was within that private sphere of individual liberty kept largely beyond the reach of the state.

The Court's focus on "constitutional privacy" doctrine obscured two other important determinants of the opinions in *Hardwick*: the Justices' underlying political philosophies and their understandings of the act for which Hardwick was arrested. The Justices disagreed about more than just the interpretation of prior cases and their application to new facts. They disagreed about the basic meaning of the terms "privacy" and "homosexuality," and, although they did not frame their dispute in these terms, they disagreed over fundamental political values. ...

THE JUSTICES' DOCTRINAL DISAGREEMENTS

Writing for the majority, Justice White announced that the constitutional right of privacy did not protect even private and consensual homosexual sodomy. White narrowly limited the Court's earlier privacy cases to their facts, and refused to extend them, arguing that substantive due process rights not found in the text of the Constitution, such as the right of privacy, should not represent merely the Justice's own values. Such rights must either be " 'deeply rooted in this Nation's history and tradition,'" or " 'implicit in the concept of ordered liberty,' such that 'neither liberty nor justice would exist if [they] were sacrificed.'" Because Justice White believed that every state that ratified the Bill of Rights and all but five of those that ratified the Fourteenth Amendment proscribed homosexual sodomy, he perceived any claim that homosexual sodomy involved a "substantive due process" right to be "facetious." White concluded that recognizing a fundamental right to "homosexual sodomy" would exceed the Court's institutional limits. Because Hardwick had no fundamental right to engage in homosexual sodomy, the Court sought merely a rational basis for Georgia's statute. White's opinion held that the "presumed belief of a majority of the electorate in Georgia that homosexual sodomy is immoral and unacceptable" was sufficient justification for the law. Writing separately, Chief Justice Burger emphasized "ancient roots" of proscriptions against "homosexual sodomy."

In dissent, Justice Blackmun rejected the majority's framing of the issue. For Blackmun, the case involved not merely a right to perform homosexual sodomy, but "the fundamental interest all individuals have in controlling the nature of their intimate associations with others," or even more broadly, " 'the right to be let alone.'" Blackmun articulated two reasons for framing the issues expansively. First, he thought that because the statute used anatomical rather than gender-based proscriptions, it should not be tested "as applied" to homosexuals alone. Selective enforcement of Georgia's statute might confer standing on a "practicing homosexual," but no enforcement pattern could narrow the language of a statute that made both gender and marital status irrelevant. Second, Justice Blackmun believed "sexual intimacy" to be "a sensitive, key relationship of human existence, central to family life, community welfare, and the development of human personality." He thought it as "central a part of an individual's life" as the activities already protected by the constitutional right of privacy. Although he would have applied a stricter test, Blackmun argued that the Georgia law lacked even a rational basis: Georgia had not proved that private, consensual homosexual sodomy caused any form of tangible harm. Blackmun also emphatically rejected the argument that "ancient" notions of immorality insulate sodomy statutes from review.

Justice Stevens' dissent took a different approach. It argued that, because prohibitions against sodomy applied historically to married and unmarried participants, of the same and of different sexes, the Court's rationale for upholding sodomy statutes must apply just as broadly. Stevens therefore considered whether Georgia could enact a neutral law prohibiting sodomy by all persons without exception, and, if not, whether it could save the statute from being found unconstitutional by selectively enforcing it against homosexuals. Stevens concluded that neither course was permissable, because the "essential 'liberty'" recognized in the Court's prior privacy cases encompassed the right of both married and unmarried heterosexual couples to engage in nonreproductive sexual conduct, and because every citizen has the same subjective interest in such liberty. Stevens could find no neutral and legitimate interest to support selectively enforcing a generally applicable sodomy law against homosexuals; he thought Georgia's asserted interest amounted to nothing more substantial than "habitual dislike...or ignorance." Indeed, Stevens argued that the statute's language demonstrated that the Georgia electorate did not believe homosexual sodomy to be either more immoral or more unacceptable than heterosexual sodomy. Similarly, the Georgia prosecutor's failure to prosecute Hardwick, even though Hardwick acknowledged that he intended to continue to engage in the prohibited conduct, showed that the prosecutor did not believe that homosexuals should necessarily be punished for violating the statute. Stevens concluded that Georgia's failure to "provide the Court with any support for the conclusion that homosexual sodomy, *simpliciter*, is considered unacceptable conduct in that State" deprived the statute of a rational basis.

COMPETING CONCEPTIONS OF "PRIVACY" AND "HOMOSEXUALITY"

The doctrinal disputes among the Justices in *Hardwick* proceeded from more basic differences regarding the meanings of "privacy" and "homosexuality." This section explores that level of disagreement.

"Privacy"

"Privacy" is an evocative word, but courts have been unable to give it precise meaning.[3] When Michael Hardwick's lawyers claimed that his arrest violated his "right to privacy," they explicitly compared his desire to be uninterrupted in sexual activity in his own bedroom to the desire of a heterosexual couple to use birth control without interference, or the desire of a woman to terminate an early pregnancy. The Court therefore faced two basic and related questions: What was the nature of the "private" activities that the Court had protected in past decisions? And what was the nature of the act for which Hardwick had been arrested? If the Court understood Hardwick's sexual act as similar to other activities protected under the "constitutional right of privacy," his challenge should have succeeded. If it saw his sexual act as dissimilar from those earlier protected activities, his claim should have failed. Yet Justice White's majority opinion did not explicitly address either question. It said only, "we think it evident that none of the rights announced in those cases bears any resemblance to the claimed constitutional right...asserted in this case."

Justice White's conclusion can be self-evident only to those who share his implicit, unarticulated assumptions about the nature of homosexuality and "homosexual sodomy." Recognizing and evaluating the diverse ways in which the Justices conceptualized homosexuality is therefore crucial to understanding their disagreements over this case. This task does not involve an assessment of judicial attitudes toward a known, objectively existing entity. Rather, the task is to discern the paradigms each Justice used to understand the essential nature of Hardwick's activity on that August morning. Although what Hardwick had done was clear, evaluating whether an arrest was a constitutionally permissible response required a more profound understanding of his activity than accurate fact-finding alone can provide.

FIVE CONCEPTIONS OF "HOMOSEXUALITY"

The majority opinion is written as if the term "homosexual" solved, rather than confused, the problem of evaluating Hardwick's actions in terms of his constitutional rights. Yet, like "privacy," "homosexuality" lacks an unambiguous, uncontroversial meaning. In the *Hardwick* opinions, one may discern at least five very different conceptions of "homosexuality": that it is (1) immoral, (2) criminally harmful, (3) a manifestation of illness, (4) an identity, and (5) a normal variation of human sexuality. The first two of these focus primarily upon actions, the last three upon desire.

The sources for the Justices' conceptions of homosexuality were equally various. Justice White and Chief Justice Burger relied upon what they claimed were historical conceptions of "homosexual sodomy" that they assumed informed the framers' vision of the Bill of Rights and the Fourteenth Amendment. Claiming to be uninfluenced by their personal preferences, these Justices also relied on the "presumed belief of a majority of the electorate in Georgia that homosexuality is immoral." By comparing "homosexual sodomy" to other crimes, and relying on other sodomy statutes in effect in 1791 and 1868, Justice White also implied that homosexual sodomy is criminally harmful. Similarly, Chief Justice Burger's references to "millennia of moral teaching" implied that homosexuality is immoral. Justice Powell's concern that a long prison sentence for a single, private, consensual act of homosexual sodomy might violate the Eighth Amendment proscription against cruel and unusual punishment may reflect a belief that homosexuality is an illness, or a perception that it is no longer generally regarded as a serious crime.

Justices Stevens and Blackmun, in contrast, discussed the case on the assumption that "homosexuality" is a normal human variation. Justice Blackmun also linked homosexuality to personality or identity, relying on the views of "mental health professionals." Stevens ironically relied on the apparent values of the Georgia electorate and prosecutor. Each of these conceptions, and the Justices' support for them, will be evaluated in turn.

1. The Majority's Historical Justifications for the Ideas of Homosexuality as Immorality, Crime, and Illness

The majority relied heavily upon history to explain and justify the result in this case. Justice White made three historical assertions: (1) "[s]odomy was...forbidden by the laws of the original thirteen States when they ratified the Bill of Rights"; (2) "[i]n 1868, when the Fourteenth Amendment was ratified, all but 5 of the 37 States in the Union had criminal sodomy laws"; and (3) "[p]roscriptions against that conduct have ancient roots." Chief Justice Burger's concurrence forcefully elaborated Justice White's third point. Yet none of these historical statements is sufficiently accurate to guide constitutional interpretation.

a. The Framers' Intentions

Justice White's and Chief Justice Burger's most important justification for viewing "homosexual" sodomy as immoral was that this view was shared by the framers. Some commentators argue that attempts to know and follow the framers' intent are necessarily misguided, whatever the method. Yet even if the goal of discerning historical attitudes in order to follow the framers' intent is accepted, the majority's depiction of eighteenth- and nineteenth-century views of sodomy is too flawed to guide constitutional interpretation.

In 1791, when the Bill of Rights was adopted, three states' criminal statutes singled out sexual acts between men for special condemnation.[4] Eight of the other states' statutes proscribed "buggery" or "sodomy" without reference to the gender of the participants.[5] Finally, in one state, no statutory proscription against sodomy may have existed in 1791,[6] and in one state the historical evidence is unclear.[7]

By 1868, when the Fourteenth Amendment was ratified, no additional states had singled out sexual acts between men for special prohibition. Many states' statutes had been bowdlerized, however, and now prohibited "the crime against nature" instead of "sodomy" or "buggery." That phrase applied to acts of anal intercourse between men and women as well as between two men. Courts in at least seven of the thirty-two states Justice White found to have "criminal sodomy statutes in effect in 1868" explicitly held that these statutes did not apply to oral-genital contact. Some treatise writers explicitly included sodomy in marriage within the statutory proscription.

Thus the evidence does not support Justice White's conclusion that the framers could not have intended the Constitution to "extend a fundamental right to homosexuals to engage in acts of consensual sodomy." American sodomy laws in force when the Bill of Rights and the Fourteenth Amendment were ratified applied to acts performed by men with women as well as with one another. Only three of the thirteen original states singled out sex acts between men for proscription; the others prohibited "sodomy" and "buggery," terms denoting sex acts between men and women as well as between two men. Moreover, in both 1791 and 1868 statutes proscribing "sodomy," "buggery," and the "crime against nature," were interpreted to proscribe anal intercourse only—not fellatio, the act for which Hardwick was arrested.

b. Ancient Prohibitions and the Concept of "Homosexuality"

The majority bolstered its inferences about the framers' intentions with the claim that "[p]roscriptions against [homosexual sodomy] have ancient roots." Although literally true, the statement is misleading in two ways. First, it oversimplifies and distorts a complex historical record; second, it misuses the relatively modern concept of "homosexuality" to depict the past.

Over the course of Western history, sexual practices between men, like other sexual practices, have been tolerated as well as condemned. In Classical Greece and Rome, sexual practices between men were not uniformly condemned, and some were widely accepted; under Roman rule, even marriage between men was possible until at least 342 A.D. Sexual acts between men were also openly tolerated by both church and state during the early Middle Ages, and among the male social elite in eighteenth-century France. By ignoring ancient tolerance to focus selectively on ancient proscriptions, the majority distorted the historical record. This distortion enabled the majority to present its choice of proscription over tolerance as if it were merely fidelity to "ancient roots" and conformity with laws in force "throughout the history of Western Civilization."

The majority's use of the concept of homosexuality is flawed as well. All of the Justices seem to have assumed that "homosexuality" has been an invariant reality, outside of history. In fact, however, like most ways of describing aspects of the human condition, "homosexuality" is a cultural and historical artifact. No attitude toward "homosexuals" or "homosexuality" can really be identified before the mid-nineteenth century, because the concept did not exist until then. Before the late 1800s, sexuality—whether tolerated or condemned—was something a person did, not what he or she was. Although both the behavior and the desires we now call "homosexual" existed in earlier eras, our currently common assumption that persons who make love with others of their own sex are fundamentally different from the rest of humanity is only about one hundred years old.[8]

Even the word "homosexual" is new. It was coined in the nineteenth century to express the new idea that a person's immanent and essential nature is revealed by the gender of his desired sex partner. The concept emerged around the time that sexuality began to seem a proper object of medical, as distinguished from clerical or judicial, concern. Before the invention of "homosexuality," sexual touchings between men were determined to be licit or illicit according to criteria that applied equally to heterosexual practices, such as the parts of the body involved, the relative status of the parties, and whether the sexual drama conformed to sex role stereotypes. Although illicit sexual acts were seen as sinful, immoral, criminal, or all three, before the 1870s illicit sexual acts between men were not seen as fundamentally different from, or necessarily worse than, illicit acts between a man and a woman.

Thus, by referring to "homosexual sodomy" in ancient times, in 1791, and even in 1868, White and Burger were inserting their modern understanding of "homosexuality" anachronistically into systems of values organized on other principles, obscuring the relative novelty of the distinction between "homosexuality" and "heterosexuality" with a myth about its antiquity. Moreover, their anachronistic myth distorted the meaning "homosexuality" had for its nineteenth-century inventors. Nineteenth-century medical theories about "homosexuality" seem to have developed out of contemporaneous theories about the dangers of sexual arousal and satisfaction and the debilitating effects of masturbation. The concept was introduced as a medical category, and was intended to rebut the idea that sex between men could be either sinful or criminal. "Homosexuality," in the nineteenth century, implied that sexual inclinations toward a person of one's own sex are beyond one's control (at least without professional treatment). Using the nineteenth-century medical category of homosexuality to justify the law's treatment of sex between men as criminal thus precisely inverts the term's historical significance.

2. *The Dissenters' Justification for the Idea of Homosexuality as Normal Variation and Identity*

In order to decide this case, the Court had to choose among inconsistent paradigms for "homosexuality." The conceptions relied on by the majority do not exhaust current thinking on this issue. Alternate conceptions adopted by the dissenters treat homosexuality as an identity and as a biologically normal variation of human sexuality. The dissenters justified these views by reference to modern scientific consensus and to one tendency among contemporary values; Justice Stevens, ironically but correctly, also relied on the beliefs of the Georgia legislature, electorate, and prosecutors, as revealed by the language of the statute and the state's pattern of nonenforcement.

Like the ideas of "immorality," "crime," and "illness" discussed above, each of the dissenters' ideas reflects a particular worldview. The idea of "homosexuality as identity" seems to have been invented for self-description. In a development related to, and roughly contemporaneous with, the invention of "homosexuality" as a medical category, some lay people adapted the idea to understand themselves and to seek societal tolerance. These self-described homosexuals did not always accept the medical assumption that their condition was an illness (or "perversion") requiring treatment, but they did agree that the gender of a person's desired sex partner revealed something essential about his nature.

In the 1950s, the nineteenth-century conception of homosexuality as an illness or identity began to be challenged by a new concept: "homosexuality as normal variation." This idea combined the pre-nineteenth-century assumption that a person's sexuality should be evaluated without considering the gender of his object choice with the twentieth-century notion that sexual expression is good and sexual repression, bad. The idea that homosexuality is a normal manifestation of human sexuality has gradually achieved scientific acceptance; the American Psychiatric Association formally adopted this position in 1973. The idea that homosexuality constitutes a normal variation is consistent with the nineteenth-century idea of homosexuality as an identity only in that both recognize the central part sexuality plays in life. The idea that homosexuality is normal, however, implies a recognition that homosexuality and heterosexuality may not be rigidly distinct, mutually exclusive categories. It is inconsistent with the nineteenth-century notion that "a homosexual" is fundamentally a different sort of person than "a heterosexual."

The various paradigms the Justices used to understand the act for which Hardwick was arrested shaped their responses to his assertion that he was protected by a constitutional right of privacy. The Justices who understood homosexuality to be immoral held it to be therefore utterly unlike the more conventional personal and family interests prior cases had protected, whereas the Justices who understood homosexuality to be normal analogized Hardwick's act to other forms of "intimate association." All of the Justices drew their conceptions of homosexuality from among paradigms current in contemporary society, although the majority's historical justification for its choice of meaning was deeply flawed.

SUBTEXT AND TEXT: THE POLITICAL PHILOSOPHIES UNDERLYING *BOWERS v. HARDWICK*

The Justices' debate over the scope of constitutional "privacy" masked not only disagreement about the nature of Hardwick's activity, but also a dispute over fundamental values. Two competing political philosophies, classical conservatism and classical liberalism, respectively, underlie the Supreme Court majority and dissenting opinions.[9] The *Hardwick* majority accepted Georgia's argument that even irrational popular prejudices should be enforced in order to preserve the very existence of society, because the prejudices may embody ancient wisdom. This argument resembles the classical conservativism of Edmund Burke and FitzJames Stephen.[10] Justice Blackmun's dissent implied that an individual's right to behave as he chooses may be limited only in order to prevent him from causing harm to others, a view reminiscent of the classical liberalism of Jeremy Bentham and John Stuart Mill.[11] Disputes over similar issues in other contexts have been framed in these terms, most notably the extended debate between Professor H.L.A. Hart[12] and Lord Patrick Devlin[13] when the Wolfenden Committee recommended in 1957 that criminal penalties for private and consensual sexual acts between men be repealed in Great Britain.[14] Thus, the Supreme Court's discussion and resolution of *Bowers v. Hardwick* was shaped by thirty years of lively public, forensic, and scholarly debate about whether consensual lovemaking between two persons of the same sex ought to be a crime....

...*Bowers v. Hardwick* reflects a battle between two incommensurable and incompatible systems of fundamental values: classical liberalism and classical conservatism.

Both liberal and conservative philosophies make single goals the touchstone of their analysis. Individual freedom is of paramount value for classical liberalism, and the continued existence of society in its present form is of paramount value for classical conservatism. However useful this technique may be for philosophical analysis, risks inhere in using either value as a rationale for deciding cases. These risks are most clearly perceived from the opposing perspective. The risks of the extreme liberal position are risks to conservative values. Taken to its logical limit, the liberal argument seems to risk anarchy, since a totally unfettered right to be left alone might undermine virtually all social control over individuals. Similarly, the risks of the extreme conservative position are risks to liberal values. At its logical limit, the conservative argument degenerates into "mere moral conservatism,"[15] preserving even manifest injustice and tyranny from change by preventing nominative criticism of traditional laws.

The disagreements between the majority and dissenting Justices in *Hardwick* demonstrate the uneasy balancing of risk characteristic of judicial decisions where these polar values dash. The resolution of any dispute pitting liberty against tradition requires a balance between potential anarchy and potential tyranny. A court's assessment of the potential risk of any result must therefore depend heavily on how the facts are construed. In *Hardwick*, each Justice's calculation of the relative dangers of a liberal or a conservative decision was determined by his or her understanding of the act for which Hardwick was arrested.

If homosexuality is intrinsically immoral, as Justice White and Chief Justice Burger implicitly asserted, a liberal decision might well be the more dangerous. Depriving the state of the power to arrest and punish an adult for engaging in intrinsically immoral behavior might undermine its power to curb other traditionally disfavored but private and consensual practices, such as suicide, drug use, adultery, and incest. The risk of a liberal decision could then be discussed in terms of a need for a limiting principle, an answer to the question: Where will it end?

If homosexuality is a normal variation, however, as the dissenters implicitly asserted, a conservative decision might easily be the more dangerous. If homosexual love is as normal as any other, a conservative decision risks government enforcement of a majority's intolerance in other sensitive areas of life as well. The relevant comparisons are then not between homosexuality and incest or suicide, but between homophobia and religious intolerance or racial animus. If a state may proscribe and punish a "sensitive, key relationship of human existence" such as sexual love, few limits remain on its control of individual autonomy, and on its imposition of majority preferences upon minorities with other values.

The Justices' assessment of the risk inherent in the classical liberal and conservative resolutions of this case in turn determined how they applied the doctrine of constitutional privacy to the facts of *Hardwick*. The Court's prior decisions invoking constitutional privacy may be interpreted in both liberal and conservative terms. One liberal interpretation of "privacy" is as "autonomy." This concept is fully consistent with the classical liberal view that individual liberty is a primary value. In contrast, one conservative interpretation of privacy is that it guarantees no more than "seclusion" for otherwise legal activities. This view is consistent with making society's unchanged continuation a primary value. Interpreting privacy as protection only for traditional relationships is conservative for the same reason. In *Hardwick*, the Justices in the majority neither explained which of these definitions of privacy they were invoking, nor articulated the understandings of homosexuality they held before they compared Hardwick's actions with the facts of prior cases. This silence obscured the underlying determinants of their opinions....

NOTES

The author thanks Howard I. Kalodner, Dean, Western New England College School of Law, for reading earlier drafts and for providing institutional support that aided in the completion of this article. She also thanks Gary Buseck, Mary Joe Frug, Molly Geraghty, James Gordon, Cathy Jones, Leora Harpaz, Kathleen Lachance, Michele Dill LaRose, Art Leavens, Stephanie Levin, Bruce Miller, Martha Minow, Dennis Pattersom, David A.J. Richards, Barry Stern, Sam Stonefield, Kathleen Sullivan, Samuel Thorne, Donna Uhlmann, and Keith Werhan for their assistance, and, above all, Zipporah B. Wiseman, without whose encouragement and support this would never have been written.

[1]Ga.Code Ann. §16–6–2(a) (1984) provides, "A person commits the offense of sodomy when he performs or submits to any sexual act involving the sex organs of one person and the mouth or anus of another. ..."

[2]Hardwick and his lover were held in a cell with about twelve other men. Jail employees repeatedly joked that they would be sexually assaulted by other inmates. See Affidavit of Michael David Hardwick, dated Sept. 19, 1982 (not filed in court; on file with the author).

[3]A "right of privacy" was first discerned in the Constitution in *Griswold v. Connecticut* (1965) (married couples' right to contraception grounded in privacy of marital relationship). Although *Griswold* cited earlier cases, it used the evocative word "privacy" to justify a new substantive due process right with only tenuous support in the text of the Constitution.

Subsequent cases have found a right of privacy in a variety of circumstances. See, e.g. *Zablocki v. Redhail* (1978) (right to remarry because marriage is "the foundation of the family"); *Moore v. City of East Cleveland* (1977) (right to live in extended family); *Planned Parenthood v. Danforth* (1976) (married woman may obtain abortion over husband's objection); *Cleveland Bd. of Educ. v. LaFeur* (1974) (mandatory maternity leave rules in public schools unconstitutional because of "freedom of personal choice in matters of marriage and family life"); *Eisenstadt v. Baird* (1972) (right to birth control); *Stanley v. Georgia* (1969) (possession of obscene matter in home protected from "unwanted governmental instrusions").

⁴These states were Connecticut, Massachusetts, and New Hampshire.

⁵These states were Delaware, New York, North Carolina, Pennsylvania, Rhode Island, South Carolina, New Jersey, and Virginia.

⁶This was Maryland.

⁷This is Georgia.

⁸Michel Foucault gave 1870 as the "convenient date" of the concept's birth. See M. Foucault, *The History of Sexuality, Volume One: An Introduction* (New York: Random House, 1978): 43.

⁹In this comment, "classical conservatism" designates the constellation of values expressed by Edmund Burke and FitzJames Stephen, based on the view that the preservation of society in its present form is of preeminent value. "Classical liberalism" designates the constellation of values expressed by Jeremy Bentham and John Stuart Mill, based on the primacy of individual freedom.

¹⁰E. Burke, *Reflections on the Revolution in France* (London: Dent/Dutton, 1935) and J.F. Stephen, *Liberty, Equality, and Fraternity* (New York: Henry Holt and Company, 1882).

¹¹J. Bentham, *An Introduction to the Principles of Morals and Legislation* (New York: Hafner Press, 1970) and J.S. Mill, *On Liberty* (Indianapolis: Hackett, 1978).

¹²H.L.A. Hart, *Law, Liberty and Morality* (Stanford, California: Stanford University Press, 1963).

¹³Lord Patrick Devlin, *The Enforcement of Morals* (London: Oxford University Press, 1965).

¹⁴*The Wolfenden Report: Report of the Committee on Homosexual Offenses and Prostitution* (American Ed. 1963).

¹⁵H.L.A. Hart: 72.

HOMOSEXUALITY AND THE "UNNATURALNESS ARGUMENT"

Burton M. Leiser

...The word "nature" has a built-in ambiguity that can lead to serious misunderstandings. When something is said to be "natural," or in conformity with "natural law" or the "law of nature," this may mean either (1) that it is in conformity with the descriptive laws of nature, or (2) that it is not artificial, that man has not imposed his will or his devices upon events or conditions as they exist or would have existed without such interference.

THE DESCRIPTIVE LAWS OF NATURE

The laws of nature, as these are understood by the scientist, differ from the laws of man. The former are purely descriptive, whereas the latter are prescriptive. When a scientist says that water boils at 212° Fahrenheit, or that the volume of a gas varies directly with the heat that is applied to it and inversely with the pressure, he means merely that as a matter of recorded and observable fact, pure water under standard conditions always boils at precisely 212° Fahrenheit, and that as a matter of observed fact, the volume of a gas rises as it is heated and falls as pressure is applied to it. These "laws" merely *describe* the manner in which physical substances *actually behave*. They differ from municipal and federal laws in that they *do not prescribe behavior*. Unlike man-made laws, natural laws are not passed by any legislator or group of legislators; they are not proclaimed or announced; they impose no obligation upon anyone or anything; their "violation" entails no penalty; and there is no reward for "following" them or "abiding by" them.... [A]ccording to the scientist, it does not make sense to speak of a natural law being violated. For if there were a true exception to a so-called law of nature, the exception would require a change in the description of those phenomena, and the "law" would have been shown to be no law at all. The laws of nature are revised as scientists discover new phenomena that require new refinements in their descriptions of the way things actually happen. In this respect they differ fundamentally from human laws, which are revised periodically by legislators who are not so interested in *describing* human behavior as they are in *prescribing* what human behavior *should be*.

THE ARTIFICIAL AS A FORM OF THE UNNATURAL

On occasion when we say that something is not natural, we mean that it is a product of human artifice. My typewriter is not a natural object, in this sense, for the substances of which it is composed have been removed from their natural state—the state in which they existed before men came along—and have been transformed by a series of chemical and physical and mechanical processes into other substances. They have been rearranged into a whole that is quite different from anything found in nature. In short, my typewriter is an artificial object.... Human laws, being artificial conventions designed to exercise a degree of control over the natural inclinations and propensities of men, may in this sense be considered to be unnatural.

Now, when theologians and moralists speak of homosexuality, contraception, abortion, and other forms of human behavior as being unnatural, and say that for that reason such behavior must be considered to be wrong, in what sense are they using the word *unnatural*? Are they saying that homosexual behavior and the use of contraceptives are contrary to the scientific laws of nature? Are they saying that they are artificial forms of behavior? Or are they using the terms *natural* and *unnatural* in some third sense?

They cannot mean that homosexual behavior (to stick to the subject presently under discussion) violates the laws of nature in the first sense, for, as we have pointed out, in *that* sense it is impossible to violate the laws of nature. Those laws, being merely descriptive of what actually does happen, would have to *include* homosexual behavior if such behavior does actually take place. Even if the defenders of the theological view that homosexuality is unnatural were to appeal to a statistical analysis by pointing out that such behavior is not normal from a statistical point of view, and therefore not what the laws of nature require, it would be open to their critics to reply that any descriptive law of nature must account for and incorporate all statistical deviations, and that the laws of nature, in this sense, do not *require anything*. These critics might also note that the best statistics available reveal that about half of all American males engage in homosexual activity at some time in their lives, and that a very large percentage of American males have exclusively homosexual relations for a fairly extensive period of time; from which it would follow that such behavior is natural, for them, at any rate, in this sense of the word *natural*.

If those who say that homosexual behavior is *unnatural* are using the term unnatural in the second sense, it is difficult to see why they should be fussing over it. Certainly nothing is intrinsically wrong with going against nature (if that is how it should be put) in this sense. That which is artificial is often far better than what is natural. Artificial homes seem, at any rate, to be more suited to human habitation and more conducive to longer life and better health than caves and other natural shelters. There are distinct advantages to the use of such unnatural (that is, artificial) amenities as clothes, furniture, and books. Although we may dream of an idyllic return to nature in our more wistful moments, we would soon discover, as Thoreau did in his attempt to escape from the artificiality of civilization, that needles and thread, knives and matches, ploughs and nails, and countless other products of human artifice are essential to human life. We would discover, as Plato pointed out in the *Republic*, that no man can be truly self-sufficient. Some of the by-products of industry are less than desirable; but neither industry itself, nor the products of industry, is intrinsically evil, even though both are unnatural in this sense of the word.

Interference with nature is not evil in itself. Nature, as some writers have put it, must be tamed. In some respects man must look upon it as an enemy to be conquered. If nature were left to its own devices, without the intervention of human artifice, men would be consumed with disease, they would be plagued by insects, they would be chained to the places where they were born with no means of swift communication or transport, and they would suffer the discomforts and the torments of wind and weather and flood and fire with no practical means of combating any of them. Interfering with nature, doing battle with nature, using human will and reason and skill to thwart what might otherwise follow from the conditions that prevail in the world, is a peculiarly human enterprise, one that can hardly be condemned merely because it does what is not natural.

Homosexual behavior can hardly be considered to be unnatural in this sense. There is nothing "artificial" about such behavior. On the contrary, it is quite natural, in this sense, to those who engage in it. And even if it were not, even if it were quite artificial, this is not in itself a ground for condemning it.

It would seem, then, that those who condemn homosexuality as an unnatural form of behavior must mean something else by the word *unnatural*, something not covered by either of the preceding definitions. A third possibility is this:

ANYTHING UNCOMMON OR ABNORMAL IS UNNATURAL

If this is what is meant by those who condemn homosexuality on the ground that it is unnatural, it is quite obvious that their condemnation cannot be accepted without further argument. For the fact that a given form of behavior is uncommon provides no justification for condemning it. Playing viola in a string quartet is no doubt an uncommon form of human behavior. I do not know what percentage of the human race engages in such behavior, or what percentage of his life any given violist devotes to such behavior, but I suspect that the number of such people must be very small indeed, and that the total number of man-hours spent in such activity would justify our calling that form of activity uncommon, abnormal (in the sense that it is statistically not the kind of thing that people are ordinarily inclined to do), and therefore unnatural, in this sense of the word. Yet there is no reason to suppose that such uncommon, abnormal behavior is, by virtue of its uncommonness, deserving of condemnation, or ethically or morally wrong. On the contrary, many forms of behavior are praised precisely because they are so uncommon. Great artists, poets, musicians, and scientists are "abnormal" in this sense; but clearly the world is better off for having them, and it would be absurd to condemn them or their activities for their failure to be common and normal. If homosexual behavior is wrong, then, it must be for some reason other than its "unnaturalness" in this sense of the word.

ANY USE OF AN ORGAN OR AN INSTRUMENT THAT IS CONTRARY TO ITS PRINCIPAL PURPOSE OR FUNCTION IS UNNATURAL

Every organ and every instrument—perhaps even every creature—has a function to perform, one for which it is particularly designed. Any use of those instruments and organs that is consonant with their purposes is natural and proper, but any use that is inconsistent with their principal functions is unnatural and improper, and to that extent, evil or harmful. Human teeth, for example, are admirably designed for their principal functions—biting and chewing the kinds of food suitable for human consumption. But they are not particularly well suited for prying the caps from beer bottles. If they are used for the latter purpose, which is not natural to them, they are liable to crack or break under the strain. The abuse of one's teeth leads to their destruction and to a consequent deterioration in one's overall health. If they are used only for their proper function, however, they may continue to serve well for many years. Similarly, a given drug may have a proper function. If used in the furtherance of that end, it can preserve life and restore health. But if it is abused, and employed for purposes for which it was never intended, it may cause serious harm and even death. The natural uses of things are good and proper, but their unnatural uses are bad and harmful.

What we must do, then, is to find the proper use, or the true purpose, of each organ in our bodies. Once we have discovered that, we will know what constitutes the natural use of each organ, and what constitutes an unnatural, abusive, and potentially harmful employment of the various parts of our bodies. If we are rational, we will be careful to confine our behavior to our proper functions and to refrain from unnatural behavior. According to those philosophers who follow this line of reasoning, the way to discover the "proper" use of any organ is to determine what it is peculiarly suited to do. The eye is suited for seeing, the ear for hearing, the nerves for transmitting impulses from one part of the body to another, and so on.

What are the sex organs peculiarly suited to do? Obviously, they are peculiarly suited to enable men and women to reproduce their own kind. No other organ in the body is capable of fulfilling that function. It follows, according to those who follow the natural-law line, that the "proper" or "natural" function of the sex organs is reproduction, and that strictly speaking, any use of those organs for other purposes is unnatural, abusive, potentially harmful, and therefore wrong. The sex organs have been given to us in order to enable us to maintain the continued existence of mankind on this earth. All perversions—including masturbation, homosexual behavior, and heterosexual intercourse that deliberately frustrates the design of the sexual organs—are unnatural and bad. As Pope Pius XI once said, "Private individuals have no other power over the members of their bodies than that which pertains to their natural ends."

But the problem is not so easily resolved. Is it true that every organ has one and only one proper function? A hammer may have been designed to pound nails, and it may perform that particular job best. But it is not sinful to employ a hammer to crack nuts if I have no other more suitable tool immediately available. The hammer, being a relatively versatile tool, may be employed in a number of ways. It has no one "proper" or "natural" function. A woman's eyes are well adapted to seeing, it is true. But they seem also to be well adapted to flirting. Is a woman's use of her eyes for the latter purpose sinful merely because she is not using them, at that moment, for their "primary" purpose of seeing? Our sexual organs are uniquely adapted for procreation, but that is obviously not the only function for which they are adapted. Human beings may—and do—use those organs for a great many other purposes, and it is difficult to see why any *one* use should be considered to be the only proper one. The sex organs, for one thing, seem to be particularly well adapted to give their owners and others intense sensations of pleasure. Unless one believes that pleasure itself is bad, there seems to be little reason to believe that the use of the sex organs for the production of pleasure in oneself or in others is evil. In view of the peculiar design of these organs, with their great concentration of nerve endings, it would seem that they were designed (if they *were* designed) with that very goal in mind, and that their use for such purposes would be no more unnatural than their use for the purpose of procreation.

Nor should we overlook the fact that human sex organs may be and are used to express, in the deepest and most intimate way open to man, the love of one person for another. Even the most ardent opponents of "unfruitful" intercourse admit that sex does serve this function. They have accordingly conceded that a man and his wife may have intercourse even though she is pregnant, or past the age of childbearing, or in the infertile period of her menstrual cycle.

Human beings are remarkably complex and adaptable creatures. Neither they nor their organs can properly be compared to hammers or to other tools. The analogy quickly breaks down. The generalization that a given organ or instrument has one and only one proper function does not hold up, even with regard to the simplest manufactured tools, for, as we have seen, a tool may be used for more than one purpose—less effectively than one especially designed for a given task, perhaps, but "properly" and certainly not *sinfully*. A woman may use her eyes not only to see and to flirt, but also to earn money—if she is, for example, an actress or a model. Though neither of the latter functions seems to have been a part of the original "design," if one may speak sensibly of *design* in this context, of the eye, it is difficult to see why such a use of the eyes of a woman should be considered sinful, perverse, or unnatural. Her sex organs have the unique capacity of producing ova and nurturing human embryos, under the right conditions; but why should any other use of those organs, including their use to bring pleasure to their owner or to someone else, or to manifest love to another person, or even, perhaps, to earn money, be regarded as perverse, sinful, or unnatural? Similarly, a man's sexual organs possess the unique capacity of causing the generation of another human being, but if a man chooses to use them for pleasure, or for the expression of love, or for some other purpose—so long as he does not interfere with the rights of some other person—the fact that his sex organs do have their unique capabilities does not constitute a convincing justification for condemning their other uses as being perverse, sinful, unnatural, or criminal. If a man "perverts" himself by wiggling his ears for the entertainment of his neighbors instead of using them exclusively for their "natural" function of hearing, no one thinks of consigning him to prison. If he abuses his teeth by using them to pull staples from memos—a function for which teeth were clearly not designed—he is not accused of being immoral, degraded, and degenerate. The fact that people are condemned for using their sex organs for their own pleasure or profit, or for that of others, may be more revealing about the prejudices and taboos of our society than it is about our perception of the true nature or purpose or "end" (whatever that might be) of our bodies.

To sum up, then, the proposition that any use of an organ that is contrary to its principal purpose or function is unnatural assumes that organs have a principal purpose or function, but this may be denied on the ground that the purpose or function of a given organ may vary according to the needs or desires of its owner. It may be denied on the ground that a given organ may have more than one principal purpose or function, and any attempt to call one use or another the only natural one seems to be arbitrary, if not question-begging. Also, the proposition suggests that what is unnatural is evil or depraved. This goes beyond the pure description of things, and enters into the problem of the evaluation of human behavior, which leads us to the fifth meaning of "natural."

THAT WHICH IS NATURAL IS GOOD, AND WHATEVER IS UNNATURAL IS BAD

When one condemns homosexuality or masturbation or the use of contraceptives on the ground that it is unnatural, one implies that whatever is unnatural is bad, wrongful, or perverse. But as we have seen, in some senses of the word, the unnatural (that is, the artificial) is often very good, whereas that which is natural (that is, that which has not been subjected to human artifice or improvement) may be very bad indeed. Of course, interference with nature may be bad. Ecologists have made us more aware than we have ever been of the dangers of unplanned and uninformed interference with nature. But this is not to say that all interference with nature is bad. Every time a man cuts down a tree to make room for a home for himself, or catches a fish to feed himself or his family, he is interfering with nature. If men did not interfere with nature, they would have no homes, they could eat no fish, and, in fact, they could not survive. What, then, can be meant by those who say that whatever is natural is good and whatever is unnatural is bad? Clearly, they cannot have intended merely to reduce the word *natural* to a synonym of *good, right,* and *proper,* and *unnatural* to a synonym of *evil, wrong, improper, corrupt,* and *depraved.* If that were all they had intended to do, there would be very little to discuss as to whether a given form of behavior might be proper even though it is not in strict conformity with someone's views of what is natural; for *good* and *natural* being synonyms, it would follow inevitably that whatever is good must be natural, and vice versa, by definition. This is certainly not what the opponents of homosexuality have been saying when they claim that homosexuality, being unnatural, is evil. For if it were, their claim would be quite empty. They would be saying merely that homosexuality, being evil, is evil—a redundancy that could as easily be reduced to the simpler assertion that homosexuality is evil. This assertion, however, is not an argument. Those who oppose homosexuality and other sexual "perversions" on the ground that they are "unnatural" are saying that there is some objectively identifiable quality in such behavior that is unnatural; and that that quality, once it has been identified by some kind of scientific observation, can be seen to be detrimental to those who engage in such behavior, or to those around them; and that *because* of the harm (physical, mental, moral, or spiritual) that results from engaging in any behavior possessing the attribute of unnaturalness, such behavior must be considered to be wrongful, and should be discouraged by society. "Unnaturalness" and "wrongfulness" are not synonyms, then, but different concepts. The problem with which we are wrestling is that we are unable to find a meaning for *unnatural* that enables us to arrive at the conclusion that homosexuality is unnatural or that if homosexuality is unnatural, it is therefore wrongful behavior. We have examined four common meanings of *natural* and *unnatural,* and have seen that none of them performs the task that it must perform if the advocates of this argument are to prevail. Without some more satisfactory explanation of the connection between the wrongfulness of homosexuality and its alleged unnaturalness, the argument must be rejected.

GAY BASICS

Richard D. Mohr

Two out of five men one passes on the street have had orgasmic sex with men. Every second family in the country has a member who is essentially homosexual, and many more people regularly have homosexual experiences. Who are homosexuals? They are your friends, your minister, your teacher, your bank teller, your doctor, your mail carrier, your secretary, your congressional representative, your sibling, parent, and spouse. They are everywhere, virtually all ordinary, virtually all unknown.

What follows? First, the country is profoundly ignorant of the actual experience of gay people. Second, social attitudes and practices that are harmful to gays have a much greater overall negative impact on society than is usually realized. Third, most gay people live in hiding—in the closet—making the "coming out" experience the central fixture of gay consciousness and invisibility the chief social characteristic of gays.

IGNORANCE, STEREOTYPE, AND MORALITY

Society's ignorance of gay people is, however, not limited to individuals' lack of personal acquaintance with gays. Stigma against gay people is so strong that even discussions of homosexuality are taboo. This taboo is particularly strong in academe, where it is reinforced by the added fear of the teacher as molester. So even within the hearth of reason irrational forces have held virtually unchallenged and largely unchallengeable sway. The usual sort of clarifying research that might be done on a stigmatized minority has, with gays, only just begun—haltingly—in history, literature, sociology, and the sciences.

Yet ignorance about gays has not stopped people from having strong opinions about them. The void which ignorance leaves has been filled with stereotypes. Society holds chiefly two groups of antigay stereotypes; the two are an oddly contradictory lot. One set of stereotypes revolves around alleged mistakes in an individual's gender identity: lesbians are women that want to be, or at least look and act like, men—bull dykes, diesel dykes; while gay men are those who want to be, or at least look and act like, women—queens, fairies, limp-wrists, nellies. Gays are "queer," which, remember, means at root not merely weird but chiefly counterfeit—"he's as queer as a three dollar bill." These stereotypes of mismatched or fraudulent genders provide the materials through which gays and lesbians become the butts of ethniclike jokes. These stereotypes and jokes, though derisive, basically view gays and lesbians as ridiculous.

Another set of stereotypes revolves around gays as a pervasive, sinister, conspiratorial, and corruptive threat. The core stereotype here is the gay person as child-molester and, more generally, as sex-crazed maniac. These stereotypes carry with them fears of the very destruction of family and civilization itself. Now, that which is essentially ridiculous can hardly have such a staggering effect. Something must be afoot in this incoherent amalgam.

Sense can be made of this incoherence if the nature of stereotypes is clarified. Stereotypes are not simply false generalizations from a skewed sample of cases examined. Admittedly, false generalizing plays a part in most stereotypes a society holds. If, for instance, one takes as one's sample homosexuals who are in psychiatric hospitals or prisons, as was done in nearly all early investigations, not surprisingly one will probably find homosexuals to be of a crazed and criminal cast. Such false generalizations, though, simply confirm beliefs already held on independent grounds, ones that likely led the investigator to the prison and psychiatric ward to begin with. Evelyn Hooker, who in the mid-fifties carried out the first rigorous studies to use nonclinical gays, found that psychiatrists, when presented with results of standard psychological diagnostic tests—but with indications of sexual orientation omitted—were able to do no better than if they had guessed randomly in their attempts to distinguish gay files from nongay ones, even though the psychiatrists believed gays to be crazy and supposed themselves to be experts in detecting craziness.[1] These studies proved a profound embarrassment to the psychiatric establishment, the financial well-being of which was substantially enhanced by "curing" allegedly insane gays. Eventually the studies contributed to the American Psychiatric Association's dropping homosexuality from its registry of mental illnesses in 1973.[2] Nevertheless, the stereotype of gays as sick continues apace in the mind of America.

False generalizations *help maintain* stereotypes; they do not *form* them. As the history of Hooker's discoveries shows, stereotypes have a life beyond facts. Their origin lies in a culture's ideology—the general system of beliefs by which it lives—and they are sustained across generations by diverse cultural transmissions, hardly any of which, including slang and jokes, even purport to have a scientific basis. Stereotypes, then, are not the products of bad science, but are social constructions that perform central functions in maintaining society's conception of itself.

On this understanding, it is easy to see that the antigay stereotypes surrounding gender identification are chiefly means of reinforcing still-powerful gender roles in society. If, as this stereotype presumes (and condemns), one is free to choose one's social roles independently of gender, many guiding social divisions, both domestic and commercial, might be threatened. The socially gender-linked distinctions would blur between breadwinner and homemaker, protector and protected, boss and secretary, doctor and nurse, priest and nun, hero and whore, saint and siren, lord and helpmate, and God and his world. The accusations "fag" and "dyke" (which recent philology has indeed shown to be rooted in slang referring to gender-bending, especially cross-dressing)[3] exist in significant part to keep women in their place and to prevent men from breaking ranks and ceding away theirs.

The stereotypes of gays as child-molesters, sex-crazed maniacs, and civilization-destroyers function to displace (socially irresolvable) problems from their actual source to a foreign (and so, it is thought, manageable) one. Thus, the stereotype of child-molester functions to give the family unit a false sheen of absolute innocence. It keeps the unit from being examined too closely for incest, child abuse, wife-battering, and the terrorism of constant threats. The stereotype teaches that the problems of the family are not internal to it, but external.

Because this stereotype has this central social function, it could not be dislodged even by empirical studies, paralleling Hooker's efforts, that showed heterosexuals to be child-molesters to a far greater extent than the actual occurrence of heterosexuals in the general population.[4] But one need not even be aware of such debunking empirical studies in order to see the same cultural forces at work in the social belief that gays are molesters as in its belief that they are crazy. For one can see them now in society's and the media's treatment of current reports of violence, especially domestic violence. When a mother kills her child or a father rapes his daughter—regular Section B fare even in major urbane papers—this is never taken by reporters, columnists, or pundits as evidence that there is something wrong with heterosexuality or with traditional families. These issues are not even raised.

But when a homosexual child molestation is reported, it is taken as confirming evidence of the way homosexuals are. One never hears of heterosexual murders, but one regularly reads of "homosexual" ones. Compare the social treatment of Richard Speck's sexually motivated mass murder in 1966 of Chicago nurses with that of John Wayne Gacy's serial murders of Chicago youths. Gacy was, in the culture's mind, taken as symbolic of gay men in general. To prevent the possibility that the Family was viewed as anything but an innocent victim in this affair, the mainstream press knowingly failed to mention that most of Gacy's adolescent victims were homeless hustlers, even though this was made obvious at his trial. That knowledge would be too much for the six o'clock news and for cherished beliefs.

The stereotype of gays as sex-crazed maniacs functions socially to keep individuals' sexuality contained. For this stereotype makes it look as though the problem of how to address one's considerable sexual drives can and should be answered with repression, for it gives the impression that the cyclone of dangerous psychic forces is *out there* where the fags are, not within one's own breast. With the decline of the stereotype of the black man as raping, pillaging marauder (found in such works as *Birth of a Nation, Gone with the Wind*, and *Soul on Ice*), the stereotype of gay men as sex-crazed maniacs has become more aggravated. The stereotype of the sex-crazed threat seems one that society desperately needs to have some-where in its sexual cosmology.

For the repressed homosexual, this stereotype has an especially power-ful allure—by hating it consciously, he subconsciously appears to save himself from himself....

By directly invoking sex acts, the second set of stereotypes is the more severe and serious of the two—one never hears child-molester jokes. These stereotypes are aimed chiefly against men, as in turn stereotypically the more sexed of the genders. They are particularly divisive for they cre-ate a very strong division between those conceived as "us" and those con-ceived as "them." This divide is not so strong in the case of the stereotype of gay men as effeminate. For women (and so the womanlike) after all do have their place. Nonstrident, nonuppity, useful ones can even be part of "us," indeed, belong, like "our children," to "us." Thus, in many cultures with overweening gender-identified social roles (like prisons, truckstops, the armed forces, Latin America, and the Islamic world) only passive partners in male couplings are derided as homosexuals.

Because "the facts" largely do not matter when it comes to the genera-tion and maintenance of stereotypes, the effects of scientific and academic research and of enlightenment generally will be, at best, slight and grad-ual in the changing fortunes of gays. If this account of stereotypes holds, society has been profoundly immoral. For its treatment of gays is a grand-scale rationalization and moral sleight of hand. The problem is not that society's usual standards of evidence and procedure in coming to judg-ments of social policy have been misapplied to gays; rather, when it comes to gays, the standards themselves have simply been ruled out of court and disregarded in favor of mechanisms that encourage unexamined fear and hatred. ...

WHY SODOMY LAWS ARE BAD

The American Civil Liberties Union is occasionally called upon to defend the civil liberties of homosexuals. It is not within the province of the Union to evaluate the social validity of laws aimed at the suppression or elimination of homosexuals.[5]

Some thirty years after this ACLU policy statement, the Supreme Court in *Bowers v. Hardwick* would assert the same of the Constitution's province, holding that gays have no constitutional privacy right to have sex: the Constitution does not "confer a fundamental right upon homosexuals to engage in sodomy." Perhaps surprisingly—but perhaps not—the Court was able to reach this conclusion without discussing gays, or privacy, or sex. The strategy of the Court was to treat privacy as only a way of denominating a series of cases—"the privacy cases"—yet not as having anything essential to do with why the cases declared various laws unconstitutional. The Court broke the privacy cases into isolated atoms—viewed them as having relevantly in common nothing more specific than being what are called Substantive Due Process cases. Then, for rights to Substantive Due Process, the Court applied a test of long-held traditions and consensus that allowed the simple citing of the illegality of gay sex to ground its continued illegality.

The aim of this [section] is not to criticize, other than incidentally, the Court's opinion in *Bowers*, but to do the work the Court majority—and even in its dissents—chose not to do: to explain why privacy should be viewed as a fundamental, substantive, and quite general constitutional right, why gay sex falls under that right, and why it is important that this should be so recognized by the courts. ... One might well ask whether the game is worth the candle. For sodomy laws are virtually never enforced.[6] ... [I] will argue that quite a lot is at stake in the elimination of even unenforced sodomy laws, but that the stakes have largely been misunderstood. The evil of unenforced sodomy laws is chiefly their assault on dignity and only secondarily their unwarranted causing of unhappiness.

THE STAKES

Sodomy laws are so little enforced that it has been difficult for civil libertarians even to bring cases under them into court for constitutional review. Previous unsuccessful challenges to such laws were mounted in Texas and Virginia by claiming that even without the laws' having been enforced, they were unconstitutional on their face. A successful attempt to overturn New York's sodomy law was occasioned by an odd series of events in which a grand jury indictment for the raping of a child was basically reconstructed by the district attorney and judge into a charge of sex between consenting adults. The challenge in *Bowers* started when a policeman came to Mr. Hardwick's home to confront him with an unpaid ticket for public drunkenness. A housemate, not knowing of Mr. Hardwick's whereabouts, admitted the policeman to see if Mr. Hardwick was in his bedroom. He was entangled with another man's anatomy in ways allegedly violating the Peach State's statute against unnatural acts. His arrest under the statute was the first in some fifty years for adult, private, consensual, gay sex.

In the absence of anything approaching routine enforcement of sodomy laws, it is not surprising that little attention was paid to them in the early 1970s at the start of the gay rights movement. Rather, civil rights legislation guarding against discrimination in employment, housing, and the like was the paramount issue on gay political agendas. More recently, and especially with the establishment of a number of gay legal defense foundations in the middle and late 1970s, the courts have become the center of serious attention as a possible source of gay justice.

Even so, arguments for bothering with such laws are cast almost entirely in terms of their practical consequences: legal reform is generally called for not because of a perception that the laws are inherently objectionable, but because of real or apparent spin-off effects in areas of public policy that do matter.

Sodomy laws are, so many current activists claim, the bedrock of discrimination against gays. The case for this position is of mixed virtue. Opponents of civil rights legislation for gays do cite the existence of sodomy laws in opposing such legislated rights—how, after all, can one legitimately force people to hire and rent to unapprehended felons? One suspects, though, that this move is in general a ruse for opposition of foreign origin. For the absence of such laws does not stop people who are otherwise opposed to civil rights for gays from continuing their opposition; at least, one never hears of people changing their views on civil rights when the status of a state's sodomy law changes. Rather the existence of sodomy laws simply gives those opposed to civil rights something to say that does not sound patently prejudicial in an area where there may not be a lot to say.

Indeed, most Americans, including gay ones, probably do not even know with any degree of certainty whether the state in which they live has a sodomy law. When Illinois legislators voted in 1961 to repeal the state's sodomy law, making it the first state to legalize gay sex, they did not even know what they were voting on. The repeal was simply one overlooked and undiscussed technical detail of an omnibus criminal law reform package adopted in entirety from the American Law Institute's Model Penal Code. Two of the toughest gay civil rights laws in the country have been passed in locales where sodomy laws were in force—Wisconsin, the only state to adopt such protections although it decriminalized gay sex only a year later, and the District of Columbia, where sodomy is still a felony.[7]

In general, little weight can be given to claims of some activists that one chief harm of these laws is that they produce severe psychological damage for many gays in states with such laws. The existence of such damage and unhappiness cannot be denied, but it is the result of a general, toxic, antigay social climate, to which sodomy laws may or may not be a concomitant. At least, sodomy laws are not the substrate or initiating cause of social hostility to gays.

More promising sources of possible indirect practical benefits from the elimination of sodomy laws are found in judicial treatments of sexual solicitation laws, which are enforced—almost always through techniques of entrapment.[8] These solicitation laws frequently have devastating personal, social, and economic effects for those arrested, even though criminal penalties typically are slight, and even if charges are ultimately dropped or a not-guilty verdict reached. Though solicitation is sometimes crabbedly viewed as a species of public nuisance or public indecency, sometimes the relation between solicitation and sodomy is viewed, reasonably enough, as that between an attempt of an act and the offense itself. If the latter is not something that can be criminal, neither, so it has been successfully argued in New York, can the former. The California Supreme Court has taken the still stronger position that even when legislative reform rather than constitutional construction has decriminalized consensual private sodomy, laws against solicitation to commit the act violate Due Process rights. Whither sodomy laws go, so too do sexual solicitation laws.

The existence of sodomy laws also significantly affects the way in which judges—who are aware of their existence—apply the law in general. Such influences are apparent when judges make determinations based on what they perceive to be public policy. It would be the rare judge that did not consider the admission of regular violations of the laws as tantamount, at a minimum, to a showing of bad moral character, which by statute or construction is then allegedly a sufficient warrant to deny one the position of schoolteacher, state licensee, or child's custodian. Such laws have had a concrete impact on many state employment opportunities for gays and lesbians and in custody suits involving lesbian and gay parties. However, as in the realm of legislated rights, the repeal of sodomy laws still might not be sufficient to eliminate blockades to correct judicial decisions in gay employment and related cases. In one of the more note-worthy antigay cases on record, Washington State's highest court, inde-pendent of the existence of the state's sodomy law, upheld the firing of a gay schoolteacher on grounds of immorality, quoting at length the *New Catholic Encyclopedia* as its rationale.[9]

Further, should sodomy laws be eliminated from the books not by leg-islation but by a judicial finding that they violate a fundamental constitu-tional right to privacy, one could reasonably hope that most discriminations against gay people *by the state* would also be declared unconstitutional. For under Equal Protection analyses, discriminations which impinge or trench on a fundamental right must pass, like laws bar-ring outright actions protected by the right, the highest standard of judi-cial review: such discrimination must be shown both to have an end that is compelling and to be necessary to that end.[10] Widespread discrimina-tion in government employment both directly, in hiring, and indirectly, through licensing procedures, would likely be eliminated, especially at the state level. Further discrimination against gays in immigration and military policy might be eliminated, though the courts have traditionally given Congress and the executive branch the greatest degree of deference in these two areas. And there is an untried possibility that laws barring gays from marrying would also be struck down on these grounds.

All of these indirect deleterious effects of sodomy laws may, when taken collectively, constitute a strong enough reason for their elimination, even if they are never enforced. But the mere existence of these laws is an evil of a kind different and greater than their damaging consequences. The basic evil of sodomy laws is that they are an affront to dignity. In con-trast, their bad indirect effects are mere mischief. An affront to dignity occurs whether the laws are enforced or not, and even whether they are known to exist or not.

Admittedly, dignity is an elusive notion, often appealed to when people have run out of moral reasons and explanations. Nevertheless, the com-mon phrase "adding insult to injury" affords an intuitive grasp of the rel-evant distinction between two types of evils. An insult is an offense against dignity, while an injury is something that reduces one's happiness or pleasure, or denies one some benefit, wealth, power, useful possession, or generally reduces one's material circumstances in the world. Insults are a graver form of evil, for they are of a class of evils that attacks a person as a person. The most common indignities—invective and name-calling, insults in a narrow sense—attack a person because of some largely irrele-vant peculiarity and without regard to anything that he has done. Thus calling someone a "nigger," "faggot," or "cunt" is a star case of insult. Such abuses attack the person as person in two ways. By focusing impor-tance on an irrelevant characteristic, they attack persons as repositories of deserved fair treatment and equal respect. And as holding a person morally accountable without regard for anything he has done, they show disrespect for persons as moral agents.

Now, an offense may be both an insult and an injury, or just one or the other. Thus simple theft without aggravating circumstances, particularly theft of a luxury item, is chiefly an injury without being an affront to dignity, unless of course one views a person essentially as a consumer and possessor of luxuries. Cutting someone is likely to be both an injury and an insult, since it will both cause pain and affront dignity by violating bodily integrity, a precondition for a person being in the world at all.

Some acts can be insults and yet provide no injury. Lying, or more particularly lying that actually benefits its hearer, provides many examples. Lying attacks persons in pretty much any conception of what a person is. On a Kantian notion of a person as a creature who has ends of his own, who can recognize others as having ends of their own, and so who is capable of respecting others, lying to a person shows a lack of respect for her by treating her merely as a means to one's own ends. The chief problem in this conception is not that the person will come to have a false belief or even act upon a false belief to her detriment, but that in lying one treats another like a found object, treating that person entirely as an instrument for one's own ends. Alternatively, if one views a person quasi-Platonically as essentially a thinker, knower, seer, poet, or contemplator, then causing a person to have false beliefs is sufficient to assault persons in that conception simply as casting the contemplated world in a false light.

Invasions of privacy typically entail disrespect and not mere harm. Admittedly some invasions of privacy produce injuries, sometimes grave ones. When police place hidden movie cameras in washroom stalls, men lose jobs, families are destroyed, men kill themselves. But invasions of privacy usually are also assaults on dignity. They are particularly grave failures to respect persons if the notion of person as thinker is fused with that of person as a creature with her own ends, into a unified view of person as chooser—a subject conscious of herself as an agent with plans, projects, and a view of her own achievements.[11] In this conception one respects a person not by treating her essentially as one who is happy or sad—that would be a ground for sympathetic joy or pity but not respect. Rather one shows respect by not manipulating the conditions in which a person makes choices.

On this account, observed uninvited scrutiny effects such disrespectful manipulation by forcing the agent to become self-reflective, to become continuously aware of what he is doing, thus forcing an alteration of an agent's perception of himself. But even covert observation—spying—is objectionable. For it, like lying, "deceives a person about his world for reasons that *cannot* be his own reasons."[12]

Thus a person need not be aware of the act that insults her in order to be insulted nonetheless. When the state, through sodomy laws, reserves for itself the power to snoop on activity that is both traditionally and inherently private, it insults gays even if gays are not harmed by the laws and even if they are unaware of the laws' existence.

Sodomy laws assault dignity in another way as well. As mentioned, the largest class of insults and assaults to dignity arises when a person is held in low esteem for widely irrelevant features and without regard to anything he himself has done. These violate a person's essential desert for equal respect and respect as a moral agent. Equal respect is violated because a person's desires, plans, aspirations, and sense of the sacred are not considered worthy of social care and concern on a par with those of others. And respect for moral agency is violated because a person is being judged without regard to her individual merits or accomplishments. Unenforced sodomy laws are invective by government.

When a state has unenforced sodomy laws on its books—not by oversight but even after the failure of law reform has drawn attention to their existence, and yet no attempt is made to enforce them though their frequent violation is a secret to no one—then insult is their main purpose. If the law is virtually never enforced, the law exists not out of a concern with the *actions* of gay people, but with their *status*. At oral argument in *Bowers*, Georgia claimed the purpose of its sodomy law was "symbolic." And that claim unwittingly is true. For sodomy laws afford an opportunity for the citizenry to express its raw hatred of gays *systematically and officially* without even having publicly to discuss and so justify that hatred. There are, of course, nonsystematic means to this end, queer-bashing, for instance. Still, unenforced sodomy laws are the chief systematic way that society as a whole tells gays they are scum.

Slandering someone behind his back is an insult, even if he never learns of the slander. So again, gays, even if unaware of sodomy laws, are insulted behind their backs by them. Even if *some* gays are unaffected by them in the sense that their happiness or fortunes do not depend upon the laws' removal, nevertheless their dignity is diminished by the laws' very existence....

In America there is a forum for the redress of those assaults to dignity that are perpetrated by government: the courts as expounders of constitutional immunities against the state's monopoly of legitimate coercive powers. To the extent that sodomy laws are an assault on dignity and to the extent that dignity is not, as it is not, something which ought morally to depend on the whims of majorities, then the courts are not just an available forum to overrun sodomy laws, but are also the proper forum. There is, I think, no effective social equivalent to an individual's heartfelt apology. There is only the assertion of rights.

NOTES

[1]Evelyn Hooker, "The Adjustment of the Male Overt Homosexual," *Journal of Protective Techniques* (1957) 21: 18–31, reprinted in Hendrik M. Ruitenbeek, ed., *The Problem of Homosexuality* (New York: Dutton, 1963): 141–161, epigram quote from 149.

[2]See Ronald Bayer, *Homosexuality and American Psychiatry* (New York: Basic Books, 1981).

[3]See Wayne Dynes, *Homolexis: A Historical and Cultural Lexicon of Homosexuality* (New York: Gay Academic Union, 1985) s.v.v. dyke, faggot.

[4]For studies showing that gay men are no more likely—indeed, are less likely—than heterosexuals to be child-molesters and that the most widespread and persistent sexual abusers of children are the children's fathers, stepfathers, or mother's boyfriends, see Vincent DeFrancis, *Protecting the Child Victim of Sex Crimes Committed by Adults* (Denver: The American Humane Association, 1969), pp. vii, 38, 69–70; A. Nicholas Groth, "Adult Sexual Orientation and Attraction to Underage Persons," *Archives of Sexual Behavior* (1978) 7: 175–181; Mary J. Spencer, "Sexual Abuse of Boys," *Pediatrics* (July 1986) 78(l): 133–138.

[5]"Homosexuality and Civil Liberties: Policy statement adopted by the Union's Board of Directors, January 7, 1957" *Civil Liberties: Monthly Publication of the ACLU*, March 1957, No. 150:3 abutting a sidebar marking the centenary of *Dred Scott*.

[6]...Currently, twenty-four states and the District of Columbia have some form of sodomy laws applying to same-sex adult couples.... The content of sodomy laws has varied widely from time to time, state to state and country to country. Laws have ranged from banning only anal penetrations of males by males to banning all permutations of contacts between mouth, genitals, and anus except kissing and genital contacts between those married to each other. The arguments of this part apply to all such variations. For one of the most broadly phrased and thus restrictive sodomy laws, see Miss. Code Ann. sect 97–29–59 (1972) ("Every person who shall be convicted of the detestable and abominable crime against nature, committed with mankind or with beast, shall be punished by imprisonment in the penitentiary for a term of not more than ten years....

[7]Wisconsin's bill protecting gays, among other classes, in employment and public accommodations was passed in 1982. Wis. Star. Ann. section III.31–.32 (West Supp. 1986). Its sodomy law was revised in 1983 to eliminate consensual adult sex in private as a crime. Wis. State. Ann. section 944.17 (West Supp. 1986) (1983 Act 17, sect. 5, effective May 12, 1983). Washington, D.C. still has a sodomy law, with ten years' imprisonment as a maximum penalty. D.C. Code Ann. sect. 22–3502 (1981). It has, however, one of the oldest and strongest gay rights laws in the country, passed in 1977. D.C. Code Ann. sections 1–2501, 1–2502, 1–2512, 1–2515, 1–2519, 1–2520 (1981).

[8]For a levelheaded treatment of the legal morality of entrapment as a law enforcement technique, see Gerald Dworkin, "The Serpent Beguiled Me and I Did Eat: Entrapment and the Creation of Crime," *Law and Philosophy* (1985) 4: 17–39. Dworkin's analysis, however, is not fine-grained enough to deal with sexual solicitation and, indeed, does not address the matter....

⁹*Gaylord v. Tacoma School District No. 10*, 88 Wash. 2d 286, 292, 295, 559 P2d 1340, 1343, 1345 (Sup. Ct. Wash., 1977) (upholding the firing of a gay teacher for being immoral), cert. denied. 434 U.S. 879 (1977); see also *Rowland v. Mad River Local School District*, 730 F.2d 444 (6th Cir. 1984) (upholding, against First Amendment and Equal Protection challenges, the permanent suspension of a school counselor for mentioning her lesbianism at school), cert. denied, 470 U.S. 1009 (1985).

¹⁰The leading case here is *Shapiro v. Thompson*, 394 U.S. 618 (1969), which invalidated year-long residency requirements for welfare recipients as impinging on the fundamental right to interstate travel. However, subsequent to the abortion funding decisions, it is unclear what counts as impinging or trenching on fundamental rights. *Maher v. Roe*, 432. U.S. 464 (1976) (prohibition of abortion funding upheld against Equal Protection challenge); *Harris v. McRae*, 448 U.S. 297 (1980) (abortion funding bar upheld). These cases upheld bans on funding abortions for indigents even when all other medical procedures for them are paid by the state. *Shapiro* suggested that any distinction made with regard to a fundamental right counted as an impingement on that right.

¹¹This definition and paragraph adapt views from Stanley I. Benn's "Privacy, Freedom, and Respect for Persons" in Ferdinand D. Schoeman, ed., *Philosophical Dimensions of Privacy: An Anthology* (Cambridge: Cambridge University Press, 1984): 228–232.

¹²*Ibid.*, 230.

A MORAL JUSTIFICATION FOR GAY AND LESBIAN CIVIL RIGHTS LEGISLATION

Vincent J. Samar

The past ten years have seen dozens of municipalities and seven states pass civil rights legislation aimed at protecting gays and lesbians from discrimination in employment, housing, and places of public accommodation such as banks, hotels, mortgage companies, restaurants, retail establishments, and schools.[1] The past fifteen years have seen several federal bills introduced to protect lesbian and gay civil rights....

In part, the successes in enacting legislation in this area at the state and local levels and in garnering support at the federal level for such legislation have been due substantially to the willingness of gay men and lesbians to come out of the closet...this has led some politicians, military officials, the media, and various other groups in the United States to engage in a debate at the federal, state, and local levels about whether discrimination against lesbians and gays is morally justified, and, if not, whether laws should be enacted to prevent this form of discrimination.

Any legislation that seeks to limit the freedom of private citizens to hire, house, or serve whom they want in their business establishments requires a moral justification. This is because a free society is predicated on the belief that individuals can choose to associate with whomever they wish. This does not mean that the existence of any restrictions necessarily renders a society unfree. What it does mean is that such restrictions must

From *Gay Ethics*, ed. Timothy F. Murphy, originally appearing in the *Journal of Homosexuality* Vol. 27, No. 3/4 (1994). Reprinted with permission from Haworth Press, Inc.

complement the freedom that the society holds dear under an applicable moral theory. Moreover, because at least some lesbians and gay men can avoid discrimination only by remaining in the closet, the justification for antidiscrimination legislation protecting this group must go beyond considerations of affiliative or affectional orientation to protect some homosexual behavior. In this sense, antidiscrimination legislation for gays and lesbians will depart from prior justifications involving racial, gender, ethnic, and age *statuses* by having to take into account statements or perceptions related to *conduct*. Consequently, the justification for such legislation does not run the easy mile of "they could not help what they are," for there is always the counterargument that one does not have to act upon any desire one may have, as well as the counterargument that society does not have to support any and all such desires.

In this essay, I will take up some of the typical arguments that have been used to try and justify discrimination against gays and lesbians in employment, housing, and public accommodations. I will, then, address them one by one, demonstrating that they are irrational or based on irrelevant information. In doing this, I will show how some of these arguments reflect ethical views under utilitarianism, rights theory, communitarianism, and natural law. Absent from this discussion will be analyses of purely religious texts and traditions, since I am presupposing the existence of a society which values personal, ethical, and religious pluralism.

GAY/LESBIAN DISCRIMINATION IS UNJUSTIFIED

Typical arguments proffered in favor of discrimination against gays and lesbians include the following:

1. In order to maintain social stability, society needs to exclude from the mainstream those groups that the majority deems to be too far different or "deviant."
2. At least in respect to the private sector, people have the right to hire, house, or serve in their business establishments whomever they want.
3. The overall good of society (as defined by its most dominant values) may be enhanced if discrimination is allowed.
4. Protecting gays and lesbians from discrimination undermines morality.
5. Protecting lesbians and gays encourages role models harmful to children.
6. Protecting gays and lesbians against discrimination opens the door to affirmative action programs for lesbians and gays.
7. The right to the free exercise of religion may conflict with the right to nondiscrimination.

Reasons one through five are theoretical. In particular, reasons one through four are purely normative in that they rely for their justification on one or another ethical theory. Reason one, for example, is usually offered in a utilitarian context, whereas reason two presupposes a rights theory. Reason three tends to be asserted from a communitarian point of view, and reason four is most often asserted on the basis of natural law. Depending on how one interprets the claim, reason five is an admixture of ethical theory and causal psychology. By contrast, reasons six and seven are practical in that they question how (if at all) legislation could be structured to avoid a broader consequence than what a minimal justification for nondiscrimination would allow.

Clearly, some discrimination in employment, such as favoring persons who are appropriately educated to practice law or medicine over those not so educated, is justified, while most discrimination based on race, religion, gender, or disability is not justified. (I am assuming here that the control of education—via controlling accreditation, curriculum or admissions policies—is neither designed nor has the effect of keeping power unfairly distributed only in the hands of one group of people.) So the question is: What is it that makes some kinds of discrimination justified, but not other kinds? Obviously, context plays a role, as when the religion of the person is relevant to whether he or she becomes a member of a particular clergy. But exactly what role context plays must itself be justified.

Although it may seem like a truism to say that discrimination based on irrational prejudice or matters unrelated to the opportunity sought (called "invidious" discrimination) is unfair, it is nevertheless true. (From hereon in I will use "discrimination" to mean only the invidious sort.) And this truth can be seen to cut across boundaries of utilitarianism, rights theory, and communitarianism once we make clear what we mean by "irrational" and "irrelevant."

By "irrational" I mean that the claim cannot be proved either by reference to physical evidence or by deduction from a noncontroversial premise or at least one that is plausible. Belief that the stars control our activities is irrational because we cannot devise an astrological test that predicts the future with a degree of accuracy higher than would be expected by random chance. The reason for the requirement of a noncontroversial premise is to recognize that the theory adopted should apply in a society that approves of pluralism in personal values and religious beliefs. By "irrelevant" I mean that the evidence chosen does not support the claim at hand. That a person knows how to drive does not prove either that he or she is a good or bad driver. "Irrational" thus attaches to a claim, while "irrelevant" goes to the evidence supporting the claim.

At this point, it should be noted that I am treating "rational" and "relevant" not as theory-specific but as ethical-area-specific, that is, what would be rational and relevant within a particular ethical tradition. My rationale for doing this is not that individual theories within a particular area might not provide more specific criteria for what is rational and relevant. Rather, it is that across the areas considered there is enough certitude on (at least) the grosser interpretations of these concepts to suggest their overall application.

In the case of gay and lesbian discrimination in housing, employment, and public accommodations much of the debate turns on irrational claims (such as "homosexuality is an abomination to God") or irrelevant evidence (such as gay sex is inferior because it cannot produce children). The few allegedly rational and potentially relevant claims made (such as the charge that gay people are more inclined to molest children and spread disease) are easily refuted by available evidence.

Applying the concepts of rationality and relevancy to the three ethical theories referred to above, we discover the grounds upon which lesbian and gay discrimination in employment, housing, and public accommodations is unjustified. We also begin to unpack some of the arguments that are often used against claims that the state has an obligation to avoid such discrimination. . . .

From a utilitarian standpoint, discrimination would be justified if it serves to maximize utility (that is, if it serves to aggregate utility by affording the greatest happiness to the greatest number). Since utilitarianism specifies no preordained "good" to be achieved, the greatest happiness principle is satisfied when, in light of the various competing goods that the members of society take to be important, there is more satisfaction to be obtained in meeting some particular social good (hopefully, in light of thought and reflection) than there is dissatisfaction from the loss of other competing goods. However, as will be argued, any form of discrimination is not to be tolerated. If the discrimination is *irrational or irrelevant*, then allowing the discrimination may create more unhappiness and less utility than would otherwise be the case. This is especially true where what is at stake is of central importance to the individual, as is where one lives or how one earns a living. Denying lesbians and gays access to housing, jobs, and places of public accommodation based on irrational prejudice or irrelevant evidence needlessly creates unhappiness for the persons whose desires are frustrated, and loss of benefits to the society from its gay and lesbian members.

First, it is economically inefficient for the society to limit anyone from buying property or participating in those professions to which they are most suited. Regarding this latter point, there may also be loss of creativity from discriminatory barriers.

Second, being free of the fear that one might be discriminated against because they are gay encourages openness, which itself is positively beneficial both to the individual and to the society. It is positively beneficial to the individual when the person can feel good about him- or herself because he or she no longer has to suppress that central element of personal identity which is the basis for decisions about whom one might love, be with, or share a life with. (In this same vein, coming out to parents and friends ensures that the love one feels—or, unfortunately, sometimes does not feel—from them is honest and not based on an artificial image of the self.) It is positively beneficial to the society when large numbers of its members begin to accept gays and lesbians, because the coming-out decision has shortened the social and political distance that previously separated lesbians and gays from the rest of society. Shortening the social and political distance may mean more attention to the battle over AIDS funding and related sex education which until recently has had a disproportionate impact on the gay male community. It may also mean more attention to issues like gay-bashings. No longer can we speak of "those people over there," for now we must also include "these people over here." This latter point is not only beneficial to the individual's need to overcome feelings of isolation but to society's interest in overcoming prejudicial and irrational fear. For the more lesbian and gay people come out in many different walks of life, the more will stereotypes be broken down and replaced with a more realistic view about the actual makeup of society. All of these potential gains are undermined, however, so long as discrimination may result in losing one's home, career, or other important public accommodations.

Still, it might be argued that adopting a policy of discrimination against gays and lesbians would provide the society with a needed scapegoat, especially at times of trouble. That is because ostracizing openly gay or lesbian persons is easier than ramming contrived accusations through a court. Moreover, the existence of such policy would not be likely to cause nongay members of society to become concerned that the policy might eventually be applied to them.

The problem with this attempt at justifying antigay/antilesbian discrimination is the level of abstraction at which the argument is offered. Discrimination against lesbians and gays is either irrational or irrelevant when there is no hard evidence that such persons as a *class* actually cause physical or mental harm to others. Consequently, a third utilitarian reason for not allowing such discrimination is that such discrimination may breed anxiety in society generally, since no one will ever be certain that a similar prejudice will not evolve against them. That is to say, no one will ever be certain that they will not be made part of some class judged worthy of discrimination. Even if the presence of gays and lesbians in the minds of people is currently underestimated, given the efforts by many activists to obtain public forums on questions of rights, there is reason to assume that this state of affairs will continue. Thus, if not now, certainly in the future, whenever one hears of someone being discriminated against, he or she will not know whether the discrimination was justified (in the sense that it was based on more than mere perception of harm) or not. Consequently, it is difficult to detect any social utility in discriminating against gays and lesbians in employment, housing, and public accommodations, when such a practice encourages an atmosphere of paranoia and irrationality harmful to society as a whole.

It might also be argued that if Western society has allowed gay/lesbian discrimination for hundreds of years, why should it change now? This argument, however, ignores the fact that benefits are additive, and that both society and the individual benefit more when the potential of each person is tapped to the maximum extent. For example, racial separation was for a long time (and to a lesser but more insidious extent still is) practiced in the schools of this country. One of the drawbacks of racial separation in the schools is that the potential of most African-American youth is stifled by a poorer quality of education and lack of self-esteem *vis-à-vis* the broader society. A similar response could be made to the military's policy of discharging openly gay and lesbian persons from the services in order to ensure the morale of the troops. Surely educating the troops about what homosexuality is, who gay people are, and what types of interpersonal conduct are appropriate while on duty could go a long way toward resolving morale problems (not only in respect to gays and lesbians but also indirectly in respect to military women) without having to engage in this form of discrimination. This is, indeed, what happened when the armed services were ordered racially integrated.

Under rights theory, invidious discrimination is never justified, because it undermines individual autonomy. However, not all cases of discrimination need be invidious. Consequently, cases in which people appear to be justified in discriminating against gays and lesbians are not really cases of invidious discrimination because the affectional orientation is relevant. An example would be a heterosexual male who chooses to marry a heterosexual female. Where rights theory becomes problematic is where there are two or more rights in conflict. For example, how should one resolve the conflict between a claim to manage one's business of housing as one pleases and the fight not to be discriminated against? Here, the right to freedom should be tolerated unless autonomy generally (in the sense of each person to decide for him- or herself what is in his or her own interest) is better served by not allowing it than by allowing it. This is because protecting liberty protects autonomy generally. More specifically, the right of freedom to do with one's business or housing as one chooses ought to win out over the right not to be discriminated against if the result would better promote overall individual autonomy for the society generally than not allowing it. On the other hand, if allowing the right to freedom would inhibit or restrict more autonomy generally than not allowing it, then the right to freedom is not justified. Where the latter is true, the maximum allowance of interference with liberty is the minimum necessary to protect autonomy generally. This appeal to maximal autonomy does not undercut any claim to a deontological basis for the right at stake. For the question here (unlike for the utilitarian) is not the good to be achieved, but affirmation of the underlying principle (in this case autonomy) that justifies the right in the first place. Thus, where the right to freedom is based in individual autonomy, a principle of equality (that seeks to further the promotion of autonomy generally) can limit exercise of that right.

Here it is important to distinguish two different extremes of rights theory: classical liberalism (or libertarianism) and egalitarian liberalism. Under the classical liberal or libertarian view, an individual's freedom to do what he or she wants with his or her own property (whether in their persons, as to whom to associate with, or other objects) is the most important value. The only limitation is that one cannot use his or her freedom so as to deprive another of a similar freedom. Consequently, under a libertarian rights theory, there is never a justification for limiting one individual's freedom to use his or her property merely for the sake of advancing the welfare of another. In contrast, the egalitarian liberal values equality above freedom. Consequently, the egalitarian liberal would support a scheme of civil liberties (as well as social and economic rights) that affords all persons the same opportunities. This difference between the two views can be seen in the different ways they would approach the question of discrimination. Because the libertarian wants to maximize individual freedom, the right not to be discriminated against (even if it is based on irrational or irrelevant criteria) is overridden in the private sector, although not in the public sector. In contrast, for the egalitarian liberal, the right not to be discriminated against, when based on irrational and irrelevant criteria, always undercuts human dignity and respect for persons and, therefore, is not overridden by the right to freedom.

Both libertarians and egalitarian liberals alike would recognize that irrational discrimination or discrimination based on irrelevant evidence against openly gay or lesbian persons restricts the autonomy of this group by limiting its opportunities to compete for the essential goods of society on the same basis as society offers to its other members. Such denial has two basic components. On the objective level, it denies lesbian and gay individuals the freedom to be openly gay and still participate in receiving the same benefits afforded other members of society. Such exclusion also has the effect of skewing occupational patterns of gay men who are unable or unwilling to hide their sexual orientation, toward certain professions which are stereotypically viewed to have less immediate, direct impact on the important questions of life or the important value aspect of property, and are often labeled "unmanly." At the subjective level, irrational discrimination or discrimination based on irrelevant information denies some gay and lesbian individuals a means to express publicly their uniqueness in a way that is self-fulfilling and likely to promote their own happiness, while not threatening the objective interests of any other person. Furthermore, failing to allow open expression can lead to development of self-doubt, lost self-esteem, and self-hatred.

Libertarians and more egalitarian liberals disagree over what should be done to correct such prejudice. Libertarians would say that laws cannot be used to restrict the use of private property or employment practices in the private sector, whereas egalitarian theorists would allow the law to prevent discrimination (based on irrational or irrelevant views about sexual orientation). This seeming impasse between libertarians and egalitarian liberals should not lead one to the conclusion that rights theory can develop no firm position on this topic. If one separates out liberty (as a system of rights defining equal citizenship) from the worth of liberty (as the capacity to advance one's ends within a system of equal rights), then one must endeavor to resolve the problem in terms of more basic principles—principles underlying both libertarian and egalitarian views—which rational persons would want guaranteed as a minimal condition for the advancement of the responsible pursuit of their ends.

Here two theories serve as possible bases for a solution. The intuitionist approach of John Rawls, for example, asks what persons would choose if they were in a position of not knowing anything about themselves but only in a position of knowing general economic and psychological facts about human beings.[2] Clearly, they would choose not to allow arbitrary discrimination, for they would be afraid of discovering that they were themselves the objects of discrimination once the veil of personal ignorance was lifted from them. A rationalist approach, as developed, for example, by Alan Gewirth, argues that every rational agent (a person who can act voluntarily for his or her own purposes) must logically accept on pain of contradiction that every other agent has the same rights as oneself to freedom and well-being, because these are the proximate necessary conditions of human agency.[3] Here, arbitrary prejudice is avoided, because such prejudice assumes that certain features (not in the definition of agency) are relevant, when all that is at stake for the establishment of moral rights is that one be a moral agent. Thus, both of these theories would condemn arbitrary discrimination, especially where individual well-being is threatened. However, both of these theories are controversial, because they raise deep philosophical questions about the nature of moral-theory justification. Pending an ultimate resolution of this controversy, one might tentatively (because it starts from a value-laden assumption) adopt the following approach toward solving the problem of discrimination.

It would seem that our democratic society generally accepts the idea that all persons should have the opportunity to discover, amidst numerous competing interests and compatible with a like freedom for all, what is in their own interests. If this is true, then gay and lesbian persons should have the same rights to discover what is in their interests as every other person, at least where there is no rational and relevant reason for their being denied these rights. But clearly, lesbians and gays are deterred from discovering who they are by the possibility of loss of jobs, housing, and other important public accommodations. If society believes that people ought to be allowed to discover what is in their own interests, then it must grant to gays and lesbians the level of autonomy (in the sense of freedom from arbitrary discrimination) that would allow this discovery to occur.

From a communitarian position, discrimination should be allowed only when it serves the interests of society treated as organic whole. Here the individual is seen as constituted by society rather than as constituting society. Discrimination is not allowed where denying someone full citizenship will produce, on balance, more of a detriment to society (perhaps in the form of a lost resource) than not. Thus, the question of whether one can discriminate from a communitarian standpoint (even as to essential elements of well-being) cannot be answered independent of the conception about the overall good of the society at stake. In this sense, a communitarian view need be neither liberal nor conservative. Modern communitarians often differ from their classical forerunners (philosophers like Plato, Rousseau, and Marx) in that the "good" to be obtained is not something eternal or outside society but is, rather, a constitutive element of the society in question. This does not mean that communitarians ignore at a fundamental level the influence of who holds power. Rather, they see actions of those who hold power as often reflecting the society's deeper values. For example, certain forms of discrimination that may be allowed in a society of fundamentalist Christians may not be allowed in a more pluralistic society, especially one which values tolerance of differing personal moral and religious points of view. The only exception to the latter would be discrimination necessary to support the very existence of the society, such as providing laws against murder, theft, and insurrection. On the other hand, why should anyone need to start from so narrow a premise in a society that avows personal, religious, and moral freedom? Clearly, in a pluralistic society one should hope to avoid supporting such discriminatory claims.

Discrimination against gays and lesbians in employment, housing, and public accommodations can create an artificial image of a homogeneous society that is not true to life, thereby sowing the seeds of discontent which could in the long run undermine social stability. (An excellent example of this problem is Patrick Buchanan's homophobic denunciation at the 1992 Republican National Convention of "the" gay and lesbian "lifestyle" as inimical to traditional American "family values." That speech played a role in galvanizing many citizens to vote Democratic.) This is especially true if gay/lesbian discrimination becomes a testing ground (because of the unpopularity of the group) for a broader-based social/political agenda for society at large. Such a domino theory of moral views exhibits itself when justifications for discriminating against lesbians and gays are based on the view that these groups fail to engage in procreative sex (a view which in addition to its questionable claim to moral authority is not always even factual). From here, it is only a short step to a more generalized criticism of the rights of women to choose abortion or even to enter into nontraditional professions. Additionally, allowing this discrimination against gays and lesbians ignores the fact that at least part of this group's contribution to pluralistic society might lie in setting examples for how persons of different sexual orientations (much like persons of different genders, races, and ethnic groups) can live and work together. At a more sophisticated level, the removal of sanctions against the acknowledgment and expression of affectionate emotional response would contribute significantly toward "a repudiation of stereotypical gender roles" which feminists, and more recently proponents of male liberation, have advocated.[4]

Looking at the issue from an approach framed by natural law theory, discrimination is justified when it promotes the inherent (or divine) purpose of nature, as discovered from nature's laws. According to Aquinas, for example, the inherent purpose of nature is discovered from the order of natural inclinations. It is in this sense that natural law theory makes a claim to moral objectivity. Specifically, three inclinations provide, in the order stated, the basis for evaluating the morality of human acts. First, since everything in nature has substance (that is, continues to exist over time), survival is the first and foremost tenet. Hence, we have laws against violence and murder, and a claim from some for laws prohibiting abortion. Next, because human beings share with all other animals a desire to procreate and rear offspring, procreation becomes a second important inclination. Herein lies natural law's traditional prohibition against all forms of sexual expression/activity (especially homosexuality) which are not procreative. Finally, human beings have as part of their unique nature the desire to seek knowledge of God. This is natural law's claimed moral basis for freedom of worship.

Natural law theory, however, does not suffice to show that the homosexuality of a person is immoral *per se*. This is because the kinds of things that should count as relevant arguments in natural law theory are themselves problematic. First, acceptance of a divinely ordered plan of nature is a controversial claim, as indicated by the fact that modern science may proceed without any assumption about the teleological design of its objects of study. Second, what constitutes the "natural" in natural law is not precise (at least) under Aquinas's formulation. For example, why is it natural to have heterosexual intercourse during an infertile period while it is unnatural to have intercourse using a contraceptive? Why is heterosexuality more natural than homosexuality? Is "natural" just a substitute for "statistically average"? In which case, the question might be: Why would one want to be statistically average? Is "natural" supposed to mean not found in nature other than in humans? If so, then it must be recognized that many of the actions that natural law is supposed to prohibit—such as homosexuality—are found in nature. It is also unclear why the concept of the natural (when employed in moral theory) should embody any broader conception of nature than what is unique to human beings. Or is natural supposed to mean morally right? In which case the concept of the natural begs the question of what is morally right.

A similar criticism applies against Kant's view of homosexuality. Kant argued, from the second version of the categorical imperative ("Act so that you treat humanity, whether in your own person or that of another, always as an end and never as a means only"), that homosexuality was universally wrong because it violates the end of humanity in respect of sexuality, which is to preserve the species without debasing the person.[5] Kant thought that the homosexual self is degraded below the level of animals and, thus, degraded in itself. No violation of the second version of the categorical imperative occurs, however, once one drops the antinatural thesis. The flaw in Kant's approach can be seen in the fact that gay and lesbian people fall in love with partners and, under any meaningful sense of that term, treat those persons as ends and not simply as means.

Obviously, not every moral theory will succumb to the same sorts of criticism. Nevertheless, regardless of the theory one chooses, discrimination against lesbians and gays in housing, employment, and public accommodations, because it is usually based on either irrational or irrelevant grounds or on a loose use of concepts, causes serious suffering to the individuals involved and a detriment to the society that loses the benefits of the full and unfettered contributions of its lesbian and gay members....

NOTES

[1]Given that the next generation of gay and lesbian civil rights activists will aim their efforts primarily at the federal and state levels, it is worth noting that antidiscrimination laws covering (at least some) housing, employment, and public accommodations have already been passed in California, Connecticut, Hawaii, Massachusetts, New Jersey, Vermont, and Wisconsin.

[2]John Rawls, *A Theory of Justice* (Cambridge, MA: Harvard University Press, 1971): 136–142.

[3]Alan Gewirth, *Political Philosophy* (London: Macmillan, 1965): 10.

[4]David E. Greenberg, *The Construction of Homosexuality* (Chicago: University of Chicago Press, 1988): 470.

[5]Immanuel Kant, *Foundations of the Metaphysics of Morals* (Indianapolis: Bobbs-Merrill, 1959), and *Lectures on Ethics* (Indianapolis: Hackett, 1963).

CHAPTER 2

Prostitution

INTRODUCTION

Unlike their attitudes towards gay and lesbian sex, few Americans feel it appropriate to subject consensual heterosexual conduct to pervasive legal scrutiny. Most believe that unleashing the full force of the criminal law to reduce or eradicate consensual conduct invariably involves unjustifiable inequities in enforcement and unacceptable intrusions into the private lives of citizens. Thus even for those finding some consensual sex wrong, legal tolerance of "objectionable-even-if-consensual" heterosexual sex seems a fair price for security and privacy in matters of sexual choice. Similarly, few wish to prohibit free economic exchanges for services desired by informed consenting adults. Admittedly, state regulation of certain exchanges are reasonable and consistent with the common good. Blanket prohibition, however, is inconsistent with both individual liberty and the fundamental mechanisms of a free market. But then, by what alchemy does the combination of these two activities—consensual sex and free economic exchange—become conduct deserving of legal prohibition? Is the legal prohibition of commercial sex unjustifiably intrusive and inconsistent with liberty and the market? Why, then, should prostitution be criminal?

In *People v. Johnson*, the Appellate Court of Illinois rejected arguments that the Illinois statute prohibiting prostitution is an unconstitutional violation of the prostitute's constitutional rights of free speech, association, and privacy. Because the state has a legitimate interest in "safeguarding the public health, safety and welfare through a law prohibiting prostitution," the court argued, prostitution can be criminalized. Hence appeals to basic constitutional rights to protect prostitution are ill-founded, for such rights are justifiably annulled when exercised for criminal purposes. The court admits that the legitimate state interests served by the criminal prohibition of prostitution might be better served if prostitution were legalized and regulated. But the decision to regulate rather than prohibit is properly that of the legislature which, the court held, had enacted a reasonable statute.

If this court intends concerns with the public welfare to embrace the "integrity and stability of family life," then their decision can be read as consistent with the argument of the majority in *Bowers v. Hardwick* (see Chapter 1) and the tradition of legal moralism found throughout American jurisprudence in matters of sex and sexuality. Defined by Rosemarie Tong as holding "that individual liberty may be limited to prevent immoral behavior," where "immoral" is identified with conventional morality, legal moralism is criticized by Tong and subjected to a sustained attack by Lars Ericsson. Ericsson contends that many of the problems attending prostitution stem not from any inherent wrongness in commercial sex, but rather from the irrational attitudes of conventional morality towards "promiscuous sexual relations in general and prostitution in particular."

However, the court seems to avoid justifying criminalization on grounds of legal paternalism, the position which permits limitations on an individual's liberty for that individual's own good. Legal paternalism certainly can justify prohibition of child prostitution and might well serve as appropriate grounds for regulating prostitution by, for example, providing medical services for prostitutes and information regarding various health risks to both prostitutes and their customers. For these measures are consistent with protecting the interests of those, for example, children, who are not capable of fully informed voluntary consent, or whose freedom of choice would be significantly augmented by relevant information. In referring only to the legislature's concern with matters of the common or public interest, this court does not endorse banning prostitution solely because of the harm which might or does result to or for the informed, consenting adults who voluntarily provide and purchase sexual services. Thus the court's decision seems to elude the serious criticisms of paternalistic prohibitions as discussed by both Tong and Ericsson.

But is the court's position sound? Ought the state be permitted to prohibit the voluntary conduct of informed adults on the basis of beliefs which, though "reasonable," are questionable? What does the evidence regarding prostitution show? Does prostitution pose a serious public health risk (like cigarette smoking, for example), or are such charges grossly exaggerated? Does prostitution cause crime or, as many who have studied societies where prostitution is legal have argued, are the crimes associated with prostitution the result of its criminalization? Indeed to what degree are the "reasonable" beliefs of legislators suspect because they are permeated by the conventional prejudices about sex and sexuality against which Ericsson issues his warnings? In the absence of unambiguous evidence of significant public harm, it might be argued, the voluntary choices of ordinary adults should prevail; otherwise the choices of prostitutes and their customers are, as claimed in the "World Whores' Congress Statement," subject to unjustifiable interference. The pertinent questions remaining, then, are those concerning the type and extent of legal regulation appropriate to commercial sex. Should prostitutes be licensed, required to obtain medical certificates, and limited to "red light zones" or, as argued by prostitutes' rights organizations such as Coyote (Call Off Your Old Tired Ethics), are such measures simply mechanisms of patriarchal control which prevent women from exercising their sexual autonomy?

Various critics of prostitution, including certain Marxists and feminists (including some socialist feminists, Marxist feminists, and radical feminists), warn against viewing prostitution independent of its actual history, a history where prostitution is but one component, though perhaps the most visible and egregious, of the systematic sexual and economic exploitation of women. For these critics, talk of prostitutes' "voluntary choice" and free exercise of sexual autonomy is profoundly suspect, for it neglects the full nature and complete extent of women's subordination in societies which are capitalistic and/or patriarchal, in short, in all societies in which prostitution has flourished. Both Ericsson and Tong offer responses to some of these concerns and consider seriously the contention of various prostitutes' rights organizations that, rather than being among the most oppressed women, prostitutes are—or at least could be in the proper social and legal circumstances—among the most liberated of women. For certainly if woman's liberation is to be meaningful, it must include all women, including prostitutes.

But Laurie Shrage pushes the discussion further. Shrage questions the commitment common to the analyses of many who both defend and criticize either the legalization or decriminalization of prostitution. That questionable commitment is that prostitution can be fully understood independent of the dominant attitudes and cultural conventions which prostitution, as it occurs in a particular society such as the United States, serves to reinforce. For Shrage, prostitution, which is tied to a particular social construction of sexuality, is not a simple effect of the myriad factors contributing to the domination of women. Rather, prostitution nourishes these factors and thus functions to sustain them. Thus there is an important sense in which discussions of the morally proper legal status of commercial sex are beside the point, for they assume that simple legal change creates social and cultural transformation. Those concerned with prostitution as a harmful, socially determined form of sexual intercourse would do better, then, to direct their energies towards the subversion of those beliefs which prostitution, as a culturally determined phenomenon of female oppression, presupposes and reinforces.

SUGGESTED READINGS

Kathleen Barry, *Female Sexual Slavery* (New York: New York University Press, 1984).

Laurie Bell, *Good Girls/Bad Girls: Feminists and Sex Trade Workers Face to Face* (Seattle: Seal Press, 1987).

Valerie Jenness, *Making It Work: The Prostitutes' Rights Movement in Perspective* (New York: Walter de Gruyter, Inc., 1993).

Laurie Shrage, *Moral Dilemmas of Feminism* (New York: Routledge, 1994).

PEOPLE v. JOHNSON

Appellate Court of Illinois
376 N.E.2d 381 (1978)

Opinion by Justice Simon

The defendant, Althea Johnson, was charged with prostitution for agreeing to perform an act of deviate sexual conduct for money. (Ill. Rev. Stat. 1975, ch. 38, par. 11–14(a)(2).) The statute provides:

"Section 11–14. Prostitution. (a) Any person who performs, offers or agrees to perform any of the following acts for money commits the act of prostitution:

1. Any act of sexual intercourse; or
2. Any act of deviate sexual conduct.

(b) Sentence.

Prostitution is a Class A misdemeanor." Ill. Rev. Stat. 1975, ch. 38, 11–14. After a bench trial she was found guilty, fined $100, and sentenced to serve 8 days in the Cook County House of Correction. The appellate court reversed the conviction (*People v. Johnson* (1975), 34 Ill. App. 3d 38, 339 N.E.2d 325), concluding that there was a fatal variance between the charge in the complaint and the proof adduced at trial. The Supreme Court reversed the appellate court's decision (*People v. Johnson* (1976), 65 Ill. 2d 332, 357 N.E.2d 1166), and remanded the case to this court to consider the other issues the defendant raised in her appeal.

The defendant now contends: (1) the prostitution statute is unconstitutional, either on its face or as applied to her case, (2) she was not proven guilty beyond a reasonable doubt,... We reject these contentions and affirm the defendant's conviction.

The complaint against the defendant, made out by Chicago Police Department vice investigator Andrew Murcia, charged that she "committed the offense of prostitution (deviate sexual conduct) in that she agreed to perform an act of deviate sexual conduct, namely oral copulation with Andrew Murcia, for the sum of $50.00 U.S.C."

At trial, Investigator Murcia, the State's sole witness, testified that at about 7 P.M., dressed in civilian clothes, he was leaving his private car at 1300 North Clark Street, on his way to a part-time job at the Ambassador East Hotel. The defendant approached him and offered to perform an act of oral copulation for $50, using a word which the witness testified was street slang for an act of oral copulation. He stated that he declined the offer, but did not arrest the defendant at that time because he was alone, and it is not considered good police policy for a lone officer to arrest a woman. He said that after he watched the defendant enter a car driven by a man, he followed them in his own car to approximately 3153 North Broadway. At this point, Investigator Murcia asked a squad car to stop the car in which the defendant was riding, and the defendant and her companion, William Kraus, were arrested and taken to police headquarters. Investigator Murcia testified that although the defendant began to talk about a lawsuit after her arrest, he did not initiate the conversation or ask her if she wanted to talk about a lawsuit.

The testimony of the defendant and Kraus established that Kraus had known the defendant for six years and owned a company which employed the defendant. Their testimony was that on the night in question Kraus picked her up at her apartment and the two of them drove to a restaurant in the 3100 block of North Broadway. The two then were stopped by two policemen, ordered out of their car, and arrested by Investigator Murcia.

The defendant denied that the incident Investigator Murcia described ever took place, or that she had walked at 1300 North Clark at any time that day, or that she ever had seen Investigator Murcia before her arrest at 3100 North Broadway. She also testified that after her arrest, Investigator Murcia said to her, "I understand you are involved in a lawsuit. You want to talk about it?"

Kraus testified that on the evening in question, he was on a date with the defendant. He agreed with her version of what happened that evening, and said that she did not have a conversation with Murcia prior to the arrest....

The defendant's first contention is that the statute defining the crime of prostitution in this State is unconstitutional on its face, or was unconstitutionally applied to her. Essentially, the defendant takes a scattershot approach, arguing that the statute violates (i) her due process rights under the Fourteenth Amendment, by being unconstitutionally vague; (ii) her First Amendment rights to freedom of speech and association; and (iii) her First, Third, Fourth, Fifth, Ninth and Fourteenth Amendment rights of privacy. These defenses are not novel. Similar ones were raised by persons charged with violating prohibitions against prostitution....

The defendant's first constitutional attack is that the prostitution statute is unconstitutionally vague because it would make a "prostitute" of a woman who offers, performs or agrees to perform sexual acts in overt or tacit exchange for an expensive dinner or a concert, an exchange the defendant contends is part of an unwritten social code. The defendant argues that the overbroad language of the statute would apply to women who perform such sexual acts in return for gifts or evenings out.

This argument is unsound. The committee which drafted the statute specifically limited its language to apply only to sex acts performed for "money," instead of for "any valuable consideration." And case law has indicated that an offer or agreement to receive money, rather than, for example, a fur coat or a night at the opera for sexual favors is essential to a prostitution conviction. Thus, the Illinois prostitution statute applies only to those who offer, perform or agree to perform a sexual act for money; the statute does not discourage exchanges of sexual acts as a part of social companionship or for gifts of material goods. The statute, then, is not an overbroad or vague attempt to regulate sexual conduct in general, or even sexual acts which result, for whatever motives, from ordinary social situations. Because the statute provides an ascertainable standard of conduct, is specifically directed at a defined evil, and is not so vague as to inhibit the exercise of constitutionally protected freedoms, it is not void for being overbroad. *Baggett v. Bullitt* (1964), 377 U.S. 360; *Beauharnais v. Illinois* (1951), 343 U.S. 250, 96. ...

We also reject the defendant's claims that the statute takes away her constitutional rights to freedom of speech and freedom of association under the First Amendment. The defendant contends that her right to freedom of speech permitted her to speak to Investigator Murcia in the way she did. Even the essential and basic freedom provided by the First Amendment which is cherished as a cornerstone of our liberty is not absolute. In *United States v. O'Brien* (1968), 391 U.S. 367, 377, 20 L. Ed. 2d 672, 680, 88 S. Ct. 1673, the Supreme Court stated that when "speech" and "nonspeech" elements are combined in the same course of conduct, governmental statutory regulation of speech is justified, "if it is within the constitutional power of the Government; if it furthers an important or substantial governmental interest...unrelated to the suppression of free expression; and if the incidental restriction on alleged First Amendment freedoms is no greater than is essential to the furtherance of that interest."

The Illinois statute meets the O'Brien tests. There is an important and substantial governmental interest in eliminating acts of prostitution because of the potential prostitution has for causing crime and spreading disease, as noted below. And the State's interest in regulating prostitution is unrelated to the suppression of free speech, for prostitution can be effectively combated only by prohibiting spoken offers and agreements to perform acts of prostitution. The complainants in prostitution cases are often, as in this case, police officers who have been solicited. If an offer standing alone were not prohibited conduct, the police could not be complainants in prostitution cases unless they first actually performed acts of intercourse with the persons they were arresting—a practice which no doubt would create a great deal of marital dissatisfaction and public criticism. Thus, the incidental restriction on speech here is not greater than is essential to further the State's interest, because the regulatory enactment is "carefully and narrowly aimed" at the forbidden conduct.

In addition, the Supreme Court has repeatedly stated that speech is not constitutionally protected when it is part of a course of criminal conduct. In *Giboney v. Empire Storage & Ice Co.* (1949), 336 U.S. 490, 498, the Supreme Court said:

"It rarely has been suggested that the constitutional freedom for speech and press extends its immunity to speech or writing used as an integral part of conduct in violation of a valid criminal statute. We reject the contention now." And in *Cox v. Louisiana* (1965), 379 U.S. 536, 554, 563, the court, recognizing the necessity for regulating types of speech aimed at furthering anti-social or criminal purposes, said:

"...The constitutional guarantee of liberty implies the existence of an organized society maintaining public order, without which liberty itself would be lost in the excesses of anarchy.... The examples are many of the application by this Court of the principle that certain forms of conduct mixed with speech may be regulated or prohibited."

Illinois courts also have recognized the danger of a purported exercise of free speech which is actually intended to circumscribe freedom by ruling that words may be prohibited where they are intended to be part of a course of criminal action. (See *Beauharnais,* at 266.) In *Chicago Real Estate Board v. City of Chicago* (1967), 36 Ill. 2d 530, the court upheld an ordinance which prohibited distribution by real estate brokers of statements designed to induce owners to sell their property because of the entry into neighborhoods of minority races. The court ruled that such statements were not protected by freedom of speech, since "[w]here speech is an integral part of unlawful conduct, it has no constitutional protection." *Chicago,* at 552–53.

The defendant in the present case was found by the trier of fact to have offered to perform an act of oral copulation for money. Thus, her spoken words were designed to lead immediately to an illegal act. Her First Amendment rights did not give her a license in the guise of free speech to use words which were an integral part of a course of criminal conduct.

Turning next to the defendant's claim that she was denied her right to associational freedom, the defendant has not demonstrated how she was prevented from or penalized for associating with anyone. In *Griswold v. Connecticut* (1965), 381 U.S. 479, 483, the Supreme Court wrote: "The right of 'association'...is more than the right to attend a meeting; it includes the right to express one's attitudes or philosophies by membership in a group or by affiliation with it or by other lawful means. Association in that context is a form of expression of opinion...." Thus, if the statute in question banned the defendant from joining a group of prostitutes, or from attending a meeting of prostitutes, or prevented her from receiving foodstamps, or speaking publicly about the merits of legalizing prostitution because she was charged with being a prostitute, the defendant might have a legitimate First Amendment associational freedom claim. But here the defendant was not prevented from talking with, or walking with, Investigator Murcia. She was merely prohibited from propositioning Investigator Murcia to engage in sexual relations with her for money. The defendant was penalized for associating with Investigator Murcia in only one specified and prohibited way—for offering, performing or agreeing to perform, an act of sexual intercourse with him for money. Thus, to argue that the defendant's First Amendment freedom of association was abridged by the statute demeans the essence of that fundamental freedom, and on its face is as demonstrably unsupportable as would be the argument that freedom of association encompasses the right to gather together to plan or commit crime.

The defendant's final constitutional argument is that her prosecution invaded her constitutionally protected right of privacy. A person's sexual life is normally highly personal and appropriately protected from unwarranted governmental intrusion. But the defendant's conduct here was utterly at odds with her claim that her privacy was impinged upon. In this case, the evidence established that the defendant approached Investigator Murcia on a public street and offered to perform a sexual act for $50. There was nothing private about her relationship with him, or about the place where she made her offer. Although several recent decisions have ruled that certain private conduct, such as the use of contraceptives (*Griswold*), possession of obscene materials in one's own home (*Stanley v. Georgia* (1969), 394 U.S. 557), or a decision to have an abortion in the early stages of pregnancy (*Roe v. Wade* (1973), 410 U.S. 113), may not be prohibited by criminal law, none of these holdings is relevant to what happened here, where a citizen's right to privacy was not at stake.

And even if we accept the dubious position that the defendant's actions were encompassed, and so protected, by her constitutional right to privacy in sexual matters, the State legislature was acting within its proper scope of authority in limiting this "right" because of the State's interest in safeguarding the public health, safety and welfare through a law prohibiting prostitution. Although many persons have urged that the State's interest in protecting the public by preventing venereal disease, cutting down prostitution-related crimes of violence and theft, and protecting the integrity and stability of family life could better be served by legalizing and regulating prostitution, rather than by prohibiting it, such an argument should be settled by the legislature, rather than by this court. The Illinois statute forbidding prostitution is a rational attempt to protect valid State interests. As such, it is a valid exercise of the legislature's authority, and must be upheld.

As the Supreme Court noted in its implicit approval of anti-prostitution statutes in *Paris Adult Theatre I v. Slaton* (1973), 413 U.S. 49, 68, "The state statute books are replete with constitutionally unchallenged laws against prostitution." In seeking to legitimize her conduct by wrapping herself in the concepts of free speech, freedom of association and right of privacy, the defendant debases these noble and fundamental legacies of our constitutional heritage. The defendant's challenge to the constitutionality of the Illinois law prohibiting prostitution must be rebuffed.

Judgment affirmed.

CHARGES AGAINST PROSTITUTION: AN ATTEMPT AT A PHILOSOPHICAL ASSESSMENT

Lars O. Ericsson

A NEGLECTED PHILOSOPHICAL TASK

The debate over prostitution is probably as old as prostitution itself. And the discussion of the oldest profession is as alive today as it ever was. New books and articles are constantly being published, new scientific reports and theories presented, and new committees and commissions formed.[1] Yet while the scientific and literary discussion is very much alive, the philosophical discussion of it seems never even to have come to life. How is this to be explained? And is there any justification for it?

Could it be that harlotry is a topic unsuitable for philosophical treatment? Or could it be that, although suitable, it does not give rise to any interesting philosophical questions? Obviously, I would not be writing this article if I thought that the answer to any of these questions was yes.

"Charges Against Prostitution," by Lars O. Ericsson in *Ethics* 90 (April 1980): 335–366. © 1980 by The University of Chicago. Reprinted by permission.

But I wish to emphasize that it seems absurd to maintain that the subject is unsuitable for philosophical treatment, since it clearly involves many normative and evaluative issues....

It is the purpose of this paper to undertake a critical assessment of the view that prostitution is an undesirable social phenomenon that ought to be eradicated. I shall do this by examining what seem to me (and to others) the most important and serious charges against prostitution. I shall try to show that mercenary love *per se* must, upon closer inspection, be acquitted of most of these charges. Instead, I shall argue, the major culprit is the hostile and punitive attitudes which the surrounding hypocritical society adopts toward promiscuous sexual relations in general and prostitution in particular.

THE CHARGE FROM CONVENTIONAL MORALITY

By far the most common ground for holding that prostitution is undesirable is that it constitutes a case of sexual immorality. Society and conventional morality condemn it. The law at best barely tolerates it; sometimes, as in most states in the United States, it downright prohibits it. In order to improve prostitution, we must first and foremost improve our attitudes toward it. Contrary to what is usually contended, I shall conclude that prostitution, although not in any way *ultimately* desirable, is still conditionally desirable because of certain ubiquitous and permanent imperfections of actual human societies.

The prostitute, according to the moralist, is a sinful creature who ought to be banned from civilized society. Whoredom is "the great social evil," representing a flagrant defiance of common decency. The harlot is a threat to the family, and she corrupts the young. To engage in prostitution signifies a total loss of character. To choose "the life"' is to choose a style of living unworthy of any decent human being. And so on.

There is also a less crude form of moralism, which mixes moral disapproval with a more "compassionate" and "concerned" attitude. The fate of a whore is "a fate worse than death." The hustler is a poor creature who has to debase herself in order to gratify the lusts of immoral men. Prostitution is degrading for all parties involved, but especially for the woman.

It might seem tempting to say that the best thing to do with respect to the moralistic critique is to ignore it. But this is exactly what moral philosophers have been doing for far too long. It appears that many otherwise sophisticated persons more or less consciously adhere to views of a rather unreflectively moralistic kind where prostitution is concerned. More important, to ignore conventional moralism would be philosophically unsatisfactory for the simple reason that the mere fact that an idea is conventional does not constitute a disproof of its validity. Thus, arguments are what we need, not silence.

How are the hostile and punitive attitudes of society toward prostitution to be explained? It seems to be an anthropological fact that sexual institutions are ranked on the basis of their relation to reproduction. Hence, in virtue of its intimate relation to reproduction, the monogamous marriage constitutes the sexual institution in society which is ranked the highest and which receives the strongest support from law and mores. On the other hand, the less a sexual practice has to do with the bearing and rearing of children, the less sanctioned it is. Therefore, when coitus is practiced for pecuniary reasons (the hooker), with pleasure and not procreation in mind (the client), we have a sexual practice that, far from being sanctioned, finds itself at the opposite extreme on the scale of social approval.[2]

Two other factors should be mentioned in this connection. First, wherever descent is reckoned solely through the male line, promiscuity in the female can hardly be approved by society. And the property relations associated with descent of course point in the same direction. Second, our Christian heritage—especially in its Lutheran and Calvinist versions—is both antisexual and antihedonistic. To indulge in sexual activities is bad enough, but to indulge in them for the sheer fun and pleasure of them is a major feat in the art of sin. Moreover, sex is consuming, and as such, quite contrary to Protestant morals with respect to work.

An explanation of our antiprostitution attitudes and their probably prehistoric roots must not, however, be confused with a *rationale* for their continuation in our own time. That we understand why the average moralist, who is a predominantly unreflecting upholder of prevailing rules and values, regards prostitution and prostitutes as immoral gives us no good reason to shield those rules and values from criticism, especially if we find, upon reflection, that they are no longer adequate to our present social conditions.

That prostitution neither is nor ever was a threat to reproduction within the nuclear family is too obvious to be worth arguing for. Nor has it ever been a threat to the family itself. People marry and visit whores for quite different reasons. In point of fact, the greatest threat to the family is also the greatest threat to prostitution, namely, complete sexual liberty for both sexes. The conclusion we must draw from this is that neither the value of future generations nor the importance of the family (if it is important) warrants the view that prostitution is bad and undesirable.

It is hardly likely, however, that the moralist would be particularly perturbed by this, for the kernel of his view is, rather, that to engage in prostitution is *intrinsically* wrong. Both whore and customer (or at least the former) act immorally, according to the moralist, even if neither of them nor anyone else gets hurt. Mercenary love *per se* is regarded as immoral.

...There is something fanatic about both of these views which I find utterly repelling. If two adults voluntarily consent to an economic arrangement concerning sexual activity and this activity takes place in private, it seems plainly absurd to maintain that there is something intrinsically wrong with it. In fact, I very much doubt that it is wrong at all. To say that prostitution is intrinsically immoral is in a way to refuse to give any arguments. The moralist simply "senses" or "sees" its immorality. And this terminates rational discussion at the point where it should begin.

THE SENTIMENTALIST CHARGE

There is also a common contention that harlotry is undesirable because the relation between whore and customer must by the nature of things be a very poor relation to nonmercenary sex. Poor, not in a moral but in a nonmoral, sense. Since the majority of the objections under this heading have to do with the quality of the feelings and sentiments involved, or with the lack of them, I shall refer to this critique as "the sentimentalist charge."

Sex between two persons who love and care for one another can of course be, and often is, a very good thing. The affection and tenderness which exists between the parties tends to create an atmosphere in which the sexual activities can take place in such a way as to be a source of mutual pleasure and satisfaction. Sexual intercourse is here a way of becoming even more intimate in a relation which is already filled with other kinds of intimacies.

Now, according to the sentimentalist, mercenary sex lacks just about all of these qualities. Coitus between prostitute and client is held to be impoverished, cold, and impersonal. The association is regarded as characterized by detachment and emotional noninvolvement. And the whole thing is considered to be a rather sordid and drab affair.

In order to answer this charge, there is no need to romanticize prostitution. Mercenary sex usually *is* of poorer quality compared with sentimental sex between lovers. To deny this would be simply foolish. But does it follow from this that hustling is undesirable? Of course not! That would be like contending that because 1955 Chateau Mouton Rothschild is a much better wine than ordinary claret, we should condemn the act of drinking the latter.

The sentimentalist's mistake lies in the comparison on which he relies. He contrasts a virtual sexual ideal with prostitutional sex, which necessarily represents an entirely different kind of erotic association and which therefore fulfills quite different social and individual functions. Only a minute share of all sex that takes place deserves to be described as romantic sex love. And if, in defending mercenary sex, we should beware of romanticizing it, the same caution holds for the sentimentalist when he is describing nonprostitutional sex. The sex lives of ordinary people often fall miles short of the sentimentalist's ideal. On the other hand, the sexual services performed by harlots are by no means always of such poor quality as we are conditioned to think. And we would most likely think better of them were we able to rid ourselves of the feelings of guilt and remorse that puritanism and conventional morality create in us....

This brings us to another aspect of the sentimentalist charge. It is not seldom a tacit and insidious presupposition of the sentimentalist's reasoning that good sex equals intramarital sex, and that bad sex equals extramarital—especially prostitutional—sex. This is just another stereotype, which deserves to be destroyed. Concerning this aspect, Benjamin and Masters make the following comment: "The experience with a prostitute is probably ethically, and may be esthetically, on a higher level than an affectionless intercourse between husband and wife, such as is all too common in our present society."[3] The demarcation line between marital and mercenary sex is not quality but the contrasting nature of the respective legal arrangements. Furthermore, we must not think that the quality —in terms of physical pleasure—of the sex services of prostitutes varies any less than the quality of "regular" sex. The best prostitutional sex available is probably much better from the customer's point of view than average marital sex....

In conclusion, I would like to counter the charge that the prostitute-customer relationship is bad on the ground that it involves the selling of something that is too basic and too elementary in human life to be sold. This is perhaps not a sentimentalist charge proper, but since it seems to be related to it I shall deal with it here.

Common parlance notwithstanding, what the hustler sells is of course not her body or vagina, but sexual services. If she actually did sell herself, she would no longer be a prostitute but a sexual slave. I wish to emphasize this simple fact, because the popular misnomer certainly contributes to and maintains our distorted views about prostitution.

But is it not bad enough to sell sexual services? To go to bed with someone just for the sake of money? To perform fellatio on a guy you neither love nor care for? In view of the fact that sex is a fundamental need, is it not wrong that anyone should have to pay to have it satisfied and that anyone should profit from its satisfaction? Is it not a deplorable fact that in the prostitute-customer relationship sexuality is completely alienated from the rest of the personality and reduced to a piece of merchandise?

In reply to these serious charges I would, first, like to confess that I have the greatest sympathy for the idea that the means necessary for the satisfaction of our most basic needs should be free, or at least not beyond the economic means of anyone. We all need food, so food should be available to us. We all need clothes and a roof over our heads, so these things should also be available to us. And since our sexual desires are just as basic, natural, and compelling as our appetite for food, this also holds for them. But I try not to forget that this is, and probably for long time will remain, an ideal state of affairs.

...That we have to pay for the satisfaction of our most basic appetites is no reason for stigmatizing those individuals whose profession it is to cater to those appetites. With this, I take it, at least the nonfanatical sentimentalist agrees. But if so, it seems to me inconsistent to hold that prostitution is undesirable on the ground that it involves the selling of something that, ideally, should not be sold but freely given away. Emotional prejudice aside, there is on *this* ground no more reason to despise the sex market and those engaged in it than there is to despise the food market and those engaged in it.

But still is there not an abyss between selling meat and selling "flesh"? Is there not something private, personal, and intimate about sex that makes it unfit for commercial purposes? Of course, I do not wish to deny that there are great differences between what the butcher does and what the whore does, but at the same time it seems to me clear that the conventional labeling of the former as "respectable" and the latter as "indecent" is not so much the result of these differences as of the influence of cultural, especially religious and sexual, taboos. That the naked human body is "obscene," that genitalia are "offending," that menstrual blood is "unclean," etc., are expressions of taboos which strongly contribute to the often-neurotic way in which sex is surrounded with mysteriousness and secrecy. Once we have been able to liberate ourselves from these taboos we will come to realize that we are no more justified devaluating the prostitute, who, for example, masturbates her customers, than we are in devaluating the assistant nurse, whose job it is to take care of the intimate hygiene of disabled patients. Both help to satisfy important human needs, and both get paid for doing so. That the harlot, in distinction to the nurse, intentionally gives her client pleasure is of course nothing that should be held against her....

THE PATERNALISTIC CHARGE

It is a well-established fact that the occupational hazards connected with prostitution constitute a serious problem. The prostitute runs the risk of being hurt, physically as well as mentally. On the physical side there is always the risk of getting infected by some venereal disease. Certain forms of urosis are known to be more common among harlots than among women in general. And then there is the risk of assault and battery from customers with sadistic tendencies. On the mental side we encounter such phenomena as depression and neurosis, compulsive behavior, self-degrading and self-destructive impulses, etc.

It is therefore not uncommon to find it argued that prostitution is undesirable because it is not in the best interest of the prostitute to be what she is. It is held that society should, for the prostitute's own good, try to prevent people from becoming prostitutes and to try to "rehabilitate" those who already are. This type of criticism I shall refer to as "the paternalistic charge."

I shall not consider the question—discussed by Mill, Devlin, Hart, and others—of whether society has the *right* to interfere with a person's liberty for his own good. I shall limit my discussion to the question of whether the fact that the hustler runs the risks that she runs is a good reason for holding that prostitution is undesirable.

A comparison with other fields clearly shows that the fact that a certain job is very hazardous is not regarded as a good reason for the view that the type of job in question is undesirable. Take, for instance, a miner: he runs considerable risks in his job, but we hardly think that this warrants the conclusion that mining should be prohibited. What we do think (or at least ought to think) is that, since the miner is doing a socially valuable job, everything possible should be done to minimize those risks by improving his working conditions, by installing various safety devices, introducing shorter working hours, etc. It seems to me, therefore, that in cases like this—and there are many of them—paternalistic considerations carry no weight. The individual is not to be protected from himself (for wanting to take risks) but from certain factors in the environment. It is not the individual who should be changed, but the milieu in which he has to place himself in order to be able to follow his occupational inclinations.

Unless the paternalist simply assumes what remains to be proven, namely, that what the prostitute does is of no value to society, a similar argument also applies in the case of prostitution. The individual whore does not need to be protected from herself if her hustling is voluntary in the same sense of "voluntary" as someone's choice of profession may be voluntary. What she does need protection from are detrimental factors in the social environment, especially the hostile, punitive, or condescending attitudes of so-called respectable citizens. It is not the hooker who should be changed, reformed, or rehabilitated, but the social milieu in which she works.

The paternalistic charge is not an independent argument against prostitution. It only seems to work because it has already given in to conventional morality. To oppose prostitution by referring to the welfare, good, happiness, needs, or interests of the prostitute may seem very noble and humanitarian, but in reality it serves the status quo by leaving the norms and values of the surrounding society intact, viewing prostitution through the unreflected spectacles of a conservative public opinion, and placing the "blame" exclusively on the individual....

To sum up: the paternalistic charge rests on two assumptions, neither of which is valid. First, it rests on the assumption that a society's scorn for whoredom is justified. Second, it rests on the assumption that the hooker is not doing a socially valuable job. From these assumptions, together with the fact that harlotry is known to be a hazardous profession, the paternalist jumps to the conclusion that prostitution is undesirable and that society should intervene against it for the prostitutes' own good.

THE MARXIST CHARGE

Generally speaking, Marxist opposition to prostitution forms part and parcel of Marxist opposition to capitalism and to the property and family relations created by it. Harlotry is regarded as the offspring of class society, and, says Engels, it "is based on private property and falls with it."[4] One of the most refreshing and original features of the Marxist analysis and critique of prostitution is that it is comparatively free from conventional moralism. At least this is true of the classics, Marx and Engels. Far from morally condemning the courtesan, they put her on a par with the woman in the holiest of bourgeois institutions, the family:

> In both cases [in Catholic and Protestant bourgeois marriage], however, marriage is determined by the class position of the participants, and to that extent, always remains marriage of convenience. In both cases, this marriage of convenience often enough turns into the crassest prostitution—sometimes on both sides, but much more generally on the part of the wife, who differs from the ordinary courtesan only in that she does not hire out her body, like a wage-worker, on piece-work, but sells it into slavery once and for all.[5]

Marxists also draw close parallels between production and wage labor. Thus, for instance, Aleksandra Kollontai contends that "bargaining over the female body is closely related to bargaining over female working power. Prostitution can only finally disappear when wage labor does."[6] In a similar vein, a contemporary socialist, Sheila Rowbotham, writes: "Just as the prostitute gives the substitute of love for money, the worker hands over his work and his life for a daily wage."[7] What these passages suggest is that the difference between, on the one hand, courtesan and the married bourgeois woman, and on the other, harlot and wageworker is one of *degree* and not one of *kind*. The general condition of women and wageworkers in capitalist society is an inhuman one. The specific condition of the prostitute does not consist in her being morally depraved or "vicious," but in her being the most degraded and miserable of her class.

The strength of the Marxist analysis is, it seems to me, twofold. First, it resolutely brushes aside the moralistic veil, which lures us to place the prostitute in a category of her own—a category that creates a barrier between her and ordinary, "decent" people. Second, it does not regard prostitution as an isolated phenomenon but places it in its socioeconomic context....

The weakness of the Marxist critique lies partly in the fact that it is so general and unspecific, and partly in the fact that, where it is specific enough to allow empirical test, it is contradicted by the data in several important respects. And since it is the theoretical analysis which constitutes the basis for the thesis that harlotry is undesirable (together with certain value premises, of course), this severely undermines the Marxist critique.

By saying that the Marxist critique is so general and unspecific, I mean that it is not a critique of whoredom *per se*. In fact, Marxist opposition to prostitution is completely derivative of Marxist opposition to capitalism. I have already conceded that this has the virtue of displaying the similarities between prostitution and other social institutions and practices like, for instance, marriage, the family, and wage labor. But at the same time, this implies that harlotry is no worse, no more undesirable, than these other institutions and practices. For if, as the Marxist contends, the wageworker and the harlot are the products of the same social conditions, and if these conditions force them both to prostitute themselves, the former to sell working power, the latter to sell sexual services, there seems to be no rational foundation left for moralizing distinctions with regard to their respective activities. They are both victims of the same inhuman social system. At most the whore is more victimized than the wageworker, but since, according to Marxist theory, if you have the one you get the other, it makes little if no sense to hold that they are unequally undesirable....

This brings us to the question of the correctness of the Marxist analysis of prostitution. To begin with, Engels's contention that prostitution is based on private property and falls with it is hardly sustained by empirical data. One of the oldest forms of prostitution, temple prostitution, was based on certain religious beliefs rather than on private property. Nor is it true that harlotry "falls" with the abolition of private property, as the evidence from countries with socialist economies clearly shows....

Furthermore, there are two sides of prostitution: supply and demand. And these two sides give rise to entirely different questions. On the supply side, first and foremost the question is: Why do women become prostitutes? As we have seen, the Marxist answer here is that women become prostitutes because their socioeconomic position in class society makes it necessary. For example, writing about the situation in the nineteenth century, Sheila Rowbotham says that "it [prostitution] became a necessary way of supplementing their wages for large numbers of urban working women."[8] And even if it is inadequate—especially within the context of a welfare society—this answer at least has some truth in it.[9] But when we come to the demand side, to the question of why men ask and are willing to pay for the sexual services of harlots, the economistic character of the Marxist analysis makes it fail completely. It is bound to fail for the simple and obvious reason that the sex drive—which constitutes a necessary condition for the demand—is neither an economic phenomenon nor a phenomenon less basic (in fact it is more basic) than any economic factor. The "economic base" is not, in other words, a base for the explanation of the ubiquitous demand for the services of whores. That Marxists cling to the myth that those who visit whores are mainly middle- and upper-class men, and that they on this ground impute to the demand a certain class character, is, on my view, nothing more than a misconceived attempt to cover the fact that Marxist theory is particularly ill suited for the analysis of the demand for prostitutes.

The Marxist portrait of prostitute and customer—she a poor, working-class female, he a lascivious, middle-class male—constitutes too gross an oversimplification to catch the essentials of so complex a phenomenon as prostitution. The class character of harlotry—and there is a class character—is in fact of a nature that is difficult to square with the simplistic view that lets the proletariat stand for the supply and the bourgeoisie for the demand of whores. What empirical data seem to show is that prostitution reflects class society in the following sense. Middle- and upper-class men tend to visit "high-class" whores (call girls and the like), while working class men tend to visit "low-class" whores (streetwalkers, bar and dance-hall prostitutes, fleabags, etc.). And "high-class" prostitutes more often than not come from a background that is not working class.

Before concluding this section I wish to point out—lest there be any misunderstanding—that I do not regard prostitution as desirable or defensible in any ultimate sense. So if Marx, Engels, and their followers are interpreted as merely saying that in the good (that is, the classless) society there is no room or need for prostitution because of the new, truly human relationship between the sexes that exists there, I do not necessarily have anything to object. For it is of course possible to envisage a society in which harlotry would indeed be superfluous. My criticism of Marxism has been exclusively directed against its theoretical analysis of the nature and causes of prostitution in society as it is known in history and against the evaluative conclusion based on that analysis....

THE FEMINIST CHARGE

...I shall in this section discuss a group of arguments in support of the thesis that prostitution is undesirable whose common feature is this fact: prostitution is held to be undesirable on the ground that it constitutes an extreme instance of the inequality between the sexes. Whoredom is regarded as displaying the male oppression of the female in its most naked form. It is contended that the relation between hooker and "John" is one of object to subject—the prostitute being reified into a mere object, a thing for the male's pleasure, lust, and contempt. The customer-man pays to use the whore-woman and consequently has the upper hand. He is the dominating figure, the master. It is the whore's task to oblige, to satisfy his most "perverse" and secret desires, desires that the male is unable to reveal to his wife or girlfriend. Prostitution, it is argued, reduces the woman to a piece of merchandise that anyone who can pay the price may buy. The unequal nature of prostitution is also contended to consist in the fact that it represents a way out of *misère sexuel* only for men. Instead of trying to solve the sexual problems together with his wife, the married man can resort to the services of the hustler; but the woman lacks the same advantage, since there are not so many male heterosexual prostitutes around. I shall refer to this group of arguments as "the feminist charge."

Like the moralist and the Marxist, the feminist is of the opinion that prostitution can and ought to be eradicated. Some feminists, like the moralist, even want to criminalize prostitution. But unlike the moralist, they want to criminalize both whore and customer.

The core of the feminist charge—that prostitution is unequal and disfavors the female sex—deserves to be taken seriously. For social inequality matters both morally and politically. And inequalities based on differences with regard to race, color of skin, religious belief, sex, and the like are particularly serious. Thus, if valid, the feminist critique would constitute powerful support for the view that prostitution is undesirable.

No one denies that a majority of prostitutes are women, and no one denies that a majority of customers are men. But it is clear from the evidence that a large portion of the prostitutes, especially in metropolitan areas, are male homosexuals. There is also lesbian prostitution, though this is not (at least not yet) sufficiently widespread to be of any great social importance. And finally, there is male heterosexual prostitution, the prevalence of which is also rather limited. We may sum up by saying that, rather than constituting a dichotomy between the sexes, prostitution has the characteristic that a considerable portion of the prostitutes are men, and a small minority of the customers are women. I mention this because I think that a rational assessment should not be based on an incomplete picture of the phenomenon under assessment, and I consider these data to have some relevance with respect to the feminist charge against prostitution.

There are at least two types of inequalities. In the one, the inequality consists in the fact that some *benefit* is withheld from some group or individual. A typical example: only white members of a society are allowed to vote. In the other, the inequality consists in the fact that some *burden* is placed only on some group or individual. A typical example: a feudal society in which peasants and artisans are the only ones who have to pay taxes. ...

Is harlotry an unequal practice? And if so, in what precisely does its inequality consist?

If it is conceded that in exchange for his money the customer receives a service—something that at least the sentimentalist seems most reluctant to concede—it could be argued that harlotry is unequal in the sense that some benefit is withheld from or denied women that is not withheld from or denied men...if this is what the feminist charge amounts to, two things appear to be eminently clear. The first is that prostitution is unequal in a less serious way than, for instance, male franchise. For in the latter, the benefit (opportunity to vote) which is withheld from women is withheld from them in the strong sense that it is not legally possible for the women to vote, while in the former, no such legal or formal obstacle stands in their way. In fact, instead of saying that the sex services of prostitutes are withheld or denied women, it would be more appropriate to say that centuries of cultural and social conditioning makes them desist from asking for them. It is after all only recently that women have begun to define their sexuality and require that their sexual needs and desires be recognized. Rowbotham reminds us that: " 'Nymphomania' was actually used in the 1840s to describe any woman who felt sexual desire, and such women were seen as necessarily abandoned, women of the streets, women of the lower classes."[10] The second point is that if, through prostitution, a benefit is "withheld" from the female sex, the best way to deal with this inequality would not be an attempt to stamp out the institution but an attempt to modify it, by making the benefit in question available to both sexes.

Could it be, then, that the inequality of whoredom consists in the fact that some burden is unequally placed on the two sexes and in disfavor of the female sex? This allegation can be interpreted in several different ways. And I shall in what follows consider those that seem to me the most important.

To begin with, this allegation can be understood in accordance with the view that it is women, and not men, who are in peril of becoming prostitutes. But first of all, this is largely untrue since...a great many prostitutes are men. Moreover, the perils of being a prostitute, although existent today, do not constitute a good reason for abolishing harlotry; rather they constitute a good reason for a social reform that will reduce the perils to a minimum tomorrow.

Another way of interpreting this allegation is to say that prostitution constitutes exploitation of the female sex, since harlots are being exploited by, *inter alia*, sex capitalists and customers, and a majority of harlots are women. This interpretation of the allegation merits careful study, and I shall therefore in the first instance limit my discussion to the capitalist exploitation of prostitutes.

There is no doubt...that practically all harlots—irrespective of whether they are high-class call girls, cheap streetwalkers, or sex-club performers—are being exploited, economically, in a much more crude sense than that in which an automobile worker at General Motors is being exploited. I am thinking here of the fact that all of them—and there are very few exceptions to this—have to pay usury rents in order to be able to operate. Many are literally being plundered by their landlord—sex capitalists who often specialize in letting out rooms, flats, or apartments to people in the racket. Not a few prostitutes also have to pay for "protection" to *mafiosi* with close connections to organized crime.

What makes all this possible? And what are the implications of the existence of conditions such as these for the question of the alleged undesirability of prostitution? With respect to the first of these questions, the answer, it seems to me, is that the major culprit is society's hypocritical attitude toward harlotry and harlots. It is this hypocrisy which creates the prerequisites for the sex-capitalist exploitation of the prostitutes. Let me exemplify what I mean by society's hypocritical—and, I might add, totally inconsistent—attitude here. On the one hand, most societies, at least in the West (one deplorable exception is the United States), have followed the U.N. declaration which recommends that prostitution in itself should not be made illegal.[11] One would therefore expect that someone who pursues a legal activity would have the right to rent the necessary premises to advertise her services, and so on—but not so. The penal code persecutes those who rent out rooms, apartments, and other premises to prostitutes. And an editor of a Swedish newspaper was recently convicted for having accepted ads from "models" and "masseuses." In what other legal field or branch would contradictions such as these be considered tolerable? None, of course.... And the most incredible of all is that the official motivation for outlawing persons prepared to provide harlots with the premises necessary for their legal activity is a paternalistic one: so doing is in the best interest of the hustlers themselves, who would otherwise be at the mercy of unscrupulous landlords! In practice, the risk of being thrown in jail of course scares away all but the unscrupulous individuals, who can charge sky-high rents (after all they take a certain risk), and who often are associated with the criminal world. How can anyone, therefore, be surprised at the fact that not so few hustlers display "antisocial tendencies"?

The conclusion I draw from this is that the crude economic exploitation of the prostitutes is not an argument against prostitution. It rather constitutes an accusation against the laws, regulations, and attitudes which create the preconditions for that exploitation. Society cannot both allow harlotry and deprive harlots of reasonable working conditions (as a concession to "common decency"), and still expect that all will be well.

A third way of interpreting the charge that prostitution is unequal, in the sense that it places a burden on women that it does not place on men, is to say that whores are being oppressed, reified, and reduced to a piece of merchandise by their male customers. To begin with the last version of this charge first, I have already pointed out the obvious, namely, that whores do not sell themselves. The individual hooker is not for sale, but her sexual services are. One could therefore with equal lack of propriety say of any person whose job it is to sell a certain service that he, as a result thereof, is reduced to a piece of merchandise. I cannot help suspecting that behind this talk of reduction to a piece of merchandise lies contempt for prostitutes and the kind of services they offer for sale.... Let me just add this: Since when does the fact that we, when visiting a professional, are not interested in him or her as a person, but only in his or her professional performance, constitute a ground for saying that the professional is dehumanized, turned into an object?...

The kind of relationship that exists between prostitute and customer is one that we find in most service professions. It is simply cultural blindness and sexual taboos that prevent so many of us from seeing this. Moreover, in virtue of the prevalence of this type of relationship—contractual relation in which services are traded—I suspect that those who talk about the badness of it in the case of prostitute-customer relationship have in fact long before decided that the relationship is bad on some other—not declared—ground. The means-ends talk is just a way of rationalizing a preconceived opinion.

I shall conclude this section by considering the charge that harlotry constitutes oppression of the female sex. Prostitution is here regarded as displaying male oppression of the female in its most overt and extreme form. The seriousness of this charge calls, to begin with, for a clarification of the meaning of the word "oppression." If A oppresses B, I take it that B's freedom of choice and action is severely reduced, against his will, as a result of actions undertaken by A against B. In the case of political oppression, for example, A thwarts B's desire to form unions and political parties, prevents B from expressing his political opinions, throws B in jail if he refuses to comply, and so on.

It can hardly be disputed that prostitutes are oppressed in this sense. They would not have chosen to become hustlers if some better alternative had been open to them. They are very much aware of the fact that to be a prostitute is to be socially devalued; to be at the bottom of society. To become a hooker is to make just the reverse of a career. It should be observed, however, that none of this warrants the charge that prostitution means the oppression of the female by the male sex. The oppression just described is not an oppression on the basis of sex, as male franchise would be. The "oppressor" is rather those social conditions—present in practically all known social systems—which offer some individuals (both men and women) no better alternative than hustling....

It is not seldom argued from feminist quarters that the liberation of women must start with the liberation of women from exploitation of their sex. Hence the crusade against prostitution, pornography, and the use of beautiful women in commercial advertising, etc. It is argued that women's lib must have as its primary goal the abolition of the (ab)use of the female sex as a commodity. As long as the female sex is up for sale, just like any other commercial object, there can be no true liberation from oppression.

To the reader who has read this far it should be obvious that, at least in part, this type of reasoning rests on or is misguided by such misnomers as "the whore sells her body," "to live by selling oneself," "to buy oneself a piece of ass," etc. So I need not say any more about that. Instead I wish to make a comparison between a typical, middle-class housewife in suburbia and her prostitute counterpart, the moderately successful call girl. And I ask, emotional prejudice aside, which of them needs to be "liberated" the most? Both are doing fairly well economically, but while the housewife is totally dependent on her husband, at least economically, the call girl in that respect stands on her own two feet. If she has a pimp, it is she, not he, who is the breadwinner in the family. Is she a traitor to her own sex? If she is (which I doubt), she is no more a traitor to her own sex than her bourgeois counterpart. For, after all, Engels was basically right when he said that the major difference between the two is that the one hires out her body on piecework while the other hires it out once and for all.

All this does not mean that I am unsympathetic toward the aspirations of the feminist movement. It rather means that I disagree with its order of priorities.

Both men and women need to be liberated from the harness of their respective sex roles. But in order to be able to do this, we must liberate ourselves from those mental fossils which prevent us from looking upon sex and sexuality with the same naturalness as upon our cravings for food and drink. And, contrary to popular belief, we may have something to learn from prostitution in this respect, namely, that coition resembles nourishment in that, if it cannot be obtained in any other way, it can always be bought. And bought meals are not always the worst.

CAN PROSTITUTION BE ABOLISHED?

...The thesis that prostitution can and ought to be eradicated is, of course, relatively independent of the thesis that it is undesirable. For, even if undesirable, it neither follows that it can nor that it should be eradicated.

But since this thesis usually forms an integral part of the set of antiprostitution postulates, I think that a critical examination of it is definitely called for in the present context. Although no entirely satisfactory scientific explanation of mercenary sex exists today, the theories and data available seem adequate enough to allow certain well-founded conclusions as regards the eradicability of prostitution. The data available, however, also seem to disconfirm some theories.

In what follows I shall argue, with Kingsley Davis, that "we can imagine a social system in which the motive for prostitution would be completely absent, but we cannot imagine that the system could ever come to pass."[12]...

To be able to advocate the suppression of commercial sex, one's outlook must, I think, be completely ahistorical. For if there is one single general truth about human societies, it is that all attempts at suppressing prostitution—and they are innumerable—have failed completely. The harder and more efficacious the coercive measures, the deeper underground the mercenaries in sex are driven, but never is prostitution stamped out. History also teaches us that the effects of attempted suppression of prostitution are usually devastating, particularly for the prostitutes. As far as I can see, it would take at least a society as repugnant as that described by Orwell in his *1984*, in terms of totalitarian and coercive measures, to suppress prostitution. And who but a fanatic antiprostitutionist would be willing to achieve this end at that price?

Since, short of absolute and complete totalitarianism, the supply of prostitutes will not cease until there is practically no demand for the services of whores, all positive and constructive measures aiming at the abolishment of harlotry must aim at abolishing the *demand* for mercenary sex. Can we envisage a social system in which this type of demand would be absent? And what would it be like? Davis answers as follows:

> It would be a regime of absolute sexual freedom, wherein intercourse were practiced solely for the pleasure of it, by both parties. This would entail at least two conditions: First, there could be no institutional control of sexual expression. Marriage, with its concomitants of engagement, jealousy, divorce, and legitimacy, could not exist. Such an institution builds upon and limits the sexual urge, making sex expression contingent upon non-sexual factors, and thereby paving the way for intercourse against one's physical inclinations. *Second*, all sexual desire would have to be mutually complementary. One person could not be erotically attracted to a non-responsive person, because such a situation would inevitably involve frustration and give a motive for using force, fraud, authority, or money to induce the unwilling person to co-operate.[13]

And it is, of course, totally unrealistic to think that this will ever happen.

It is also naïve to think that an open, honest, and equal relationship between partners would do away with the demand for prostitution. Sexual attraction and the lack of it are largely irrational phenomena, and as such they are only marginally influenceable (thank heaven!) by open, honest discussions between equal men and women. Moreover, it is my guess that when equality between the sexes is achieved, we will see an increase in the demand for male heterosexual prostitutes. The degree of female frustration that exists today (but is rarely spoken of) will then no longer be tolerated, rationalized, or sublimated, but channeled into a demand for, *inter alia*, mercenary sex. An outlet which always has been the privilege of men will then also be available to women.[14]...

...But from the fact that prostitution can neither be suppressed (short of a brave new world) nor rendered superfluous (short of utopia), it does not follow that we must give in to the conservative notion that we live in the best of all worlds as far as prostitution is concerned. For it is hardly an exaggeration to say that the situation of today is highly unsatisfactory, especially with respect to those most primarily concerned: the prostitutes.

Given all this, the only reasonable conclusion is that prostitution ought not to be eradicated, but reformed. How? A few words will be said about this vast subject in the next section.

SOME POLICY SUGGESTIONS

...I admit, of course, that a change in our attitudes toward prostitution must be regarded as a long-range goal that it will take a long time to realize. In the meantime, a great many prostitutes will continue to suffer from our present prejudices. A program for more immediate action is therefore also called for. In this section I shall, to begin with, make some suggestions with respect to this more immediate reform program. I shall also have something to say about those values and attitudes which have negative effects on, *inter alia*, prostitution and prostitutes. I shall finally suggest in outline, my conception of a sound prostitution, a prostitution which is allowed to function in a social climate freed from prejudice.

The first and most urgent step to take is to decriminalize prostitution in those places where it is still a crime to be or to visit a whore. For as long as harlotry is lumped together with crime, there are hardly any chances of improvement. Fortunately, most societies have taken this step....

The second step is to improve the housing situation for prostitutes. The prostitute must be given the right to rent a suitable location in her or his capacity as a prostitute. The same legal rules that prohibit a landlord from refusing a tenant *in spe* should be made to apply in the case of the prostitute. Thus, that the tenant *in spe* is a harlot should not constitute adequate ground for refusal. It should also be made impossible for a landlord to evict a person simply because she or he is a hustler. Nor should it be allowed to refuse or evict someone on the ground that other tenants do not wish to live next door to a whore....

What positive effects would this have? First, it would greatly reduce crude economic exploitation of harlots. Being able to rent a flat without pretense, they would no longer have to pay usury rents to unscrupulous landlords. Second, it would tend to diminish some of the occupational hazards, notably those related to the feeling of insecurity, of being secluded, and of being deprived of the rights of ordinary citizens. Third, it would tend to weaken the association between prostitution and organized crime....

A third urgent step is to develop a program intended to get rid of child and teenage prostitution. Minors should as far as possible be prevented from entrance into prostitution, not on moralistic but on paternalistic grounds. For in the case of minors, paternalistic measures seem justified for the same reasons as they are justified in other social matters....

As for adult prostitution, I have suggested that it should be reformed rather than abolished. But the most important part of that reform does not concern prostitution and prostitutes, but our *attitudes* toward them. For it seems to me impossible to come to grips with the negative aspects of harlotry without a change of our values and attitudes....

Our attitudes toward sexual expression in general, and mercenary sex in particular, ought to be modified or abandoned, partly because of the damage that they do, partly because they represent prejudices in the sense that they are rooted in false beliefs. Women are not partial men, nor is the female sex a deformity. And the distinction between body and soul, with all its metaphysical and religious ramifications, apart from being philosophically highly dubious, is the source of more human misery than almost any other.

A sound prostitution is, first of all, a prostitution that is allowed to function in a social climate freed from emotional prejudice of the kind described above. Prostitution can never be rid of its most serious negative aspects (primarily the suffering the prostitutes have to endure) in a society where females are regarded as inferior to males and where man's physical nature is regarded as inferior to his spiritual nature.

A sound prostitution is, furthermore, a prostitution such that those who become prostitutes are adults who are not compelled to prostitute themselves but who freely choose to do so, in the same sense of "freely" as anyone's trade or occupation may be said to be freely chosen. A sound prostitution is, in other words, a prostitution of voluntary, not compulsive, hustlers.

A sound prostitution is, third, a prostitution that is legal, and where the prostitutes are not persecuted, but attributed the same rights as ordinary citizens, as a recognition of the fact that they fulfill a socially valuable function by, *inter alia*, decreasing the amount of sexual misery in society.

A sound prostitution is, fourth, a prostitution such that the prostitutes are no more economically exploited than wageworkers in general.

A sound prostitution is, finally, a prostitution that is equally available to both sexes.

Of these conditions I regard the first as the most fundamental. Without it being at least partially satisfied, the satisfaction of the others seems most difficult. Thus, if I were to sum up the principal view put forward in this concluding section, it would be formulated as follows: *in order to improve prostitution, we must first and foremost improve our attitudes toward it. ...*

NOTES

I wish to acknowledge my indebtedness to Harry Benjamin and R.E.L. Masters. Their well-argued plea for a rational reevaluation of prostitution and for an assessment of it freed from emotional prejudice has been a great source of inspiration. Their empirical studies have also provided me with a large share of my factual insights concerning mercenary sex. I also want to thank Harald Ofstad for his valuable criticism of an earlier version of this essay.

[1] For a comprehensive bibliography, see Vern Bullough et al., eds., *A Bibliography of Prostitution* (New York and London: Garland Publishers, 1977).

[2] Here I am indebted to Kingsley Davis (see his "The Sociology of Prostitution," in *Deviance, Studies in the Process of Stigmatization and Social Reaction*, eds. A.C. Clarke, S. Dinitz (New York: Oxford University Press, 1975).

[3] See Harry Benjamin and R.E.L. Masters, *Prostitution and Morality* (New York: Julian Press, 1964): 208.

[4] Frederich Engels, *Principles of Communism* (the draft of the Communist Manifesto), quoted in Sheila Rowbotham, *Women, Resistance, and Revolution* (London: Penguin Press, 1972): 64.

[5] Frederich Engels, "The Origin of the Family, Private Property and the State," in *Selected Works*, by Karl Marx and Frederich Engels (Moscow: Progress Publishers, 1970): 3:245.

[6] A. Kollontai, *Brak i semeinaja problema* [Marriage and the family problem] (1909); author's translation.

[7] Rowbotham, 65.

[8] *Ibid.*

[9] In the sense that starvation, poverty, or more generally the fact that one is economically underprivileged, often is a *predisposing* factor. But obviously being poor, etc., is neither a necessary nor a sufficient condition for someone to become a prostitute.

[10] Rowbotham, 66.

[11] United Nations, *Study on Traffic in Persons and Prostitution* (New York, 1959).

[12] Davis, 391.

[13] *Ibid.*

[14]That the lack of male heterosexual prostitutes is due to physiological factors is, of course, a myth. That inability to achieve erection would constitute an obstacle is gainsaid by the practices of male homosexual prostitutes (see Benjamin and Masters, *Prostitution and Morality,* chap. 10). Moreover, actual intercourse is only one type of sexual service, among many others, that a prostitute typically sells.

PROSTITUTION

Rosemarie Tong

...Although there are male as well as female prostitutes, and although we are seeing a dramatic increase in males offering their sexual services to other males,[1] the type of prostitution that concerns feminists as feminists is female prostitution. Next to pornography, prostitution is the most difficult sex-related legal issue for feminists to address. This is because there is considerable confusion as to whether prostitutes are the paradigm of sexual liberation, the epitome of sexual oppression, or something in between. Coupled with the fact that society in general has treated prostitution as everything from an utterly condemnable evil to an unfortunate but unavoidable reality, we begin to see why so few of us understand either what prostitution is, and what, if anything, should be done about it. Is a prostitute an evil and immoral woman, a victim of unjust social and economic opportunity structures, or an enterprising business woman? Is she a criminal from whom society needs protection, or a provider of an essential service whose work should be actively supported by the state? Should the law criminalize, legalize, or decriminalize her activities?...

...The fact that men tend to conceive of women as persons who exist to serve them helps explain not only the long history of prostitution but also the law's strange ambivalence about prostitution. On the one hand, Anglo-American thought is dominated by the image of prostitutes as bad girls, as temptresses who lure men away from their duties and who cause them to walk other than the straight and narrow path of virtue. On the other hand, Anglo-American thought has always expressed special sympathy for the

"Prostitution" in *Women, Sex, and the Law* by Rosmarie Tong (Totowa, NJ: Roman and Littlefield, 1984), reprinted by permission.

sexual wants and needs of men, and the law's desire to punish bad girls has often been moderated by its wish to save nice boys from harm, inconvenience, or embarrassment. Indeed, standard arguments both for and against the criminalization, legalization, and decriminalization of prostitution are heavily skewed in ways that favor men over women.

ARGUMENTS FOR CRIMINALIZATION, LEGALIZATION, AND DECRIMINALIZATION

Individual liberty may not be justifiably restricted unless one's actions violate at least one of the principles that have been advanced as legitimate liberty-limiting principles. Traditionally, those in favor of the criminalization of prostitution have relied primarily on the principle of legal moralism and only secondarily on the harm, legal paternalism, and offense principles. In contrast, those in favor of the decriminalization of prostitution either with licensing (legalization) or without have relied primarily on the harm principle and to a lesser extent on the offense principle. In both cases, however, the arguments are influenced by an image of the prostitute as a bad girl.

Arguments in Favor of Criminalization

1. Arguments Invoking the Principle of Legal Moralism

Given the power of the bad-girl image, it stands to reason that the principle of legal moralism—individual liberty may be limited to prevent immoral behavior—has loomed so large in arguments for the criminalization of prostitution. Invocations of this much controverted principle are based on two assumptions: (1) that a social consensus on what is immoral can be reached; and (2) that the health of a society rests on its firm adherence to a binding moral code. In the latter case, the entire system of conventional moral beliefs may in principle be subject to legal enforcement, even when violations of these moral beliefs are neither harmful nor offensive in any straightforward way.

Not surprisingly, both of these assumptions encounter serious philosophical obstacles. First, it is highly unlikely that a melting-pot society could produce a consensus on what is moral or immoral, especially regarding prostitution and other so-called morals offenses (homosexuality, lesbianism, drinking, gambling). Second, and more crucially, even if there were a consensus about the immorality of prostitution—even if 90 percent of the population agreed that prostitution was immoral—it is not clear that society has a right to punish conduct simply because its members strongly disapprove of it or believe it is wrong. Of course there are those who insist that society does have this right. Lord Patrick Devlin, for example, argues that although there are some moral principles we may adopt for our own private guidance, there are other moral principles we must adopt for public guidance. That is, a society that does not have a public, shared morality, limiting and illuminating the personal moralities of its members, is charting a perilous course. Devlin insists that no society can survive for long without some degree of moral conformity. Therefore, since every society has a right to preserve its own existence, every society also has the right to insist on some moral conformity, and to enforce legally that conformity: "Society may use the law to preserve morality in the same way it uses it to safeguard anything else if it is essential to its existence."[2]

As Devlin sees it, the common morality of a society at any time is "a blend of custom and conviction, of reason and feeling, of experience and prejudice."[3] Indeed, he goes farther than this: what makes x immoral is that reasonable persons feel or believe that x is immoral. Says Devlin: "If the reasonable man believes that a practice is immoral and believes also —no matter whether the belief is right or wrong...—that no right-minded member of his society could think otherwise, then for the purposes of the law it is immoral."[4] If Devlin is correct, then what makes prostitution immoral is not its intrinsic "wrongness," but the fact that the community of "right-minded" persons feels or believes that it is wrong.

But against Devlin it may be reasonably argued that morality is not a matter of mere belief or feeling, and that what makes a position moral is not the fact that it is "passionately and sincerely held." It is not that a position has "a certain emotional depth," or that it is "the view of one's father or mother," or that it is "conventional" that gives it its steering authority, but rather that one can provide reasons for holding such a position.[5] Plausible reasons presuppose or invoke some general moral principle (treat others as you would like to be treated in comparable circumstances) or some general moral theory (utilitarianism, contractarianism, deontology). If a man's reasons are sound, he should be able to convince any other rational, open-minded, unbiased person that his reasons are more viable and consistent than those of his opponents. Therefore, even if society does have a right to enforce a public morality, each item of that morality must be rationally defensible.

Most of those who insist that prostitution is immoral have advanced not reasons, but pseudoreasons for their claim: expressions of prejudice ("prostitutes are fallen women"), or expressions of emotion ("prostitutes make me sick"), or instances of rationalization ("acts of prostitution render prostitutes sterile"), or instances of parroting ("everyone knows that prostitution is sinful"). In particular, some have advanced the argument that prostitution is immoral because it is an instance of nonprocreational sex. A long tradition of moralists has argued that the purpose of sexuality is the procreation of children within marriage. All other functions of sexuality—the expression of love or the experience of pleasure—are abuses of sexuality, which will lead to the decay of one's rationality and the emergence of one's previously controlled animality. But this argument may be turned on its axis: It seems that procreational sex rather than nonprocreational sex represents an abuse of human sexuality. Unlike animal sexuality, human sexual activity is not bound to the female reproductive cycle. Human sexuality is a "continually available resource, upon which are built long-standing and intense personal relationships resting on reciprocal sensual delight."[6] In short, the procreational model is a description not of the human world, but of the animal world, and if anything is wrong with prostitution, it is not that it is nonprocreational....

2. Arguments Involving the Harm Principle

If none of the standard reasons advanced to justify the claim that "prostitution is immoral" is convincing, the claim fails, and prostitution may not be criminalized on the grounds that it is immoral. However, the argument that prostitution should be criminalized on the grounds that it is harmful to others remains to be tested. It has been argued, for example, that prostitution contributes significantly to venereal disease, and that prostitution is the cause of a number of crimes, such as theft and assault of patrons, beating and raping of prostitutes, trafficking in heroin, and the enlarged scope of organized crime activities.

As it turns out, however, none of these claims is empirically substantiated. First, recent studies indicate that prostitution accounts for less than ten percent of the current incidence of venereal disease. Moreover, the venereal disease rate is the highest in those age groups (fifteen to thirty) in which patronage of prostitutes is rather low. Consider for example, the current herpes epidemic. Prostitutes are not being blamed for spreading this disease; rather, sexually active middle-class men and women are being chastised—although gently—for bringing this disease upon themselves. Second, prostitution's links with organized crime have been exaggerated. In 1967 the President's Committee on Law Enforcement and the Administration of Justice reported that prostitution plays "a small and declining role in organized crime operations."[7] As for ancillary crime, much of it arises from the fact that prostitutes and patrons cannot report crimes perpetrated upon them without admitting their involvement in prostitution. Were prostitution decriminalized, prostitutes and patrons would be more likely to report ancillary crime and, as a result, the rate of ancillary crime would decrease. In short, it seems that prostitution is not in itself harmful to others and therefore cannot be legitimately restricted by invoking the harm principle.

3. Arguments Invoking the Principle of Legal Paternalism

Those who continue to favor the criminalization of prostitution may invoke yet another purported liberty-limiting principle: the principle of legal paternalism. According to this principle, the law rightfully serves in the role of a benevolent father who restricts his child's liberty in order to save the child from self-harm. Those who accept this principle begin their argument by pointing out that prostitutes are subjected to all types of physical as well as psychological harm. Depending on how much business a prostitute does, she may contract certain diseases that otherwise she would not contract, as well as unwanted pregnancies. Her hours can be long and exhausting, and she runs the risk of assault, battery, and even permanent injury or death either from customers with sadistic or homicidal tendencies, or from pimps unsatisfied with her job performance or displeased by her attitudes. On the psychological side, many prostitutes are said to suffer from depression, neurotic impulses, and self-degrading—even self-destructive—behavior. Therefore, or so the argument goes, the state should criminalize prostitution in the same way as it criminalizes self-maiming. Arguably, society would do some prostitutes a favor by criminalizing prostitution. As M. Anne Jennings puts it: "To the extent that arrest does allow prostitutes to receive medical attention, counseling and respite from the rigors of their life, it may have positive effects."[8]

But, queries the objector, is prostitution really harmful to the prostitute herself?…[P]rostitutes do harm themselves. Yet this is not to articulate it precisely enough. What prostitutes do is *risk* harm to themselves, for not all prostitutes are physically or psychologically harmed during the course of their activities. So the question becomes: Is the state warranted in preventing a woman from assuming these risks to self? If it is, then it should consider criminalizing dentistry (dentists have the highest suicide rate of all professions) as well as assembly-line work (people who work on assembly lines are more prone to depressions caused by tedium than are people who are challenged by their jobs). Indeed, the state should contemplate criminalizing many other jobs that are taken at great risk to oneself—police work, bomb-squad work, contagious-disease work—but are nevertheless needed by the public to preserve it from harm.

According to many legal theorists, however, the principle of legal paternalism does not generate such ludicrous programs of action. The state is not warranted in preventing a person from assuming any or all risks to self. If it were, it could prevent each of us from getting out of bed in the morning. What the state is warranted in preventing is personal assumptions of risk that are either unreasonable or the reflection of choices that fail to meet the criteria for full or nearly full voluntariness.[9]

Whether the assumption of a risk is reasonable or unreasonable depends on several factors. Joel Feinberg articulates at least five of these factors:

(1) the degree of probability that harm to oneself will result from a given course of action; (2) the seriousness of the harm being risked; (3) the degree of probability that the goal inclining one to shoulder the risk

will in fact result from the course of action; (4) the value or importance of achieving that goal, that is, just how worthwhile it is to one; and (5) the necessity of the risk, that is, the availability or absence of alternative, less risky means to the desired goal.[10]

A woman could come to the conclusion that if she played her cards right—if she got a fairly decent pimp or madam and obeyed his or her instructions faithfully—she could make a lot of money as a prostitute without risking anything near the injuries a professional athlete risks. Of course, even if a life of prostitution is one of *reasonable* risk, the state may still intervene if a woman has entered this profession as a result of a choice that is neither fully voluntary nor nearly fully voluntary.

As Feinberg sees it, what makes the assumption of a risk fully voluntary is that one assumes it with informed consent—aware of all relevant facts and known contingencies, and without any external coercive pressure or internal compulsion. Among the factors that tend to defeat ascriptions of full responsibility are: "neurotic compulsion, misinformation, excitement or impetuousness, clouded judgment (as from alcohol or drug), or immature or defective faculties or reasoning."[11] Given that virtually every person lacks something in the way of knowledge and power, it is doubtful that any choice is fully voluntary. Nevertheless, this does not make it impossible for us to distinguish between nearly fully voluntary choices and those that are nearly involuntary. So, for example, it is possible to distinguish between a half-starved, teenaged runaway who "decides" to be a prostitute because she is fed a steady diet of alcohol and narcotics by a ruthless pimp, and a college-educated, reasonably well-employed woman who decides to be a prostitute because she can make a lot of money quickly. In the former case, most persons are inclined to think that the state may intervene, at least temporarily, for the teenager's own good. In the latter case, however, many persons are inclined to think otherwise, observing that a competent, well-informed, calm, mature, unconstrained, adult woman is the best judge of her own good....

Arguments in Favor of Decriminalization with Regulation or Licensing

...Instead of incarcerating prostitutes for solicitation, the state could respond either by adopting an English or European system of regulation or by expanding the Nevada system. Whereas solicitation takes place through ambiguously worded advertisements in England, in continental Europe the form of regulation is some form of zoning, whereby solicitation is confined to certain well-known urban districts.[12] In Nevada, the form of regulation consists in confining prostitutes to brothels. Any one of these approaches would solve the offense problem without invoking the criminal sanction. No one whose sensibilities are likely to be wounded or aroused need read the advertisements for prostitution, go to the "red light" districts, or patronize the brothels.

If uncertainty about the harmfulness of prostitution to others renders any imposition of the criminal sanction unwarranted, the state may still be justified in licensing prostitution if there is a *risk* of harm to others. That is, it may not be overstepping its bounds by demanding that, in order to engage in commercial sex, a woman must secure a legal permit that entails having her name entered in a public record, various regulations of dress, price, and place of business and solicitation, and even regular medical inspections for venereal disease. In short, proponents of regulation/licensing argue that an ounce of prevention is worth a pound of cure.

Arguments for Laissez-Faire Decriminalization

In response to this cautious approach, those in favor of a laissez-faire regime of decriminalization argue that neither licensing of prostitution nor regulation of public solicitation is necessary. Licensing is unnecessary because the risk of contracting venereal disease from prostitutes is relatively slim, and because were prostitutes offered cheap and noncoercive medical inspections, they would voluntarily take advantage of them. Similarly, regulation of public solicitation is not necessary either. Comments David A.J. Richards:

> For all practical purposes, solicitations for prostitution occur in familiar locations where no reasonable person can claim surprise. Furthermore, the presence of prostitution is, on balance, one of the colorful amenities of life in large urban centers. It should not be hidden and isolated, but robustly accepted as what in fact it is: an inextricable part of human life.[13]

However, most feminists struggle with the suggestion that prostitution is a "colorful amenity" that should be "robustly accepted," if not by all, then by the liberal and the rational.

FEMINIST CONCEPTS OF PROSTITUTION

...[T]wentieth-century feminists have approached the issue of prostitution with considerable humility. Nevertheless, because most contemporary feminists find it difficult to understand why any woman would freely choose to be a "sex object" (prostitute, pornography model, go-go girl, *Playboy* bunny), they have sometimes constructed barriers between themselves and women who engage in commercial sex. In this connection, one porn model complains:

I've never had anybody from a poor or working-class background give me the "How could you have done anything like that?" question, but middle class feminists have no consciousness about what it is like out there. You have to remember who's the real enemy—who has the power—who you're selling it to, who you're looking up at and trying to please. It's not other women.[14]

The sentiments of this model are echoed by many prostitutes, some of whom reveal their real need for respect. Says one prostitute: "Somehow their pity deprives me of my freedom of choice. I don't want to be saved; saved by the Christians or saved by the shrink. Whatever their rationale is, it's the same: condescending, patronizing. Something in me just resents this moralism."[15] In a wholehearted effort to obviate all such criticism, contemporary feminists are beginning to cast their discussion of prostitution in terms of determinism versus freedom. Is the prostitute the quintessential oppressed woman or the quintessential liberated woman? Or is the prostitute simply a woman who, like all women in this society, is struggling to understand and live her own sexuality?

The Prostitute as Quintessential Oppressed Woman

Although they provide different reasons for their position, classical Marxist feminists, socialist feminists, and radical feminists agree that the prostitute is the quintessential oppressed woman.

1. The Classical Marxist Feminist Interpretation

With some slight variations, classical Marxist feminists adopt the Marx/Engels's analysis of prostitution: no woman under capitalism, be she a prostitute or not, can transcend the conditions that determine her and which prevent her transformation into a subject, a person who is in charge of her own destiny. Try as she might, social and economic conditions are such that she must remain an object, a plaything in the hands of those who control the contours of her existence. This is why, as Marx and Engels see it, the difference between a married woman and a prostitute—upper-, middle-, or lower-class—is one of degree and not of kind. In the course of discussing the bourgeois family, Engels asserts that in a capitalist society who one marries is determined by the class to which one belongs. This "marriage of convenience" often turns into "the crassest prostitution"—"sometimes on both sides, but much more generally on the part of the wife, who differs from the ordinary courtesan only in that she does not hire out her body, like a wage-worker, on piece-work, but sells it into slavery once and for all."[16]

Nevertheless, Marx adds that it is somehow worse to be a prostitute than a wife, not only because the prostitute is reminded anew of her bondage each time she hires out her body, but also because her situation is strictly analogous to that of the proletarian worker: "Prostitution is only a *specific* expression of the general prostitution of the laborer, and since it is a relationship in which falls not the prostitute alone, but also the one who prostitutes—and the latter's abomination is still greater—the capitalist, etc., also comes under this head."[17] In short, the prostitute is doubly oppressed by capitalism: first as a woman, and then as a worker who must make her living by hiring out not her hands, but her genitals and orifices.

This is precisely why not only Engels and Marx, but most Marxist feminists insist that "to fight prostitution is to fight the foundations of capitalist society," especially the institution of private property and the class system it generates. According to classical Marxist analysis, the typical prostitute is a working-class female and the typical patron is an upper- or middle-class male—only these men have enough money to purchase the sexual services of women other than their wives. As long as there is a bourgeois demand for whores, and as long as working-class women are paid less-than-adequate wages for less-than-interesting work, working-class women will continue to supply their bodies to meet the bourgeois demand for female flesh. The simplest way to break this cycle is to destroy the supply of prostitutes by giving working-class women jobs that provide them with a living wage and a sense of satisfaction or accomplishment. Arguably, if women are given such jobs, they will no longer be forced to choose degrading work (prostitution).[18]

...Capitalists will criminalize, legalize, or decriminalize prostitution in accordance with self-interest. For example, were capitalists to legalize prostitution, they would do so not out of concern for the prostitute, but out of a desire either to fill the state's coffers with tax revenues or to line the pockets of those who would operate the legitimate "cathouses." In neither of these latter events would the condition of the prostitute herself be ameliorated.

2. The Socialist Feminist Interpretation

By emphasizing the economic determinants of prostitution, classical Marxism rightly points out that an individual's freedom is limited in a capitalist society, especially if that individual is a working-class woman. Nonetheless, despite the accuracy of its main contention, socialist feminists claim that the Marxist analysis is flawed, that it is too eager to prove its central thesis about women; namely, that were it not for capitalism, women would be the sexual as well as economic equals of men. As socialist feminists see it, however, women's condition is considerably more complex.

First, unless capitalism and patriarchy are inextricably intertwined, women need not be exploited under capitalism any more than men are. As a result of having achieved a measure of economic independence and legal recognition, some capitalist women no longer have to hand their bodies over to men in return for long-term financial security (marriage) or in return for short-term financial security (prostitution). Nevertheless, socialist feminists admit that it may be the case under capitalism that only upper- and middle-class women can attain rough parity with men, and then not with the best, brightest, and richest of men. That is, capitalism may be able to treat a few exceptional women like men, but it may not be able to treat the majority of women (working-class women) like men. But this is an empirical hypothesis, and, in principle, it may be possible for capitalism to eliminate gender inequalities even if, by definition, it cannot eliminate class inequalities.

Second, *if* prostitution reflects class lines in capitalist society, these lines are considerably more complex than those traced by classical Marxists. Empirical data indicate that working-class men patronize prostitutes just as much, if not more than, middle- and upper-class men. But because working-class men do not have as much money as middle- and upper-class men, they are forced to take what they can get; namely, inexpensive hookers who have entered the life of prostitution as a way out of bleak economic circumstances. In contrast, upper- and middle-class men have the means to pay for "quality merchandise," expensive call girls who are generally drawn from "bourgeois" backgrounds.

Third, socialist feminists note the embarrassing fact that prostitution appears in noncapitalist systems as well as capitalist systems. Admittedly, it does not seem to be as prevalent in mainland China or Russia as it is in the United States, but this may be because the People's Republic of China engages in forms of "aggressive rehabilitation"[19] directed at the patrons of prostitutes as well as the prostitutes themselves, and because the Soviets stigmatize patrons by name in a public bulletin called "Buyers of the Bodies of Women."[20] Available evidence indicates that if socialist societies were to loosen legal controls on prostitution, it would flourish there as well as in capitalist societies.

Fourth, the demand for and supply of prostitutes is not always or only a function of economics. Indeed, according to socialist feminists, the crucial error of classical Marxist feminists is to overemphasize the role the mode of production plays in women's lives without stressing enough the role other structures such as reproduction, the socialization of children, and sexuality play in women's lives.[21] Many socialist feminists agree with Lars O. Ericsson that "the classical Marxist analysis...is bound to fail for the simple and obvious reason that the sex drive—which constitutes a necessary condition for the demand for prostitutes—is neither an economic phenomenon nor a phenomenon less basic (in fact it is more basic) than any economic factor."[22] In other words, no matter what economic system reigns, as long as a patriarchal ideology prevails according to which women exist for men, men will continue to demand prostitutes and women will continue to meet this demand.

3. The Radical Feminist Interpretation

Significantly, this previous argument is one radical feminists echo, but with some variations. As they see it, what accounts for the persistence of prostitution is not the sex drive *per se*, but the sex drive as it is institutionalized by society, in this case any advanced Western society, capitalist or socialist. On the one hand, radical feminists explain that men are socialized to have a certain set of sexual wants and needs, and to feel entitled, as a matter of right, to these wants and needs. On the other hand, women are socialized to meet male sexual wants and needs, and to feel obligated as a matter of duty to meet these wants and needs. Because male sexual requirements range from a desire to be emotionally nurtured to a desire to be erotically aroused, and because men find few women versatile enough to meet all of their sexual requirements, men divide the world of women into two: the good, or domesticated, women (wives, mothers, aunts, lovers) and the bad, or exotic, women (whores, tramps, sluts). The good women are supposed to supply men with security and the bad women are supposed to supply men with stimulation. Within this schema, prostitutes are supposed to fulfill those male sexual fantasies that would otherwise go unfulfilled.

...Stripped of its clinical gloss, this piece of contemporary enlightenment simply states that men are allowed to use whores in ways that they are not allowed to use madonnas. This view is continuous with the "prostitution is society's sewer" line of reasoning, according to which the whore is the one who does the madonna's dirty work. In other words, were it not for the whore, the madonna would have to satisfy all of her man's sexual yearnings, even the kinky and cruel ones. But fortunately, for the madonnas, that is, there are enough whores to go around. In the same way that society reproduces women who will be wives and mothers, it reproduces women who will be prostitutes, even if their basic economic needs are met elsewhere. According to several studies, girl-children who have been sexually abused or raped are much more likely to become prostitutes than girl-children who have not been subjected to such manhandling. In one study, 65 percent of adolescent prostitutes were forced into sexual activities as children; 57 percent had been raped, and one-third of those had been raped more than once.[23] These studies also suggest that girl-children who have been rewarded for entering into sexual relations with their fathers, brothers, uncles, neighbors, and so on are even more prone than girl-children who have been forced into such relations to enter the life of prostitution.[24]

...Bluntly stated, prostitutes are not born. They are made by a society that teaches girls that, if all else fails, a woman can always gain attention or money by offering her body to men who both want and need it.

The Prostitute as Quintessential Liberated Woman

In contrast to classical Marxist, socialist, and radical feminists, there are those feminists who paint an alternative portrait of the prostitute: one that focuses neither on the working-class woman nor on the sexually abused girl, but on the woman who insists that she has chosen to be a prostitute. According to these existentialist feminists, the prostitute is an exceptional woman who dares to challenge the sexual mores of her society....

...Simone de Beauvoir observes that...today's common prostitute... may...find a certain liberation in the money or other benefits that she gains from men. Provided that she is not dominated by a pimp, the money she makes need not be enslaving. It can, says de Beauvoir, have a "purifying role" to the extent that, for her, it does away with the battle of the sexes:

> If many women who are not professionals insist on extracting checks and presents from their lovers, it is not from cupidity alone, for to make the man pay...is to change him into an instrument. In this way the woman avoids being one. The man may perhaps think he "has" her, but his sexual possession is an illusion; it is she who has *him*...she will not be "taken," since she is being paid.[25]

Interestingly, de Beauvoir's thoughts are shared by members of COYOTE (Cast Off Your Old Tired Ethics), a San Francisco-based union of prostitutes. According to members of this group, their decisions to enter the life were fully or nearly fully voluntary. Among the options open to them, they chose to be prostitutes. Indeed, as they see it, their choices make better sense than those of women who choose not to be prostitutes....

What COYOTE, Simone de Beauvoir, and existentialist feminists may be overlooking, however, is that the only freedom women currently have is the freedom to choose that form of bondage (prostitution, marriage) that most suits them. But this type of freedom cannot be compared to the freedom to choose initially the institutions (patriarchal, matriarchal, androgynous) that will shape one's subsequent decisions. It is one thing to say that under patriarchy women may choose either a life of prostitution or a life of marriage. It is quite another to say that in the best possible world women would want to have their choices restricted to either prostitution or heterosexual marriage. The issue is not whether a woman is free in a technical, psychological sense to choose between prostitution and marriage, but what values she chooses and why. If her values are not her own, if she simply parrots the values of her culture, then her choice is a limited one indeed.

FEMINIST LEGAL APPROACHES TO PROSTITUTION

From what has been said so far, it seems clear that if the prostitute is free, then she is not much more or much less free than her married counterpart. At the same time that the prostitute proclaims her freedom, she may, like her nonprostitute counterpart, also admit its fragility and limited nature. One former prostitute comments: "I'd like so much to have the illusion that I had some freedom of choice. Maybe it's just an illusion, but I need to think I had some freedom. Yet then I realize how much was determined in the way I got into prostitution."[26] But whether or not prostitutes are more or less free (determined) than other women in this society, virtually all feminists agree that prostitution should be decriminalized, because present antiprostitution laws discriminate against prostitutes in at least three ways.

First, in some jurisdictions the laws against prostitution apply only to women and not to men. This means that these laws apply neither to males who prostitute themselves nor to males who patronize male or female prostitutes. Although some states have addressed these equal-protection problems by redefining a prostitute as any female or male who sells her or his sexual services, and by enacting laws aimed at male patrons as well as female prostitutes, the police continue to enforce these statutes selectively against women. In 1974 in San Francisco there were 768 arrests for heterosexual prostitution, of which 756 were women. And in nearby Oakland 3,663 prostitutes were arrested while only 21 clients were apprehended.[27] Indeed, in some cases there were no male clients to pick up because police decoys had masqueraded as "johns" in order to arrest women for solicitation—however discreet. Although such police methods verge on entrapment, which is illegal, police have argued that such methods do not constitute entrapment because, *per definiens,* you cannot entrap a woman who *would* have prostituted herself to a real "john" had she not been fooled by a police decoy. In other words, she was in the process of soliciting when she was arrested.

Second, in some jurisdictions the police enforce prostitution laws in ways that invade the prostitute's privacy. Surveillance strategies are frequently excessive, as in cases where police stake out a call girl's apartment and use spying equipment to record her activities before intruding on her and her patron in the midst of sexual intercourse. Prostitution laws that make this possible are being challenged on the grounds that they violate the right to privacy. Increasingly, this right has been invoked to protect consensual sexual activities, and there seems little reason not to extend this right to the act of prostitution *per se*: "Prostitution, both in the preliminary solicitation and negotiations and in the act itself, is overwhelmingly a private, consensual affair between individuals who wish to make their own decisions as how to control their sexual lives and use their bodies."[28]

The point is that sexual intercourse is a private affair even if it involves a preliminary business transaction on the street. The fact that money is exchanged does not necessarily bring the act of prostitution into the public domain, unless said exchange is universally offensive *and* not reasonably avoidable by unwilling spectators.

Finally, in some jurisdictions vague "antiloitering" or "repeated beckoning" laws, aimed at controlling public solicitation, have violated the due process rights not only of prostitutes but also of nonprostitutes. In making their sweeps down the streets of New York, for example, the police have arrested "known prostitutes" who were simply taking a stroll that day. And in some instances they have even arrested women who "looked like" prostitutes but were in fact simply women visiting the "red light" districts or doing business there.

One begins to appreciate just how discriminatory antiprostitution laws are when one couples these three facts with a further, even more distressing fact: most women who are in prison are there because they are prostitutes. Significantly, the prostitutes' pimps and patrons are not likely to be incarcerated alongside them—as if the crime (if it is a crime) of prostitution is women's alone. Antiprostitution laws should be enforced against men as well as against women or they should not be enforced at all. One thing is certain, the prostitute does not deserve to be treated in a way stricter than her patrons or promoters.

Arguments for Decriminalization with Licensing (Legalization)

Even if most feminists agree that prostitution should be decriminalized, and even if they also agree that *public* solicitation for prostitution may be regulated, provided that it is universally offensive and not reasonably avoidable, they remain divided on the issue of licensing (although the majority do not favor licensing).

That only a small minority of feminists should support licensing is not surprising. Traditionally, feminists have been strident opponents of legalized or state-supervised prostitution. Nineteenth-century feminists were adamantly opposed to the state licensing of prostitutes because it imposed demoralizing and demeaning conditions on prostitutes, including public records that stigmatized them for life, intrusive medical inspections that stripped them of certain dignities, and arbitrary regulations that confined them to their brothel rooms for excessively long periods of time.[29]

Unfortunately, as a result of their attempts to help prostitutes, nineteenth-century feminists inadvertently worsened the lot of their prostitute sisters. Their campaign to end legalized prostitution resulted not in the decriminalization of prostitution, but in the criminalization of prostitution. As soon as their profession was criminalized, prostitutes were treated as lepers and exiled from their neighborhoods. Deprived of their network of community support, they were increasingly forced to rely on pimps for protection against police authorities as well as for emotional security. . . .

Those prostitutes who support legalized prostitution do so because, as they see it, state licensing would improve their health, give them protection from abusive pimps and patrons, and ensure them a steady income. Rightly conceived, state licensing could, they point out, be beneficial to prostitutes. When and where state schemes of licensing have worked against women's interests, they have been guided by the state's misguided desire to protect the male patron from venereal disease, to save him from force and fraud, and to provide him with the most pleasure possible for the least price possible. In Nevada, for example, where prostitution has been legalized, women must not only register as prostitutes, but also be fingerprinted, checked over by medical officials, and licensed. They must agree to what amounts to an informal incarceration that requires them to stay in the publicly run brothels for as long as three weeks at a time. Moreover, some Nevada locations establish strict regulations governing not only the times when prostitutes may be in town and the places where they may go (no bars, casinos, residential areas permitted), but also those with whom they may be seen (no boyfriends or husbands).[30]

Yet despite the shortcomings of Nevada-like experiments, some prostitutes continue to believe that state schemes of legalization are not necessarily pernicious. As these women see it, the state could ensure prostitutes adequate and fair protection in their business dealings "without making regulatory authorities moralistic and often sadistically retributive police."[31] It could also forge programs that would facilitate a woman's decision to exit as well as enter the "oldest profession."

Arguments for Laissez-Faire Decriminalization

It is at this point in the discussion that feminists opposed to legalization ask a pointed question: Why should prostitutes trust the state, which after all is largely male-dominated, to come up with women-centered systems of state licensing? Instead, why not simply decriminalize prostitution and leave prostitutes to control their own lives? Provided the state dispenses inexpensive, noncoercive, quality medical treatment to all victims and carriers of venereal disease, and provided that the police enforce current fraud as well as assault and battery statutes against abusive patrons and exploitative pimps, it seems likely that prostitutes can take care of themselves better than the state can. Indeed, this is the viewpoint of not only most feminists, but of COYOTE, the San Francisco prostitutes who have unionized in order to bring the support of collective organizational self-protection to what has been an atomistic, each-woman-out-on-her-own profession. Should COYOTE's efforts succeed, it may serve as a paradigm model for prostitutes elsewhere.

Yet there are reasons to oppose legalization other than the fact that the state may skew its terms in ways that favor patrons rather than prostitutes. That is, feminists who oppose legalization have ideological as well as pragmatic reasons for their point of view. Like their nineteenth-century counterparts, most twentieth-century feminists find the notion of state-operated houses of prostitution an *endorsement* of the institution of prostitution itself. Unlike their predecessors, however, contemporary feminists do not base their objections to state-endorsed prostitution on the grounds that it maintains a double standard that holds women up to higher moral norms than men. Were they to make such an objection, one could predict the following response: "Ladies, your argument is with merit. Henceforward the state, in addition to supplying men with female prostitutes, shall supply women with male prostitutes." But...male prostitution is not the solution to female prostitution. What feminists want is not a stable of male prostitutes, but the elimination of an ideology that teaches that women's sexuality is for men, and that there are two types of girls: good and bad. Indeed, what angers feminists most about some rationales for legalized prostitution is the suggestion that it is a good way to curb criminal rape: Supposedly if men are provided with readily accessible and reasonably priced prostitutes, they will not be tempted to rape other women.

That feminists find this rationale so irrational is not surprising. First, legalized prostitution would not necessarily serve as a rape deterrent. The behavior of the American military in Vietnam, where "officially sanctioned" brothels for GIs were "incorporated into the base-camp recreation areas," indicates that the availability of sex for a small price is not always a deterrent to rape.[32] Many GIs adopted a both-and rather than an either-or approach to prostitution and rape. At the base they paid for Vietnamese women's sexual favors; on the front they simply took them for free. Second, and more significant, far from being a deterrent to rape, legalized prostitution may serve as a propaedeutic to rape. Comments Susan Brownmiller:

> My horror at the idea of legalized prostitution is not that it does not function as a rape deterrent, but that it institutionalizes the concept that it is a man's monetary right, if not his divine right, to gain access to the female body and that sex is a female service that should not be denied the civilized male. Perpetuation of the concept that the "powerful male impulse" must be satisfied with immediacy by a cooperative class of women, set apart and licensed for this purpose, is part and parcel of the mass psychology of rape.[33]

Finally, even if Brownmiller is wrong, even if prostitution and rape are not connected in the ways she thinks they are connected, there is something reprehensible about conceiving of prostitutes as a class of sacrificial victims. I, for one, do not like to think that somewhere a prostitute is offering up her body so that I and "my kind" can be spared from rape. I do not want to be privileged in any way that a prostitute is not, since she is no less or no more a person than I; and, therefore, I do not wish to cast my vote in favor of legalization if it promotes a state of affairs in which burdens are placed upon her that are not placed upon me.

CONCLUSION

When the ideological objections against legalization are coupled with the pragmatic arguments for laissez-faire decriminalization, the latter policy prevails for feminist as well as nonfeminist reasons. By decriminalizing prostitution, we do not add unnecessary burdens to those who would not be prostitutes if more attractive lifestyles were available to them. And we remove unnecessary burdens from those who would still choose to be prostitutes even if other, equally attractive lifestyles were available to them. But this is all we do, and it may not be enough.

It may not be enough in one sense because many women become prostitutes at an extremely young age, at a time when their knowledge is limited, and when they are especially vulnerable to coercion. Here the portrait of the runaway teenager looms large. Each year 600,000 to 1,000,000 young girls and boys, aged nine to seventeen, run away from home and a sizable percentage of them become prostitutes. In New York City alone there are about 20,000 youngsters under sixteen fending for themselves on the streets, and girls as young as nine years old provide easy prey for pimps.[34] Decriminalization will not help these girls achieve autonomy unless it is accompanied by extralegal remedies in the form of needed social services and by laws that prohibit the sexual exploitation of minors. The former remedies will increase the adolescent's general ability to understand both the nature and consequences of prostitution and its alternatives. The latter laws will free her from the individual coercion pimps and others exert on her—a coercion that ranges from the enticement of being the best-paid and most-pampered pony in the pimp's stable to threats of beatings and worse.

Of course, this makes it sound as if young girls who enter prostitution, appraised of its nature and consequences and without any sign of individual coercion, always do so voluntarily. This may not be the case, however. In addition to *individual coercion*, the phenomenon of *institutional coercion* often plays a role in lessening the adolescent's ability to choose voluntarily the life of a prostitute. Institutional coercion is the type of pressure that flows from the structures of capitalism and patriarchy; and laissez-faire decriminalization leaves these structures untouched. Therefore, unless poor women are given opportunities for education and employment, they will not be able to withstand the institutional pressures of capitalism. Likewise, unless sexually abused adolescents are given emotional support and psychological help, they will remain convinced that they are tainted, and they will not be able to withstand the institutional pressures of patriarchy. In short, unless one has the concrete means to transcend the institutions that work to limit one's freedom, chances are that one will submit to their constraints.

But the situation is even more complex than this. So far we have considered the institutions of capitalism and patriarchy as separate phenomena, but if we consider them as an amalgam, as capitalist-patriarchy, we will come to understand why even the woman who chooses prostitution freely is not likely to remain free for long. Says Jeffrey Bloustein: "The relation between man and woman is at present characterized by great disparities of social, economic, and political power, and the pervasive powerlessness of women often subverts sexual relations into relations of dominance and submission, regardless of the wishes and choices of the particular persons involved."[35] This suggests that the prostitute boasts idly when she insists that, because she has the "goods," the buyer is in her power. In point of fact, it is not at all certain that she is ever in charge, since the buyer is probably "purchasing" something other than her sexuality....

...If the prostitute is, by her thoughts, words, and deeds, reinforcing a conception of woman according to which *being for man* is the whole of her sexual identity, then like the rest of womankind, she must ask herself how free her choice to participate in the oldest profession is. If the prostitute can honestly say not only that her lifestyle is sexually liberating for herself, but that she wishes a similar sexual liberation for her daughter, then that nearly settles matters. But I doubt that any prostitute wishes to reproduce the current institution of prostitution for future generations of women: Like her nonprostitute sisters, who suffer from other, but equally confusing, sexual unfreedoms, she wishes a better life for her daughter, one in which sexual relations between persons, but especially between men and women, will be guided not by some subject-object dichotomy, but by a vision of multiplicity liberating enough to allow each person celebration of her or his own unique sexual identity.

NOTES

[1] Says Lars O. Ericsson in "Charges Against Prostitution: An Attempt at a Philosophical Assessment," *Ethics* 90 (April 1980): 349:

> No one denies that a majority of prostitutes are women, and no one denies that a majority of customers are men. But it is clear from the evidence that a large portion of the prostitutes, especially in metropolitan areas, are male homosexuals. There is also lesbian prostitution, though this is not (at least

not yet) sufficiently widespread to be of any great social importance. And finally, there is male heterosexual prostitution, the prevalence of which is also rather limited. We may sum up by saying that, rather than constituting a dichotomy between the sexes, prostitution has the characteristic that a considerable portion of the prostitutes are men, and small minority of the customers are women.

[2]Lord Patrick Devlin, *The Enforcement of Morals* (New York: Oxford University Press, 1965): 11.

[3]Eugene V. Rostow, "The Enforcement of Morals," *Cambridge Law Journal* 174 (November 1960): 197.

[4]Devlin, 22–23.

[5]David A. J. Richards, "Commercial Sex and the Rights of the Person: A Moral Argument for the Decriminalization of Prostitution," *University of Pennsylvania Law Review* 127 (May 1979): 1233.

[6]*Ibid.*, 1240–1244.

[7]President's Commission on Law Enforcement and Administration of Justice, *The Challenge of Crime in a Free Society: A Report* (Washington, D.C.: U.S. Government Printing Office, 1967): 189.

[8]M. Anne Jennings, "The Victim as Criminal: A Consideration of California Prostitution Law," *California Law Review* 64 (July 1976): 1248.

[9]John Stuart Mill, *On Liberty* (New York: Liberal Arts Press, 1956): 117.

[10]Joel Feinberg, *Social Philosophy* (Englewood Cliffs, N. J.: Prentice-Hall, 1973): 47.

[11]*Ibid.*, 48.

[12]Richards, 1282.

[13]*Ibid.*, 1285.

[14]Laura Lederer, "Then and Now: An Interview with a Former Pornography Model," in *Take Back the Night*, Laura Lederer, ed. (New York: William Morrow, 1980): 69.

[15]Voice "J" in Kate Millett, "A Quartet for Female Voices," in *Women in Sexist Society*, Vivian Gornick and Barbara K. Moran, eds. (New York: Basic Books, 1971): 69.

[16]Ericsson, 344.

[17]Karl Marx, *Economic and Philosophical Manuscripts of 1844*, trans. M. Mulligan (New York: International Publishers, 1964): 133n.

[18]Ericsson, 345.

[19]Ruth Sidel, *Women and Child Care in China* (New York: Hill & Wang, 1972): 50–51.

[20]Leo Kanowitz, *Women and the Law* (Albuquerque: University of New Mexico Press, 1969): 17–18.

[21]Juliet Mitchell, *Women's Estate* (New York: Pantheon Books, 1971): 144–145.

[22]Ericsson, 347.

[23]Jennifer James and Jane Myerding, "Early Sexual Experiences and Prostitution," *American Journal of Psychiatry* 134 (December 1977): 1383.

[24]*Ibid.*

[25]Simone de Beauvoir, *The Second Sex* (New York: Vintage Books, 1974): 632.

[26]Voice "J" in Millett, "A Quartet for Female Voices,"69.

[27]M. Shiels et al., "Flatfoot Floozies," *Newsweek*, June 28, 1976: 27–28.

[28]Charles Rosenbleet and Barbara J. Puriente, "The Prostitution of the Criminal Law," *American Criminal Law Review* 11 (Winter 1973): 373.

[29]Judith R. Walkowitz, "The Politics of Prostitution," *Signs: Journal of Women in Culture and Society* 6, No. I (Autumn 1980): 128.

[30]Richards, 1284, n. 440.

[31]*Ibid.*, 1281.

[32]Susan Brownmiller, *Against Our Will: Men, Women and Rape* (New York: Bantam, 1976): 440.

[33]*Ibid.*

[34]"Youth for Sale on the Streets," *Time*, November 28, 1977: 23.

[35]In an unpublished paper by Jeffrey Bloustein, Department of Philosophy, Barnard College, New York City.

WORLD WHORES' CONGRESS STATEMENTS

Draft Statements from the Second World Whores' Congress (1986)

PROSTITUTION AND FEMINISM

The International Committee for Prostitutes' Rights (ICPR) realizes that up until now the women's movement in most countries has not, or has only marginally, included prostitutes as spokeswomen and theorists. Historically, women's movements (like socialist and communist movements) have opposed the institution of prostitution while claiming to support prostitute women. However, prostitutes reject support that requires them to leave prostitution; they object to being treated as symbols of oppression and demand recognition as workers. Due to feminist hesitation or refusal to accept prostitution as legitimate work and to accept prostitutes as working women, the majority of prostitutes have not identified as feminists; nonetheless, many prostitutes identify with feminist values such as independence, financial autonomy, sexual self-determination, personal strength, and female bonding.

During the last decade, some feminists have begun to reevaluate the traditional antiprostitution stance of their movement in light of the actual experiences, opinions, and needs of prostitute women. The ICPR can be considered a feminist organization in that it is committed to giving voice and respect to all women, including the most invisible, isolated, degraded, and/or idealized. The development of prostitution analyses and strategies within women's movements which link the condition of prostitutes to the condition of women in general and which do justice to the integrity of prostitute women is therefore an important goal of the committee.

FINANCIAL AUTONOMY

Financial autonomy is basic to female survival, self-determination, self-respect, and self-development. Unlike men, women are often scorned and/or pitied for making life choices primarily in the interest of earning money. True financial independence includes the means to earn money (or the position to have authority over money) and the freedom to spend it as one needs or desires. Such means are rarely available to women even with compromise and struggle. Financial dependency or despair is the condition of a majority of women, depending upon class, culture, race, education, and other differences and inequalities. Female compromises and struggles are traditionally considered reflections of immorality and misfortune rather than of responsibility, intelligence, and courage. The financial initiative of prostitutes is stigmatized and/or criminalized as a warning to women in general against such sexually explicit strategies for financial independence. Nonetheless, "being sexually attractive" and "catching a good man" are traditional female strategies for survival, strategies which may provide financial sustenance but rarely financial independence. All women, including prostitutes, are entitled to the same commercial rights as other citizens in any given society. *The ICPR affirms the right of women to financial initiative and financial gain, including the right to commercialize sexual service or sexual illusion (such as erotic media), and to save and spend their earnings according to their own needs and priorities.*

OCCUPATIONAL CHOICE

The lack of educational and employment opportunities for women throughout the world has been well documented. Occupational choice for women (especially for women of color and working-class women), and also for men oppressed by class and race prejudice, is usually a choice between different subordinate positions. Once employed, women are often stigmatized and harassed. Furthermore, they are commonly paid according to their gender rather than their worth. Female access to jobs traditionally reserved for men and adequate pay and respect to women in jobs traditionally reserved for women are necessary conditions of true occupational choice. Those conditions entail an elimination of the sexual division of labor. Prostitution is a traditional female occupation. Some prostitutes report job satisfaction, others job repulsion; some consciously chose prostitution as the best alternative open to them; others rolled into prostitution through male force or deceit. Many prostitutes abhor the conditions and social stigma attached to their work, but not the work itself. *The ICPR affirms the right of women to the full range of education and employment alternatives and to due respect and compensation in every occupation, including prostitution.*

ALLIANCE BETWEEN WOMEN

Women have been divided into social categories on the basis of their sexual labor and/or sexual identity. Within the sex industry, the prostitute is the most explicitly oppressed by legal and social controls. Pornography models, striptease dancers, sexual masseuses, and prostitutes euphemistically called escorts or sexual surrogates often avoid association with prostitution labels and workers in an effort to elevate their status. Also among self-defined prostitutes, a hierarchy exists with street workers on the bottom and call girls on the top. Efforts to distance oneself from explicit sex work reinforce prejudice against prostitutes and reinforce sexual shame among women. Outside the sex industry, women are likewise divided by status, history, identity, and appearance. Nonprostitutes are frequently pressured to deliver sexual services in the form of sex, smiles, dress, or affection; those services are rarely compensated with pay and may even diminish female status. In general, a whore-madonna division is imposed upon women wherein those who are sexually assertive are considered whores and those who are sexually passive are considered madonnas. *The ICPR calls for alliance between all women within and outside the sex industry and especially affirms the dignity of street prostitutes and of women stigmatized for their color, class, ethnic difference, history of abuse, marital or motherhood status, sexual preference, disability, or weight. The ICPR is in solidarity with homosexual male, transvestite, and transsexual prostitutes.*

SEXUAL SELF-DETERMINATION

The right to sexual self-determination includes women's right to set the terms of their own sexuality, including the choice of partner(s), behaviors, and outcomes (such as pregnancy, pleasure, or financial gain). Sexual self-determination includes the right to refuse sex and to initiate sex as well as the right to use birth control (including abortion), the right to have lesbian sex, the right to have sex across lines of color or class, the right to engage in sadomasochistic sex, and the right to offer sex for money. Those possibly self-determining acts have been stigmatized and punished by law or custom. Necessarily, no one is entitled to act out a sexual desire that includes another party unless that party agrees under conditions of total free will. The feminist task is to nurture self-determination both by increasing women's sexual consciousness and courage and also by demanding conditions of safety and choice. *The ICPR affirms the right of all women to determine their own sexual behavior, including commercial exchange, without stigmatization or punishment.*

HEALTHY CHILDHOOD DEVELOPMENT

Children are dependent upon adults for survival, love, and development. Pressure upon children, either with kindness or force, to work for money or to have sex for adult satisfaction, is a violation of rights to childhood development. Often the child who is abused at home runs away but can find no subsistence other than prostitution, which perpetuates the violation of childhood integrity. Some research suggests that a higher percentage of prostitutes were victims of childhood abuse than of nonprostitutes. Research also suggests that 50 percent of prostitutes were not abused and that 25 percent of nonprostitutes were abused. Child abuse in private and public spheres is a serious violation of human rights, but it does not mean that the victims cannot survive and recover, especially given support and resources for development. A victim deserves no stigmatization either in childhood or adulthood. *The ICPR affirms the right of children to shelter, education, medical or psychological or legal services, safety, and sexual self-determination. Allocation of government funds to guarantee the above rights should be a priority in every country.*

INTEGRITY OF ALL WOMEN

Violence against women and girls has been a major feminist preoccupation for the past decade. Specifically, rape, sexual harassment at work, battering, and denial of motherhood rights have been targeted as focal areas for concern, research, and activism. Within the context of prostitution, women are sometimes raped or sexually harassed by the police, by their clients, by their managers, and by strangers who know them to be whores. Prostitute women, like nonprostitute women, consider rape to be any sexual act forced upon them. The fact that prostitutes are available for sexual negotiation does not mean that they are available for sexual harassment or rape. *The ICPR demands that the prostitute be given the same protection from rape and the same legal recourse and social support following rape that should be the right of any woman or man.*

Battering of prostitutes, like battering of nonprostitutes, reflects the subordination of women to men in personal relationships. Laws against such violence are often discriminately and/or arbitrarily enforced. Boyfriends and husbands of prostitutes, in addition to anyone else assumed to profit from prostitution earnings (such as family and room-mates), are often fined or imprisoned in various countries on charges of "pimping" regardless of whether they commit a violent offense or not. Boyfriends and husbands of nonprostitute women are rarely punished for battering, even when the woman clearly presses charges against them. *The ICPR affirms the right of all women to relational choice and to recourse against violence within any personal or work setting.*

Women known to be prostitutes or sex workers, like women known to be lesbians, are regularly denied custody of their children in many countries. The assumption that prostitute women or lesbian women are less responsible, loving, or deserving than other women is a denial of human rights and human dignity. The laws and attitudes which punish sexually stigmatized women function to punish their children as well by stigmatizing them and by denying them their mothers. *The ICPR considers the denial of custodial rights to prostitutes and lesbians to be a violation of the social and psychological integrity of women.*

MIGRATION OF WOMEN THROUGH PROSTITUTION ("TRAFFICKING")

Trafficking of women and children, an international issue among both feminists and nonfeminists, usually refers to the transport of women and children from one country to another for purposes of prostitution under conditions of force or deceit. The ICPR has a clear stand against child prostitution under any circumstances. In the case of adult prostitution, it must be acknowledged that prostitution both within and across national borders can be an individual decision to which an adult woman has a right. Certainly, force or deceit are crimes which should be punished whether in the context of prostitution or not. Women who choose to migrate as prostitutes should not be punished or assumed to be victims of abuse. They should enjoy the same rights as other immigrants. For many women, female migration through prostitution is an escape from an economically and socially impossible situation in one country to hopes for a better situation in another. The fact that many women find themselves in another awful situation reflects the lack of opportunities for financial independence and employment satisfaction for women, especially for

Third World women, throughout the world. Given the increased internationalization of industry, including prostitution, the rights and specific needs of foreign women workers must be given special attention in all countries.

The ICPR objects to policies which give women the status of children and which assume migration through prostitution among women to be always the result of force or deceit. Migrant women, also those who work as prostitutes, deserve both worker rights and worker protections. Women who are transported under conditions of deceit or force should be granted choice of refuge status or return to their country of origin.

A MOVEMENT FOR ALL WOMEN'S RIGHTS

It is essential that feminist struggle include the rights of all women. Prostitutes (especially those also oppressed by racism and classism) are perhaps the most silenced and violated of all women; the inclusion of their rights and their own words in feminist platforms for change is necessary. *The ICPR urges existing feminist groups to invite whore-identified women into their leading ranks and to integrate a prostitution consciousness in their analyses and strategies.*

SHOULD FEMINISTS OPPOSE PROSTITUTION?

Laurie Shrage

Because sexuality is a social construction, individuals as individuals are not free to experience eros just as they choose. Yet just as the extraction and appropriation of surplus value by the capitalist represents a choice available, if not to individuals, to society as a whole, so too sexuality and the forms taken by eros must be seen as at some level open to change.[1]

INTRODUCTION

Prostitution raises difficult issues for feminists. On the one hand, many feminists want to abolish discriminatory criminal statutes that are mostly used to harass and penalize prostitutes, and rarely to punish johns and pimps—laws which, for the most part, render prostitutes more vulnerable to exploitation by their male associates.[2] On the other hand, most feminists find the prostitute's work morally and politically objectionable. In their view, women who provide sexual services for a fee submit to sexual domination by men, and suffer degradation by being treated as sexual commodities.[3]

"Should Feminists Oppose Prostitution?" by Laurie Shrage in *Ethics* 99 (January 1989): 347–361. © 1989 by The University of Chicago. Reprinted by permission.

My concern in this paper is whether persons opposed to the social subordination of women should seek to discourage commercial sex. My goal is to marshal the moral arguments needed to sustain feminists' condemnation of the sex industry in our society. In reaching this goal, I reject accounts of commercial sex which posit cross-cultural and transhistorical causal mechanisms to explain the existence of prostitution or which assume that the activities we designate as "sex" have a universal meaning and purpose. By contrast, I analyze mercenary sex in terms of culturally specific beliefs and principles that organize its practice in contemporary American society. I try to show that the sex industry, like other institutions in our society, is structured by deeply ingrained attitudes and values which are oppressive to women. The point of my analysis is not to advocate an egalitarian reformation of commercial sex, nor to advocate its abolition through state regulation. Instead, I focus on another political alternative: that which must be done to subvert widely held beliefs that legitimate this institution in our society. Ultimately, I argue that nothing closely resembling prostitution, as we currently know it, will exist, once we have undermined these cultural convictions.

WHY PROSTITUTION IS PROBLEMATIC

A number of recent papers on prostitution begin with the familiar observation that prostitution is one of the oldest professions.[4] Such "observations" take for granted that "prostitution" refers to a single transhistorical, transcultural activity. By contrast, my discussion of prostitution is limited to an activity that occurs in modern Western societies—a practice which involves the purchase of sexual services from women by men....

...In this paper, I use the term "prostitute" as shorthand for "provider of commercial sexual services," and correspondingly, I use the term "prostitution" interchangeably with "commercial sex." By employing these terms in this fashion, I hope to appear consistent with colloquial English, and not to be taking for granted that a person who provides commercial sexual services "prostitutes" her- or himself....

...I do not attempt to construct an account of the psychological, social, and economic forces that presumably cause men to demand commercial sex, or of the factors which cause a woman to market her sexual services. Instead, I first consider whether prostitution, in all cultural contexts, constitutes a degrading and undesirable form of sexuality. I argue that, although the commercial availability of sexuality is not in every existing or conceivable society oppressive to women, in our society this practice depends upon the general acceptance of principles which serve to marginalize women socially and politically. Because of the cultural context in which prostitution operates, it epitomizes and perpetuates pernicious patriarchal beliefs and values and, therefore, is both damaging to the women who sell sex and, as an organized social practice, to all women in our society.

HISTORICAL AND CROSS-CULTURAL PERSPECTIVES

In describing Babylonian temple prostitution, Gerda Lerner reports: "For people who regarded fertility as sacred and essential to their own survival, the caring for the gods included, in some cases, offering them sexual services. Thus, a separate class of temple prostitutes developed. What seems to have happened was that sexual activity for and in behalf of the god or goddesses was considered beneficial to the people and sacred."[5] Similarly, according to Emma Goldman, the Babylonians believed that "the generative activity of human beings possessed a mysterious and sacred influence in promoting the fertility of Nature."[6] When the rationale for the impersonal provision of sex is conceived in terms of the promotion of nature's fecundity, the social meaning this activity has may differ substantially from the social significance it has in our own society.

In fifteenth-century France, as described by Jacques Rossiaud, commercial sex appears likewise to have had an import that contrasts with its role in contemporary America. According to Rossiaud:

> By the age of thirty, most prostitutes had a real chance of becoming reintegrated into society.... Since public opinion did not view them with disgust, and since they were on good terms with priests and men of the law, it was not too difficult for them to find a position as servant or wife.... Marriage was definitely the most frequent end to the career of communal prostitutes who had roots in the town where they have publicly offered their bodies.[7]

The fact that prostitutes were regarded by medieval French society as eligible for marriage, and were desired by men for wives, suggests that the cultural principles which sustained commercial exchanges of sex in this society were quite different than those which shape our own sex industry. Consequently, the phenomenon of prostitution requires a distinct political analysis and moral assessment *vis-à-vis* fifteenth-century France. This historically specific approach is justified, in part, because commercial sexual transactions may have different consequences for individuals in an alien society than for individuals similarly placed in our own. Indeed, it is questionable whether, in two quite different cultural settings, we should regard a particular outward behavior—the impersonal provision of sexual services for fees or their equivalent—as the same practice, that is, as prostitution.

Another cross-cultural example may help to make the last point clear. Anthropologists have studied a group in New Guinea, called the Etoro, who believe that young male children need to ingest male fluid or semen in order to develop properly into adult males, much like we believe that young infants need their mother's milk, or some equivalent, to be properly nurtured. Furthermore, just as our belief underlies our practice of breast-feeding, the Etoro's belief underlies their practice of penis-feeding, where young male children fellate older males, often their relatives.[8] From the perspective of our society, the Etoro's practice involves behaviors which are highly stigmatized—incest, sex with children, and homosexuality. Yet, for an anthropologist who is attempting to interpret and translate these behaviors, to assume that the Etoro practice is best subsumed under the category of "sex," rather than, for example, "child rearing," would reflect ethnocentrism. Clearly, our choice of one translation scheme or the other will influence our attitude toward the Etoro practice. The point is that there is no practice, such as "sex," which can be morally evaluated apart from a cultural framework.

In general, historical and cross-cultural studies offer little reason to believe that the dominant forms of sexual practice in our society reflect psychological, biological, or moral absolutes that determine human sexual practice. Instead, such studies provide much evidence that, against a different backdrop of beliefs about the world, the activities we designate as "sex"—impersonal or otherwise—have an entirely different meaning and value. Yet, while we may choose not to condemn the "child-rearing" practices of the Etoro, we can nevertheless recognize that "penis-feeding" would be extremely damaging to children in our society. Similarly, though we can appreciate that making an occupation by the provision of sex may not have been oppressive to women in medieval France or ancient Babylon, we should nevertheless recognize that in our society it can be extremely damaging to women. What then are the features which, in our culture, render prostitution oppressive?

THE SOCIAL MEANING OF PROSTITUTION

Let me begin with a simple analogy. In our society there exists a taboo against eating cats and dogs. Now, suppose a member of our society wishes to engage in the unconventional behavior of ingesting cat or dog meat. In evaluating the moral and political character of this person's behavior, it is somewhat irrelevant whether eating cats and dogs "really" is or is not healthy, or whether it "really" is or is not different than eating cows, pigs, and chickens. What is relevant is that, by including cat and dog flesh in one's diet, a person may really make others upset and, therefore, do damage to them as well as to oneself. In short, how actions are widely perceived and interpreted by others, even if wrongly or seemingly irrational, is crucial to determining their moral status because, though such interpretations may not hold up against some "objective reality," they are part of the "social reality" in which we live.

I am not using this example to argue that unconventional behavior is wrong but, rather, to illustrate the relevance of cultural convention to how our outward behaviors are perceived. Indeed, what is wrong with prostitution is not that it violates deeply entrenched social conventions—ideals of feminine purity, and the noncommoditization of sex—but precisely that it epitomizes other cultural assumptions—beliefs which, reasonable or not, serve to legitimate women's social subordination. In other words, rather than subvert patriarchal ideology, the prostitute's actions, and the industry as a whole, serve to perpetuate this system of values. By contrast, lesbian sex and egalitarian heterosexual economic and romantic relationships do not. In short, female prostitution oppresses women, not because some women who participate in it "suffer in the eyes of society" but because its organized practice testifies to and perpetuates socially hegemonic beliefs which oppress all women in many domains of their lives.

What, then, are some of the beliefs and values which structure the social meaning of the prostitute's business in our culture—principles which are not necessarily consciously held by us but are implicit in our observable behavior and social practice? First, people in our society generally believe that human beings naturally possess, but socially repress, powerful, emotionally destabilizing sexual appetites. Second, we assume that men are naturally suited for dominant social roles. Third, we assume that contact with male genitals in virtually all contexts is damaging and polluting to women. Fourth, we assume that a person's sexual practice renders her or him a particular "kind" of person, for example, "a homosexual," "a bisexual," "a whore," "a virgin," "a pervert," and so on. I will briefly examine the nature of these four assumptions, and then discuss how they determine the social significance and impact of prostitution in our society.…

The Universal Possession of a Potent Sex Drive

…The assumption of a potent "sex drive" is implicit in Lars Ericsson's relatively recent defense of prostitution: "We must liberate ourselves from those mental fossils which prevent us from looking upon sex and sexuality with the same naturalness as upon our cravings for food and drink. And, contrary to popular belief, we may have something to learn from prostitution in this respect, namely, that coition resembles nourishment in that if it cannot be obtained in any other way it can always be bought. And bought meals are not always the worst."[9] More explicitly, he argues that the "sex drive" provides a noneconomic, natural basis for explaining the demand for commercial sex.[10] Moreover, he claims that because of the irrational nature of this impulse, prostitution will exist until all persons are granted sexual access upon demand to all other persons.[11] In a society where individuals lack such access to others, but where women are the social equals of men, Ericsson predicts that "the degree of female frustration that exists today…will no longer be tolerated, rationalized, or sublimated, but channeled into a demand for, *inter alia*, mercenary sex."[12] Consequently, Ericsson favors an unregulated sex industry, which can respond spontaneously to these natural human wants…

…By contrast, consider a group of people in New Guinea, called the Dani, as described by Karl Heider: "Especially striking is their five year postpartum sexual abstinence, which is uniformly observed and is not a subject of great concern or stress. This low level of sexuality appears to be a purely cultural phenomenon, not caused by any biological factors."[13] The moral of this anthropological tale is that our high level of sexuality is also "a purely cultural phenomenon," and not the inevitable result of human biology. Though the Dani's disinterest in sex need not lead us to regard our excessive concern as improper, it should lead us to view one of our cultural rationalizations for prostitution as just that—a cultural rationalization.

The "Natural" Dominance of Men

One readily apparent feature of the sex industry in our society is that it caters almost exclusively to a male clientele. Even the relatively small number of male prostitutes at work serve a predominantly male consumer group. Implicit in this particular division of labor, and also the predominant division of labor in other domains of our society, is the cultural principle that men are naturally disposed to dominate in their relations with others.

Ironically, this cultural conviction is implicit in some accounts of prostitution by feminist writers, especially in their attempts to explain the social and psychological causes of the problematic demand by men for impersonal, commercial sex. For example, Marxist feminists have argued that prostitution is the manifestation of the unequal class position of women *vis-à-vis* men: women who do not exchange their domestic and sexual services with the male ruling class for their subsistence are forced to market these services to multiple masters outside marriage.[14] The exploitation of female sexuality is a ruling-class privilege, an advantage which allows those socially identified as "men" to perpetuate their economic and cultural hegemony. In tying female prostitution to patriarchy and capitalism, Marxist accounts attempt to tie it to particular historical forces rather than to biological or natural ones. However, without the assumption of men's biological superiority, Marxist feminist analyses cannot explain why women, at this particular moment under capitalism, have evolved as an economic underclass, that is, why capitalism gives rise to patriarchy. Why did women's role in production and reproduction not provide them a market advantage, a basis upon which they could subordinate men or assert their political equality?....

In appealing to the principle that men naturally assume dominant roles in all social systems, feminists uncritically accept a basic premise of patriarchy. In my view such principles do not denote universal causal mechanisms, but represent naturally arbitrary, culturally determined beliefs which serve to legitimate certain practices.

Sexual Contact Pollutes Women

To say that extensive sexual experience in a woman is not prized in our society is to be guilty of indirectness and understatement. Rather, a history of sexual activity is a negative mark that is used to differentiate kinds of women. Instead of being valued for their experience in sexual matters, women are valued for their "innocence."

That the act of sexual intercourse with a man is damaging to a woman is implicit in the vulgar language we use to describe this act. As Robert Baker has pointed out, a woman is "fucked," "screwed," "banged," "had," and so forth, and it is a man (a "prick") who does it to her.[15] The metaphors we use for the act of sexual intercourse are similarly revealing. Consider, for example, Andrea Dworkin's description of intercourse: "The thrusting is persistent invasion. She is opened up, split down the center. She is occupied—physically, internally, in her privacy."[16] Dworkin invokes both images of physical assault and imperialist domination in her characterization of heterosexual copulation. Women are split, penetrated, entered, occupied, invaded, and colonized by men. Though aware of the nonliteralness of this language, Dworkin appears to think that these metaphors are motivated by natural, as opposed to arbitrary, cultural features of the world. According to Ann Garry, "Because in our culture we connect sex with harm that men do to women, and because we think of the female role in sex as that of harmed object, we can see that to treat a woman as a sex object is automatically to treat her as less than fully human."[17] As the public vehicles for "screwing," "penetration," "invasion," prostitutes are reduced to the status of animals or things—mere instruments for human ends.

The Reification of Sexual Practice

Another belief that determines the social significance of prostitution concerns the relationship between a person's social identity and her or his sexual behavior. For example, we identify a person who has sexual relations with a person of the same gender as a "homosexual," and we regard a woman who has intercourse with multiple sexual partners as being of a particular type—for instance, a "loose woman," "slut," or "prostitute." As critics of our society, we may find these categories too narrow or the values they reflect objectionable. If so, we may refer to women who are sexually promiscuous, or who have sexual relations with other women, as "liberated women," and thereby show a rejection of double (and homophobic) standards of sexual morality. However, what such linguistic iconoclasm generally fails to challenge is that a person's sexual practice makes her a particular "kind" of person.

I will now consider how these cultural convictions and values structure the meaning of prostitution in our society. Our society's tolerance for commercially available sex, legal or not, implies general acceptance of principles which perpetuate women's social subordination. Moreover, by their participation in an industry which exploits the myths of female social inequality and sexual vulnerability, the actions of the prostitute and her clients imply that they accept a set of values and beliefs which assign women to marginal social roles in all our cultural institutions, including marriage and waged employment. Just as an Uncle Tom exploits noxious beliefs about blacks for personal gain, and implies through his actions that blacks can benefit from a system of white supremacy, the prostitute and her clients imply that women can profit economically from patriarchy....

Because members of our society perceive persons in terms of their sexual orientation and practice, and because sexual contact in most settings—but especially outside the context of a "secure" heterosexual relationship—is thought to be harmful to women, the prostitute's work may have social implications that differ significantly from the work of persons in other professions. For instance, women who work or have worked in the sex industry may find their future social prospects severely limited. By contrast to medieval French society, they are not desired as wives or domestic servants in our own. And unlike other female subordinates in our society, the prostitute is viewed as a defiled creature; nonetheless, we rationalize and tolerate prostitutional sex out of the perceived need to mollify men's sexual desires.

In sum, the woman who provides sex on a commercial basis and the man who patronizes her epitomize and reinforce the social principles I have identified: these include beliefs that attribute to humans potent subjugating sex drives that men can satisfy without inflicting self-harm through impersonal sexual encounters. Moreover, the prostitute cannot alter the political implications of her work by simply supplying her own rationale for the provision of her services. For example, Margo St. James has tried to represent the prostitute as a skilled sexual therapist, who serves a legitimate social need.[18] According to St. James, while the commercial sex provider may be unconventional in her sexual behavior, her work may be performed with honesty and dignity. However, this defense is implausible since it ignores the possible adverse impact of her behavior on herself and others, and the fact that by participating in prostitution her behavior does little to subvert the cultural principles that make her work harmful.... Although the prostitute may want the meaning of her actions assessed relative to her own idiosyncratic beliefs and values, the political and social meaning of her actions must be assessed in the political and social context in which they occur.

One can imagine a society in which individuals sought commercial sexual services from women in order to obtain high-quality sexual experiences. In our society, people pay for medical advice, meals, education in many fields, and so on, in order to obtain information, services, or goods that are superior to or in some respect more valuable than those they can obtain noncommercially. A context in which the rationale for seeking a prostitute's services was to obtain sex from a professional—from a person who knows what she is doing—is probably not a context in which women are thought to be violated when they have sexual contact with men. In such a situation, those who supplied sex on a commercial basis would probably not be stigmatized but, instead, granted ordinary social privileges. The fact that prostitutes have such low social status in our society indicates that the society in which we live is not congruent with this imaginary one; that is, the prostitute's services in our society are not generally sought as a gourmet item. In short, if commercial sex was sought as a professional service, then women who provided sex commercially would probably not be regarded as "prostituting" themselves—as devoting their bodies or talents to base purposes, contrary to their true interests.

SUBVERTING THE STATUS QUO

Let me reiterate that I am not arguing for social conformism. Rather, my point is that not all nonconformist acts equally challenge conventional morality. For example, if a person wants to subvert the belief that eating cats and dogs is bad, it is not enough to simply engage in eating them. Similarly, it is unlikely that persons will subvert prevalent attitudes toward gender and sexuality by engaging in prostitution.

Consider another example. Suppose that I value high-quality child care and am willing to pay a person well to obtain it. Because of both racial and gender oppression, the persons most likely to be interested in and suitable for such work are bright Third World and minority First World women who cannot compete fairly for other well-paid work. Suppose, then, I hire a person who happens to be a woman and a person of color to provide child care on the basis of the belief that such work requires a high level of intelligence and responsibility. Though the belief on which this act is based may be unconventional, my action of hiring a "sitter" from among the so-called lower classes of society is not politically liberating.

What can a person who works in the sex industry do to subvert widely held attitudes toward her work? To subvert the beliefs which currently structure commercial sex in our society, the female prostitute would need to assume the role not of a sexual subordinate but of a sexual equal or superior. For instance, if she were to have the authority to determine what services the customer could get, under what conditions the customer could get them, and what they would cost, she would gain the status of a sexual professional. Should she further want to establish herself as a sexual therapist, she would need to represent herself as having some type of special technical knowledge for solving problems having to do with human sexuality. In other words, experience is not enough to establish one's credentials as a therapist or professional. However, if the industry were reformed so that all these conditions were met, what would distinguish the prostitute's work from that of a bona fide "sexual therapist"? If her knowledge was thought to be only quasi-legitimate, her work might have the status of something like the work of a chiropractor, but this would certainly be quite different than the current social status of her work.[19] In sum, the political alternatives of reformation and abolition are not mutually exclusive: if prostitution were sufficiently transformed to make it completely nonoppressive to women, though commercial transactions involving sex might still exist, prostitution as we now know it would not.

If our tolerance for marriage fundamentally rested on the myth of female subordination, then the same arguments which apply to prostitution would apply to it. Many theorists, including Simone de Beauvoir and Friedrich Engels, have argued that marriage, like prostitution, involves female sexual subservience. In addition, Lars Ericsson contends that marriage, unlike prostitution, involves economic dependence for women: "While the housewife is totally dependent on her husband, at least economically, the call girl in that respect stands on her own two feet. If she has a pimp, it is she, not he, who is the breadwinner in the family."[20]

Since the majority of marriages in our society render the wife the domestic and sexual subordinate of her husband, marriage degrades the woman who accepts it (or perhaps only the woman who accepts marriage on unequal terms), and its institutionalization in its present form oppresses all women. However, because marriage can be founded on principles which do not involve the subordination of women, we can challenge oppressive aspects of this institution without radically altering it....

CONCLUSIONS

If my analysis is correct, then prostitution is not a social aberration or disorder but, rather, a consequence of well-established beliefs and values that form part of the foundation of all our social institutions and practices.

Therefore, by striving to overcome discriminatory structures in all aspects of society—in the family, at work outside the home, and in our political institutions—feminists will succeed in challenging some of the cultural presuppositions which sustain prostitution. In other words, prostitution needs no unique remedy, legal or otherwise; it will be remedied as feminists make progress in altering patterns of belief and practice that oppress women in all aspects of their lives. Yet, while prostitution requires no special social cure, some important strategic and symbolic feminist goals may be served by selecting the sex industry for criticism at this time. In this respect, a consumer boycott of the industry is especially appropriate....

NOTES

I am grateful to Sandra Bartky, Alison Jaggar, Elizabeth Segal, Richard Arneson, and the anonymous reviewers for *Ethics* for their critical comments and suggestions. Also, I am indebted to Daniel Segal for suggesting many anthropological and historical examples relevant to my argument. In addition, I would like to thank the Philosophy Department of the Claremont Graduate School for the opportunity to present an earlier draft of this paper for discussion.

[1] Nancy Hartsock, *Money, Sex and Power* (Boston: Northeastern University Press, 1985): 178.

[2] See Rosemarie Tong, *Women, Sex, and the Law* (Totowa, N. J.: Rowman & Allanheld, 1984): 37–64.

[3] See Carole Pateman, "Defending Prostitution: Charges against Ericsson," *Ethics* 93 (1983): 561–565; and Kathleen Barry, *Female Sexual Slavery* (New York: Avon, 1979).

[4] For example, see Gerda Lerner, "The Origin of Prostitution in Ancient Mesopotamia," *Signs: Journal of Women in Culture and Society* 11 (1986): 236–254; Lars Ericsson, "Charges against Prostitution: An Attempt at a Philosophical Assessment," *Ethics* 90 (1980): 335–366; and James Brundage, "Prostitution in the Medieval Canon Law," *Signs: Journal of Women in Culture and Society* I (1976): 825–845.

[5] Lerner, 239.

[6] Emma Goldman, "The Traffic in Women," in *Red Emma Speaks*, ed. Alix Kates Shulman (New York: Schocken, 1983): 180.

[7] Jacques Rossiaud, "Prostitution, Youth, and Society in the Towns of Southeastern France in the Fifteenth Century," in *Deviants and the Abandoned in French Society: Selections from the Annales Economies, Société, Civilisations*, eds. Robert Forster and Orest Ranum (Baltimore: Johns Hopkins University Press, 1978): 21.

[8] See Gilbert H. Herdt, ed., *Rituals of Manhood* (Berkeley and Los Angeles: University of California Press, 1982). Also see Harriet Whitehead, "The Varieties of Fertility Cultism in New Guinea: Part I," *American Ethnologist* 13 (1986): 80–99. In comparing penis-feeding to breast-feeding rather than to oral sex, some anthropologists point out that both involve the use of a culturally erotic bodily part for parental nurturing.

[9]Ericsson, 355.

[10]*Ibid.*, 347.

[11]*Ibid.*, 359–360.

[12]*Ibid.*, 360.

[13]Karl Heider, "Dani Sexuality: A Low Energy System," *Man* 11 (1976): 188–201.

[14]See Friedrich Engels, *The Origins of the Family, Private Property and the State* (New York: Penguin, 1985); Goldman, *op. cit.*; Allison Jagger, "Prostitution," in *The Philosophy of Sex*, ed. Alan Soble (Totowa, N.J.: Rowman & Littlefield, 1980): 353–358.

[15]Robert Baker, " 'Pricks' and 'Chicks': A Plea for 'Persons,' " in *Philosophy and Sex*, eds. R. Baker and F. Elliston (Buffalo, N.Y.: Prometheus, 1984): 260–266. In this section, Baker provides both linguistic and nonlinguistic evidence that intercourse, in our cultural mythology, hurts women.

[16]Andrea Dworkin, *Intercourse* (New York: Free Press, 1987): 122.

[17]Ann Garry, "Pornography and Respect for Women," in Baker and Elliston, eds., *op. cit.*, 318.

[18]Margo St. James, Speech to the San Diego County National Organization for Women, La Jolla, California, February 27, 1982, and from private correspondence with St. James (1983). Margo St. James is the founder of COYOTE (Call Off Your Old Tired Ethics) and the editor of *Coyote Howls*. COYOTE is a civil rights organization which seeks to change the sex industry from within by getting better working conditions for prostitutes.

[19]I am grateful to Richard Arneson for suggesting this analogy to me.

[20]Ericsson, 354.

CHAPTER 3

Pornography

INTRODUCTION

Historically, concerns with pornographic materials have raised a variety of interrelated questions. Conceptually, questions have been raised about what makes a particular sexually explicit representation pornographic, how pornography is similar to or different from obscenity or erotica, and what the relationship is between representation and reality. Legally, the debate has traditionally been one of interpreting the scope of the First Amendment right to freedom of expression. If the conceptual questions can be answered, that is, if it is possible to define pornography, then what role, if any, should the state have in controlling its production, distribution, and consumption? Does the constitutional right to freedom of expression extend to protect those words and images that are offensive to community standards of decency? The right to privacy is also often invoked in the legal debates about pornography. Do state-imposed restrictions on the production and consumption of pornography violate an individual's right to choose what career to pursue or what entertainment to enjoy? Morally, pornography also raises interesting and difficult questions. Does pornography cause harm? If so, to whom and how? How are we to weigh the values of expression and choice against the offense or harm pornography may cause?

Some of these questions were considered in 1973 by the Supreme Court in *Paris Adult Theatre I v. Slaton.* In that ruling, the majority determined that the state has a legitimate interest in restricting the production and distribution of obscene material. In order to determine whether material is obscene, the court looked for the coalescence of three elements: (1) the material, on the whole, appeals to a "prurient interest in sex"; (2) the material is offensive to "contemporary community standards"; and (3) the material is devoid of social value. These standards did not receive unanimous support from the Justices. In his dissent, Justice Brennan, joined by Justice Stewart and Justice Marshall, noted that all of the existing formulas for determining when a state can legitimately regulate sexually explicit material contain intolerable vagueness and will be applied unpredictably depending on the disposition of the person or persons making the determination. Citing the often-repeated, and in his view inadequate, "we know it when we see it" criterion, Brennan argues that "the concept of obscenity cannot be defined with sufficient specificity and clarity to provide fair notice to persons who create and distribute sexually oriented material" and "to prevent substantial erosion of protected speech." Ultimately, the dissent maintains that appeals to public morality cannot override fundamental First Amendment protections.

Irving Kristol considers the conflict between public morality on the one hand, and individual rights or liberties on the other. He argues that interest in pornography and obscenity appeals to an "infantile" and "masturbatory" sexuality that is in opposition to the flourishing of an advanced democratic society. He further suggests that democratic arguments for absolute self-government based on autonomous choices fail to examine the character of those making the choices, an examination which is necessary to promote the highest quality of public life. Kristol concludes that censorship of pornography will serve the interests of society. Mindful of concerns, such as those expressed in the dissent of *Paris Adult Theatre*, that once censorship starts there is a danger of inhibiting free thought and expression, Kristol claims that censorship has been going on for almost two centuries without diminishing significant freedoms. This response is compelling against slippery-slope arguments warning that once some censorship is allowed, it cannot be stopped. But in the face of Brennan's concerns about the changing, and potentially idiosyncratic, beliefs of the censors, this response appears inadequate. In addition, Kristol's appeal to tradition runs the risk of curtailing full human flourishing. We will never know what the quality of our public life might have become in the absence of hundreds of years of censorship.

A different but related argument against pornography and in favor of state control of its production, distribution, and consumption is one that is based on the harm it causes not to society in general, but to particular and identifiable individuals. This sort of argument is made by many feminists who maintain that pornography harms women, individually and as a group. According to the leading proponents of this view, pornography harms individual women because it leads to violence against them, and it harms women in general by sexualizing gender subordination. Catharine A. MacKinnon who, with Andrea Dworkin, authored the Indianapolis ordinance that is the subject of *American Booksellers v. Hudnut*, argues that pornography promotes the idea that women are inferior and unequal to men. As such, pornography is a form of sex discrimination, and is thus in direct conflict with women's civil rights.

This view of pornography significantly alters the traditional terms of the debate. Instead of viewing the conflict as the *Paris Adult Theatre* and earlier courts did, in terms of weighing the interest in public morality with individual liberty, on MacKinnon's view a direct conflict of individual rights lies at the root of the problem. These conflicting rights are the rights of women to equal respect and opportunities, and the rights of pornographers to express themselves as they choose. As Ronald Dworkin frames it, the conflict is not just one between negative liberties, the liberty to be free from interference, but with positive liberties, the freedom to participate in public life, as well. In *Hudnut*, Circuit Judge Easterbrook allows that pornography can function as a component of domination as it helps to shape the way men see women as inferior sexual objects. But he nonetheless rules against the ordinance as written because without strong protections for speech, the most effective means for ending domination are eliminated.

MacKinnon and others have claimed that pornographers abduct and abuse women in their films and that such violence occurs to the girlfriends and wives of the men who consume pornography. If women are not directly victimized by pornography, they are injured socially and politically. Women cannot exercise their right to expression, because pornography renders their own speech inaudible. It thus seems that until the institution of pornography is eliminated, women will not be able to achieve equality. But is it true that as long as pornography exists, women cannot escape victimization and will remain subordinated? Many feminists think not. Some feminists argue that the industry in pornography serves them well. A large number of women—heterosexual, bisexual, and lesbian—are actively involved in the production of pornography and, as Nina Hartley makes clear, in her own case it is a choice which is fully consistent with her feminism. As the star of hundreds of pornographic videos, Hartley sees herself as a reformer, altering stereotypes of women and presenting positive, self-satisfying portrayals of female sexuality.

Other feminists, while not directly participating in the production and distribution of pornography, nonetheless support its existence, or at least are opposed to efforts to censor it. In their Amici Brief presented to the *Hudnut* court, the Feminist Anti-Censorship Taskforce (F.A.C.T.), the Women's Legal Defense Fund, and eighty individual feminists present various reasons why feminists oppose censorship. Some of these include denying women like Hartley the right to pursue the career of their choosing; denying women access to valuable feminist materials and ways of developing their own sexual expression; discriminating against minority sexualities; perpetuating the ideas that sex is bad for women and that women are victims in need of special protections; and distracting from immediate efforts to end violence against women. With MacKinnon, these feminists agree that the gender inequality which characterizes our society is unacceptable and must be eliminated. Deep disagreements arise when considering whether to allow a historically gender-biased state to determine what should and should not be censored. The F.A.C.T. brief concludes, with Easterbrook, that women, and all those working to change society, must preserve the system of free expression.

But if MacKinnon is right, the system of free expression that condones pornography effectively denies women access to the marketplace of ideas as it silences women's voices. Dworkin argues that rather than censoring pornography, the state's role is to allow every voice to be heard. According to his analysis, a more effective legal and moral way of addressing the issue of pornography would be to create mechanisms whereby full free expression is promoted. The inequality that women suffer must be addressed, he argues, but it is a mistake to think that the positive values of equality and justice can be promoted by curtailing negative freedoms, such as those protected under the First Amendment.

SUGGESTED READINGS

Susan G. Cole, *Pornography and the Sex Crisis* (Toronto: Amanita Enterprises, 1989).

David Copp and Susan Wendell, *Pornography and Censorship* (Buffalo, NY: Prometheus Books, 1983).

Susan Dwyer, *The Problem of Pornography* (Belmont, CA: Wadsworth Publishing Company, 1995).

Susan Easton, *The Problem of Pornography: Regulation and the Right to Free Speech* (New York: Routledge, 1994).

Joel Feinberg, *Offense to Others* (New York: Oxford University Press, 1985).

Nadine Strossen, *Defending Pornography: Free Speech, Sex and the Fight for Women's Rights* (New York: Scribner, 1995).

Linda Williams, *Hardcore: Power, Pleasure and the Frenzy of the Visible* (Berkeley, CA: University of California Press, 1989).

PARIS ADULT THEATRE I v. SLATON

413 U.S. 49 (1973)
Argued October 19, 1972,
Decided June 21, 1973

Chief Justice Berger delivered the opinion of the Court.

Petitioners are two Atlanta, Georgia, movie theaters and their owners and managers, operating in the style of "adult" theaters. On December 28, 1970, respondents, the local state district attorney and the solicitor for the local state trial court, filed civil complaints in that court alleging that petitioners were exhibiting to the public for paid admission two allegedly obscene films, contrary to Georgia Code Ann. §26–2101.[1] The two films in question, "Magic Mirror" and "It All Comes Out in the End," depict sexual conduct characterized by the Georgia Supreme Court as "hard-core pornography" leaving "little to the imagination."

Respondents' complaints, made on behalf of the State of Georgia, demanded that the two films be declared obscene and that petitioners be enjoined from exhibiting the films....

Certain photographs, also produced at trial, were stipulated to portray the single entrance to both Paris Adult Theatre I and Paris Adult Theatre II as it appeared at the time of the complaints. These photographs show a conventional, inoffensive theater entrance, without any pictures, but with signs indicating that the theaters exhibit "Atlanta's Finest Mature Feature Films." On the door itself is a sign saying: "Adult Theatre—You must be 21 and able to prove it. If viewing the nude body offends you, Please Do Not Enter."

The two films were exhibited to the trial court. The only other state evidence was testimony by criminal investigators that they had paid admission to see the films and that nothing on the outside of the theater indicated the full nature of what was shown. In particular, nothing indicated that the films depicted—as they did—scenes of simulated fellatio, cunnilingus, and group sex intercourse. There was no evidence presented that minors had ever entered the theaters. Nor was there evidence presented that petitioners had a systematic policy of barring minors, apart from posting signs at the entrance. On April 12, 1971, the trial judge dismissed respondents' complaints. He assumed "that obscenity is established," but stated:

> It appears to the Court that the display of these films in a commercial theatre, when surrounded by requisite notice to the public of their nature and by reasonable protection against the exposure of these films to minors, is constitutionally permissible.

On appeal, the Georgia Supreme Court unanimously reversed. It assumed that the adult theaters in question barred minors and gave a full warning to the general public of the nature of the films shown, but held that the films were without protection under the First Amendment.... After viewing the films, the Georgia Supreme Court held that their exhibition should have been enjoined, stating:

> The films in this case leave little to the imagination. It is plain what they purport to depict, that is, conduct of the most salacious character. We hold that these films are also hard core pornography, and the showing of such films should have been enjoined since their exhibition is not protected by the First Amendment. *Id.*, at 347.

I

It should be clear from the outset that we do not undertake to tell the States what they must do, but rather to define the area in which they may chart their own course in dealing with obscene material. This Court has consistently held that obscene material is not protected by the First Amendment as a limitation on the state police power by virtue of the Fourteenth Amendment.... While this procedure is civil in nature, and does not directly involve the state criminal statute proscribing exhibition of obscene material, the Georgia case law permitting civil injunction does adopt the definition of "obscene materials" used by the criminal statute. Today, in *Miller v. California* 413 U.S. 15 (1973), we have sought to clarify the constitutional definition of obscene material subject to regulation by the States, and we vacate and remand this case for reconsideration in light of Miller....

II

We categorically disapprove the theory, apparently adopted by the trial judge, that obscene, pornographic films acquire constitutional immunity from state regulation simply because they are exhibited for consenting adults only. This holding was properly rejected by the Georgia Supreme Court. Although we have often pointedly recognized the high importance of the state interest in regulating the exposure of obscene materials to juveniles and unconsenting adults,... this Court has never declared these to be the only legitimate state interests permitting regulation of obscene material. The States have a long-recognized legitimate interest in regulating the use of obscene material in local commerce and in all places of public accommodation, as long as these regulations do not run afoul of specific constitutional prohibitions....

In particular, we hold that there are legitimate state interests at stake in stemming the tide of commercialized obscenity, even assuming it is feasible to enforce effective safeguards against exposure to juveniles and to passersby.[2] Rights and interests "other than those of the advocates are involved." *Breard v. Alexandria*, 341 U.S. 622, 642 (1951). These include the interest of the public in the quality of life and the total community environment, the tone of commerce in the great city centers, and, possibly, the public safety itself. The Hill-Link Minority Report of the Commission on Obscenity and Pornography indicates that there is at least an arguable correlation between obscene material and crime.[3] Quite apart from sex crimes, however, there remains one problem of large proportions aptly described by Professor Bickel:

> It concerns the tone of the society, the mode, or to use terms that have perhaps greater currency, the style and quality of life, now and in the future. A man may be entitled to read an obscene book in his room, or expose himself indecently there...We should protect his privacy. But if he demands a right to obtain the books and pictures he wants in the market, and to foregather in public places—discreet, if you will, but accessible to all—with others who share his tastes, *then to grant him his right is to affect the world about the rest of us, and to impinge on other privacies.* Even supposing that each of us can, if he wishes, effectively avert the eye and stop the ear (which, in truth, we cannot), what is commonly read and seen and heard and done intrudes upon us all, want it or not. 22 *The Public Interest* 25–26 (Winter 1971).[4] (Emphasis added.)

As Mr. Chief Justice Warren stated, there is a "right of the Nation and of the States to maintain a decent society,... "...But, it is argued, there are no scientific data which conclusively demonstrate that exposure to obscene material adversely affects men and women or their society. It is urged on behalf of the petitioners that, absent such a demonstration, any kind of state regulation is "impermissible." We reject this argument. It is not for us to resolve empirical uncertainties underlying state legislation, save in the exceptional case where that legislation plainly impinges upon rights protected by the Constitution itself.

...From the beginning of civilized societies, legislators and judges have acted on various unprovable assumptions. Such assumptions underlie much lawful state regulation of commercial and business affairs.... On the basis of these assumptions both Congress and state legislatures have, for example, drastically restricted associational rights by adopting antitrust laws, and have strictly regulated public expression by issuers of and dealers in securities, profit-sharing "coupons," and "trading stamps," commanding what they must and must not publish and announce.... Understandably those who entertain an absolutist view of the First Amendment find it uncomfortable to explain why rights of association, speech, and press should be severely restrained in the marketplace of goods and money, but not in the marketplace of pornography.

Likewise, when legislatures and administrators act to protect the physical environment from pollution and to preserve our resources of forests, streams, and parks, they must act on such imponderables as the impact of a new highway near or through an existing park or wilderness area.... The fact that a congressional directive reflects unprovable assumptions about what is good for the people, including imponderable aesthetic assumptions, is not a sufficient reason to find that statute unconstitutional.

If we accept the unprovable assumption that a complete education requires the reading of certain books,... and the well-nigh universal belief that good books, plays, and art lift the spirit, improve the mind, enrich the human personality, and develop character, can we then say that a state legislature may not act on the corollary assumption that commerce in obscene books, or public exhibitions focused on obscene conduct, have a tendency to exert a corrupting and debasing impact leading to antisocial behavior?... The sum of experience, including that of the past two decades, affords an ample basis for legislatures to conclude that a sensitive, key relationship of human existence, central to family life, community welfare, and the development of human personality, can be debased and distorted by crass commercial exploitation of sex. Nothing in the Constitution prohibits a State from reaching such a conclusion and acting on it legislatively simply because there is no conclusive evidence or empirical data.

It is argued that individual "free will" must govern, even in activities beyond the protection of the First Amendment and other constitutional guarantees of privacy, and that government cannot legitimately impede an individual's desire to see or acquire obscene plays, movies, and books. We do indeed base our society on certain assumptions that people have the capacity for free choice. Most exercises of individual free choice—those in politics, religion, and expression of ideas—are explicitly protected by the Constitution. Totally unlimited play for free will, however, is not allowed in our or any other society. We have just noted, for example, that neither the First Amendment nor "free will" precludes States from having "blue sky" laws to regulate what sellers of securities may write or publish about their wares.... Such laws are to protect the weak, the uninformed, the unsuspecting, and the gullible from the exercise of their own volition. Nor do modern societies leave disposal of garbage and sewage up to the individual "free will," but impose regulation to protect both public health and the appearance of public places. States are told by some that they must await a "laissez-faire" market solution to the obscenity-pornography problem, paradoxically "by people who have never otherwise had a kind word to say for laissez-faire," particularly in solving urban, commercial, and environmental pollution problems. See I. Kristol, *On the Democratic Idea in America* 37 (1972).

The States, of course, may follow such a "laissez-faire" policy and drop all controls on commercialized obscenity, if that is what they prefer, just as they can ignore consumer protection in the marketplace, but nothing in the Constitution compels the States to do so with regard to matters falling within state jurisdiction.

It is asserted, however, that standards for evaluating state commercial regulations are inapposite in the present context, as state regulation of access by consenting adults to obscene material violates the constitutionally protected right to privacy enjoyed by petitioners' customers. Even assuming that petitioners have vicarious standing to assert potential customers' rights, it is unavailing to compare a theater open to the public for a fee with the private home of *Stanley v. Georgia*, 394 U.S., at 568 (1969), and the marital bedroom of *Griswold v. Connecticut*, 381 U.S., at 485–486 (1965). This Court has, on numerous occasions, refused to hold that commercial ventures such as a motion-picture house are "private" for the purpose of civil rights litigation and civil rights statutes.... The Civil Rights Act of 1964 specifically defines motion-picture houses and theaters as places of "public accommodation" covered by the Act as operations affecting commerce....

Our prior decisions recognizing a right to privacy guaranteed by the Fourteenth Amendment included "only personal rights that can be deemed 'fundamental' or 'implicit in the concept of ordered liberty.'" *Palko v. Connecticut*, 302 U.S. 319, 325 (1937)...*Roe v. Wade*, 410 U.S. 113, 152 (1973).... This privacy right encompasses and protects the personal intimacies of the home, the family, marriage, motherhood, procreation, and child rearing.... Nothing, however, in this Court's decisions intimates that there is any "fundamental" privacy right "implicit in the concept of ordered liberty" to watch obscene movies in places of public accommodation.

If obscene material unprotected by the First Amendment in itself carried with it a "penumbra" of constitutionally protected privacy, this Court would not have found it necessary to decide *Stanley* on the narrow basis of the "privacy of the home," which was hardly more than a reaffirmation that "a man's home is his castle." Cf. *Stanley v. Georgia, supra,* at 564.[5] Moreover, we have declined to equate the privacy of the home relied on in *Stanley* with a "zone" of "privacy" that follows a distributor or a consumer of obscene materials wherever he goes.... The idea of a "privacy" right and a place of public accommodation are, in this context, mutually exclusive. Conduct or depictions of conduct that the state police power can prohibit on a public street do not become automatically protected by the Constitution merely because the conduct is moved to a bar or a "live" theater stage, any more than a "live" performance of a man and woman locked in a sexual embrace at high noon in Times Square is protected by the Constitution because they simultaneously engage in a valid political dialogue.

It is also argued that the State has no legitimate interest in "control [of] the moral content of a person's thoughts," *Stanley v. Georgia, supra,* at 565, and we need not quarrel with this. But we reject the claim that the State of Georgia is here attempting to control the minds or thoughts of those who patronize theaters. Preventing unlimited display or distribution of obscene material, which by definition lacks any serious literary, artistic, political, or scientific value as communication, *Miller v. California, ante,* at 24, 34, is distinct from a control of reason and the intellect.... Where communication of ideas, protected by the First Amendment, is not involved, or the particular privacy of the home protected by *Stanley,* or any of the other "areas or zones" of constitutionally protected privacy, the mere fact that, as a consequence, some human "utterances" or "thoughts" may be incidentally affected does not bar the State from acting to protect legitimate state interests.... The fantasies of a drug addict are his own and beyond the reach of government, but government regulation of drug sales is not prohibited by the Constitution....

Finally, petitioners argue that conduct which directly involves "consenting adults" only has, for that sole reason, a special claim to constitutional protection. Our Constitution establishes a broad range of conditions on the exercise of power by the States, but for us to say that our Constitution incorporates the proposition that conduct involving consenting adults only is always beyond state regulation[6] is a step we are unable to take.[7] Commercial exploitation of depictions, descriptions, or exhibitions of obscene conduct on commercial premises open to the adult public falls within a State's broad power to regulate commerce and protect the public environment. The issue in this context goes beyond whether someone, or even the majority, considers the conduct depicted as "wrong" or "sinful." The States have the power to make a morally neutral judgment that public exhibition of obscene material, or commerce in such material, has a tendency to injure the community as a whole, to endanger the public safety, or to jeopardize, in Mr. Chief Justice Warren's words, the States' "right...to maintain a decent society."...

To summarize, we have today reaffirmed the basic holding of *Roth v. United States, supra,* that obscene material has no protection under the First Amendment. See *Miller v. California, supra....* We have directed our holdings, not at thoughts or speech, but at depiction and description of specifically defined sexual conduct that States may regulate within limits designed to prevent infringement of First Amendment rights.... In this case we hold that the States have a legitimate interest in regulating commerce in obscene material and in regulating exhibition of obscene material in places of public accommodation, including so-called "adult" theaters from which minors are excluded. In light of these holdings, nothing precludes the State of Georgia from the regulation of the allegedly obscene material exhibited in Paris Adult Theatre I or II, provided that the applicable Georgia law, as written or authoritatively interpreted by the Georgia courts, meets the First Amendment standards set forth in *Miller v. California....*

Justice Brennan with whom Justice Stewart and Justice Marshall join, dissenting.

This case requires the Court to confront once again the vexing problem of reconciling state efforts to suppress sexually oriented expression with the protections of the First Amendment, as applied to the States through the Fourteenth Amendment. No other aspect of the First Amendment has, in recent years, demanded so substantial a commitment of our time, generated such disharmony of views, and remained so resistant to the formulation of stable and manageable standards. I am convinced that the approach initiated 16 years ago in *Roth v. United States,* 354 U.S. 476 (1957), and culminating in the Court's decision today, cannot bring stability to this area of the law without jeopardizing fundamental First Amendment values, and I have concluded that the time has come to make a significant departure from that approach....

II

In *Roth v. United States,* the Court held that obscenity, although expression, falls outside the area of speech or press constitutionally protected under the First and Fourteenth Amendments against state or federal infringement. But at the same time we emphasized in *Roth* that "sex and obscenity are not synonymous," *id.,* at 487, and that matter which is sexually oriented but not obscene is fully protected by the Constitution. For we recognized that "sex, a great and mysterious motive force in human life, has indisputably been a subject of absorbing interest to mankind through the ages; it is one of the vital problems of human interest and public concern." *Ibid. Roth* rested, in other words, on what has been termed a two-level approach to the question of obscenity. While much criticized,[8] that approach has been endorsed by all but two members of this Court who have addressed the question since *Roth*. Yet our efforts to implement that approach demonstrate that agreement on the existence of something called "obscenity" is still a long and painful step from agreement on a workable definition of the term.

Recognizing that "the freedoms of expression...are vulnerable to gravely damaging yet barely visible encroachments," *Bantam Books, Inc. v. Sullivan*, 372 U.S. 58, 66 (1963), we have demanded that "sensitive tools" be used to carry out the "separation of legitimate from illegitimate speech." *Speiser v. Randall*, 357 U.S. 513, 525 (1958). The essence of our problem in the obscenity area is that we have been unable to provide "sensitive tools" to separate obscenity from other sexually oriented but constitutionally protected speech, so that efforts to suppress the former do not spill over into the suppression of the latter....

The view that, until today, enjoyed the most, but not majority, support was an interpretation of *Roth....* We expressed the view that Federal or State Governments could control the distribution of material where "three elements...coalesce: it must be established that (a) the dominant theme of the material taken as a whole appeals to a prurient interest in sex; (b) the material is patently offensive because it affronts contemporary community standards relating to the description or representation of sexual matters; and (c) the material is utterly without redeeming social value."...

III

Our experience with the *Roth* approach has certainly taught us that the outright suppression of obscenity cannot be reconciled with the fundamental principles of the First and Fourteenth Amendments. For we have failed to formulate a standard that sharply distinguishes protected from unprotected speech....

Of course, the vagueness problem would be largely of our own creation if it stemmed primarily from our failure to reach a consensus on any one standard. But after sixteen years of experimentation and debate I am reluctantly forced to the conclusion that none of the available formulas, including the one announced today, can reduce the vagueness to a tolerable level while at the same time striking an acceptable balance between the protections of the First and Fourteenth Amendments, on the one hand, and on the other the asserted state interest in regulating the dissemination of certain sexually oriented materials. Any effort to draw a constitutionally acceptable boundary on state power must resort to such indefinite concepts as "prurient interest," "patent offensiveness," "serious literary value," and the like. The meaning of these concepts necessarily varies with the experience, outlook, and even idiosyncrasies of the person defining them. Although we have assumed that obscenity does exist and that we "know it when [we] see it," *Jacobellis v. Ohio*, 378 U.S. at 197 (1964), we are manifestly unable to describe it in advance except by reference to concepts so elusive that they fail to distinguish clearly between protected and unprotected speech....

V

Our experience since *Roth* requires us not only to abandon the effort to pick out obscene materials on a case-by-case basis, but also to reconsider a fundamental postulate of *Roth*: that there exists a definable class of sexually oriented expression that may be totally suppressed by the Federal and State Governments. Assuming that such a class of expression does in fact exist, I am forced to conclude that the concept of "obscenity" cannot be defined with sufficient specificity and clarity to provide fair notice to persons who create and distribute sexually oriented materials, to prevent substantial erosion of protected speech as a byproduct of the attempt to suppress unprotected speech, and to avoid very costly institutional harms. Given these inevitable side effects of state efforts to suppress what is assumed to be unprotected speech, we must scrutinize with care the state interest that is asserted to justify the suppression. For in the absence of some very substantial interest in suppressing such speech, we can hardly condone the ill effects that seem to flow inevitably from the effort.

Obscenity laws have a long history in this country. Most of the States that had ratified the Constitution by 1792 punished the related crime of blasphemy or profanity despite the guarantees of free expression in their constitutions.... Although the number of early obscenity laws was small and their enforcement exceedingly lax, the situation significantly changed after about 1870 when Federal and State Governments, mainly as a result of the efforts of Anthony Comstock, took an active interest in the suppression of obscenity. By the end of the nineteenth century at least thirty States had some type of general prohibition on the dissemination of obscene materials, and by the time of our decision in *Roth* no State was without some provision on the subject. The Federal Government meanwhile had enacted no fewer than 20 obscenity laws between 1842 and 1956....

This history caused us to conclude in *Roth* "that the unconditional phrasing of the First Amendment [that 'Congress shall make no law... abridging the freedom of speech, or of the press...'] was not intended to protect every utterance." 354 U.S., at 483. It also caused us to hold, as numerous prior decisions of this Court had assumed, see *id.*, at 481, that obscenity could be denied the protection of the First Amendment and hence suppressed because it is a form of expression "utterly without redeeming social importance," *id.*, at 484, as "mirrored in the universal judgment that [it] should be restrained..." *Id.*, at 485.

Because we assumed—incorrectly, as experience has proved—that obscenity could be separated from other sexually oriented expression without significant costs either to the First Amendment or to the judicial machinery charged with the task of safeguarding First Amendment freedoms, we had no occasion in *Roth* to probe the asserted state interest in curtailing unprotected, sexually oriented speech. Yet, as we have increasingly come to appreciate the vagueness of the concept of obscenity, we have begun to recognize and articulate the state interests at stake....

The opinions in *Redrup* 386 U.S. 767 and *Stanley* reflected our emerging view that the state interests in protecting children and in protecting unconsenting adults may stand on a different footing from the other asserted state interests. It may well be, as one commentator has argued, that "exposure to [erotic material] is for some persons an intense emotional experience. A communication of this nature, imposed upon a person contrary to his wishes, has all the characteristics of a physical assault.... [And it] constitutes an invasion of his privacy...."[9] ...Similarly, if children are "not possessed of that full capacity for individual choice which is the presupposition of the First Amendment guarantees," *Ginsberg v. New York*, 390 U.S., at 649–650 (Stewart, J., concurring), then the State may have a substantial interest in precluding the flow of obscene materials even to consenting juveniles....

But, whatever the strength of the state interests in protecting juveniles and unconsenting adults from exposure to sexually oriented materials, those interests cannot be asserted in defense of the holding of the Georgia Supreme Court in this case. That court assumed for the purposes of its decision that the films in issue were exhibited only to persons over the age of 21 who viewed them willingly and with prior knowledge of the nature of their contents. And on that assumption the state court held that the films could still be suppressed. The justification for the suppression must be found, therefore, in some independent interest in regulating the reading and viewing habits of consenting adults.

At the outset it should be noted that virtually all of the interests that might be asserted in defense of suppression, laying aside the special interests associated with distribution to juveniles and unconsenting adults, were also posited in *Stanley v. Georgia, supra,* where we held that the State could not make the "mere private possession of obscene material a crime." *Id.,* at 568. That decision presages the conclusions I reach here today.

In *Stanley* we pointed out that "there appears to be little empirical basis for" the assertion that "exposure to obscene materials may lead to deviant sexual behavior or crimes of sexual violence." *Id.,* at 566 and n. 9.[10] In any event, we added that "if the State is only concerned about printed or filmed materials inducing antisocial conduct, we believe that in the context of private consumption of ideas and information we should adhere to the view that 'among free men, the deterrents ordinarily to be applied to

prevent crime are education and punishment for violations of the law....'
Whitney v. California, 274 U.S. 357, 378 (1927) (Brandeis, J., concurring)."
Id., at 566–567.

Moreover, in *Stanley* we rejected as "wholly inconsistent with the philosophy of the First Amendment," *id.,* at 566, the notion that there is a legitimate state concern in the "control [of] the moral content of a person's thoughts," *id.,* at 565, and we held that a State "cannot constitutionally premise legislation on the desirability of controlling a person's private thoughts." *Id.,* at 566. That is not to say, of course, that a State must remain utterly indifferent to—and take no action bearing on—the morality of the community. The traditional description of state police power does embrace the regulation of morals as well as the health, safety, and general welfare of the citizenry. See, e.g., *Village of Euclid v. Ambler Realty Co.,* 272 U.S. 365, 395 (1926). And much legislation—compulsory public education laws, civil rights laws, even the abolition of capital punishment—is grounded, at least in part, on a concern with the morality of the community. But the State's interest in regulating morality by suppressing obscenity, while often asserted, remains essentially unfocused and ill defined. And, since the attempt to curtail unprotected speech necessarily spills over into the area of protected speech, the effort to serve this speculative interest through the suppression of obscene material must tread heavily on rights protected by the First Amendment.

In *Roe v. Wade,* 410 U.S. 113 (1973), we held constitutionally invalid a state abortion law, even though we were aware of

> the sensitive and emotional nature of the abortion controversy, of the vigorous opposing views, even among physicians, and of the deep and seemingly absolute convictions that the subject inspires. One's philosophy, one's experiences, one's exposure to the raw edges of human existence, one's religious training, one's attitudes toward life and family and their values, and the moral standards one establishes and seeks to observe, are all likely to influence and to color one's thinking and conclusions about abortion. *Id.,* at 116.

Like the proscription of abortions, the effort to suppress obscenity is predicated on unprovable, although strongly held, assumptions about human behavior, morality, sex, and religion. The existence of these assumptions cannot validate a statute that substantially undermines the guarantees of the First Amendment, any more than the existence of similar assumptions on the issue of abortion can validate a statute that infringes the constitutionally protected privacy interests of a pregnant woman....

Even a legitimate, sharply focused state concern for the morality of the community cannot, in other words, justify an assault on the protections of the First Amendment. Cf. *Griswold v. Connecticut,* 381 U.S. 479 (1965); *Eisenstadt v. Baird,* 405 U.S. 438 (1972); *Loving v. Virginia,* 388 U.S. 1 (1967).

Where the state interest in regulation of morality is vague and ill defined, interference with the guarantees of the First Amendment is even more difficult to justify.

In short, while I cannot say that the interests of the State—apart from the question of juveniles and unconsenting adults—are trivial or nonexistent, I am compelled to conclude that these interests cannot justify the substantial damage to constitutional rights and to this Nation's judicial machinery that inevitably results from state efforts to bar the distribution even of unprotected material to consenting adults.... I would hold, therefore, that at least in the absence of distribution to juveniles or obtrusive exposure to unconsenting adults, the First and Fourteenth Amendments prohibit the State and Federal Governments from attempting wholly to suppress sexually oriented materials on the basis of their allegedly "obscene" contents....

NOTES

[1]...Georgia Code Ann. §26–2101 reads in relevant part: Distributing obscene materials. (a) A person commits the offense of distributing obscene materials when he sells, lends, rents, leases, gives, advertises, publishes, exhibits or otherwise disseminates to any person any obscene material of any description, knowing the obscene nature thereof, or who offers to do so, or who possesses such material with the intent so to do.... (b) Material is obscene if considered as a whole, applying community standards, its predominant appeal is to prurient interest, that is, a shameful or morbid interest in nudity, sex or excretion, and utterly without redeeming social value and if, in addition, it goes substantially beyond customary limits of candor in describing or representing such matters.... (d) A person convicted of distributing obscene material shall for the first offense be punished as for a misdemeanor, and for any subsequent offense shall be punished by imprisonment for not less than one nor more than five years, or by a fine not to exceed $5,000, or both....

[2]It is conceivable that an "adult" theater can—if it really insists—prevent the exposure of its obscene wares to juveniles. An "adult" bookstore, dealing in obscene books, magazines, and pictures, cannot realistically make this claim. The Hill-Link Minority Report of the Commission on Obscenity and Pornography emphasizes evidence (the Abelson National Survey of Youth and Adults) that, although most pornography may be bought by elders, "the heavy users and most highly exposed people to pornography are adolescent females (among women) and adolescent and young adult males (among men)." The Report of the Commission on Obscenity and Pornography 401 (1970). The legitimate interest in preventing exposure of juveniles to obscene material cannot be fully served by simply barring juveniles from the immediate physical premises of "adult" bookstores, when there is a flourishing "outside business" in these materials.

[3]The Report of the Commission on Obscenity and Pornography, 390–412 (1970).

[4]See also Berns, "Pornography vs. Democracy: The Case for Censorship," in 22 *The Public Interest* 3 (Winter 1971); van den Haag, in *Censorship: For & Against* 156–157 (H. Hart, ed., 1971).

[5]The protection afforded by *Stanley v. Georgia*, 394 U.S. 557 (1969), is restricted to a place, the home. In contrast, the constitutionally protected privacy of family, marriage, motherhood, procreation, and child rearing is not just concerned with a particular place, but with a protected intimate relationship. Such protected privacy extends to the doctor's office, the hospital, the hotel room, or as otherwise required to safeguard the right to intimacy involved. Cf. *Roe v. Wade*, 410 U.S. 113, 152–154 (1973); *Griswold v. Connecticut*, 381 U.S. 479, 485–486 (1965). Obviously, there is no necessary or legitimate expectation of privacy which would extend to marital intercourse on a street corner or a theater stage.

[6]Cf. J. Mill, *On Liberty* 13 (1955 ed.).

[7]The state statute books are replete with constitutionally unchallenged laws against prostitution, suicide, voluntary self-mutilation, brutalizing "bare fist" prize fights, and duels, although these crimes may only directly involve "consenting adults." Statutes making bigamy a crime surely cut into an individual's freedom to associate, but few today seriously claim such statutes violate the First Amendment or any other constitutional provision. See also the summary of state statutes prohibiting bearbaiting, cockfighting, and other brutalizing animal "sports," in Stevens, "Fighting and Baiting," in *Animals and Their Legal Rights* 112–127 (Leavitt ed. 1970). As Professor Irving Kristol has observed: "Bearbaiting and cockfighting are prohibited only in part out of compassion for the suffering animals; the main reason they were abolished was because it was felt that they debased and brutalized the citizenry who flocked to witness such spectacles." *On the Democratic Idea in America* 33 (1972).

[8]See, e.g., T. Emerson, *The System of Freedom of Expression* 487 (1970).

[9]T. Emerson, *The System of Freedom of Expression* 496 (1970).

[10]Indeed, since Stanley was decided, the President's Commission on Obscenity and Pornography has concluded:

> In sum, empirical research designed to clarify the question has found no evidence to date that exposure to explicit sexual materials plays a significant role in the causation of delinquent or criminal behavior among youth or adults. The Commission cannot conclude that exposure to erotic materials is a factor in the causation of sex crime or sex delinquency. Report of the Commission on Obscenity and Pornography 27 (1970) (footnote omitted).

To the contrary, the Commission found that "on the positive side, explicit sexual materials are sought as a source of entertainment and information by substantial numbers of American adults. At times, these materials also appear to serve to increase and facilitate constructive communication about sexual matters within marriage." *Id.*, at 53.

AMERICAN BOOKSELLERS ASSN., INC. v. HUDNUT

United States Court of Appeals for the Seventh Circuit
771 F.2d 323 (1985)
Argued June 14, 1985,
Decided August 27, 1985

Judge Easterbrook, Circuit Judge .

Indianapolis enacted an ordinance defining "pornography" as a practice that discriminates against women. "Pornography" is to be redressed through the administrative and judicial methods used for other discrimination...."Pornography" under the ordinance is "the graphic sexually explicit subordination of women, whether in pictures or in words, that also includes one or more of the following:"

(1) Women are presented as sexual objects who enjoy pain or humiliation; or

(2) Women are presented as sexual objects who experience sexual pleasure in being raped; or

(3) Women are presented as sexual objects tied up or cut up or mutilated or bruised or physically hurt, or as dismembered or truncated or fragmented or severed into body parts; or

(4) Women are presented as being penetrated by objects or animals; or

(5) Women are presented in scenarios of degradation, injury, abasement, torture, shown as filthy or inferior, bleeding, bruised, or hurt in a context that makes these conditions sexual; or

(6) Women are presented as sexual objects for domination, conquest, violation, exploitation, possession, or use, or through postures or positions of servility or submission or display. Indianapolis Code §16–3(q).

The statute provides that the "use of men, children, or transsexuals in the place of women in paragraphs (1) through (6) above shall also constitute pornography under this section." The ordinance as passed in April 1984 defined "sexually explicit" to mean actual or simulated intercourse or the uncovered exhibition of the genitals, buttocks or anus. An amendment in June 1984 deleted this provision, leaving the term undefined.

The Indianapolis ordinance does not refer to the prurient interest, to offensiveness, or to the standards of the community. It demands attention to particular depictions, not to the work judged as a whole. It is irrelevant under the ordinance whether the work has literary, artistic, political, or scientific value. The City and many *amici* point to these omissions as virtues. They maintain that pornography influences attitudes, and the statute is a way to alter the socialization of men and women rather than to vindicate community standards of offensiveness. And as one of the principal drafters of the ordinance has asserted, "if a woman is subjected, why should it matter that the work has other value?" Catharine A. MacKinnon, "Pornography, Civil Rights, and Speech," 20 *Harv. Civ. Rts.—Civ. Lib. L. Rev.* 1, 21 (1985).

Civil rights groups and feminists have entered this case as amici on both sides. Those supporting the ordinance say that it will play an important role in reducing the tendency of men to view women as sexual objects, a tendency that leads to both unacceptable attitudes and discrimination in the workplace and violence away from it. Those opposing the ordinance point out that much radical feminist literature is explicit and depicts women in ways forbidden by the ordinance and that the ordinance would reopen old battles. It is unclear how Indianapolis would treat works from James Joyce's Ulysses to Homer's Iliad; both depict women as submissive objects for conquest and domination.

We do not try to balance the arguments for and against an ordinance such as this. The ordinance discriminates on the ground of the content of the speech. Speech treating women in the approved way—in sexual encounters "premised on equality" (MacKinnon, *supra*, at 22)—is lawful no matter how sexually explicit. Speech treating women in the disapproved way—as submissive in matters sexual or as enjoying humiliation—is unlawful no matter how significant the literary, artistic, or political qualities of the work taken as a whole. The state may not ordain preferred viewpoints in this way. The Constitution forbids the state to declare one perspective right and silence opponents.

I

The ordinance contains four prohibitions. People may not "traffic" in pornography, "coerce" others into performing in pornographic works, or "force" pornography on anyone. Anyone injured by someone who has seen or read pornography has a right of action against the maker or seller.

Trafficking is defined in §16–3(g)(4) as the "production, sale, exhibition, or distribution of pornography." The offense excludes exhibition in a public or educational library, but a "special display" in a library may be sex discrimination. Section 16–3(g)(4)(C) provides that the trafficking paragraph "shall not be construed to make isolated passages or isolated parts actionable."

"Coercion into pornographic performance" is defined in §16–3(g)(5) as "coercing, intimidating or fraudulently inducing any person…into performing for pornography. …" The ordinance specifies that proof of any of the following "shall not constitute a defense: I. That the person is a woman;… VI. That the person has previously posed for sexually explicit pictures…with anyone…; …VIII. That the person actually consented to a use of the performance that is changed into pornography;… IX. That the person knew that the purpose of the acts or events in question was to make pornography;… XI. That the person signed a contract, or made statements affirming a willingness to cooperate in the production of pornography; XII. That no physical force, threats, or weapons were used in the making of the pornography; or XIII. That the person was paid or otherwise compensated."

"Forcing pornography on a person," according to §16–3(g)(5), is the "forcing of pornography on any woman, man, child, or transsexual in any place of employment, in education, in a home, or in any public place." The statute does not define forcing, but one of its authors states that the definition reaches pornography shown to medical students as part of their education or given to language students for translation. MacKinnon, supra, at 40–41.

Section 16–3(g)(7) defines as a prohibited practice the "assault, physical attack, or injury of any woman, man, child, or transsexual in a way that is directly caused by specific pornography."

For purposes of all four offenses, it is generally "not…a defense that the respondent did not know or intend that the materials were pornography. …" Section 16–3(g)(8). But the ordinance provides that damages are unavailable in trafficking cases unless the complainant proves "that the respondent knew or had reason to know that the materials were pornography." It is a complete defense to a trafficking case that all of the materials in question were pornography only by virtue of category (6) of the definition of pornography. In cases of assault caused by pornography, those who seek damages from "a seller, exhibitor or distributor" must show that the defendant knew or had reason to know of the material's status as pornography. By implication, those who seek damages from an author need not show this.

A woman aggrieved by trafficking in pornography may file a complaint "as a woman acting against the subordination of women" with the office of equal opportunity. Section 16–17(b)....

The office investigates and within 30 days makes a recommendation to a panel of the equal opportunity advisory board. The panel then decides whether there is reasonable cause to proceed (§16–24(2)) and may refer the dispute to a conciliation conference or to a complaint adjudication committee for a hearing (§§16–24(3), 16–26 (a)). The committee uses the same procedures ordinarily associated with civil rights litigation. It may make findings and enter orders, including both orders to cease and desist and orders "to take further affirmative action...including but not limited to the power to restore complainant's losses...." Section 16–26 (d)....

The district court held the ordinance unconstitutional. 598 F. Supp. 1316 (S.D. Ind. 1984). The court concluded that the ordinance regulates speech rather than the conduct involved in making pornography. The regulation of speech could be justified, the court thought, only by a compelling interest in reducing sex discrimination, an interest Indianapolis had not established. The ordinance is also vague and overbroad, the court believed, and establishes a prior restraint of speech.

II

The plaintiffs are a congeries of distributors and readers of books, magazines, and films. The American Booksellers Association comprises about 5,200 bookstores and chains.... Collectively the plaintiffs (or their members, whose interests they represent) make, sell, or read just about every kind of material that could be affected by the ordinance, from hard-core films to W.B. Yeats's poem "Leda and the Swan"...to the collected works of James Joyce, D.H. Lawrence, and John Cleland....

III

"If there is any fixed star in our constitutional constellation, it is that no official, high or petty, can prescribe what shall be orthodox in politics, nationalism, religion, or other matters of opinion or force citizens to confess by word or act their faith therein." *West Virginia State Board of Education v. Barnette*, 319 U.S. 624, 642, (1943). Under the First Amendment the government must leave to the people the evaluation of ideas. Bald or subtle, an idea is as powerful as the audience allows it to be. A belief may be pernicious—the beliefs of Nazis led to the death of millions, those of the Klan to the repression of millions. A pernicious belief may prevail. Totalitarian governments today rule much of the planet, practicing suppression of billions and spreading dogma that may enslave others. One of the things that separates our society from theirs is our absolute right to propagate opinions that the government finds wrong or even hateful.

The ideas of the Klan may be propagated. *Brandenburg v. Ohio*, 395 U.S. 444 (1969). Communists may speak freely and run for office. *DeJonge v. Oregon*, 299 U.S. 353, (1937). The Nazi Party may march through a city with a large Jewish population. *Collin v. Smith*, 578 F.2d 1197 (7th Cir.), cert. denied, 439 U.S. 916 (1978). People may criticize the President by misrepresenting his positions, and they have a right to post their misrepresentations on public property. *Lebron v. Washington Metropolitan Area Transit Authority*, 242 U.S. App. D.C. 215, 749 (1984) (Bork, J.). People may seek to repeal laws guaranteeing equal opportunity in employment or to revoke the constitutional amendments granting the vote to blacks and women. They may do this because "above all else, the First Amendment means that government has no power to restrict expression because of its message [or] its ideas...." *Police Department v. Mosley*, 408 U.S. 92, 95, (1972). See also Geoffrey R. Stone, "Content Regulation and the First Amendment," 25 *William & Mary L. Rev.* 189 (1983); Paul B. Stephan, *The First Amendment and Content Discrimination*, 68 Va. L. Rev. 203, 233–236 (1982).

Under the ordinance graphic sexually explicit speech is "pornography" or not depending on the perspective the author adopts. Speech that "subordinates" women and also, for example, presents women as enjoying pain, humiliation, or rape, or even simply presents women in "positions of servility or submission or display" is forbidden, no matter how great the literary or political value of the work taken as a whole. Speech that portrays women in positions of equality is lawful, no matter how graphic the sexual content. This is thought control. It establishes an "approved" view of women, of how they may react to sexual encounters, of how the sexes may relate to each other. Those who espouse the approved view may use sexual images; those who do not, may not.

Indianapolis justifies the ordinance on the ground that pornography affects thoughts. Men who see women depicted as subordinate are more likely to treat them so. Pornography is an aspect of dominance.[1] It does not persuade people so much as change them. It works by socializing, by establishing the expected and the permissible. In this view pornography is not an idea; pornography is the injury.

There is much to this perspective. Beliefs are also facts. People often act in accordance with the images and patterns they find around them. People raised in a religion tend to accept the tenets of that religion, often without independent examination. People taught from birth that black people are fit only for slavery rarely rebelled against that creed; beliefs coupled with the self-interest of the masters established a social structure that inflicted great harm while enduring for centuries. Words and images act at the level of the subconscious before they persuade at the level of the conscious. Even the truth has little chance unless a statement fits within the framework of beliefs that may never have been subjected to rational study.

Therefore we accept the premises of this legislation. Depictions of subordination tend to perpetuate subordination. The subordinate status of women in turn leads to affront and lower pay at work, insult and injury at home, battery and rape on the streets.[2] In the language of the legislature, "pornography is central in creating and maintaining sex as a basis of discrimination. Pornography is a systematic practice of exploitation and subordination based on sex which differentially harms women. The bigotry and contempt it produces, with the acts of aggression it fosters, harm women's opportunities for equality and rights [of all kinds]." Indianapolis Code §16–1(a)(2).

Yet this simply demonstrates the power of pornography as speech. All of these unhappy effects depend on mental intermediation. Pornography affects how people see the world, their fellows, and social relations. If pornography is what pornography does, so is other speech. Hitler's orations affected how some Germans saw Jews. Communism is a world view, not simply a Manifesto by Marx and Engels or a set of speeches. Efforts to suppress communist speech in the United States were based on the belief that the public acceptability of such ideas would increase the likelihood of totalitarian government. Religions affect socialization in the most pervasive way. The opinion in *Wisconsin v. Yoder*, 406 U.S. 205 (1972), shows how a religion can dominate an entire approach to life, governing much more than the relation between the sexes. Many people believe that the existence of television, apart from the content of specific programs, leads to intellectual laziness, to a penchant for violence, to many other ills. The Alien and Sedition Acts passed during the administration of John Adams rested on a sincerely held belief that disrespect for the government leads to social collapse and revolution—a belief with support in the history of many nations. Most governments of the world act on this empirical regularity, suppressing critical speech. In the United States, however, the strength of the support for this belief is irrelevant. Seditious libel is protected speech unless the danger is not only grave but also imminent. See *New York Times Co. v. Sullivan*, 376 U.S. 254 (1964)....

Racial bigotry, anti-Semitism, violence on television, reporters' biases—these and many more influence the culture and shape our socialization.

None is directly answerable by more speech, unless that speech too finds its place in the popular culture. Yet all is protected as speech, however insidious. Any other answer leaves the government in control of all of the institutions of culture, the great censor and director of which thoughts are good for us.

Sexual responses often are unthinking responses, and the association of sexual arousal with the subordination of women therefore may have a substantial effect. But almost all cultural stimuli provoke unconscious responses. Religious ceremonies condition their participants. Teachers convey messages by selecting what not to cover; the implicit message about what is off limits or unthinkable may be more powerful than the messages for which they present rational argument. Television scripts contain unarticulated assumptions. People may be conditioned in subtle ways. If the fact that speech plays a role in a process of conditioning were enough to permit governmental regulation, that would be the end of freedom of speech.

It is possible to interpret the claim that the pornography is the harm in a different way. Indianapolis emphasizes the injury that models in pornographic films and pictures may suffer. The record contains materials depicting sexual torture, penetration of women by red-hot irons and the like. These concerns have nothing to do with written materials subject to the statute, and physical injury can occur with or without the "subordination" of women...a state may make injury in the course of producing a film unlawful independent of the viewpoint expressed in the film.

The more immediate point, however, is that the image of pain is not necessarily pain. In *Body Double*, a suspense film directed by Brian DePalma, a woman who has disrobed and presented a sexually explicit display is murdered by an intruder with a drill. The drill runs through the woman's body. The film is sexually explicit and a murder occurs—yet no one believes that the actress suffered pain or died. In *Barbarella* a character played by Jane Fonda is at times displayed in sexually explicit ways and at times shown "bleeding, bruised, [and] hurt in a context that makes these conditions sexual"—and again no one believes that Fonda was actually tortured to make the film. In *Carnal Knowledge* a woman grovels to please the sexual whims of a character played by Jack Nicholson; no one believes that there was a real sexual submission, and the Supreme Court held the film protected by the First Amendment. *Jenkins v. Georgia*, 418 U.S. 153, (1974). And this works both ways. The description of women's sexual domination of men in *Lysistrata* was not real dominance. Depictions may affect slavery, war, or sexual roles, but a book about slavery is not itself slavery, or a book about death by poison a murder.

Much of Indianapolis's argument rests on the belief that when speech is "unanswerable," and the metaphor that there is a "marketplace of ideas" does not apply, the First Amendment does not apply either. The metaphor is honored; Milton's *Aeropagitica* and John Stuart Mill's *On Liberty* defend freedom of speech on the ground that the truth will prevail, and many of the most important cases under the First Amendment recite this position. The Framers undoubtedly believed it. As a general matter it is true. But the Constitution does not make the dominance of truth a necessary condition of freedom of speech. To say that it does would be to confuse an outcome of free speech with a necessary condition for the application of the amendment.

A power to limit speech on the ground that truth has not yet prevailed and is not likely to prevail implies the power to declare truth. At some point the government must be able to say (as Indianapolis has said): "We know what the truth is, yet a free exchange of speech has not driven out falsity, so that we must now prohibit falsity." If the government may declare the truth, why wait for the failure of speech? Under the First Amendment, however, there is no such thing as a false idea, *Gertz v. Robert Welch, Inc.*, 418 U.S. 323 (1974), so the government may not restrict speech on the ground that in a free exchange truth is not yet dominant.

At any time, some speech is ahead in the game; the more numerous speakers prevail. Supporters of minority candidates may be forever "excluded" from the political process because their candidates never win, because few people believe their positions. This does not mean that freedom of speech has failed.

The Supreme Court has rejected the position that speech must be "effectively answerable" to be protected by the Constitution.... In *Mills v. Alabama*, 384 U.S. 214 (1966), the Court held unconstitutional a statute prohibiting editorials on election day—a statute the state had designed to prevent speech that came too late for answer. In cases from *Eastern Railroad Presidents Conference v. Noerr Motor Freight, Inc.*, 365 U.S. 127 (1961), through *NAACP v. Claiborne Hardware Co.*, 458 U.S. 886 (1982), the Court has held that the First Amendment protects political stratagems—obtaining legislation through underhanded ploys and outright fraud in *Noerr*, obtaining political and economic ends through boycotts in *Clairborne Hardware*—that may be beyond effective correction through more speech.

We come, finally, to the argument that pornography is "low-value" speech, that it is enough like obscenity that Indianapolis may prohibit it. Some cases hold that speech far removed from politics and other subjects at the core of the Framers' concerns may be subjected to special regulation. E.g., *FCC v. Pacifica Foundation*, 438 U.S. 726 (1978); *Young v. American Mini Theatres, Inc.*, 427 U.S. 50, 67–70 (1976) (plurality opinion); *Chaplinsky v. New Hampshire*, 315 U.S. 568, 571–572 (1942). These cases do not sustain statutes that select among viewpoints, however. In *Pacifica* the FCC sought to keep vile language off the air during certain times. The Court held that it may; but the Court would not have sustained a regulation prohibiting scatological descriptions of Republicans but not scatological descriptions of Democrats, or any other form of selection among view-points. See *Planned Parenthood Ass'n v. Chicago Transit Authority*, 767 F.2d 1225 (7th Cir. 1985), *slip op.* 13–14.

At all events, "pornography" is not low-value speech within the meaning of these cases. Indianapolis seeks to prohibit certain speech because it believes this speech influences social relations and politics on a grand scale, that it controls attitudes at home and in the legislature. This precludes a characterization of the speech as low-value. True, pornography and obscenity have sex in common. But Indianapolis left out of its definition any reference to literary, artistic, political, or scientific value. The ordinance applies to graphic sexually explicit subordination in works great and small. The Court sometimes balances the value of speech against the costs of its restriction, but it does this by category of speech and not by the content of particular works. ...

Any rationale we could imagine in support of this ordinance could not be limited to sex discrimination. Free speech has been on balance an ally of those seeking change. Governments that want stasis start by restricting speech. Culture is a powerful force of continuity; Indianapolis paints pornography as part of the culture of power. Change in any complex system ultimately depends on the ability of outsiders to challenge accepted views and the reigning institutions. Without a strong guarantee of freedom of speech, there is no effective right to challenge what is. ...

IV

The definition of "pornography" is unconstitutional. No construction or excision of particular terms could save it...and we cannot find a sensible way to repair the defect without seizing power that belongs elsewhere. Indianapolis might choose to have no ordinance if it cannot be limited to viewpoint-specific harms, or it might choose to extend the scope to all speech, just as the law of libel applies to all speech. An attempt to repair this ordinance would be nothing but a blind guess.

No amount of struggle with particular words and phrases in this ordinance can leave anything in effect. The district court came to the same conclusion. Its judgment is therefore affirmed.

NOTES

[1]"Pornography constructs what a woman is in terms of its view of what men want sexually. ... Pornography's world of equality is a harmonious and balanced place. Men and women are perfectly complementary and perfectly bipolar. ... All the ways men love to take and violate women, women love to be taken and vio-

lated. . . . What pornography does goes beyond its content: It eroticizes hierarchy, it sexualizes inequality. It makes dominance and submission sex. Inequality is its central dynamic; the illusion of freedom coming together with the reality of force is central to its working. . . . Pornography is neither harmless fantasy nor a corrupt and confused misrepresentation of an otherwise neutral and healthy sexual situation. It institutionalizes the sexuality of male supremacy, fusing the erotization of dominance and submission with the social construction of male and female. . . . Men treat women as who they see women as being. Pornography constructs who that is. Men's power over women means that the way men see women defines who women can be. Pornography...is a sexual reality." MacKinnon, supra, at 17–18 (note omitted). See also Andrea Dworkin, *Pornography: Men Possessing Women* (1981). A national commission in Canada recently adopted a similar rationale for controlling pornography. Special Commission on Pornography and Prostitution, 1 *Pornography and Prostitution in Canada* 49–59 (Canadian Government Publishing Centre 1985).

[2]MacKinnon's article collects empirical work that supports this proposition. The social science studies are very difficult to interpret, however, and they conflict. Because much of the effect of speech comes through a process of socialization, it is difficult to measure incremental benefits and injuries caused by particular speech. Several psychologists have found, for example, that those who see violent, sexually explicit films tend to have more violent thoughts. But how often does this lead to actual violence? National commissions on obscenity here, in the United Kingdom, and in Canada have found that it is not possible to demonstrate a direct link between obscenity and rape or exhibitionism. The several opinions in *Miller v. California* discuss the U.S. commission. See also Report of the Committee on Obscenity and Film Censorship 61–95 (Home Office, Her Majesty's Stationary Office, 1979); Special Committee on Pornography and Prostitution, 1 *Pornography and Prostitution in Canada* 71–73, 95–103 (Canadian Government Publishing Centre 1985). In saying that we accept the finding that pornography as the ordinance defines it leads to unhappy consequences, we mean only that there is evidence to this effect, that this evidence is consistent with much human experience, and that as judges we must accept the legislative resolution of such disputed empirical questions. See *Gregg v. Georgia*, 428 U.S. 153, 184–187, 49 L. Ed. 2d 859, 96 S. Ct. 2909 (1976) (opinion of Stewart, Powell, and Stevens, JJ.).

PORNOGRAPHY, OBSCENITY, AND THE CASE FOR CENSORSHIP

Irving Kristol

Being frustrated is disagreeable, but the real disasters in life begin when you get what you want. For almost a century now, a great many intelligent, well-meaning, and articulate people—of a kind generally called liberal or intellectual, or both—have argued eloquently against any kind of censorship of art and/or entertainment. And within the past ten years, the courts and the legislatures of most Western nations have found these arguments persuasive—so persuasive that hardly a man is now alive who clearly remembers what the answers to these arguments were. Today, in the United States and other democracies, censorship has to all intents and purposes ceased to exist.

Is there a sense of triumphant exhilaration in the land? Hardly. There is, on the contrary, a rapidly growing unease and disquiet. Somehow, things have not worked out as they were supposed to, and many notable civil libertarians have gone on record as saying this was not what they meant at all. They wanted a world in which *Desire Under the Elms* could be produced, or *Ulysses* published, without interference by philistine busybod-

Originally appeared in *The New York Times Magazine*, March 28, 1971. Reprinted by permission of the author.

ies holding public office. They have got that, of course; but they have also got a world in which homosexual rape takes place on the stage, in which the public flocks during lunch hours to witness varieties of professional fornication, in which Times Square has become little more than a hideous market for the sale and distribution of printed filth that panders to all known (and some fanciful) sexual perversions.

But disagreeable as this may be, does it really matter? Might not our unease and disquiet be merely a cultural hangover—a "hang-up," as they say? What reason is there to think that anyone was ever corrupted by a book?

This last question, oddly enough, is asked by the very same people who seem convinced that advertisements in magazines or displays of violence on television do indeed have the power to corrupt. It is also asked, incredibly enough and in all sincerity, by people—e.g., university professors and school teachers—whose very lives provide all the answers one could want. After all, if you believe that no one was ever corrupted by a book, you have also to believe that no one was ever improved by a book (or a play or a movie). You have to believe, in other words, that all art is morally trivial and that, consequently, all education is morally irrelevant. No one, not even a university professor, really believes that.

To be sure, it is extremely difficult, as social scientists tell us, to trace the effects of any single book (or play or movie) on an individual reader or any class of readers. But we all know, and social scientists know it too, that the ways in which we use our minds and imaginations do shape our characters and help define us as persons. That those who certainly know this are nevertheless moved to deny it merely indicates how a dogmatic resistance to the idea of censorship can—like most dogmatism—result in a mindless insistence on the absurd.

I have used these harsh terms—"dogmatism" and "mindless"—advisedly. I might also have added "hypocritical." For the plain fact is that none of us is a complete civil libertarian. We all believe that there is some point at which the public authorities ought to step in to limit the "self-expression" of an individual or a group, even where this might be seriously intended as a form of artistic expression, and even where the artistic transaction is between consenting adults. A playwright or theatrical director might, in this crazy world of ours, find someone willing to commit suicide on the stage, as called for by the script. We would not allow that—any more than we would permit scenes of real physical torture on the stage, even if the victim were a willing masochist. And I know of no one, no matter how free in spirit, who argues that we ought to permit gladiatorial contests in Yankee Stadium, similar to those once performed in the Coliseum at Rome—even if only consenting adults were involved.

The basic point that emerges is one that Professor Walter Berns has powerfully argued: no society can be utterly indifferent to the ways its citizens publicly entertain themselves.[1] Bearbaiting and cockfighting are prohibited only in part out of compassion for the suffering animals; the main reason they were abolished was because it was felt that they debased and brutalized the citizenry who flocked to witness such spectacles. And the question we face with regard to pornography and obscenity is whether, now that they have such strong legal protection from the Supreme Court, they can or will brutalize and debase our citizenry. We are, after all, not dealing with one passing incident—one book, or one play, or one movie. We are dealing with a general tendency that is suffusing our entire culture.

I say pornography and obscenity because, though they have different dictionary definitions and are frequently distinguishable as "artistic" genres, they are nevertheless in the end identical in effect. Pornography is not objectionable simply because it arouses sexual desire or lust or prurience in the mind of the reader or spectator; this is a silly Victorian notion.... Pornography differs from erotic art in that its whole purpose is to treat human beings obscenely, to deprive human beings of their specifically human dimension. That is what obscenity is all about. To quote Susan Sontag: "What pornographic literature does is precisely to drive a wedge between one's existence as a full human being and one's existence as a sexual being—while in ordinary life a healthy person is one who prevents such a gap from opening up." This definition occurs in an essay *defending* pornography—Miss Sontag is a candid as well as gifted critic—so the definition, which I accept, is neither tendentious nor censorious....

It may well be that Western society, in the latter half of the twentieth century, is experiencing a drastic change in sexual mores and sexual relationships. We have had many such "sexual revolutions" in the past—and the bourgeois family and bourgeois ideas of sexual propriety were themselves established in the course of a revolution against eighteenth-century "licentiousness"—and we shall doubtless have others in the future. It is, however, highly improbable (to put it mildly) that what we are witnessing is the Final Revolution which will make sexual relations utterly unproblematic, permit us to dispense with any kind of ordered relationships between the sexes, and allow us freely to redefine the human condition. And so long as humanity has not reached that utopia, obscenity will remain a problem.

One of the reasons it will remain a problem is that obscenity is not merely about sex, any more than science fiction is about science. Science fiction, as every student of the genre knows, is a peculiar vision of power: what it is really about is politics. And obscenity is a peculiar vision of humanity: what it is really about is ethics and metaphysics.

Imagine a man—a well-known man, much in the public eye—in a hospital ward, dying an agonizing death. He is not in control of his bodily functions, so that his bladder and his bowels empty themselves of their own accord. His consciousness is overwhelmed and extinguished by pain, so that he cannot communicate with us, nor we with him. Now, it would be, technically, the easiest thing in the world to put a television camera in his hospital room and let the whole world witness this spectacle. We don't do it—at least we don't do it as yet—because we regard this as an *obscene* invasion of privacy. And what would make the spectacle obscene is that we would be witnessing the extinguishing of humanity in a human animal.

Sex—like death—is an activity that is both animal and human. There are human sentiments and human ideals involved in this animal activity. But when sex is public, the viewer does not see—cannot see—the sentiments and the ideals. He can only see the animal coupling. And that is why, when men and women make love, as we say, they prefer to be alone—because it is only when you are alone that you can make love, as distinct from merely copulating in an animal and casual way. And that, too, is why those who are voyeurs, if they are not irredeemably sick, also feel ashamed at what they are witnessing. When sex is a public spectacle, a human relationship has been debased into a mere animal connection.

It is also worth noting that this making of sex into an obscenity is not a mutual and equal transaction, but is rather an act of exploitation by one of the partners—the male partner. I do not wish to get into the complicated question as to what, if any, are the essential differences—as distinct from conventional and cultural differences—between male and female. I do not claim to know the answer to that. But I do know—and I take it as a sign which has meaning—that pornography is, and always has been, a man's work; that women rarely write pornography; and that women tend to be indifferent consumers of pornography.[2] My own guess, by way of explanation, is that a woman's sexual experience is ordinarily more suffused with human emotion than is man's, that men are more easily satisfied with autoerotic activities, and that men can therefore more easily take a more "technocratic" view of sex and its pleasures. Perhaps this is not correct. But whatever the explanation, there can be no question that pornography is a form of "sexism," as the Women's Liberation Movement calls it, and that the instinct of Women's Lib has been unerring in perceiving that, when pornography is perpetrated, it is perpetrated against them, as part of a conspiracy to deprive them of their full humanity.

But even if all this is granted, it might be said—and doubtless will be said—that I really ought not to be unduly concerned. Free competition in the cultural marketplace—it is argued by people who have never otherwise had a kind word to say for laissez-faire—will automatically dispose of the problem. The present fad for pornography and obscenity, it will be asserted, is just that, a fad. It will spend itself in the course of time; people will get bored with it, will be able to take it or leave it alone in a casual way, in a "mature way," and, in sum, I am being unnecessarily distressed about the whole business....

I would like to be able to go along with this line of reasoning, but I cannot. I think it is false, and for two reasons, the first psychological, the second political.

The basic psychological fact about pornography and obscenity is that it appeals to and provokes a kind of sexual regression. The sexual pleasure one gets from pornography and obscenity is autoerotic and infantile; put bluntly, it is a masturbatory exercise of the imagination, when it is not masturbation pure and simple. Now, people who masturbate do not get bored with masturbation, just as sadists don't get bored with sadism, and voyeurs don't get bored with voyeurism.

In other words, infantile sexuality is not only a permanent temptation for the adolescent or even the adult—it can quite easily become a permanent, self-reinforcing neurosis. It is because of an awareness of this possibility of regression toward the infantile condition, a regression which is always open to us, that all the codes of sexual conduct ever devised by the human race take such a dim view of autoerotic activities and try to discourage autoerotic fantasies. Masturbation is indeed a perfectly natural autoerotic activity, as so many sexologists blandly assure us today. And it is precisely because it is so perfectly natural that it can be so dangerous to the mature or maturing person, if it is not controlled or sublimated in some way. That is the true meaning of Portnoy's complaint. Portnoy, you will recall, grows up to be a man who is incapable of having an adult sexual relationship with a woman; his sexuality remains fixed in an infantile mode, the prison of his autoerotic fantasies. Inevitably, Portnoy comes to think, in a perfectly *infantile* way, that it was all his mother's fault....

What is at stake is civilization and humanity, nothing less. The idea that "everything is permitted," as Nietzsche put it, rests on the premise of nihilism and has nihilistic implications. I will not pretend that the case against nihilism and for civilization is an easy one to make. We are here confronting the most fundamental of philosophical questions, on the deepest levels. But that is precisely my point—that the matter of pornography and obscenity is not a trivial one, and that only superficial minds can take a bland and untroubled view of it....

I am touching upon a political aspect of pornography when I suggest that it is inherently and purposefully subversive of civilization and its institutions. But there is another and more specifically political aspect, which has to do with the relationship of pornography and/or obscenity to democracy, and especially to the quality of public life on which democratic government ultimately rests.

Though the phrase "the quality of life," trips easily from so many lips these days, it tends to be one of those clichés with many trivial meanings and no large, serious one. Sometimes it merely refers to such externals as the enjoyment of cleaner air, cleaner water, cleaner streets. At other times it refers to the merely private enjoyment of music, painting or literature.

Rarely does it have anything to do with the way the citizen in a democracy views himself—his obligations, his intentions, his ultimate self-definition.

Instead, what I would call the "managerial" conception of democracy is the predominant opinion among political scientists, sociologists and economists, and has, through the untiring efforts of these scholars, become the conventional journalistic opinion as well. The root idea behind this "managerial" conception is that democracy is a "political system" (as they say) which can be adequately defined in terms of—can be fully reduced to—its mechanical arrangements. Democracy is then seen as a set of rules and procedures, *and nothing but* a set of rules and procedures, whereby majority rule and minority rights are reconciled into a state of equilibrium. If everyone follows these rules and procedures, then a democracy is in working order....

I cannot help but feel that there is something ridiculous about being this kind of a democrat, and I must further confess to having a sneaking sympathy for those of our young radicals who also find it ridiculous. The absurdity is the absurdity of idolatry—of taking the symbolic for the real, the means for the end. The purpose of democracy cannot possibly be the endless functioning of its own political machinery. The purpose of any political regime is to achieve some version of the good life and the good society. It is not at all difficult to imagine a perfectly functioning democracy which answers all questions except one—namely, why should anyone of intelligence and spirit care a fig for it?

There is, however, an older idea of democracy—one which was fairly common until about the beginning of this century—for which the conception of the quality of public life is absolutely crucial. This idea starts from the proposition that democracy is a form of self-government, and that if you want it to be a meritorious polity, you have to care about what kind of people govern it. Indeed, it puts the matter more strongly and declares that, if you want self-government, you are only entitled to it if that "self" is worthy of governing. There is no inherent right to self-government if it means that such government is vicious, mean, squalid, and debased. Only a dogmatist and a fanatic, an idolater of democratic machinery, could approve of self-government under such conditions.

And because the desirability of self-government depends on the character of the people who govern, the older idea of democracy was very solicitous of the condition of this character. It was solicitous of the individual self, and felt an obligation to educate it into what used to be called "republican virtue." And it was solicitous of that collective self which we call public opinion and which, in a democracy, governs us collectively. Perhaps in some respects it was nervously oversolicitous—that would not be surprising. But the main thing is that it cared, cared not merely about the machinery of democracy but about the quality of life that this machinery might generate.

And because it cared, this older idea of democracy had no problem in principle with pornography and/or obscenity. It censored them—and it did so with a perfect clarity of mind and a perfectly clear conscience. It was not about to permit people capriciously to corrupt themselves. Or, to put it more precisely: in this version of democracy, the people took some care not to let themselves be governed by the more infantile and irrational parts of themselves.

I have, it may be noticed, uttered that dreadful word, "censorship." And I am not about to back away from it. If you think pornography and/or obscenity is a serious problem, you have to be for censorship. I'll go even further and say that if you want to prevent pornography and/or obscenity from becoming a problem, you have to be for censorship. And lest there be any misunderstanding as to what I am saying, I'll put it as bluntly as possible: if you care for the quality of life in our American democracy, then you have to be for censorship.

But can a liberal be for censorship? Unless one assumes that being a liberal *must* mean being indifferent to the quality of American life, then the answer has to be: yes, a liberal can be for censorship—but he ought to favor a liberal form of censorship.

Is that a contradiction in terms? I don't think so. We have no problem in contrasting *repressive* laws governing alcohol and drugs and tobacco with laws *regulating* (that is, discouraging the sale of) alcohol and drugs and tobacco. Laws encouraging temperance are not the same thing as laws that have as their goal prohibition or abolition. We have not made the smoking of cigarettes a criminal offense. We have, however, and with good liberal conscience, prohibited cigarette advertising on television, and may yet, again with good liberal conscience, prohibit it in newspapers and magazines. The idea of restricting individual freedom, in a liberal way, is not at all unfamiliar to us.

I therefore see no reason why we should not be able to distinguish repressive censorship from liberal censorship of the written and spoken word. In Britain, until a few years ago, you could perform almost any play you wished—but certain plays, judged to be obscene, had to be performed in private theatrical clubs which were deemed to have a "serious" interest in theater. In the U.S., all of us who grew up using public libraries are familiar with the circumstances under which certain books could be circulated only to adults, while still other books had to be read in the library reading room, under the librarian's skeptical eye. In both cases, a small minority that was willing to make a serious effort to see an obscene play or read an obscene book could do so. But the impact of obscenity was circumscribed and the quality of public life was only marginally affected.[3]

I am not saying it is easy in practice to sustain a distinction between liberal and repressive censorship, especially in the public realm of a democracy, where popular opinion is so vulnerable to demagoguery. Moreover,

an acceptable system of liberal censorship is likely to be exceedingly difficult to devise in the United States today, because our educated classes,
upon whose judgment a liberal censorship must rest, are so convinced
that there is no such thing as a problem of obscenity, or even that there is
no such thing as obscenity at all. But, to counterbalance this, there is the
further, fortunate truth that the tolerable margin for error is quite large,
and single mistakes or single injustices are not all that important.

This possibility, of course, occasions much distress among artists and
academics. It is a fact, one that cannot and should not be denied, that any
system of censorship is bound, upon occasion, to treat unjustly a particular work of art—to find pornography where there is only gentle eroticism,
to find obscenity where none really exists, or to find both where its existence ought to be tolerated because it serves a larger moral purpose.
Though most works of art are not obscene, and though most obscenity has
nothing to do with art, there are some few works of art that are, at least in
part, pornographic and/or obscene. There are also some few works of art
that are in the special category of the comic-ironic "bawdy" (Boccaccio,
Rabelais). It is such works of art that are likely to suffer at the hands of the
censor. That is the price one has to be prepared to pay for censorship—
even liberal censorship.

But just how high is this price? If you believe, as so many artists seem to
believe today, that art is the only sacrosanct activity in our profane and
vulgar world—that any man who designates himself an artist thereby
acquires a sacred office—then obviously censorship is an intolerable form
of sacrilege. But for those of us who do not subscribe to this religion of art,
the costs of censorship do not seem so high at all.

If you look at the history of American or English literature, there is precious little damage you can point to as a consequence of the censorship
that prevailed throughout most of that history. Very few works of literature—of real literary merit, I mean—ever were suppressed; and those that
were, were not suppressed for long. Nor have I noticed, now that censorship of the written word has to all intents and purposes ceased in this
country, that hitherto suppressed or repressed masterpieces are flooding
the market. Yes, we can now read *Fanny Hill* and the Marquis de Sade. Or,
to be more exact, we can now openly purchase them, since many people
were able to read them even though they were publicly banned, which is
as it should be under a liberal censorship. So how much have literature
and the arts gained from the fact that we can all now buy them over the
counter, that, indeed, we are all now encouraged to buy them over the
counter? They have not gained much that I can see....

Just one last point which I dare not leave untouched. If we start censoring pornography or obscenity, shall we not inevitably end up censoring
political opinion? A lot of people seem to think this would be the case—
which only shows the power of doctrinaire thinking over reality. We had

censorship of pornography and obscenity for 150 years, until almost yesterday, and I am not aware that freedom of opinion in this country was in any way diminished as a consequence of this fact. Fortunately for those of us who are liberal, freedom is not indivisible. If it were, the case for liberalism would be indistinguishable from the case for anarchy; and they are two very different things.

But I must repeat and emphasize: what kind of laws we pass governing pornography and obscenity, what kind of censorship—or, since we are still a federal nation—what kinds of censorship we institute in our various localities may indeed be difficult matters to cope with; nevertheless the real issue is one of principle. I myself subscribe to the liberal view of the enforcement problem: I think that pornography should be illegal and available to anyone who wants it so badly as to make a pretty strenuous effort to get it. We have lived with under-the-counter pornography for centuries now, in a fairly comfortable way. But the issue of principle, of whether it should be over or under the counter, has to be settled before we can reflect on the advantages and disadvantages of alternative modes of censorship. I think the settlement we are living under now, in which obscenity and democracy are regarded as equals, is wrong; I believe it is inherently unstable; I think it will, in the long run, be incompatible with any authentic concern for the quality of life in our democracy.

NOTES

[1] This is as good a place as any to express my profound indebtedness to Walter Berns's superb essay, "Pornography vs. Democracy," in the Winter, 1971, issue of *The Public Interest*.

[2] There are, of course, a few exceptions but of a kind that prove the rule. *L'Histoire d'O*, for instance, written by a woman, is unquestionably the most *melancholy* work of pornography ever written. And its theme is precisely the dehumanization accomplished by obscenity.

[3] It is fairly predictable that some one is going to object that this point of view is "elitist"—that, under a system of liberal censorship, the rich will have privileged access to pornography and obscenity. Yes, of course they will—just as at present, the rich have privileged access to heroin if they want it. But one would have to be an egalitarian maniac to object to this state of affairs on the grounds of equality.

PORNOGRAPHY, CIVIL RIGHTS, AND SPEECH

Catharine A. MacKinnon

...Once power constructs social reality, as I will show pornography constructs the social reality of gender, the force behind sexism, the subordination in gender inequality, is made invisible; dissent from it becomes inaudible as well as rare. What a woman is, is defined in pornographic terms; this is what pornography *does*. If the law then looks neutrally on the reality of gender so produced, the harm that has been done will *not be perceptible as harm*. It becomes just the way things are. Refusing to look at what has been done substantively institutionalizes inequality in law and makes it look just like principle.

In the philosophical terms of classical liberalism, an equality-freedom dilemma is produced: freedom to make or consume pornography weighs against the equality of the sexes. Some people's freedom hurts other people's equality. There is something to this, but my formulation, as you might guess, comes out a little differently. If one asks whose freedom pornography represents, a tension emerges that is not a dilemma among abstractions so much as it is a conflict between groups. Substantive interests are at stake on *both* sides of the abstract issues, and women are allowed to matter in neither. If women's freedom is as incompatible with pornography's construction of our freedom as our equality is incompatible with pornography's construction of our equality, we get neither freedom nor equality under the liberal calculus. Equality for women is incompatible with a definition of men's freedom that is at our expense. What can freedom for women mean, so long as we remain unequal? Why should men's freedom to use us in this way be purchased with our second-class civil status?

Substantively considered, the situation of women is *not really like anything else*. Its specificity is not just the result of our numbers—we are half the human race—and our diversity, which at times has obscured that we are a group with an interest at all. It is, in part, that our status as a group relative to men has almost never, if ever, been much changed from what it is. Women's roles do vary enough that gender, the social form sex takes, cannot be said to be biologically determined. Different things are valued in different cultures, but whatever is valued, women are not that. If bottom is bottom, look across time and space, and women are who you will find there. Together with this, you will find, in as varied forms as there are cultures, the belief that women's social inferiority to men is not that at all but is merely the sex difference.

Doing something legal about a situation that is not really like anything else is hard enough in a legal system that prides itself methodologically on reasoning by analogy. Add to this the specific exclusion or absence of women and women's concerns from the definition and design of this legal system since its founding, combined with its determined adherence to precedent, and you have a problem of systemic dimension. The best attempt at grasping women's situation in order to change it by law has centered on an analogy between sex and race in the discrimination context. This gets a lot, since inequalities are alike on some levels, but it also misses a lot. It gets the stigmatization and exploitation and denigration of a group of people on the basis of a condition of birth. It gets that difference, made an issue of, is an excuse for dominance, and that if forced separation is allowed to mean equality in a society where the line of separation also divides top from bottom in a hierarchy, the harm of that separation is thereby made invisible. It also gets that defining neutrality as principle, when reality is not neutral, prevents change in the guise of promoting it. But segregation is not the central practice of the inequality of the sexes. Women are as often forcibly integrated with men, if not on an equal basis. And it did help the struggle against white supremacy that blacks had not always been in bondage to white people.

Most important, I think it never was a central part of the ideology of racism that the system of chattel slavery of Africans really was designed for their enjoyment and benefit. The system *was* defended as an expression of their true nature and worth. They *were* told to be grateful for good treatment and kind masters. Their successful struggle to organize resistance and avoid complicity while still surviving is instructive to all of us. But although racism *has* been defended by institutionalizing it in law, and then calling that legal; although it *has* been cherished not just as a system of exploitation of labor but as a way of life; and although it *is* based on force, changes in its practices are opposed by implying that they are really only a matter of choice of personal values. For instance: "You can't legislate morality." And slave owners did say they couldn't be racist—they loved their slaves. Nonetheless, few people pretended that the entire system existed *because* of its basis in love and mutual respect and veneration, that white supremacy really treated blacks in many cases *better* than whites, and that the primary intent and effect of their special status was and is their protection, pleasure, fulfillment, and liberation. Crucially, many have believed, and some actually still do, that black people were not the equals of whites. But at least since *Brown v. Board of Education*, few have pretended, much less authoritatively, that the social system, as it was, *was equality for them.*

There is a belief that this is a society in which women and men are basically equals. Room for marginal corrections is conceded, flaws are known to exist, attempts are made to correct what are conceived as occasional lapses from the basic condition of sex equality. Sex discrimination law has concentrated most of its focus on these occasional lapses. It is difficult to overestimate the extent to which this belief in equality is an article of faith for most people, including most women, who wish to live in self-respect in an internal universe, even (perhaps especially) if not in the world. It is also partly an expression of natural law thinking: if we are inalienably equal, we can't "really" be degraded.

…Feminism is the discovery that women do not live in this world, that the person occupying this realm is a man, so much more a man if he is white and wealthy. This world of potential credibility, authority, security, and just rewards, recognition of one's identity and capacity, is a world that some people do inhabit as a condition of birth, with variations among them. It is not a basic condition accorded humanity in this society, but a prerogative of status, a privilege, among other things, of gender.

I call this a discovery because it has not been an assumption. Feminism is the first theory, the first practice, the first movement, to take seriously the situation of all women from the point of view of all women, both on our situation and on social life as a whole. The discovery has therefore been made that the implicit social content of humanism, as well as the standpoint from which legal method has been designed and injuries have been defined, has not been women's standpoint…this discovery can be summed up by saying that women live in another world: specifically, a world of not-equality, a world of inequality.

Looking at the world from this point of view, a whole shadow-world of previously invisible silent abuse has been discerned. Rape, battery, sexual harassment, forced prostitution, and the sexual abuse of children emerge as common and systematic. We find that rape happens to women in all contexts, from the family, including rape of girls and babies, to students and women in the workplace, on the streets, at home, in their own bedrooms by men they do not know and by men they do know, by men they are married to, men they have had a social conversation with, and, least often, men they have never seen before. Overwhelmingly, rape is something that men do or attempt to do to women (44 percent of American women according to a recent study)[1] at some point in our lives. Sexual harassment of women by men is common in workplaces and educational institutions. Based on reports in one study of the federal workforce, up to 85 percent of women will experience it, many in physical forms.[2] Between a quarter and a third of women are battered in their homes by men.[3] Thirty-eight percent of little girls are sexually molested inside or outside the family.[4] Until women listened to women, this world of sexual abuse was *not spoken of*. It was the unspeakable. What I am saying is, if you *are* the tree falling in the epistemological forest, your demise doesn't make a sound if no one is listening. Women did not "report" these events, and overwhelmingly do not today, because no one is listening, because no one believes us....

[P]eople don't really believe that the things I have just said are true, though there really is little question about their empirical accuracy. The data are extremely simple, like women's pay figure of fifty-nine cents on the dollar.[5] People don't really seem to believe that either. Yet there is no question of its empirical validity. This is the workplace story: what women do is seen as not worth much, or what is not worth much is seen as something for women to do. Women are seen as not worth much, is the thing. Now why are these basic realities of the subordination of women to men, for example, that only 7.8 percent of women have never been sexually assaulted, not effectively believed, not perceived as real in the face of all this evidence? Why don't *women* believe our own experiences? In the face of all this evidence, especially of systematic sexual abuse—subjection to violence with impunity is one extreme expression, although not the only expression, of a degraded status—the view that basically the sexes are equal in this society remains unchallenged and unchanged. The day I got this was the day I understood its real message, its real coherence: *this is equality for us.*

I could describe this, but I couldn't explain it until I started studying a lot of pornography. In pornography, there it is, in one place, all of the abuses that women had to struggle so long even to begin to articulate, all the *unspeakable* abuse: the rape, the battery, the sexual harassment, the prostitution, and the sexual abuse of children. Only in the pornography it is called something else: sex, sex, sex, sex, and sex, respectively. Pornography sexualizes rape, battery, sexual harassment, prostitution, and child sexual abuse; it thereby celebrates, promotes, authorizes, and legitimizes them. More generally it eroticizes the dominance and submission that is the dynamic common to them all. It makes hierarchy sexy, and calls that "the truth about sex" or just a mirror of reality. Through this process pornography constructs what a woman is as what men want from sex. This is what the pornography means.

Pornography constructs what a woman is in terms of its view of what men want sexually, such that acts of rape, battery, sexual harassment, prostitution, and sexual abuse of children become acts of sexual equality. Pornography's world of equality is a harmonious and balanced place. Men and women are perfectly complementary and perfectly bipolar. Women's desire to be fucked by men is equal to men's desire to fuck women. All the ways men love to take and violate women, women love to be taken and violated. The women who most love this are most men's equals, the most liberated; the most participatory child is the most grown-up, the most equal to an adult. Their consent merely expresses or ratifies these preexisting facts.

The content of pornography is one thing. There, women substantively desire dispossession and cruelty. We desperately want to be bound, battered, tortured, humiliated, and killed. Or, to be fair to the soft core, merely taken and used. This is erotic to the male point of view. Subjection itself, with self-determination ecstatically relinquished, is the content of women's sexual desire and desirability. Women are there to be violated and possessed, men to violate and possess us, either on screen, or by camera or pen, on behalf of the consumer. On a simple descriptive level, the inequality of hierarchy, of which gender is the primary one, seems necessary for sexual arousal to work. Other added inequalities identify various pornographic genres or subthemes, although they are always added through gender: age, disability, homosexuality, animals, objects, race (including anti-Semitism), and so on. Gender is never irrelevant.

What pornography *does* goes beyond its content: it eroticizes hierarchy, it sexualizes inequality. It makes dominance and submission into sex. Inequality is its central dynamic; the illusion of freedom coming together with the reality of force is central to its working. Perhaps because this is a bourgeois culture, the victim must look free, appear to be freely acting. Choice is how she got there. Willing is what she is when she is being equal. It seems equally important that then and there she actually be forced and that forcing be communicated on some level, even if only through still photos of her in postures of receptivity and access, available for penetration. Pornography in this view is a form of forced sex, a practice of sexual politics, an institution of gender inequality.

From this perspective, pornography is neither harmless fantasy nor a corrupt and confused misrepresentation of an otherwise natural and healthy sexual situation. It institutionalizes the sexuality of male supremacy, fusing the erotization of dominance and submission with the social construction of male and female. To the extent that gender is sexual, pornography is part of constituting the meaning of that sexuality. Men treat women as who they see women as being. Pornography constructs who that is. Men's power over women means that the way men see women defines who women can be. Pornography is that way. Pornography is not imagery in some relation to a reality elsewhere constructed. It is not a distortion, reflection, projection, expression, fantasy, representation, or symbol either. It is a sexual reality.

In Andrea Dworkin's definitive work, *Pornography: Men Possessing Women*, sexuality itself is a social construct gendered to the ground. Male dominance here is not an artificial overlay upon an underlying inalterable substratum of uncorrupted essential sexual being. Dworkin presents a sexual theory of gender inequality of which pornography is a constitutive practice. The way pornography produces its meaning constructs and defines men and women as such. Gender has no basis in anything other than the social reality its hegemony constructs. Gender is what gender means. The process that gives sexuality its male-supremacist meaning is the same process through which gender inequality becomes socially real.

In this approach, the experience of the (overwhelmingly) male audiences who consume pornography is therefore not fantasy or simulation or catharsis but sexual reality, the level of reality on which sex itself largely operates. Understanding this dimension of the problem does not require noticing that pornography models are real women to whom, in most cases, something real is being done; nor does it even require inquiring into the systematic infliction of pornography and its sexuality upon women, although it helps. What matters is the way in which the pornography itself provides what those who consume it want. Pornography *participates* in its audience's eroticism through creating an accessible sexual object, the possession and consumption of which *is* male sexuality, as socially constructed; to be consumed and possessed as which, is female sexuality, as socially constructed; pornography is a process that constructs it that way. ...

Obscenity law provides a very different analysis and conception of the problem of pornography. In 1973 the legal definition of obscenity became that which the average person, applying contemporary community standards, would find that, taken as a whole, appeals to the prurient interest; that which depicts or describes in a patently offensive way... sexual conduct specifically defined by the applicable state law; and that which, taken as a whole, lacks serious literary, artistic, political, or scientific value.[6] Feminism doubts whether the average person gender-neutral exists; has more questions about the content and process of defining what community standards are than it does about deviations from them; wonders why prurience counts but powerlessness does not, and why sensibilities are better protected from offense than women are from exploitation; defines sexuality, and thus its violation and expropriation, more broadly than does state law; and questions why a body of law that has not in practice been able to tell rape from intercourse should, without further guidance, be entrusted with telling pornography from anything less. Taking the work "as a whole" ignores that which the victims of pornography have long known: legitimate settings diminish the perception of injury done to those whose trivialization and objectification they contextualize. Besides, and this is a heavy one, if a woman is subjected, why should it matter that the work has other value?...

...At the request of the city of Minneapolis, Andrea Dworkin and I conceived and designed a local human rights ordinance in accordance with our approach to the pornography issue. We define pornography as a practice of sex discrimination, a violation of women's civil rights, the opposite of sexual equality. Its point is to hold those who profit from and benefit from that injury accountable to those who are injured. It means that women's injury—our damage, our pain, our enforced inferiority—should outweigh their pleasure and their profits, or sex equality is meaningless.

We define pornography as the graphic sexually explicit subordination of women through pictures or words that also includes women dehumanized as sexual objects, things, or commodities—enjoying pain or humiliation or rape; being tied up, cut up, mutilated, bruised, or physically hurt; in postures of sexual submission or servility or display; reduced to body parts, penetrated by objects or animals, or presented in scenarios of degradation, injury, torture; shown as filthy or interior; bleeding, bruised, or hurt in a context that makes these conditions sexual. Erotica, defined by distinction as not this, might be sexually explicit materials premised on equality.[7] We also provide that the use of men, children, or transsexuals in the place of women is pornography. The definition is substantive in that it is sex-specific, but it covers everyone in a sex-specific way, so is gender-neutral in overall design....

This law aspires to guarantee women's rights consistent with the First Amendment by making visible a conflict of rights between the equality guaranteed to all women and what, in some legal sense, is now the freedom of the pornographers to make and sell, and their consumers to have access to, the materials this ordinance defines. Judicial resolution of this conflict, if the judges do for women what they have done for others, is likely to entail a balancing of the rights of women, arguing that our lives and opportunities, including our freedom of speech and action, are constrained by—and in many cases flatly precluded by, in, and through—pornography, against those who argue that the pornography is harmless, or harmful only in part but not in the whole of the definition; or that it is more important to preserve the pornography than it is to prevent or remedy whatever harm it does.

In predicting how a court would balance these interests, it is important to understand that this ordinance cannot now be said to be either conclusively legal or illegal under existing law or precedent, although I think the weight of authority is on our side. This ordinance enunciates a new form of the previously recognized governmental interest in sex equality. Many laws make sex equality a governmental interest. Our law is designed to further the equality of the sexes, to help make sex equality real. Pornography is a practice of discrimination on the basis of sex, on one level because of its role in creating and maintaining sex as a basis for discrimination. It harms many women one at a time, and helps keep all women in an inferior status by defining our subordination as our sexuality and equating that with our gender. It is also sex discrimination because its victims, including men, are selected for victimization on the basis of their gender. But for their sex, they would not be so treated.

The harm of pornography, broadly speaking, is the harm of the civil inequality of the sexes made invisible as harm because it has become accepted as the sex difference. Consider this analogy with race: if you see black people as different, there is no harm to segregation; it is merely a recognition of that difference. To neutral principles, separate but equal was equal. The injury of racial separation to blacks arises "solely because [they] choose to put that construction upon it."[8] Epistemologically translated: how you see it is not the way it is. Similarly, if you see women as just different, even or especially if you don't know that you do, subordination will not look like subordination at all, much less like harm. It will merely look like an appropriate recognition of the sex difference.

Pornography does treat the sexes differently, so the case for sex differentiation can be made here. But men as a group do not tend to be (although some individuals may be) treated the way women are treated in pornography. As a social group, men are not hurt by pornography the way women as a social group are. Their social status is not defined as *less* by it. So the major argument does not turn on mistaken differentiation, particularly since the treatment of women according to pornography's dictates makes it all too often accurate. The salient quality of a distinction between the top and the bottom in a hierarchy is not difference, although top is certainly different from bottom; it is power. So the major argument is: subordinate but equal is not equal. ...

Specific pornography does directly cause some assaults. Some rapes are performed by men with paperback books in their pockets. One young woman testified in our hearings about walking through a forest at thirteen and coming across a group of armed hunters reading pornography. As they looked up and saw her, one said "There is a live one."[9] They gang-raped her at gunpoint for several hours. ...

Now I'm going to talk about causality in its narrowest sense. Recent experimental research on pornography shows that the materials covered by our definition cause measurable harm to women through increasing men's attitudes and behaviors of discrimination in both violent and non-violent forms. Exposure to some of the pornography in our definition increases the immediately subsequent willingness of normal men to aggress against women under laboratory conditions. It makes normal men more closely resemble convicted rapists attitudinally, although as a group they don't look all that different from them to start with. Exposure to pornography also significantly increases attitudinal measures known to correlate with rape and self-reports of aggressive acts, measures such as hostility toward women, propensity to rape, condoning rape, and predicting that one would rape or force sex on a woman if one knew one would not get caught. On this latter measure, by the way, about a third of all men predict that they would rape, and half would force sex on a woman.[10]

As to that pornography covered by our definition in which normal research subjects seldom perceive violence, long-term exposure still makes them see women as more worthless, trivial, nonhuman, and object-like, that is, the way those who are discriminated against are seen by those who discriminate against them. Crucially, all pornography by our definition acts dynamically over time to diminish the consumer's ability to distinguish sex from violence. The materials work behaviorally to diminish the capacity of men (but not women) to perceive that an account of a rape is an account of a rape. The so-called sex-only materials, those in which subjects perceive no force, also increase perceptions that a rape victim is worthless and decrease the perception that she was harmed. The overall direction of current research suggests that the more expressly violent materials accomplish with less exposure what the less overtly violent—that is, the so-called sex-only materials—accomplish over the longer term. Women are rendered fit for use and targeted for abuse. The only thing that the research cannot document is which individual women will be next on the list. (This cannot be documented experimentally because of ethics constraints on the researchers—constraints that do not operate in life.) Although the targeting is systematic on the basis of sex, for individuals it is random. They are selected on a roulette basis. Pornography can no longer be said to be just a mirror. It does not just reflect the world or some people's perceptions. It *moves* them. It increases attitudes that are lived out, circumscribing the status of half the population....

In our hearings women spoke, to my knowledge for the first time in history in public, about the damage pornography does to them. We learned that pornography is used to break women, to train women to sexual submission, to season women, to terrorize women, and to silence their dissent. It is this that has previously been termed "having no effect." The way men inflict on women the sex they experience through the pornography gives women no choice about seeing the pornography or doing the sex. Asked if anyone ever tried to inflict unwanted sex acts on them that they knew came from pornography, 10 percent of women in a recent random study said yes. Among married women, 24 percent said yes. That is a lot of women. A lot more don't know. Some of those who do testified in Minneapolis. One wife said of her ex-husband, "He would read from the pornography like a textbook, like a journal. In fact when he asked me to be bound, when he finally convinced me to do it, he read in the magazine how to tie the knots."[11] Another woman said of her boyfriend, "[H]e went to this party, saw pornography, got an erection, got me...to inflict his erection on.... There is a direct causal relationship there."[12] One woman, who said her husband had rape and bondage magazines all over the house, discovered two suitcases full of Barbie dolls with rope tied on their arms and legs and with tape across their mouths.[13] Now think about the silence of women....

It is worth considering what evidence has been enough when other harms involving other purported speech interests have been allowed to be legislated against. By comparison to our trafficking provision, analytically similar restrictions have been allowed under the First Amendment, with a legislative basis far less massive, detailed, concrete, and conclusive. Our statutory language is more ordinary, objective, and precise, and covers a harm far narrower than the legislative record substantiates. Under *Miller*, obscenity was allowed to be made criminal in the name of the "danger of offending the sensibilities of unwilling recipients, or exposure to juveniles."[14] Under our law, we have direct evidence of harm, not just a conjectural danger, that unwilling women in considerable numbers are not simply offended in their sensibilities, but are violated in their persons and restricted in their options. Obscenity law also suggests that the applicable standard for legal adequacy in measuring such connections may not be statistical certainty. The Supreme Court has said that it is not their job to resolve empirical uncertainties that underlie state obscenity legislation.[15] Rather, it is for them to determine whether a legislature could reasonably have determined that a connection might exist between the prohibited material and harm of a kind in which the state has legitimate interest. Equality should be such an area. The Supreme Court recently recognized that prevention of sexual exploitation and abuse of children is, in their words, "a governmental objective of surpassing importance."[16] This might also be the case for sexual exploitation and abuse of women, although I think a civil remedy is initially more appropriate to the goal of empowering adult women than a criminal prohibition would be.

Other rubrics provide further support for the argument that this law is narrowly tailored to further a legitimate governmental interest consistent with the goals underlying the First Amendment. Exceptions to the First Amendment—you may have gathered from this—exist. The reason they exist is that the harm done by some speech outweighs its expressive value, if any. In our law a legislature recognizes that pornography, as defined and made actionable, undermines sex equality. One can say—and I have—that pornography is a causal factor in violations of women; one can also say that women will be violated so long as pornography exists; but one can also say simply that pornography violates women. Perhaps this is what the woman had in mind who testified at our hearings that for her the question is not just whether pornography causes violent acts to be perpetrated against some women. "Porn is already a violent act against women. It is our mothers, our daughters, our sisters, and our wives that are for sale for pocket change at the newsstands in this country."[17] *Chaplinsky v. New Hampshire* recognized the ability to restrict as "fighting words" speech which, "by [its] very utterance inflicts injury."[18] Perhaps the only reason that pornography has not been "fighting words"—in the sense of words that by their utterance tend to incite immediate breach of the peace—is that women have seldom fought back, yet. ...

The situation in which women presently find ourselves with respect to the pornography is one in which more *pornography* is inconsistent with rectifying or even counterbalancing its damage through speech, because so long as the pornography exists in the way it does, there *will not be more speech by women.* Pornography strips and devastates women of credibility, from our accounts of sexual assault to our everyday reality of sexual subordination. We are stripped of authority and reduced and devalidated and silenced. Silenced here means that the purposes of the First Amendment, premised upon conditions presumed and promoted by protecting free speech, do not pertain to women because they are not our conditions. Consider them: individual self-fulfillment—how does pornography promote our individual self-fulfillment? How does sexual inequality even permit it? Even if she can form words, who listens to a woman with a penis in her mouth? Facilitating consensus—to the extent pornography does so, it does so one-sidedly by silencing protest over the injustice of sexual subordination. Participation in civic life—central to Professor Meiklejohn's theory[19]—how does pornography enhance women's participation in civic life? Anyone who cannot walk down the street or even lie down in her own bed without keeping her eyes cast down and her body clenched against assault is unlikely to have much to say about the issues of the day, still less will she become Tolstoy. Facilitating change—this law facilitates the change that existing First Amendment theory had been used to throttle. Any system of freedom of expression that does not address a problem where the free speech of men silences the free speech of women, a real conflict between speech interests as well as between people, is not serious about securing freedom of expression in this country.

For those of you who still think pornography is only an idea, consider the possibility that obscenity law got one thing right. Pornography is more actlike than thoughtlike. The fact that pornography, in a feminist view, furthers the idea of the sexual inferiority of women, which is a political idea, doesn't make the pornography itself into a political idea. One can express the idea a practice embodies. That does not make that practice into an idea. Segregation expresses the idea of the inferiority of one group to another on the basis of race. That does not make segregation an idea. A sign that says "Whites Only" is only words. Is it therefore protected by the First Amendment? Is it not an act, a practice, of segregation because what it means is inseparable from what it does? *Law* is only words.

The issue here is whether the fact that words and pictures are the central link in the cycle of abuse will immunize that entire cycle, about which we cannot do anything without doing something about the pornography. As Justice Stewart said in *Ginsburg*, "When expression occurs in a setting where the capacity to make a choice is absent, government regulation of that expression may coexist with and even implement First Amendment guarantees."[20] I would even go so far as to say that the pattern of evidence we have closely approaches Justice Douglas' requirement that "freedom of expression can be suppressed if, and to the extent that, it is so closely brigaded with illegal action as to be an inseparable part of it."[21] Those of you who have been trying to separate the acts from the speech—that's an act, that's an act, there's a law against that act, regulate that act, don't touch the speech—notice here that the illegality of the acts involved doesn't mean that the speech that is "brigaded with" it *cannot* be regulated....

The most basic assumption underlying First Amendment adjudication is that, socially, speech is free. The First Amendment says Congress shall not abridge the freedom of speech. Free speech, get it, *exists*. Those who wrote the First Amendment had speech—they wrote the Constitution. Their problem was to keep it free from the only power that realistically threatened it: the federal government. They designed the First Amendment to prevent government from constraining that which, if unconstrained by government, was free, *meaning accessible to them*. At the same time, we can't tell much about the intent of the Framers with regard to the question of women's speech, because I don't think we crossed their minds. It is consistent with this analysis that their posture toward freedom of speech tends to presuppose that whole segments of the population are not systematically silenced socially, prior to government action. If everyone's power were equal to theirs, if this were a nonhierarchical society, that might make sense. But the place of pornography in the inequality of the sexes makes the assumption of equal power untrue.

This is a hard question. It involves risks. Classically, opposition to censorship has involved keeping government off the backs of people. Our law is about getting some people off the backs of other people. The risks that it will be misused have to be measured against the risks of the status quo. Women will never have that dignity, security, or compensation that is the promise of equality so long as the pornography exists as it does now. The situation of women suggests that the urgent issue of our freedom of speech is not primarily the avoidance of state intervention as such, but getting affirmative access to speech for those to whom it has been denied....

NOTES

[1]See Diana Russell, "The Prevalence of Rape in the United States Revisited," *Signs: The Journal of Women in Culture and Society* 8 (1983): 689.

[2]See U.S. Merit Systems Protection Board, *Sexual Harassment in the Federal Workplace: Is It a Problem?* (1981).

[3]See R. Emerson Dobash and Russell Dobash, *Violence against Wives: A Case against the Patriarchy* (1979); R. Langley and R. Levy, *Wife Beating: The Silent Crisis* (1977); D. Martin, *Battered Wives* (rev.ed. 1981); and L. Walker, *The Battered Woman* (1979).

[4]See Diana Russell, "Incidence and Prevalence of Intrafamilial and Extrafamilial Sexual Abuse of Female Children," *Child Abuse and Neglect: The International Journal* 7 (1983): 2.

[5]See Employment Standards Administration, U.S. Department of Labor, *Handbook on Women Workers* (1975); U.S. Department of Labor, *Women's Bureau Bulletin* 297 (1975 and 1982 update).

[6]*Miller v. California*, 413 U.S. 15, 24 (1973).

[7]See e.g., Gloria Steinem, "Erotica v. Pornography," in *Outrageous Acts and Everyday Rebellions* (1983): 219.

[8]See *Plessy v. Ferguson*, 163 U.S. at 551 (1896).

[9]See II Hearing 43 (testimony of Rita M.).

[10][There is a tremendous amount of literature on this topic. For full information refer to MacKinnon's original notes 116–120 pages 295–297 in *Feminism Unmodified*—eds.]

[11]See II Hearings 68 (testimony of Ruth M.).

[12] See II Hearings (testimony of Nancy C.).

[13]III Hearings (testimony of Sharon Rice Vaughn, reading statement by Donna Dunn of Women's Shelter, Inc., in Rochester, MN, which describes events reported by a woman at the shelter.)

[14]See *Miller v. California*, 413 U.S. 15, 19 (1973).

[15]See *Kaplan v. California* 413 U.S. 115, 120 (1973); *Paris Adult Theatre I v. Slaton*, 413 U.S. 49, 60 (1973); *Roth v. United States*, 354 U.S. 476, 501 (1957).

[16]*New York v. Ferber*, 458 U.S. 742, 757 (1982).

[17]III Hearings 53.

[18]315 U.S. 568, 572 (1941).

[19]A. Meiklejohn, *Political Freedom* (1960): 24–28.

[20]*Ginsberg v. New York*, 390 U.S. 629, 649 (1968).

[21]*Roth v. United States*, 354 U.S. 476, 514 (Douglas, J., dissenting). See also *Memoirs v. Massachusetts*, 383 U.S. 413, 426 (1966) (Douglas, J., concurring).

CONFESSIONS OF A FEMINIST PORNO STAR

Nina Hartley

"A feminist porno star?" Right, tell me another one, I can hear some feminists saying. I hear a chorus of disbelief, a lot like the two crows in the Disney movie *Dumbo*—"I thought I'd seen everything till I saw an elephant fly." On the surface, contradictions seem to abound. But one of the most basic tenets of feminism, a tenet with which I was inculcated by the age of ten, was the *right* to sexual free expression, without being told by society (or men) what was right, wrong, good, or bad. But why porno? Simple—I'm an exhibitionist with a cause: to make sexually graphic (hard-core) erotica, and today's porno is the only game in town. But it's a game where there is a possibility of the players, over time, getting some of the rules changed.

As I examine my life, I uncover the myriad influences that led me to conclude that it was perfectly natural for me to choose a career in adult films. I find performing in sexually explicit material satisfying on a number of levels. First, it provides a physically and psychically safe environment for me to live out my exhibitionistic fantasies. Secondly, it provides a surprisingly flexible and supportive arena for me to grow in as a performer, both sexually and nonsexually. Thirdly, it provides me with erotic material that I like to watch for my own pleasure. Finally, the medium

From *Sex Work*, edited by Frederique Delacoste and Priscilla Alexander © 1987. Reprinted by permission from Cleis Press.

allows me to explore the theme of celebrating a positive female sexuality—a sexuality that has heretofore been denied us. In choosing my roles and characterizations carefully, I strive to show, always, women who thoroughly enjoy sex and are forceful, self-satisfying, and guilt-free without also being neurotic, unhappy, or somehow unfulfilled.

In order to understand why I can be so happily involved in a business that is anathema to so many feminists today, it's important for me to explain the uniqueness of my early life experiences....

My parents were very liberal, and never censored my reading material. By the time I was twelve, I was checking out books on the subjects of puberty, pregnancy, and sex. I was doubly lucky to live in Berkeley, California, during the sixties and seventies, as the librarians never tried to discourage me from checking out "unsuitable" books. This access to factual, nonjudgmental, biological information is the basis now for my "surprising" lack of shame and guilt: since sex is so natural, and since I demystified sex early on, having sex on screen, if that's what I wanted to do, was not traumatic at all.

Once I passed puberty, two books in particular were very influential in the continuing development of my personal sexual philosophy: *Our Bodies, Ourselves*, and *The Happy Hooker*. The former taught me that women deserved to be happy sexually, that their bodies were wonderful and strong, and that all sexual fantasies were natural and okay as long as coercion was not involved. The latter book taught me that an intelligent, sexual woman could choose a job in the sex industry and not be a victim, but instead emerge even stronger and more self-confident, with a feeling, even, of self-actualization.

High school was uneventful—I became deeply involved in the excellent drama department at Berkeley High, exploring a long-standing interest in the theater arts. Contrary to a lot of adolescents' experiences with peer pressure in the realm of sex and drugs, I was lucky to have no pressure placed on me one way or another, because that was the norm in Berkeley in the seventies. Consequently, I had a more active fantasy life than sex life, and was very ripe when I lost my virginity at eighteen to a man with whom I had my first long-term relationship. This, unfortunately, had more forgettable moments than memorable ones. The sex and intimacy were mediocre at best, and I realized that my libido was not to have a good future with this man. My present husband is just the opposite. He gave full support for my long-dormant lesbian side; for the past four years I have lived with him and his long-term woman lover in a close-knit, loving, supportive, and intellectually stimulating *ménage à trois*.

I stripped once a week while getting my bachelor's degree in nursing, *magna cum laude*, enjoying it to the fullest, and using the performance opportunity to develop the public side of my sexuality. I went into full-time movie work immediately following graduation, having done a few movies while still in school.

I know there are people who wonder, "Is she naïve or something? What kind of a cause is porno?" But let's face it, folks: while the sex drive may be innate, modes of sexual behavior are learned.... If the media can have an effect on people's behavior, and I believe it does, why is it assumed that sex movies must always reinforce the most negative imagery of women? That certainly isn't what I'm about. From my very first movie I have always refused to portray rape, coercion, pain-as-pleasure, woman-as-victim, domination, humiliation, and other forms of nonconsensual sex.

I can look back on all of my performances and see that I have not contributed to any negative images or depictions of women; and the feedback I get from men and women of all ages supports my contention. I get a lot of satisfaction from my job—for me it is a job of choice. As feminists, we must all fight to change our society so that women who don't want to do gender-stereotyped jobs can be free to work, support their families decently, and fulfill their potential in whatever job they choose. This includes not feeling compelled to do sex work because other well-paying options are severely limited.

Each of us has some idea or action that we hate but that is still protected by the First Amendment. I consider myself a reformer, and as a reformer I need a broad interpretation of the First Amendment to make my point. As a feminist I have principles that won't allow me to take license with that precious right to free speech. There have always been, and to some degree will always be, extremists who see the First Amendment as their license to do or say whatever, and not as a right which has implied responsibilities. Of course the sexual entertainment medium is no exception to this. I say censure them, but do not censor me.

BRIEF *AMICI CURIAE* OF FEMINIST ANTI-CENSORSHIP TASKFORCE, ET AL., IN *AMERICAN BOOKSELLERS ASSOCIATION v. HUDNUT*

Nan D. Hunter and Sylvia A. Law

The document that follows represents both a legal brief and a political statement. It was written for two purposes: to mobilize, in a highly visible way, a broad spectrum of feminist opposition to the enactment of laws expanding state suppression of sexually explicit material; and to place before the Court of Appeals for the Seventh Circuit a cogent legal argument for the constitutional invalidity of an Indianapolis municipal ordinance that would have permitted private civil suits to ban such material, purportedly to protect women....[1]

The brief was written on behalf of the Feminist Anti-Censorship Taskforce (FACT) and was co-signed by the Women's Legal Defense Fund

(WLDF) and eighty individual feminists. The analysis of sexuality underlying the brief flows directly from a long tradition of nineteenth-century women's rights activists who sought sexual self-determination as an essential aspect of full liberation. From the beginning, others within the early feminist movement opposed this understanding of feminism because they viewed sexuality as a realm in which women often suffered. To protect women, they sought to restrict male sexual freedom by imposing on men the standard of sexual purity already applied to women.[2]

The modern feminist movement has continued this divergence of viewpoint. Simone de Beauvoir, for example, saw the erotic as an aspect of human liberty and insisted that sexual self-determination constitutes a fundamental part of women's liberation. Since 1966, women's demands have included calls for greater sexual freedom for women and an end to double standards. At the same time, the movement has fought for and won a number of reforms to curb rape and other violence directed pointedly at women. A part of the feminist antiviolence movement evolved first into a campaign aimed at depictions of violence against women in a variety of media and then into a campaign aimed at all pornographic imagery, whether violent or not.

Meanwhile, as feminist discourse on issues of sexuality became more elaborate, conservative forces also mobilized around issues of sexual imagery. An alliance of traditional moralists, the New Right, and some feminists promoted and defended the Indianapolis ordinance. In the current political environment, the conservative voices are plainly more powerful than those of the feminists. For conservatives, the current interest in suppression of pornography forms part of a larger agenda to reverse recent feminist gains through a moral crusade against abortion, lesbian and gay rights, contraceptive education and services, and women's fragile economic achievements. Conservatives and religious fundamentalists oppose pornography because it appears to depict and approve of sex outside marriage and procreation. The Right seeks to use legitimate feminist concern about sexual violence and oppression to reinstate traditional sexual arrangements and the formerly inexorable link between reproduction and sexuality....

The feminists of FACT have helped to transform the contemporary dialogue about pornography. That debate no longer pits victimized women and conventional moralists against pornographers and civil libertarians. FACT affirms that sexuality is, for women, a source of pleasure and power, as well as a realm of danger and oppression. As a consequence, discussion of pornography and sexuality is more intricately contextualized and appropriately complex. The brief that follows aspires to keep open the discussion about sexual explicitness and to assert that sexually explicit materials have both liberating and repressive qualities. The feminist analysis of these issues remains far from complete. As Carole S.

Vance, one of the founders of FACT, observes, "The hallmark of sexuality is its complexity: its multiple meanings, sensations, and connections."[3]

Despite the contradictory strands in the feminist approach, the empirical and intellectual exploration of sexuality remains a central enterprise for the contemporary feminist movement. Sexual ideas, images, and practices have been dominated by and oriented toward men and are often not responsive to women. Many women experience sexual failure and frustration, rather than ecstasy and pleasure. Furthermore, feminism's core insight emphasizes that gender is socially defined. Social and sexual role acculturation largely determine gender differences; accordingly, these differences are not natural or immutable. In Simone de Beauvoir's classic words, "One is not born, but rather becomes, a woman."[4] Social ideas and material arrangements give deep meaning to masculinity and femininity. The social significance of gender is fabricated to favor men systematically through economic, political, and legal structures that rest upon and reinforce gender. Sexual desire, both powerful and pliable, forms a part of that gender system. Discovering, describing, and analyzing the complex interaction of gender and sexuality, of representation and reality, thus remains a key project of feminist theory and lives.

BRIEF *AMICI CURIAE* OF FEMINIST ANTI-CENSORSHIP TASKFORCE, ET AL.

…Amici are feminists who sign this brief as a statement of our opposition to the Indianapolis ordinance. We believe that the ordinance reinforces rather than undercuts central sexist stereotypes in our society and would result in state suppression of sexually explicit speech, including feminist images and literature, which does not in any way encourage violence against women. We condemn acts of violence against women; incitement to that violence; and misogyny, racism, and anti-Semitism in all media. We believe, however, that the Indianapolis ordinance will not reduce violence against women and will censor speech and imagery that properly belong in the public realm. Some proponents of this ordinance genuinely believed that it would assist women to overcome disabling sex role stereotypes and promote greater equality for women. We who sign this brief are deeply concerned that it will have precisely the opposite effect.…

THE ORDINANCE SUPPRESSES CONSTITUTIONALLY PROTECTED SPEECH IN A MANNER PARTICULARLY DETRIMENTAL TO WOMEN.

Although Appellants argue that the ordinance is designed to restrict images which legitimate violence and coercion against women, the definition of pornography in the ordinance is not limited to images of violence or of coercion, or to images produced by women who were coerced. Nor is it limited to materials which advocate or depict the torture or rape of women as a form of sexual pleasure. It extends to any sexually explicit material which an agency or court finds to be "subordinating" to a claimant acting on behalf of women and which fits within one of the descriptive categories which complete the definition of pornography.

For purposes of the trafficking cause of action, the ordinance defines pornography as the "graphic sexually explicit subordination of women, whether in pictures or in words, that also includes one or more" of the depictions described in six categories.[5] The violent and brutal images which Appellants use as illustrative examples cannot obscure the fact that the ordinance authorizes suppression of material that is sexually explicit, but in no way violent. The language of the definition mixes phrases that have clear meanings and thus ascertainable applications (e.g., "cut up or mutilated") with others which are sufficiently elastic to encompass almost any sexually explicit image that someone might find offensive (e.g., "scenarios of degradation" or "abasement"). The material that could be suppressed under the latter category is virtually limitless.

While the sweep of the ordinance is breathtaking, it does not address (nor would *Amici* support state suppression of) the far more pervasive commercial images depicting women as primarily concerned with the whiteness of their wash, the softness of their toilet tissue, and whether the lines of their panties show when wearing tight slacks. Commercial images, available to the most impressionable young children during prime time, depict women as people interested in inconsequential matters who are incapable of taking significant, serious roles in societal decision-making.

The constitutionality of the ordinance depends on the assumption that state agencies and courts can develop clear legal definitions of terms like "sexually explicit subordination," "sexual object," and "scenarios of degradation" and "abasement." In truth, these terms are highly contextual and of varying meanings. Worse, many of their most commonly accepted meanings would, if applied in the context of this ordinance, reinforce rather than erode archaic and untrue stereotypes about women's sexuality.

1. Historically the Law Has Incorporated a Sexual Double Standard Denying Women's Interest in Sexual Expression.

Traditionally, laws regulating sexual activity were premised upon and reinforced a gender-based double standard which assumed that women are delicate, that voluntary sexual intercourse may harm them in certain circumstances, and that they may be seriously injured by words as well as deeds. The statutes also suggest that, despite the generally delicate nature of most women, there exists a class of women who are not delicate or who are not worthy of protection. [By contrast, the law's treatment of male sexuality reflected] the underlying assumption that only males have aggressive sexual desires [and] hence they must be restrained. The detail and comprehensiveness of [such] laws suggest that men are considered almost crazed by sex.

The Indianapolis ordinance is squarely within the tradition of the sexual double standard. It allows little room for women to openly express certain sexual desires and resurrects the notion that sexually explicit materials are subordinating and degrading to women. Because the "trafficking" cause of action allows one woman to obtain a court order suppressing images which fall within the ordinance's definition of pornography, it implies that individual women are incapable of choosing for themselves what they consider to be enjoyable, sexually arousing material without being degraded or humiliated.

The legal system has used many vehicles to enforce the sexual double standard which protected "good" women from both sexual activity and explicit speech about sex. For example, the common law of libel held that "an oral imputation of unchastity to a woman is actionable without proof of damage.... Such a rule never has been applied to a man, since the damage to his reputation is assumed not to be as great."[6]...

The sexual double standard is applied with particular force to young people. Statutory rape laws often punished men for consensual intercourse with a female under a certain age. Such laws reinforce the stereotype that in sex the man is the offender and the woman the victim, and that young men may legitimately engage in sex, at least with older people, while a young woman may not legally have sex with anyone.

The suppression of sexually explicit material most devastating to women was the restriction on dissemination of birth control information, common until 1971. In that year, the Supreme Court held that the constitutional right to privacy protects an unmarried person's right to access to birth control information.[7] To deny women access to contraception "prescribe[s] pregnancy and the birth of an unwanted child as punishment for fornication."[8] For the previous century, the federal Comstock law, passed in 1873, had prohibited mailing, transporting or importing "obscene, lewd or lascivious" items, specifically including all devices and information pertaining to "preventing contraception and producing abortion."[9] Women were jailed for distributing educational materials regarding birth control to other women because the materials were deemed sexually explicit in that they "contain[ed] pictures of certain organs of women" and because the materials were found to be "detrimental to public morals and welfare."[10]

The Mann Act also was premised on the notion that women require special protection from sexual activity.[11] It forbids interstate transportation of women for purposes of "prostitution, debauchery, or any other immoral purposes," and was enacted to protect women from reportedly widespread abduction by bands of "white slavers" coercing them into prostitution. As the legislative history reveals, the Act reflects the assumption that women have no will of their own and must be protected against themselves. Like the premises underlying this ordinance, the Mann Act assumed that women were naturally chaste and virtuous, and that no woman became a whore unless she had first been raped, seduced, drugged or deserted. [Its] image of the prostitute...was of a lonely and confused female.... [Its proponents] maintained that prostitutes were the passive victims of social disequilibrium and the brutality of men.... [Its] conception of female weakness and male domination left no room for the possibility that prostitutes might consciously choose their activities.[12]...

Society's attempts to "protect" women's chastity through criminal and civil laws have resulted in restrictions on women's freedom to engage in sexual activity, to discuss it publicly, and to protect themselves from the risk of pregnancy. These disabling restrictions reinforced the gender roles which have oppressed women for centuries. The Indianapolis ordinance resonates with the traditional concept that sex itself degrades women, and its enforcement would reinvigorate those discriminatory moral standards which have limited women's equality in the past.

2. The Ordinance Is Unconstitutionally Vague Because Context Inescapably Determines the Effect of Sexual Texts and Images.

The ordinance authorizes court orders removing from public or private availability "graphic sexually explicit" words and images which "subordinate" women. A judge presented with a civil complaint filed pursuant to this law would be required to determine whether the material in question "subordinated" women. To equate pornography with conduct having the power to "subordinate" living human beings, whatever its value as a rhetorical device, requires a "certain sleight of hand" to be incorporated as a doctrine of law. Words and images do influence what people think, how they feel, and what they do, both positively and negatively.

Thus pornography may have such influence. But the connection between fantasy or symbolic representation and actions in the real world is not direct or linear. Sexual imagery is not so simple to assess. In the sexual realm, perhaps more so than in any other, messages and their impact on the viewer or reader are often multiple, contradictory, layered and highly contextual.

The film *Swept Away* illustrates that serious problems of context and interpretation confound even the categories which on first reading might seem reasonably easy to apply. Made in 1975 by Italian director Lina Wertmuller, *Swept Away* tells a powerful story of dominance and submission. A rich attractive woman and a younger working class man are first shown as class antagonists during a yachting trip on which the man is a deckhand and the woman a viciously rude boss, and then as sexual antagonists when they are stranded on a Mediterranean island and the man exacts his revenge. During the second part of the film, the man rapes the woman and repeatedly assaults her. She initially resists, then falls in love with him, and he with her.

Scenes in *Swept Away* clearly present the woman character as "experienc[ing] sexual pleasure" during rape. In addition, she is humiliated, graphically and sexually, and appears to grow to enjoy it. Although sexually explicit depictions are not the majority of scenes, the film as a whole has an active sexual dynamic. Given the overall and pervasive theme of sexual dominance and submission, it is improbable that the explicit scenes could be deemed "isolated." It is virtually certain that the film could be suppressed under the ordinance…

Swept Away is an example of graphic, sexually explicit images and characterizations used to treat themes of power imbalance, to push at the edges of what is thought to be acceptable or desirable, and to shock. Critical and popular opinions of the film varied, ranging from admiration to repulsion. Whatever one's interpretation of the film, however, its profoundly important themes entitle it to a place in the realm of public discourse.

Context often determines meaning. Whether a specific image could be found to "subordinate" or "degrade" women may depend entirely on such factors as the purpose of the presentation; the size and nature of the audience; the surrounding messages; the expectation and attitude of the viewer; and where the presentation takes place, among others. Yet the trafficking provision allows blanket suppression of images based on highly subjective criteria which masquerade as simple, delineating definitions.

3. The Ordinance Is Unconstitutionally Vague Because Its Central Terms Have No Fixed Meaning, and the Most Common Meanings of These Terms Are Sexist and Damaging to Women.

The ordinance's definition of pornography, essential to each cause of action, is fatally flawed. It relies on words often defined in ways that reinforce a constricted and constricting view of women's sexuality. Thus Amici fear that experimentations in feminist art which deal openly and explicitly with sexual themes will be easily targeted for suppression under this ordinance.

The central term "sexually explicit subordination" is not defined. Appellants argue that "subordination" means that which "places women in positions of inferiority, loss of power, degradation and submission, among other things." The core question, however, is left begging: what kinds of sexually explicit acts place a woman in an inferior status? Appellants argued in their brief to the District Court that "[t]he mere existence of pornography in society degrades and demeans all women." To some observers, any graphic image of sexual acts is "degrading" to women and hence would subordinate them. To some, the required element of subordination or "positions of...submission" might be satisfied by the image of a woman lying on her back inviting intercourse, while others might view the same image as affirming women's sexual pleasure and initiative. Some might draw the line at acts outside the bounds of marriage or with multiple partners. Others might see a simple image of the most traditional heterosexual act as subordinating in presenting the man in a physical position of superiority and the woman in a position of inferiority.

In any of these contexts, it is not clear whether the ordinance is to be interpreted with a subjective or an objective standard. If a subjective interpretation of "subordination" is contemplated, the ordinance vests in individual women a power to impose their views of politically or morally correct sexuality upon other women by calling for repression of images consistent with those views. The evaluative terms—subordination, degradation, abasement—are initially within the definitional control of the plaintiff, whose interpretation, if colorable, must be accepted by the court. An objective standard would require a court to determine whether plaintiff's reaction to the material comports with some generalized notion of which images do or do not degrade women. It would require the judiciary to impose its views of correct sexuality on a diverse community. The inevitable result would be to disapprove of those images that are least conventional and privilege those that are closest to majoritarian beliefs about proper sexuality.

Whether subjective or objective, the inquiry is one that plainly and profoundly threatens First Amendment freedoms and is totally inconsistent with feminist principles, as they are understood by *Amici*. Sexuality is particularly susceptible to extremely charged emotions, including feelings of vulnerability and power. The realm of image judgment opened by the ordinance is too contested and sensitive to be entrusted to legislative categorization and judicial enforcement.

The danger of discrimination is illustrated by the probability that some women would consider any explicit lesbian scene as subordinating, or as causing "[their] dignity [to] suffer." Appellants plainly intend to include same-sex depictions, since their carefully selected trial court exhibits include such materials. Lesbians and gay men encounter massive discrimination based on prejudice related to their sexuality. The trafficking provision of the ordinance virtually invites new manifestations of this prejudice by means of civil litigation against the erotica of sexual minorities.

The six subsections of the definition applicable to a trafficking complaint provide no clarification. The term "sexual object," for example, appears frequently in the definition. Appellants are confident that "the common man knows a sex object when he sees one." Yet, although "sex object" may be a phrase which has begun to enjoy widened popular usage, its precise meaning is far from clear. Some persons maintain that any detachment of women's sexuality from procreation, marriage, and family objectifies it, removing it from its "natural" web of association and context. When sex is detached from its traditional moorings, men allegedly benefit and women are the victims. Feminists, on the other hand, generally use the term "sex object" to mean the absence of any indicia of personhood, a very different interpretation.

Appellants argue that the meaning of "subordination" and "degradation" can be determined in relation to "common usage and understanding." But as we have seen, the common understanding of sexuality is one that incorporates a sexual double standard. Historically, virtually all sexually explicit literature and imagery has been thought to be degrading or abasing or humiliating, especially to women....

The ordinance requires enforcement of "common understandings" of culturally loaded terms. It perpetuates beliefs which undermine the principle that women are full, equal, and active agents in every realm of life, including the sexual.

4. Sexually Explicit Speech Does Not Cause or Incite Violence in a Manner Sufficiently Direct to Justify Its Suppression Under the First Amendment.

To uphold this ordinance and the potential suppression of all speech which could be found to fall within its definition of pornography, this court must invent a new exception to the First Amendment. To justify that, Appellants must show that the speech to be suppressed will lead to immediate and concrete harm.... Only a small number of social science studies which purport to show a connection between violent pornography and negative attitudes and behavior toward women have been offered to support this position. For many reasons, their effort must fail.

Substantively, the studies relied upon do not justify the sweeping suppression authorized by the ordinance. Appellants cite the social science data in highly selective and grossly distorting ways. They fail to acknowledge that most of it is limited to studies of a narrow class of violent imagery. The ordinance, by contrast, both leaves untouched most of the images which may be said to cause negative effects and would allow the suppression of many images which have not been shown to have any harmful effect. Appellants also fail to mention that the "debriefing" phase of the cited experiments suggests that negative changes in attitudes may be corrected through further speech. They seek to create the false impression that new social science data have completely refuted the finding in 1971 by the Presidential Commission on Obscenity and Pornography that pornography was not harmful. However, as Professor Edward Donnerstein wrote in the study placed before the District Court by Appellants as Exh. T. at 127–128,

> One should not assume...that all the research since the commission's time has indicated negative effects [of pornographic materials] on individuals. In fact, this is quite to the contrary.... [A] good amount of research strongly supports the position that exposure to certain types of erotica can reduce aggressive responses in people who are predisposed to aggression....

Lastly, whatever Appellants' claims, numerous methodological problems make these studies too unreliable as predictors of real world behavior to sustain the withdrawal of constitutional protection from what is now permitted speech....

Although the ordinance authorizes suppression of far more than simply violent images, the limited findings of a linkage between sexually explicit materials and a willingness to aggress against women under laboratory conditions have occurred only in studies of "aggressive pornography," defined as a particular scenario: "depictions in which physical force is used or threatened to coerce a woman to engage in sexual acts (e.g. rape)." This limiting definition is used by both Professor Donnerstein and Professor Neil Malamuth in the recently published book, *Pornography and Sexual Aggression....* Where nonaggressive pornography is studied, no effect on aggression against women has been found; it is the violent, and not the sexual, content of the depiction that is said to produce the effects.[13] Further, all of the aggression studies have used visual imagery; none has studied the impact of only words. Finally, even as to violent "aggressive pornography," the results of the studies are not uniform.[14]

Violent and misogynist images are pervasive in our culture. Nothing in the research cited by Appellants proves their hypothesis that these messages are believed in a qualitatively different way when they are communicated through the medium of sexually explicit material. Both Professors Donnerstein and Malamuth have noted that regulation of imagery targeted at the sexually explicit misses the core of the problem:

> Images of violence against women are not the sole property of aggressive or violent pornography. Such images are quite pervasive in our society. Images outside of the pornographic or X-rated market may in fact be of more concern, since they are imbued with a certain "legitimacy" surrounding them and tend to have much wider acceptance.

Sexist attitudes, callous attitudes about rape, and other misogynist values are just as likely to be reinforced by non-sexualized violent symbols as they are by violent pornography.

Attempts to alter the content of mass media...cannot be limited to pornography, since research has documented similar effects from mainstream movies. In addition, other mass media forms, such as advertisements, television soap operas, and detective magazines, to name a few, also contain undesirable images of violence against women. The most pertinent question on the issue of changing mass media content may not be where we draw the line between pornography and non-pornography but how we can best combat violence against women in its myriad forms.

When "more speech" can be an effective means of countering prejudicial and discriminatory messages, the First Amendment forbids the use of censorship to suppress even the most hateful content. The social science data upon which Appellants rely so heavily indicate that further speech can remove the negative effects on attitude registered after viewing certain kinds of violent pornography. Malamuth and Donnerstein both conduct "debriefing" sessions at the conclusion of their experiments. In these sessions, the purposes of the studies are explained to the subjects, and information is presented to dispel rape myths. The effectiveness of the debriefing sessions is then tested up to four months later. "The findings of these studies indicated consistently that the education interventions were successful in counteracting the effects of aggressive pornography and in reducing beliefs in rape myths."[15]

Censorship is not the solution. Education, however, is a viable alternative. Early sex education programs which dispel myths about sexual violence and early training in critical viewing skills could mitigate the influence of these films. This debriefing effect demonstrates that the changes in attitude shown from pornography are not permanent or, as Appellants contend, conditioned....

Appellants claim a causal connection between the availability of pornography and rape. Such a claim is implausible on its face. Acts of rape and coercion long preceded the mass distribution of pornography, and in many cultures pornography is unavailable, yet the incidence of rape, and of discrimination against women generally, is high.[16] The converse is also true; that is, there are places where pornography is widely available, and the incidence of rape is low compared to the United States. ...

5. Constitutional Protection for Sexually Explicit Speech Should Be Enhanced, Not Diminished.

Sexually explicit speech which is judged "obscene" is not protected under the First Amendment. *Miller v. California*, 413 U.S. 15 (1973). Appellants seek to vitiate the protection currently afforded non-obscene sexual speech on the ground that any expression falling within the scope of this ordinance "is not the free exchange of ideas." They ask this Court to rule that all sexually explicit speech is disfavored:

> It is essential to look at the nature of the material regulated to measure the importance of the chilling effect. The Supreme Court has determined that "there is...a less vital interest in the uninhibited exhibition of material that is on the borderline between pornography and artistic expression than in the free dissemination of ideas of social and political significance."[17] ...

The argument that the First Amendment provides less protection for sexual images than for speech which is "political" misunderstands both the value of free expression and the political content of sexually explicit speech. Many justifications support free expression: our incapacity to determine truth without open discussion; the need for people to communicate to express self-identity and determine how to live their lives; the inability of the censor to wield power wisely.

Further, sexual speech is political. One core insight of modern feminism is that the personal is political. The question of who does the dishes and rocks the cradle affects both the nature of the home and the composition of the legislature. The dynamics of intimate relations are likewise political, both to the individuals involved and by their multiplied effects to the wider society. To argue, as Appellants do, that sexually explicit speech is less important than other categories of discourse reinforces the conceptual structures that have identified women's concerns with relationships and intimacy as less significant and valuable precisely because those concerns are falsely regarded as having no bearing on the structure of social and political life.

Depictions of ways of living and acting that are radically different from our own can enlarge the range of human possibilities open to us and help us grasp the potentialities of human behavior, both good and bad. Rich fantasy imagery allows us to experience in imagination ways of being that we may not wish to experience in real life. Such an enlarged vision of possible realities enhances our human potential and is highly relevant to our decision-making as citizens on a wide range of social and ethical issues.

For sexual minorities, speech describing conduct can be a means of self-affirmation in a generally hostile world. Constrictions on that speech can deny fundamental aspects of self-identity.[18]

Thus, sexually explicit expression, including much that is covered by the ordinance, carries many more messages than simply the misogyny described by Appellants. It may convey the message that sexuality need not be tied to reproduction, men, or domesticity. It may contain themes of sex for no reason other than pleasure, sex without commitment, and sexual adventure—all of which are surely ideas. *Cf. Kingsley Corp. v. Regents*, 360 U.S. 684 (1959).

Even pornography which is problematic for women can be experienced as affirming of women's desires and of women's equality:

> Pornography can be a psychic assault, both in its content and in its public intrusions on our attention, but for women as for men it can also be a source of erotic pleasure. A woman who is raped is a victim; a woman who enjoys pornography (even if that means enjoying a rape fantasy) is in a sense a rebel, insisting on an aspect of her sexuality that has been defined as a male preserve. Insofar as pornography glorifies male supremacy and sexual alienation, it is deeply reactionary. But in rejecting sexual repression and hypocrisy—which have inflicted even more damage on women than on men—it expresses a radical impulse.[19]

The range of feminist imagination and expression in the realm of sexuality has barely begun to find voice. Women need the freedom and the socially recognized space to appropriate for themselves the robustness of what traditionally has been male language. Laws such as the one under challenge here would constrict that freedom.... *Amici* fear that as more women's writing and art on sexual themes emerge which are unladylike, unfeminine, aggressive, power-charged, pushy, vulgar, urgent, confident, and intense, the traditional foes of women's attempts to step out of their "proper place" will find an effective tool of repression in the Indianapolis ordinance.

THE ORDINANCE UNCONSTITUTIONALLY DISCRIMINATES ON THE BASIS OF SEX AND REINFORCES SEXIST STEREOTYPES.

The challenged ordinance posits a great chasm—a categorical difference—between the make-up and needs of men and of women. It goes far beyond acknowledgment of the differences in life experiences which are inevitably produced by social structures of gender inequality. The ordinance presumes women as a class (and only women) are subordinated by virtually any sexually explicit image. It presumes women as a class (and only women) are incapable of making a binding agreement to participate in the creation of sexually explicit material. And it presumes men as a class (and only men) are conditioned by sexually explicit depictions to commit acts of aggression and to believe misogynist myths.

Such assumptions reinforce and perpetuate central sexist stereotypes; they weaken, rather than enhance, women's struggles to free themselves of archaic notions of gender roles. In so doing, this ordinance itself violates the equal protection clause of the Fourteenth Amendment. In treating women as a special class, it repeats the error of earlier protectionist legislation which gave women no significant benefits and denied their equality.

1. The District Court Erred in Accepting Appellants' Assertion That Pornography Is a Discriminatory Practice Based on Sex.

The ordinance is predicated on a finding that:
Pornography is a discriminatory practice based on sex which denies women equal opportunities in society. Pornography is central in creating and maintaining sex as a basis for discrimination.... [It harms] women's opportunities for equality of rights in employment, education, access to and use of public accommodations, and acquisition of real property; promote[s] rape, battery, child abuse, kidnapping and prostitution and inhibit[s] just enforcement of laws against such acts....

The District Court accepted that finding, but held that First Amendment values outweighed the asserted interest in protecting women. *American Booksellers Ass'n v. Hudnut*, 598 F. Supp. 1316, 1335–1337 (S.D. Ind. 1984).

Amici dispute the City and County's "finding" that "pornography is central in creating and maintaining sex as a basis for discrimination."...

It is true that sex discrimination takes multiple forms, which are reflected in the media. But the finding that "pornography is central in creating and maintaining sex as a basis for discrimination" does not represent our best understanding of the complex, deep-seated and structural causes of gender inequality. In the past decade, many people have grappled with the question of causation.... The factors they find most significant include: the sex segregated wage labor market; systematic devaluation of work traditionally done by women; sexist concepts of marriage and family; inadequate income maintenance programs for women unable to find wage work; lack of day care services and the premise that child care is an exclusively female responsibility; barriers to reproductive freedom; and discrimination and segregation in education and athletics.[20] Numerous feminist scholars have written major works tracing the cultural, economic, and psychosocial roots of women's oppression.[21]

Misogynist images, both those which are sexually explicit and the far more pervasive ones which are not, reflect and may help to reinforce the inferior social and economic status of women. But none of these studies and analyses identifies sexually explicit material as the central factor in the oppression of women. History teaches us that the answer is not so simple. Factors far more complex than pornography produced the English common law treatment of women as chattel property and the enactment of statutes allowing a husband to rape or beat his wife with impunity. In short, the claim that "pornography is central in creating and maintaining sex as a basis of discrimination" is flatly inconsistent with the conclusions of most who have studied the question.

Amici also dispute the "finding" that pornography, as defined by the ordinance, is "a discriminatory practice...which denies women equal opportunities." Images and fictional text are not the same thing as subordinating conduct. The ordinance does not target discriminatory actions denying access to jobs, education, public accommodations, or real property. It prohibits images. Although ideas have impact, images of discrimination are not the discrimination....

...the District Court misperceived this case as one requiring the assignment of rank in a constitutional hierarchy. It is not necessary to rule that either gender equality or free speech is more important. The ordinance is fatally flawed not only because it authorizes suppression of speech protected by the First Amendment but also because it violates the constitutional guarantee of sex-based equality.

2. The Ordinance Classifies on the Basis of Sex and Perpetuates Sexist Stereotypes.

The ordinance defines pornography in gender specific terms as "the graphic sexually explicit subordination of women" that also presents "women" in particular ways proscribed by the law. The District Court found:

> [t]he Ordinance seeks to protect adult women, as a group, from the diminution of the legal and sociological status as women, that is from

the discriminatory stigma which befalls women as women as a result of pornography.

The ordinance authorizes any woman to file a complaint against those trafficking in pornography "as a woman acting against the subordination of women." A man, by contrast, may obtain relief only if he can "prove injury in the same way that a woman is injured." Again the ordinance assumes that women as a class are subordinated and hurt by depictions of sex, and men are not.

The ordinance reinforces yet another sexist stereotype of men as aggressive beasts. Appellants assert:

> By conditioning the male orgasm to female subordination, pornography…makes the subordination of women pleasurable and seemingly legitimate. Each time men are sexually aroused by pornography, they learn to connect a woman's sexual pleasure to abuse and a woman's sexual nature to inferiority. They learn this in their bodies, not just their minds, so that it becomes a natural physiological response. At this point pornography leaves no more room for further debate than does shouting "kill" to an attack dog.[22]

Men are not attack dogs, but morally responsible human beings. The ordinance reinforces a destructive sexist stereotype of men as irresponsible beasts, with "natural physiological responses" which can be triggered by sexually explicit images of women, and for which the men cannot be held accountable. Thus, men are conditioned into violent acts or negative beliefs by sexual images; women are not. Further, the ordinance is wholly blind to the possibility that men could be hurt and degraded by images presenting them as violent or sadistic.

The ordinance also reinforces sexist images of women as incapable of consent. It creates a remedy for people "coerced" to participate in the production of pornography. Unlike existing criminal, tort, and contract remedies against coercion, the ordinance provides:

> proof of the following facts or conditions shall not constitute a defense: that the person actually consented…; or, knew that the purpose of the acts or events in question was to make pornography; or demonstrated no resistance or appeared to cooperate actively in the photographic sessions or in the sexual events that produced the pornography; or… signed a contract, or made statements affirming a willingness to cooperate in the production of pornography.

In effect, the ordinance creates a strong presumption that women who participate in the creation of sexually explicit material are coerced. A woman's manifestation of consent—no matter how plain, informed, or even self-initiated—does not constitute a defense to her subsequent claim of coercion. Women are judged incompetent to consent to participation in the creation of sexually explicit material and condemned as "bad" if they do so. ...

This provision does far more than simply provide a remedy to women who are pressured into the creation of pornography which they subsequently seek to suppress. It functions to make all women incompetent to enter into legally binding contracts for the production of sexually explicit material. When women are legally disabled from making binding agreements, they are denied power to negotiate for fair treatment and decent pay. Enforcement of the ordinance would drive production of sexually explicit material even further into an underground economy, where the working conditions of women in the sex industry would worsen, not improve.

3. The Ordinance Is Unconstitutional Because It Reinforces Sexist Stereotypes and Classifies on the Basis of Sex.

In recent years, the Supreme Court has firmly and repeatedly rejected gender-based classifications, such as that embodied in the ordinance. The constitutionally protected right to sex-based equality under law demands that:

> the party seeking to uphold a statute that classifies individuals on the basis of their gender must carry the burden of showing an "exceedingly persuasive justification" for the classification. ... The burden is met only by showing at least that the classification serves "important governmental objectives and that the discriminatory means employed" are "substantially related to the achievement of those objectives."[23]

The sex-based classifications embodied in the statute are justified on the basis of stereotypical assumptions about women's vulnerability to sexually explicit images and their production and men's latent uncontrollability. But the Supreme Court has held that, "[This standard] must be applied free of fixed notions concerning the roles and abilities of males and females. Care must be taken in ascertaining whether the statutory objective itself reflects archaic and stereotypic notions." Gender-based classifications cannot be upheld if they are premised on "'old notions' and 'archaic and overbroad' generalizations about the roles and relative abilities of men and women."[24]

The ordinance damages individuals who do not fit the stereotypes it embodies. It delegitimates and makes socially invisible women who find sexually explicit images of women "in positions of display" or "penetrated by objects" to be erotic, liberating, or educational. These women are told that their perceptions are a product of "false consciousness" and that such images are so inherently degrading that they may be suppressed by the state. At the same time, it stamps the imprimatur of state approval on the belief that men are attack dogs triggered to violence by the sight of a sexually explicit image of a woman. It delegitimates and makes socially invisible those men who consider themselves gentle, respectful of women, or inhibited about expressing their sexuality.

Even worse, the stereotypes of the ordinance perpetuate traditional social views of sex-based difference. By defining sexually explicit images of woman as subordinating and degrading to them, the ordinance reinforces the stereotypical view that "good" women do not seek and enjoy sex. As applied, it would deny women access to sexually explicit material at a time in our history when women have just begun to acquire the social and economic power to develop our own images of sexuality. Stereotypes of hair-trigger male susceptibility to violent imagery can be invoked as an excuse to avoid directly blaming the men who commit violent acts.

Finally, the ordinance perpetuates a stereotype of women as helpless victims, incapable of consent, and in need of protection. A core premise of contemporary sex equality doctrine is that if the objective of the law is to "'protect' members of one gender because they are presumed to suffer from an inherent handicap or to be innately inferior, the objective itself is illegitimate."[25] We have learned through hard experience that gender-based classifications protecting women from their own presumed innate vulnerability reflect "an attitude of 'romantic paternalism' which, in practical effect, puts women not on a pedestal but in a cage."[26]...

...Women were, and continue to be, in a position of social and economic vulnerability that inhibits their ability to negotiate fair terms and conditions of wage labor. Further, the pervasive sexism and violence of our culture make women vulnerable to exploitation and inhibit their ability to enter into sexual or other relationships on a free and voluntary basis.

Slavery and free self-actualization are opposite poles on a continuum. Both free agency and response to external pressure are simultaneous aspects of human action. In the 1930s, employers challenged minimum wage and hour laws saying that laborers "freely consented" to work twelve hours a day, under dangerous and harmful conditions, for wages that did not provide minimal subsistence. We understand today that this concept of voluntary consent is self-serving and empty. Similarly, many women engage in sex or in the production of sexually explicit materials in response to pressures so powerful that it would be cynical to characterize their actions as simply voluntary and consensual.

Still, the laws that "protected" only women from exploitation in wage labor hurt them. Many employers responded by barring women from the best paying jobs with the greatest opportunity for advancement. Further, the protective labor laws reinforced general beliefs about women's vulnerability and incompetence. Similarly here, the protection of the ordinance reinforces the idea that women are incompetent, particularly in relation to sex.

The pervasive sexism and violence of our culture create a social climate—in the home, workplace, and street—that is different for women than for men. But even accurate generalizations about women's need for help do not justify sex-based classifications such as those in this ordinance. It is also true that women generally are still the ones who nurture young children. Yet we understand that laws giving mothers an irrebuttable "tender years" presumption for custody, or offering child rearing leaves only to mothers but not to fathers, ultimately hurt women and are unconstitutional.

Some of the proponents of the ordinance believe that it will empower women, while others support it for more traditional, patriarchal reasons. But many gender-based classifications are premised on a good faith intent to help or protect women. Good intent does not justify an otherwise invidious gender-based law. "Our nation has had a long and unfortunate history of sex discrimination."[27] The clearest lesson of that history is that sex-based classifications hurt women.

Thus, the District Court was correct to reject Appellants' claim that women are like children who need special protection from sexually explicit material. The Court found that:

> adult women as a group do not, as a matter of public policy or applicable law, stand in need of the same type of protection which has long been afforded children.... Adult women generally have the capacity to protect themselves from participating in and being personally victimized by pornography....

The gender-based classification embodied in the ordinance is unconstitutional because it assumes and perpetuates classic sexist concepts of separate gender-defined roles, which carry "the inherent risk of reinforcing the stereotypes about the 'proper place' of women and their need for special protection."[28]

4. The Sex-Based Classification and Stereotypes Created by the Ordinance Are Not Carefully Tailored to Serve Important State Purposes.

Appellants claim that the ordinance serves the "governmental interest in promoting sex equality." Certainly preventing the violent subordination of women is the sort of compelling public purpose that might justify sex-based classification. But, as is often true of classifications justified on grounds that they protect women, the benefits actually provided are minimal. The ordinance thus also fails the requirement for a "substantial relationship" between its classification and the achievement of its asserted goal.

Supporters of the ordinance describe acts of violence against women and claim that the ordinance would provide a remedy for those injuries. But the only new remedy it provides is suppression of sexually explicit materials, a wholly inadequate and misdirected response to real violence....

Individuals who commit acts of violence must be held legally and morally accountable. The law should not displace responsibility onto imagery. Amicus Women Against Pornography describe as victims of pornography married women coerced to perform sexual acts depicted in pornographic works, working women harassed on the job with pornographic images, and children who have pornography forced on them during acts of child abuse. Each of these examples describes victims of violence and coercion, not of images. The acts are wrong, whether or not the perpetrator refers to an image. The most wholesome sex education materials, if shown to a young child as an example of what people do with those they love, could be used in a viciously harmful way. The law should punish the abuser, not the image. Title VII of the Civil Rights Act provides remedies for working women injured by sexual taunts or slurs, including sexually explicit pictures...and for those injured by misogynist imagery.... These legal principles apply to any images or texts which people put to discriminatory use, whether pornography or the Bible. But no law has or should assume that the same woman harassed by pornographic images in the workplace might not enjoy those very images if given the opportunity to put them to her own use.

To resist forced sex and violence, women need the material resources to enable them to reject jobs or marriages in which they are abused or assaulted and the internal and collective strength to fight the conditions of abuse. The ordinance does nothing to enhance the concrete economic and social power of women. Further, its stereotype of women as powerless victims undermines women's ability to act affirmatively to protect themselves.

Suppression of sexually explicit material will not eliminate the pervasive sexist images of the mainstream culture or the discriminatory economic and social treatment that maintains women's second class status. Such suppression will not empower women to enter into sexual relationships on a voluntary, consensual basis. Empowering women requires something more than suppression of texts and images. It demands "concrete material changes that enable women and men to experience sexuality less attached to and formed by gender."[29] These changes include social and economic equality; access to jobs, day care and education; more equal sharing of responsibility for children; recognition of the social and economic value of the work that women have traditionally done in the home; and access to birth control, abortion, and sex education.

CONCLUSION

Sexually explicit speech is not per se sexist or harmful to women. Like any mode of expression, it can be used to attack women's struggle for equal rights, but it is also a category of speech from which women have been excluded. The suppression authorized by the Indianapolis ordinance of a potentially enormous range of sexual imagery and texts reinforces the notion that women are too fragile, and men too uncontrollable, absent the aid of the censor, to be trusted to reject or enjoy sexually explicit speech for themselves. By identifying "subordination of women" as the concept that distinguishes sexually explicit material which is tolerable from that to be condemned, the ordinance incorporates a vague and asymmetric standard for censorship that can as readily be used to curtail feminist speech about sexuality, or to target the speech of sexual minorities, as to halt hateful speech about women. Worse, perpetuation of the concept of gender-determined roles in regard to sexuality strengthens one of the main obstacles to achieving real change and ending sexual violence.

NOTES

[1] ...It appears that the Feminist Anti-Censorship Taskforce (FACT) analysis had some influence on Judge Easterbrook's approach to the constitutional issues presented. The opinion discusses concrete examples illustrating the difficulty of distinguishing images that liberate women from those that subordinate women. It addresses the relationship between images, ideas, and behavior, and the distinction between fantasy and reality, in terms that are unusually rich and thoughtful for a judicial opinion. The court rightly rejects the state's claim that pornography is "low value" speech, entitled to lesser constitutional protection than "serious" talk about public issues.

[2] Ellen DuBois and Linda Gordon, "Seeking Ecstasy on the Battlefield: Danger and Pleasure in Nineteenth-Century Feminist Sexual Thought," in *Pleasure and Danger: Exploring Female Sexuality*, C. Vance (ed.) (Boston: Routledge & Kegan Paul, 1984): 31 [hereinafter *Pleasure and Danger*].

[3] C. Vance, "Pleasure and Danger: Toward a Politics of Sexuality," in *Pleasure and Danger*: 5.

[4] Simone de Beauvoir, *The Second Sex* (New York: Bantam Books, 1968) translated by H.M. Parshley: 273.

[5] (1) Women are presented as sexual objects who enjoy pain or humiliation; or (2) Women are presented as sexual objects who experience sexual pleasure in being raped; or (3) Women are presented as sexual objects tied up or cut up or mutilated or bruised or physically hurt, or as dismembered or truncated or fragmented or severed into body parts; or (4) Women are presented being penetrated by objects or animals; or (5) Women are presented in scenarios of degradation, injury, abasement, torture, shown as filthy or inferior, bleeding, bruised, or hurt in a context that makes these conditions sexual; or (6) Women are presented as sexual objects

for domination, conquest, violation, exploitation, possession, or use, or through postures or positions of servility or submission or display. Indianapolis, Ind., Code § 16–3(q) (1984).

[6]W. Prosser, Law of Torts, 759–760 (1971).

[7]Eisenstadt v. Baird, 405 U.S. 438 (1972).

[8]*Ibid*: 448.

[9]18 U.S.C.A. §§ 1461–1462 (West 1984); 19 U.S.C.A. § 1305 (West 1980 & Supp. 1984); see United States v. One Obscene Book Entitled "Married Love", 48 F.2d 821 (S.D.N.Y. 1931); United States v. One Book Entitled "Contraceptions", 51 F.2d 525 (S.D.N.Y. 1931) (prosecution for distribution of books by Marie Stopes on contraception); United States v. Dennett, 39 F.2d 564 (2d Cir. 1930) (prosecution of Mary Ware Dennett for publication of pamphlet explaining sexual physiology and functions to children); and Bours v. United States, 229 F. 960 (7th Cir. 1915) (prosecution of physician for mailing a letter indicating that he might perform a therapeutic abortion). It was not until 1971 that an amendment was passed deleting the prohibition as to contraception, Pub. L. No. 91–662, 84 Stat. 1973 (1971); and the ban as to abortion remains in the current codification of the law.

[10]People v. Byrne, 99 Misc. 1, 6 (N.Y. 1917).

[11]35 Stat. 825 (1910), 18 U.S.C. §§ 2421-2422.

[12]The White Slave Traffic Act: The Historical Impact of a Criminal Law Policy on Women, 72 Geo. L.J. 1111 (1984). The Mann Act initially defined a "white slave" to include "only those women or girls who are literally slaves—those women who are owned and held as property and chattels...those women and girls who, if given a fair chance, would, in all human probability, have been good wives and mothers," H.R. Rep. No. 47, 61st Cong., 2d Sess., at 9–10 (1910). Over the years, the interpretation and use of the Act changed drastically to punish voluntary "immoral" acts even when no commercial intention or business profit was involved. See Caminetti v. United States, 242 U.S. 470 (1917); Cleveland v. United States, 329 U.S. 14 (1946). The term "other immoral acts" was held to apply to a variety of activities: the interstate transportation of a woman to work as a chorus girl in a theatre where the woman was exposed to smoking, drinking, and cursing; a dentist who met his young lover in a neighboring state and shared a hotel room to discuss her pregnancy; two students at the University of Puerto Rico who had sexual intercourse on the way home from a date; and a man and woman who had lived together for four years and traveled around the country as man and wife while the man sold securities.

[13]Studies have indicated that if you take out the explicit sexual content from aggressive pornographic films, leaving just the violence (which could be shown on any network television show), you find desensitization to violent acts in some subjects. However, if you take out the aggressive component and leave just the sexual, you do not seem to observe negative effects of desensitization to violence against women. Thus, violence is at issue here. That is why restrictions or censorship solutions are problematical. Donnerstein & Linz, "Debate on Pornography," *Film Comment*, Dec. 1984: 34, 35.

[14]Malamuth describes a study he did in which no evidence was found of changes in perceptions or attitudes following exposure to this type of pornography: One group of male and female subjects looked at issues of *Penthouse* and *Playboy* magazines that showed incidents of sadomasochism and rape. A second

group examined issues of these magazines that contained only non-aggressive pornography and a third group was given only neutral materials. Shortly afterward, subjects watched an actual videotaped interview with a rape victim and responded to a questionnaire assessing their perceptions of a rape victim and her experience. Weeks later…subjects indicated their views on rape in response to a newspaper article. Exposure to the aggressive pornography did not affect perceptions of rape either in response to the videotaped interview with a rape victim or to the newspaper article.

[15]Malamuth: 46.

[16]Even the Baron and Strauss chapter, "Sexual Stratification, Pornography, and Rape in the United States," in *Pornography and Sexual Aggression*, cited by the W.A.P. amicus brief at 16, which found, in a state-by-state analysis, a positive correlation between circulation rates for mainstream pornographic magazines (e.g., *Playboy*) and incidents of rape, could not explain some strikingly anomalous results, such as, for example, Utah, which ranked 51st (last) in per capita readership of sex magazines, but 25th in per capita rate of rape.

[17]Appelant's brief at 53.

[18]Cf. *Gay Law Students Ass'n v. Pacific Tel. & Tel.*, 24 Cal. 3d 458, 488, 594 P.2d 592, 611, 156 Cal. Rptr. 14, 33 (1979). In *Rowland v. Mad River Local School District*, 730 F.2d 444 (6th Cir. 1984), cert. denied, 53 U.S.L.W. 3614 (U.S. Feb. 26, 1985), a public employee was fired from her job because she confided in coworkers that she was bisexual. Although her statement resulted in no disruption of the workplace, the Court of Appeals ruled that it was constitutionally permissible to fire her "for talking about it." Id. at 450. Yet, as in Gay Law Students Association, the speech should have been considered political: I think it is impossible not to note that a…public debate is currently ongoing regarding the rights of homosexuals. The fact of petitioner's bisexuality, once spoken, necessarily and ineluctably involved her in that debate. Speech that "touches upon" this explosive issue is no less deserving of constitutional attention than speech relating to more widely condemned forms of discrimination. *Rowland v. Mad River Local School Dist.*, 53 U.S.L.W. at 3615 (Brennan and Marshall, JJ., dissenting from denial of certiorari).

[19]Ellen Willis, "Feminism, Moralism and Pornography," in *Powers of Desire: The Politics of Sexuality*, A. Snitow, C. Stansell & S. Thompson (eds.) (New York: Monthly Review Press, 1983): 460, 464. Fantasy is not the same as wish fulfillment. See N. Friday, *My Secret Garden: Women's Secret Fantasies* (New York: Trident, 1973) and *Forbidden Flowers: More Women's Sexual Fantasies* (1975). But one cannot fully discuss or analyze fantasy if the use of explicit language is precluded.

[20]See, for example, U.S. Commission on Civil Rights, *Women and Poverty* (1974); *Women Still in Poverty* (1979); and *Child Care and Equal Opportunity for Women* (1981) and National Advisory Council on Economic Opportunity, *Final Report: The American Promise: Equal Justice and Economic Opportunity* (1981).

[21]See, e.g., *Toward an Anthropology of Women*, R. Reiter (ed.) (New York: Monthly Review Press, 1975); *Women, Culture and Society*, M. Rosaldo & L. Lamphere (eds.) (Stanford, CA.: Stanford University Press, 1974); N. Chodorow, *The Reproduction of Mothering: Psychoanalysis and the Sociology of Gender* (Berkeley, CA: University of California, 1978); D. Dinnerstein, *The Mermaid and the Minotaur: Sexual Arrangements and Human Malaise* (New York: Harper & Row, 1976); J. Mitchell, *Women's Estate* (New York: Vintage Books, 1972).

[22]Appellants brief at 21.

[23]*Mississippi Univ. for Women v. Hogan*, 458 U.S. 718, 724–725 (1982).

[24]*Califano v. Goldfarb*, 430 U.S. 199, 217 (1977).

[25]*Mississippi Univ. for Women v. Hogan*, 458 U.S. at 725.

[26]*Frontiero v. Richardson*, 411 U.S. 677, 684 (1973).

[27]*Frontiero v. Richardson*, 411 U.S. at 684.

[28]*Orr v. Orr*, 440 U.S. 268, 283 (1979).

[29]C. Vance & A. Snitow, "Toward a Conversation About Sex in Feminism: A Modest Proposal," *Signs: Journal of Women in Culture and Society.* 10 (1984): 126, 131.

LIBERTY AND PORNOGRAPHY

Ronald Dworkin

...[Isaiah] Berlin's lecture, "Two Concepts of Liberty,"...provoked immediate, continuing, heated, and mainly illuminating controversy.... Its
scope and erudition, its historical sweep and evident contemporary force,
its sheer interest, made political ideas suddenly seem exciting and fun. Its
main polemical message—that it is fatally dangerous for philosophers to
ignore either the complexity or the power of those ideas—was both compelling and overdue. But chiefly, or so I think, its importance lay in the
force of its central argument. For though Berlin began by conceding to the
disdaining philosophers that political philosophy could not match logic
or the philosophy of language as a theater for "radical discoveries," in
which "talent for minute analyses is likely to be rewarded," he continued
by analyzing subtle distinctions that, as it happens, are even more important now, in the Western democracies at least, than when he first called
our attention to them.

I must try to describe two central features of his argument, though for
reasons of space I shall have to leave out much that is important to them.
The first is the celebrated distinction described in the lecture's title:
between two (closely allied) senses of liberty. Negative liberty (as Berlin
came later to restate it) means not being obstructed by others in doing
what one might wish to do. We count some negative liberties—like the
freedom to speak our minds without censorship—as very important and

---

others—like driving at very fast speeds—as trivial. But they are both instances of negative freedom, and though a state may be justified in imposing speed limits, for example, on grounds of safety and convenience, that is nevertheless an instance of restricting negative liberty.

Positive liberty, on the other hand, is the power to control or participate in public decisions, including the decision of how far to curtail negative liberty. In an ideal democracy—whatever that is—the people govern themselves. Each is master to the same degree, and positive liberty is secured for all.

In his inaugural lecture Berlin described the historical corruption of the idea of positive liberty, a corruption that began in the idea that someone's true liberty lies in control by his rational self rather than his empirical self, that is, in control that aims at securing goals other than those the person himself recognizes. Freedom, on that conception, is possible only when people are governed, ruthlessly if necessary, by rulers who know their true, metaphysical will. Only then are people truly free, albeit against their will. That deeply confused and dangerous, but nevertheless potent, chain of argument had in many parts of the world turned positive liberty into the most terrible tyranny. Of course, by calling attention to this corruption of positive liberty, Berlin did not mean that negative liberty was an unalloyed blessing, and should be protected in all its forms in all circumstances at all costs. He said later that, on the contrary, the vices of excessive and indiscriminate negative liberty were so evident, particularly in the form of savage economic inequality, that he had not thought it necessary to describe them in much detail.

The second feature of Berlin's argument that I have in mind is a theme repeated throughout his writing on political topics. He insists on the complexity of political value, and the fallacy of supposing that all the political virtues that are attractive in themselves can be realized in a single political structure. The ancient Platonic ideal of some master accommodation of all attractive virtues and goals, combined in institutions satisfying each in the right proportion and sacrificing none, is in Berlin's view, for all its imaginative power and historical influence, only a seductive myth. He later summed this up:

> One freedom may abort another; one freedom may obstruct or fail to create conditions which make other freedoms, or a larger degree of freedom, or freedom for more persons, possible; positive and negative freedom may collide; the freedom of the individual or the group may not be fully compatible with a full degree of participation in a common life, with its demands for cooperation, solidarity, fraternity. But beyond all these there is an acuter issue: the paramount need to satisfy the claims of other, no less ultimate, values: justice, happiness, love, the realization of capacities to create new things and experiences and ideas, the dis-

covery of the truth. Nothing is gained by identifying freedom proper, in either of its senses, with these values, or with the conditions of freedom, or by confounding types of freedom with one another.[1]

Berlin's warnings about conflating positive and negative liberty, and liberty itself, with other values seemed, to students of political philosophy in the great Western democracies in the 1950s, to provide important lessons about authoritarian regimes in other times and places. Though cherished liberties were very much under attack in both America and Britain in that decade, the attack was not grounded in or defended through either form of confusion. The enemies of negative liberty were powerful, but they were also crude and undisguised. Joseph McCarthy and his allies did not rely on any Kantian or Hegelian or Marxist concept of metaphysical selves to justify censorship or blacklists. They distinguished liberty not from itself, but from security; they claimed that too much free speech made us vulnerable to spies and intellectual saboteurs, and ultimately to conquest.

In both Britain and America, in spite of limited reforms, the state still sought to enforce conventional sexual morality about pornography, contraception, prostitution, and homosexuality. Conservatives who defended these invasions of negative liberty appealed not to some higher or different sense of freedom, however, but to values that were plainly distinct from, and in conflict with, freedom: religion, true morality, and traditional and proper family values. The wars over liberty were fought, or so it seemed, by clearly divided armies. Liberals were for liberty, except, in some circumstances, for the negative liberty of economic entrepreneurs. Conservatives were for that liberty, but against other forms when these collided with security or their view of decency and morality.

But now the political maps have radically changed, and some forms of negative liberty have acquired new opponents. Both in America and in Britain, though in different ways, conflicts over race and gender have transformed old alliances and divisions. Speech that expresses racial hatred or a degrading attitude toward women has come to seem intolerable to many people whose convictions are otherwise traditionally liberal. It is hardly surprising that they should try to reduce the conflict between their old liberal ideals and their new acceptance of censorship by adopting some new definition of what liberty, properly understood, really is. It is hardly surprising, but the result is dangerous confusion, and Berlin's warnings, framed with different problems in mind, are directly in point.

I shall try to illustrate that point with a single example: a lawsuit arising out of the attempt by certain feminist groups in America to outlaw what they consider a particularly objectionable form of pornography. I select this example not because pornography is more important or dangerous or objectionable than racist invective or other highly distasteful kinds of speech, but because the debate over pornography has been the subject of the fullest and most comprehensive scholarly discussion.

Through the efforts of Catharine MacKinnon, a professor of law at the University of Michigan, and other prominent feminists, Indianapolis, Indiana, enacted an antipornography ordinance. The ordinance defined pornography as "the graphic sexually explicit subordination of women, whether in pictures or words..." and it specified, as among pornographic materials falling within that definition, those that present women as enjoying pain or humiliation or rape, or as degraded or tortured, or as filthy, bruised or bleeding, or in postures of servility or submission or display. It included no exception for literary or artistic value, and opponents claimed that applied literally it would outlaw James Joyce's *Ulysses*, John Cleland's *Memoirs of a Woman of Pleasure*, various works of D.H. Lawrence, and even Yeats's "Leda and the Swan." But the groups who sponsored the ordinance were anxious to establish that their objection was not to obscenity or indecency as such, but to the consequences for women of a particular kind of pornography, and they presumably thought that an exception for artistic value would undermine that claim.[2]

The ordinance did not simply regulate the display of pornography so defined, or restrict its sale or distribution to particular areas, or guard against the exhibition of pornography to children. Regulation for those purposes does restrain negative liberty, but if reasonable, it does so in a way compatible with free speech. Zoning and display regulations may make pornography more expensive or inconvenient to obtain, but they do not offend the principle that no one must be prevented from publishing or reading what he or she wishes on the ground that its content is immoral or offensive.[3] The Indianapolis ordinance, on the other hand, prohibited any "production, sale, exhibition, or distribution" whatever of the material it defined as pornographic.

Publishers and members of the public who claimed a desire to read the banned material arranged a prompt constitutional challenge. The federal district court held that the ordinance was unconstitutional because it violated the First Amendment to the United States Constitution, which guarantees the negative liberty of free speech. The Circuit Court for the Seventh Circuit upheld the district court's decisions, and the Supreme Court of the United States declined to review that holding. The Circuit Court's decision, in an opinion by Judge Easterbrook, noticed that the ordinance did not outlaw obscene or indecent material generally but only material reflecting the opinion that women are submissive, or enjoy being dominated, or should be treated as if they did. Easterbrook said that the central point of the First Amendment was exactly to protect speech from content-based regulation of that sort. Censorship may on some occasions be permitted if it aims to prohibit directly dangerous speech—crying fire in a crowded theater or inciting a crowd to violence, for example—or speech particularly and unnecessarily inconvenient—broadcasting from sound trucks patrolling residential streets at night, for instance. But nothing must be censored, Easterbrook wrote, because the message it seeks to deliver is a bad one, or because it expresses ideas that should not be heard at all.

It is by no means universally agreed that censorship should never be based on content. The British Race Relations Act, for example, forbids speech of racial hatred, not only when it is likely to lead to violence, but generally, on the grounds that members of minority races should be protected from racial insults. In America, however, it is a fixed principle of constitutional law that such regulation is unconstitutional unless some compelling necessity, not just official or majority disapproval of the message, requires it. Pornography is often grotesquely offensive; it is insulting, not only to women but to men as well. But we cannot consider that a sufficient reason for banning it without destroying the principle that the speech we hate is as much entitled to protection as any other. The essence of negative liberty is freedom to offend, and that applies to the tawdry as well as the heroic.

Lawyers who defend the Indianapolis ordinance argue that society does have a further justification for outlawing pornography: that it causes great harm as well as offense to women. But their arguments mix together claims about different types or kinds of harm, and it is necessary to distinguish these. They argue, first, that some forms of pornography significantly increase the danger that women will be raped or physically assaulted. If that were true, and the danger were clear and present, then it would indeed justify censorship of those forms, unless less stringent methods of control, such as restricting pornography's audience, would be feasible, appropriate, and effective. In fact, however, though there is some evidence that exposure to pornography weakens people's critical attitudes toward sexual violence, there is no persuasive evidence that it causes more actual incidents of assault. ...

Some feminist groups argue, however, that pornography causes not just physical violence, but a more general and endemic subordination of women. In that way, they say, pornography makes for inequality. But even if it could be shown, as a matter of causal connection, that pornography is in part responsible for the economic structure in which few women attain top jobs or equal pay for the same work, that would not justify censorship under the Constitution. It would plainly be unconstitutional to ban speech directly *advocating* that women occupy inferior roles, or none at all in commerce and the professions, even if that speech fell on willing male ears and achieved its goals. So it cannot be a reason for banning pornography that it contributes to an unequal economic or social structure, even if we think that it does.

But the most imaginative feminist literature for censorship makes a further and different argument: that negative liberty for pornographers conflicts not just with equality but with positive liberty as well, because pornography leads to women's *political* as well as economic or social subordination. Of course pornography does not take the vote from women, or somehow make their votes count less. But it produces a climate, according to this argument, in which women cannot have genuine political power or authority because they are perceived and understood unauthentically—that is, they are made over by male fantasy into people very different from, and of much less consequence than, the people they really are. Consider, for example, these remarks from the work of the principal sponsor of the Indianapolis ordinance. "[Pornography] institutionalizes the sexuality of male supremacy, fusing the eroticization of dominance and submission with the social construction of male and female. . . . Men treat women as who they see women as being. Pornography constructs who that is. Men's power over women means that the way men see women defines who women can be."[4]

Pornography, on this view, denies the positive liberty of women; it denies them the right to be their own masters by recreating them, for politics and society, in the shapes of male fantasy. That is a powerful argument, even in constitutional terms, because it asserts a conflict not just between liberty and equality but within liberty itself, that is, a conflict that cannot be resolved simply on the ground that liberty must be sovereign. What shall we make of the argument understood that way? We must notice, first, that it remains a causal argument. It claims not that pornography is a consequence or symptom or symbol of how the identity of women has been reconstructed by men, but an important cause or vehicle of that reconstruction.

That seems strikingly implausible. Sadistic pornography is revolting, but it is not in general circulation, except for its milder, soft-porn manifestations. It seems unlikely that it has remotely the influence over how women's sexuality or character or talents are conceived by men, and indeed by women, that commercial advertising and soap operas have. Television and other parts of popular culture use sexual display and sexual innuendo to sell virtually everything, and they often show women as experts in domestic detail and unreasoned intuition and nothing else. The images they create are subtle and ubiquitous, and it would not be surprising to learn, through whatever research might establish this, that they indeed do great damage to the way women are understood and allowed to be influential in politics. Sadistic pornography, though much more offensive and disturbing, is greatly overshadowed by these dismal cultural influences as a causal force.

Judge Easterbrook's opinion for the Seventh Circuit assumed, for the sake of argument, however, that pornography did have the consequences the defenders of the ordinance claimed. He said that the argument never-theless failed because the point of free speech is precisely to allow ideas to have whatever consequences follow from their dissemination, including undesirable consequences for positive liberty. "Under the First Amend-ment," he said, "the government must leave to the people the evaluation of ideas. Bald or subtle, an idea is as powerful as the audience allows it to be.... [The assumed result] simply demonstrates the power of pornography as speech. All of these unhappy effects depend on mental intermediation."

That is right as a matter of American constitutional law. The Ku Klux Klan and the American Nazi Party are allowed to propagate their ideas in America, and the British Race Relations Act, so far as it forbids abstract speech of racial hatred, would be unconstitutional in the U.S. But does the American attitude represent the kind of Platonic absolutism Berlin warned against? No, because there is an important difference between the idea he thinks absurd, that all ideals attractive in themselves can be per-fectly reconciled within a single utopian political order, and the different idea he thought essential, that we must, as individuals and nations, choose, among possible combinations of ideals, a coherent, even though inevitably and regrettably limited, set of these to define our own individ-ual or national way of life. Freedom of speech, conceived and protected as a fundamental negative liberty, is the core of the choice modern democra-cies have made, a choice we must now honor in finding our own ways to combat the shaming inequalities women still suffer.

This reply depends, however, on seeing the alleged conflict within lib-erty as a conflict between the negative and positive senses of that virtue. We must consider yet another argument which, if successful, could not be met in the same way, because it claims that pornography presents a con-flict within the negative liberty of speech itself. Berlin said that the charac-ter, at least, of negative liberty was reasonably clear, that although excessive claims of negative liberty were dangerous, they could at least always be seen for what they were. But the argument I have in mind, which has been offered by, among others, Frank Michelman of the Har-vard Law School, expands the idea of negative liberty in an unanticipated way. He argues that some speech, including pornography, may be itself "silencing," so that its effect is to prevent other people from exercising their negative freedom to speak.

Of course it is fully recognized in First Amendment jurisprudence that some speech has the effect of silencing others. Government must indeed balance negative liberties when it prevents heckling or other demonstra-tive speech designed to stop others from speaking or being heard. But Michelman has something different in mind. He says that a woman's speech may be silenced not just by noise intended to drown her out but also by argument and images that change her audience's perceptions of her character, needs, desires, and standing, and also, perhaps, change her own sense of who she is and what she wants. Speech with that consequence silences her, Michelman supposes, by making it impossible for her effectively to contribute to the process Judge Easterbrook said the First Amendment protected, the process through which ideas battle for the public's favor. "[It] is a highly plausible claim," Michelman writes, "[that] pornography [is] a cause of women's subordination and silencing.... It is a fair and obvious question why our society's openness to challenge does not need protection against repressive private as well as public action."[5]

He argues that if our commitment to negative freedom of speech is consequentialist—if we want free speech in order to have a society in which no idea is barred from entry—then we must censor some ideas in order to make entry possible for other ones. He protests that the distinction that American constitutional law makes between the suppression of ideas by the effect of public criminal law and by the consequences of private speech is arbitrary, and that a sound concern for openness would be equally worried about both forms of control. But the distinction the law makes is not between public and private power as such, but between negative liberty and other virtues, including positive liberty. It would indeed be contradictory for a constitution to prohibit official censorship while protecting the right of private citizens physically to prevent other citizens from publishing or broadcasting specified ideas. That would allow private citizens to violate the negative liberty of other citizens by preventing them from saying what they wish.

But there is no contradiction in insisting that every idea must be allowed to be heard, even those whose consequence is that other ideas will be misunderstood, or given little consideration, or even not be spoken at all because those who might speak them are not in control of their own public identities and therefore cannot be understood as they wish to be. They are very bad consequences, and they must be resisted by whatever means our Constitution permits. But acts that have these consequences do not, for that reason, deprive others of their negative liberty to speak and the distinction, as Berlin insisted, is very far from arbitrary or inconsequential.

It is of course understandable why Michelman and others should want to expand the idea of negative liberty in the way they try to do. Only by characterizing certain ideas as themselves "silencing" ideas—only by supposing that censoring pornography is the same thing as stopping people from drowning out other speakers—can they hope to justify censorship within the constitutional scheme that assigns a preeminent place to free speech. But the assimilation is nevertheless a confusion, exactly the kind of confusion Berlin warned against in his original lecture, because it obscures the true political choice that must be made. I return to Berlin's lecture, which put the point with that striking combination of clarity and sweep I have been celebrating:

I should be guilt-stricken, and rightly so, if I were not, in some circumstances, ready to make [some] sacrifice [of freedom]. But a sacrifice is not an increase in what is being sacrificed, namely freedom, however great the moral need or the compensation for it. Everything is what it is: liberty is liberty, not equality or fairness or justice or culture, or human happiness or a quiet conscience.

NOTES

[1] Isaiah Berlin, *Four Essays on Liberty* (Oxford University Press, 1968): lvi.

[2] MacKinnon explained that "if a woman is subjected, why should it matter that the work has other value?" See her article "Pornography, Civil Rights, and Speech," reprinted in this volume.

[3] See my article "Do We Have a Right to Pornography?" reprinted as Chapter 17 in my book *A Matter of Principle* (Harvard University Press, 1985).

[4] See MacKinnon's article in this volume.

[5] Frank Michelman, "Conceptions of Democracy in American Constitutional Argument: The Case of Pornography Regulation," *Tennessee Law Review*, 56 (1989): 303–304.

CHAPTER 4

Abortion

INTRODUCTION

Beginning in 1973, and extending for a period of nearly twenty years, women in the United States enjoyed an essentially no-questions-asked legal right to abortion during the first trimester of pregnancy. This right, affirmed by the Supreme Court in *Roe v. Wade*, was taken as an implication of the fundamental right to privacy, a right which, though never mentioned explicitly in the Constitution, was held, in *Griswold v. Connecticut*, to be encompassed by several constitutional guarantees. In acknowledging a right to abortion, the *Roe* court extended dramatically the range of individual choice in matters of reproduction. But the court never took the right to abortion to be absolute. States could justifiably restrict or prohibit second- and third-trimester abortions for compelling reasons regarding maternal health and safety and the protection of prenatal life. But because these concerns were taken to be significantly less weighty during the first trimester, wherein abortion procedures are exceptionally safe and fetuses are yet another trimester from viability, a pregnant woman's first-trimester right to terminate a pregnancy was protected from state interference.

Within only a few years and in certain states and municipalities, opponents of a right to abortion as found in *Roe* attempted to weaken or eliminate the right by placing legislative restrictions on its exercise. Examples of these restrictions include requirements of informed consent, spousal and parental notification and consent, and determinations of fetal viability. But not until 1989 (in *Webster v. Reproductive Health Services* [492 U.S. 490, 524]), with only three members of the seven-to-two majority in *Roe* remaining, did significant restrictions on the exercise of the right to abortion find favor with the Supreme Court. And by 1992, in *Planned Parenthood v. Casey*, even though the basic holding of *Roe*—that a woman's rights to privacy entails a right to abortion—was reaffirmed, the court found that Pennsylvania could require the following restrictions on the exercise of that right: a twenty-four-hour waiting period during which certain information about fetal development and abortion is provided, the consent of at least one parent (with a provision for judicial bypass) where the woman is a minor, and specific reporting requirements on abortion clinics. While spousal consent was found to unconstitutionally infringe upon the right to abortion, only those restrictions placing an "undue burden" on a women's choices would be rejected.

Leaving "undue burden" vaguely defined, the court opened previability abortions to legislative restrictions which could vary considerably from state to state and have far greater impact on the young and the poor. Such an inequitable distribution of a meaningful fundamental right seems plainly objectionable in terms of the fair and equal treatment of all women. But no matter the inequities and inconsistencies which characterize a post-*Casey* America, some believe that *any* legal right to abortion wholly lacks moral justification and thus ought to be eliminated. This belief, rooted in a commitment which the court consistently resisted—that fetuses are persons with rights and thus abortion is murder—has formed the ground for aggressive antiabortion activism, ranging from the obstruction of abortion clinics, to firebombings and the killing of clinic workers and physicians.

The abortion controversy has focused attention on the issue of who has which rights and how these rights ought to be interpreted and implemented as a matter of law. Moral philosophers have asked whether in fact fetuses are persons with a right to life and, if so, precisely what this actually implies. In her famous article, "A Defense of Abortion," Judith Jarvis Thomson grants, for the sake of argument, precisely what the court resisted: fetuses are persons with the right to life. Yet by exploiting a set of engaging but controversial analogies, Thomson denies that this right implies an additional fetal right always to be kept alive, especially if this requires the nonconsensual use of woman's body. One can imagine moral grounds for a fetal right to dwell within a woman's womb, and a woman might have a moral duty to bear a fetus to term if she consented to her pregnancy. But unless this consent is free and informed, a woman has no duty that the fetus enjoy the use of her womb. Absent consent, abortion is morally permissible, though certainly not required. So if Thomson's argument is correct, granting fetuses the right to life does not provide adequate grounds for denying women the right to abortion. That a fetus has a right to life does not mean that all abortions are unjust killings. And any contrary position seems tantamount to denying women fundamental rights to their bodies, health, and privacy.

Mary Anne Warren denies that Thomson's analogy is morally apt. Except in cases of pregnancy due to rape, Warren contends that *if* one ascribes rights to fetuses, thereby including them in the moral community, then women have far greater duties to fetuses than Thomson allows. But given the ambiguities haunting the issue of whether simply engaging in consensual sex counts as grounds for duties to fetuses, Warren contends that only if fetuses are denied the status of beings with moral rights—"persons"—can women lay claim to extensive abortion rights. But Warren provides criteria for inclusion in the moral category of personhood which fetuses cannot meet. While fetuses are genetically human, they are not persons in the moral sense. Thus on her view, because fetuses do not count as persons at all, laws restricting or denying access to abortion violate women's moral and constitutional rights, and are thus wholly unjustified.

But are Warren's criteria for moral personhood reasonable? And perhaps more troublesome still, is the moral permissibility of abortion reducible solely to the issue of whether fetuses have a right to life to which pregnant women must almost always yield? Don Marquis argues that abortion is indeed immoral, as immoral as killing any ordinary mature innocent human being, but his argument for this does not rely on appeals to a fetal right to life. Rather, Marquis contends that because abortion denies to fetuses the value of their future, "a future-like-ours," and because such a denial ultimately constitutes what is wrong with killing *per se*, then abortion is generally wrong. Of course Marquis' belief that fetuses possess a "future-like-ours" in the morally relevant sense is quite contentious, as is his omitting consideration of whether and to what extent pregnant women must endure a pregnancy, no matter how it occurred, to protect such a future. But Marquis' emphasis on the moral value of fetal life forces the question of whether the abortion debate is best resolved when the moral value of fetal life is taken to overpower women's reproductive rights.

Drawing on recent developments in feminist ethics, Susan Sherwin contends that, in taking the morality of abortion to be a kind of winner-take-all contest between isolated individuals (fetuses, women), critical components of women's real-world lives, choices, and moral intuitions are grotesquely neglected. Sherwin acknowledges the moral value of fetuses, but she understands this value in the context of the dependent relationship of fetuses to women, for whom the right to obtain an abortion constitutes an indispensable element of sexual and political liberation. Interestingly enough, this view is affirmed by Justice Blackmun in his dissent in *Casey*. Now, Sherwin admits that, while recognizing women as full, responsible, moral agents requires recognizing the right to choose, not every woman's choice to obtain an abortion is beyond moral scrutiny. But how can this be? Can one contend that, as a matter of public policy, the private choice to obtain an abortion must be both a legally protected and socially supported right even though such a choice can be morally wrong?

Daniel Callahan addresses this question by raising objections to the moral assumptions of both those favoring and those opposing legal rights to abortion. Callahan also agrees that fetal life is morally valuable, but denies that this value trumps the value of individual choice. Thus while he believes it would be a grave error to overturn the basic holding of *Roe v. Wade*, Callahan contends that it would be an equally grave error to eliminate public debate on whether and in what cases individual choices to obtain an abortion are morally tolerable. Thus, if Callahan is correct, endorsing a legally protected right to obtain an abortion can be taken as logically distinct from endorsing morally each and every choice which this right would protect.

SUGGESTED READINGS

Dan Drucker, *Abortion Decisions of the Supreme Court, 1973 through 1989: A Comprehensive Review with Historical Commentary* (Jefferson, NC: McFarland and Company, 1990).

Ronald Dworkin, *Life's Dominion: An Argument About Abortion, Euthanasia and Individual Freedom* (New York: Alfred Knopf, 1993).

Louis P. Pojman and Francis J. Beckwith, *The Abortion Controversy*, (Boston, MA: Jones and Bartlett Publishers, 1994).

Laurence H. Tribe, *Abortion: The Clash of Absolutes* (New York: W. W. Norton & Company, 1992).

GRISWOLD v. CONNECTICUT

381 U.S. 479 (1965)
Argued March 29–30, 1965,
Decided June 7, 1965

Mr. Justice Douglas delivered the opinion of the Court.

Appellant Griswold is Executive Director of the Planned Parenthood League of Connecticut. Appellant Buxton is a licensed physician and a professor at the Yale Medical School who served as Medical Director for the League at its Center in New Haven—a center open and operating from November 1 to November 10, 1961, when appellants were arrested.

They gave information, instruction, and medical advice to married persons as to the means of preventing conception. They examined the wife and prescribed the best contraceptive device or material for her use. Fees were usually charged, although some couples were serviced free.

The statutes whose constitutionality is involved in this appeal are §§ 53–32 and 54–196 of the General Statutes of Connecticut (1958 rev.). The former provides:

> Any person who uses any drug, medicinal article or instrument for the purpose of preventing conception shall be fined not less than fifty dollars or imprisoned not less than sixty days nor more than one year or be both fined and imprisoned.

Section 54–196 provides:

Any person who assists, abets, counsels, causes, hires or commands another to commit any offense may be prosecuted and punished as if he were the principal offender.

The appellants were found guilty as accessories and fined $100 each, against the claim that the accessory statute as so applied violated the Fourteenth Amendment. The Appellate Division of the Circuit Court affirmed. The Supreme Court of Errors affirmed that judgment....

Coming to the merits, we are met with a wide range of questions that implicate the Due Process Clause of the Fourteenth Amendment.... We do not sit as a super-legislature to determine the wisdom, need, and propriety of laws that touch economic problems, business affairs, or social conditions. This law, however, operates directly on an intimate relation of husband and wife and their physician's role in one aspect of that relation.

The association of people is not mentioned in the Constitution nor in the Bill of Rights. The right to educate a child in a school of the parents' choice—whether public or private or parochial—is also not mentioned. Nor is the right to study any particular subject or any foreign language. Yet the First Amendment has been construed to include certain of those rights....

In other words, the State may... not, consistently with the spirit of the First Amendment, contract the spectrum of available knowledge. The right of freedom of speech and press includes not only the right to utter or to print, but the right to distribute, the right to receive, the right to read...and freedom of inquiry, freedom of thought, and freedom to teach...—indeed the freedom of the entire university community. Without those peripheral rights the specific rights would be less secure....

In *NAACP v. Alabama*, 357 U.S. 449, 462, we protected the "freedom to associate and privacy in one's associations," noting that freedom of association was a peripheral First Amendment right. Disclosure of membership lists of a constitutionally valid association, we held, was invalid "as entailing the likelihood of a substantial restraint upon the exercise by petitioner's members of their right to freedom of association." *Ibid*. In other words, the First Amendment has a penumbra where privacy is protected from governmental intrusion....

The right of "association," like the right of belief,... is more than the right to attend a meeting; it includes the right to express one's attitudes or philosophies by membership in a group or by affiliation with it or by other lawful means. Association in that context is a form of expression of opinion; and while it is not expressly included in the First Amendment its existence is necessary in making the express guarantees fully meaningful.

...[S]pecific guarantees in the Bill of Rights have penumbras, formed by emanations from those guarantees that help give them life and substance.

See *Poe v. Ullman,* 367 U.S. 497, 516–522 (dissenting opinion). Various guarantees create zones of privacy. The right of association contained in the penumbra of the First Amendment is one, as we have seen. The Third Amendment in its prohibition against the quartering of soldiers "in any house" in time of peace without the consent of the owner is another facet of that privacy. The Fourth Amendment explicitly affirms the "right of the people to be secure in their persons, houses, papers, and effects, against unreasonable searches and seizures." The Fifth Amendment in its Self-Incrimination Clause enables the citizen to create a zone of privacy which government may not force him to surrender to his detriment. The Ninth Amendment provides: "The enumeration in the Constitution, of certain rights, shall not be construed to deny or disparage others retained by the people."...

The present case, then, concerns a relationship lying within the zone of privacy created by several fundamental constitutional guarantees. And it concerns a law which, in forbidding the use of contraceptives rather than regulating their manufacture or sale, seeks to achieve its goals by means having a maximum destructive impact upon that relationship. Such a law cannot stand in light of the familiar principle, so often applied by this Court, that a "governmental purpose to control or prevent activities constitutionally subject to state regulation may not be achieved by means which sweep unnecessarily broadly and thereby invade the area of protected freedoms." *NAACP v. Alabama,* 377 U.S. 288, 307. Would we allow the police to search the sacred precincts of marital bedrooms for telltale signs of the use of contraceptives? The very idea is repulsive to the notions of privacy surrounding the marriage relationship.

We deal with a right of privacy older than the Bill of Rights—older than our political parties, older than our school system. Marriage is a coming together for better or for worse, hopefully enduring, and intimate to the degree of being sacred. It is an association that promotes a way of life, not causes; a harmony in living, not political faiths; a bilateral loyalty, not commercial or social projects. Yet it is an association for as noble a purpose as any involved in our prior decisions.

Reversed.

Mr. Justice Goldberg, whom The Chief Justice and Mr. Justice Brennan join, concurring.

I agree with the Court that Connecticut's birth control law unconstitutionally intrudes upon the right of marital privacy, and I join in its opinion and judgment.... In reaching the conclusion that the right of marital privacy is protected, as being within the protected penumbra of specific guarantees of the Bill of Rights, the Court refers to the Ninth Amendment,... I add these words to emphasize the relevance of that Amendment to the Court's holding....

The Court stated many years ago that the Due Process Clause protects those liberties that are "so rooted in the traditions and conscience of our people as to be ranked as fundamental." *Snyder v. Massachusetts*, 291 U.S. 97....

This Court, in a series of decisions, has held that the Fourteenth Amendment absorbs and applies to the States those specifics of the first eight amendments which express fundamental personal rights. The language and history of the Ninth Amendment reveal that the Framers of the Constitution believed that there are additional fundamental rights, protected from governmental infringement, which exist alongside those fundamental rights specifically mentioned in the first eight constitutional amendments.

The Ninth Amendment reads, "The enumeration in the Constitution, of certain rights, shall not be construed to deny or disparage others retained by the people." The Amendment is almost entirely the work of James Madison. It was introduced in Congress by him and passed the House and Senate with little or no debate and virtually no change in language. It was proffered to quiet expressed fears that a bill of specifically enumerated rights could not be sufficiently broad to cover all essential rights and that the specific mention of certain rights would be interpreted as a denial that others were protected....

In presenting the proposed Amendment, Madison said:

It has been objected also against a bill of rights, that, by enumerating particular exceptions to the grant of power, it would disparage those rights which were not placed in that enumeration; and it might follow by implication, that those rights which were not singled out, were intended to be assigned into the hands of the General Government, and were consequently insecure. This is one of the most plausible arguments I have ever heard urged against the admission of a bill of rights into this system; but, I conceive, that it may be guarded against. I have attempted it, as gentlemen may see by turning to the last clause of the fourth resolution [the Ninth Amendment]." I Annals of Congress 439 (Gales and Seaton ed. 1834)....

The Ninth Amendment to the Constitution may be regarded by some as a recent discovery and may be forgotten by others, but since 1791 it has been a basic part of the Constitution which we are sworn to uphold. To hold that a right so basic and fundamental and so deep-rooted in our society as the right of privacy in marriage may be infringed because that right is not guaranteed in so many words by the first eight amendments to the Constitution is to ignore the Ninth Amendment and to give it no effect whatsoever. Moreover, a judicial construction that this fundamental right is not protected by the Constitution because it is not mentioned in explicit terms by one of the first eight amendments or elsewhere in the Constitution would violate the Ninth Amendment, which specifically states that "the enumeration in the Constitution, of certain rights, shall not be *construed* to deny or disparage others retained by the people." (Emphasis added.)....

In determining which rights are fundamental, judges are not left at large to decide cases in light of their personal and private notions. Rather, they must look to the "traditions and [collective] conscience of our people" to determine whether a principle is "so rooted [there]...as to be ranked as fundamental." *Snyder v. Massachusetts*, 291 U.S. 97, 105. The inquiry is whether a right involved "is of such a character that it cannot be denied without violating those 'fundamental principles of liberty and justice which lie at the base of all our civil and political institutions'...." *Powell v. Alabama*, 287 U.S. 45, 67. "Liberty" also "gains content from the emanations of...specific [constitutional] guarantees" and "from experience with the requirements of a free society." *Poe v. Ullman*, 367 U.S. 497, 517 (dissenting opinion of Mr. Justice Douglas)....

Although the Constitution does not speak in so many words of the right of privacy in marriage, I cannot believe that it offers these fundamental rights no protection. The fact that no particular provision of the Constitution explicitly forbids the State from disrupting the traditional relation of the family—a relation as old and as fundamental as our entire civilization—surely does not show that the Government was meant to have the power to do so. Rather, as the Ninth Amendment expressly recognizes, there are fundamental personal rights such as this one, which are protected from abridgment by the Government though not specifically mentioned in the Constitution.

My Brother Stewart, while characterizing the Connecticut birth control law as "an uncommonly silly law," would nevertheless let it stand on the ground that it is not for the courts to "'substitute their social and economic beliefs for the judgment of legislative bodies, who are elected to pass laws.'" Elsewhere, I have stated that "while I quite agree with Mr. Justice Brandeis that...'a...State may...serve as a laboratory; and try novel social and economic experiments,' *New State Ice Co. v. Liebmann*, 285 U.S. 262, 280, 311 (dissenting opinion), I do not believe that this includes the power to experiment with the fundamental liberties of citizens...." ...The vice of the dissenters' views is that it would permit such experimentation by the States in the area of the fundamental personal rights of its citizens. I cannot agree that the Constitution grants such power either to the States or to the Federal Government.

The logic of the dissents would sanction federal or state legislation that seems to me even more plainly unconstitutional than the statute before us. Surely the Government, absent a showing of a compelling subordinating state interest, could not decree that all husbands and wives must be sterilized after two children have been born to them. Yet by their reasoning such an invasion of marital privacy would not be subject to constitutional challenge because, while it might be "silly," no provision of the Constitution specifically prevents the Government from curtailing the marital right to bear children and raise a family. While it may shock some of my Brethren that the Court today holds that the Constitution protects the right of marital privacy, in my view it is far more shocking to believe that the personal liberty guaranteed by the Constitution does not include protection against such totalitarian limitation of family size, which is at complete variance with our constitutional concepts. Yet, if upon a showing of a slender basis of rationality, a law outlawing voluntary birth control by married persons is valid, then, by the same reasoning, a law requiring compulsory birth control also would seem to be valid. In my view, however, both types of law would unjustifiably intrude upon rights of marital privacy which are constitutionally protected....

Finally, it should be said of the Court's holding today that it in no way interferes with a State's proper regulation of sexual promiscuity or misconduct. As my Brother Harlan so well stated in his dissenting opinion in *Poe v. Ullman, supra,* at 553.

> Adultery, homosexuality and the like are sexual intimacies which the State forbids...but the intimacy of husband and wife is necessarily an essential and accepted feature of the institution of marriage, an institution which the State not only must allow, but which always and in every age it has fostered and protected. It is one thing when the State exerts its power either to forbid extra-marital sexuality...or to say who may marry, but it is quite another when, having acknowledged a marriage and the intimacies inherent in it, it undertakes to regulate by means of the criminal law the details of that intimacy.

In sum, I believe that the right of privacy in the marital relation is fundamental and basic—a personal right "retained by the people" within the meaning of the Ninth Amendment. Connecticut cannot constitutionally abridge this fundamental right, which is protected by the Fourteenth Amendment from infringement by the States. I agree with the Court that petitioners' convictions must therefore be reversed....

Dissent: Mr. Justice Black, with whom Mr. Justice Stewart joins, dissenting.

I agree with my Brother Stewart's dissenting opinion. And like him I do not to any extent whatever base my view that this Connecticut law is constitutional on a belief that the law is wise or that its policy is a good one. In order that there may be no room at all to doubt why I vote as I do, I feel constrained to add that the law is every bit as offensive to me as it is to my

Brethren of the majority and my Brothers Harlan, White and Goldberg who, reciting reasons why it is offensive to them, hold it unconstitutional....

Had the doctor defendant here, or even the nondoctor defendant, been convicted for doing nothing more than expressing opinions to persons coming to the clinic that certain contraceptive devices, medicines or practices would do them good and would be desirable, or for telling people how devices could be used, I can think of no reasons at this time why their expressions of views would not be protected by the First and Fourteenth Amendments, which guarantee freedom of speech.... But speech is one thing; conduct and physical activities are quite another.... The two defendants here were active participants in an organization which gave physical examinations to women, advised them what kind of contraceptive devices or medicines would most likely be satisfactory for them, and then supplied the devices themselves, all for a graduated scale of fees, based on the family income. Thus these defendants admittedly engaged with others in a planned course of conduct to help people violate the Connecticut law. Merely because some speech was used in carrying on that conduct—just as in ordinary life some speech accompanies most kinds of conduct—we are not in my view justified in holding that the First Amendment forbids the State to punish their conduct. Strongly as I desire to protect all First Amendment freedoms, I am unable to stretch the Amendment so as to afford protection to the conduct of these defendants in violating the Connecticut law....

One of the most effective ways of diluting or expanding a constitutionally guaranteed right is to substitute for the crucial word or words of a constitutional guarantee another word or words, more or less flexible and more or less restricted in meaning. This fact is well illustrated by the use of the term "right of privacy" as a comprehensive substitute for the Fourth Amendment's guarantee against "unreasonable searches and seizures." "Privacy" is a broad, abstract and ambiguous concept which can easily be shrunken in meaning but which can also, on the other hand, easily be interpreted as a constitutional ban against many things other than searches and seizures.... For these reasons I get nowhere in this case by talk about a constitutional "right of privacy" as an emanation from one or more constitutional provisions. I like my privacy as well as the next one, but I am nevertheless compelled to admit that government has a right to invade it unless prohibited by some specific constitutional provision. For these reasons I cannot agree with the Court's judgment and the reasons it gives for holding this Connecticut law unconstitutional....

My Brother Goldberg has adopted the recent discovery that the Ninth Amendment as well as the Due Process Clause can be used by this Court as authority to strike down all state legislation which this Court thinks violates "fundamental principles of liberty and justice," or is contrary to the "traditions and [collective] conscience of our people." He also states, without proof satisfactory to me, that in making decisions on this basis judges will not consider "their personal and private notions." One may ask how they can avoid considering them. Our Court certainly has no machinery with which to take a Gallup Poll. And the scientific miracles of this age have not yet produced a gadget which the Court can use to determine what traditions are rooted in the "[collective] conscience of our people." Moreover, one would certainly have to look far beyond the language of the Ninth Amendment to find that the Framers vested in this Court any such awesome veto powers over lawmaking, either by the States or by the Congress. Nor does anything in the history of the Amendment offer any support for such a shocking doctrine....

Mr. Justice Stewart, whom Mr. Justice Black joins, dissenting.

Since 1879 Connecticut has had on its books a law which forbids the use of contraceptives by anyone. I think this is an uncommonly silly law. As a practical matter, the law is obviously unenforceable, except in the oblique context of the present case. As a philosophical matter, I believe the use of contraceptives in the relationship of marriage should be left to personal and private choice, based upon each individual's moral, ethical, and religious beliefs. As a matter of social policy, I think professional counsel about methods of birth control should be available to all, so that each individual's choice can be meaningfully made. But we are not asked in this case to say whether we think this law is unwise, or even asinine. We are asked to hold that it violates the United States Constitution. And that I cannot do.

In the course of its opinion the Court refers to no less than six Amendments to the Constitution: the First, the Third, the Fourth, the Fifth, the Ninth, and the Fourteenth. But the Court does not say which of these Amendments, if any, it thinks is infringed by this Connecticut law.

We are told that the Due Process Clause of the Fourteenth Amendment is not, as such, the "guide" in this case. With that much I agree. There is no claim that this law, duly enacted by the Connecticut Legislature, is unconstitutionally vague. There is no claim that the appellants were denied any of the elements of procedural due process at their trial, so as to make their convictions constitutionally invalid.

As to the First, Third, Fourth, and Fifth Amendments, I can find nothing in any of them to invalidate this Connecticut law, even assuming that all those Amendments are fully applicable against the States. It has not even been argued that this is a law "respecting an establishment of religion, or prohibiting the free exercise thereof." And surely, unless the solemn process of constitutional adjudication is to descend to the level of a play on words, there is not involved here any abridgment of "the freedom of speech, or of the press; or the right of the people peaceably to assemble, and to petition the Government for a redress of grievances." No soldier has been quartered in any house. There has been no search, and no seizure. Nobody has been compelled to be a witness against himself....

What provision of the Constitution, then, does make this state law invalid? The Court says it is the right of privacy "created by several fundamental constitutional guarantees." With all deference, I can find no such general right of privacy in the Bill of Rights, in any other part of the Constitution, or in any case ever before decided by this Court....

...It is the essence of judicial duty to subordinate our own personal views, our own ideas of what legislation is wise and what is not. If, as I should surely hope, the law before us does not reflect the standards of the people of Connecticut, the people of Connecticut can freely exercise their true Ninth and Tenth Amendment rights to persuade their elected representatives to repeal it. That is the constitutional way to take this law off the books.

ROE v. WADE

410 U.S. 113 (1973)
Argued December 13, 1971,
Reargued October 11, 1972,
Decided January 22, 1973

A pregnant single woman (Roe) brought a class action challenging the constitutionality of the Texas criminal abortion laws, which proscribe procuring or attempting an abortion except on medical advice for the purpose of saving the mother's life. She also sought an injunction against their continued enforcement. A licensed physician (Hallford), who had two state abortion prosecutions pending against him, was permitted to intervene. A childless married couple (the Does), the wife not being pregnant, separately attacked the laws, basing alleged injury on the future possibilities of contraceptive failure, pregnancy, unpreparedness for parenthood, and impairment of the wife's health. A three-judge District Court, which consolidated the actions, held that Roe and Hallford, and members of their classes, had standing to sue and presented justiciable controversies. Ruling that declaratory, though not injunctive, relief was warranted, the court declared the abortion statutes void as vague and overbroadly infringing those plaintiffs' Ninth and Fourteenth Amendment rights. The court ruled the Does' complaint not justiciable. Appellants directly appealed to this Court on the injunctive rulings, and appellee cross-appealed from the District Court's grant of declaratory relief to Roe and Hallford.

Mr. Justice Blackmun delivered the opinion of the Court....

VI

It perhaps is not generally appreciated that the restrictive criminal abortion laws in effect in a majority of States today are of relatively recent vintage. Those laws, generally proscribing abortion or its attempt at any time during pregnancy except when necessary to preserve the pregnant woman's life, are not of ancient or even of common-law origin. Instead, they derive from statutory changes effected, for the most part, in the latter half of the nineteenth century....

The American law.

In this country, the law in effect in all but a few States until mid-nineteenth century was the pre-existing English common law. Connecticut, the first State to enact abortion legislation, adopted in 1821 that part of Lord Ellenborough's Act that related to a woman "quick with child."... The death penalty was not imposed. Abortion before quickening was made a crime in that State only in 1860.... In 1828, New York enacted legislation...that, in two respects, was to serve as a model for early anti-abortion statutes. First, while barring destruction of an unquickened fetus as well as a quick fetus, it made the former only a misdemeanor, but the latter second-degree manslaughter. Second, it incorporated a concept of therapeutic abortion by providing that an abortion was excused if it "shall have been necessary to preserve the life of such mother, or shall have been advised by two physicians to be necessary for such purpose." By 1840, when Texas had received the common law,...only eight American States had statutes dealing with abortion.... It was not until after the War Between the States that legislation began generally to replace the common law. Most of these initial statutes dealt severely with abortion after quickening but were lenient with it before quickening. Most punished attempts equally with completed abortions. While many statutes included the exception for an abortion thought by one or more physicians to be necessary to save the mother's life, that provision soon disappeared and the typical law required that the procedure actually be necessary for that purpose....

In the past several years, however, a trend toward liberalization of abortion statutes has resulted in adoption, by about one-third of the States, of less stringent laws, most of them patterned after the ALI Model Penal Code....

It is thus apparent that at common law, at the time of the adoption of our Constitution, and throughout the major portion of the nineteenth century, abortion was viewed with less disfavor than under most American statutes currently in effect. Phrasing it another way, a woman enjoyed a substantially broader right to terminate a pregnancy than she does in most States today. At least with respect to the early stage of pregnancy, and very possibly without such a limitation, the opportunity to make this choice was present in this country well into the nineteenth century....

The position of the American Medical Association.

The anti-abortion mood prevalent in this country in the late nineteenth century was shared by the medical profession. Indeed, the attitude of the profession may have played a significant role in the enactment of stringent criminal abortion legislation during that period....

Except for periodic condemnation of the criminal abortionist, no further formal AMA action took place until 1967. In that year, the Committee on Human Reproduction urged the adoption of a stated policy of opposition to induced abortion, except when there is "documented medical evidence" of a threat to the health or life of the mother, or that the child "may be born with incapacitating physical deformity or mental deficiency," or that a pregnancy "resulting from legally established statutory or forcible rape or incest may constitute a threat to the mental or physical health of the patient," two other physicians "chosen because of their recognized professional competence have examined the patient and have concurred in writing," and the procedure "is performed in a hospital accredited by the Joint Commission on Accreditation of Hospitals."...

In 1970, after the introduction of a variety of proposed resolutions, and of a report from its Board of Trustees, a reference committee noted "polarization of the medical profession on this controversial issue"; division among those who had testified; a difference of opinion among AMA councils and committees; "the remarkable shift in testimony" in six months, felt to be influenced "by the rapid changes in state laws and by the judicial decisions which tend to make abortion more freely available"; and a feeling "that this trend will continue."

VII

Three reasons have been advanced to explain historically the enactment of criminal abortion laws in the nineteenth century and to justify their continued existence.

It has been argued occasionally that these laws were the product of a Victorian social concern to discourage illicit sexual conduct. Texas, however, does not advance this justification in the present case, and it appears that no court or commentator has taken the argument seriously. The appellants and amici contend, moreover, that this is not a proper state purpose at all and suggest that, if it were, the Texas statutes are overbroad in protecting it since the law fails to distinguish between married and unwed mothers.

A second reason is concerned with abortion as a medical procedure. When most criminal abortion laws were first enacted, the procedure was a hazardous one for the woman. This was particularly true prior to the development of antisepsis. Antiseptic techniques, of course, were based on discoveries by Lister, Pasteur, and others first announced in 1867, but were not generally accepted and employed until about the turn of the century. Abortion mortality was high. Even after 1900, and perhaps until as late as the development of antibiotics in the 1940s, standard modern techniques such as dilation and curettage were not nearly so safe as they are today. Thus, it has been argued that a State's real concern in enacting a criminal abortion law was to protect the pregnant woman, that is, to restrain her from submitting to a procedure that placed her life in serious jeopardy.

Modern medical techniques have altered this situation. Appellants and various *amici* refer to medical data indicating that abortion in early pregnancy, that is, prior to the end of the first trimester, although not without its risk, is now relatively safe. Mortality rates for women undergoing early abortions, where the procedure is legal, appear to be as low as or lower than the rates for normal childbirth.... Consequently, any interest of the State in protecting the woman from an inherently hazardous procedure, except when it would be equally dangerous for her to forgo it, has largely disappeared. Of course, important state interests in the areas of health and medical standards do remain. The State has a legitimate interest in seeing to it that abortion, like any other medical procedure, is performed under circumstances that insure maximum safety for the patient. This interest obviously extends at least to the performing physician and his staff, to the facilities involved, to the availability of after-care, and to adequate provision for any complication or emergency that might arise. The prevalence of high mortality rates at illegal "abortion mills" strengthens, rather than weakens, the State's interest in regulating the conditions under which abortions are performed. Moreover, the risk to the woman increases as her pregnancy continues. Thus, the State retains a definite interest in protecting the woman's own health and safety when an abortion is proposed at a late stage of pregnancy.

The third reason is the State's interest—some phrase it in terms of duty—in protecting prenatal life. Some of the argument for this justification rests on the theory that a new human life is present from the moment of conception.... The State's interest and general obligation to protect life then extends, it is argued, to prenatal life. Only when the life of the pregnant mother herself is at stake, balanced against the life she carries within her, should the interest of the embryo or fetus not prevail. Logically, of course, a legitimate state interest in this area need not stand or fall on acceptance of the belief that life begins at conception or at some other point prior to live birth. In assessing the State's interest, recognition may be given to the less rigid claim that as long as at least potential life is involved, the State may assert interests beyond the protection of the pregnant woman alone....

VIII

The Constitution does not explicitly mention any right of privacy. In a line of decisions, however, going back perhaps as far as *Union Pacific R. Co. v. Botsford*, 141 U.S. 250, 251 (1891), the Court has recognized that a right of personal privacy, or a guarantee of certain areas or zones of privacy, does exist under the Constitution. In varying contexts, the Court or individual Justices have, indeed, found at least the roots of that right in the First Amendment, *Stanley v. Georgia*, 394 U.S. 557, 564 (1969); in the Fourth and Fifth Amendments, *Terry v. Ohio*, 392 U.S. 1, 8–9 (1968), *Katz v. United States*, 389 U.S. 347, 350 (1967),…in the penumbras of the Bill of Rights, *Griswold v. Connecticut*, 381 U.S., at 484–485; in the Ninth Amendment, id., at 486 (Goldberg, J., concurring); or in the concept of liberty guaranteed by the first section of the Fourteenth Amendment, see *Meyer v. Nebraska*, 262 U.S. 390, 399 (1923). These decisions make it clear that only personal rights that can be deemed "fundamental" or "implicit in the concept of ordered liberty," *Palko v. Connecticut*, 302 U.S. 319, 325 (1937), are included in this guarantee of personal privacy.…

This right of privacy, whether it be founded in the Fourteenth Amendment's concept of personal liberty and restrictions upon state action, as we feel it is, or, as the District Court determined, in the Ninth Amendment's reservation of rights to the people, is broad enough to encompass a woman's decision whether or not to terminate her pregnancy. The detriment that the State would impose upon the pregnant woman by denying this choice altogether is apparent. Specific and direct harm medically diagnosable even in early pregnancy may be involved. Maternity, or additional offspring, may force upon the woman a distressful life and future. Psychological harm may be imminent. Mental and physical health may be taxed by child care. There is also the distress, for all concerned, associated with the unwanted child, and there is the problem of bringing a child into a family already unable, psychologically and otherwise, to care for it. In other cases, as in this one, the additional difficulties and continuing stigma of unwed motherhood may be involved. All these are factors the woman and her responsible physician necessarily will consider in consultation.

On the basis of elements such as these, appellant and some amici argue that the woman's right is absolute and that she is entitled to terminate her pregnancy at whatever time, in whatever way, and for whatever reason she alone chooses. With this we do not agree.… The Court's decisions recognizing a right of privacy also acknowledge that some state regulation in areas protected by that right is appropriate. As noted above, a State may properly assert important interests in safeguarding health, in maintaining medical standards, and in protecting potential life. At some point in pregnancy, these respective interests become sufficiently compelling to sustain regulation of the factors that govern the abortion decision. The privacy right involved, therefore, cannot be said to be absolute. In fact, it is not clear to us that the claim asserted by some *amici* that one has an unlimited right to do with one's body as one pleases bears a close relationship to the right of privacy previously articulated in the Court's decisions. The Court has refused to recognize an unlimited right of this kind in the past....

We, therefore, conclude that the right of personal privacy includes the abortion decision, but that this right is not unqualified and must be considered against important state interests in regulation....

Although the results are divided, most of these courts have agreed that the right of privacy, however based, is broad enough to cover the abortion decision; that the right, nonetheless, is not absolute and is subject to some limitations; and that at some point the state interests as to protection of health, medical standards, and prenatal life, become dominant. We agree with this approach.

IX

A.

The appellee and certain *amici* argue that the fetus is a "person" within the language and meaning of the Fourteenth Amendment. In support of this, they outline at length and in detail the well-known facts of fetal development. If this suggestion of personhood is established, the appellant's case, of course, collapses, for the fetus' right to life would then be guaranteed specifically by the Amendment. The appellant conceded as much on reargument. On the other hand, the appellee conceded on reargument that no case could be cited that holds that a fetus is a person within the meaning of the Fourteenth Amendment.

The Constitution does not define "person" in so many words. Section 1 of the Fourteenth Amendment contains three references to "person." The first, in defining "citizens," speaks of "persons born or naturalized in the United States." The word also appears both in the Due Process Clause and in the Equal Protection Clause. "Person" is used in other places in the Constitution.... But in nearly all these instances, the use of the word is such that it has application only postnatally. None indicates, with any assurance, that it has any possible pre-natal application.[1]

All this, together with our observation, supra, that throughout the major portion of the nineteenth century prevailing legal abortion practices were far freer than they are today, persuades us that the word "person," as used in the Fourteenth Amendment, does not include the unborn....

This conclusion, however, does not of itself fully answer the contentions raised by Texas, and we pass on to other considerations.

B.

The pregnant woman cannot be isolated in her privacy. She carries an embryo and, later, a fetus, if one accepts the medical definitions of the developing young in the human uterus.... The situation therefore is inherently different from marital intimacy, or bedroom possession of obscene material, or marriage, or procreation, or education, with which *Eisenstadt* and *Griswold, Stanley, Loving, Skinner*, and *Pierce* and *Meyer* were respectively concerned. As we have intimated above, it is reasonable and appropriate for a State to decide that at some point in time another interest, that of health of the mother or that of potential human life, becomes significantly involved. The woman's privacy is no longer sole and any right of privacy she possesses must be measured accordingly.

Texas urges that, apart from the Fourteenth Amendment, life begins at conception and is present throughout pregnancy, and that, therefore, the State has a compelling interest in protecting that life from and after conception. We need not resolve the difficult question of when life begins. When those trained in the respective disciplines of medicine, philosophy, and theology are unable to arrive at any consensus, the judiciary, at this point in the development of man's knowledge, is not in a position to speculate as to the answer....

X

In view of all this, we do not agree that, by adopting one theory of life, Texas may override the rights of the pregnant woman that are at stake. We repeat, however, that the State does have an important and legitimate interest in preserving and protecting the health of the pregnant woman, whether she be a resident of the State or a nonresident who seeks medical consultation and treatment there, and that it has still another important and legitimate interest in protecting the potentiality of human life. These interests are separate and distinct. Each grows in substantiality as the woman approaches term and, at a point during pregnancy, each becomes "compelling."

With respect to the State's important and legitimate interest in the health of the mother, the "compelling" point, in the light of present medical knowledge, is at approximately the end of the first trimester. This is so because of the now-established medical fact.... that until the end of the first trimester, mortality in abortion may be less than mortality in normal childbirth. It follows that, from and after this point, a State may regulate the abortion procedure to the extent that the regulation reasonably relates to the preservation and protection of maternal health. Examples of permissible state regulation in this area are requirements as to the qualifications of the person who is to perform the abortion; as to the licensure of that person; as to the facility in which the procedure is to be performed, that is, whether it must be a hospital or may be a clinic or some other place of less-than-hospital status; as to the licensing of the facility; and the like.

This means, on the other hand, that, for the period of pregnancy prior to this "compelling" point, the attending physician, in consultation with his patient, is free to determine, without regulation by the State, that, in his medical judgment, the patient's pregnancy should be terminated. If that decision is reached, the judgment may be effectuated by an abortion free of interference by the State.

With respect to the State's important and legitimate interest in potential life, the "compelling" point is at viability. This is so because the fetus then presumably has the capability of meaningful life outside the mother's womb. State regulation protective of fetal life after viability thus has both logical and biological justifications. If the State is interested in protecting fetal life after viability, it may go so far as to proscribe abortion during that period, except when it is necessary to preserve the life or health of the mother.

Measured against these standards, Art. 1196 of the Texas Penal Code, in restricting legal abortions to those "procured or attempted by medical advice for the purpose of saving the life of the mother," sweeps too broadly. The statute makes no distinction between abortions performed early in pregnancy and those performed later, and it limits to a single reason, "saving" the mother's life, the legal justification for the procedure. The statute, therefore, cannot survive the constitutional attack made upon it here....

Dissent: Mr. Justice White
...With all due respect, I dissent. I find nothing in the language or history of the Constitution to support the Court's judgment. The Court simply fashions and announces a new constitutional right for pregnant mothers and, with scarcely any reasons or authority for its actions, invests that right with sufficient substance to override most existing abortion statutes....As an exercise of raw judicial power, the Court perhaps has authority to do what it does today; but in my view its judgment is an improvident and extravagant exercise of the power of judicial review that the Constitution extends to this Court....

Mr. Justice Rehnquist, dissenting.
The Court's opinion brings to the decision of this troubling question both extensive historical fact and a wealth of legal scholarship. While the opinion thus commands my respect, I find myself nonetheless in fundamental disagreement with those parts of it that invalidate the Texas statute in question, and therefore dissent....

...I have difficulty in concluding, as the Court does, that the right of "privacy" is involved in this case. Texas, by the statute here challenged, bars the performance of a medical abortion by a licensed physician on a plaintiff such as Roe. A transaction resulting in an operation such as this is not "private" in the ordinary usage of that word. Nor is the "privacy" that the Court finds here even a distant relative of the freedom from searches and seizures protected by the Fourth Amendment to the Constitution, which the Court has referred to as embodying a right to privacy. *Katz v. United States*, 389 U.S. 347 (1967).

If the Court means by the term "privacy" no more than that the claim of a person to be free from unwanted state regulation of consensual transactions may be a form of "liberty" protected by the Fourteenth Amendment, there is no doubt that similar claims have been upheld in our earlier decisions on the basis of that liberty. I agree with the statement of Mr. Justice Stewart in his concurring opinion that the "liberty," against deprivation of which without due process the Fourteenth Amendment protects, embraces more than the rights found in the Bill of Rights. But that liberty is not guaranteed absolutely against deprivation, only against deprivation without due process of law. The test traditionally applied in the area of social and economic legislation is whether or not a law such as that challenged has a rational relation to a valid state objective. *Williamson v. Lee Optical Co.*, 348 U.S. 483, 491 (1955). The Due Process Clause of the Fourteenth Amendment undoubtedly does place a limit, albeit a broad one, on legislative power to enact laws such as this. If the Texas statute were to prohibit an abortion even where the mother's life is in jeopardy, I have little doubt that such a statute would lack a rational relation to a valid state objective under the test stated in Williamson, *supra*. But the Court's sweeping invalidation of any restrictions on abortion during the first trimester is impossible to justify under that standard, and the conscious weighing of competing factors that the Court's opinion apparently substitutes for the established test is far more appropriate to a legislative judgment than to a judicial one....

The fact that a majority of the States reflecting, after all, the majority sentiment in those States, have had restrictions on abortions for at least a century is a strong indication, it seems to me, that the asserted right to an abortion is not "so rooted in the traditions and conscience of our people as to be ranked as fundamental," *Snyder v. Massachusetts*, 291 U.S. 97, 105 (1934). Even today, when society's views on abortion are changing, the very existence of the debate is evidence that the "right" to an abortion is not so universally accepted as the appellant would have us believe....

For all of the foregoing reasons, I respectfully dissent.

NOTE

[1]When Texas urges that a fetus is entitled to Fourteenth Amendment protection as a person, it faces a dilemma. Neither in Texas nor in any other State are all abortions prohibited. Despite broad proscription, an exception always exists. The exception contained in Art. 1196, for an abortion procured or attempted by medical advice for the purpose of saving the life of the mother, is typical. But if the fetus is a person who is not to be deprived of life without due process of law, and if the mother's condition is the sole determinant, does not the Texas exception appear out of line with the Amendment's command?... There are other inconsistencies between Fourteenth Amendment status and the typical abortion statute. ...[In] Texas the woman is not a principal or an accomplice with respect to an abortion upon her. If the fetus is a person, why is the woman not a principal or an accomplice? Further, the penalty for criminal abortion specified by Art. 1195 is significantly less than the maximum penalty for murder prescribed by Art. 1257 of the Texas Penal Code. If the fetus is a person, may the penalties be different?

PLANNED PARENTHOOD v. CASEY

112 S.Ct. 2791 (1992)
Argued, April 22, 1992,
Decided June 29, 1992

Justice O'Connor, Justice Kennedy, and Justice Souter announced the judgment of the Court....

I

Liberty finds no refuge in a jurisprudence of doubt. Yet nineteen years after our holding that the Constitution protects a woman's right to terminate her pregnancy in its early stages, *Roe v. Wade*, 410 U.S. 113 (1973), that definition of liberty is still questioned. Joining the respondents as amicus curiae, the United States, as it has done in five other cases in the last decade, again asks us to overrule Roe.

At issue in these cases are five provisions of the Pennsylvania Abortion Control Act of 1982 as amended in 1988 and 1989. 18 Pa. Cons. Stat. §§ 3203–3220 (1990).... The Act requires that a woman seeking an abortion give her informed consent prior to the abortion procedure, and specifies that she be provided with certain information at least 24 hours before the abortion is performed. §3205. For a minor to obtain an abortion, the Act requires the informed consent of one of her parents, but provides for a judicial bypass option if the minor does not wish to or cannot obtain a parent's consent. §3206. Another provision of the Act requires that, unless certain exceptions apply, a married woman seeking an abortion must sign a statement indicating that she has notified her husband of her intended abortion. §3209. The Act exempts compliance with these three requirements in the event of a "medical emergency," which is defined in §3203 of the Act.... In addition to the above provisions regulating the performance of abortions, the Act imposes certain reporting requirements on facilities that provide abortion services. §§3207(b), 3214(a), 3214(f).

Before any of these provisions took effect, the petitioners, who are five abortion clinics and one physician representing himself as well as a class of physicians who provide abortion services, brought this suit seeking declaratory and injunctive relief. Each provision was challenged as unconstitutional on its face. The District Court entered a preliminary injunction against the enforcement of the regulations, and, after a three-day bench trial, held all the provisions at issue here unconstitutional, entering a permanent injunction against Pennsylvania's enforcement of them. 744 F. Supp 1323 (ED Pa 1990)... The Court of Appeals for the Third Circuit affirmed in part and reversed in part, upholding all of the regulations except for the husband notification requirement. 947 F.2d 682 (1991)....

The Court of Appeals found it necessary to follow an elaborate course of reasoning even to identify the first premise to use to determine whether the statute enacted by Pennsylvania meets constitutional standards.... And at oral argument in this Court, the attorney for the parties challenging the statute took the position that none of the enactments can be upheld without overruling *Roe v. Wade*.... We disagree with that analysis; but we acknowledge that our decisions after *Roe* cast doubt upon the meaning and reach of its holding. Further, the Chief Justice admits that he would overrule the central holding of *Roe* and adopt the rational relationship test as the sole criterion of constitutionality.... State and federal courts as well as legislatures throughout the Union must have guidance as they seek to address this subject in conformance with the Constitution. Given these premises, we find it imperative to review once more the principles that define the rights of the woman and the legitimate authority of the State respecting the termination of pregnancies by abortion procedures.

After considering the fundamental constitutional questions resolved by *Roe*, principles of institutional integrity, and the rule of stare decisis, we are led to conclude this: the essential holding of *Roe v. Wade* should be retained and once again reaffirmed.

II

...It is a promise of the Constitution that there is a realm of personal liberty which the government may not enter. We have vindicated this principle before. Marriage is mentioned nowhere in the Bill of Rights and interracial marriage was illegal in most States in the nineteenth century, but the Court was no doubt correct in finding it to be an aspect of liberty protected against state interference by the substantive component of the Due Process Clause in *Loving v. Virginia*, 388 U.S. 1, 12 (1967).... In *Griswold*, we held that the Constitution does not permit a State to forbid a married couple to use contraceptives. That same freedom was later guaranteed, under the Equal Protection Clause, for unmarried couples. See *Eisenstadt v. Baird*, 405 U.S. 438 (1972). Constitutional protection was extended to the sale and distribution of contraceptives in *Carey v. Population Services International*, supra. It is settled now, as it was when the Court heard arguments in *Roe v. Wade*, that the Constitution places limits on a State's right to interfere with a person's most basic decisions about family and parenthood,...

Men and women of good conscience can disagree, and we suppose some always shall disagree, about the profound moral and spiritual implications of terminating a pregnancy, even in its earliest stage. Some of us as individuals find abortion offensive to our most basic principles of morality, but that cannot control our decision. Our obligation is to define the liberty of all, not to mandate our own moral code. The underlying constitutional issue is whether the State can resolve these philosophic questions in such a definitive way that a woman lacks all choice in the matter, except perhaps in those rare circumstances in which the pregnancy is itself a danger to her own life or health, or is the result of rape or incest.

Our law affords constitutional protection to personal decisions relating to marriage, procreation, contraception, family relationships, child rearing, and education.... These matters, involving the most intimate and personal choices a person may make in a lifetime, choices central to personal dignity and autonomy, are central to the liberty protected by the Fourteenth Amendment. At the heart of liberty is the right to define one's own concept of existence, of meaning, of the universe, and of the mystery of human life. Beliefs about these matters could not define the attributes of personhood were they formed under compulsion of the State.

These considerations begin our analysis of the woman's interest in terminating her pregnancy but cannot end it, for this reason: though the abortion decision may originate within the zone of conscience and belief, it is more than a philosophic exercise. Abortion is a unique act. It is an act fraught with consequences for others: for the woman who must live with the implications of her decision; for the persons who perform and assist in the procedure; for the spouse, family, and society which must confront the knowledge that these procedures exist, procedures some deem nothing short of an act of violence against innocent human life; and, depending on one's beliefs, for the life or potential life that is aborted. Though abortion is conduct, it does not follow that the State is entitled to proscribe it in all instances. That is because the liberty of the woman is at stake in a sense unique to the human condition and so unique to the law. The mother who carries a child to full term is subject to anxieties, to physical constraints, to pain that only she must bear. That these sacrifices have from the beginning of the human race been endured by woman with a pride that ennobles her in the eyes of others and gives to the infant a bond of love cannot alone be grounds for the State to insist she make the sacrifice. Her suffering is too intimate and personal for the State to insist, without more, upon its own vision of the woman's role, however dominant that vision has been in the course of our history and our culture. The destiny of the woman must be shaped to a large extent on her own conception of her spiritual imperatives and her place in society. . . .

While we appreciate the weight of the arguments made on behalf of the State in the case before us, arguments which in their ultimate formulation conclude that *Roe* should be overruled, the reservations any of us may have in reaffirming the central holding of *Roe* are outweighed by the explication of individual liberty we have given combined with the force of stare decisis. We turn now to that doctrine.

III

A

The obligation to follow precedent begins with necessity, and a contrary necessity marks its outer limit. With Cardozo, we recognize that no judicial system could do society's work if it eyed each issue afresh in every case that raised it. See B. Cardozo, *The Nature of the Judicial Process* 149 (1921). Indeed, the very concept of the rule of law underlying our own Constitution requires such continuity over time that a respect for precedent is, by definition, indispensable. See Powell, "Stare Decisis and Judicial Restraint," 1991 *Journal of Supreme Court History* 13, 16. At the other extreme, a different necessity would make itself felt if a prior judicial ruling should come to be seen so clearly as error that its enforcement was for that very reason doomed.

Even when the decision to overrule a prior case is not, as in the rare, latter instance, virtually foreordained, it is common wisdom that the rule of stare decisis is not an "inexorable command," and certainly it is not such in every constitutional case. . . . Rather, when this Court reexamines a prior holding, its judgment is customarily informed by a series of prudential and pragmatic considerations designed to test the consistency of overruling a prior decision with the ideal of the rule of law, and to gauge the respective costs of reaffirming and overruling a prior case. . . .

So in this case we may inquire whether *Roe*'s central rule has been found unworkable; whether the rule's limitation on state power could be removed without serious inequity to those who have relied upon it or significant damage to the stability of the society governed by the rule in question; whether the law's growth in the intervening years has left *Roe*'s central rule a doctrinal anachronism discounted by society; and whether *Roe*'s premises of fact have so far changed in the ensuing two decades as to render its central holding somehow irrelevant or unjustifiable in dealing with the issue it addressed.

3

. . .No evolution of legal principle has left *Roe*'s doctrinal footings weaker than they were in 1973. No development of constitutional law since the case was decided has implicitly or explicitly left *Roe* behind as a mere survivor of obsolete constitutional thinking. . . .

The sum of the precedential inquiry to this point shows Roe's underpinnings unweakened in any way affecting its central holding. While it has engendered disapproval, it has not been unworkable. An entire generation has come of age free to assume *Roe*'s concept of liberty in defining the capacity of women to act in society, and to make reproductive decisions; no erosion of principle going to liberty or personal autonomy has left *Roe*'s central holding a doctrinal remnant; *Roe* portends no developments at odds with other precedent for the analysis of personal liberty; and no changes of fact have rendered viability more or less appropriate as the point at which the balance of interests tips. Within the bounds of normal stare decisis analysis, then, and subject to the considerations on which it customarily turns, the stronger argument is for affirming *Roe*'s central holding, with whatever degree of personal reluctance any of us may have, not for overruling it. . . .

IV

From what we have said so far it follows that it is a constitutional liberty of the woman to have some freedom to terminate her pregnancy. We conclude that the basic decision in *Roe* was based on a constitutional analysis which we cannot now repudiate. The woman's liberty is not so unlimited, however, that from the outset the State cannot show its concern for the life of the unborn, and at a later point in fetal development the State's interest in life has sufficient force so that the right of the woman to terminate the pregnancy can be restricted.

That brings us, of course, to the point where much criticism has been directed at *Roe*, a criticism that always inheres when the Court draws a specific rule from what in the Constitution is but a general standard. We conclude, however, that the urgent claims of the woman to retain the ultimate control over her destiny and her body, claims implicit in the meaning of liberty, require us to perform that function. Liberty must not be extinguished for want of a line that is clear. And it falls to us to give some real substance to the woman's liberty to determine whether to carry her pregnancy to full term.

We conclude the line should be drawn at viability, so that before that time the woman has a right to choose to terminate her pregnancy. We adhere to this principle for two reasons. First, as we have said, is the doctrine of stare decisis. Any judicial act of line-drawing may seem somewhat arbitrary, but *Roe* was a reasoned statement, elaborated with great care. We have twice reaffirmed it in the face of great opposition....

The second reason is that the concept of viability, as we noted in *Roe*, is the time at which there is a realistic possibility of maintaining and nourishing a life outside the womb, so that the independent existence of the second life can in reason and all fairness be the object of state protection that now overrides the rights of the woman.... Consistent with other constitutional norms, legislatures may draw lines which appear arbitrary without the necessity of offering a justification. But courts may not. We must justify the lines we draw. And there is no line other than viability which is more workable. To be sure, as we have said, there may be some medical developments that affect the precise point of viability,...but this is an imprecision within tolerable limits given that the medical community and all those who must apply its discoveries will continue to explore the matter. The viability line also has, as a practical matter, an element of fairness. In some broad sense it might be said that a woman who fails to act before viability has consented to the State's intervention on behalf of the developing child.

The woman's right to terminate her pregnancy before viability is the most central principle of *Roe v. Wade*. It is a rule of law and a component of liberty we cannot renounce....

Yet it must be remembered that *Roe v. Wade* speaks with clarity in establishing not only the woman's liberty but also the State's "important and legitimate interest in potential life."...That portion of the decision in *Roe* has been given too little acknowledgment and implementation by the Court in its subsequent cases....

Roe established a trimester framework to govern abortion regulations. Under this elaborate but rigid construct, almost no regulation at all is permitted during the first trimester of pregnancy; regulations designed to protect the woman's health, but not to further the State's interest in potential life, are permitted during the second trimester; and during the third trimester, when the fetus is viable, prohibitions are permitted provided the life or health of the mother is not at stake....

The trimester framework no doubt was erected to ensure that the woman's right to choose not become so subordinate to the State's interest in promoting fetal life that her choice exists in theory but not in fact. We do not agree, however, that the trimester approach is necessary to accomplish this objective. A framework of this rigidity was unnecessary and in its later interpretation sometimes contradicted the State's permissible exercise of its powers.

Though the woman has a right to choose to terminate or continue her pregnancy before viability, it does not at all follow that the State is prohibited from taking steps to ensure that this choice is thoughtful and informed. Even in the earliest stages of pregnancy, the State may enact rules and regulations designed to encourage her to know that there are philosophic and social arguments of great weight that can be brought to bear in favor of continuing the pregnancy to full term and that there are procedures and institutions to allow adoption of unwanted children as well as a certain degree of state assistance if the mother chooses to raise the child herself.... It follows that States are free to enact laws to provide a reasonable framework for a woman to make a decision that has such profound and lasting meaning....

...A logical reading of the central holding in *Roe* itself, and a necessary reconciliation of the liberty of the woman and the interest of the State in promoting prenatal life, require, in our view, that we abandon the trimester framework as a rigid prohibition on all previability regulation aimed at the protection of fetal life. The trimester framework suffers from these basic flaws: in its formulation it misconceives the nature of the pregnant woman's interest; and in practice it undervalues the State's interest in potential life, as recognized in *Roe*.

As our jurisprudence relating to all liberties save perhaps abortion has recognized, not every law which makes a right more difficult to exercise is, ipso facto, an infringement of that right. An example clarifies the point. We have held that not every ballot access limitation amounts to an infringement of the right to vote. Rather, the States are granted substantial flexibility in establishing the framework within which voters choose the candidates for whom they wish to vote. *Anderson v. Celebrezze*, 460 U.S. 780, 788 (1983)....

The abortion right is similar. Numerous forms of state regulation might have the incidental effect of increasing the cost or decreasing the availability of medical care, whether for abortion or any other medical procedure. The fact that a law which serves a valid purpose, one not designed to strike at the right itself, has the incidental effect of making it more difficult or more expensive to procure an abortion cannot be enough to invalidate it. Only where state regulation imposes an undue burden on a woman's ability to make this decision does the power of the State reach into the heart of the liberty protected by the Due Process Clause....

For the most part, the Court's early abortion cases adhered to this view. In *Maher v. Roe*, 432 U.S. 464, 473–474 (1977), the Court explained: "*Roe* did not declare an unqualified 'constitutional right to an abortion,' as the District Court seemed to think. Rather, the right protects the woman from unduly burdensome interference with her freedom to decide whether to terminate her pregnancy."...

Roe v. Wade was express in its recognition of the State's "important and legitimate interests in preserving and protecting the health of the pregnant woman [and] in protecting the potentiality of human life" 410 US. at 162. The trimester framework, however, does not fulfill *Roe*'s own promise that the State has an interest in protecting fetal life or potential life. *Roe* began the contradiction by using the trimester framework to forbid any regulation of abortion designed to advance that interest before viability. *Id.*, at 163. Before viability, *Roe* and subsequent cases treat all governmental attempts to influence a woman's decision on behalf of the potential life within her as unwarranted. This treatment is, in our judgment, incompatible with the recognition that there is a substantial state interest in potential life throughout pregnancy.... Cf. *Webster*, 492 U.S., at 519....

The very notion that the State has a substantial interest in potential life leads to the conclusion that not all regulations must be deemed unwarranted. Not all burdens on the right to decide whether to terminate a pregnancy will be undue. In our view, the undue burden standard is the appropriate means of reconciling the State's interest with the woman's constitutionally protected liberty....

A finding of an undue burden is a shorthand for the conclusion that a state regulation has the purpose or effect of placing a substantial obstacle in the path of a woman seeking an abortion of a nonviable fetus. A statute with this purpose is invalid because the means chosen by the State to further the interest in potential life must be calculated to inform the woman's free choice, not hinder it. And a statute which, while furthering the interest in potential life or some other valid state interest, has the effect of placing a substantial obstacle in the path of a woman's choice cannot be considered a permissible means of serving its legitimate ends. To the extent that the opinions of the Court or of individual Justices use the undue burden standard in a manner that is inconsistent with this analysis, we set out what in our view should be the controlling standard.... In our considered judgment, an undue burden is an unconstitutional burden....

...What is at stake is the woman's right to make the ultimate decision, not a right to be insulated from all others in doing so. Regulations which do no more than create a structural mechanism by which the State, or the parent or guardian of a minor, may express profound respect for the life of the unborn are permitted, if they are not a substantial obstacle to the woman's exercise of the right to choose....

We give this summary:

(a) To protect the central right recognized by *Roe v. Wade* while at the same time accommodating the State's profound interest in potential life, we will employ the undue burden analysis as explained in this opinion. An undue burden exists, and therefore a provision of law is invalid, if its purpose or effect is to place a substantial obstacle in the path of a woman seeking an abortion before the fetus attains viability.

(b) We reject the rigid trimester framework of *Roe v. Wade*. To promote the State's profound interest in potential life, throughout pregnancy the State may take measures to ensure that the woman's choice is informed, and measures designed to advance this interest will not be invalidated as long as their purpose is to persuade the woman to choose childbirth over abortion. These measures must not be an undue burden on the right.

(c) As with any medical procedure, the State may enact regulations to further the health or safety of a woman seeking an abortion. Unnecessary health regulations that have the purpose or effect of presenting a substantial obstacle to a woman seeking an abortion impose an undue burden on the right.

(d) Our adoption of the undue burden analysis does not disturb the central holding of *Roe v. Wade*, and we reaffirm that holding. Regardless of whether exceptions are made for particular circumstances, a State may not prohibit any woman from making the ultimate decision to terminate her pregnancy before viability.

(e) We also reaffirm *Roe*'s holding that "subsequent to viability, the State in promoting its interest in the potentiality of human life may, if it chooses, regulate, and even proscribe, abortion except where it is necessary, in appropriate medical judgment, for the preservation of the life or health of the mother." *Roe v. Wade*, 410 U.S., at 164–165.

These principles control our assessment of the Pennsylvania statute, and we now turn to the issue of the validity of its challenged provisions.

V

The Court of Appeals applied what it believed to be the undue burden standard and upheld each of the provisions except for the husband notification requirement. We agree generally with this conclusion, but refine the undue burden analysis in accordance with the principles articulated above....

B

We next consider the informed consent requirement. Except in a medical emergency, the statute requires that at least 24 hours before performing an abortion a physician inform the woman of the nature of the procedure, the health risks of the abortion and of childbirth, and the "probable gestational age of the unborn child." The physician or a qualified nonphysician must inform the woman of the availability of printed materials published by the State describing the fetus and providing information about medical assistance for childbirth, information about child support from the father, and a list of agencies which provide adoption and other services as alternatives to abortion. An abortion may not be performed unless the woman certifies in writing that she has been informed of the availability of these printed materials and has been provided them if she chooses to view them.

Our prior decisions establish that as with any medical procedure, the State may require a woman to give her written informed consent to an abortion. See *Planned Parenthood of Central Mo. v. Danforth*, 428 U.S., at 67. In this respect, the statute is unexceptional. Petitioners challenge the statute's definition of informed consent because it includes the provision of specific information by the doctor and the mandatory 24-hour waiting period. The conclusions reached by a majority of the Justices in the separate opinions filed today and the undue burden standard adopted in this opinion require us to overrule in part some of the Court's past decisions, decisions driven by the trimester framework's prohibition of all previability regulations designed to further the State's interest in fetal life. ...

It cannot be questioned that psychological well-being is a facet of health. Nor can it be doubted that most women considering an abortion would deem the impact on the fetus relevant, if not dispositive, to the decision. In attempting to ensure that a woman apprehend the full consequences of her decision, the State furthers the legitimate purpose of reducing the risk that a woman may elect an abortion, only to discover later, with devastating psychological consequences, that her decision was not fully informed. If the information the State requires to be made available to the woman is truthful and not misleading, the requirement may be permissible.

We also see no reason why the State may not require doctors to inform a woman seeking an abortion of the availability of materials relating to the consequences to the fetus, even when those consequences have no direct relation to her health. An example illustrates the point. We would think it constitutional for the State to require that in order for there to be informed consent to a kidney transplant operation the recipient must be supplied with information about risks to the donor as well as risks to himself or herself. ...

Our analysis of Pennsylvania's 24-hour waiting period between the provision of the information deemed necessary to informed consent and the performance of an abortion under the undue burden standard requires us to reconsider the premise behind the decision in *Akron I* invalidating a parallel requirement. In *Akron I* we said: "Nor are we convinced that the State's legitimate concern that the woman's decision be informed is reasonably served by requiring a 24-hour delay as a matter of course." 462 U.S., at 450. We consider that conclusion to be wrong. The idea that important decisions will be more informed and deliberate if they follow some period of reflection does not strike us as unreasonable, particularly where the statute directs that important information become part of the background of the decision.... In theory, at least, the waiting period is a reasonable measure to implement the State's interest in protecting the life of the unborn, a measure that does not amount to an undue burden.

Whether the mandatory 24-hour waiting period is nonetheless invalid because in practice it is a substantial obstacle to a woman's choice to terminate her pregnancy is a closer question. The findings of fact by the District Court indicate that because of the distances many women must travel to reach an abortion provider, the practical effect will often be a delay of much more than a day because the waiting period requires that a woman seeking an abortion make at least two visits to the doctor. The District Court also found that in many instances this will increase the exposure of women seeking abortions to "the harassment and hostility of anti-abortion protesters demonstrating outside a clinic." 744 F. Supp., at 1351. As a result, the District Court found that for those women who have the fewest financial resources, those who must travel long distances, and those who have difficulty explaining their whereabouts to husbands, employers, or others, the 24-hour waiting period will be "particularly burdensome." *Id.*, at 1352.

These findings are troubling in some respects, but they do not demonstrate that the waiting period constitutes an undue burden. We do not doubt that, as the District Court held, the waiting period has the effect of "increasing the cost and risk of delay of abortions," *id.*, at 1378, but the District Court did not conclude that the increased costs and potential delays amount to substantial obstacles....

We also disagree with the District Court's conclusion that the "particularly burdensome" effects of the waiting period on some women require its invalidation. A particular burden is not of necessity a substantial obstacle. Whether a burden falls on a particular group is a distinct inquiry from whether it is a substantial obstacle even as to the women in that group. And the District Court did not conclude that the waiting period is such an obstacle even for the women who are most burdened by it. Hence, on the record before us, and in the context of this facial challenge, we are not convinced that the 24-hour waiting period constitutes an undue burden.

C

Section 3209 of Pennsylvania's abortion law provides, except in cases of medical emergency, that no physician shall perform an abortion on a married woman without receiving a signed statement from the woman that she has notified her spouse that she is about to undergo an abortion. The woman has the option of providing an alternative signed statement certifying that her husband is not the man who impregnated her; that her husband could not be located; that the pregnancy is the result of spousal sexual assault which she has reported; or that the woman believes that notifying her husband will cause him or someone else to inflict bodily injury upon her. A physician who performs an abortion on a married woman without receiving the appropriate signed statement will have his or her license revoked, and is liable to the husband for damages.

The District Court heard the testimony of numerous expert witnesses, and made detailed findings of fact regarding the effect of this statute.... findings supported by studies of domestic violence. The American Medical Association (AMA) has published a summary of the recent research in this field, which indicates that in an average 12-month period in this country, approximately two million women are the victims of severe assaults by their male partners. In a 1985 survey, women reported that nearly one of every eight husbands had assaulted their wives during the past year. The AMA views these figures as "marked underestimates," because the nature of these incidents discourages women from reporting them, and because surveys typically exclude the very poor, those who do not speak English well, and women who are homeless or in institutions or hospitals when the survey is conducted....

This information and the District Court's findings reinforce what common sense would suggest. In well-functioning marriages, spouses discuss important intimate decisions such as whether to bear a child. But there are millions of women in this country who are the victims of regular physical and psychological abuse at the hands of their husbands. Should these women become pregnant, they may have very good reasons for not wishing to inform their husbands of their decision to obtain an abortion. Many may have justifiable fears of physical abuse, but may be no less fearful of the consequences of reporting prior abuse to the Commonwealth of Pennsylvania. Many may have a reasonable fear that notifying their husbands will provoke further instances of child abuse; these women are not exempt from [the] notification requirement. Many may fear devastating forms of psychological abuse from their husbands, including verbal harassment, threats of future violence, the destruction of possessions, physical confinement to the home, the withdrawal of financial support, or the disclosure of the abortion to family and friends. These methods of psychological abuse may act as even more of a deterrent to notification than the possibility of physical violence, but women who are the victims of the abuse are not exempt from [the] notification requirement....

The spousal notification requirement is thus likely to prevent a significant number of women from obtaining an abortion. It does not merely make abortions a little more difficult or expensive to obtain; for many women, it will impose a substantial obstacle. We must not blind ourselves to the fact that the significant number of women who fear for their safety and the safety of their children are likely to be deterred from procuring an abortion as surely as if the Commonwealth had outlawed abortion in all cases....

The husband's interest in the life of the child his wife is carrying does not permit the State to empower him with this troubling degree of authority over his wife. The contrary view leads to consequences reminiscent of the common law. A husband has no enforceable right to require a wife to advise him before she exercises her personal choices. If a husband's interest in the potential life of the child outweighs a wife's liberty, the State could require a married woman to notify her husband before she uses a postfertilization contraceptive. Perhaps next in line would be a statute requiring pregnant married women to notify their husbands before engaging in conduct causing risks to the fetus. After all, if the husband's interest in the fetus' safety is a sufficient predicate for state regulation, the State could reasonably conclude that pregnant wives should notify their husbands before drinking alcohol or smoking. Perhaps married women should notify their husbands before using contraceptives or before undergoing any type of surgery that may have complications affecting the husband's interest in his wife's reproductive organs.... Women do not lose their constitutionally protected liberty when they marry. The Constitution protects all individuals, male or female, married or unmarried, from the abuse of governmental power, even where that power is employed for the supposed benefit of a member of the individual's family. These considerations confirm our conclusion that §3209 is invalid.

D

We next consider the parental consent provision. Except in a medical emergency, an unemancipated young woman under 18 may not obtain an abortion unless she and one of her parents (or guardian) provides informed consent as defined above. If neither a parent nor a guardian provides consent, a court may authorize the performance of an abortion upon a determination that the young woman is mature and capable of giving informed consent and has in fact given her informed consent, or that an abortion would be in her best interests.

We have been over most of this ground before. Our cases establish, and we reaffirm today, that a State may require a minor seeking an abortion to obtain the consent of a parent or guardian, provided that there is an adequate judicial bypass procedure....

Dissent: Justice Stevens, concurring in part and dissenting in part....

II

My disagreement with the joint opinion begins with its understanding of the trimester framework established in *Roe*. Contrary to the suggestion of the joint opinion,...it is not a "contradiction" to recognize that the State may have a legitimate interest in potential human life and, at the same time, to conclude that that interest does not justify the regulation of abortion before viability (although other interests, such as maternal health, may). The fact that the State's interest is legitimate does not tell us when, if ever, that interest outweighs the pregnant woman's interest in personal liberty. It is appropriate, therefore, to consider more carefully the nature of the interests at stake.

First, it is clear that, in order to be legitimate, the State's interest must be secular; consistent with the First Amendment the State may not promote a theological or sectarian interest. See *Thornburgh v. American College of Obstetricians and Gynecologists*, 476 U.S. 747, 778 (1986) (Stevens, J., concurring); see generally *Webster v. Reproductive Health Services*, 492 U.S. 490, 563–572 (1989) (Stevens, J., concurring in part and dissenting in part). Moreover, as discussed above, the state interest in potential human life is not an interest in *loco parentis*, for the fetus is not a person.

Identifying the State's interests—which the States rarely articulate with any precision—makes clear that the interest in protecting potential life is not grounded in the Constitution. It is, instead, an indirect interest supported by both humanitarian and pragmatic concerns. Many of our citizens believe that any abortion reflects an unacceptable disrespect for potential human life and that the performance of more than a million abortions each year is intolerable; many find third-trimester abortions performed when the fetus is approaching personhood particularly offensive. The State has a legitimate interest in minimizing such offense. The State may also have a broader interest in expanding the population,... believing society would benefit from the services of additional productive citizens—or that the potential human lives might include the occasional Mozart or Curie. These are the kinds of concerns that comprise the State's interest in potential human life.

In counterpoise is the woman's constitutional interest in liberty. One aspect of this liberty is a right to bodily integrity, a right to control one's person. See e.g., *Rochin v. California*, 342 U.S. 165 (1952); *Skinner v. Oklahoma*, 316 U.S. 535 (1942). This right is neutral on the question of abortion:

The Constitution would be equally offended by an absolute requirement that all women undergo abortions as by an absolute prohibition on abortions. "Our whole constitutional heritage rebels at the thought of giving government the power to control men's minds." *Stanley v. Georgia*, 394 U.S. 557, 565 (1969). The same holds true for the power to control women's bodies....

III

The 24-hour waiting period required by §§3205(a)(1)–(2) of the Pennsylvania statute raises even more serious concerns. Such a requirement arguably furthers the State's interests in two ways, neither of which is constitutionally permissible....

First, it may be argued that the 24-hour delay is justified by the mere fact that it is likely to reduce the number of abortions, thus furthering the State's interest in potential life. But such an argument would justify any form of coercion that placed an obstacle in the woman's path. The State cannot further its interests by simply wearing down the ability of the pregnant woman to exercise her constitutional right.

Second, it can more reasonably be argued that the 24-hour delay furthers the State's interest in ensuring that the woman's decision is informed and thoughtful. But there is no evidence that the mandated delay benefits women or that it is necessary to enable the physician to convey any relevant information to the patient. The mandatory delay thus appears to rest on outmoded and unacceptable assumptions about the decision-making capacity of women. While there are well-established and consistently maintained reasons for the State to view with skepticism the ability of minors to make decisions...none of those reasons applies to an adult woman's decision-making ability....

...The decision to terminate a pregnancy is profound and difficult. No person undertakes such a decision lightly—and States may not presume that a woman has failed to reflect adequately merely because her conclusion differs from the State's preference. A woman who has, in the privacy of her thoughts and conscience, weighed the options and made her decision cannot be forced to reconsider all, simply because the State believes she has come to the wrong decision.

Part of the constitutional liberty to choose is the equal dignity to which each of us is entitled. A woman who decides to terminate her pregnancy is entitled to the same respect as a woman who decides to carry the fetus to term. The mandatory waiting period denies women that equal respect.

IV

In my opinion, a correct application of the "undue burden" standard leads to the same conclusion concerning the constitutionality of these requirements. A state-imposed burden on the exercise of a constitutional right is measured both by its effects and by its character: a burden may be "undue" either because the burden is too severe or because it lacks a legitimate, rational justification.

The 24-hour delay requirement fails both parts of this test. The findings of the District Court establish the severity of the burden that the 24-hour delay imposes on many pregnant women. Yet even in those cases in which the delay is not especially onerous, it is, in my opinion, "undue" because there is no evidence that such a delay serves a useful and legitimate purpose. As indicated above, there is no legitimate reason to require a woman who has agonized over her decision to leave the clinic or hospital and return again another day. While a general requirement that a physician notify her patients about the risks of a proposed medical procedure is appropriate, a rigid requirement that all patients wait 24 hours or (what is true in practice) much longer to evaluate the significance of information that is either common knowledge or irrelevant is an irrational and, therefore, "undue" burden....

Justice Blackmun, concurring in part, concurring in the judgment in part, and dissenting in part....

II

Today, no less than yesterday, the Constitution and decisions of this Court require that a State's abortion restrictions be subjected to the strictest of judicial scrutiny. Our precedents and the joint opinion's principles require us to subject all non-de minimis abortion regulations to strict scrutiny. Under this standard, the Pennsylvania statute's provisions requiring content-based counseling, a 24-hour delay, informed parental consent, and reporting of abortion-related information must be invalidated.

A

...State restrictions on abortion violate a woman's right of privacy in two ways. First, compelled continuation of a pregnancy infringes upon a woman's right to bodily integrity by imposing substantial physical intrusions and significant risks of physical harm. During pregnancy, women experience dramatic physical changes and a wide range of health consequences. Labor and delivery pose additional health risks and physical demands. In short, restrictive abortion laws force women to endure physical invasions far more substantial than those this Court has held to violate the constitutional principle of bodily integrity in other contexts. See, e.g., *Winston v. Lee*, 470 U.S. 753 (1985) (invalidating surgical removal of bullet from murder suspect); *Rochin v. California*, 342 U.S. 165 (1952) (invalidating stomach-pumping)....

A State's restrictions on a woman's right to terminate her pregnancy also implicate constitutional guarantees of gender equality. State restrictions on abortion compel women to continue pregnancies they otherwise might terminate. By restricting the right to terminate pregnancies, the State conscripts women's bodies into its service, forcing women to continue their pregnancies, suffer the pains of childbirth, and in most instances, provide years of maternal care. The State does not compensate women for their services; instead, it assumes that they owe this duty as a matter of course....

B

The Court has held that limitations on the right of privacy are permissible only if they survive "strict" constitutional scrutiny—that is, only if the governmental entity imposing the restriction can demonstrate that the limitation is both necessary and narrowly tailored to serve a compelling governmental interest. *Griswold v. Connecticut*...*Roe* identified two relevant State interests: "an interest in preserving and protecting the health of the pregnant woman" and an interest in "protecting the potentiality of human life."... With respect to the State's interest in the health of the mother, "the 'compelling' point...is at approximately the end of the first trimester," because it is at that point that the mortality rate in abortion approaches that in childbirth.... With respect to the State's interest in potential life, "the 'compelling' point is at viability," because it is at that point that the fetus "presumably has the capability of meaningful life outside the mother's womb." In order to fulfill the requirement of narrow tailoring, "the State is obligated to make a reasonable effort to limit the effect of its regulations to the period in the trimester during which its health interest will be furthered." *Akron*, 462 U.S. at 434.

In my view, application of this analytical framework is no less warranted than when it was approved by seven Members of this Court in *Roe*. Strict scrutiny of state limitations on reproductive choice still offers the most secure protection of the woman's right to make her own reproductive decisions, free from state coercion. No majority of this Court has ever agreed upon an alternative approach. The factual premises of the trimester framework have not been undermined, see *Webster*, 492 U.S. at 553 (Blackmun, J., dissenting), and the *Roe* framework is far more administrable, and far less manipulable, than the "undue burden" standard adopted by the joint opinion....

...[w]hile a State has "legitimate interests from the outset of the pregnancy in protecting the health of the woman and the life of the fetus that may become a child,"...legitimate interests are not enough. To overcome the burden of strict scrutiny, the interests must be compelling. The question then is how best to accommodate the State's interest in potential human life with the constitutional liberties of pregnant women. Again, I stand by the views I expressed in *Webster*:

> I remain convinced, as six other Members of this Court sixteen years ago were convinced, that the *Roe* framework, and the viability standard in particular, fairly, sensibly, and effectively functions to safeguard the constitutional liberties of pregnant women while recognizing and accommodating the State's interest in potential human life. The viability line reflects the biological facts and truths of fetal development; it marks that threshold moment prior to which a fetus cannot survive separate from the woman and cannot reasonably and objectively be regarded as a subject of rights or interests distinct from, or paramount to, those of the pregnant woman. At the same time, the viability standard takes account of the undeniable fact that as the fetus evolves into its postnatal form, and as it loses its dependence on the uterine environment, the State's interest in the fetus' potential human life, and in fostering a regard for human life in general, becomes compelling. As a practical matter, because viability follows "quickening"—the point at which a woman feels movement in her womb—and because viability occurs no earlier than twenty-three weeks gestational age, it establishes an easily applicable standard for regulating abortion while providing a pregnant woman ample time to exercise her fundamental right with her responsible physician to terminate her pregnancy." 492 U.S. at 553–554.

In sum, *Roe*'s requirement of strict scrutiny as implemented through a trimester framework should not be disturbed. No other approach has gained a majority, and no other is more protective of the woman's fundamental right. Lastly, no other approach properly accommodates the woman's constitutional right with the State's legitimate interests. ...

III

...The Chief Justice's criticism of Roe follows from his stunted conception of individual liberty. While recognizing that the Due Process Clause protects more than simple physical liberty, he then goes on to construe this Court's personal-liberty cases as establishing only a laundry list of particular rights, rather than a principled account of how these particular rights are grounded in a more general right of privacy.... This constricted view is reinforced by the Chief Justice's exclusive reliance on tradition as a source of fundamental rights.... In the Chief Justice's world, a woman considering whether to terminate a pregnancy is entitled to no more protection than adulterers, murderers, and so-called "sexual deviates." The Chief Justice's exclusive reliance on tradition, people using contraceptives seem the next likely candidate for his list of outcasts.

Even more shocking than the Chief Justice's cramped notion of individual liberty is his complete omission of any discussion of the effects that compelled childbirth and motherhood have on women's lives. The only expression of concern with women's health is purely instrumental...only women's psychological health is a concern, and only to the extent that he assumes that every woman who decides to have an abortion does so without serious consideration of the moral implications of their decision. In short, the Chief Justice's view of the State's compelling interest in maternal health has less to do with health than it does with compelling women to be maternal....

But, we are reassured, there is always the protection of the democratic process. While there is much to be praised about our democracy, our country since its founding has recognized that there are certain fundamental liberties that are not to be left to the whims of an election. A woman's right to reproductive choice is one of those fundamental liberties. Accordingly, that liberty need not seek refuge at the ballot box....

Chief Justice Rehnquist, with whom Justice White, Justice Scalia, and Justice Thomas join, concurring in the judgment in part and dissenting in part.

...We believe that *Roe* was wrongly decided, and that it can and should be overruled consistently with our traditional approach to stare decisis in constitutional cases. We would adopt the approach of the plurality in *Webster v. Reproductive Health Services*, 492 U.S. 490 (1989), and uphold the challenged provisions of the Pennsylvania statute in their entirety.

I

...We have held that a liberty interest protected under the Due Process Clause of the Fourteenth Amendment will be deemed fundamental if it is "implicit in the concept of ordered liberty." *Palko v. Connecticut*, 302 U.S. 319, 325 (1937). Three years earlier, in *Snyder v. Massachusetts*, 291 U.S. 97 (1934), we referred to a "principle of justice so rooted in the traditions and conscience of our people as to be ranked as fundamental." *Id.* ... These expressions are admittedly not precise, but our decisions implementing this notion of "fundamental" rights do not afford any more elaborate basis on which to base such a classification....

We think, therefore, both in view of this history and of our decided cases dealing with substantive liberty under the Due Process Clause, that the Court was mistaken in *Roe* when it classified a woman's decision to terminate her pregnancy as a "fundamental right" that could be abridged only in a manner which withstood "strict scrutiny." In so concluding, we repeat the observation made in *Bowers v. Hardwick,* 478 U.S. 186 (1986):

> Nor are we inclined to take a more expansive view of our authority to discover new fundamental rights imbedded in the Due Process Clause. The Court is most vulnerable and comes nearest to illegitimacy when it deals with judge-made constitutional law having little or no cognizable roots in the language or design of the Constitution. *Id.,* at 194....

...Because the undue burden standard is plucked from nowhere, the question of what is a "substantial obstacle" to abortion will undoubtedly engender a variety of conflicting views. For example, in the very matter before us now, the authors of the joint opinion would uphold Pennsylvania's 24-hour waiting period, concluding that a "particular burden" on some women is not a substantial obstacle. But the authors would at the same time strike down Pennsylvania's spousal notice provision, after finding that in a "large fraction" of cases the provision will be a substantial obstacle. And, while the authors conclude that the informed consent provisions do not constitute an "undue burden," Justice Stevens would hold that they do....

We have stated above our belief that the Constitution does not subject state abortion regulations to heightened scrutiny. Accordingly, we think that the correct analysis is that set forth by the plurality opinion in *Webster.* A woman's interest in having an abortion is a form of liberty protected by the Due Process Clause, but States may regulate abortion procedures in ways rationally related to a legitimate state interest....

Justice Scalia, with whom the Chief Justice, Justice White, and Justice Thomas join, concurring in the judgment in part and dissenting in part.

My views on this matter are unchanged from those I set forth in my separate opinions in *Webster v. Reproductive Health Services,* 492 U.S. 490, 532 (1989) (Scalia, A.J., concurring in part and concurring in judgment), and *Ohio v. Akron Center for Reproductive Health,* 497 U.S. 502, 520 (1990) (*Akron II*) (Scalia, A.J., concurring). The States may, if they wish, permit abortion on demand, but the Constitution does not require them to do so. The permissibility of abortion, and the limitations upon it, are to be resolved like most important questions in our democracy: by citizens trying to persuade one another, and then voting. As the Court acknowledges, "where reasonable people disagree the government can adopt one position or the other." The Court is correct in adding the qualification that this "assumes a state of affairs in which the choice does not intrude upon a protected liberty"—but the crucial part of that qualification is the penultimate word. A State's choice between two positions on which reasonable people can disagree is constitutional even when (as is often the case) it intrudes upon a "liberty" in the absolute sense. Laws against bigamy, for example—which entire societies of reasonable people disagree with—intrude upon men and women's liberty to marry and live with one another. But bigamy happens not to be a liberty specially "protected" by the Constitution.

That is, quite simply, the issue in this case: not whether the power of a woman to abort her unborn child is a "liberty" in the absolute sense; or even whether it is a liberty of great importance to many women. Of course it is both. The issue is whether it is a liberty protected by the Constitution of the United States. I am sure it is not. I reach that conclusion not because of anything so exalted as my views concerning the "concept of existence, of meaning, of the universe, and of the mystery of human life." Rather, I reach it for the same reason I reach the conclusion that bigamy is not constitutionally protected—because of two simple facts: (1) the Constitution says absolutely nothing about it, and (2) the longstanding traditions of American society have permitted it to be legally proscribed. *Akron II*, supra, at 520 (Scalia J., concurring).

Beyond that brief summary of the essence of my position, I will not swell the United States Reports with repetition of what I have said before; and applying the rational basis test, I would uphold the Pennsylvania statute in its entirety. I must, however, respond to a few of the more outrageous arguments in today's opinion, which it is beyond human nature to leave unanswered....

The joint opinion frankly concedes that the amorphous concept of "undue burden" has been inconsistently applied by the Members of this Court in the few brief years since that "test" was first explicitly propounded by Justice O'Connor in her dissent in *Akron I*, supra. See *ante*, at 34. Because the three Justices now wish to "set forth a standard of general application," the joint opinion announces that "it is important to clarify what is meant by an undue burden," I certainly agree with that, but I do not agree that the joint opinion succeeds in the announced endeavor. To the contrary, its efforts at clarification make clear only that the standard is inherently manipulable and will prove hopelessly unworkable in practice....

The joint opinion explains that a state regulation imposes an "undue burden" if it "has the purpose or effect of placing a substantial obstacle in the path of a woman seeking an abortion of a nonviable fetus." An obstacle is "substantial," we are told, if it is "calculated, [not] to inform the woman's free choice, [but to] hinder it." This latter statement cannot possibly mean what it says. Any regulation of abortion that is intended to advance what the joint opinion concedes is the State's "substantial" interest in protecting unborn life will be "calculated [to] hinder" a decision to have an abortion. It thus seems more accurate to say that the joint opinion would uphold abortion regulations only if they do not unduly hinder the woman's decision. That, of course, brings us right back to square one: defining an "undue burden" as an "undue hindrance" (or a "substantial obstacle") hardly "clarifies" the test. Consciously or not, the joint opinion's verbal shell game will conceal raw judicial policy choices concerning what is "appropriate" abortion legislation....

...The joint opinion is flatly wrong in asserting that "our jurisprudence relating to all liberties save perhaps abortion has recognized" the permissibility of laws that do not impose an "undue burden."... It argues that the abortion right is similar to other rights in that a law "not designed to strike at the right itself, [but which] has the incidental effect of making it more difficult or more expensive to [exercise the right,]" is not invalid.... I agree, indeed I have forcefully urged, that a law of general applicability which places only an incidental burden on a fundamental right does not infringe that right, see *R.A.V. v. St. Paul*, 505 U.S. (1992) (slip op., at 11); *Employment Division, Dept. of Human Resources of Ore. v. Smith*, 494 U.S. 872, 878–882 (1990), but that principle does not establish the quite different (and quite dangerous) proposition that a law which directly regulates a fundamental right will not be found to violate the Constitution unless it imposes an "undue burden." It is that, of course, which is at issue here: Pennsylvania has consciously and directly regulated conduct that our cases have held is constitutionally protected. The appropriate analogy, therefore, is that of a state law requiring purchasers of religious books to endure a 24-hour waiting period, or to pay a nominal additional tax of one cent. The joint opinion cannot possibly be correct in suggesting that we would uphold such legislation on the ground that it does not impose a "substantial obstacle" to the exercise of First Amendment rights. The "undue burden" standard is not at all the generally applicable principle the joint opinion pretends it to be; rather, it is a unique concept created specially for this case, to preserve some judicial foothold in this ill-gotten territory. In claiming otherwise, the three Justices show their willingness to place all constitutional rights at risk in an effort to preserve what they deem the "central holding in *Roe*,"...

I do not, of course, have any objection to the notion that, in applying legal principles, one should rely only upon the facts that are contained in the record or that are properly subject to judicial notice.... But what is remarkable about the joint opinion's fact-intensive analysis is that it does not result in any measurable clarification of the "undue burden" standard. Rather, the approach of the joint opinion is, for the most part, simply to highlight certain facts in the record that apparently strike the three Justices as particularly significant in establishing (or refuting) the existence of an undue burden; after describing these facts, the opinion then simply announces that the provision either does or does not impose a "substantial obstacle" or an "undue burden."… We do not know whether the same conclusions could have been reached on a different record, or in what respects the record would have had to differ before an opposite conclusion would have been appropriate. The inherently standardless nature of this inquiry invites the district judge to give effect to his personal preferences about abortion. By finding and relying upon the right facts, he can invalidate, it would seem, almost any abortion restriction that strikes him as "undue"—subject, of course, to the possibility of being reversed by a Circuit Court or Supreme Court that is as unconstrained in reviewing his decision as he was in making it.

We should get out of this area, where we have no right to be, and where we do neither ourselves nor the country any good by remaining.

A DEFENSE OF ABORTION

Judith Jarvis Thomson

Most opposition to abortion relies on the premise that the fetus is a human being, a person, from the moment of conception. The premise is argued for, but, as I think, not well. Take, for example, the most common argument. We are asked to notice that the development of a human being from conception through birth into childhood is continuous; then it is said that to draw a line, to choose a point in this development and say "before this point the thing is not a person; after this point it is a person" is to make an arbitrary choice, a choice for which, in the nature of things, no good reason can be given. It is concluded that the fetus is, or anyway, that we had better say it is, a person from the moment of conception. But this conclusion does not follow. Similar things might be said about the development of an acorn into an oak tree, and it does not follow that acorns are oak trees, or that we had better say they are. Arguments of this form are sometimes called "slippery slope arguments"—the phrase is perhaps self-explanatory—and it is dismaying that opponents of abortion rely on them so heavily and uncritically....

...I think that the premise is false, that the fetus is not a person from the moment of conception. A newly fertilized ovum, a newly implanted clump of cells, is no more a person than an acorn is an oak tree. But I shall not discuss any of this. For it seems to me to be of great interest to ask what happens if, for the sake of argument, we allow the premise. How,

Reprinted from *Philosophy & Public Affairs*, Vol. 1, No. 1 (1971): 47–66, with permission of the author and the publisher, Princeton University Press.

precisely, are we supposed to get from there to the conclusion that abortion is morally impermissible? Opponents of abortion commonly spend most of their time establishing that the fetus is a person, and hardly any time explaining the step from there to the impermissibility of abortion. Perhaps they think the step too simple and obvious to require much comment....

I propose, then, that we grant that the fetus is a person from the moment of conception. How does the argument go from here? Something like this, I take it. Every person has a right to life. So the fetus has a right to life. No doubt the mother has a right to decide what shall happen in and to her body; everyone would grant that. But surely a person's right to life is stronger and more stringent than the mother's right to decide what happens in and to her body, and so outweighs it. So the fetus may not be killed; an abortion may not be performed.

It sounds plausible. But now let me ask you to imagine this. You wake up in the morning and find yourself back to back in bed with an unconscious violinist. A famous violinist. He has been found to have a fatal kidney ailment, and the Society of Music Lovers has canvassed all the available medical records and found that you alone have the right blood type to help. They have therefore kidnapped you, and last night the violinist's circulatory system was plugged into yours, so that your kidneys can be used to extract poisons from his blood as well as your own. The director of the hospital now tells you, "Look, we're sorry the Society of Music Lovers did this to you—we would never have permitted it if we had known. But still, they did it, and the violinist is now plugged into you. To unplug you would be to kill him. But never mind, it's only for nine months. By then he will have recovered from his ailment, and can safely be unplugged from you." Is it morally incumbent on you to accede to this situation? No doubt it would be very nice of you if you did, a great kindness. But do you *have* to accede to it? What if it were not nine months, but nine years? Or longer still? What if the director of the hospital says, "Tough luck, I agree, but you've now got to stay in bed with the violinist plugged into you for the rest of your life. Because remember this. All persons have a right to life, and violinists are persons. Granted you have a right to decide what happens in and to your body, but a person's right to life outweighs your right to decide what happens in and to your body. So you cannot ever be unplugged from him." I imagine you would regard this as outrageous, which suggests that something really is wrong with that plausible sounding argument I mentioned a moment ago.

In this case, of course, you were kidnapped; you didn't volunteer for the operation that plugged the violinist into your kidneys. Can those who oppose abortion on the ground I mentioned make an exception for a pregnancy due to rape? Certainly. They can say that persons have a right to life only if they didn't come into existence because of rape; or they can say that all persons have a right to life, but that some have less of a right to life than others; in particular, that those who came into existence because of rape have less. But these statements have a rather unpleasant sound. Surely the question of whether you have a right to life at all, or how much of it you have, shouldn't turn on the question of whether or not you are the product of a rape. And in fact, the people who oppose abortion on the ground I mentioned do not make this distinction, and hence do not make an exception in case of rape.

Nor do they make an exception for a case in which the mother has to spend the nine months of her pregnancy in bed. They would agree that would be a great pity, and hard on the mother; but all the same, all persons have a right to life, the fetus is a person, and so on. I suspect, in fact, that they would not make an exception for a case in which, miraculously enough, the pregnancy went on for nine years, or even the rest of the mother's life.

Some won't even make an exception for a case in which continuation of the pregnancy is likely to shorten the mother's life; they regard abortion as impermissible even to save the mother's life. Such cases are nowadays very rare, and many opponents of abortion do not accept this extreme view. All the same, it is a good place to begin: a number of points of interest come out in respect to it.

1.

Let us call the view that abortion is impermissible even to save the mother's life "the extreme view." I want to suggest first that it does not issue from the argument I mentioned earlier without the addition of some fairly powerful premises. Suppose a woman has become pregnant, and now learns that she has a cardiac condition such that she will die if she carries the baby to term. What may be done for her? The fetus, being a person, has a right to life, but as the mother is a person too, so has she a right to life. Presumably they have an equal right to life. How is it supposed to come out that an abortion may not be performed? If mother and child have an equal right to life, shouldn't we perhaps flip a coin? Or should we add to the mother's right to life her right to decide what happens in and to her body, which everybody seems to be ready to grant—the sum of her rights now outweighing the fetus' right to life?

The most familiar argument here is the following. We are told that performing the abortion would be directly killing the child,[1] whereas doing nothing would not be killing the mother, but only letting her die. Moreover, in killing the child, one would be killing an innocent person, for the child has committed no crime, and is not aiming at his mother's death. And then there are a variety of ways in which this might be continued. (1) But as directly killing an innocent person is always and absolutely impermissible, an abortion may not be performed. Or, (2) as directly killing an innocent person is murder, and murder is always and absolutely imper-missible, an abortion may not be performed. Or, (3) as one's duty to refrain from directly killing an innocent person is more stringent than one's duty to keep a person from dying, an abortion may not be per-formed. Or, (4) if one's only options are directly killing an innocent person or letting a person die, one must prefer letting the person die, and thus an abortion may not be performed.

Some people seem to have thought that these are not further premises which must be added if the conclusion is to be reached, but that they fol-low from the very fact that an innocent person has a right to life. But this seems to me to be a mistake, and perhaps the simplest way to show this is to bring out that while we must certainly grant that innocent persons have a right to life, the theses in (1) through (4) are all false. Take (2), for exam-ple. If directly killing an innocent person is murder, and thus is impermis-sible, then the mother's directly killing the innocent person inside her is murder, and thus is impermissible. But it cannot seriously be thought to be murder if the mother performs an abortion on herself to save her life. It cannot seriously be said that she must refrain, that she must sit passively by and wait for her death. Let us look again at the case of you and the vio-linist. There you are, in bed with the violinist, and the director of the hos-pital says to you, "It's all most distressing, and I deeply sympathize, but you see this is putting an additional strain on your kidneys, and you'll be dead within the month. But you *have* to stay where you are all the same. Because unplugging you would be directly killing an innocent violinist, and that's murder, and that's impermissible." If anything in the world is true, it is that you do not commit murder, you do not do what is imper-missible, if you reach around your back and unplug yourself from that violinist to save your life....

I should perhaps stop to say explicitly that I am not claiming that peo-ple have a right to do anything whatever to save their lives. I think, rather, that there are drastic limits to the right of self-defense. If someone threat-ens you with death unless you torture someone else to death, I think you have not the right, even to save your own life, to do so. But the case under consideration here is very different. In our case there are only two people involved, one whose life is threatened, and one who threatens it. Both are innocent: the one who is threatened is not threatened because of any fault, the one who threatens does not threaten because of any fault. For this rea-son we may feel that we bystanders cannot intervene. But the person threatened can.

In sum, a woman surely can defend her life against the threat to it posed by the unborn child, even if doing so involves its death. And this shows not merely that the theses in (1) through (4) are false; it shows also that the extreme view of abortion is false, and so we need not canvass any other possible ways of arriving at it from the argument I mentioned at the outset.

2.

The extreme view, could, of course, be weakened to say that, while abortion is permissible to save the mother's life, it may not be performed by a third party, but only by the mother herself. But this cannot be right either. For what we have to keep in mind is that the mother and the unborn child are not like two tenants in a small house which has, by an unfortunate mistake, been rented to both: the mother owns the house. The fact that she does adds to the offensiveness of deducing that the mother can do nothing from the supposition that third parties can do nothing. But it does more than this: it casts a bright light on the supposition that third parties can do nothing. Certainly it lets us see that a third party who says "I cannot choose between you" is fooling himself if he thinks this is impartiality. If Jones has found and fastened on a certain coat, which he needs to keep him from freezing, but which Smith also needs to keep him from freezing, then it is not impartiality that says "I cannot choose between you" when Smith owns the coat. Women have said again and again "This body is my body!" and they have reason to feel angry, reason to feel that it has been like shouting into the wind. Smith, after all, is hardly likely to bless us if we say to him, "Of course it's your coat, anybody would grant that it is. But no one may choose between you and Jones who is to have it."

We should really ask what it is that says "no one may choose" in the face of the fact that the body that houses the child is the mother's body. It may be simply a failure to appreciate this fact. But it may be something more interesting, namely the sense that one has a right to refuse to lay hands on people, even where it would be just and fair to do so, even where justice seems to require that somebody do so. Thus justice might call for somebody to get Smith's coat back from Jones, and let you have a right to refuse to be the one to lay hands on Jones, a right to refuse to do physical violence to him. This, I think, must be granted. But then what should be said is not "no one may choose," but only "*I* cannot choose," and indeed not even this, but "*I* will not *act*," leaving it open that somebody else can or should, and in particular that anyone in a position of authority, with the job of securing people's rights, both can and should. So this is no difficulty. I have not been arguing that any given third party must accede to the mother's request that he perform an abortion to save her life, but only that he may.

I suppose that in some views of human life the mother's body is only on loan to her, the loan not being one which gives her any prior claim to it. One who held this view might well think it impartiality to say "I cannot choose." But I shall simply ignore this possibility. My own view is that if a human being has any just, prior claim to anything at all, he has a just, prior claim to his own body. And perhaps this needn't be argued for here anyway, since, as I mentioned, the arguments against abortion we are looking at do grant that the woman has a right to decide what happens in and to her body.

But although they do grant it, I have tried to show that they do not take seriously what is done in granting it. I suggest the same thing will reappear even more clearly when we turn away from cases in which the mother's life is at stake, and attend, as I propose we now do, to the vastly more common cases in which a woman wants an abortion for some less weighty reason than preserving her own life.

3.

Where the mother's life is not at stake, the argument I mentioned at the outset seems to have a much stronger pull. "Everyone has a right to life, so the unborn person has a right to life." And is not the child's right to life weightier than anything other than the mother's own right to life, which she might put forward as a ground for an abortion?

This argument treats the right to life as if it were unproblematic. It is not, and this seems to me to be precisely the source of the mistake.

For we should now, at long last, ask what it comes to, to have a right to life. In some views, having a right to life includes having a right to be given at least the bare minimum one needs for continued life. But suppose that what in fact *is* the bare minimum a man needs for continued life is something he has no right at all to be given? If I am sick unto death, and the only thing that will save my life is the touch of Henry Fonda's cool hand on my fevered brow, then all the same, I have no right to be given the touch of Henry Fonda's cool hand on my fevered brow. It would be frightfully nice of him to fly in from the West Coast to provide it. It would be less nice, though no doubt well meant, if my friends flew out to the West Coast and carried Henry Fonda back with them. But I have no right at all against anybody that he should do this for me. Or again, to return to the story I told earlier, the fact that for continued life that violinist needs the continued use of your kidneys does not establish that he has a right to be given the continued use of your kidneys. He certainly has no right against you that *you* should give him continued use of your kidneys. For nobody has any right to use your kidneys unless you give him such a right; and nobody has the right against you that you shall give him this right—if you do allow him to go on using your kidneys this is a kindness on your part, and not something he can claim from you as his due. Nor has he any right against anybody else that they should give him continued use of your kidneys. Certainly he had no right against the Society of Music Lovers that they should plug him into you in the first place. And if you now start to unplug yourself, having learned that you will otherwise have to spend nine years in bed with him, there is nobody in the world who must try to prevent you, in order to see to it that he is given something he has a right to be given.

Some people are rather stricter about the right to life. In their view it does not include the right to be given anything, but amounts to, and only to, the right not to be killed by anybody. But here a related difficulty arises. If everybody is to refrain from killing that violinist, then everybody must refrain from doing a great many different sorts of things. Everybody must refrain from slitting his throat, everybody must refrain from shooting him—and everybody must refrain from unplugging you from him. But does he have a right against everybody that they shall refrain from unplugging you from him? To refrain from doing this is to allow him to continue to use your kidneys. It could be argued that he has a right against us that we should allow him to continue to use your kidneys. That is, while he had no right against us that we should give him the use of your kidneys, it might be argued that he anyway has a right against us that we shall not now intervene and deprive him of the use of your kidneys. I shall come back to third-party interventions later. But certainly the violinist has no right against you that you shall allow him to continue to use your kidneys. As I said, if you do allow him to use them, it is a kindness on your part, and not something you owe him.

…I would stress that I am not arguing that people do not have a right to life—quite to the contrary, it seems to me that the primary control we must place on the acceptability of an account of rights is that it should turn out, in that account, to be a truth that all persons have a right to life. I am arguing only that having a right to life does not guarantee having either a right to be given the use of or a right to be allowed continued use of another person's body—even if one needs it for life itself. So the right to life will not serve the opponents of abortion in the very simple and clear way in which they seem to have thought it would.

4.

There is another way to bring out the difficulty. In the most ordinary sort of case, to deprive someone of what he has a right to is to treat him unjustly. Suppose a boy and his small brother are jointly given a box of chocolates for Christmas. If the older boy takes the box and refuses to give his brother any of the chocolates, he is unjust to him, for the brother has been given a right to half of them. But suppose that, having learned that otherwise it means nine years in bed with that violinist, you unplug yourself from him. You surely are not being unjust to him, for you gave him no right to use your kidneys, and no one else can have given him any such right. But we have to notice that in unplugging yourself, you are killing him; and violinists, like everybody else, have a right to life, and thus in the view we are considering just now, the right not to be killed. So here you do what he supposedly has a right you shall not do, but do not act unjustly to him in doing it.

The emendation which may be made at this point is this: the right to life consists not in the right not to be killed, but rather in the right not to be killed unjustly. This runs a risk of circularity, but never mind: it would enable us to square the fact that the violinist has a right to life with the fact that you do not act unjustly toward him in unplugging yourself, thereby killing him. For if you do not kill him unjustly, you do not violate his right to life, and so it is no wonder you do him no injustice.

But if this emendation is accepted, the gap in the argument against abortion stares us plainly in the face: it is by no means enough to show that the fetus is a person, and to remind us that all persons have a right to life—we need to be shown also that killing the fetus violates its right to life, that is, that abortion is unjust killing. And is it?

I suppose we may take it as a datum that in a case of pregnancy due to rape the mother has not given the unborn person a right to the use of her body for food and shelter. Indeed, in what pregnancy could it be supposed that the mother has given the unborn person such a right? It is not as if there were unborn persons drifting about the world, to whom a woman who wants a child says "I invite you in."

But it might be argued that there are other ways one can have acquired a right to the use of another person's body than by having been invited to use it by that person. Suppose a woman voluntarily indulges in intercourse, knowing of the chance it will issue in pregnancy, and then she does become pregnant, is she not in part responsible for the presence, in fact the very existence of the unborn person inside her? No doubt she did not invite it in. But doesn't her partial responsibility for its being there itself give it a right to the use of her body? If so, then her aborting it would be more like the boy's taking the chocolates, and less like your unplugging yourself from the violinist—doing so would be depriving it of what it does have a right to, and thus would be doing it an injustice.

And then, too, it might be asked whether or not she can kill it even to save her own life: If she voluntarily called it into existence, how can she now kill it, even in self-defense?

The first thing to be said about this is that it is something new. Opponents of abortion have been so concerned to make out the independence of the fetus, in order to establish that it has a right to life, just as its mother does, that they have tended to overlook the possible support they might gain from making out that the fetus is *dependent* on the mother, in order to establish that she has a special kind of responsibility for it, a responsibility that gives it rights against her which are not possessed by any independent person—such as an ailing violinist who is a stranger to her.

On the other hand, this argument would give the unborn person a right to its mother's body only if her pregnancy resulted from a voluntary act, undertaken in full knowledge of the chance a pregnancy might result from it. It would leave out entirely the unborn person whose existence is due to rape. Pending the availability of some further argument, then, we would be left with the conclusion that unborn persons whose existence is due to rape have no right to the use of their mothers' bodies, and thus that aborting them is not depriving them of anything that they have a right to and hence is not unjust killing.

And we should also notice that it is not at all plain that this argument really does go even as far as it purports to. For there are cases and cases, and the details make a difference. If the room is stuffy, and I therefore open a window to air it, and a burglar climbs in, it would be absurd to say, "Ah, now he can stay, she's given him a right to the use of her house—for she is partially responsible for his presence there, having voluntarily done what enabled him to get in, in full knowledge that there are such things as burglars, and that burglars burgle." It would be still more absurd to say this if I had had bars installed outside my windows, precisely to prevent burglars from getting in, and a burglar got in only because of a defect in the bars. It remains equally absurd if we imagine it is not a burglar who climbs in, but an innocent person who blunders or falls in. Again, suppose it were like this: people-seeds drift about in the air like pollen, and if you open your windows, one may drift in and take root in your carpets or upholstery. You don't want children, so you fix up your windows with fine mesh screens, the very best you can buy. As can happen, however, and on very, very rare occasions does happen, one of the screens is defective; and a seed drifts in and takes root. Does the person-plant who now develops have a right to the use of your house? Surely not—despite the fact that you voluntarily opened your windows, you knowingly kept carpets and upholstered furniture, and you knew that screens were sometimes defective. Someone may argue that you are responsible for its rooting, that it does have a right to your house, because after all you *could* have lived out your life with bare floors and furniture, or with sealed windows and doors. But this won't do—for by the same token anyone can avoid a pregnancy due to rape by having a hysterectomy, or anyway by never leaving home without a (reliable!) army.

It seems to me that the argument we are looking at can establish at most that there are some cases in which the unborn person has a right to the use of its mother's body, and therefore some cases in which abortion is unjust killing...the argument certainly does not establish that all abortion is unjust killing.

5.

There is room for yet another argument here, however. We surely must all grant that there may be cases in which it would be morally indecent to detach a person from your body at the cost of his life. Suppose you learn that what the violinist needs is not nine years of your life, but only one hour: all you need to do to save his life is to spend one hour in that bed with him. Suppose also that letting him use your kidneys for that one hour would not affect your health in the slightest. Admittedly you were kidnapped. Admittedly you did not give anyone permission to plug him into you. Nevertheless it seems to me plain you ought to allow him to use your kidneys for that hour—it would be indecent to refuse.

Again, suppose pregnancy lasted only an hour, and constituted no threat to life or health. And suppose that a woman becomes pregnant as a result of rape. Admittedly she did not voluntarily do anything to bring about the existence of a child. Admittedly she did nothing at all which would give the unborn person a right to the use of her body. All the same it might well be said, as in the newly emended violinist story, that she ought to allow it to remain for that hour—that it would be indecent in her to refuse.

Now some people are inclined to use the term "right" in such a way that it follows from the fact that you ought to allow a person to use your body for the hour he needs, that he has a right to use your body for the hour he needs, even though he has not been given that right by any person or act. They may say that it follows also that if you refuse, you act unjustly toward him. This use of the term is perhaps so common that it cannot be called wrong; nevertheless it seems to me to be an unfortunate loosening of what we would do better to keep a tight rein on....

A further objection to so using the term "right" that from the fact that A ought to do a thing for B, it follows that B has a right against A that A do it for him, is that it is going to make the question of whether or not a man has a right to a thing turn on how easy it is to provide him with it; and this seems not merely unfortunate, but morally unacceptable. Take the case of Henry Fonda again. I said earlier that I had no right to the touch of his cool hand on my fevered brow, even though I needed it to save my life. I said it would be frightfully nice of him to fly in from the West Coast to provide me with it, but that I had no right against him that he should do so. But suppose he isn't on the West Coast. Suppose he has only to walk across the room, place a hand briefly on my brow—and lo, my life is saved. Then surely he ought to do it, it would be indecent to refuse. Is it to be said "Ah, well, it follows that in this case she has a right to the touch of his hand on her brow, and so it would be an injustice in him to refuse"? So that I have a right to it when it is easy for him to provide it, though no right when it's hard? It's rather a shocking idea that anyone's rights should fade away and disappear as it gets harder and harder to accord them to him.

So my own view is that even though you ought to let the violinist use your kidneys for the one hour he needs, we should not conclude that he has a right to do so—we should say that if you refuse, you are...self-centered and callous, indecent in fact, but not unjust. And similarly, that even supposing a case in which a woman pregnant due to rape ought to allow the unborn person to use her body for the hour he needs, we should not conclude that he has a right to do so; we should conclude that she is self-centered, callous, indecent, but not unjust, if she refuses. The complaints are no less grave; they are just different. However, there is no need to insist on this point. If anyone does wish to deduce "he has a right" from "you ought," then all the same he must surely grant that there are cases in which it is not morally required of you that you allow that violinist to use your kidneys, and in which he does not have a right to use them, and in which you do not do him an injustice if you refuse. And so also for mother and unborn child. Except in such cases as the unborn person has a right to demand it—and we were leaving open the possibility that there may be such cases—nobody is morally *required* to make large sacrifices, of health, of all other interests and concerns, of all other duties and commitments, for nine years, or even for nine months, in order to keep another person alive.

6.

We have in fact to distinguish between two kinds of Samaritan: the Good Samaritan and what we might call the Minimally Decent Samaritan. The story of the Good Samaritan, you will remember, goes like this:

> A certain man went down from Jerusalem to Jericho, and fell among thieves, which stripped him of his raiment, and wounded him, and departed, leaving him half-dead.
> And by chance there came down a certain priest that way; and when he saw him, he passed by on the other side.
> And likewise a Levite, when he was at the place, came and looked on him, and passed by on the other side.
> But a certain Samaritan, as he journeyed, came where he was; and when he saw him he had compassion on him.
> And went to him, and bound up his wounds, pouring in oil and wine, and set him on his own beast, and brought him to an inn, and took care of him.
> And on the morrow, when he departed, he took out two pence, and gave them to the host, and said unto him, "Take care of him; and whatsoever thou spendest more, when I come again, I will repay thee." (Luke 10: 30–35)

The Good Samaritan went out of his way at some cost to himself, to help one in need of it. We are not told what the options were, that is, whether or not the priest and the Levite could have helped by doing less than the Good Samaritan did, but assuming they could have, then the fact they did nothing at all shows they were not even Minimally Decent Samaritans, not because they were not Samaritans, but because they were not even minimally decent.

These things are a matter of degree, of course, but there is a difference, and it comes out perhaps most clearly in the story of Kitty Genovese, who, as you will remember, was murdered while thirty-eight people watched or listened, and did nothing at all to help her. A Good Samaritan would have rushed out to give direct assistance against the murderer. Or perhaps we had better allow that it would have been a Splendid Samaritan who did this, on the ground that it would have involved a risk of death for himself. But the thirty-eight not only did not do this, they did not even trouble to pick up a phone to call the police. Minimally Decent Samaritanism would call for doing at least that, and their not having done it was monstrous.

After telling the story of the Good Samaritan, Jesus said "Go, and do thou likewise." Perhaps he meant that we are morally required to act as the Good Samaritan did. Perhaps he was urging people to do more than is morally required of them. At all events it seems plain that it was not morally required of any of the thirty-eight that he rush out to give direct assistance at the risk of his own life, and that it is not morally required of anyone that he give long stretches of his life—nine years or nine months—to sustaining the life of a person who has no special right (we were leaving open the possibility of this) to demand it.

Indeed, with one rather striking class of exceptions, no one in any country in the world is legally required to do anywhere near as much as this for anyone else. The class of exceptions is obvious. My main concern here is not the state of the law in respect to abortion, but it is worth drawing attention to the fact that in no state in this country is any man compelled by law to be even a Minimally Decent Samaritan to any person; there is no law under which charges could be brought against the thirty-eight who stood by while Kitty Genovese died. By contrast, in most states in this country, women are compelled by law to be not merely Minimally Decent Samaritans, but Good Samaritans to unborn persons inside them. This doesn't by itself settle anything one way or the other, because it may well be argued that there should be laws in this country—as there are in many European countries—compelling at least Minimally Decent Samaritanism. But it does show that there is a gross injustice in the existing state of the law. And it shows also that the groups currently working against liberalization of abortion laws, in fact working toward having it declared unconstitutional for a state to permit abortion, had better start working for the adoption of Good Samaritan laws generally, or earn the charge that they are acting in bad faith.

I should think, myself, that Minimally Decent Samaritan laws would be one thing, Good Samaritan laws quite another, and in fact highly improper. But we are not here concerned with the law. What we should ask is not whether anybody should be compelled by law to be a Good Samaritan, but whether we must accede to a situation in which somebody is being compelled—by nature, perhaps—to be a Good Samaritan. We have, in other words, to look now at third-party interventions. I have been arguing that no person is morally required to make large sacrifices to sustain the life of another who has no right to demand them, and this even where the sacrifices do not include life itself, we are not morally required to be Good Samaritans or anyway, Very Good Samaritans to one another. But what if a man cannot extricate himself from such a situation? What if he appeals to us to extricate him? It seems to me plain that there are cases in which we can, cases in which a Good Samaritan would extricate him. There you are, you were kidnapped, and nine years in bed with that violinist lie ahead of you. You have your own life to lead. You are sorry but you simply cannot see giving up so much of your life to the sustaining of his. You cannot extricate yourself, and ask us to do so. I should have thought that—in light of his having no right to the use of your body—it was obvious that we do not have to accede to your being forced to give up so much. We can do what you ask. There is no injustice to the violinist in our doing so.

7.

Following the lead of the opponents of abortion, I have throughout been speaking of the fetus merely as a person, and what I have been asking is whether or not the argument we began with, which proceeds only from the fetus' being a person, really does establish its conclusion. I have argued that it does not.

But of course there are arguments and arguments, and it may be said that I have simply fastened on the wrong one. It may be said that what is important is not merely the fact that the fetus is a person, but that it is a person for whom the woman has a special kind of responsibility issuing from the fact that she is its mother. And it might be argued that all my analogies are therefore irrelevant, for you do not have that special kind of responsibility for that violinist, Henry Fonda does not have that special kind of responsibility for me. And our attention might be drawn to the fact that men and women both are compelled by law to provide support for their children.

I have in effect dealt (briefly) with this argument in Section 4 above; but a (still briefer) recapitulation now may be in order. Surely we do not have any such "special responsibility" for a person unless we have assumed it, explicitly or implicitly. If a set of parents do not try to prevent pregnancy, do not obtain an abortion, and then at the time of birth of the child do not put it out to adoption, but rather take it home with them, then they have assumed responsibility for it, they have given it rights, and they cannot now withdraw support from it at the cost of its life because they now find it difficult to go on providing for it. But if they have taken all reasonable precautions against having a child, they do not, simply by virtue of their biological relationship to the child who comes into existence, have a special responsibility for it. They may wish to assume responsibility for it, or they may not wish to. And I am suggesting that if assuming responsibility for it would require large sacrifices, then they may refuse. A Good Samaritan would not refuse—or anyway, a Splendid Samaritan, if the sacrifices that had to be made were enormous. But then so would a Good Samaritan assume responsibility for that violinist; so would Henry Fonda, if he is a Good Samaritan, fly in from the West Coast and assume responsibility for me.

8.

My argument will be found unsatisfactory on two counts by many of those who want to regard abortion as morally permissible. First, while I do argue that abortion is not impermissible, I do not argue that it is always permissible. There may well be cases in which carrying the child to term requires only Minimally Decent Samaritanism of the mother, and this is a standard we must not fall below. I am inclined to think it a merit of my account precisely that it does *not* give a general yes or a general no. It allows for and supports our sense that, for example, a sick and desperately frightened fourteen-year-old schoolgirl, pregnant due to rape, may *of course* choose abortion, and that any law which rules this out is an insane law. And it also allows for and supports our sense that in other cases resort to abortion is even positively indecent. It would be indecent in the woman to request an abortion, and indecent in a doctor to perform it, if she is in her seventh month, and wants the abortion just to avoid the nuisance of postponing a trip abroad. The very fact that the arguments I have been drawing attention to treat all cases of abortion, or even all cases of abortion in which the mother's life is not at stake, as morally on a par ought to have made them suspect at the outset.

Secondly, while I am arguing for the permissibility of abortion in some cases, I am not arguing for the right to secure the death of the unborn child. It is easy to confuse these two things in that, up to a certain point in the life of the fetus, it is not able to survive outside the mother's body; hence removing it from her body guarantees its death. But they are importantly different. I have argued that you are not morally required to spend nine months in bed, sustaining the life of that violinist; but to say this is by no means to say that if, when you unplug yourself, there is a miracle and he survives, you then have a right to turn round and slit his throat. You may detach yourself even if this costs him his life: you have no right to be guaranteed his death, by some other means, if unplugging yourself does not kill him. There are some people who will feel dissatisfied by this feature of my argument. A woman may be utterly devastated by the thought of a child, a bit of herself, put out for adoption and never seen or heard of again. She may therefore want not merely that the child be detached from her, but more, that it die. Some opponents of abortion are inclined to regard this as beneath contempt—thereby showing insensitivity to what is surely a powerful source of despair. All the same, I agree that the desire for the child's death is not one which anybody may gratify, should it turn out to be possible to detach the child alive.

At this place, however, it should be remembered that we have only been pretending throughout that the fetus is a human being from the moment of conception. A very early abortion is surely not the killing of a person, and so is not dealt with by anything I have said here.

NOTES

I am very much indebted to James Thomson for discussion, criticism, and many helpful suggestions.

[1]The term "direct" in the arguments I refer to is a technical one. Roughly, what is meant by *direct killing* is either killing as an end in itself, or killing as a means to some end, for example, the end of saving someone else's life....

ON THE MORAL AND LEGAL STATUS OF ABORTION

Mary Anne Warren

We will be concerned with both the moral status of abortion, which for our purposes we may define as the act which a woman performs in voluntarily terminating, or allowing another person to terminate, her pregnancy, and the legal status which is appropriate for this act. I will argue that, while it is not possible to produce a satisfactory defense of a woman's right to obtain an abortion without showing that a fetus is not a human being, in the morally relevant sense of that term, we ought not to conclude that the difficulties involved in determining whether or not a fetus is human make it impossible to produce any satisfactory solution to the problem of the moral status of abortion. For it is possible to show that, on the basis of intuitions which we may expect even the opponents of abortion to share, a fetus is not a person, and hence not the sort of entity to which it is proper to ascribe full moral rights.

Of course, while some philosophers would deny the possibility of any such proof,[1] others will deny that there is any need for it, since the moral permissibility of abortion appears to them to be too obvious to require proof. But the inadequacy of this attitude should be evident from the fact that both the friends and the foes of abortion consider their position to be morally self-evident. Because proabortionists have never adequately come to grips with the conceptual issues surrounding abortion, most if not all, of the arguments which they advance in opposition to laws restricting access to abortion fail to refute or even weaken the traditional antiabortion argument, that is, that a fetus is a human being, and therefore abortion is murder.

These arguments are typically of one of two sorts. Either they point to the terrible side effects of the restrictive laws, e.g., the deaths due to illegal abortions, and the fact that it is poor women who suffer the most as a result of these laws, or else they state that to deny a woman access to abortion is to deprive her of her right to control her own body. Unfortunately, however, the fact that restricting access to abortion has tragic side effects does not, in itself, show that the restrictions are unjustified, since murder is wrong regardless of the consequences of prohibiting it; and the appeal to the right to control one's body, which is generally construed as a property right, is at best a rather feeble argument for the permissibility of abortion. Mere ownership does not give me the right to kill innocent people whom I find on my property, and indeed I am apt to be held responsible if such people injure themselves while on my property. It is equally unclear that I have any moral right to expel an innocent person from my property when I know that doing so will result in his death. ...

But however we wish to construe the right to abortion, we cannot hope to convince those who consider abortion a form of murder of the existence of any such right unless we are able to produce a clear and convincing refutation of the traditional antiabortion argument, and this has not, to my knowledge, been done. With respect to the two most vital issues which that argument involves, that is, the humanity of the fetus, and its implication for the moral status of abortion, confusion has prevailed on both sides of the dispute. ...

[R]ecent papers, ...one by Judith Thomson,[2] have attempted to settle the question of whether abortion ought to be prohibited apart from the question of whether or not the fetus is human. ...

Judith Thomson is, in fact, the only writer I am aware of who has... argued that, even if we grant the antiabortionist his claim that a fetus is a human being, with the same right to life as any other human being, we can still demonstrate that in at least some and perhaps most cases, a woman is under no moral obligation to complete an unwanted pregnancy. Her argument is worth examining, since if it holds up it may enable us to establish the moral permissibility of abortion without becoming involved in problems about what entitles an entity to be considered human, and accorded full moral rights. To be able to do this would be a great gain in the power and simplicity of the proabortion position, since, although I will argue that these problems can be solved at least as decisively as can any other moral problem, we should certainly be pleased to be able to avoid having to solve them as part of the justification of abortion. ...

Our own inquiry will also have two stages. In Section I, we will consider whether or not it is possible to establish that abortion is morally permissible even on the assumption that a fetus is an entity with a full-fledged right to life. I will argue that in fact this cannot be established, at least not with the conclusiveness which is essential to our hopes of convincing those who are skeptical about the morality of abortion, and that we therefore cannot avoid dealing with the question of whether or not a fetus really does have the same right to life as a (more fully developed) human being.

In Section II, I will propose an answer to this question, namely, that a fetus cannot be considered a member of the moral community, the set of beings with full and equal moral rights, for the simple reason that it is not a person, and that it is personhood, and not genetic humanity…which is the basis for membership in this community. I will argue that a fetus, whatever its stage of development, satisfies none of the basic criteria of personhood, and is not even enough *like* a person to be accorded even some of the same rights on the basis of this resemblance. Nor, as we will see, is a fetus's *potential* personhood a threat to the morality of abortion, since, whatever the rights of potential people may be, they are invariably overridden in any conflict with the moral rights of actual people.

I

We turn now to Professor Thomson's case for the claim that even if a fetus has full moral rights, abortion is still morally permissible, at least sometimes, and for some reasons other than to save the woman's life. Her argument is based upon a clever, but I think faulty, analogy. She asks us to picture ourselves waking up one day in bed with a famous violinist. Imagine that you have been kidnapped, and your bloodstream hooked up to that of the violinist, who happens to have an ailment which will certainly kill him unless he is permitted to share your kidneys for a period of nine months.…

Now then, she continues, what are your obligations in this situation? The antiabortionist, if he is consistent, will have to say that you are obligated to stay in bed with the violinist: for all people have a right to life, and violinists are people, and therefore it would be murder for you to disconnect yourself from him and let him die. But this is outrageous, and so there must be something wrong with the same argument when it is applied to abortion. It would certainly be commendable of you to agree to save the violinist, but it is absurd to suggest that your refusal to do so would be murder. His right to life does not obligate you to do whatever is required to keep him alive; nor does it justify anyone else in forcing you to do so. A law which required you to stay in bed with the violinist would clearly be an unjust law, since it is no proper function of the law to force unwilling people to make huge sacrifices for the sake of other people toward whom they have no such prior obligation.

Thomson concludes that, if this analogy is an apt one, then we can grant the antiabortionist his claim that a fetus is a human being, and still hold that it is at least sometimes the case that a pregnant woman has the right to refuse to be a Good Samaritan towards the fetus, that is, to obtain an abortion. For there is a great gap between the claim that x has a right to life, and the claim that y is obligated to do whatever is necessary to keep x alive, let alone that he ought to be forced to do so. It is y's duty to keep x alive only if he has somehow contracted a special obligation to do so; and a woman who is unwillingly pregnant, e.g., who was raped, has done nothing which obligates her to make the enormous sacrifice which is necessary to preserve the conceptus.

This argument is initially quite plausible, and in the extreme case of pregnancy due to rape it is probably conclusive. Difficulties arise, however, when we try to specify more exactly the range of cases in which abortion is clearly justifiable even on the assumption that the fetus is human. Professor Thomson considers it a virtue of her argument that it does not enable us to conclude that abortion is always permissible. It would, she says, be "indecent" for a woman in her seventh month to obtain an abortion just to avoid having to postpone a trip to Europe. On the other hand, her argument enables us to see that "a sick and desperately frightened schoolgirl, pregnant due to rape, may *of course* choose abortion, and that any law which rules this out is an insane law" (p. 294). So far, so good; but what are we to say about the woman who becomes pregnant not through rape but as a result of her own carelessness, or because of contraceptive failure, or who gets pregnant intentionally and then changes her mind about wanting a child? With respect to such cases, the violinist analogy is of much less use to the defender of the woman's right to obtain an abortion.

Indeed, the choice of a pregnancy due to rape, as an example of a case in which abortion is permissible even if a fetus is considered a human being, is extremely significant; for it is only in the case of pregnancy due to rape that the woman's situation is adequately analogous to the violinist case for our intuitions about the latter to transfer convincingly. The crucial difference between a pregnancy due to rape and the *normal* case of an unwanted pregnancy is that in the normal case we cannot claim that the woman is in no way responsible for her predicament; she could have remained chaste, or taken her pills more faithfully, or abstained on dangerous days, and so on. If, on the other hand, you are kidnapped by strangers, and hooked up to a strange violinist, then you are free of any shred of responsibility for the situation on the basis of which it could be argued that you are obligated to keep the violinist alive. Only when her pregnancy is due to rape is a woman clearly just as nonresponsible....

Consequently, there is room for the antiabortionist to argue that in the normal case of unwanted pregnancy a woman has, by her own actions, assumed responsibility for the fetus. For if x behaves in a way which he could have avoided, and which he knows involves, let us say, a one percent chance of bringing into existence a human being, with a right to life, and does so knowing that, if this should happen, then that human being will perish unless x does certain things to keep him alive, then it is by no means clear that, when it does happen, x is free of any obligation to what he knew in advance would be required to keep that human being alive.

The plausibility of such an argument is enough to show that the Thomson analogy can provide a clear and persuasive defense of a woman's right to obtain an abortion only with respect to those cases in which the woman is in no way responsible for her pregnancy, e.g., where it is due to rape. In all other cases, we would almost certainly conclude that it was necessary to look carefully at the particular circumstances in order to determine the extent of the woman's responsibility, and hence the extent of her obligation. This is an extremely unsatisfactory outcome, from the viewpoint of the opponents of restrictive abortion laws, most of whom are convinced that a woman has a right to obtain an abortion regardless of how and why she got pregnant....

Perhaps we can make this point more clear by altering the violinist story just enough to make it more analogous to a normal unwanted pregnancy and less to a pregnancy due to rape, and then seeing whether it is still obvious that you are not obligated to stay in bed with the fellow.

Suppose, then, that violinists are peculiarly prone to the sort of illness the only cure for which is the use of someone else's bloodstream for nine months, and that because of this there has been formed a society of music lovers who agree that whenever a violinist is stricken they will draw lots and the loser will, by some means, be made the one and only person capable of saving him. Now then, would you be obligated to cooperate in curing the violinist if you had voluntarily joined this society, knowing the possible consequences, and then your name had been drawn and you had been kidnapped? Admittedly, you did not promise ahead of time that you would, but you did deliberately place yourself in a position in which it might happen that a human life would be lost if you did not. Surely this is at least a *prima facie* reason for supposing that you have an obligation to stay in bed with the violinist. Suppose that you had gotten your name drawn deliberately; surely *that* would be quite a strong reason for thinking that you had such an obligation....

...[O]nce we allow the assumption that a fetus has full moral rights, it becomes an extremely complex and difficult question whether and when abortion is justifiable. Thus the Thomson analogy cannot help us produce a clear and persuasive proof of the moral permissibility of abortion....

II

The question which we must answer in order to produce a satisfactory solution to the problem of the moral status of abortion is this: How are we to define the moral community, the set of beings with full and equal moral rights, such that we can decide whether a human fetus is a member of this community or not? What sort of entity, exactly, has the inalienable rights to life, liberty, and the pursuit of happiness? Jefferson attributed these rights to all *men*, and it may or may not be fair to suggest that he intended to attribute them *only* to men. Perhaps he ought to have attributed them to all human beings.... What reason is there for identifying the moral community with the set of all human beings, in whatever way we have chosen to define that term?

On the Definition of "Human"

One reason why this vital second question is so frequently overlooked in the debate over the moral status of abortion is that the term "human" has two distinct, but not often distinguished, senses. This fact results in a slide of meaning, which serves to conceal the fallaciousness of the traditional argument that since (1) it is wrong to kill innocent human beings, and (2) fetuses are innocent human beings, then (3) it is wrong to kill fetuses. For if "human" is used in the same sense in both (1) and (2) then, whichever of the two senses is meant, one of these premises is question-begging. And if it is used in two different senses, then of course the conclusion does not follow.

Thus, (1) is a self-evident moral truth, and avoids begging the question about abortion, only if "human being" is used to mean something like "a full-fledged member of the moral community." (It may or may not also be meant to refer exclusively to members of the species *Homo sapiens*.) We may call this the *moral* sense of "human." It is not to be confused with what we will call the *genetic* sense, that is, the sense in which any member of the species is a human being, and no member of any other species could be. If (1) is acceptable only if the moral sense is intended, (2) is non-question-begging only if what is intended is the genetic sense.

...[I]n the absence of any argument showing that whatever is genetically human is also morally human...nothing more than genetic humanity can be demonstrated by the presence of the human genetic code. And, as we will see, the *potential* capacity for rational thought can at most show that an entity has the potential for *becoming* human in the moral sense.

Defining the Moral Community

Can it be established that genetic humanity is sufficient for moral humanity? I think that there are very good reasons for not defining the moral community in this way. I would like to suggest an alternative way of defining the moral community, which I will argue for only to the extent of explaining why it is, or should be, self-evident. The suggestion is simply that the moral community consists of all and only people, rather than all and only human beings;[3] and probably the best way of demonstrating its self-evidence is by considering the concept of personhood to see what sorts of entity are and are not persons, and what the decision that a being is or is not a person implies about its moral rights.

What characteristics entitle an entity to be considered a person?... All we need is a rough and approximate list of the most basic criteria of personhood, and some idea of which, or how many, of these an entity must satisfy in order to properly be considered a person.

In searching for such criteria, it is useful to look beyond the set of people with whom we are acquainted, and ask how we would decide whether a totally alien being was a person or not. (For we have no right to assume that genetic humanity is necessary for personhood.) Imagine a space traveler who lands on an unknown planet and encounters a race of beings utterly unlike any he has ever seen or heard of. If he wants to be sure of behaving morally toward these beings, he has to somehow decide whether they are people, and hence have full moral rights, or whether they are the sort of thing which he need not feel guilty about treating as, for example, a source of food.

How should he go about making this decision?...

I suggest that the traits which are most central to the concept of personhood are, very roughly, the following:

1. consciousness (of objects and events external and/or internal to the being), and in particular the capacity to feel pain;
2. reasoning (the *developed* capacity to solve new and relatively complex problems);
3. self-motivated activity (activity which is relatively independent of either genetic or direct external control);
4. the capacity to communicate, by whatever means, messages of an indefinite variety of types, that is, not just with an indefinite number of possible contents, but on indefinitely many possible topics;
5. the presence of self-concepts and self-awareness, either individual or racial, or both.

Admittedly, there are apt to be a great many problems involved in formulating precise definitions of these criteria, let alone in developing universally valid behavioral criteria for deciding when they apply. But I will assume that both we and our explorer know approximately what (1) to (5) mean, and that he is also able to determine whether or not they apply. How, then, should he use his findings to decide whether or not the alien beings are people? We need not suppose that an entity must have *all* of these attributes to be properly considered a person; (1) and (2) alone may well be sufficient for personhood, and quite probably (1) to (3) are sufficient. Neither do we need to insist that any one of these criteria is *necessary* for personhood, although once again (1) and (2) look like fairly good candidates for necessary conditions, as does (3), if "activity" is construed so as to include the activity of reasoning.

All we need to claim, to demonstrate that a fetus is not a person, is that any being which satisfies *none* of (1) to (5) is certainly not a person. I consider this claim to be so obvious that I think anyone who denied it, and claimed that a being which satisfied none of (1) to (5) was a person all the same, would thereby demonstrate that he had no notion at all of what a person is—perhaps because he had confused the concept of a person with that of genetic humanity. If the opponents of abortion were to deny the appropriateness of these five criteria, I do not know what further arguments would convince them. We would probably have to admit that our conceptual schemes were indeed irreconcilably different, and that our dispute could not be settled objectively....

Now if (1) to (5) are indeed the primary criteria of personhood, then it is clear that genetic humanity is neither necessary nor sufficient for establishing that an entity is a person. Some human beings are not people, and there may well be people who are not human beings. A man or woman whose consciousness has been permanently obliterated but who remains alive is a human being which is no longer a person; defective human beings, with no appreciable mental capacity, are not and presumably never will be people; and a fetus is a human being which is not yet a person, and which therefore cannot coherently be said to have full moral rights....

Fetal Development and the Right to Life

Two problems arise in the application of these suggestions for the definition of the moral community to the determination of the precise moral status of a human fetus. Given that the paradigm example of a person is a normal adult human being, then (1) how like this paradigm, in particular how far advanced since conception, does a human being need to be before it begins to have a right to life by virtue, not of being fully a person as of yet, but of being *like* a person? And (2) to what extent, if any, does the fact that a fetus has the *potential* for becoming a person endow it with some of the same rights?...

In answering the first question, we need not attempt a detailed consideration of the moral rights of organisms which are not developed enough, aware enough, intelligent enough, etc., to be considered people, but which resemble people in some respects. It does seem reasonable to suggest that the more like a person, in the relevant respects, a being is, the stronger is the case for regarding it as having a right to life, and indeed the stronger its right to life is. Thus we ought to take seriously the suggestion that insofar as "the human individual develops biologically in a continuous fashion...the rights of a human person might develop in the same way."[4] But we must keep in mind that the attributes which are relevant in determining whether or not an entity is enough like a person to be regarded as having some of the same moral rights are no different from those which are relevant to determining whether or not it is fully a person—that is, are no different from (1) to (5)—and that being genetically human, or having recognizably human facial and other physical features, or detectable brain activity, or the capacity to survive outside the uterus, are simply not among these relevant attributes.

Thus it is clear, that even though a seven- or eight-month fetus has features which make it apt to arouse in us almost the same powerful protective instinct as is commonly aroused by a small infant, nevertheless it is not significantly more personlike than is a very small embryo. It is *somewhat* more personlike; it can apparently feel and respond to pain, and it may even have a rudimentary form of consciousness, insofar as its brain is quite active. Nevertheless, it seems safe to say that it is not fully conscious, in the way that an infant of a few months is, and that it cannot reason, or communicate messages of indefinitely many sorts, does not engage in self-motivated activity, and has no self-awareness. Thus, in the *relevant* respects, a fetus, even a fully developed one, is considerably less personlike than is the average mature mammal, indeed the average fish. And I think that a rational person must conclude that if the right to life of a fetus is to be based upon its resemblance to a person, then it cannot be said to have any more right to life than, let us say, a newborn guppy (which also seems to be capable of feeling pain), and that a right of that magnitude could never override a woman's right to obtain an abortion, at any stage of her pregnancy....

Thus, since the fact that even a fully developed fetus is not personlike enough to have any significant right to life on the basis of its personlikeness shows that no legal restrictions upon the stage of pregnancy in which an abortion may be performed can be justified on the grounds that we should protect the rights of the older fetus; and since there is no other apparent justification for such restrictions, we may conclude that they are entirely unjustified....

Potential Personhood and the Right to Life

We have seen that a fetus does not resemble a person in any way which can support the claim that it has even some of the same rights. But what about its *potential*, the fact that, if nurtured and allowed to develop naturally, it will very probably become a person? Does not that alone give it at least some right to life? It is hard to deny that the fact that an entity is a potential person is a strong *prima facie* reason for not destroying it; but we need not conclude from this that a potential person has a right to life, by virtue of that potential. It may be that our feeling that it is better, other things being equal, not to destroy a potential person, is better explained by the fact that potential people are still (felt to be) an invaluable resource, not to be lightly squandered. …

Still, we do not need to insist that a potential person has no right to life whatever. There may well be something immoral, and not just imprudent, about wantonly destroying potential people, when doing so is not necessary to protect anyone's rights. But even if a potential person does have some *prima facie* right to life, such a right could not possibly outweigh the right of a woman to obtain an abortion, since the rights of any actual person invariably outweigh those of any potential person whenever the two conflict. Since this may not be immediately obvious in the case of a human fetus, let us look at another case.

Suppose that our space explorer falls into the hands of an alien culture, whose scientists decide to create a few hundred thousand or more human beings by breaking his body into its component cells, and using these to create fully developed human beings with, of course, his genetic code. We may imagine that each of these newly created men will have all of the original man's abilities, skills, knowledge, and so on, and also have an individual self-concept, in short that each of them will be a bona fide (though hardly unique) person. Imagine that the whole project will take only seconds, and that its chances of success are extremely high, and that our explorer knows all of this, and also knows that these people will be treated fairly. I maintain that in such a situation he would have every right to escape if he could, and thus to deprive all of these potential people of their potential lives: for his right to life outweighs all of theirs together, in spite of the fact that they are all genetically human, all innocent, and all have a very high probability of becoming people very soon, if only he refrains from acting. …

Thus, neither a fetus's resemblance to a person nor its potential for becoming a person provides any basis whatever for the claim that it has any significant right to life. Consequently, a woman's right to protect her health, happiness, freedom, and even her life…by terminating an unwanted pregnancy will always override whatever right to life it may be appropriate to ascribe to a fetus, even a fully developed one. And thus, in the absence of any overwhelming social need for every possible child, the laws which restrict the right to obtain an abortion, or limit the period of pregnancy during which an abortion may be performed, are a wholly unjustified violation of a woman's most basic moral and constitutional rights.

POSTSCRIPT ON INFANTICIDE

Since the publication of this article, many people have written to point out that my argument appears to justify not only abortion, but infanticide as well. For a newborn infant is not significantly more personlike than an advanced fetus, and consequently it would seem that if the destruction of the latter is permissible, so, too, must be that of the former. Inasmuch as most people, regardless of how they feel about the morality of abortion, consider infanticide a form of murder, this might appear to represent a serious flaw in my argument.

Now, if I am right in holding that it is only people who have a full-fledged right to life, and who can be murdered, and if the criteria of personhood are as I have described them, then it obviously follows that killing a newborn infant is not murder. It does *not* follow, however, that infanticide is permissible, for two reasons. In the first place, it would be wrong, at least in this country and in this period of history, and other things being equal, to kill a newborn infant, because even if its parents do not want it and would not suffer from its destruction, there are other people who would like to have it, and would, in all probability, be deprived of a great deal of pleasure by its destruction. Thus, infanticide is wrong for reasons analogous to those which make it wrong to wantonly destroy natural resources, or great works of art.

Secondly, most people, at least in this country, value infants, and would much prefer that they be preserved, even if foster parents are not immediately available. Most of us would rather be taxed to support orphanages than allow unwanted infants to be destroyed. So long as there are people who want an infant preserved, and who are willing and able to provide the means of caring for it, under reasonably humane conditions, it is, *ceteris parabis*, wrong to destroy it.

But, it might be replied, if this argument shows that infanticide is wrong, at least at this time and in this country, does it not also show that abortion is wrong? After all, many people value fetuses, are disturbed by their destruction, and would much prefer that they be preserved, even at some cost to themselves. Furthermore, as a potential source of pleasure to some foster family, a fetus is just as valuable as an infant. There is, however, a crucial difference between the two cases: so long as the fetus is unborn, its preservation contrary to the wishes of the pregnant woman, violates her rights to freedom, happiness, and self-determination. Her rights override the rights of those who would like the fetus preserved, just as, if someone's life or limb is threatened by a wild animal, his right to protect himself by destroying the animal overrides the rights of those who would prefer that the animal not be harmed.

The minute the infant is born, however, its preservation no longer violates any of its mother's rights, even if she wants it destroyed, because she is free to put it up for adoption. Consequently, while the moment of birth does not mark any sharp discontinuity in the degree to which an infant possesses the right to life, it does mark the end of its mother's right to determine its fate. Indeed, if abortion could be performed without killing the fetus, she would never possess the right to have the fetus destroyed, for the same reasons that she has no right to have an infant destroyed.

On the other hand, it follows from my argument that when an unwanted or defective infant is born into a society which cannot afford and/or is not willing to care for it, then its destruction is permissible. This conclusion will, no doubt, strike many people as heartless and immoral; but remember that the very existence of people who feel this way, and who are willing and able to provide care for unwanted infants, is reason enough to conclude that they should be preserved.

NOTES

My thanks to the following people, who were kind enough to read and criticize an earlier version of this paper: Herbert Gold, Gene Glass, Anne Lauterbach, Judith Thomson, Mary Mothersill, and Timothy Binkley.

[1] For example, Roger Wertheimer, who, in "Understanding the Abortion Argument" (*Philosophy and Public Affairs*, 1, No. I [Fall 1971]: 67–95), argues that the problem of the moral status of abortion is insoluble, in that the dispute over the status of the fetus is not a question of fact at all, but only a question how one responds to the facts.

[2] Judith Jarvis Thomson, "A Defense of Abortion," *Philosophy and Public Affairs*, 1, No. 1 (Fall 1971): 47–66.

[3] From here on, we will use "human" to mean genetically human, since the moral sense seems closely connected to, and perhaps derived from, the assumption that genetic humanity is sufficient for membership in the moral community.

[4] Thomas L. Hayes, "A Biological View," *Commonweal*, 85 (March 17, 1967): 677–678; quoted by Daniel Callahan, in *Abortion: Law, Choice and Morality* (London: Macmillan & Co., 1970).

WHY ABORTION IS IMMORAL

Don Marquis

The view that abortion is, with rare exceptions, seriously immoral has received little support in the recent philosophical literature.... This essay sets out an argument that purports to show, as well as any argument in ethics can show, that abortion is, except possibly in rare cases, seriously immoral, that it is in the same moral category as killing an innocent adult human being.

The argument is based on a major assumption. Many of the most insightful and careful writers on the ethics of abortion...believe that whether or not abortion is morally permissible stands or falls on whether or not a fetus is the sort of being whose life it is seriously wrong to end. The argument of this essay will assume, but not argue, that they are correct.

Also, this essay will neglect issues of great importance to a complete ethics of abortion. Some antiabortionists will allow that certain abortions, such as abortion before implantation or abortion when the life of a woman is threatened by a pregnancy or abortion after rape, may be morally permissible. This essay will not explore the casuistry of these hard cases. The purpose of this essay is to develop a general argument for the claim that the overwhelming majority of deliberate abortions are seriously immoral....

Reprinted from the *Journal of Philosophy* LXXXVI (April 1989): 183–202 with permission of the publisher and author.

II

...[W]e can start from the following unproblematic assumption concerning our own case: it is wrong to kill us. Why is it wrong? Some answers can be easily eliminated. It might be said that what makes killing us wrong is that a killing brutalizes the one who kills. But the brutalization consists of being inured to the performance of an act that is hideously immoral; hence, the brutalization does not explain the immorality. It might be said that what makes killing us wrong is the great loss others would experience due to our absence. Although such hubris is understandable, such an explanation does not account for the wrongness of killing hermits, or those whose lives are relatively independent and whose friends find it easy to make new friends.

A more obvious answer is better. What primarily makes killing wrong is neither its effect on the murderer nor its effect on the victim's friends and relatives, but its effect on the victim. The loss of one's life is one of the greatest losses one can suffer. The loss of one's life deprives one of all the experiences, activities, projects, and enjoyments that would otherwise have constituted one's future. Therefore, killing someone is wrong primarily because the killing inflicts (one of) the greatest possible losses on the victim. To describe this as the loss of life can be misleading, however. The change in my biological state does not by itself make killing me wrong. The effect of the loss of my biological life is the loss to me of all those activities, projects, experiences, and enjoyments which would otherwise have constituted my future personal life. These activities, projects, experience, and enjoyments are either valuable for their own sakes or are means to something else that is valuable for its own sake. Some parts of my future are not valued by me now, but will come to be valued by me as I grow older and as my values and capacities change. When I am killed, I am deprived both of what I now value which would have been part of my future personal life, but also what I would come to value. Therefore, when I die, I am deprived of all of the value of my future. Inflicting this loss on me is ultimately what makes killing me wrong. This being the case, it would seem that what makes killing any adult human being *prima facie* seriously wrong is the loss of his or her future.[1]...

The claim that what makes killing wrong is the loss of the victim's future is directly supported by two considerations. In the first place, this theory explains why we regard killing as one of the worst of crimes. Killing is especially wrong because it deprives the victim of more than perhaps any other crime. In the second place, people with AIDS or cancer who know they are dying believe, of course, that dying is a very bad thing for them. They believe that the loss of a future to them that they would otherwise have experienced is what makes their premature death a very bad thing for them. ...

The view that what makes killing wrong is the loss to the victim of the value of the victim's future gains additional support when some of its implications are examined. In the first place, it is incompatible with the view that it is wrong to kill only beings who are biologically human; it is possible that there exists a different species from another planet whose members have a future like ours. Since having a future like that is what makes killing someone wrong, this theory entails that it would be wrong to kill members of such a species. Hence, this theory is opposed to the claim that only life that is biologically human has great moral worth, a claim which many antiabortionists have seemed to adopt. This opposition, which this theory has in common with personhood theories, seems to be a merit of the theory.

In the second place, the claim that the loss of one's future is the wrong-making feature of one's being killed entails the possibility that the futures of some actual nonhuman mammals on our own planet are sufficiently like ours that it is seriously wrong to kill them also. Whether some animals do have the same right to life as human beings depends on adding to the account of the wrongness of killing some additional account of just what it is about my future or the futures of other adult human beings which makes it wrong to kill us. No such additional account will be offered in this essay....

In the third place, the claim that the loss of one's future is the wrong-making feature of one's being killed does not entail, as sanctity of human life theories do, that active euthanasia is wrong. Persons who are severely and incurably ill, who face a future of pain and despair, and who wish to die will not have suffered a loss if they are killed. It is, strictly speaking, the value of a human's future which makes killing wrong in this theory. This being so, killing does not necessarily wrong some persons who are sick and dying. Of course, there may be other reasons for a prohibition of active euthanasia, but that is another matter. Sanctity-of-human-life theories seem to hold that active euthanasia is seriously wrong even in an individual case where there seems to be good reason for it independently of public policy considerations. This consequence is most implausible, and it is a plus for the claim that the loss of a future of value is what makes killing wrong that it does not share this consequence.

In the fourth place, the account of the wrongness of killing defended in this essay does straightforwardly entail that it is *prima facie* seriously wrong to kill children and infants, for we do presume that they have futures of value. Since we do believe that it is wrong to kill defenseless little babies, it is important that a theory of the wrongness of killing easily account for this. Personhood theories of the wrongness of killing, on the other hand, cannot straightforwardly account for the wrongness of killing infants and young children. Hence, such theories must add special ad hoc accounts of the wrongness of killing the young. The plausibility of such ad hoc theories seems to be a function of how desperately one wants such theories to work. The claim that the primary wrong-making feature of a killing is the loss to the victim of the value of its future accounts for the wrongness of killing young children and infants directly; it makes the wrongness of such acts as obvious as we actually think it is. This is a further merit of this theory. Accordingly, it seems that this value of a future-like-ours theory of the wrongness of killing shares strengths of both sanctity-of-life and personhood accounts, while avoiding weaknesses of both. In addition, it meshes with a central intuition concerning what makes killing wrong.

The claim that the primary wrong-making feature of a killing is the loss to the victim of the value of its future has obvious consequences for the ethics of abortion. The future of a standard fetus includes a set of experiences, projects, activities, and such which are identical with the futures of adult human beings and are identical with the futures of young children. Since the reason that is sufficient to explain why it is wrong to kill human beings after the time of birth is a reason that also applies to fetuses, it follows that abortion is *prima facie* seriously morally wrong.

This argument does not rely on the invalid inference that, since it is wrong to kill persons, it is wrong to kill potential persons also. The category that is morally central to this analysis is the category of having a valuable future like ours; it is not the category of personhood. The argument to the conclusion that abortion is *prima facie* seriously morally wrong proceeded independently of the notion of person or potential person or any equivalent....

The structure of this antiabortion argument can be both illuminated and defended by comparing it to what appears to be the best argument for the wrongness of the wanton infliction of pain on animals. This latter argument is based on the assumption that it is *prima facie* wrong to inflict pain on me (or you, reader). What is the natural property associated with the infliction of pain which makes such infliction wrong? The obvious answer seems to be that the infliction of pain causes suffering, and that suffering is a misfortune. The suffering caused by the infliction of pain is what makes the wanton infliction of pain on me wrong. The wanton infliction of pain on other adult humans causes suffering. The wanton infliction of pain on animals causes suffering. Since causing suffering is what makes the wanton infliction of pain wrong, and since the wanton infliction of pain on animals causes suffering, it follows that the wanton infliction of pain on animals is wrong.

This argument for the wrongness of the wanton infliction of pain on animals shares a number of structural features with the argument for the serious *prima facie* wrongness of abortion. Both arguments start with an obvious assumption concerning what it is wrong to do to me (or you, reader). Both then look for the characteristic or the consequence of the wrong action which makes the action wrong. Both recognize that the wrong-making feature of these immoral actions is a property of actions sometimes directed at individuals other than postnatal human beings. If the structure of the argument for the wrongness of the wanton infliction of pain on animals is sound, then the structure of the argument for the *prima facie* serious wrongness of abortion is also sound, for the structure of the two arguments is the same. The structure common to both is the key to the explanation of how the wrongness of abortion can be demonstrated without recourse to the category of person. In neither argument is that category crucial....

Of course, this value of a future-like-ours argument, if sound, shows only that abortion is *prima facie* wrong, not that it is wrong in any and all circumstances. Since the loss of the future to a standard fetus, if killed, is, however, at least as great a loss as the loss of the future to a standard adult human being who is killed, abortion, like ordinary killing, could be justified only by the most compelling reasons. The loss of one's life is almost the greatest misfortune that can happen to one. Presumably abortion could be justified in some circumstances, only if the loss consequent on failing to abort would be at least as great. Accordingly, morally permissible abortions will be rare indeed unless, perhaps, they occur so early in pregnancy that a fetus is not yet definitely an individual. Hence, this argument should be taken as showing that abortion is presumptively very seriously wrong, where the presumption is very strong—as strong as the presumption that killing another adult human being is wrong.

III

How complete an account of the wrongness of killing does the value of a future-like-ours account have to be in order that the wrongness of abortion is a consequence? This account does not have to be an account of the necessary conditions for the wrongness of killing. Some persons in nursing homes may lack valuable human futures, yet it may be wrong to kill them for other reasons. Furthermore, this account does not obviously have to be the sole reason killing is wrong where the victim did have a valuable future. This analysis claims *only* that, for any killing where the victim did have a valuable future like ours, having that future by itself is sufficient to create the strong presumption that the killing is seriously wrong.

One way to overturn the value of a future-like-ours argument would be to find some account of the wrongness of killing which is at least as intelligible and which has different implications for the ethics of abortion. Two rival accounts possess at least some degree of plausibility. One account is based on the obvious fact that people value the experience of living and wish for that valuable experience to continue. Therefore, it might be said, what makes killing wrong is the discontinuation of that experience for the victim. Let us call this the *discontinuation account*.[2] Another rival account is based upon the obvious fact that people strongly desire to continue to live. This suggests that what makes killing us so wrong is that it interferes with the fulfillment of a strong and fundamental desire, the fulfillment of which is necessary for the fulfillment of any other desires we might have. Let us call this the *desire account*.

Consider first the desire account as a rival account of the ethics of killing which would provide the basis for rejecting the antiabortion position. Such an account will have to be stronger than the value of a future-like-ours account of the wrongness of abortion if it is to do the job expected of it. To entail the wrongness of abortion, the value of a future-like-ours account has only to provide a sufficient, but not a necessary, condition for the wrongness of killing. The desire account, on the other hand, must provide us also with a necessary condition for the wrongness of killing in order to generate a prochoice conclusion on abortion. The reason for this is that presumably the argument from the desire account moves from the claim that what makes killing wrong is interference with a very strong desire to the claim that abortion is not wrong because the fetus lacks a strong desire to live. Obviously, this inference fails if someone's having the desire to live is not a necessary condition of its being wrong to kill that individual.

One problem with the desire account is that we do regard it as seriously wrong to kill persons who have little desire to live or who have no desire to live or, indeed, have a desire not to live. We believe it is seriously wrong to kill the unconscious, the sleeping, those who are tired of life, and those who are suicidal. The value-of-a-human-future account renders standard morality intelligible in these cases; these cases appear to be incompatible with the desire account.

The desire account is subject to a deeper difficulty. We desire life, because we value the goods of this life. The goodness of life is not secondary to our desire for it. If this were not so, the pain of one's own premature death could be done away with merely by an appropriate alteration in the configuration of one's desires. This is absurd. Hence, it would seem that it is the loss of the goods of one's future, not the interference with the fulfillment of a strong desire to live, which accounts ultimately for the wrongness of killing.

It is worth noting that, if the desire account is modified so that it does not provide a necessary, but only a sufficient, condition for the wrongness of killing, the desire account is compatible with the value of a future-like-ours account. The combined accounts will yield an antiabortion ethic. This suggests that one can retain what is intuitively plausible about the desire account without a challenge to the basic argument of this paper....

The discontinuation account looks more promising as an account of the wrongness of killing. It seems just as intelligible as the value of a future-like-ours account, but it does not justify an antiabortion position. Obviously, if it is the continuation of one's activities, experiences, and projects, the loss of which makes killing wrong, then it is not wrong to kill fetuses for that reason, for fetuses do not have experiences, activities, and projects to be continued or discontinued. Accordingly, the discontinuation account does not have the antiabortion consequences that the value of a future-like-ours account has. Yet, it seems as intelligible as the value of a future-like-ours account, for when we think of what would be wrong with our being killed, it does seem as if it is the discontinuation of what makes our lives worthwhile which makes killing us wrong.

Is the discontinuation account just as good an account as the value of a future-like-ours account? The discontinuation account will not be adequate at all, if it does not refer to the *value* of the experience that may be discontinued. One does not want the discontinuation account to make it wrong to kill a patient who begs for death and who is in severe pain that cannot be relieved short of killing. (I leave open the question of whether it is wrong for other reasons.) Accordingly, the discontinuation account must be more than a bare discontinuation account. It must make some reference to the positive value of the patient's experiences. But, by the same token, the value of a future-like-ours account cannot be a bare future account either. Just having a future surely does not itself rule out killing the above patient. This account must make some reference to the value of the patient's future experiences and projects also. Hence, both accounts involve the value of experiences, projects, and activities. So far we still have symmetry between the accounts.

The symmetry fades, however, when we focus on the time period of the value of the experiences, etc., which has moral consequences. Although both accounts leave open the possibility that the patient in our example may be killed, this possibility is left open only in virtue of the utterly bleak future for the patient. It makes no difference whether the patient's immediate past contains intolerable pain, or consists in being in a coma (which we can imagine is a situation of indifference), or consists in a life of value. If the patient's future is a future of value, we want our account to make it wrong to kill the patient. If the patient's future is intolerable, whatever his or her immediate past, we want our account to allow killing the patient. Obviously, then, it is the value of that patient's future which is doing the work in rendering the morality of killing the patient intelligible.

This being the case, it seems clear that whether one has immediate past experiences or not does no work in the explanation of what makes killing wrong. The addition the discontinuation account makes to the value of a human future account is otiose. Its addition to the value-of-a-future account plays no role at all in rendering intelligible the wrongness of killing. Therefore, it can be discarded with the discontinuation account of which it is a part.

IV

The analysis of the previous section suggests that alternative general accounts of the wrongness of killing are either inadequate or unsuccessful in getting around the antiabortion consequences of the value of a future-like-ours argument. A different strategy for avoiding these antiabortion consequences involves limiting the scope of the value-of-a-future argument. More precisely, the strategy involves arguing that fetuses lack a property that is essential for the value-of-a-future argument (or for any antiabortion argument) to apply to them.

One move of this sort is based upon the claim that a necessary condition of one's future being valuable is that one values it. Value implies a valuer. Given this one might argue that, since fetuses cannot value their futures, their futures are not valuable to them. Hence, it does not seriously wrong them deliberately to end their lives.

This move fails, however, because of some ambiguities. Let us assume that something cannot be of value unless it is valued by someone. This does not entail that my life is of no value unless it is valued by me. I may think, in a period of despair, that my future is of no worth whatsoever, but I may be wrong because others rightly see value—even great value—in it. Furthermore, my future can be valuable to me even if I do not value it. This is the case when a young person attempts suicide, but is rescued and goes on to significant human achievements. Such young people's futures are ultimately valuable to them, even though such futures do not seem to be valuable to them at the moment of attempted suicide. A fetus's future can be valuable to it in the same way. Accordingly, this attempt to limit the antiabortion argument fails. ...

Finally, Paul Bassen[3] has argued that, even though the prospects of an embryo might seem to be a basis for the wrongness of abortion, an embryo cannot be a victim and therefore cannot be wronged. An embryo cannot be a victim, he says, because it lacks sentience. His central argument for this seems to be that, even though plants and the permanently unconscious are alive, they clearly cannot be victims. What is the explanation of this? Bassen claims that the explanation is that their lives consist of mere metabolism and mere metabolism is not enough to ground victimizability. Mentation is required.

The problem with this attempt to establish the absence of victimizability is that both plants and the permanently unconscious clearly lack what Bassen calls "prospects" or what I have called "a future life like ours." Hence, it is surely open to one to argue that the real reason we believe plants and the permanently unconscious cannot be victims is that killing them cannot deprive them of a future life like ours; the real reason is not their absence of present mentation.

Bassen recognizes that his view is subject to this difficulty, and he recognizes that the case of children seems to support this difficulty, for "much of what we do for children is based on prospects." He argues, however, that, in the case of children and in other such cases, "potentiality comes into play only where victimizability has been secured on other grounds."[4]

Bassen's defense of his view is patently question-begging, since what is adequate to secure victimizability is exactly what is at issue. His examples do not support his own view against the thesis of this essay. Of course, embryos can be victims: when their lives are deliberately terminated, they are deprived of their futures of value, their prospects. This makes them victims, for it directly wrongs them....

V

In this essay, it has been argued that the correct ethic of the wrongness of killing can be extended to fetal life and used to show that there is a strong presumption that any abortion is morally impermissible. If the ethic of killing adopted here entails, however, that contraception is also seriously immoral, then there would appear to be a difficulty with the analysis of this essay.

But this analysis does not entail that contraception is wrong. Of course, contraception prevents the actualization of a possible future of value. Hence, it follows from the claim that futures of value should be maximized that contraception is *prima facie* immoral. This obligation to maximize does not exist, however; furthermore, nothing in the ethics of killing in this paper entails that it does. The ethics of killing in this essay would entail that contraception is wrong only if something were denied a human future of value by contraception. Nothing at all is denied such a future by contraception, however.

Candidates for a subject of harm by contraception fall into four categories: (1) some sperm or other, (2) some ovum or other, (3) a sperm and an ovum separately, and (4) a sperm and an ovum together. Assigning the harm to some sperm is utterly arbitrary, for no reason can be given for making a sperm the subject of harm rather than an ovum. Assigning the harm to some ovum is utterly arbitrary, for no reason can be given for making an ovum the subject of harm rather than a sperm. One might attempt to avoid these problems by insisting that contraception deprives both the sperm and the ovum separately of a valuable future like ours. On this alternative, too many futures are lost. Contraception was supposed to be wrong because it deprived us of one future of value, not two. One might attempt to avoid this problem by holding that contraception deprives the combination of sperm and ovum of a valuable future like ours. But here the definite article misleads. At the time of contraception, there are hundreds of millions of sperm, one (released) ovum and millions of possible combinations of all of these. There is no actual combination at all. Is the subject of the loss to be a merely possible combination? Which one? This alternative does not yield an actual subject of harm either. Accordingly, the immorality of contraception is not entailed by the loss-of-a-future-like-ours argument, simply because there is no nonarbitrarily identifiable subject of the loss in the case of contraception.

VI

The purpose of this essay has been to set out an argument for the serious presumptive wrongness of abortion subject to the assumption that the moral permissibility of abortion stands or falls on the moral status of the fetus. Since a fetus possesses a property, the possession of which in adult human beings is sufficient to make killing an adult human being wrong, abortion is wrong. This way of dealing with the problem of abortion seems superior to other approaches to the ethics of abortion, because it rests on an ethics of killing which is close to self-evident, because the crucial morally relevant property clearly applies to fetuses, and because the argument avoids the usual equivocations on "human life," "human being," or "person." The argument rests neither on religious claims nor on Papal dogma. It is not subject to the objection of "speciesism." Its soundness is compatible with the moral permissibility of euthanasia and contraception. It deals with our intuitions concerning young children.

Finally, this analysis can be viewed as resolving a standard problem—indeed, the standard problem—concerning the ethics of abortion. Clearly, it is wrong to kill adult human beings. Clearly, it is not wrong to end the life of some arbitrarily chosen single human cell. Fetuses seem to be like arbitrarily chosen human cells in some respects, and like adult humans in other respects. The problem of the ethics of abortion is the problem of determining the fetal property that settles this moral controversy. The thesis of this essay is that the problem of the ethics of abortion, so understood, is solvable.

NOTES

[1] I have been most influenced on this matter by Jonathan Glover, *Causing Death and Saving Lives* (New York: Penguin, 1977): ch. 3; and Robert Young, "What Is So Wrong With Killing People?" *Philosophy*, LIV, 210 (1979): 515–528.

[2] I am indebted to Jack Bricke for raising this objection.

[3] Paul Bassen, "Present Sakes and Future Prospects: The Status of Early Abortion," *Philosophy and Public Affairs*, XI, 4 (1982): 322–326.

[4] *Ibid.*, 333.

ABORTION THROUGH A FEMINIST ETHICS LENS

Susan Sherwin

Abortion has long been a central issue in the arena of applied ethics, but the distinctive analysis of feminist ethics is generally overlooked in most philosophic discussions. Authors and readers commonly presume a familiarity with the feminist position and equate it with liberal defenses of women's right to choose abortion, but, in fact, feminist ethics yields a different analysis of the moral questions surrounding abortion than that usually offered by the more familiar liberal defenders of abortion rights. Most feminists can agree with some of the conclusions that arise from certain nonfeminist arguments on abortion, but they often disagree about the way the issues are formulated and the sorts of reasons that are invoked in the mainstream literature.

Among the many differences found between feminist and nonfeminist arguments about abortion is the fact that most nonfeminist discussions of abortion consider the questions of the moral or legal permissibility of abortion in isolation from other questions, ignoring (and thereby obscuring) relevant connections to other social practices that oppress women.

From "Abortion through a Feminist Ethics Lens," *Dialogue* 30 (1991): 327–342. Reprinted by permission of *Dialogue*, Canadian Philosophical Review.

They are generally grounded in masculinist conceptions of freedom (e.g., privacy, individual choice, individuals' property rights in their own bodies) that do not meet the needs, interests, and intuitions of many of the women concerned. In contrast, feminists seek to couch their arguments in moral concepts that support their general campaign of overcoming injustice in all its dimensions, including those inherent in moral theory itself.[1] There is even disagreement about how best to understand the moral question at issue: nonfeminist arguments focus exclusively on the morality and/or legality of performing abortions, whereas feminists insist that other questions, including ones about accessibility and delivery of abortion services, must also be addressed.

Although feminists welcome the support of nonfeminists in pursuing policies that will grant women control over abortion decisions, they generally envision very different sorts of policies for this purpose than those considered by nonfeminist sympathizers.... Here, I propose one conception of the shape such an analysis should take.

WOMEN AND ABORTION

The most obvious difference between feminist and nonfeminist approaches to abortion can be seen in the relative attention each gives to the interests and experiences of women in its analysis. Feminists consider it self-evident that the pregnant woman is a subject of principal concern in abortion decisions. In most nonfeminist accounts, however, not only is she not perceived as central, she is rendered virtually invisible. Nonfeminist theorists, whether they support or oppose women's right to choose abortion, focus almost all their attention on the moral status of the developing embryo or the fetus.

In pursuing a distinctively feminist ethics, it is appropriate to begin with a look at the role of abortion in women's lives. Clearly, the need for abortion can be very intense; women have pursued abortions under appalling and dangerous conditions, across widely diverse cultures and historical periods. No one denies that if abortion is not made legal, safe, and accessible, women will seek out illegal and life-threatening abortions to terminate pregnancies they cannot accept. Antiabortion activists seem willing to accept this price, but feminists judge the inevitable loss of women's lives associated with restrictive abortion policies to be a matter of fundamental concern.

Although antiabortion campaigners imagine that women often make frivolous and irresponsible decisions about abortion, feminists recognize that women have abortions for a wide variety of reasons. Some women, for instance, find themselves seriously ill and incapacitated throughout pregnancy; they cannot continue in their jobs and may face enormous difficulties in fulfilling their responsibilities at home. Many employers and schools will not tolerate pregnancy in their employees or students, and not every woman is able to put her job, career, or studies on hold. Women of limited means may be unable to take adequate care of children they have already borne, and they may know that another mouth to feed will reduce their ability to provide for their existing children.... Some who are homeless, or addicted to drugs, or who are diagnosed as carrying the AIDS virus may be unwilling to allow a child to enter the world under such circumstances....

Whatever the reason, most feminists believe that a pregnant woman is in the best position to judge whether abortion is the appropriate response to her circumstances. Since she is usually the only one able to weigh all the relevant factors, most feminists reject attempts to offer any general abstract rules for determining when abortion is morally justified. Women's personal deliberations about abortion include contextually defined considerations reflecting her commitment to the needs and interests of everyone concerned—including herself, the fetus she carries, other members of her household, etc. Because there is no single formula available for balancing these complex factors through all possible cases, it is vital that feminists insist on protecting each woman's right to come to her own conclusions. Abortion decisions are, by their very nature, dependent on specific features of each woman's experience; theoretically dispassionate philosophers and other moralists should not expect to set the agenda for these considerations in any universal way. Women must be acknowledged as full moral agents with the responsibility for making moral decisions about their own pregnancies.[2] Although I think that it is possible for a woman to make a mistake in her moral judgment on this matter (that is, it is possible that a woman may come to believe that she was wrong about her decision to continue or terminate a pregnancy), the intimate nature of this sort of decision makes it unlikely that anyone else is in a position to arrive at a more reliable conclusion; it is, therefore, improper to grant others the authority to interfere in women's decisions to seek abortions.

Feminist analysis regards the effects of unwanted pregnancies on the lives of women individually and collectively as a central element in the moral evaluation of abortion. Even without patriarchy, bearing a child would be a very important event in a woman's life. It involves significant physical, emotional, social, and (usually) economic changes for her. The ability to exert control over the incidence, timing, and frequency of childbearing is often tied to her ability to control most other things she values. Since we live in a patriarchal society, it is especially important to ensure that women have the authority to control their own reproduction.[3] Despite the diversity of opinion among feminists on most other matters, virtually all feminists seem to agree that women must gain full control over their own reproductive lives if they are to free themselves from male dominance. Many perceive the commitment of the political right wing to opposing abortion as part of a general strategy to reassert patriarchal control over women in the face of significant feminist influence.[4]

Women's freedom to choose abortion is also linked with their ability to control their own sexuality. Women's subordinate status often prevents them from refusing men sexual access to their bodies. If women cannot end the unwanted pregnancies that result from male sexual dominance, their sexual vulnerability to particular men can increase, because caring for an(other) infant involves greater financial needs and reduced economic opportunities for women.[5] As a result, pregnancy often forces women to become dependent on men. Since a woman's dependence on a man is assumed to entail that she will remain sexually loyal to him, restriction of abortion serves to channel women's sexuality and further perpetuates the cycle of oppression.

In contrast to most nonfeminist accounts, feminist analyses of abortion direct attention to the question of how women get pregnant. Those who reject abortion seem to believe that women can avoid unwanted pregnancies by avoiding sexual intercourse. Such views show little appreciation for the power of sexual politics in a culture that oppresses women. Existing patterns of sexual dominance mean that women often have little control over their sexual lives. They may be subject to rape by strangers, or by their husbands, boyfriends, colleagues, employers, customers, fathers, brothers, uncles, and dates. Often the sexual coercion is not even recognized as such by the participants, but is the price of continued "goodwill"—popularity, economic survival, peace, or simple acceptance. Few women have not found themselves in circumstances where they do not feel free to refuse a man's demands for intercourse, either because he is holding a gun to her head or because he threatens to be emotionally hurt if she refuses (or both). Women are socialized to be compliant and accommodating, sensitive to the feelings of others, and frightened of physical power; men are socialized to take advantage of every opportunity to engage in sexual intercourse and to use sex to express dominance and power. Under such circumstances, it is difficult to argue that women could simply "choose" to avoid heterosexual activity if they wish to avoid pregnancy. Catharine MacKinnon neatly sums it up: "the logic by which women are supposed to consent to sex [is]: preclude the alternatives, then call the remaining option 'her choice.'"[6]

From a feminist perspective, a central moral feature of pregnancy is that it takes place in *women's bodies*, and has profound effects on *women's* lives. Gender-neutral accounts of pregnancy are not available; pregnancy is explicitly a condition associated with the female body.[7] Because the need for abortion is experienced only by women, policies about abortion affect women uniquely. Thus, it is important to consider how proposed policies on abortion fit into general patterns of oppression for women. Unlike nonfeminist accounts, feminist ethics demands that the effects on the oppression of women be a principal consideration when evaluating abortion policies.

THE FETUS

In contrast, most nonfeminist analysts believe that the moral acceptability of abortion turns on the question of the moral status of the fetus. Even those who support women's right to choose abortion tend to accept the central premise of the antiabortion proponents that abortion can only be tolerated if it can be proved that the fetus is lacking some criterion of full personhood.[8] Opponents of abortion have structured the debate so that it is necessary to define the status of the fetus as either valued the same as other humans (and hence entitled not to be killed) or as lacking in all value. Rather than challenging the logic of this formulation, many defenders of abortion have concentrated on showing that the fetus is indeed without significant value;[9] others, such as Wayne Sumner,[10] offer a more subtle account that reflects the gradual development of fetuses, whereby there is some specific criterion that determines the degree of protection to be afforded them which is lacking in the early stages of pregnancy but present in the later stages. Thus the debate often rages between abortion opponents who describe the fetus as an "innocent," vulnerable, morally important, separate being whose life is threatened and who must be protected at all costs, and abortion supporters who try to establish some sort of deficiency inherent to fetuses which removes them from the scope of the moral community.

The woman on whom the fetus depends for survival is considered as secondary (if she is considered at all) in these debates. The actual experiences and responsibilities of real women are not perceived as morally relevant (unless they, too, can be proved innocent by establishing that their pregnancies are a result of rape or incest). It is a common assumption of both defenders and opponents of women's right to choose abortion that many women will be irresponsible in their choices. The important question, though, is whether fetuses have the sort of status that justifies interfering in women's choices at all. In some contexts, women's role in gestation is literally reduced to that of "fetal containers": the individual women disappear or are perceived simply as mechanical life-support systems....

Within antiabortion arguments, fetuses are identified as individuals; in our culture, which views the (abstract) individual as sacred, fetuses *qua* individuals should be honored and preserved. Extraordinary claims are made to try to establish the individuality and moral agency of fetuses. At the same time, the women who carry these fetal individuals are viewed as passive hosts whose only significant role is to refrain from aborting or harming their fetuses. Since it is widely believed that the woman does not actually have to do anything to protect the life of the fetus, pregnancy is often considered (abstractly) to be a tolerable burden to protect the life of an individual so like us.

Medicine has played its part in supporting these sorts of attitudes. Fetal medicine is a rapidly expanding specialty, and it is commonplace in professional medical journals to find references to pregnant women as "fetal environments." Fetal surgeons now have at their disposal a repertory of sophisticated technology that can save the lives of dangerously ill fetuses; in light of such heroic successes, it is perhaps understandable that women have disappeared from their view. These specialists see fetuses as their patients, not the women who nurture them. Doctors perceive themselves as the *active* agents in saving fetal lives and, hence, believe that they are the ones in direct relationship with the fetuses they treat.

Perhaps even more distressing than the tendency to ignore the woman's agency altogether and view her as a purely passive participant in the medically controlled events of pregnancy and childbirth is the growing practice of viewing women as genuine threats to the well-being of the fetus. Increasingly, women are viewed as irresponsible or hostile towards their fetuses, and the relationship between them is characterized as adversarial.[11] Concern for the well-being of the fetus is taken as license for doctors to intervene to ensure that women comply with medical "advice." Courts are called upon to enforce the doctors' orders when moral pressure alone proves inadequate, and women are being coerced into undergoing unwanted Caesarean deliveries and technologically monitored hospital births. Some states have begun to imprison women for endangering their fetuses through drug abuse and other socially unacceptable behaviors. An Australian state recently introduced a bill that makes women liable to criminal prosecution "if they are found to have smoked during pregnancy, eaten unhealthful foods, or taken any other action which can be shown to have adversely affected the development of the fetus."[12]

In other words, physicians have joined with antiabortionist activists in fostering a cultural acceptance of the view that fetuses are distinct individuals who are physically, ontologically, and socially separate from the women whose bodies they inhabit, and who have their own distinct interests. In this picture, pregnant women are either ignored altogether, or are viewed as deficient in some crucial respect and hence subject to coercion for the sake of their fetuses. In the former case, the interests of the women concerned are assumed to be identical with those of the fetus; in the latter, the women's interests are irrelevant because they are perceived as immoral, unimportant, or unnatural. Focus on the fetus as an independent entity has led to presumptions which deny pregnant women their roles as active, independent, moral agents with a primary interest in what becomes of the fetuses they carry. Emphasis on the fetus's status has led to an assumed license to interfere with women's reproductive freedom.

A FEMINIST VIEW OF THE FETUS

Because the public debate has been set up as a competition between the rights of women and those of fetuses, feminists have often felt pushed to reject claims of fetal value in order to protect women's claims. Yet, as Addelson has argued, viewing abortion in this way "tears [it] out of the context of women's lives."[13] There are other accounts of fetal value that are more plausible and less oppressive to women.

On a feminist account, fetal development is examined in the context in which it occurs, within women's bodies, rather than in the imagined isolation implicit in many theoretical accounts. Fetuses develop in specific pregnancies which occur in the lives of particular women. They are not individuals housed in generic female wombs, nor are they full persons at risk only because they are small and subject to the whims of women. Their very existence is relational, developing as they do within particular women's bodies, and their principal relationship is to the women who carry them.

On this view, fetuses are morally significant, but their status is relational rather than absolute. Unlike other human beings, fetuses do not have any independent existence; their existence is uniquely tied to the support of a specific other. Most nonfeminist commentators have ignored the relational dimension of fetal development, and have presumed that the moral status of fetuses could be resolved solely in terms of abstract metaphysical criteria of personhood. They imagine that there is some set of properties (such as genetic heritage, moral agency, self-consciousness, language use, or self-determination) which will entitle all who possess them to be granted the moral status of persons.[14] They seek some particular feature by which we can neatly divide the world into the dichotomy of moral persons (who are to be valued and protected) and others (who are not entitled to the same group privileges); it follows that it is a merely empirical question whether or not fetuses possess the relevant properties.

But this vision misinterprets what is involved in personhood and what it is that is especially valued about persons. Personhood is a social category, not an isolated state. Persons are members of a community; they develop as concrete, discrete, and specific individuals. To be a morally significant category, personhood must involve personality as well as biological integrity. It is not sufficient to consider persons simply as Kantian atoms of rationality; persons are all embodied, conscious beings with particular social histories. Annette Baier has developed a concept of persons as "second persons" which helps explain the sort of social dimension that seems fundamental to any moral notion of personhood:

> A person, perhaps, is best seen as one who was long enough dependent upon other persons to acquire the essential arts of personhood. Persons essentially are *second* persons, who grow up with other persons.... The fact that a person has a life *history*, and that a people collectively have a history, depends upon the humbler fact that each person has a childhood in which a cultural heritage is transmitted, ready for adolescent rejection and adult discriminating selection and contribution. Persons come after and before other persons.[15]

Persons, in other words, are members of a social community which shapes and values them, and personhood is a relational concept that must be defined in terms of interactions and relationships with others.

A fetus is a unique sort of being in that it cannot form relationships freely with others, nor can others readily form relationships with it. A fetus has a primary and particularly intimate relationship with the woman in whose womb it develops; any other relationship it may have is indirect, and must be mediated through the pregnant woman. The relationship that exists between a woman and her fetus is clearly asymmetrical, since she is the only party to the relationship who is capable of making a decision about whether the interaction should continue, and since the fetus is wholly dependent on the woman who sustains it, while she is quite capable of surviving without it.

However much some might prefer it to be otherwise, no one else can do anything to support or harm a fetus without doing something to the woman who nurtures it. Because of this inexorable biological reality, she bears a unique responsibility and privilege in determining her fetus's place in the social scheme of things. Clearly, many pregnancies occur to women who place very high value on the lives of the particular fetuses they carry and choose to see their pregnancies through to term despite the possible risks and costs involved; hence, it would be wrong of anyone to force such a woman to terminate her pregnancy under these circumstances. Other women, or some of these same women at other times, value other things more highly (e.g., their freedom, their health, or previous responsibilities which conflict with those generated by the pregnancies), and choose not to continue their pregnancies. The value that women ascribe to individual fetuses varies dramatically from case to case, and may well change over the course of any particular pregnancy. There is no absolute value that attaches to fetuses apart from their relational status, determined in the context of their particular development.

FEMINIST POLITICS AND ABORTION

Feminist ethics directs us to look at abortion in the context of other issues of power and not to limit discussion to the standard questions about its moral and legal acceptability. Because coerced pregnancy has repercussions for women's oppressed status generally, it is important to ensure that abortion not only be made legal but that adequate services be made accessible to all women who seek them.... Ethical study of abortion involves understanding and critiquing the economic, age, and social barriers that currently restrict access to medically acceptable abortion services.

Moreover, it is also important that abortion services be provided in an atmosphere that fosters women's health and well-being; hence, the care offered should be in a context that is supportive of the choices women make. Abortions should be seen as part of women's overall reproductive health, and could be included within centers that deal with all matters of reproductive health in an open, patient-centered manner where effective counseling is offered for a wide range of reproductive decisions. Providers need to recognize that abortion is a legitimate option, so that services will be delivered with respect and concern for the physical, psychological, and emotional effects on a patient. All too frequently, hospital-based abortions are provided by practitioners who are uneasy about their role, and treat the women involved with hostility and resentment. Increasingly, many antiabortion activists have personalized their attacks and focused their attention on harassing the women who enter and leave abortion clinics. Surely requiring a woman to pass a gauntlet of hostile protesters on her way to and from an abortion is not conducive to effective health care. Ethical exploration of abortion raises questions about how women are treated when they seek abortions. Achieving legal permission for women to dispose of their fetuses if they are determined enough to manage the struggle should not be accepted as the sole moral consideration....

Feminists support abortion on demand because they know that women must have control over their reproduction. For the same reason, they actively oppose forced abortion and coerced sterilization, practices that are sometimes inflicted on the most powerless women, especially those in the Third World. Feminist ethics demands that access to voluntary, safe, effective birth control be part of any abortion discussion, so that women have access to other means of avoiding pregnancy.

Feminist analysis addresses the context as well as the practice of abortion decisions. Thus feminists also object to the conditions which lead women to abort wanted fetuses because there are not adequate financial and social supports available to care for a child. Because feminist accounts value fetuses that are wanted by the women who carry them, they oppose practices which force women to abort because of poverty or intimidation.

Yet the sorts of social changes necessary if we are to free women from having abortions out of economic necessity are vast; they include changes not only in legal and health care policy, but also in housing, child care, employment, etc.[16] Nonetheless, feminist ethics defines reproductive freedom as the condition under which women are able to make truly voluntary choices about their reproductive lives, and these many dimensions are implicit in the ideal.

Clearly, feminists are not "proabortion," for they are concerned to ensure the safety of each pregnancy to the greatest degree possible; wanted fetuses should not be harmed or lost. Therefore, adequate pre- and postnatal care and nutrition are also important elements of any feminist position on reproductive freedom. Where antiabortionists direct their energies to trying to prevent women from obtaining abortions, feminists seek to protect the health of wanted fetuses. They recognize that far more could be done to protect and care for fetuses if the state directed its resources at supporting women who continue their pregnancies, rather than draining away resources in order to police women who find that they must interrupt their pregnancies. Caring for the women who carry fetuses is not only a more legitimate policy than is regulating them; it is probably also more effective at ensuring the health and well-being of more fetuses.

Feminist ethics also explores how abortion policies fit within the politics of sexual domination. Most feminists are sensitive to the fact that many men support women's right to abortion out of the belief that women will be more willing sexual partners if they believe that they can readily terminate an unwanted pregnancy. Some men coerce their partners into obtaining abortions the women may not want. Feminists understand that many women oppose abortion for this very reason, being unwilling to support a practice that increases women's sexual vulnerability.[17] Thus, it is important that feminists develop a coherent analysis of reproductive freedom that includes sexual freedom (as women choose to define it). That requires an analysis of sexual freedom that includes women's right to refuse sex; such a right can only be assured if women have equal power to men and are not subject to domination by virtue of their sex.

In sum, then, feminist ethics demands that moral discussions of abortion be more broadly defined than they have been in most philosophic discussions. Only by reflecting on the meaning of ethical pronouncements on actual women's lives and the connections between judgments on abortion and the conditions of domination and subordination can we come to an adequate understanding of the moral status of abortion in our society. As Rosalind Petchesky argues, feminist discussion of abortion "must be moved beyond the framework of a 'woman's right to choose' and connected to a much broader revolutionary movement that addresses all of the conditions of women's liberation."[18]

NOTES

Earlier versions of this paper were read to the Department of Philosophy, Dalhousie University and to the Canadian Society for Women in Philosophy in Kingston. I am very grateful for the comments received from colleagues in both forums; particular thanks go to Lorraine Code, David Braybrooke, Richmond Campbell, Sandra Taylor, Terry Tomkow and Kadri Vihvelin for their patience and advice.

[1] For some idea of the ways in which traditional moral theory oppresses women, see Kathryn Pauly Morgan "Women and Moral Madness," in *Science, Morality and Feminist Theory*, Marsha Hanen and Kai Nielsen, eds., *Canadian Journal of Philosophy* Supplementary Vol. 13 (1987): 201–226.

[2] Critics continue to want to structure the debate around the *possibility* of women making frivolous abortion decisions, and hence want feminists to agree to setting boundaries on acceptable grounds for choosing abortion. Feminists ought to resist this injunction, though. There is no practical way of drawing a line fairly in the abstract; cases that may appear "frivolous" at a distance often turn out to be substantive when the details are revealed, i.e., frivolity is in the eyes of the beholder. There is no evidence to suggest that women actually make the sorts of choices worried critics hypothesize about: e.g., a woman eight months pregnant who chooses to abort because she wants to take a trip or gets in "a tiff" with her partner. These sorts of fantasies, on which demands to distinguish between legitimate and illegitimate personal reasons for choosing abortion chiefly rest, reflect on offensive conceptions of women as irresponsible; they ought not to be perpetuated....

[3] In her monumental historical analysis of the early roots of Western patriarchy, Gerda Lerner (*The Creation of Patriarchy* [New York: Oxford University Press, 1986]) determined that patriarchy began in the period from 3100 to 600 B.C. when men appropriated women's sexual and reproductive capacity; the earliest states entrenched patriarchy by institutionalizing the sexual and procreative subordination of women to men.

[4] Rosalind Pollack Petchesky, "Reproductive Freedom: Beyond "A Woman's Right to Choose,'" in *Women: Sex and Sexuality*, Catharine R. Stimpson and Ethel Spector Person, eds., (Chicago: University of Chicago Press, 1980): 112.

[5] There is a lot the state could do to ameliorate this condition. If the state provided women with adequate financial support, removed the inequities in the labor market, and provided affordable and reliable child care, pregnancy would not need so often to lead to a woman's dependence on a particular man. The fact that it does not do so is evidence of the state's complicity in maintaining women's subordinate position with respect to men.

[6] Catharine MacKinnon, *Toward a Feminist Theory of the State* (Cambridge, MA: Harvard University Press, 1989): 192.

[7] See Zillah Eisenstein, *The Female Body and the Law* (Berkeley: University of California Press, 1988) for a comprehensive theory of the role of the pregnant body as the central element in the cultural subordination of women.

[8] Judith Jarvis Thomson, "A Defense of Abortion," *Philosophy and Public Affairs*, 1, 1 (1971): 47–76 is a notable exception to this trend.

[9]Michael Tooley, "Abortion and Infanticide," *Philosophy and Public Affairs*, 2, 1 (Fall, 1972): 37–65 and Mary Anne Warren, "On the Moral and Legal Status of Abortion," *The Monist*, 57 (1973): 43–65.

[10]L.W. Sumner, *Abortion and Moral Theory* (Princeton: Princeton University Press, 1981).

[11]Christine Overall, *Ethics and Human Reproduction: A Feminist Analysis* (Winchester, MA: Allen & Unwin, 1987): 60.

[12]Mary Anne Warren, "The Moral Significance of Birth," *Hypatia*, 4, 2 (Summer, 1989): 46–65.

[13]Kathryn Pyne Addelson, "Moral Passages," in *Women and Moral Theory*, Eva Feder Kittay and Diana T. Meyers, eds., (Totowa, N.J.: Roman & Littlefield, 1987): 107.

[14]See Warren and Tooley.

[15]Annette Baier, *Postures of the Mind: Essays on Mind and Morals* (Minneapolis: University of Minnesota Press, 1985): 84–85, emphasis in original.

[16]Petchesky, 112.

[17]Kristin Luker, *Abortion and the Politics of Motherhood* (Berkeley: University of California Press, 1984): 209–215.

[18]Petchesky, 113.

AN ETHICAL CHALLENGE TO PROCHOICE ADVOCATES: ABORTION AND THE PLURALISTIC PROPOSITION

Daniel Callahan

At the heart of much moral debate in America lies a simple and popular conviction: the law should leave to the individual conscience choice about those acts that are private, do not command a moral consensus, and are not harmful to others. I will call this the pluralistic proposition. The abortion debate of the past three decades has, in great part, been about this proposition. Those who call themselves "prochoice" argue that the abortion choice is private and personal to women, and should thus be left to them without the interference of the law. The "prolife" side, by contrast, has held that the decisive harm abortion does to the fetus and its right to life removes it from the private realm and makes it a matter of legitimate government regulation....

I want...to look at the subject of abortion as a case study of the problems and paradoxes of the pluralistic proposition, particularly as it has manifested itself in the logic and politics of the prochoice position. One question, above all, troubles me. Is it possible, simultaneously and with equal seriousness, to hold that abortion should (a) be left to the individual and private choice of women, and (b) that each such decision should be understood as a genuine moral choice, one that can be good or bad, right or wrong?...

Over twenty years ago I published a book on abortion, *Abortion: Law, Choice and Morality.*[1] Reversing my own earlier convictions, I concluded that the universality of a resort to abortion even if illegal and dangerous, the inherently uncertain moral status of the fetus (at least the relatively early fetus), and the value in a pluralistic society of keeping the law out of controverted and delicate moral issues whenever possible made the "prochoice" position morally and politically compelling. I have not changed my view on the legal issue in any significant way.

I also argued, no less strongly, that even though the choice should be the woman's, and that it should be a private choice, it was still a serious moral choice. Once women had the choice, it would then become important for them in their private lives to give thought to what could count as a morally justifiable choice; and it would be no less appropriate to have some public discussion about the standards and criteria appropriate for such choices, much as we might about other moral matters not subject to law but of common interest and importance.... The goal that I proposed seemed, then, perfectly compatible with what I understand the pluralistic proposition to be: leave the choice to women, but understand the choice to be a grave one, worthy of public no less than private reflection.

I could not have been more naïve, more hopelessly optimistic in thinking that such reflection would be acceptable. The prochoice movement has in fact never known quite what to do with the moral issue. For most of its leaders, it is simply set aside altogether, left to the opaque sphere of personal morality, itself a subject of uncertainty and discomfort. Is it not the nature of personal morality, many seem to think, that it is so unique and idiosyncratic to the individual, so subject to private, self-determined moral standards, that nothing meaningful can be said about it, and certainly not enough for public debate? The tacit answer to this question is clear enough....

Yet if silence or uneasiness is the predominant response to the moral problem, there are others in the prochoice movement—a small but seemingly growing minority—for whom even the idea of discussion of the moral choice is repugnant.... They either want to declare that abortion is not, in its substance, a moral question at all (only the woman's *right* to choose an abortion is taken to be a moral issue); or that women should not have to struggle and suffer over the choice even if it is; or that, in any case, to concede that it is a *serious* moral choice and to have a public discussion about that choice is politically hazardous, the opening wedge of a discussion that could easily lead once again to a restriction of a woman's right to an abortion. Better to declare the whole topic of the morality of abortion off limits.

One way or another, then, the prochoice movement has not been able to tolerate the fullness of the pluralistic proposition. It can support the choice side more readily than the morality side. At best it is uneasy about the moral issue, at worst dismissive and hostile toward it. ...

If, for some people, to have choice is itself the beginning and end of morality, for most people it is just the beginning. It does not end until a supportable, justifiable choice has been made, one that can be judged right or wrong by the individual herself, based on some reasonably serious, not patently self-interested way of thinking about ethics. That standard—central to every major ethical system and tradition—applies to the moral life generally, whether it be a matter of abortion or any other grave matter. An unwillingness to come to grips with that standard not only puts the prochoice movement in jeopardy as a political force. It has a still more deleterious effect: it is a basic threat to moral honesty and integrity. The cost of failing to take seriously the personal moral issues is to court self-deception, and to be drawn to employ arguments of expediency and evasion. I want to show how that has happened in at least some strands of the prochoice movement, and why it reduces the moral strength of that position.

Before I develop that thesis, however, a caution is in order. Despite the harsh things I have to say about elements of the prochoice position, I think in the end it is the only one that is viable in our society. For all of its faults, it is the position I embrace. ... I am searching for two things simultaneously: a *permanent* and *secure* place in American law for the right of women to make their own choice, and a far richer, more sensitive notion of the nature of that choice than is now commonly the case.

Let me begin that task by looking, first, at the history of arguments used by the prochoice movement. ...

During the 1950s and into the late 1960s, the movement to legalize abortion rested on a number of contentions: that a vast number of illegal abortions was doing great harm to the health of women, killing and maiming them; that women should have available a backup to ineffective contraception, though the latter should always remain the primary method of birth control; that the number of unwanted pregnancies, thought to be large, should be reduced and only wanted children should be born—the welfare of children was as much at stake as that of women; that, while an abortion decision is and must be difficult morally and psychologically, a woman should have a right to make such a decision; and that, while abortion should be legally available and financially affordable, everything possible should be done to change those economic and domestic circumstances that force women into unwanted pregnancies.

While this set of arguments looked strongly to the freedom and welfare of women, it was not exclusively a feminist argument by any means. It stressed the common benefits of abortion reform, particularly to children and the society, and it drew heavily on the pluralistic proposition, which bears on a wide range of personal choices for men and women, not simply the abortion choice for women....

But there have been a number of developments since the early 1970s, some political, some scientific, and some ideological. The most obvious political change has been the emergence of a strong, well-organized, and well-financed prolife movement. It has been able to press its case effectively in legislatures and with the general public (even though public opinion has remained remarkably stable and stationary on abortion for nearly two decades). While this movement has often been stereotyped by its opponents as nothing but religious conservatism, that is hardly accurate. It has grassroots support among many who are otherwise politically liberal. It has also of late gained the support of many women who are feminists. They see in abortion a resort to violence similar to that used for centuries by men against women: the use of power by the strong against the weak, both the physical power of violence and the cultural power to define the unwanted out of the human community altogether.[2] More generally, the prolife movement has found its greatest strength in its focus on precisely that issue that the prochoice movement has found most discomforting and awkward: the moral status of the fetus....

The most striking ideological development has been the emergence into leadership positions in the prochoice movement of some feminists who have scanted many of the original arguments for abortion reform. They have shifted the emphasis almost entirely to a woman's right to an abortion, whatever her reasons and whatever the consequences. Much less is heard about the social harm of unwanted pregnancies, much less about the terrible or tragic choice posed by an abortion, much less about the moral nature of the choice, and practically nothing about the need to reduce the number of abortions, now running at a rate of 1.6 million a year. No number of abortions seems to be too many.

...If the prolife movement exclusively stresses the rights of the fetus, then the prochoice movement must exclusively stress the rights of women. If the prolife movement says that abortion is oppressive and murderous, the prochoice movement must then say it is liberating and morally unimportant. If the prolife movement says that every abortion choice is wrong whatever the reason, then the prochoice leadership implies that every choice is right, whatever the choice. From a movement that in the 1950s and 1960s was measured, careful, open to larger concerns, it now runs the risk of becoming narrow and ideologically rigid....

Why has this shift taken place? The most obvious reasons are the growing pressures and successes of the prolife movement, forcing a more defensive, intransigent position; the prospect of a Supreme Court gutting or reversal of *Roe v. Wade*; and the impact of the media, with its predilection for polarized positions, encouraging one-dimensionality on both sides of the debate. Yet we might speculate on a more subtle additional possibility: that of the actual difficulty of managing the pluralistic proposition in the face of insistent moral issues that cannot be successfully denatured by exclusive reduction to choice.

Public opinion polls over the years have persistently displayed two distinctive features. When asked a *general* question about the right of women to have an abortion, a majority favors such a right; it has been steadily supportive of *Roe v. Wade*. At the same time, when questioned more precisely, a majority also wants morally to distinguish among abortion choices. In that respect, the public has never been unambiguously prochoice or prolife; some 60 percent of the public falls in a zone of ambivalence and nuance....

The prochoice movement is unable effectively to respond to these findings, partly because of its own ideology (which wants no such distinctions) and partly because of deficiencies in the pluralistic proposition on which it relies to make its general case....

Why has this happened? I offer a hypothesis. To make its advocacy case, the prochoice movement has partially relied on a set of beliefs and assertions that are either false or highly misleading. It has had to do that because, if looked at too closely, the actual complexity of the abortion situation raises disturbing questions about both the political realities and issues of personal morality. To admit that complexity would be to admit the importance of some portions of the prolife argument, a highly distressing prospect. I offer a partial list of those assertions, counterpoised against what I take to be the more complex truth of the matter.

1. Abortion restrictions represent a war of men against women, with men intent upon keeping women in reproductive thralldom.

Yet every survey for nearly twenty years shows women themselves divided on the issue, marginally but consistently more opposed to fully permissive abortion than men. The strongest supporters of legal abortion over the years have been young males....

2. Abortion should not be promoted as a primary means of birth control, but as a backup to a contraceptive failure.

Yet some 40 percent of all abortions are now repeat abortions, a figure that has steadily grown over the years. There are, moreover, some 1.6 million abortions a year, with no diminution in sight. Those figures suggest, though do not prove, a primary and growing dependence for many upon abortion as the first line of defense against unwanted pregnancy....

3. Abortion will diminish the dependence of women upon men, giving them full control over their reproduction.

If legal abortion has given women more choice, it has also given men more choice as well. They now have a potent new weapon in the old business of manipulating and abandoning women. For if women can have abortions, then there is no compelling leverage for women to use in demanding that men take responsibility for the children they procreate. That men have long coerced women into abortion when it suits their purposes is well known but rarely mentioned....

4. Given freedom of choice, women will make free choices.

Why is it, then, that many women feel coerced economically into having an abortion? (Poor black women, mainly young, are proportionately the largest group to choose abortion.) Why is it, then, that there is now a whole genre of literature and reports of women who regret their abortions, who felt coerced by others or their social circumstances into having an abortion they would not otherwise have chosen?[3]

5. It does not matter what choice women make as long as they have the freedom to make their own choice.

But that is a hard position to sustain, even for the single-minded, when the choice is to abort a female fetus simply because it is female; or to have an abortion to please (or spite) a husband or boyfriend; or to have repeat abortions because of a casual attitude toward the use of contraceptives; or to conceive fetuses for experimental purposes or commercial profit.

I cite that list of arguments to show that "choice" covers a multitude of realities, not all of them quite so tidy as some mainline prochoice ideology would have it. Those realities reveal a disturbingly obvious point: not all opponents of abortion are men, not all arguments against abortion are antiwoman, and not each and every abortion choice is equally justifiable, either because of the social circumstances or setting of the choice, or because of the actual content of the choice.

Of course to concede even the moral possibility that some abortion choices could be reprehensible, to admit that some choices can be morally wrong, would be to agree that choice itself is not the end of the moral matter. As a theoretical issue, the pluralistic proposition surely encompasses that possibility. To admit that much in the case of particular abortion choices, however, would be to show the hazards of the pluralistic proposition in its actual political usage. At the least it would be to concede implicitly that the fetus has enough moral status to force a judgment that not all reasons for its destruction are morally defensible. There are good choices, and there are bad choices....

Note an interesting parallel. A number of prominent feminists—including Betty Friedan and Gloria Steinem, it might be recalled—came to reject a pure choice ideology in the case of surrogate motherhood (during the debate over the Baby M case). The choice of becoming a surrogate mother, they argued, is not necessarily a good choice or beneficial to women, however much it may have the virtue of being a choice that a woman can legally make. That was a little-noted revolution in feminist thinking, though it was foreshadowed by those feminists who have condemned pornography and prostitution even in cases where women freely choose to take part. The same kind of thinking applied to the abortion debate would represent a genuine upheaval—asking not just whether it is good for women to have choice, but to ask also what constitutes a good choice. How can it make sense to favor the right to choice, but to be morally indifferent about the use of that right?...

I conclude that only the second alternative noted above is tenable, to admit the moral seriousness of the abortion choice. I have already suggested one set of reasons for moving in that direction: the high price paid in credibility for evasion of problems of real moral concern to probably a majority of prochoice supporters (and surely of great concern to those who are not certain just where they stand). Such a move will surely be risky. Once they start taking the moral choice seriously, some people are likely to change their position on abortion in general. Yet in the long run, if the prochoice position is to prevail, it will have to run such risks.... More generally, the pluralism proposition cannot itself well endure unless it finds a stronger place for a consideration of private moral choices. A strong commitment to legal freedom and choice combined with a weak commitment to substantive moral examination and ethical choice is an unsatisfactory combination. The latter simply goes underground, eating away corrosively at the commitment to legal freedom.

Is it possible in the case of abortion to combine legal freedom and seriousness about the moral questions? That would require the meeting of at least four conditions: (1) recognizing that the prochoice position represents only one important moral tradition in our culture, and must exist in tension with and appreciation of the no-less-important tradition embodied in the prolife movement, that of a respect for life; (2) accepting the need for active public debate about individual moral choices and the likelihood that some will be judged more negatively than others; (3) accepting the necessity for some compromise in the law as a way of taking seriously the objections of the prolife position; (4) agreeing on the need to make every effort to change those economic and social circumstances that lead women to make coerced abortion choices, and on the need for meaningful counseling of women who are considering abortion.

1. Abortion and the traditions of morality.

One reason for the intensity and intractability of the abortion debate is that it pits two important moral traditions against each other, that of respect for choice, and that of respect for life. The prolife position speaks eloquently and meaningfully about the value of nascent, defenseless life. It is a morally serious position, one compatible with a wide range of other values that seek to protect and preserve life.

Where it fails in the eyes of many of us, however, is in moving from its premise of respect for life to its conclusion that embryonic or fetal life merits the same protection as life after birth. At the least, that is a difficult question, not so perspicuously self-evident as prolife advocates would have us believe.

A prolife position that would resolutely put to one side the value of free choice in grappling with and acting upon that question must fail to make a fully persuasive case. It assumes that it has solved a moral problem for everyone that has, in actuality, never found any single and enduring historical solution. It confuses moral fervor and noble intentions with ethical justification. It would impose upon the unwilling a position that does not command their moral agreement, and would force them to act against their conscience. . . .

A prochoice position that would make the value of early human life depend solely upon private choice and the individual exercise of power—the view that a woman confers value on a fetus by her decision to accept it—fails to understand the importance of communal safeguards against capricious power over life and death. It is no less insensitive to the all-too-common tendency to define out of the human community those lives that are threatening or burdensome. It is prone morally to confuse being unwanted with being valueless, a blurring of categories that puts the value of all human life at risk. . . .

Why is there, as public opinion polls suggest, a broad agreement on the general right of women to make an abortion choice, yet considerable disagreement on morally acceptable reasons for abortion? The most plausible reason is that most people are trying to find a suitable balance between the traditions of choice and those of respect for life. . . .

2. Moral choice and moral judgment.

Only a willingness to make room for an ongoing—and no doubt never-ending—debate about the morality of individual abortion choices can preserve the status of abortion as a serious moral issue. A prochoice movement unwilling or unable to do that will be forever in jeopardy, hiding from itself but not from others its underlying moral insecurity. In practice that kind of openness will mean accepting the likelihood that some reasons for abortion will be judged reasonable and acceptable, and others unreasonable and unacceptable. It no less means that women will and should have a difficult and highly troubling debate with themselves about their own abortions and will, if the public discussion has been full and rich, have to struggle with the conflicting moral views. ...

I take it to be a good rule of ethical thinking that an important moral choice is one that can give a principled defense of itself and that is not, under most circumstances, simply a self-interested defense of personal preference (called ethical egoism in the philosophical literature). In this case, that would at the least require some sensitive reflection of the values encompassed in that moral tradition that presses for a respect for life. It should not, moreover, be assumed that, just because there is psychological anguish or ambivalence about abortion, there is moral seriousness present; they are not necessarily the same. Anguish and ambivalence can result from trying to decide what one really wants to do, fear of the procedure itself, worry about the reaction of others. Serious ethical reflection goes beyond those matters. It requires thinking carefully about the moral status of the fetus, and about the best way to live a life and to shape a set of moral values and ideals.

3. Compromise and accommodation.

The Supreme Court, in its 1989 *Webster* decision, gave to the states the right to set some conditions on abortion, and it will probably allow even further restrictions in the future. ... An immediate response of the pro-choice leadership to *Webster* was hostility to the decision and to any and all compromise. ... That kind of stance is a mistake. The *Webster* decision already assures that there will be such ground, like it or not. More importantly, it seems increasingly clear that, *with some compromise*, an accommodation might be developed that would have a good chance of both enduring and allowing for the great majority of present abortions.

What accommodations might be reasonable? A restriction on late abortions, already made more difficult by the *Webster* decision, would meet widespread approval. A large number of hospitals have, for some years, established an informal cutoff point of twenty weeks, so a restriction of this kind would not have a major impact. A parental notification requirement for minors seeking abortion would win widespread support as well (even if, as I believe, it would have some unhappy, damaging results). A continuing limitation on the use of federal facilities, while also troublesome, is doubtless likely in the future. Most abortions are not carried out for strictly medical or health reasons, but for private and personal reasons. It is hard, then, to see how a strong case can be made for the use of federal or federally supported facilities in the face of widespread public opposition, and in the light of the prochoice definition of abortion as a private matter, outside the scope of government intervention.

I do not claim that such compromises will be without pain. A number of women might in the future be denied abortions, for economic or other reasons, that are now available. I am only saying that compromises of this sort are most likely to find a middle ground that will be acceptable to public opinion, to be sustainable by the legislatures and courts, and yet also to be most likely to insure that women will still be left with a wide range of choice in the future.

4. Taking choice seriously.

There are three major obstacles to taking choice seriously. The first I have already discussed at length, that of the fear of, and reluctance to, even discuss openly what might count as an unjustifiable moral choice. The morality of the choice is thereby trivialized. The second obstacle is the absence of serious counseling on abortion, particularly in the clinics that do such a larger number of abortions. They rarely explore with women their own thinking, the implications for their lives of their choice, or the possibility that they are being influenced or coerced into abortions they would not otherwise want. There can be no serious choice apart from those conditions. If one believes in real choice—in abortion or any other serious matter that requires reflection and psychological freedom—then the proposal in many states that there be a mandatory waiting period of a few days seems a reasonable accommodation for the prochoice movement to make. A flat rejection of that possibility suggests a desire to maximize abortion rather than to increase choice.

I would be considerably less reassured about going in this direction, I should stress, unless good counseling services were in place. There will, it is true, be practical problems here. Good counseling programs are never easy to organize. But then the present situation is hardly adequate either. It allows women little occasion for considered and assisted reflection, and inadequate help in implementing a range of different choices. This is even more true of the poor than the affluent....

At stake here...is the future of the pluralistic proposition. A pluralism that tries to buy social peace at the expense of moral probity, or considers public issues of far greater importance than private moral issues, cannot long endure. It will be beset from within by those who give thought to their private choices and who wonder about the meaning and impact of those choices in their lives and the lives of others. It will and should be troubled when it recognizes that many so-called private choices are shaped, even determined, by social circumstances and mores. The idea that we can draw a sharp line between the public and the private sphere, between public and private choices, is a great myth. They constantly influence and reflect each other....

NOTES

[1]Daniel Callahan, *Abortion: Law, Choice and Morality* (New York: Macmillan, 1970).

[2]See Sidney Callahan, "Abortion and the Sexual Agenda," *Commonweal*, April 25, 1986: 232–238.

[3]See David C. Reardon, *Aborted Women: Silent No More* (Chicago: Loyola University Press, 1987).

CHAPTER 5

Sexual Harassment

INTRODUCTION

According to Anita Hill, testifying in October 1991 before the Senate confirmation hearings for Justice Clarence Thomas, Thomas had sexually harassed her some ten years earlier. This nationally televised event prompted a much needed discussion about relations between men and women in the workplace and on college campuses. Women began speaking of incidents they had experienced: the boss who fondles women employees in the office, the professor who offers women students better grades for sleeping with him, the coworkers who continually joke about various parts of the female body. In this national dialogue, some spoke as if these incidents were clearly offensive, and many nodded in recognition; others, however, were perplexed—particularly those who might "flirt" in the office or the classroom, but who mean no harm or offense.

As is the case with pornography, defining sexual harassment has proven difficult. There are obvious clear cases—for instance, what has been called *quid pro quo* sexual harassment, in which a threat is made or a benefit offered in order to obtain sex. The boss who tells his office manager that she will receive a promotion if she has sex with him, and the professor who informs his student that she will not pass the class unless she goes on a date with him are engaging in this type of sexual harassment. In these situations, certain individuals use their positions of relative power to coerce or intimidate others in positions of lesser power to engage in sexual interactions. Since the 1970s, the courts have determined that this type of behavior constitutes sex discrimination and is thus in violation of Title VII of the Civil Rights Act of 1964. In order to prove a claim of sexual harassment in the workplace that individual must show that they were the subject of "unwelcome sexual advances, requests for sexual favors, and other verbal or physical conduct of a sexual nature," and that this conduct was "either explicitly or implicitly a term or condition of an individual's employment" and "submission to or rejection of such conduct [was] used as a basis for employment decisions affecting such individual." In addition to the clear-cut cases of obvious and objectionable sexual harassment, the courts have also recognized instances of sexual harassment in which an individual is subjected to an intimidating, offensive, or hostile work environment.

But what exactly counts as an intimidating, offensive, or hostile work environment? What offends one person may be humorous to another; what some find intimidating others find stimulating or challenging. Determining what constitutes an intimidating or offensive environment, as an abstract matter, may appear to be as difficult as determining what counts as the right shade of red. But in the context of sex discrimination, the matter becomes less abstract. In *Meritor v. Vinson*, the Supreme Court argued that the language of Title VII includes not only economic or tangible damage that results from discriminatory behavior, but also the right of individuals not to be subjected to sexist or racist abuse which impairs their ability to perform their jobs. Importantly, the *Meritor* Court also determined that even though Mechelle Vinson, an employee of a branch of the Meritor Bank for four years, "voluntarily" had sex with her supervisor on forty or fifty occasions, in the sense that she was not forced to participate against her will, this did not undermine her claim that she was subjected to a hostile work environment and therefore was sexually harassed by her supervisor.

But what exactly made this case, and the countless others like it, a case of sexual harassment on which legal action can be taken? Does one's ability or inability to perform one's duties determine whether or not sexual harassment has occurred? Does one's feeling offended or intimidated constitute sexual harassment? Anita Superson argues that this way of understanding sexual harassment is wrongheaded. She argues that the definitions of sexual harassment found in U.S. policy and law not only are inadequate because they contribute to a climate of tolerance for sexual harassment, but they also fail to see sexual harassment for what it is. Superson argues that sexual harassment is "an attack on the group of all women, not just the immediate victim." This particular feminist position which argues for understanding sexual harassment as a "group harm" has a number of interesting implications. First, one cannot, at least in contemporary society, locate incidents of sexual harassment outside the context of male dominance. Sexual harassment, on this view, can be carried out only by members of a group that maintains the social and economic power, namely men, while the victims are all those who are members of the disempowered group, namely women, because it is the individual acts of sexual harassment that serve to keep the whole group of women disempowered. Thus only women can be sexually harassed. Superson maintains that the subjective features that are used by the courts in determining whether or not sexual harassment has occurred must be abandoned in favor of objective criteria. According to the law, a victim of sexual harassment must be bothered by some comment or behavior.

According to Superson, due to the nature of the power imbalance that exists between women and men, many women are taught not to be bothered by certain inappropriate behaviors or are taught not to express it when they are. This may be one explanation why Anita Hill waited ten years, and only then reluctantly stepped forward to reveal her experiences. Superson claims that the only remedy for these problems is to define sexual harassment in objective terms: a behavior counts as sexual harassment when "it expresses and perpetuates the attitude that the victim and members of her sex are inferior because of their sex."

But if one man harasses one woman, does it follow that his actions perpetuate a negative attitude towards all women? Does not this definition ignore the damage a victim of sexual harassment might experience not as a representative of the group of all women, but as an individual? Do all women, of all races, ethnicities, classes, and sexual orientations experience sexual harassment in the same way, and are not these experiences important to understanding sexual harassment? And what of the awkward or clumsy perpetrator who actually believes he is being complimentary or flattering to the woman with whom he interacts? When he honestly claims he did not mean any harm, should it be assumed that he is disingenuous? Laurence Thomas argues that to understand sexual harassment as a series of actions taken by one group against another is to succumb to "oppression anxiety." He recommends, rather, that the context in which a particular comment or behavior occurs be taken into account and the actual intentions of the person making the comments be scrutinized. Not every innocent comment about a woman's attire should be heard as an instance of sexual harassment. He argues that while "sexual harassment is indeed offensive, not everything that is offensive to a woman or which causes her discomfort is an instance of sexual harassment." A world of full equality between the sexes is a world in which "goodwill" flourishes, and, Thomas suggests, goodwill facilitates progress to such a world.

Susan Dodds and her coauthors argue that having goodwill and understanding the attitudes of the would-be sexual harasser is not helpful in determining whether a given act is a case of sexual harassment. A man may fully see a particular woman as a sex object, and the woman may actually prefer it that way. Here, or as Dodds and her coauthors point out, in prostitution, women are often reduced to sexual providers, but we would not want to call such a reduction sexual harassment. Similarly, they note, as does Superson, that relying on the attitudes of women will not be likely to provide us with a useful understanding of sexual harassment. Unlike Superson, however, Dodds and her coauthors argue against understanding sexual harassment as a misuse of power, including gender power. That is, they deny that only women can be harassed (a bisexual harasser could harass both men and women) and that only those in power in the workplace can harass (coworkers can and have engaged in quite serious harassment). Dodds and her coauthors suggest that a behavioral account of sexual harassment is best, both in terms of conceptual clarity and for policy purposes. The behavioral account says that sexual harassment occurs when a harasser acts in a certain way towards a harassee—what the harasser meant by it, what the harassee thought the harasser meant, what the outcome of the interactions is, what the power relations between the two are, all have no bearing on whether or not sexual harassment has occurred. But what is the behavior in question? Though Dodds and her coauthors leave this question relatively unanswered because more empirical work is needed, their proposed account, which looks to instances of other types of harassment—for instance, police harassment, the harassment of women seeking abortions by right-to-life activists, etc.—could provide a promising model for future policy on sexual harassment.

SUGGESTED READINGS

Edmund Wall, *Sexual Harassment* (Buffalo, N.Y.: Prometheus Books, 1992).

Ellen Bravo and Ellen Cassedy, *The 9 to 5 Guide to Combatting Sexual Harassment* (New York: John Wiley & Sons, 1992).

Michele A. Paludi, *Academic and Workplace Sexual Harassment: A Resource Manual* (Albany, N.Y.: SUNY Press, 1991).

MERITOR SAVINGS BANK, FSB v. VINSON ET AL.

Argued March 25, 1996, Decided June 19, 1986

Justice Rehnquist delivered the opinion of the Court.

This case presents important questions concerning claims of workplace "sexual harassment" brought under Title VII of the Civil Rights Act of 1964, 78 Stat. 253, as amended, 42 U.S.C. §2000e et seq.

I

In 1974, respondent Mechelle Vinson met Sidney Taylor, a vice president of what is now petitioner Meritor Savings Bank and manager of one of its branch offices. When respondent asked whether she might obtain employment at the bank, Taylor gave her an application, which she completed and returned the next day; later that same day Taylor called her to say that she had been hired. With Taylor as her supervisor, respondent started as a teller-trainee, and thereafter was promoted to teller, head teller, and assistant branch manager. She worked at the same branch for four years, and it is undisputed that her advancement there was based on merit alone. In September 1978, respondent notified Taylor that she was taking sick leave for an indefinite period. On November 1, 1978, the bank discharged her for excessive use of that leave.

Respondent brought this action against Taylor and the bank, claiming that during her four years at the bank she had "constantly been subjected to sexual harassment" by Taylor in violation of Title VII. She sought injunctive relief, compensatory and punitive damages against Taylor and the bank, and attorney's fees.

At the 11-day bench trial, the parties presented conflicting testimony about Taylor's behavior during respondent's employment. Respondent testified that during her probationary period as a teller-trainee, Taylor treated her in a fatherly way and made no sexual advances. Shortly thereafter, however, he invited her out to dinner and, during the course of the meal, suggested that they go to a motel to have sexual relations. At first she refused, but out of what she described as fear of losing her job she eventually agreed. According to respondent, Taylor thereafter made repeated demands upon her for sexual favors, usually at the branch, both during and after business hours; she estimated that over the next several years she had intercourse with him some forty or fifty times. In addition, respondent testified that Taylor fondled her in front of other employees, followed her into the women's restroom when she went there alone, exposed himself to her, and even forcibly raped her on several occasions. These activities ceased after 1977, respondent stated, when she started going with a steady boyfriend.

Respondent also testified that Taylor touched and fondled other women employees of the bank, and she attempted to call witnesses to support this charge. But while some supporting testimony apparently was admitted without objection, the District Court did not allow her "to present wholesale evidence of a pattern and practice relating to sexual advances to other female employees in her case in chief, but advised her that she might well be able to present such evidence in rebuttal to the defendants' cases." *Vinson v. Taylor*, 22 E.P.D. para. 30, 708, p. 14, 693, n. 1, 23 F.E.P. Cases 37, 38–39, n. 1 (D.C. 1980). Respondent did not offer such evidence in rebuttal. Finally, respondent testified that because she was afraid of Taylor she never reported his harassment to any of his supervisors and never attempted to use the bank's complaint procedure.

Taylor denied respondent's allegations of sexual activity, testifying that he never fondled her, never made suggestive remarks to her, never engaged in sexual intercourse with her, and never asked her to do so. He contended instead that respondent made her accusations in response to a business-related dispute. The bank also denied respondent's allegations and asserted that any sexual harassment by Taylor was unknown to the bank and engaged in without its consent or approval....

II

Title VII of the Civil Rights Act of 1964 makes it "an unlawful employment practice for an employer…to discriminate against any individual with respect to his compensation, terms, conditions, or privileges of employment, because of such individual's race, color, religion, sex, or national origin." 42 U.S.C. §2000e–2(a)(1)….

Respondent argues, and the Court of Appeals held, that unwelcome sexual advances that create an offensive or hostile working environment violate Title VII. Without question, when a supervisor sexually harasses a subordinate because of the subordinate's sex, that supervisor "discriminate[s]" on the basis of sex. Petitioner apparently does not challenge this proposition. It contends instead that in prohibiting discrimination with respect to "compensation, terms, conditions, or privileges" of employment, Congress was concerned with what petitioner describes as "tangible loss" of "an economic character," not "purely psychological aspects of the workplace environment." Brief for Petitioner 30–31, 34. In support of this claim petitioner observes that in both the legislative history of Title VII and this Court's Title VII decisions, the focus has been on tangible, economic barriers erected by discrimination.

We reject petitioner's view. First, the language of Title VII is not limited to "economic" or "tangible" discrimination. The phrase "terms, conditions, or privileges of employment" evinces a congressional intent "'to strike at the entire spectrum of disparate treatment of men and women'" in employment. *Los Angeles Dept. of Water and Power v. Manhart,* 435 U.S. 702, 707, n. 13 (1978), quoting *Sprogis v. United Air Lines, Inc.,* 444 F.2d 1194, 1198 (C.A. 7 1971). Petitioner has pointed to nothing in the Act to suggest that Congress contemplated the limitation urged here.

Second, in 1980 the E.E.O.C. issued Guidelines specifying that "sexual harassment," as there defined, is a form of sex discrimination prohibited by Title VII. As an "administrative interpretation of the Act by the enforcing agency," *Griggs v. Duke Power Co.,* 401 U.S. 424, 433–434 (1971), these Guidelines, "'while not controlling upon the courts by reason of their authority, do constitute a body of experience and informed judgment to which courts and litigants may properly resort for guidance,'" *General Electric Co. v. Gilbert,* 429 U.S. 125, 141–142 (1976), quoting *Skidmore v. Swift & Co.,* 323 U.S. 134, 140 (1944). The E.E.O.C. Guidelines fully support the view that harassment leading to noneconomic injury can violate Title VII.

In defining "sexual harassment," the Guidelines first describe the kinds of workplace conduct that may be actionable under Title VII. These include "[unwelcome] sexual advances, requests for sexual favors, and other verbal or physical conduct of a sexual nature." 29 C.F.R. §1604.11(a) (1985). Relevant to the charges at issue in this case, the Guidelines provide that such sexual misconduct constitutes prohibited "sexual harassment," whether or not it is directly linked to the grant or denial of an economic *quid pro quo,* where "such conduct has the purpose or effect of unreasonably interfering with an individual's work performance or creating an intimidating, hostile, or offensive working environment." §1604.11(a)(3).

In concluding that so-called "hostile environment" (i. e., *non quid pro quo*) harassment violates Title VII, the E.E.O.C. drew upon a substantial body of judicial decisions and E.E.O.C. precedent holding that Title VII affords employees the right to work in an environment free from discriminatory intimidation, ridicule, and insult. See generally 45 Fed. Reg. 74676 (1980). *Rogers v. E.E.O.C.,* 454 F.2d 234 (C.A. 5 1971), cert. denied, 406 U.S. 957 (1972), was apparently the first case to recognize a cause of action based upon a discriminatory work environment. In *Rogers,* the Court of Appeals for the Fifth Circuit held that a Hispanic complainant could establish a Title VII violation by demonstrating that her employer created an offensive work environment for employees by giving discriminatory service to its Hispanic clientele. The court explained that an employee's protections under Title VII extend beyond the economic aspects of employment:

> [The] phrase "terms, conditions or privileges of employment" in [Title VII] is an expansive concept which sweeps within its protective ambit the practice of creating a working environment heavily charged with ethnic or racial discrimination.... One can readily envision working environments so heavily polluted with discrimination as to destroy completely the emotional and psychological stability of minority group workers.... 454 F.2d, at 238.

Courts applied this principle to harassment based on race, e.g., *Firefighters Institute for Racial Equality v. St. Louis,* 549 F.2d 506, 514–515 (C.A. 8), cert. denied *sub nom. Banta v. United States,* 434 U.S. 819 (1977); *Gray v. Greyhound Lines, East,* 178 U.S. App. D.C. 91, 98, 545 F.2d 169, 176 (1976), religion, e.g., *Compston v. Borden, Inc.,* 424 F. Supp. 157 (S.D. Ohio 1976), and national origin, e.g., *Cariddi v. Kansas City Chiefs Football Club,* 568 F.2d 87, 88 (C.A. 8 1977). Nothing in Title VII suggests that a hostile environment based on discriminatory sexual harassment should not be likewise prohibited. The Guidelines thus appropriately drew from, and were fully consistent with, the existing case law.

Since the Guidelines were issued, courts have uniformly held, and we agree, that a plaintiff may establish a violation of Title VII by proving that discrimination based on sex has created a hostile or abusive work environment. As the Court of Appeals for the Eleventh Circuit wrote in *Henson v. Dundee,* 682 F.2d 897, 902 (1982):

Sexual harassment which creates a hostile or offensive environment for members of one sex is every bit the arbitrary barrier to sexual equality at the workplace that racial harassment is to racial equality. Surely, a requirement that a man or woman run a gauntlet of sexual abuse in return for the privilege of being allowed to work and make a living can be as demeaning and disconcerting as the harshest of racial epithets.

Of course, as the courts in both *Rogers* and *Henson* recognized, not all workplace conduct that may be described as "harassment" affects a "term, condition, or privilege" of employment within the meaning of Title VII. See *Rogers v. E.E.O.C., supra,* at 238 ("mere utterance of an ethnic or racial epithet which engenders offensive feelings in an employee" would not affect the conditions of employment to sufficiently significant degree to violate Title VII); *Henson,* 682 F.2d, at 904 (quoting same). For sexual harassment to be actionable, it must be sufficiently severe or pervasive "to alter the conditions of [the victim's] employment and create an abusive working environment." *Ibid.* Respondent's allegations in this case—which include not only pervasive harassment but also criminal conduct of the most serious nature—are plainly sufficient to state a claim for "hostile environment" sexual harassment.

...The District Court's conclusion that no actionable harassment occurred might have rested on its earlier "finding" that "[if] [respondent] and Taylor did engage in an intimate or sexual relationship..., that relationship was a voluntary one." *Id.,* at 14,692, 23 F.E.P. Cases, at 42. But the fact that sex-related conduct was "voluntary," in the sense that the complainant was not forced to participate against her will, is not a defense to a sexual harassment suit brought under Title VII. The gravamen of any sexual harassment claim is that the alleged sexual advances were "unwelcome." 29 C.F.R. §1604.11(a) (1985). While the question whether particular conduct was indeed unwelcome presents difficult problems of proof and turns largely on credibility determinations committed to the trier of fact, the District Court in this case erroneously focused on the "voluntariness" of respondent's participation in the claimed sexual episodes. The correct inquiry is whether respondent by her conduct indicated that the alleged sexual advances were unwelcome, not whether her actual participation in sexual intercourse was voluntary.

Petitioner contends that even if this case must be remanded to the District Court, the Court of Appeals erred in one of the terms of its remand. Specifically, the Court of Appeals stated that testimony about respondent's "dress and personal fantasies," 243 U.S. App. D.C., at 328, n. 36, 753 F.2d, at 146, n. 36, which the District Court apparently admitted into evidence, "had no place in this litigation." *Ibid.* The apparent ground for this conclusion was that respondent's voluntariness *vel non* in submitting to Taylor's advances was immaterial to her sexual harassment claim. While "voluntariness" in the sense of consent is not a defense to such a claim, it does not follow that a complainant's sexually provocative speech or dress is irrelevant as a matter of law in determining whether he or she found particular sexual advances unwelcome. To the contrary, such evidence is obviously relevant. The E.E.O.C. Guidelines emphasize that the trier of fact must determine the existence of sexual harassment in light of "the record as a whole" and "the totality of circumstances, such as the nature of the sexual advances and the context in which the alleged incidents occurred." 29 C.F.R. §1604.11(b) (1985)....

III

...Petitioner argues that respondent's failure to use its established grievance procedure, or to otherwise put it on notice of the alleged misconduct, insulates petitioner from liability for Taylor's wrongdoing. A contrary rule would be unfair, petitioner argues, since in a hostile environment harassment case the employer often will have no reason to know about, or opportunity to cure, the alleged wrongdoing....

This debate over the appropriate standard for employer liability has a rather abstract quality about it given the state of the record in this case. We do not know at this stage whether Taylor made any sexual advances toward respondent at all, let alone whether those advances were unwelcome, whether they were sufficiently pervasive to constitute a condition of employment, or whether they were "so pervasive and so long continuing...that the employer must have become conscious of [them]," *Taylor v. Jones*, 653 F.2d 1193, 1197–1199 (C.A. 8 1981) (holding employer liable for racially hostile working environment based on constructive knowledge).

We therefore decline the parties' invitation to issue a definitive rule on employer liability, but we do agree with the E.E.O.C. that Congress wanted courts to look to agency principles for guidance in this area. While such common-law principles may not be transferable in all their particulars to Title VII, Congress' decision to define "employer" to include any "agent" of an employer, 42 U.S.C. §2000e(b), surely evinces an intent to place some limits on the acts of employees for which employers under Title VII are to be held responsible.... For the same reason, absence of notice to an employer does not necessarily insulate that employer from liability. *Ibid.*

Finally, we reject petitioner's view that the mere existence of a grievance procedure and a policy against discrimination, coupled with respondent's failure to invoke that procedure, must insulate petitioner from liability. While those facts are plainly relevant, the situation before us demonstrates why they are not necessarily dispositive. Petitioner's general nondiscrimination policy did not address sexual harassment in particular, and thus did not alert employees to their employer's interest in correcting that form of discrimination. Moreover, the bank's grievance procedure apparently required an employee to complain first to her supervisor, in this case Taylor. Since Taylor was the alleged perpetrator, it is not altogether surprising that respondent failed to invoke the procedure and report her grievance to him. Petitioner's contention that respondent's failure should insulate it from liability might be substantially stronger if its procedures were better calculated to encourage victims of harassment to come forward.

IV

In sum, we hold that a claim of "hostile environment" sex discrimination is actionable under Title VII. ... As to employer liability, we conclude that the Court of Appeals was wrong to entirely disregard agency principles and impose absolute liability on employers for the acts of their supervisors, regardless of the circumstances of a particular case.

...the case is remanded for further proceedings consistent with this opinion.

It is so ordered.

A FEMINIST DEFINITION OF SEXUAL HARASSMENT

Anita M. Superson

INTRODUCTION

By far the most pervasive form of discrimination against women is sexual harassment (SH). Women in every walk of life are subject to it, and I would venture to say, on a daily basis.[1] Even though the law is changing to the benefit of victims of SH, the fact that SH is still so pervasive shows that there is too much tolerance of it, and that victims do not have sufficient legal recourse to be protected.

The main source for this problem is that the way SH is defined by various titles and other sources does not adequately reflect the social nature of SH, or the harm it causes all women. As a result, SH comes to be defined in subjective ways. One upshot is that when subjective definitions infuse the case law on SH, the more subtle but equally harmful forms of SH do not get counted as SH and thus are not afforded legal protection.

My primary aim in this paper is to offer an objective definition of SH that accounts for the group harm all forms of SH have in common.

From "A Feminist Definition of Sexual Harassment," *Journal of Social Philosophy*, Vol. 24, No. 1 (1994). Reprinted by permission of the *Journal of Social Philosophy*.

Though my aim is to offer a moral definition of SH, I offer it in hopes that it will effect changes in the law. It is only by defining SH in a way that covers all of its forms and gets at the heart of the problem that legal protection can be given to all victims in all circumstances....

I define SH in the following way:

> Any behavior (verbal or physical) caused by a person, A, in the dominant class directed at another, B, in the subjugated class, that expresses and perpetuates the attitude that B or members of B's sex is/are inferior because of their sex, thereby causing harm to either B and/or members of B's sex.

CURRENT LAW ON SEXUAL HARASSMENT

Currently, victims of SH have legal recourse under Title VII of the Civil Rights Act of 1964, Title IX of the 1972 Education Amendments, and tort law.

The Civil Rights Act of 1964 states:

> (a) It shall be an unlawful employment practice for an employer—
> (1) to fail or refuse to hire or to discharge any individual, or otherwise to discriminate against any individual with respect to his compensation, terms, conditions, or privileges of employment because of such individual's race, color, religion, sex, or national origin....

Over time, the courts came to view SH as a form of sex discrimination. The main advocate for this was Catharine MacKinnon, whose book, *Sexual Harassment of Working Women*,[2] greatly influenced court decisions on the issue. Before it was federally legislated, some courts appealed to the Equal Employment Opportunity Commission (E.E.O.C.) *Guidelines on Discrimination Because of Sex* to establish that SH was a form of sex discrimination. The guidelines (amended in 1980 to include SH) state that:

> Harassment on the basis of sex is a violation of Sec. 703 of Title VII. Unwelcome sexual advances, requests for sexual favors, and other verbal or physical conduct of a sexual nature constitute sexual harassment when (1) submission to such conduct is made either explicitly or implicitly a term or condition of an individual's employment, (2) submission to or rejection of such conduct by an individual is used as the basis for employment decisions affecting such individual, or (3) such conduct has the purpose or effect of unreasonably interfering with an individual's work performance or creating an intimidating, hostile, or offensive working environment.

In a landmark case,[3] *Meritor Savings Bank v. Vinson*, the Supreme Court, relying on the E.E.O.C. guidelines, established that SH was a form of sex discrimination prohibited under Title VII. . . .

Sexual harassment extends beyond the workplace. To protect students who are not employees of their learning institution, Congress enacted Title IX of the Education Amendments of 1972, which states:

> No person in the The United States shall, on the basis of sex, be excluded from participation in, be denied the benefits of, or be subjected to discrimination under any educational program or activity receiving federal financial assistance.

Cases of litigation under Title IX have been influenced by *Meritor* so that SH in educational institutions is construed as a form of sex discrimination.

The principles that came about under Title VII apply equally to Title IX. Under either title, a person can file two different kinds of harassment charges: *quid pro quo*, or hostile environment. *Quid pro quo* means "something for something." *Quid pro quo* harassment occurs when "an employer or his agent explicitly ties the terms, conditions, and privileges of the victim's employment to factors which are arbitrary and unrelated to job performance."[4] Plaintiffs must show they "suffered a tangible economic detriment as a result of the harassment."[5] In contrast, hostile environment harassment occurs when the behavior of supervisors or coworkers has the effect of "unreasonably interfering with an individual's work performance or creating an intimidating, hostile, or offensive environment." Hostile environment harassment established that Title VII (and presumably Title IX) were not limited to economic discrimination, but applied to emotional harm, as well. The E.E.O.C. guidelines initiated the principle of hostile environment harassment which was used by the courts in many cases, including *Meritor*. . . .

Despite major advances made in the last few decades in the law on SH, I believe the law is still inadequate. The main problem in my view is that the law, reflecting the view held by the general public, fails to see SH for what it is: an attack on the group of all women, not just the immediate victim. Because of this, there is a failure to recognize the group harm that all instances of SH, not just the more blatant ones, cause all women. As a result, the law construes SH as a subjective issue, that is, one that is determined by what the victim feels and (sometimes) what the perpetrator intends. As a result, the burden of proof is wrongly shifted to the victim and off the perpetrator, with the result that many victims are not legally protected.

For instance, victims filing complaints under Title VII (and presumably Title IX) are not protected unless they have a fairly serious case. They have to show, under hostile environment harassment, that the behavior unreasonably interfered with their work performance, and that there was a pattern of behavior on the defendant's behalf. Regarding the latter point, the E.E.O.C. guidelines say that:

> In determining whether alleged conduct constitutes sexual harassment, the Commission will look at the record as a whole and at the totality of the circumstances, such as the nature of the sexual advances and the context in which the alleged incidents occurred.

It seems unlikely that the victim of isolated incidents of SH could have her complaint taken seriously under this assessment....

Victims not protected include the worker who is harassed by a number of different people, the worker who suffers harassment but in small doses, the person who is subjected to a slew of catcalls on her two-mile walk to work, the female professor who is subjected to leering from one of her male students, and the woman who does not complain out of fear. The number of cases is huge, and many of them are quite common.

To protect all victims in all circumstances, the law ought to treat SH as it is beginning to treat racial discrimination. In her very interesting paper, Mari Matsuda has traced the history of the law regarding racist speech.[6] Article 4 of the International Convention on the Elimination of All Forms of Racial Discrimination, which was unanimously adopted by the General Assembly on December 21, 1965, prohibits not only acts of violence, but also the "mere dissemination of racist ideas, without requiring proof of incitement." Apparently many states have signed and ratified the signing of the convention, though the United States has not yet done so because of worries about freedom of speech protected by the First Amendment. Aside from the convention, the United Nations Charter, the Universal Declaration of Human Rights, the European Convention for the Protection of Human Rights and Fundamental Freedoms, the American Declaration of the Rights and Duties of Man, as well as the domestic law of several nations, have all recognized the right to equality and freedom from racism. In these and other codes, racist ideas are banned if they are discriminatory, or related to violence, or express inferiority, hatred, or persecution. On my view, some forms of SH are related to violence, and they all express inferiority, whether or not they express hatred. At the root of the standard on racism that is gaining worldwide recognition is the view that racist speech "interferes with the rights of subordinated group members to participate equally in society, maintaining their basic sense of security and worth as human beings."[7] Sexual harassment has the same effect, so it, too, should be prohibited.... The worldwide standard against racist speech recognizes the group harm of racism by realizing that racist speech expresses inferiority; a similar standard against SH should be adopted.

THE SOCIAL NATURE OF SEXUAL HARASSMENT

Sexual harassment, a form of sexism, is about domination, in particular, the domination of the group of men over the group of women.[8] Domination involves control or power which can be seen in the economic, political, and social spheres of society. Sexual harassment is not simply an assertion of power, for power can be used in beneficial ways. The power men have over women has been wielded in ways that oppress women. The power expressed in SH is oppression, power used wrongly.

Sexual harassment is integrally related to sex roles. It reveals the belief that a person is to be relegated to certain roles on the basis of her sex, including not only women's being sex objects, but also their being caretakers, mothers, nurturers, sympathizers, etc. In general, the sex roles women are relegated to are associated with the body (versus mind) and emotions (versus reason).

When A sexually harasses B, the comment or behavior is really directed at the group of all women, not just a particular woman, a point often missed by the courts. After all, many derogatory behaviors are issued at women the harasser does not even know (e.g., scanning a stranger's body). Even when the harasser knows his victim, the behavior is directed at the particular woman because she happens to be "available" at the time, though its message is for all women. For instance, a catcall says not (merely) that the perpetrator likes a woman's body but that he thinks women are at least primarily sex objects, and he—because of the power he holds by being in the dominant group—acts to rate them according to how much pleasure they give him. The professor who refers to his female students as "chicks" makes a statement that women are intellectually inferior to men as they can be likened to nonrational animals, perhaps even soft, cuddly ones that are to serve as the objects of (men's) pleasure. Physicians using *Playboy* centerfolds in medical schools to "spice up their lectures" send the message that women lack the competence to make it in a "man's world" and should perform the "softer tasks" associated with bearing and raising children.

…Hughes and May claim that women are a disadvantaged group because:

1. they are a social group having a distinct identity and existence apart from their individual identities,
2. they occupy a subordinate position in American society, and
3. their political power is severely circumscribed.[9]

They continue:

> Once it is established that women qualify for special disadvantaged group status, all practices tending to stigmatize women as a group, or

which contribute to the maintenance of their subordinate social status, would become legally suspect.[10]

This last point, I believe, should be central to the definition of SH.

Because SH has as its target the group of all women, this group suffers harm as a result of the behavior. Indeed, when any one woman is in any way sexually harassed, all women are harmed. The group harm SH causes is different from the harm suffered by particular women as individuals: it is often more vague in nature, as it is not easily causally tied to any particular incident of harassment. The group harm has to do primarily with the fact that the behavior reflects and reinforces sexist attitudes that women are inferior to men and that they do and ought to occupy certain sex roles. For example, comments and behavior that relegate women to the role of sex objects reinforce the belief that women are sex objects and that they *ought to* occupy this sex role. Similarly, when a female professor's cogent comments at department colloquia are met with frowns and rolled eyes from her colleagues, this behavior reflects and reinforces the view that women are not fit to occupy positions men arrogate to themselves.

The harm women suffer as a group from any single instance of SH is significant. It takes many forms. A Kantian analysis would show what is wrong with being solely a sex object. Though there is nothing wrong with being a caretaker or nurturer, etc., *per se*, it is sexist—and so wrong—to assign such roles to women. In addition, it is wrong to assign a person to a role she may not want to occupy. Basically women are not allowed to decide for themselves which roles they are to occupy, but this gets decided for them, no matter what they do.... The belief that women must occupy certain sex roles is both a cause and an effect of their oppression. It is a cause because women are believed to be more suited for certain roles, given their association with body and emotions. It is an effect because, once they occupy these roles and are victims of oppression, the belief that they must occupy these sex roles is reinforced.

Women are harmed by SH in yet another way. The belief that they are sex objects, caretakers, etc., is reflected in social and political practices in ways that are unfair to women. It has undoubtedly meant many lost opportunities that are readily available to men. Women are not likely to be hired for jobs that require them to act in ways other than the ways the sex roles dictate, and if they are, what is expected of them is different from what is expected of men....

Another harm SH causes all women is that the particular form sex stereotyping takes promotes two myths: (1) that male behavior is normally and naturally predatory, and (2) that females naturally (because they are taken to be primarily bodily and emotional) and even willingly acquiesce despite the appearance of protest.[11] Because the behavior perpetuated by these myths is taken to be normal, it is not seen as sexist, and in turn is not counted as SH.

The first myth is that men have stronger sexual desires than women, and harassment is just a natural venting of these desires, which men are unable to control. The truth is, first, that women are socialized *not* to vent their sexual desires in the way men do, but this does not mean these desires are weaker or less prevalent.... But second, SH has nothing to do with men's sexual desires, nor is it about seduction; instead, it is about oppression of women. Indeed, harassment generally does not lead to sexual satisfaction, but it often gives the harasser a sense of power.

The second myth is that women either welcome, ask for, or deserve the harassing treatment. Case law reveals this mistaken belief. In *Lipsett v. Rive-Mora*,[12] the plaintiff was discharged from a medical residency program because she "did not react favorably to her professor's requests to go out for drinks, his compliments about her hair and legs, or to questions about her personal and romantic life."[13] The court exonerated the defendant because the plaintiff initially reacted favorably by smiling when shown lewd drawings of herself and when called sexual nicknames, as she thought she had to appease the physician. The court said that "given the plaintiff's admittedly favorable responses to these flattering comments, there was no way anyone could consider them as 'unwelcome.'"[14]...

Both myths harm all women as they sanction SH by shifting the burden on the victim and all members of her sex: women must either go out of their way to avoid "natural" male behavior, or establish conclusively that they did not in any way want the behavior. Instead of the behavior being seen as sexist, it is seen as women's problem to rectify.

Last, but certainly not least, women suffer group harm from SH because they come to be stereotyped as victims. Many men see SH as something they can do to women, and in many cases, get away with. Women come to see themselves as victims, and come to believe that the roles they can occupy are only the sex roles men have designated for them. Obviously these harms are quite serious for women, so the elimination of all forms of SH is warranted.

I have spoken so far as if it is only men who can sexually harass women, and I am now in a position to defend this controversial view. When a woman engages in the very same behavior harassing men engage in, the underlying message implicit in male-to-female harassment is missing. For example, when a woman scans a man's body, she might be considering him to be a sex object, but all the views about domination and being relegated to certain sex roles are absent. She cannot remind the man that he is inferior because of his sex, since given the way things are in society, he is not. In general, women cannot harm or degrade or dominate men *as a group*, for it is impossible to send the message that one dominates (and so cause group harm) if one does not dominate. Of course, if the sexist roles predominant in our society were reversed, women could sexually harass men. The way things are, any bothersome behavior a woman engages in, even though it may be of a sexual nature, does not constitute SH, because it lacks the social impact present in male-to-female harassment....

SUBJECTIVE v. OBJECTIVE DEFINITIONS OF SEXUAL HARASSMENT

Most definitions of "sexual harassment" make reference to the behavior's being "unwelcome" or "annoying" to the victim.... In their philosophical account of SH, Hughes and May define "harassment" as "a class of annoying or unwelcome acts undertaken by one person (or group of persons) against another person (or group of persons).[15] And Rosemarie Tong takes the feminists' definition of noncoercive SH to be that which "denotes sexual misconduct that merely annoys or offends the person to whom it is directed."[16]

The criterion of "unwelcomeness" or "annoyance" is reflected in the way the courts have handled cases of SH, as in *Lipsett*...and *Meritor*, though in the latter case the court said that the voluntariness of the victim's submission to the defendant's sexual conduct did not mean that she welcomed the conduct. The criterion of unwelcomeness or annoyance present in these subjective accounts of harassment puts the burden on the victim to establish that she was sexually harassed. There is no doubt that many women are bothered by this behavior, often with serious side effects including anything from anger, fear, and guilt to lowered self-esteem and decreased feelings of competence and confidence, to anxiety disorders, alcohol and drug abuse, coronary disturbances, and gastrointestinal disorders.

Though it is true that many women are bothered by the behavior at issue, I think it is seriously mistaken to say that whether the victim is bothered determines whether the behavior constitutes SH. This is so for several reasons.

First, we would have to establish that the victim was bothered by it, either by the victim's complaints, or by examining the victim's response to the behavior. The fact of the matter is that many women are quite hesitant to report being harassed, for a number of reasons. Primary among them is that they fear negative consequences from reporting the conduct. As is often the case, harassment comes from a person in a position of institutional power, whether he be a supervisor, a company president, a member of a dissertation committee, the chair of the department, and so on. Unfortunately for many women, as a review of the case law reveals, their fears are warranted.[17] Women have been fired, their jobs have been made miserable forcing them to quit, professors have handed out unfair low grades, and so on. Worries about such consequences means that complaints are not filed, or are filed years after the incident, as in the Anita

Hill versus Clarence Thomas case. But this should not be taken to imply that the victim was not harassed....

Further, some women do not recognize harassment for what it is, and so will not complain. Sometimes this is because they are not aware of their own oppression, or actually seem to endorse sexist stereotypes. I recall a young woman who received many catcalls on the streets of Daytona Beach, Florida during spring break, and who was quite proud that her body could draw such attention. Given that women are socialized into believing their bodies are the most important feature of themselves, it is no surprise that a fair number of them are complacent about harassing behavior directed at them....

Moreover, women's *behavior* is not an accurate indicator of whether they are bothered. More often than not, women try to ignore the perpetrator's behavior in an attempt not to give the impression they are encouraging it. They often cover up their true feelings so that the perpetrator does not have the satisfaction that his harassing worked. Since women are taught to smile and put up with this behavior, they might actually appear to enjoy it to some extent. Often they have no choice but to continue interacting with the perpetrator, making it very difficult to assert themselves. Women often make up excuses for not "giving in" instead of telling the perpetrator to stop. The fact that their behavior does not indicate they are bothered should not be used to show they were not bothered. In reality, women are fearful of defending themselves in the face of men's power and physical strength. Given the fact that the courts have decided that a lot of this behavior should just be tolerated, it is no wonder that women try to make the best of their situation.

It would be wrong to take a woman's behavior to be a sign that she is bothered also because doing so implies the behavior is permissible if she does not seem to care. This allows the perpetrator to be the judge of whether a woman is harassed, which is unjustifiable given the confusion among men about whether their behavior is bothersome or flattering. Sexual harassment should be treated no differently than crimes where harm to the victim is assessed in some objective way, independent of the perpetrator's beliefs. To give men this power in the case of harassment is to perpetuate sexism from all angles.

An *objective* view of SH avoids the problems inherent in a subjective view. According to the objective view defended here, what is decisive in determining whether behavior constitutes SH is not whether the victim is bothered, but whether the behavior is an instance of a practice that expresses and perpetuates the attitude that the victim and members of her sex are inferior because of their sex. Thus the Daytona Beach case counts as a case of SH, because the behavior is an instance of a practice that reflects men's domination of women in that it relegates women to the role of sex objects.

The courts have to some extent tried to incorporate an objective notion of SH by invoking the "reasonable person" standard. The E.E.O.C. guidelines, as shown earlier, define SH partly as behavior that "has the purpose or effect of *unreasonably* interfering with an individual's work performance."...

In various cases, the courts have invoked a reasonable man (or person) standard, but not to show that women who are not bothered still suffer harassment. Instead, they used the standard to show that even though a particular woman was bothered, she would have to tolerate such behavior because it was behavior a reasonable person would not have been affected by. In *Rabidue v. Osceola Refining Co.*,[18] a woman complained that a coworker made obscene comments about women in general and her in particular. The court ruled that "a reasonable person would not have been significantly affected by the same or similar circumstances," and that "women must expect a certain amount of demeaning conduct in certain work environments."

But the reasonable man standard will not work, since men and women perceive situations involving SH quite differently. The reasonable person standard fares no better, as it becomes the reasonable man standard when it is applied by male judges seeing things through male eyes. Studies have shown that sexual overtures that men find flattering are found by women to be insulting. And even when men recognize behavior as harassment, they think women will be flattered by it.[19] The differences in perception only strengthen my point about the group harm that SH cause all women: unlike women, men can take sexual overtures directed at them to be complimentary, because the overtures do not signify the stereotyping that underlies SH of women. A reasonable man standard would not succeed as a basis upon which to determine SH, as its objectivity is outweighed by the disparity found in the way the sexes assess what is "reasonable."

Related to this last topic is the issue of the harasser's intentions. In subjective definitions, this is the counterpart to the victim's being bothered....

But like the victim's feelings, the harasser's intentions are irrelevant to whether his behavior is harassment. As I just pointed out, many men do not take their behavior to be bothersome, and sometimes even mistakenly believe that women enjoy crude compliments about their bodies, ogling, pinching, etc. From perusing cases brought before the courts, I have come to believe that many men have psychological feelings of power over women, feelings of being in control of their world, and the like, when they harass. These feelings might be subconscious, but this should not be admitted as a defense of the harasser. Also, as I have said, many men believe women encourage SH, either by their dress or language or simply by the fact that they tolerate the abuse without protest (usually out of fear of repercussions). In light of these facts, it would be wrongheaded to allow the harasser's intentions to count in assessing harassment, though they might become relevant in determining punishment. I am arguing for an objective definition of SH: it is the attitudes embedded and reflected in the *practice* the behavior is an instance of, not the attitudes or intentions of the *perpetrator*, that make the behavior SH.

Yet the idea that the behavior must be directed at a certain person in order for it to count as harassment seems to suggest that intentions *do* count in assessing harassments.... If conduct is directed at a particular individual, it seems that the person expressing himself must be intentionally singling out that individual, wanting to cause her harm.

I think this is mistaken. Since the harasser can subconsciously enjoy the feeling of power harassing gives him, or might even consider his behavior to be flattering, his behavior can be directed at a specific person (or group of persons) without implying any ill intention on his part. By "directed at a particular individual," I mean that the behavior is in some way observed by a particular person (or persons). This includes, for example, sexist comments a student hears her professor say, pornographic pictures a worker sees, etc. I interpret it loosely enough to include a person's overhearing sexist comments, even though the speaker has no idea the person is within earshot (sometimes referred to as "nondirected behavior"). But I interpret it to exclude the bare knowledge that sexist behavior is going on (e.g., female employees knowing that there are pornographic pictures hidden in their boss's office). If it did not exclude such behavior it would have to include knowledge of any sexist behavior, even if no person who can be harmed by it ever observes it (e.g., pornographic magazines strewn on a desert island). Though such behavior is sexist, it fails to constitute SH.

IMPLICATIONS OF THE OBJECTIVE DEFINITION

One implication of my objective definition is that it reflects the correct way power comes into play in SH. Traditionally, SH has been taken to exist only between persons of unequal power, usually in the workplace or an educational institution. It is believed that SH in universities occurs only when a professor harasses a student, but not vice versa. It is said that students can cause "sexual hassle," because they cannot "destroy (the professor's) self-esteem or endanger his intellectual self-confidence," and professors "seldom suffer the complex psychological effects of sexual harassment victims."[20] MacKinnon, in her earlier book, defines SH as "the unwanted imposition of sexual requirements in the context of a relationship of unequal power."[21]

Though it is true that a lot of harassment occurs between unequals, it is false that harassment occurs *only* between unequals: equals and subordinates can harass....

The one sense in which it is true that the harasser must have power over his victim is that men have power—social, political, and economic—over women as a group. This cannot be understood by singling out individual men and showing that they have power over women or any particular woman for that matter. It is power that all men have, in virtue of being men. Defining SH in the objective way I do allows us to see that this is the sense in which power exists in SH, in all of its forms. The benefit of not restricting SH to cases of unequal institutional power is that all victims are afforded protection.

A second implication of my definition is that it gives the courts a way of distinguishing SH from sexual attraction. It can be difficult to make this distinction, since "traditional courtship activities" are often quite sexist and frequently involve behavior that is harassment. The key is to examine the practice the behavior is an instance of. If the behavior reflects the attitude that the victim is inferior because of her sex, then it is SH. Sexual harassment is not about a man's attempting to date a woman who is not interested, as the courts have tended to believe; it is about domination, which might be reflected, of course, in the way a man goes about trying to get a date. My definition allows us to separate cases of SH from genuine sexual attraction by forcing the courts to focus on the social nature of SH....

Finally, defining SH in a subjective way means that the victim herself must come forward and complain, as it is her response that must be assessed. But given that most judges, law enforcement officers, and even superiors are men, it is difficult for women to do so. They are embarrassed, afraid to confront someone of the same sex as the harasser who is likely not to see the problem. They do not feel their voices will be heard. Working with my definition will, I hope, assuage this. Recognizing SH as a group harm will allow women to come to each other's aid as cocomplainers, thereby alleviating the problem of reticence. Even if the person the behavior is directed at does not feel bothered, other women can complain, as they suffer the group harm associated with SH.

CONCLUSION

The definition of SH I have defended in this paper has as its main benefit that it acknowledges the group harm SH causes all women, thereby getting to the heart of what is wrong with SH. By doing so, it protects all victims in all cases from even the most subtle kinds of SH, since all cases of SH have in common group harm.

Of course, as with any definition, problems exist. Though space does not allow that I deal with them, a few are worth mentioning. One is that many behaviors will count as SH, leading perhaps to an unmanageable number of claims. Another is that it will still be a matter of interpretation whether a given behavior meets the criteria for SH. Perhaps the most crucial objection is that since so many kinds of behavior count as SH, the right to free speech will be curtailed in unacceptable ways.

I believe there are at least partial solutions to these problems. My proposal is only programmatic, and a thorough defense of it would include working through these and other problems. Such a defense will have to wait.

NOTES

I would like to thank John Exdell and Lois Pineau for helpful discussions and many insightful comments on an earlier draft of this paper.

[1]Rosemarie Tong, *Women, Sex and the Law* (Maryland: Rowman & Littlefield Publishers, 1984). Tong cites a *Redbook* study reporting that 88 percent of 9,000 readers sampled experienced some sort of sexual harassment.

[2]Catharine MacKinnon, *Sexual Harassment of Working Women: A Case of Sex Discrimination* (New Haven: Yale University Press, 1979).

[3]The case is a landmark because it established (1) federal legislation that SH is a form of sex discrimination, (2) that just because the victim "voluntarily" submitted to advances from her employer, it did not mean she welcomed the conduct, (3) that victims could appeal on grounds of emotional harm, not merely economic harm....

[4]...In the case of students, *quid pro quo* harassment can take the form of a professor threatening the student with a lower grade if she does not comply with his demands.

[5]Ellen Frankel Paul, "Sexual Harassment as Sex Discrimination: A Defective Paradigm," *Yale Law and Policy Review* 8 (1990): 341.

[6]Mari J. Matsuda, "Public Response to Racist Speech: Considering the Victim's Story," *Michigan Law Review* 87 (August 1989): 2320–2381.

[7]*Ibid*, 2348.

[8]This suggests that only men can sexually harass women. I will defend this view later in the paper.

[9]John C. Hughes and Larry May, "Sexual Harassment," *Social Theory and Practice* 6 (Fall 1980): 264–265.

[10]*Ibid*.

[11]These same myths surround the issue of rape. (See Pineau in this volume.)

[12]*Lipsett v. Rive-Mora*, 669 F. Supp 1188 (D. Puerto Rico 1987).

[13]Dawn D. Bennett-Alexander, "Hostile Environment, Sexual Harassment: A Clearer View," *Labor Law Journal* 42 (March 1991): 135.

[14]*Lipsett*, Sec. 15.

[15]Hughes and May, 250.

[16]Tong: 67.

[17]See Catharine MacKinnon, *Feminism Unmodified* (Cambridge, MA: Harvard University Press, 1987), Ch. 9. See also Ellen Frankel Paul, *op. cit.*

[18]*Rabidue v. Osceola Refining Co.*, 805 F.2nd (1986), Sixth Circuit Court.

[19]Stephanie Riger, "Gender Dilemmas in Sexual Harassment Policies and Proce-dures," *American Psychologist* 46 (May 1991): 499.

[20]Billie Wright Dziech and Linda Weiner, *The Lecherous Professor: Sexual Harass-ment on Campus* (Boston: Beacon Press, 1984): 24.

[21]MacKinnon, *Sexual Harassment of Working Women*, 1. It is actually not clear that MacKinnon endorses this definition throughout this book, as what she says seems to suggest that harassment can occur at least between equals....

LOST INNOCENCE

Laurence Thomas

We live in an age of lost innocence. To be sure, the world has never been perfect. All the same, there was a time in the workplace when not every offense that a person might cause another was seen as flowing from a corrupt and reprehensible character. Indeed, it used to be allowed that a person could, in fact, be unaware of a having caused offense. Or perhaps better: it used to be allowed that a person acted with goodwill, although the action itself was inappropriate, perhaps even harmful.[1] Not so any more. The prevailing mood seems to be that if a person feels offended or threatened by what another individual has done, then it is as if that individual had willfully set out to offend or threaten. Not only that, the person's objectionable act proceeds from a corresponding corrupt character, it being disallowed that the individual could have offended with nonreprehensible intentions and motives. The utter unwillingness to allow for this possibility is what I mean by lost innocence.

To focus specifically upon men harassing women: is the assumption of lost innocence in the workplace warranted in the interaction between women and men with respect to sexual harassment? When one considers the extent to which men have exploited and sexually harassed women, invaded the personal space of women, and referred to them in degrading ways, all in the name of having a little "innocent" fun, and the extent to which men have displayed brazen insensitivity to the feelings of women, it would seem that the answer to this question can be nothing but a resounding "yes."

Reprinted by permission of the *Stanford Law and Policy Review*. Originally appeared in Vol. 5, No. 2 (Spring 1994).

I would like to challenge the assumption of lost innocence, not because I want to diminish the wrong of sexual harassment, but because I believe that any attempt to assess human behavior independent of motives and character is misguided. Sexual harassment is offensive, but the converse is false. Not all male behavior that a woman finds offensive is rightly construed as sexual harassment. The analogous point holds for any form of "X-ism" (racism, anti-Semitism, and so on). Current discussions of sexual harassment seem to run roughshod over this truth, as illustrated by the examples offered in the section which follows. What is more, there is the phenomenon of oppression anxiety. This is when prudence makes being wary and suspicious of a person's beliefs and motives a natural way of life, because of the history of oppression of the group to which that person belongs. I develop this point later in the essay.

Throughout this essay, I shall focus upon communication, because it is relatively clear nowadays that, among adults, bodily contact without consent is inappropriate behavior that would constitute sexual harassment, in whatever context such contact might occur, but especially in the workplace.

As a final introductory remark, it should be mentioned that, although it is highly unlikely that in the examples which I offer the male could be held legally accountable for his actions, I am interested in the moral climate that prevails among individuals working together. The moral climate of a workplace or institution pertains not just to the letter of the law, but the spirit as well, regarding what is and is not appropriate behavior. There can be substantial difference in policy renderings of the spirit of the law.[2] Thus, whether or not a charge would hold up in the courts, a woman can feel that she has been sexually harassed, and others may share her conviction. Feelings in this regard are not independent of the moral climate in which things occur, with some being far more protective of women than others. I want to shed some light on the issue of where the baseline should be drawn in terms of how we think about sexual harassment.

THE MARY AND JOHN SCENARIO

Suppose John tells Mary, a colleague, that she is wearing an absolutely lovely outfit. Wanting desperately to fit in, Mary smiles demurely and says nothing. However, Mary is a person who feels extremely uncomfortable when complimented on her attire by a man. For good reason, Mary considers it nearly axiomatic that a man who compliments a woman on her attire is up to no good. Not knowing that, the next time John sees Mary in an outfit that he considers lovely, he again remarks that she is wearing a lovely outfit. Is John guilty of sexually harassing Mary?

Despite the fact that John would almost certainly not be legally liable for sexual harassment under *Meritor v. Vinson* and the recent *Harris v.*

Forklift Systems decision,[3] this does not, as I indicated in my introductory remarks, mean that society does not view John as a harasser; nor does it mean that there are not serious consequences for John in being labeled such. After all, a charge of sexual harassment that is eventually dropped or thrown out can still do serious damage to a person's reputation.

Consider, for example, Syracuse University's definition of sexual harassment:

> Any unwelcome conduct of a sexual nature, on or off campus, that relates to the gender or sexual identity of an individual or group, and that has the purpose or effect of creating an intimidating or hostile environment for work or study.[4]

Since John's remarks make Mary feel uncomfortable, under this policy they create a hostile work environment. Assume that if a man had worn a suit to work that John judged to be particularly sharp-looking, John would not have complimented him. John's complimenting behavior may then be said to be gender-related. Under the Syracuse definition, then, John is guilty of sexual harassment.

But surely that is too swift. For suppose that John believes Mary has exquisite taste in professional style, and that he had no more than that in mind when he complimented her. Furthermore, he naturally assumed that she would interpret his compliment in just that way, since it was plain that she was not wearing sexually appealing attire to begin with. Indeed, nothing was more obvious than that she was wearing what some would consider to be a woman's version of a man's suit. In any case, had Mary indicated her discomfort in any way, John would have respected her wishes and apologized profusely for having caused her such discomfort. Besides, John does not believe that it is somehow "natural" for a woman to enjoy a compliment from a man. True, John would not have complimented a man who was exquisitely attired, and this may reflect poorly upon John. But how does this differential turn his complimenting Mary into an intentional offense directed at her?

Yet John's behavior either fully satisfies Syracuse University's definition of sexual harassment, or comes dangerously close to doing so. This is precisely because we have a hostile environment generated through gender-linked behavior. But as shown by the Mary-John example, it is possible for a male to unwittingly create such an environment although his motivations are not in the least salacious. A male who causes a woman sincere discomfort in the workplace is not necessarily a male who intended to cause discomfort. Recall that, had Mary given John any indication of her discomfort, he would have sincerely apologized, and that would have been the end of such behavior on his part toward her.

It may be that no court of law in the United States would deem John guilty of sexual harassment if, at Syracuse University, he were brought up on such charges and took the matter to court. But the lack of legal ramifications does not diminish the potential consequences of the university policy.

THE BOMBASTIC MACHO MALE VERSUS
THE TIMOROUS HETEROSEXUAL MALE

To illustrate further, I would like to offer two crass models of men: Bombastic Macho Male (BMM) and Timorous Heterosexual Male (THM). Both wrestle with their male identities and see having sex with women as an inextricable part of their male identities; accordingly, each is alert to opportunities that present themselves. The difference, however, is in how each conceives of his initial interaction with a woman. BMM supposes that a brazen display of sexual interest, however crude, reveals his manliness and helps to ensure his success with a woman. He is often oblivious to how he actually comes across to women, and he has great difficulty understanding why any woman would bristle at being called "a sweet little thing." BMM is insecure and compensates for his insecurity in this bombastic macho manner.

Then there is Timorous Heterosexual Male (THM). He finds BMMs to be about as offensive as women generally do. THM would not dream of expressing his attraction to a woman unless he first noticed that she found him to be sexually attractive. Even then, his remarks are not brazen in any way, for he himself has never liked to be pressured by others. Thus he is especially careful not to pressure others. In fact, women have been known to get a little frustrated with THM, wondering is he is ever going to pick up on the avalanche of signs that they have left him. Let me be clear: I do not claim that THMs never overstep their bounds. What I do claim is that the motivational structure of THMs differs radically from that of BMMs. Specifically, the motivational structure of the former, when it comes to interacting with women, is not morally obnoxious.

Most men fall between these two extremes. Importantly, not all men are BMMs. Therefore, it is wrong to treat all men as if they are BMMs or BMMs-in-waiting. Morally obnoxious motives are characteristic of the Bombastic Macho Male's behavior towards women. In this regard, he may be incorrigible, and the objective of sexual harassment policies is simply to get him to keep his thoughts, and most certainly his hands, to himself. Nothing short of the arm of the law will suffice.

My fear, however, is that most analyses of sexual harassment assume that all men have the motivational structure associated with the model of the Bombastic Macho Male. But some men, like the Timorous Heterosexual Male, are not like that. The very point of distinguishing between the Bombastic Macho Male and the Timorous Heterosexual Male is to show that all males cannot be assumed to have obnoxious moral motives when it comes to interacting with women. To treat a THM as if he were a BMM is to do the THM an injustice. And to suppose it is justifiable to treat all men as though they belong to the class of men who are particularly obnoxious solely because one finds their words offensive or discomforting is to commit the moral error of reckless disregard.

A question that naturally arises then is this: To what extent must women (or for that matter members of any historically oppressed group) share the responsibility for diffusing a potentially uncomfortable work environment? I shall offer and develop only one answer.

OPPRESSION ANXIETY

With any group that has been the victim of systematic oppression, the members of the group will, in general, experience oppression anxiety. There will be the mistreatment (be it verbal or physical) that one can regularly anticipate, and one must somehow manage not to let that very anticipation take too great a toll. And there will be the mistreatment that one must endure from those whom one had hoped would be different, but turn out not to be. Accordingly, prudence makes being suspicious and weary of the other a natural way of life. Finally, though one could go on at considerable length in this vein, there is the weariness that comes from trying to maintain one's integrity in a world that insists on compromising a person, where prudence and integrity seem to be on a collision course most of the time. It will not always be obvious whether one has compromised one's integrity or whether, for the moment, one is simply too bruised to put up a fight. And to add insult to injury, one must often contend with the internalization of the oppression by members of one's own group. This multiplicity of concerns make being anxiety-ridden a natural way of life for the oppressed.

One of the most important things an oppressed group can do as it becomes empowered, and as social attitudes change for the better, is to bear in mind the difference between oppressive behavior and oppression anxiety. Not surprisingly, and quite understandably, oppression anxiety can manifest itself even in contexts where oppressive behavior is absent.[5]

Returning to the Mary and John scenario will be helpful. Recall that John complimented Mary on her outfit, and that this can be seen as gender-related, since he would not have complimented a man on his outfit. It goes without saying that, owing to the prevalence of sexism, women have had to endure lascivious comments from men. So women are rightly on their guard when it comes to being complimented by men. A lascivious comment is certainly out of order in the workplace.

Now, while it may be that a concern to avoid even the appearance of sexual harassment is a reason why men should avoid complimenting a female colleague on her outfit, there is nonetheless the separate question of whether the compliment is lascivious. Presumably, what the woman is wearing is quite relevant to how "that is a lovely outfit" should be taken. If she is wearing loose-fitting jeans, a baggy, discolored blouse, and tennis shoes, then "that is a lovely outfit" is just a bit of sarcastic humor.

Suppose for a moment, however, that Mary is wearing—and she has every right to wear—a low-cut blouse, a very short skirt, and spiked heels. In this case, there is a strong presumption that John's compliment is laced with sexual innuendo. The issue here is not whether Mary has a right to dress in that manner without being sexually harassed by John. As I have just indicated, there can be no question but that she has every right to do so; rather, the issue is what is what is the reasonable interpretation to put on John's remark, "that is a lovely outfit." Depending upon what she is wearing, some interpretations are more reasonable than others.

On the other hand, suppose that Mary is wearing a full-length pleated skirt, with matching jacket, and a blouse buttoned up to the neck—for I did remark at the beginning that she was attired in an exquisite business outfit. In this case, there is a very good chance that John's compliment "that is a lovely outfit" is about just that—Mary's outfit. It is in instances such as this that it is important to bear in mind the reality of oppression anxiety. At least part of the meaning of remarks is given by the social context in which they are uttered, which includes the attire of the person to whom the remarks are addressed. It is probably inappropriate for any man to tell a nun wearing a full flowing habit—but in maroon, instead of the customary black—that she has on a lovely outfit. All the same, it is quite unlikely, indeed, that such a remark would have any salacious sentiment behind it. And this the nun should recognize, though she might rightly call attention to the inappropriateness of his remark. The situation is much the same when John compliments Mary in her full-length pleated skirt.

An interesting, if not poignant fact about the world, is that things are considerably less ambiguous when oppression is in full force. With rare exception, a remark can have only one meaning, because social contexts and modes of interaction are so rigorously defined. The road to equality is rough to begin with; however, part of what accounts for that roughness is that there is much ambiguity along the way, precisely because social contexts and modes of interaction are not rigorously defined. To be sure, such ambiguity can be exploited, but ambiguity that can be exploited is still ambiguity. What is more, to assume that everyone would exploit that ambiguity for wrongful gain is, in effect, to assume away the ambiguity by wronging the innocent. Worse, it is to deny the possibility of the very social reality to which one is aspiring. In that world, presumably, it will be possible for a man to compliment a woman on the quality of her business outfit, as well as the quality of her mind, without being considered a lecher.

I cannot emphasize too much that the point being made in this section applies to all historical victims of oppression. Time was when a black in America could just assume that racism was behind a white's assessment that her or his work was below the desired standards. This is not true nowadays, although in race relations America remains quite the imperfect society. But any given situation may be fraught with ambiguity. Oppression anxiety may readily lead a hardworking black who is disappointed with an assessment of his or her work to conclude that the assessment was fueled by racism. In some instances, this conclusion will surely be false, given the assumption that society has made some progress towards the goal of racial equality. It may turn out that if the black had attended to other factors, as opposed to merely focusing upon the negative assessment, it would have been evident enough that the assumption of racism was implausible.

In the march towards equality, the situation of women is exactly parallel. In the Mary and John scenario, Mary could let oppression anxiety carry the day and focus upon just the fact that John complimented her; and if she does, then his remarks will seem on a par with the salacious comments that women in the workplace have endured in times past, even though she is wearing a full-length pleated skirt rather than a low-cut blouse and a short skirt. On the other hand, if she also attends to both John's words "that is a lovely outfit" and the fact of her attire, then she might have considerably less reason to suppose that John meant anything untoward by his remark. As I told the story of Mary, it is nearly axiomatic that any man complimenting a woman on her attire is up to no good. In race matters, the analog would be that any behavior on the part of a white towards a minority is racist, including helping behavior since that can be paternalistic. Such axioms pretty much ensure that the other is in a no-win situation in terms of having wronged the individual in question. Such is the case with oppression anxiety.

No doubt it has already occurred to some to wonder whether, in asking women to have a more discerning eye in social contexts, and so to consider the possibility that a judgment of sexual harassment is owing more to oppression anxiety than a fact of oppressive behavior, another burden is being placed upon those who have been historically oppressed. Perhaps. But is it an unfair burden? That too has to be asked. Recognizing the reality of oppression anxiety not only acknowledges that there have been gains in equality, it is also empowering. This recognition is a more precise way of grasping the other, and greater precision in this regard never puts one at a disadvantage; rather, it is always to one's greater advantage.

THE "FIGHTING WORDS" DOCTRINE REVISITED IN THE HOSTILE ENVIRONMENT CONTEXT

At this juncture, a look at the fighting words doctrine would be instructive. As originally set out by the New Hampshire Supreme Court:

> The test is what men of common intelligence would understand what would be words likely to cause an average addressee to fight.... The English language has a number of words and expressions which by general consent are "fighting words" when said without a disarming smile.... Such words, as ordinary men know, are likely to cause a fight.... The statute, as construed, does no more than prohibit the face-to-face words plainly likely to cause a breach of the peace by the addressee.[6]

The Supreme Court affirmed the New Hampshire decision in *Chaplinsky v. New Hampshire*.[7] The Court did not deny that one could offend and provoke a person to fight in extremely subtle ways, but rather, pointed out that some words could be deemed highly offensive and provoking to any person to whom they were directly addressed. What is more, the Court held that any person could plainly recognize what such words were, which in effect was to say that there could be no excuse for their utterance. Neither a plea of ignorance nor lack of intent was admissible. For it was as if a person had the intent, since it was plain to any speaker what effect the utterance of such words would have upon the listener. The Court drew a distinction; it did not obliterate one. The Court's position, of course, presupposes cultural familiarity and psychological competence. A citizen of England, with no firsthand cultural experience in America, could not be expected to know just what words count as "fighting words" in America, and would not, in the first instance at least, be held accountable for using them. Nor would a psychologically incompetent person be held accountable for using "fighting words." Any analysis of sexual harassment should take a cue from the reasoning behind this doctrine.

Without a doubt, there are "sexual harassment words." In uttering them to a woman colleague, a man straightforwardly engages in inappropriate behavior toward the woman and creates a hostile work environment. More to the point, a man knows or should have known that his behavior is inappropriate. Indeed, even when such utterances were considered permissible, no one denied that they were used to pressure women. There is, therefore, an exceedingly strong presumption that a man acts with objectionable motives when he utters "sexual harassment words" directly to a woman. Unlike "fighting words," a disarming smile, far from diminishing the force of "sexual harassment words," serves only to seal their horrific offensiveness in the mind of the listener.

I want to emphasize that, just as the doctrine of "fighting words" assumes a morally obnoxious motive on the part of the speaker, the idea of "sexual harassment words" assumes a similar morally obnoxious motive on the part of the utterer. That is, the victim's anger and discomfort stem in large measure, if not entirely, from the fact that the speaker is presumed to have spoken with a morally obnoxious motive, and not simply from the fact that the words were spoken. The motives are not secondary to the words being offensive. Thus, any attempt to understand "sexual harassment words" independent of motives is misguided, and any policy or remedy that does so makes an egregious error.

Naturally, there is also the issue of being threatened. But this observation only strengthens the point being made, for a threat from a person presupposes a malicious moral motive. A threat is not just a matter of being made worse off.

So if any man, including the THM referred to earlier, should utter a string of "sexual harassment words," he should be made to feel the full brunt of the law, as with any BMM, for it is agreed that no reasonable speaker can directly utter such words to a woman without realizing the impact that they will have upon her. Hence, when any man utters such words to a woman his motives are presumed to be morally obnoxious. But not all words carry this presumption, though a woman might find them offensive or otherwise experience discomfort over them.

While an offense-free work environment for both women and men would no doubt be ideal, sexual harassment is not about eliminating any and every offense against a woman that might occur. More precisely, while sexual harassment is indeed offensive, not everything that is offensive to a woman or which causes her discomfort is an instance of sexual harassment.

OBJECTIONS TO THE IDEA OF "SEXUAL HARASSMENT WORDS"

There are two obvious, perhaps related, objections to my argument. The first is that any list of "sexual harassment words" will fail to be exhaustive, if only because language constantly evolves. The second objection is that a man may engage in sexual harassment without using "sexual harassment words."

The first objection is easily met, as the case of racial harassment shows. Imagine someone arguing that there are no obvious racial slurs against minorities, since language is fluid, and what is a racial slur today may not be that tomorrow. Thirty-five years ago, calling a Negro "black" was highly offensive. Today, calling a black a "Negro" can be offensive, although not to the same degree. Tomorrow, "black" may be offensive, as

"African-American" gains ascendancy. Clearly, the fluidity of language has not been a bar to recognizing racial slurs against blacks. Nor has it diminished the importance of identifying at least some of the words that a minority group generally regards as racial slurs during a given time period. Likewise, the fact that a list of "sexual harassment words" cannot be exhaustive should not prevent us from recognizing some or most of the words that, at any given time, women find most offensive and threatening.

As to the second objection, I have hardly denied that a man may engage in the most egregious displays of verbal sexual harassment without using "sexual harassment words"; suppose, for example, that an employee installs cameras in the women's rest room. One can lynch a black without calling her or him "nigger." This hardly makes it any less meaningful to recognize "nigger" as a very offensive racial slur. So the fact that there can be sexual harassment without "sexual harassment words" hardly obliterates the need to distinguish between "sexual harassment words" and words that fall outside this category, just as the fact that one may offend mightily without using "fighting words" does not show that "fighting words" do not exist. However, that verbal sexual harassment can occur without the use of "sexual harassment words" is hardly a reason to hold a man guilty of sexual harassment whenever a woman finds his gender-linked words to be offensive or discomforting.

CONCLUSION

Social interaction is rich and complex. In truth, progress towards equality makes it so, precisely because social interaction across changing diversity is necessarily fraught with ambiguity and a mixture of feelings. Not least among these is what I have called oppression anxiety. It is tempting to think that, in a diverse world, nothing matters more than that persons behave towards one another just as they should. In the long run, what matters even more is that goodwill is the basis for such behavior. For goodwill is the social lubricant without which social interaction between people disintegrates, as hostility increasingly becomes the order of the day. Equality without goodwill is fragile, indeed. After all, the law itself is only as good as the character of those who interpret and enforce it. But no workplace can be as efficient and as amiable as it should be without goodwill.

Of course, goodwill is compatible with a wealth of mistakes and a considerable amount of lethargy. There is nothing like the long arm of the law to galvanize people (without resorting to violence), and to rid them of their moral laziness. I am very much in favor of the law serving the purpose. But the point of this essay is simply that a certain moral shortsightedness is to be avoided. In the name of ensuring that historically oppressed peoples receive their due, we must not as a general strategy assume away the goodwill that, in the end, is needed if the equality desperately sought after is to survive. For that strategy may prove to be prophetic in that we will not have to assume any more: goodwill will be gone, and so too will be innocence. And when these things are truly gone, or at any rate, sufficiently diminished, equality will be no more.

NOTES

[1]Katie Roiphe used the expression "lost innocence" to contrast today's teenagers, whose exposure to sexual matters is in overdrive, with teenagers of an earlier time, who were literally naïve about much. "Date Rape's Other Victim," *New York Times*, June 13, 1993, at 26. She then suggests that much of the talk about date rape is more than a little disingenuous, since today's teenage female cannot plead the sort of ignorance that a teenage female of only two generations ago could plead. Although I think that Roiphe overstates her case, I am not here concerned to argue the matter.

By lost innocence, I am inspired by Immanuel Kant's idea of goodwill, where it is allowed that a person could have good intentions even if his actions fall short of the mark. See Immanuel Kant, *The Groundwork of the Metaphysic of Morals,* H.J. Paton trans., (New York: Harper Torch Book, 1964): 61–65.

[2]The Supreme Court has recognized two forms of sexual harassment: *quid pro quo*, which is the conditioning of employment benefits on sexual favors, and hostile environment, which is harassment that, whether or not affecting economic benefits, creates a hostile or offensive working environment. *Meritor v. Vinson*, 477 U.S. 57 (1986). This paper deals only with sexual harassment stemming from a hostile environment.

[3]*Harris v. Forklift Systems, Inc.*, 114 S. Ct. 367 (1993), defines a sexually harassing environment as one which "is permeated with 'discriminatory intimidation, ridicule, and insult,' that is 'sufficiently severe or pervasive to alter the conditions of the victim's employment and create an abusive working environment.'" *Id.*, at 370 (quoting *Meritor*, 477 U.S. at 64, 67).

[4]This policy was adopted by the Syracuse University Faculty Senate on November 15, 1993, but has not yet been published.

[5]As I have made clear, some members of every oppressed group suffer from oppression anxiety. A white student applying to graduate school once asked me whether a letter of recommendation from me would be taken seriously by other members of my profession. For just a fleeting moment, I heard this as "Are you, a black man, competent to assess the philosophical abilities of me, a white student?" when, in fact, the student was asking a quite different question: "Is your profession still sufficiently racist that a letter from you, whose judgment I enormously value, would not be taken seriously?" Had I allowed oppression anxiety to run its course, I would never have heard the latter question. Ironically, the latter question proved to be quite painful in its own right, as I could not offer a resounding "No." Not only that, I have since put that student's question to various well-placed members of my profession, only to find that no one could muster a resounding "No." A nonracist white student in a racist society could make just the distinction

that this student made, and doing so would be very much to her or his credit. Alas, a black suffering from oppression anxiety might fail to see that this distinction was being drawn.

⁶*State v. Chaplinsky*, 18 A.2d 754, 762 (N.H. 1941), aff'd 315 U.S. 568 (1942). This doctrine is now judged to be rather quaint. One reason might be that there can be no excuse for engaging in physical combat over provocative words. Another might be that it has become far less plain which words have this status. I suggest that the quaintness of the doctrine is owing more to the first than the latter. Time was when it was perfectly acceptable for men to challenge one another to a duel when their dignity had been insulted, but not any longer. What has changed, though, is not the sense that vastly provocative words can be recognized, but the method for settling the insult of being an object of such words.

A Kantian interpretation of the "fighting words" doctrine would be that there are some words the utterance of which (by a person of sound mind and the requisite cultural familiarity) presupposes the absence of goodwill. This is compatible with the Kantian view that there is some logical space between a person's goodwill and her or his actions. For the Kantian position is not that acting with goodwill is compatible with anything a person might do (or say) that is inappropriate or harmful to another. Contrast, for instance, the difference between "kike" and "nigger." There are no contexts in which the word "kike" is used in an amiable way, while there are contexts in which the word "nigger" is so used. So, while the use of "nigger" does not, as matter of social usage, entail the absence of goodwill, the use of "kike" does. "He is one bad nigger" is acceptable usage, and possibly a compliment, among blacks in some circles, though it is debatable whether any white can use this term without offending. By contrast, the use of the term "kike" is thought to be offensive in all contexts. Jews have not reserved a positive or, at any rate, acceptable meaning of this term for use among themselves. For a partial account of how I understand the differences between blacks and Jews, see generally Laurence M. Thomas, *Vessels of Evil: American Slavery and the Holocaust* (Philadelphia: Temple University Press, 1993).

⁷315 U.S. 568 (1942).

SEXUAL HARASSMENT

Susan M. Dodds, Lucy Frost,
Robert Pargetter, and Elizabeth W. Prior

Mary has a problem. Her boss, Bill, gives her a bad time. He is constantly making sexual innuendoes, and seems always to be blocking her way and brushing against her. He leers at her, and on occasions has made it explicitly clear that it would be in her own best interests to go to bed with him. She is the one woman in the office now singled out for this sort of treatment, although she hears that virtually all other attractive women who have in the past worked for Bill have had similar experiences. On no occasion has Mary encouraged Bill. His attentions have all been unwanted. She has found them threatening, unpleasant, and objectionable. When on some occasions she has made these reactions too explicit, she has been subjected to unambiguously detrimental treatment. Bill has no genuinely personal feelings for Mary, is neither truly affectionate nor loving: his motivation is purely sexual.

Surely this is a paradigmatic case of sexual harassment. Bill discriminates against Mary, and it seems that he would also discriminate against any other attractive woman who worked for him. He misuses his power as an employer when he threatens Mary with sex she does not want. His actions are clearly against her interests. He victimizes her at present and will probably force her to leave the office, whatever the consequences to her future employment.

From "Sexual Harassment," *Social Theory and Practice* Vol. 14, No. 2 (Summer 1988). Reprinted by permission.

Not all cases of sexual harassment are so clear. Indeed, each salient characteristic of the paradigmatic case may be missing and yet sexual harassment still occur. Even if all the features are missing, it could still be a case of sexual harassment.

We aim to explicate the notion of sexual harassment. We note that our aim is not to provide an analysis of the ordinary-language concept of sexual harassment. Rather we aim to provide a theoretical rationale for a more behavioral, stipulative definition of sexual harassment. For it is an account of this kind which proves to be clearly superior for policy purposes. It provides the basis for a clear, just, and enforceable policy, suitable for the workplace and for society at large. Of course ordinary-language intuitions provide important touchstones. What else could we use to broadly determine the relevant kind of behavior? But this does not mean that all ordinary-language considerations are to be treated as sacrosanct. Sexual harassment is a concept with roots in ordinary language, but we seek to develop the concept as one suitable for more theoretical purposes, particularly those associated with the purposes of adequate policy development.

In brief we aim to provide an account which satisfies three desiderata. The account should:

a. show the connection between harassment in general and sexual harassment;
b. distinguish between sexual harassment and legitimate sexual interaction;
c. be useful for policy purposes.

SEXUAL HARASSMENT AND SEXUAL DISCRIMINATION

It seems plausible that, minimally, harassment involves discrimination, and more particularly, sexual harassment involves sexism. Sexual discrimination was clearly part of the harassment in the case of Mary and Bill.

The pull towards viewing sexual harassment as tied to sexual discrimination is strengthened by consideration of the status of most harassers and most harassees. In general, harassers are men in a position of power over female harassees. The roles of these men and women are reinforced by historical and cultural features of systematic sexual discrimination against women. Generally, men have control of greater wealth and power in our society, while women are economically dependent on men. Men are viewed as having the (positive) quality of aggression in sexual and social relations, while women are viewed as (appropriately) passive. These entrenched attitudes reflect an even deeper view of women as fundamentally unequal, that is, in some sense less fully persons than men. Sexual harassment, then, seems to be just one more ugly manifestation of the sexism and sexual inequality which is rampant in public life....

Closer consideration reveals, however, that while discrimination may be present in cases of harassment, it need not be. More specifically, while sexual discrimination may be (and often is) present in cases of sexual harassment, it is not a necessary feature of sexual harassment. The fact that in most cases women are (statistically, though not necessarily) the objects of sexual harassment, is an important feature of the issue of sexual harassment, and it means that in many cases where women are harassed, the harassment will involve sexual discrimination. However, sexual harassment need not entail sexual discrimination.

Consider the case of Mary A and Bill A, a case very similar to that of Mary and Bill. The only relevant difference is that Bill A is bisexual and is sexually attracted to virtually everyone regardless of sex, appearance, age or attitude. Perhaps all that matters is that he feels that he has power over them (which is the case no matter who occupies the position now occupied by Mary A). Mary A or anyone who filled her place would be subjected to sexual harassment.

The point of this variant case is that there appears to be no discrimination, even though there clearly is harassment. Even if it is argued that there is discrimination against the class of those over whom Bill A has power, we can still describe a case where no one is safe. Bill A could sexually harass anyone. This particular case clearly defeats both of MacKinnon's conceptual approaches to sexual discrimination; it is neither the case that Bill A treats a man in Mary A's position differently from the way in which he treats Mary A, nor is it the case that (in Bill A's office) the burden of Bill A's advances is placed disproportionately on one sex, because of that person's sex (for the purpose of sex, perhaps, but not on account of chromosomes).[1]

A different point, but one worth making here, is that there is a difference between sexual harassment and sexist harassment. A female academic whose male colleagues continually ridicule her ideas and opinions may be the object of sexist harassment, and this sexist harassment will necessarily involve sexual discrimination. But she is not, on this basis, the object of sexual harassment.

NEGATIVE CONSEQUENCES AND INTERESTS

Perhaps sexual harassment always involves action by the harasser which is against the interests of the harassee, or has overall negative consequences for the harassee. However, consider Mary B, who is sexually harassed by Bill B. Mary B gives in, but as luck would have it, things turn out extremely well; Mary B is promoted by Bill B to another department.

The long-term consequences are excellent, so clearly it has been in Mary B's best interests to be the object of Bill B's attentions. One could also imagine a case where Mary B rejects Bill B, with the (perhaps unintentional) effect that the overall consequences for Mary B are very good.

Crosthwaite and Swanton argue for a modification of this view. They urge that, in addition to being an action of a sexual nature, an act of sexual harassment is an action where there is no adequate consideration of the interests of the harassee. They in fact suggest that this is both a necessary and sufficient condition for sexual harassment.

We think it is not sufficient. Consenting to sex with an AIDS carrier is not in an antibody-negative individual's best interests. If the carrier has not informed the other party, the antibody-positive individual has not given adequate consideration to those interests. But this case need not be one of sexual harassment.

Nor is this condition necessary for sexual harassment. Of course, Bill B may believe that it is in Mary B's interests to come across. (A sexual harasser can be deceitful or just intensely egotistical.) Bill B may believe that it would conform with Mary B's conception of her interests. And, as we noted earlier, it may even be objectively in her own best interests. Yet still we think this would not prevent the action of Bill B against Mary B, which is in other ways similar to Bill's actions against Mary, being a case of sexual harassment.

In general, harassment need not be against the interests of the harassee. You can be harassed to stop smoking, and harassed to give up drugs. In these cases the consequences may well be good, and the interests of the harassee adequately considered and served, yet it is still harassment. This general feature seems equally applicable to sexual harassment.

MISUSE OF POWER

Bill has power over Mary, and it is the misuse of this power which plays an important role in making his treatment of Mary particularly immoral. For, on almost any normative theory, to misuse power is immoral. But is this misuse of power what makes this action one of sexual harassment? If it is, then it must not be restricted to the formal power of the kind which Bill has over Mary—the power to dismiss her, demote her, withhold benefits from her, and so on. We also usually think of this sort of formal power in cases of police harassment. But consider the harassment of women at an abortion clinic by right-to-lifers. They cannot prevent the women having abortions, and indeed lack any formal power over them. Nonetheless, they do possess important powers—to dissuade the fainthearted (or even the oversensitive), and to increase the unpleasantness of the experience of women attending the clinic.

Now consider the case of Mary C. Bill C and Mary C are coworkers in the office, and Bill C lacks formal power over Mary C. He sexually harasses her—with sexual innuendoes, touches, leers, jokes, suggestions, and unwanted invitations. To many women, Bill C's actions would be unpleasant. But Mary C is a veteran—this has happened to her so many times before that she no longer responds. It is not that she desires or wants the treatment, but it no longer produces the unpleasant mental attitudes it used to produce—it just rolls off her. She gives the negative responses automatically, and goes on as though nothing had happened.

It would still seem to us that Mary C has been sexually harassed. But what power has Bill C misused against Mary C? He has used not even some informal power which has caused her some significantly unpleasant experience.... Misuse of power cannot in itself, therefore, constitute sexual harassment.

ATTITUDES, INTENTIONS, AND EXPERIENCES

In our discussions so far, it seems that we have not taken into account, to any significant extent, how Mary and Bill feel about things. It may be argued that what defines or characterizes sexual harassment is the mental state of the harasser, or harassee, or both.

Bill wanted to have sex with Mary. He perceived her as a sex object. He failed to have regard for her as a person. He failed to have regard for how she might feel about things. And his actions gave him egotistical pleasure. These attitudes, intentions, and experiences may help constitute Bill's action as a case of sexual harassment.

Mary also had very specific kinds of mental states. She found Bill's actions unpleasant, and unwanted. She wished Bill would not act in that way towards her, and she disliked him for it. She was angry that someone would treat her in that way, and she resented being forced to cope with the situation. So again, we have attributed attitudes and mental experiences to Mary in describing this case as one of sexual harassment.

We do not want to have to label as sexual harassment all sexual actions or approaches between people in formally structured relationships. Cases of sexual harassment and nonharassing sexual interaction may appear very similar (at least over short time intervals). It seems that in the two kinds of cases, only the mental features differ. That is, we refer to attitudes, intentions, or experiences in explaining the difference between the two cases. But attention to this feature of sexual harassment is not enough in itself to identify sexual harassment.

We will now consider one of the more salient features of the mental attitudes of Bill and Mary, and show that sexual harassment is not dependent on these or similar features. Then we shall describe a case where the mental experiences are very different, but where sexual harassment does, in fact, still occur.

Consider the claim that Bill uses (or tries to use) Mary as a sex object. The notion of sex object is somewhat vague and ill-defined, but we accept that it is to view her as merely an entity for sexual activity or satisfaction, with no interest in her attributes as a person and without any intention of developing any personal relationship with her.

This will not do as a sufficient condition for sexual harassment. We normally do not think of a client sexually harassing a prostitute. And surely there can be a relationship between two people where each sees the other merely as a sex object without there being harassment. Nor is viewing her merely as a sex object a necessary condition. For surely Bill could love Mary deeply, and yet by pursuing her against her wishes, still harass her.

Now consider the claim that what is essential is that Mary not want the attentions of Bill. This is not a sufficient condition. Often the most acceptable of sexual approaches is not wanted. Also, a woman may not want certain attentions, and even feel sexually harassed, in situations which we would not want to accept as ones of sexual harassment.

Imagine that Mary D is an abnormally sensitive person. She feels harassed when Bill D comments that the color she is wearing suits her very well, or even that it is a cold day. Bill D is not in the habit of making such comments, nor is he in the habit of harassing anyone. He is just making conversation and noting something (seemingly innocuous) that has caught his attention. Mary D feels harassed even though she is not being harassed.

Perhaps this condition is a necessary one. But this, too, seems implausible. Remember Mary C, the veteran. She is now so immune to Bill C that she has no reaction at all to his approaches. He does not cause unpleasantness for her; she does not care what he does. Yet nonetheless Bill C is harassing Mary C.

Mary E and Bill E interact in a way which shows that sexual harassment is not simply a matter of actual attitudes, intentions, or experiences. Bill E is infatuated with Mary E and wants to have sex with her. In addition to this, he genuinely loves her and generally takes an interest in her as a person. But he is hopeless on technique. He simply copies the brash actions of those around him and emulates to perfection the actions of the sexual harasser. Most women who were the object of his infatuation (for instance, someone like our original Mary) would feel harassed and have all the usual emotions and opinions concerning the harasser. But Mary E is different. Outwardly, to all who observe the public interactions between them, she seems the typical harassee—doing her best to politely put off Bill E, seeming not to want his attentions, looking as though she is far from enjoying it. That is how Bill E sees it too, but he thinks that that is the way women are.

Inwardly Mary E's mental state is quite different. Mary E is indifferent about Bill E personally, and is a veteran like Mary C, in that she is not distressed by his actions. But she decides to take advantage of the situation and make use of Bill E's attentions. By manipulating the harassing pressures and invitations, she believes she can obtain certain benefits that she wants, and can gain certain advantages over others. The attention from Bill E is thus not unwanted, nor is the experience for her unpleasant. In this case, neither the harasser nor the harassee have mental states in any way typical of harassers and harassees, yet it is a case of sexual harassment.

Such a case, as hypothetical and unlikely as it is, demonstrates that the actual mental states of the people involved cannot be what is definitive of sexual harassment. They are not even necessary for sexual harassment.

A BEHAVIORAL ACCOUNT OF SEXUAL HARASSMENT

The case of Mary E and Bill E persuades us that we require a behavioral account of sexual harassment. For a harasser to sexually harass a harassee is for the harasser to behave in a certain way towards the harassee. The causes of that behavior are not important, and what that behavior in turn causes is not important. The behavior itself constitutes the harassment.

But how then are we to specify the behavior that is to count as sexual harassment?…

Consider the behavior which is typically associated with a mental state representing an attitude which seeks sexual ends without any concern for the person from whom those ends are sought, and which typically produces an unwanted and unpleasant response in the person who is the object of the behavior. Such behavior, we suggest, is what constitutes sexual harassment. Instances of the behavior are instances of sexual harassment, even if the mental states of the harasser or harassee (or both) are different from those typically associated with such behavior. The behavior constitutes a necessary and sufficient condition for sexual harassment.

According to this view, the earlier suggestion that attitudes, intentions, and experience are essential to an adequate characterization of sexual harassment is correct. It is correct to the extent that we need to look at the mental states typical of the harasser, rather than those present in each actual harasser, and at those typical of the harassee, rather than those present in each actual harassee. The empirical claim is that connecting these typical mental states is a kind of behavior—behavior not incredibly different from instance to instance, but with a certain sameness to it. Thus it is a behavior of a definite characteristic type. This type of behavior is sexual harassment.…

…[A]s the account focuses on behavior, rather than mental states, it explains why we feel so skeptical about someone who behaves as Bill behaves, yet pleads innocence and claims he had no bad intentions. The intentions are not essential for the harassment, and such a person has an obligation to monitor the responses of the other person so that he has an accurate picture of what is going on. Moreover, he has an obligation to be aware of the character of his own behavior. He also has an obligation to give due consideration to the strength and the weight of the beliefs upon which he is operating before he makes a decision to act in a manner that may have unpleasant consequences for others. ...

In the case of Mary E and Bill E, Bill E relies on the harassing behavior of other men as a guide to his actions regarding Mary E. Mary E has displayed standard forms of avoidance behavior (although she has ulterior motives). Bill E does not pay sufficient heed to the strength and weight of the beliefs which guide his actions, and it is just fortunate that Mary E is not harmed by what he does. Given Bill E's total disregard of Mary E's interests and reactions, it seems that his behavior could have caused, just as easily, significant distress to any other Mary who might have filled that role. A policy intended to identify sexual harassment should not rely on such luck, although the actual mental states (where they are as a typical as Mary E's) may mitigate blameworthiness. Bill E's harassing behavior should be checked and evaluated, regardless of any of Mary's actual mental states.[2]

Consider an example taken from an actual case which highlights this obligation.[3] Suppose Tom is married to Jane. He invites Dick (an old friend who has never met Jane) home to have sex with Jane. He tells Dick that Jane will protest, but that this is just part of the game (a game she very much enjoys). Dick forces Jane, who all the time protests violently, to have sex with him. Jane later claims to have been raped. Dick has acted culpably because he has acted without giving due consideration to the weight of the belief which guided his action, that is, to how rational it was to act on the belief given such a minimal evidential base. The only evidence he had that Jane did consent was Tom's say-so, and the consequences of acting on the belief were very serious. All of Jane's actions indicated that she did not consent.

In the case of Bill E and Mary E, Bill has an obligation to consider the strength and weight of the beliefs which guide his action before he acts. He is not justified in claiming that he is innocent, when he has been provided with signals that indicate that Mary does not welcome his attentions.

We acknowledge that it will be difficult in many situations to obtain sufficient evidence that a proposed act will not be one of sexual harassment. This will be true especially in cases where the potential harassee may believe that any outward indication of her displeasure would have bad consequences for her. The awareness of this difficulty is probably what has led others to promote the policy of a total ban on sexual relationships at the office or workplace. While we acknowledge the problem, we feel that such a policy is both unrealistic and overrestrictive.

[This] account allows an interesting stance on the connection between sexual harassment and morality. For consequentialist theories of morality, it is possible (though unlikely) that an act of sexual harassment may be, objectively, morally right. This would be the case if the long-term good consequences outweighed the bad effects (including those on the harassee at the time of the harassment). For other moral theories it is not clear that this is a possibility, except where there are sufficiently strong overriding considerations present, such as to make the sexual harassment morally permissible. From the agent's point of view, it would seem that the probable consequences of sexual harassment (given the typical attitude of the typical harasser and the typical effects on the typical harassee) will be bad. Hence it is very likely, on any moral theory, that the agent evaluation for a harasser will be negative. The possible exceptions are where the harasser's actual mental state is not typical of a harasser, or the harassee's is not typical of a harassee.

Further, on this account, many of the salient features of the case of Mary and Bill—such as misuse of power, discrimination, unfair distribution of favors, and so on—are not essential features of sexual harassment. They are usually immoral in their own right, and their immorality is not explained by their being part of the harassment. But the behavior characteristic of sexual harassment will be constituted by features which we commonly find in particular instances of sexual harassment. For sexual harassment must supervene on the behavioral features which constitute its instances, but there is a range of such behavior, no one element of which need be present on any particular occasion. Similarly the morality of an instance of sexual harassment (at least for the consequentialist) will supervene on the morality of those same features of behavior.

OBJECTIONS TO THE BEHAVIORAL ACCOUNT

It may be objected that we have made no significant progress. We acknowledged at the beginning of the paper that many different kinds of behavior were instances of sexual harassment, even though there seemed to be no specific kind of behavior commonly present in all these instances.

Our reply is to concede the point that there is no first order property commonly possessed by all the behaviors. However, other important similarities do exist.

The property of being an instance of sexual harassment is a second-order property of a particular complex piece of behavior. It is a property of the relevant specific behavioral features, and these features may be from a list of disjunctive alternatives (which may be altered as norms of behavior change). Also, the behavior of a typical harassee will possess the property of being an instance of avoidance behavior. Avoidance behavior is a disposition. Hence, even if two lots of behavior are descriptively similar, they may differ in their dispositional properties. Finally the behavior of the typical harasser will possess the property of being sexually motivated, which again is dispositional in nature.

A second objection goes as follows: Couldn't we have the very same piece of behavior and yet have no sexual harassment? To take the kind of example well tried as an objection to behaviorism, what would we say about the case of two actors acting out a sexual harassment sequence?

There are a variety of replies we may make here. We could "bite the bullet" and admit the case to be one of sexual harassment. On the model proposed, we may do this while still maintaining that the behavior in this case is not morally wrong. Or instead, we could insist that certain kinds of behavior only become harassment when they are carried on over a sufficiently lengthy time interval, the circumstances surrounding the behavior also being relevant. The case of the actors would not count as an instance of harassment because the behavior has not been recurrent over a sufficiently long period of time, especially as the behavior before and after the acting period are significantly different. Also the circumstances surrounding an acting exercise would be typically different from those of an instance of sexual harassment.

Still another response to the acting example is to argue that if the actual mental states of "harasser" and "harassee" are sufficiently different from those of the prototypical harasser and harassee, there can be no sexual harassment, as there will be behavioral differences. This is not a logical necessity, but a physical one, given the causal relations which hold between the mental states and the behavior. We should also keep in mind that many of the features of sexual harassment are dispositional. Thus, even if such features of sexual harassment are not manifested in particular circumstances, they would be in other circumstances, and it is in these other circumstances that the observable behavior would be significantly different, if it is the manifestation of harassment, from that which would be associated with nonharassment.

A third objection to our behavioral account focuses on our use of the mental state *typical* of harassers and harassees. We have noted that it is possible that some instances of harassment will involve a harasser or harassee with mental states significantly different from those of the typical harasser or harassee. So it is possible that the harassee is not even offended or made to feel uncomfortable, and it is possible that the harasser did not have intentions involving misuse of power against, and disregard for the interests of, the harassee. It is even possible that one or both of the harasser and harassee could know about the atypical mental states of the other. Why, at least in this last case, insist that the behavior is sufficient for sexual harassment?

From our concern to provide an account of sexual harassment adequate for policy purposes, we would be inclined to resist this kind of objection, given the clear advantage in policy matters of a behavioral account. But there is more to say in reply to this objection. Policy is directed at the action of agents, and in all cases except where at least one of the agents involved has justified beliefs about the atypical actual mental states of the agents involved, it is clearly appropriate to stipulate behavior associated with the states of mind typical of harassers and harassees as sexual harassment. For agents ought to be guided by what it is reasonable to predict, and rational prediction as to the mental states of those involved in some kind of behavior will be determined by the mental states typically associated with that behavior. So only in cases where we have reliable and justified knowledge of atypical mental states does the objection have any substance at all.

But even in these cases, it seems the behavior should not be regarded as innocuous. Instances of behavior all form parts of behavioral patterns. People are disposed to behave similarly in similar circumstances. Hence we ought not to overlook instances of behavior which would typically be instances of sexual harassment. Agents ought not be involved in such patterns of behavior. It is for similar reasons that, while we allow for cultural relativity in the behavior constitutive of sexual harassment, this relativity should not be taken to legitimate patterns of behavior which do constitute sexual harassment but which are taken as the standard mode of behavior by a culture....

NOTES

We acknowledge useful comments from Robert Young and various readers for this journal.

[1]Given that sexual harassment is possible between men, by a woman harassing a man, among coworkers, and so on, [Catharine] MacKinnon's view of sexual harassment as nothing but one form of sexual discrimination is even less persuasive. It is also interesting that the problems which MacKinnon recognizes in trying to characterize the "offense" of sexual harassment [in *Sexual Harassment of Working Women* (New Haven: Yale University Press, 1979): 162 ff.], indicate a need for a behavioral analysis of sexual harassment, like the one we offer.

[2]Some might say that this behavioristic account of sexual harassment is similar to having strict liability for murder, that is to say, that mental states do need to be taken into account when judging and penalizing someone's actions. What we are arguing for is a way of *identifying* sexual harassment, not how (or even if) it should be *penalized*....

[3]This example is based on the British case, *D.P.P. v Morgan* (1975) 2 All E.R. (House of Lords)....

CHAPTER 6

Rape

INTRODUCTION

In the criminal statutes, rape, in particular aggravated rape between strangers, is a very serious offense. Thus if a woman claims she was raped by a stranger and if the man charged is legally found to have used physical force or the threat of force to compel her to engage in sex, severe punishment is likely to ensue. In such cases, relatively few defense strategies are available to men who can be shown to have employed physical force to compel a woman to engage in sex. Here, attempts to demonstrate that a woman is in any sense a willful sexual partner are commonly greeted with great skepticism. Indeed, because of the patent incompatibility of coercive physical force and consent, a defendant who denied that a rape had occurred would probably be viewed either as a bald-faced liar or as not understanding the ordinary meaning of his own words. So, at least on the paradigm of an unambiguous, aggravated stranger-rape, the criminal law recognizes rape as a significant wrong deserving efficient treatment and a harsh response.

But once consideration of rape moves away from the paradigm of aggravated stranger-rape to include cases where, for example, clear evidence of forcible compulsion is absent and the persons involved are known to each other, a complex network of moral, legal, and conceptual controversies arise. These controversies begin with the root question, considered in *Commonwealth v. Mlinarich*, of how the crime of rape ought to be defined. Must a fully conscious woman be subjected to force in the form of a physical assault or the threat thereof in order to be coerced to the degree warranting a charge of rape? Or should the relevant standard of coercion be considerably lower, as argued in the dissent, so as to include coercive proposals such as those faced by Mlinarich's victim, a fourteen-year-old girl who feared Mlinarich would do as he threatened: return her to a detention home unless she engaged in sex with him. Women routinely chose unwanted sex rather than some less wanted alternative. Have they, then, not given the relevant kind of consent to intercourse—have they all been raped? Lowering the standard of coercion to include non-physical harm or loss (or threats thereof) can expand dramatically the number and kinds of sexual encounters which might count as rape. Will this result, as the majority in *Mlinarich* feared, in a hopeless blurring of the distinction between rape and seduction? Is it possible to protect adequately the rights of criminal defendants when a reduced standard of coercion is employed?

In reviewing *Mlinarich* and other pertinent court decisions, including the controversial *State v. Rusk*, Susan Estrich argues that judicial reluctance to adopt a lowered standard of coercion reveals a profound male bias in rape law. For so long as a strong force standard of coercion—one appealing to physical injury or the threat thereof—is sustained, then unimpeachable determinations of rape will be limited to those in which there is evidence of physical resistance. Did the woman fight back? Then there should be evidence of injury. If she did not fight back, was it because to do so would result in serious injury? But how easily can this be shown without evidence of physical injury? So the actual measure for determining guilt in a rape case remains whether a woman is willing to engage in physical resistance. And this just is to measure consent and coercion in male terms. Real men, men of virtue, fight back. Thus the absence of physical resistance shows that a woman does not have enough "virtue," that she is just like those men who do not fight back: they are "sissies" who deserve what they get. Furthermore, given the male bias, adopting a lowered standard of coercion or nonconsent empowers women intolerably; it provides them legal weaponry—to both bring and sustain a charge of rape—with which they quite simply cannot be trusted. A standard of consent and coercion consistent with the sensibilities of women and a view to what women find reasonable threatens male control of the very terms of sex and seduction. Small wonder, then, that male resistance to rape law reform remains great.

Catharine MacKinnon takes the male bias in rape law and the resistance to rape law reform as crucial indications of the nature and extent of male supremacy. Rape, delimited in terms of the heterosexual penetration of females, constitutes a mechanism of political control, of subjugation. Because, on MacKinnon's view, male supremacy, *cum* male heterosexuality, is ubiquitous, both politically and ideologically, the concepts and distinctions employed to cast the controversies surrounding rape and rape law are unstable. Hence the idea that *any* intercourse occurs in the absence of force becomes suspect; the idea that *any* consent to intercourse can be uncoerced triggers ambiguity. The bedrock issue seems to be *not* how one determines when rape has occurred, but rather how one determines when it has not. Women thus confront conceptual quandaries in distinguishing sex from rape, and come to regard the law of rape, rather as do men, as comprised of a set of regulations rather than prohibitions.

Now, MacKinnon's hypotheses concerning the pervasiveness of male supremacy and its effects on the abilities of ordinary persons, especially women, to properly understand their own decisions and conduct remain highly controversial. But when conjoined with the analysis provided by Estrich, MacKinnon's views force a careful examination of the role played by traditional rape law in maintaining men's power over and access to women. Thus only if rape law were to undergo a self-consciously feminist reconstruction would there be any hope of just rape law reform.

Lois Pineau offers such a reconstruction in the area of nonaggravated sexual assault. In these cases, in order to determine whether or not the offense has occurred, evidence of consent must be obtained. Here, however, the predominant standard for establishing consent is that of whether a man reasonably believes the woman consented. But without clear evidence of resistance, it is difficult, if not impossible, should he lie, to show a man's claims about whether consent has been provided to be unreasonable. If widely accepted assumptions regarding the culture of seduction are maintained, and the belief that at least some resistance to sexual advances is a normal component of a woman's response, then men might reasonably believe that they are expected *by women* to be aggressors. That men can on occasion make an error in judgment as to whether resistance was sincere should thus not be construed as showing their belief in consent unreasonable. Pineau objects, however, that so long as the standard of reasonableness remains a male standard—a standard of what is reasonable from a man's point of view—arrests and convictions for date or acquaintance rape are likely to remain rare.

Pineau defends a different standard of consent, a standard based on the kind of sex to which women can be reasonably expected to agree. On this standard, women can be presumed (absent evidence to the contrary) to consent only to a kind of highly communicative sex in which persons display both respect and a high degree of personal regard for each other. Thus if a charge of rape is brought, a burden would likely fall on the accused to show why he believed, in the face of resistance, the sex to be consensual. If the sex is not of a kind to which a woman would agree, then why should his belief that consent had been provided be taken as reasonable? Now this proposal might well entail highly controversial (if not unconstitutional) procedures where, for example, defendants could be required to testify on their own behalf and where the presumption of innocence might be endangered. But can rape law reform eliminate male bias without adopting a standard of consent such as that argued for by Pineau?

Douglas Husak and George Thomas are deeply suspicious of rape law reform which begins with radical changes in the legal standard of consent. While men must be held responsible for determining whether their partners have consented to intercourse, they must also be legally excused when they reasonably, but mistakenly, believe consent to be present. On Husak's and Thomas' view, the reasonableness of such beliefs is properly grounded in extant social conventions governing sexual activity. But given available empirical information regarding the current state of these conventions, it is unreasonable to impose upon men a standard of reasonableness based, as some rape law reformers would, on various models of ideal sex. Thus rape law reform should not precede changes in sexual conventions. However, this is not an endorsement of current social conventions regarding sexual activity. Moral education of precisely the sort which engenders responsible sexual communication between men and women ought to be encouraged and sustained. For only when persons correctly understand each other's sexuality can reasonable but harmful beliefs be avoided.

SUGGESTED READINGS

Timothy Benecke, *Men on Rape* (New York: St. Martin, 1982).

Katie Roiphe, *The Morning After: Sex, Fear, and Feminism on Campus* (Boston: Little, Brown, 1993).

Patricia Searles and Ronald Berger, *Rape and Society: Readings on the Problem of Sexual Assault* (Boulder, CO: Westview Press, 1995).

COMMONWEALTH v. MLINARICH

345 Pa. Super. 269;
498 A.2d 395 (1985)
Argued, July 23, 1984,
Decided, August 30, 1985

Opinion by Judge Wieand

The issue in this appeal is the interpretation to be placed upon the phrase "forcible compulsion" as it was used to define the crime of rape. What did the legislature intend when it defined rape as sexual intercourse with another person "by forcible compulsion" or "by threat of forcible compulsion that would prevent resistance by a person of reasonable resolution"? Did the legislature intend to include within the crime of rape acts of sexual intercourse induced by threats to do non-violent acts? After a careful review of the legislative history of Section 3121 of the Crimes Code, 18 Pa. C.S. §3121, and the legal decisions in this and other jurisdictions, we conclude that the legislature intended the term "forcible compulsion" to mean "physical compulsion or violence."

The complainant in this case had been committed to the Cambria County Detention Home at the age of thirteen after admitting the theft of her brother's ring. Joseph Mlinarich was a neighbor of the child's father. Mlinarich and his wife agreed to assume custody of the juvenile, who was then placed in their home. Shortly thereafter, on the occasion of the child's fourteenth birthday, Mlinarich allegedly asked her to undress and, when she complied, fondled her while she sat on his lap. When the juvenile asked him to stop, Mlinarich did so. The same scenario was repeated four or five times during the succeeding two weeks. Thereafter, on five separate dates, events occurred which led to criminal charges and convictions which are the subject of appellate review.

Because of events occurring on June 15, 1981, Mlinarich was convicted of attempted rape. The testimony of the juvenile was that appellant had threatened to send her back to the detention home if she refused to undress and engage in sexual intercourse. Although she undressed on that occasion, appellant's efforts to achieve penetration were unsuccessful. A similar incident occurred on June 19, 1981. Again, in response to a threat by appellant to send her back to the detention home and amidst her own tears, the juvenile submitted to appellant's unsuccessful attempts to penetrate her vagina. The events of this day were the basis for appellant's second conviction of attempted rape. By virtue of similar threats made on June 26, 1981, appellant was finally able to achieve penetration. For this he was convicted of rape. Because of events occurring on June 29 and July 1, appellant was also convicted of involuntary deviate sexual intercourse. Mlinarich was convicted additionally on five counts of corrupting the morals of a child for his conduct on all five dates and on two counts of indecent exposure for conduct occurring on June 29 and July 1. On appeal, he contends that the Commonwealth failed to prove that he engaged in sexual acts with another person by forcible compulsion or threat of forcible compulsion.

The crime of rape, a felony of the first degree, is defined at 18 Pa. C.S. §3121 as follows:

A person commits a felony of the first degree when he engages in sexual intercourse with another person...:

(1) by forcible compulsion;
(2) by threat of forcible compulsion that would prevent resistance by a person of reasonable resolution;
(3) who is unconscious; or
(4) who is so mentally deranged or deficient that such person is incapable of consent.

This provision, we are admonished, "shall be construed according to the fair import of [its] terms." 18 Pa. C.S. §105. Because it is a penal statute, however, it must be strictly construed. *Commonwealth v. Driscoll*, 485 Pa. 99, 107, 401 A.2d 312, 316 (1979) (plurality opinion);... Strict construction is necessary to avoid the injustice of convicting a person without clear notice to him that contemplated conduct is unlawful. It also serves to prevent courts from creating offenses which the legislature did not intend to create....

Our task in this case is made more difficult because the victim of appellant's sexual advances was a fourteen-year-old child. The definition which we adopt, however, will know no age limitation. It is with a view to general application, therefore, that we attempt to define the parameters of the legislative proscription against sexual intercourse by forcible compulsion or threat of forcible compulsion.

At common law, rape was defined as unlawful carnal knowledge of a woman, not a spouse, forcibly and against her will. This common law definition was incorporated into the statutory law of Pennsylvania from earliest times. It is the same definition which was included in Section 721 of the Penal Code of 1939.... The phrase "against her will" was held by the courts to be synonymous with absence of consent. The decided cases placed great emphasis on the presence or absence of consent in determining whether the crime of rape had been committed. Force, however, was also a necessary ingredient. "The only relaxation of this rule [was] that this force [might] be constructive. Under this relaxation, it [was] held that where the female was an idiot, or had been rendered insensible by the use of drugs or intoxicating drinks, and, in one case, where she was under the age of ten years, she was incapable of consenting, and the law implied force." *Commonwealth v. Stephens, supra,* 143 Pa. at 399, 17 A.2d at 921.

The common law definition of rape was determined to be unsatisfactory. It was found inadequate not because of its insistence that force or violence be an essential element but because of its inordinate emphasis on "lack of consent." This element of the offense had been construed to require a woman to resist to the utmost. Therefore, whether she resisted sufficiently was deemed an issue for the jury in most cases where the charge was rape. The rule worked to the unfair disadvantage of the woman who, when threatened with violence, chose quite rationally to submit to her assailant's advances rather than risk death or serious bodily injury.

Because of the often unjust result achieved by the common law definition, the American Law Institute determined to find a more satisfactory approach. The original draft of the Model Penal Code proposed the establishment of separate crimes of "rape" and "intercourse without legally effective consent." The proposed crimes were defined as follows:

Section 207.4. Rape and Related Offenses.

(1) Rape by Force or Its Equivalent. A male who has carnal knowledge of a female not his wife commits a felony of the second degree if:
    (a) He compels her to submit by force or violence or out of fear that death or serious physical injury or extreme pain is about to be inflicted on her or a member of her family, or by threat to commit any felony of the first degree; or
    (b) For the purpose of preventing resistance he administers to her or employs, without her knowledge or consent, drugs, intoxicants, or other substance or force resulting in a major deficiency of the victim's power to appraise or control behavior; or

    (c) The female is unconscious or physically powerless to resist; or

    (d) The female is less than 10 years old (whether or not the actor is aware of that).

An offense within this subsection shall constitute a felony of the first degree if the actor inflicts serious physical injury upon the victim, or if the victim is not a voluntary social companion of the actor and has not previously permitted him sexual liberties.

(2) Intercourse Without Legally Effective Consent. A male who has carnal knowledge of a female not his wife, in situations not covered by subsection (1), commits a felony of the third degree if:

    (a) He compels her to submit by any intimidation [which would prevent resistance by a woman of ordinary resolution] [reasonably calculated to prevent resistance]; or

    (b) He knows that her submission is due to substantially complete incapacity to appraise or control her own behavior, but this paragraph shall not apply where a woman over 18 years of age loses that capacity as a result of voluntary use of [intoxicants or] drugs in the company of the actor; or

    (c) He knows that the female submits because she is unaware that a sexual act is being committed upon her or because she falsely supposes that he is her husband; or

    (d) The female is less than 16 years old and the actor is at least 5 years older than she is; but it shall be a defense under this paragraph if the actor proves that the girl was a prostitute. Model Penal Code, §207.4 (Tentative Draft No. 4 1955).

The Commentary explained that paragraph (a) of subsection (1) was intended to cover "the classic rape cases, where the woman [had been] overpowered by violence or the threat of it." By requiring only that the victim be "compelled to submit," and not that she resist "to the utmost," it was intended to eliminate to a great extent the requirement that a woman struggle when struggle would be useless and dangerous. Subsection (2), on the other hand, was designed to emphasize the absence of voluntary consent. The Comment stated:

> As the gravity of the threat diminishes, the situation gradually changes from one where compulsion overwhelms the will of the victim to a situation where she can make a deliberate choice to avoid some alternative evil. The man may threaten to disclose an illicit affair, to foreclose the mortgage on her parent's farm, to cause her to lose her job, or to deprive her of a valued possession. The situation may move into a shadow area between coercion and bargain. A bargain for gain is not within the present section; but subsection 2(a) is designed to reach all situations of actual compulsion, i.e., where the female's submission is

determined by fear of harm, with an objective test of the efficiency of the coercive element. Under this proposed statute, subsection (1) was designed to cover sexual intercourse accomplished by physical force or by threats which instilled fear of grave physical consequences to the victim or a member of her family, or fear of the perpetration of a serious crime. Subsection (2), on the other hand, sought to criminalize intercourse obtained by psychological duress rather than physical violence or threats thereof.

These definitions were modified when a corresponding provision was inserted into the Proposed Official Draft of the Model Penal Code....

This draft continued the distinction between "classic rape cases" involving force and situations where force was not present but the other person had not freely consented. The latter situation, which the proposed statute designated as "Gross Sexual Imposition," was defined as intercourse compelled "by any threat that would prevent resistance by a woman of ordinary resolution."...

In Pennsylvania, the Joint State Government Commission drafted a proposal similar to the Official Draft of the Model Penal Code. The proposed draft did not receive favorable action by the legislature, which, in 1972, enacted a Crimes Code containing the present definition of rape. The Crimes Code did not divide sex crimes into rape and gross sexual imposition. It did, however, divide rape under the Model Penal Code into two separate crimes. The statutory provision defining forcible rape eliminated language which would have defined rape to include intercourse with a child less than ten years of age. Instead, the legislature created a separate offense of statutory rape, a felony of the second degree, which it defined as sexual intercourse by a person eighteen years of age with a person not a spouse who is less than fourteen years of age....

Instead of creating a separate crime of "gross sexual imposition," the legislature in Pennsylvania created one offense of forcible rape, a felony of the first degree. In defining this offense, the legislature substituted for the language of the Model Penal Code, which had spoken of "force or...threat of imminent death, serious bodily injury, extreme pain or kidnapping, to be inflicted upon anyone," the words "forcible compulsion" or "the threat of forcible compulsion." It is significant that the legislature did not incorporate into the definition of rape those circumstances which, under the Model Penal Code, would have constituted "gross sexual imposition." This appears to have been intentional. Thus, where the Model Penal Code had spoken of "any threat that would prevent resistance by a woman of ordinary resolution" and had used those words to define the crime of gross sexual imposition, the legislature in Pennsylvania, in defining rape, spoke of sexual intercourse by forcible compulsion or "threat of forcible compulsion that would prevent resistance by a person of reasonable resolution."

The conclusion which must be drawn from this legislative progression is that the legislature in Pennsylvania intended to exclude from its definition of rape those acts of intercourse where the victim's will was not overwhelmed by physical compulsion or violence or a threat thereof and where the victim had made a deliberate choice in order to avoid some alternative evil not amounting to bodily harm....

The term "force" and its derivative, "forcible," when used to define the crime of rape, have historically been understood by the courts and legal scholars to mean physical force or violence. Thus, *American Jurisprudence* in its second edition uses the terms "force" and "violence" synonymously while defining rape:

> The term "by force" does not necessarily imply the use of actual physical force to compel submission of the victim to sexual intercourse, but it may mean threatened force or violence if the female does not comply. The threat of such force or violence may create a real apprehension of dangerous consequences, or bodily harm, in order to prevent resistance or extort the consent of the victim, and if it so overpowers the mind of the victim that she dare not resist, it must be regarded in all respects equivalent to force actually exerted....

To constitute rape, where there is no force used, the woman must have been unconscious, or unable fairly to comprehend the nature and consequence of the sexual act. If not, there is no distinction between rape, where the force used is constructive, and seduction. 65 Am. Jur. 2d Rape §4 (1972) (footnotes omitted).

The legislatures of at least nine other states have employed the term "forcible compulsion" to define the crime of rape....

The Supreme Court of Pennsylvania has defined "forcible compulsion" consistently with the definition followed by sister jurisdictions. The Court has done so in the context of interpreting the section of the Crimes Code which defines involuntary deviate sexual intercourse. In *Commonwealth v. Perrin*, 484 Pa. 188, 398 (1979), the appellant argued that the evidence was insufficient to sustain a conviction for involuntary deviate sexual intercourse. The Supreme Court said: "The crime of involuntary deviate sexual intercourse is committed when a person forces another person by actual physical compulsion or threats thereof to engage in acts of anal or oral intercourse." *Id.* This interpretation of the statute, even though it must be deemed dictum in view of the facts of the case, is worthy of weighty consideration.... It represents an expression by the highest court of this Commonwealth that "forcible compulsion" is equivalent to "physical compulsion" rather than "psychological duress." As an intermediate appellate court we adopt the Supreme Court's interpretation of "forcible compulsion" and apply it to the issue now before us....

This Court has also considered the intent of the legislature in using the term "forcible compulsion." In *Commonwealth v. Biggs*, 320 Pa. Super. 265, 467 (1983), a unanimous panel of this Court held that sexual intercourse induced by moral persuasion, in the form of a biblical admonition, was not rape. The Court said: "We cannot ignore the clear import of the language of section 3121 by upholding defendant's conviction in the absence of any evidence that Marion Biggs submitted to intercourse out of fear of an exercise of force by her father." *Id.* The definition of "forcible compulsion" which we adopt today is consistent with the holding in Biggs.

The interpretations of "forcible compulsion" advocated by the writers of the separate dissenting opinions are inconsistent not only with the fair import of the word "force" but also with all legally recognized definitions of the term. President Judge Spaeth would define "forcible compulsion" as any "compulsion by physical, moral, or intellectual means or by the exigencies of the circumstances." This definition of "forcible compulsion," however, is sufficiently broad to include "threats." If the threat is itself the forcible compulsion necessary to constitute rape, then the requirement that a threat be such as "would prevent resistance by a person of reasonable resistance" has been rendered unnecessary verbiage and has, for practical purposes, been removed from the statutory definition of the offense. This is illustrated by the facts of the instant case where, according to President Judge Spaeth's definition, appellant's "threat" to return the juvenile to the detention home would itself be the "forcible compulsion" required by the statute for a conviction of rape. Judge Popovich, on the other hand, would simply eliminate the words "of forcible compulsion" as used by the legislature to modify the noun "threat" and would define rape to include sexual intercourse induced by "any threat." In construing a statute, however, a court must assume the legislature intended that every word is to be given effect....

To define "forcible compulsion" so as to permit a conviction for rape whenever sexual intercourse is induced by "any threat" or by "physical, moral or intellectual means or by the exigencies of the circumstances" will undoubtedly have unfortunate consequences. If a man takes a destitute widow into his home and provides support for her and her family, such a definition of forcible compulsion will convict him of attempted rape if he threatens to withdraw his support and compel her to leave unless she engages in sexual intercourse. Similarly, a person may be guilty of rape if he or she extorts sexual favors from another person upon threat of discharging the other or his or her spouse from a position of employment, or upon threat of foreclosing the mortgage on the home of the other's parents, or upon threat of denying a loan application, or upon threat of disclosing the other's adultery or submission to an abortion. An interpretation of forcible compulsion which employs an ambiguous, generic definition of force will create the potential for a veritable parade of threats, express and implied, in support of accusations of rape and attempted rape. To make it even more troublesome, such an interpretation of forcible compulsion will place in the hands of jurors almost unlimited discretion to determine which acts, threats or promises will transform sexual intercourse into rape. Without intending to condone any of the foregoing, reprehensible acts, our use of them serves to illustrate the intolerable uncertainty which a wholly elastic definition of rape will create.

The legislature, we conclude, did not intend to equate seduction, whether benign or sinister, with rape and make it a felony of the first degree. To allow a conviction for rape where the alleged victim has deliberately chosen intercourse in preference to some other unpleasant sensation not amounting to physical injury or violence would be to trivialize the plight of the helpless victim of a violent rape. The latter is truly a felony of the first degree. The former is not....

...We hold that rape, as defined by the legislature at 18 Pa. C.S. §3121(1) and (2), requires actual physical compulsion or violence or a threat of physical compulsion or violence sufficient to prevent resistance by a person of reasonable resolution. Applying that definition to the facts of the instant case, a threat to withdraw custodial care and return a juvenile to a detention home was not "forcible compulsion" sufficient to make rape out of appellant's act of sexual intercourse. It does not imply condonation of appellant's conduct to suggest that, although reprehensible, it did not constitute the crime of forcible rape as defined by the legislature....

The judgments of sentence imposed for convictions of rape and attempted rape are reversed and set aside. The judgments of sentence imposed for involuntary deviate sexual intercourse and corrupting the morals of a child are affirmed. The convictions for indecent exposure merged into the convictions for involuntary deviate sexual intercourse; and the separate sentences imposed for those convictions, therefore, are vacated and set aside.

Dissent by President Judge Spaeth

A majority of the court today holds that the term "forcible compulsion" contained in the Crimes Code definitions of rape and involuntary deviate sexual intercourse, 18 Pa. C.S. §§3121, 3123, means "physical compulsion or violence." Proceeding from the same legislative history that the majority has analyzed, I am led to quite a different conclusion: by the term "physical compulsion" the General Assembly meant "compulsion by physical, moral, or intellectual means or by the exigencies of the circumstances." That we begin at the same point and end so far apart suggests not so much the difficulty of the issue, or its importance, neither of which may be discounted, as a fundamental clash over how the law is to regard the crime of rape and its victims. I regret that we have been unable to provide a unified response to the question before us. I hope, however, that in the several opinions filed today we have at least provided the basis for a debate that will resolve the question. ...

The information charges that on or about June 15, 19, and 26, 1981, appellant engaged in sexual intercourse with the complainant by threat of forcible compulsion that would prevent resistance by a person of reasonable resolution. The complainant testified that appellant's wife was never home during the incidents in question. She said that the first incident began with appellant asking her to take her clothes off. When she did not remove her bra and underwear, "he [appellant] said, 'Take them off.' I said, 'No.' He said, 'Yes, or he would send me back to the DH' [detention home]. So, I took them off. Then, he took his clothes off." After they had their clothes off, the complainant told appellant she did not want to do anything, and cried, but "[h]e said, 'You did it before, you can do it now,'" and that "[i]f I didn't do it, he would send me back." Appellant then got on the sofa bed next to the complainant and tried to penetrate her. Since appellant does not challenge the sufficiency of the evidence of intercourse, I shall not describe those aspects of the complainant's testimony except to note that she testified that she felt pain and was "screaming and hollering" and "crying." The second and third incidents happened in much the same way, with the complainant crying and saying that she did not want to participate because she did not think that it was right, and with appellant threatening to send her back to the detention home. The complainant testified that she was afraid of going back to the detention home.

The information also charges that on or about June 29 and July 1, 1981, appellant engaged in involuntary deviate sexual intercourse with the complainant. The complainant testified that during the first incident appellant kept pushing her head down to his penis and that she was struggling, crying and yelling at him to quit it. She told appellant that she was going to tell her father and he replied that "[h]e would send me to the DH", and that "[h]e wouldn't let my dad see me because he had me now." N.T. 1/21/82, 168, 169. The second incident was similar. ...

Appellant argues that he must be discharged because the foregoing evidence was insufficient to prove the degree of compulsion that must be proved before one may be convicted of rape. Specifically, he argues that "although the courts no longer require [proof of] actual physical violence they do require [proof] that the actions of the defendant create[d] a reasonable fear of physical harm." In appellant's view, his threat to send the complainant back to the detention home if she did not submit to his demands "[did] not give rise to the level of force or threat contemplated by the courts. ... [citing cases]." ...

Appellant concedes—by not arguing otherwise—that the evidence was sufficient to prove that he "engage[d] in sexual intercourse with another person not his spouse."... Therefore, we are left with two questions: First, was the jury entitled to find from the evidence that appellant's threat to send the complainant back to the detention home if she did not submit to his demands constituted a "threat of forcible compulsion." And second, if so, was the jury further entitled to find that the threat was such as "would prevent resistance by a person of reasonable resolution"?...

It is frequently said that the words of a statute are to be "given their plain meaning," or are to be "understood according to their common and approved usage." These maxims, however, will not yield the meaning of the phrase, "threat of forcible compulsion," for "force" has more than one plain, or common and approved, meaning. *Webster's Third New International Dictionary* (1968) provides eleven definitions of "force," some of these being subdivided....

As one considers the range and tone of these several definitions it becomes evident that appellant's threat to send the complainant back to the detention home if she did not submit to his demands might, or might not, have been a "threat of forcible compulsion." It was not such a threat if "forcible" is to be considered as limited to meaning "to do violence to"; it might have been such a threat if "forcible" is to be construed as meaning "to constrain or compel by physical, moral, or intellectual means or by the exigencies of the circumstances," or as meaning "to press, impose, or thrust urgently, importunately, inexorably."

The same possibility of reaching conflicting conclusions—"forcible compulsion" or no "forcible compulsion"—becomes evident upon examining the synonyms of "force." As the editors of *Webster's* observe, in commenting on these synonyms: "Force is a general term indicating use of strength, power, weight, stress, duress in overcoming resistance." Appellant did not threaten "to do violence to" the complainant in the same way as often occurs in rape cases—for example, he made no threat to kill or beat her. However, the jury was entitled to find, if not a threat of "violence," then a threat of some sort of application of "strength"; for the complainant did not want to return to the detention home and therefore in some way would have had to have been "forced" to return. The jury was also entitled to find that appellant had used the "power" and "weight" of his authority over the complainant, and had subjected her to "stress" and "duress," in order to overcome her resistance to his demands.

Our problem, therefore, is not to choose the "plain meaning" of the phrase, "threat of forcible compulsion," but, rather, to decide which of several plain meanings the legislature had in mind when it used the phrase in enacting the Crimes Code....

Gradually, but with increasing momentum, it became apparent that the common law conception of rape was simply inadequate. The proven reluctance of victims to report rape, the dramatic increase in the incidence of the crime, and the low conviction rates for defendants [were] all indices of a law...gone awry....

The fundamental flaws in the common law conception were summarized in the commentary to the Model Penal Code. In the first place, the common law oversimplified to the point of falsifying the victim's response to her situation, failing to recognize that the victim's failure to resist might be, not because she had consented to the intercourse, but because she was "frozen by fear and panic."... In addition, the common law demanded inordinately dangerous conduct on the part of the victim; resistance might invite death or serious bodily harm, and rather than risk either, she might "quite rationally decide to 'consent' to the intercourse." And finally, it is wrong to excuse the male assailant on the ground that his victim failed to protect herself with the dedication and intensity that a court might expect of a reasonable person in her situation. As a practical matter, juries may require resistance to show that the male compelled her to submit, but there is little reason to encase this generalization in a rule of law....

In recognition of the fundamentally flawed nature, and consequent inadequacy, of the common law, the American Law Institute "determined that an essentially fresh approach should be undertaken." The essence of this approach, as embodied in the Model Penal Code, was to define rape in terms of the actor's use of force, with no reference to the victim's refusal to consent. As the authors explained:

> By focusing upon the actor who "compels" the victim "to submit by force" and by omitting express language of consent and resistance, the Model Code casts away encrusted precedents and strikes a fresh approach. This is not to say that consent by the victim is irrelevant or that inquiry into the level of resistance by the victim cannot or should not be made. Compulsion plainly implies non-consent, just as resistance is evidence of non-consent. By the same token, the lack of resistance on a particular occasion will not preclude a conviction of rape if the jury can be convinced by the context and degree of force employed by the actor that the submission was by compulsion....

When one recognizes that in enacting the Crimes Code, the legislature followed the Model Penal Code's "fresh approach," it becomes clear that the meaning of "forcible compulsion" is not limited to compulsion accomplished by force, or by threat of force, in the sense of "to do violence to." For if rape could be proved only by evidence of violence, or threat of violence, the very questions would arise under the Crimes Code that arose at common law, and that led to the criticism and rejection of the common law, that is to say, the inquiry would continue to focus, instead of on the actor, on the victim: What violence was done to the victim? Was she beaten, for example, or choked? Was she threatened with death? The very essence of the Model Penal Code's, and the legislature's, rejection of the common law is that this should not be the inquiry—that while rape can of course be accomplished by violence, or threat of violence, it also can be accomplished by compulsion arising from something less than violence, or threat of violence.

Returning, then, to the question with which I started—which plain meaning of "force" did the legislature have in mind when it used the phrase "forcible compulsion" in the Crimes Code?—I have no hesitancy in concluding that the legislature did not mean force in the limited sense of "to do violence to," and did mean force in the more general sense of "to constrain or compel by physical, moral, or intellectual means or by the exigencies of the circumstances." Only this conclusion is consistent with the legislature's manifested agreement with the Model Penal Code that a "fresh approach" should be taken, and the focus of inquiry shifted away from the victim's consent to the actor's force....

In conclusion, then: Appellant's argument that the evidence was insufficient depends upon the fact that the evidence fails to show either that he did, or threatened to do, any violence to the complainant. Were this prosecution a prosecution at common law, this argument would prevail. However, it is a prosecution under the Crimes Code, which rejects the common law and only requires that the evidence show that the complainant submitted to appellant's demands because he made such a "threat of forcible compulsion [as] would prevent resistance by a person of reasonable resolution." By "forcible compulsion" the legislature meant "compulsion by physical, moral, or intellectual means or by the exigencies of the circumstances." By this standard, the evidence, viewed in the light most favorable to the Commonwealth, was sufficient. Appellant threatened the complainant, a 14-year-old girl, with being returned to the detention home, and with not seeing her father again. Complainant was afraid of going back to the detention home. Her father and brother, with whom she had been living, had filed charges against her, with the result that she had spent three days there, and then been placed in appellant's home by court order. I believe that the jury was entitled to find that the complainant was compelled to submit to appellant's demands by the exigencies of her circumstances, and, further, that in submitting, she acted as a person of reasonable resolution.[1]

Resisting this conclusion, appellant relies heavily on, and the majority cites with approval, *Commonwealth v. Biggs*. In *Biggs* the defendant had sexual intercourse, over a period of two years, on several occasions with his 17-year-old daughter. She complied because her father told her that the Bible said it was the oldest daughter's duty to have intercourse with her father when the mother could no longer provide as a mother. He also told her that if she told anyone, he would show nude pictures of her. He never did any violence to her, nor did he threaten to do so. We reversed the defendant's conviction of rape, holding that there was "no evidence that the intercourse was accomplished through threat of forcible compulsion.... Rather, [the defendant] asserted a biblical basis for the intercourse and assured his daughter's silence by threats, not of force, but of humiliation." To the extent that *Biggs* holds that threats of humiliation are insufficient as a matter of law to constitute a threat of forcible compulsion, it should be overruled....

NOTE

[1]The differences between the foregoing interpretation of the Crimes Code and the majority's interpretation are instructive. In my view, the majority's interpretation of the Crimes Code continues to keep women in a position subordinate to men: a woman's testimony in a rape case that she was compelled to submit is not to be trusted; she must be able to prove that the man used physical force. Neither, in the majority's view, is a jury to be trusted: Although the Crimes Code requires that in submitting, the woman must have acted as a woman of reasonable resolution, a jury cannot be relied upon to apply this standard; instead it will convict as a rapist one who was only a seducer. It is, I suggest, those different convictions, regarding a woman's appropriate status and a jury's competence and appropriate function, that underlie the majority's and my different interpretations of the Crimes Code.

ENDURING DISTRUST: THE MODERN LAW OF FORCE

Susan Estrich

In 1984 the Superior Court of Pennsylvania set about to define "with a view to general application" the rape statute enacted by its legislature in the 1970s. In describing the history of that statute, the court detailed why the previous common law definition was deemed unsatisfactory. It was found inadequate "because of its inordinate emphasis on 'lack of consent,'" an element of the offense which had "been construed to require a woman to resist to the utmost."[1] The rule "worked to the unfair disadvantage of the woman who, when threatened with violence, chose quite rationally to submit to her assailant's advances rather than risk death or serious bodily injury."[2]

The authors of the Modern Penal Code saw similar flaws in the common law approach; their alternative was highly influential in Pennsylvania and elsewhere. Criticizing the traditional approach that placed "disproportionate emphasis upon objective manifestations by the woman," they emphasized that female nonconsent was not even an element in their proposed definition of rape (although the code's general

From Chapter 4 of Susan Estrich, *Real Rape* (Cambridge, MA.: Harvard University Press) Copyright © 1987 by the President and Fellows of Harvard College.

consent defense would be applicable). Rather, rape was defined as sexual intercourse where the man "compels her to submit by force or by threat of imminent death, serious bodily injury, extreme pain or kidnapping, to be afflicted on anyone." The focus, the code emphasized, was properly placed not on the manifestations of female nonconsent, but on the prohibited acts of the defendant.[3]

Many jurisdictions followed suit. Some copied the code's language verbatim. Others, like Pennsylvania itself, followed the basic approach, but worded their prohibitions in terms of "forcible compulsion" and the threat of "forcible compulsion." Only a minority followed what was then New York's approach, criticized by the code, of statutorily defining forcible compulsion in terms of the "earnest resistance" of the victim.

The requirement of force is not new to the law of rape; virtually every jurisdiction has traditionally made "force" or "threat of force" an element of the crime. Yet so long as the focus was on female nonconsent, defined as utmost or at least reasonable resistance, force was a decidedly secondary issue and remained essentially unaddressed. One commentator even said that the cases had established that "force" is not truly speaking an element of the crime itself, but if great force was not needed to accomplish the act, the necessary lack of consent has been disproved in other than exceptional situations.[4]

Force, like nonconsent, is required in other crimes besides rape. But rape *is* different from other crimes in at least two respects that affect the definition given to force. First, whereas in noncriminal theft (philanthropy), for example, no contact at all is required, in noncriminal sex, physical contact, if not "force," is inherent. Certainly if a thief stripped his victim, flattened that victim on the floor, lay down on top, and took the victim's wallet or jewelry, few would pause before concluding forcible robbery.

Second, we are not dealing here with "one person" and "another person." We are dealing with a male person using "force" against a female person. In one of his most memorable essays, Oliver Wendell Holmes explained that the law does not exist to tell the good man what to do, but rather to tell the bad man what not to do.[5] Holmes was interested in distinguishing between the good and bad man; I cannot help but notice that both are men. Most of the time a criminal law that reflects male views and male standards imposes its judgment on men who have injured other men. It is "boys' rules" applied to a boy's fight.[6] In rape the male standard defines a crime that, traditionally by law and still predominantly in practice, is committed only by men against women. The question of whose definition of "force" should apply, of whose understanding should govern, is critical.

The distinction between the "force" incidental to the act of intercourse and the "force" required to convict of rape is one commonly drawn by courts. Once drawn, however, the distinction would seem to require the courts to define what additional acts are needed to constitute prohibited as opposed to merely incidental force. That is not a problem in the aggravated case: guns, knives, or threats of injury are all easily accepted as force. Simple rapes are another matter. For many courts, force is the key to making a simple rape criminal, but force—even force that goes far beyond the physical contact necessary to accomplish penetration—is not itself prohibited. What is required, and prohibited, is force used to overcome female nonconsent. The prohibition of "force" or "forcible compulsion" ends up being defined in terms of a woman's resistance.

State v. Alston, a 1984 decision of the North Carolina Supreme Court, is one of the most striking examples of this.[7] Mr. Alston and the victim had been involved in a "consensual" relationship for six months. That relationship admittedly involved "some violence" by the defendant and some passivity by the victim. The defendant would strike the victim when she refused to give him money or refused to do what he wanted. As for sex, the court noted that "she often had sex with the defendant just to accommodate him. On those occasions, she would stand still and remain entirely passive while the defendant undressed her and had intercourse with her."[8] This was their "consensual" relationship. It ended when, after being struck by the defendant, the victim left the apartment she shared with him and moved in with her mother.

A month later the defendant came to the school the victim attended, blocked her path, demanded to know where she was living, and, when she refused to tell him, grabbed her arm and stated that she was coming with him. The victim told the defendant she would walk with him if he released her arm. Then they walked around the school and talked about their relationship. At one point the defendant told the victim he was going to "fix" her face to show her he "was not playing." When told that their relationship was over, the defendant stated that he had a "right" to have intercourse with her again. The two went to the house of a friend of the defendant. The defendant asked her if she was "ready" and the victim told him she did not want to have sexual relations. The defendant pulled her up from the chair, undressed her, pushed her legs apart, and penetrated her. She cried.

The defendant was convicted of rape, and his conviction was affirmed by the intermediate court of appeals. The North Carolina Supreme Court reversed. The state supreme court held that the victim was not required to resist physically to establish nonconsent; it described the victim's testimony that she did not consent as "unequivocal" and held that her testimony provided substantial evidence that the act of sexual intercourse was against her will.[9]

Consent was not the problem. Force was. The North Carolina Supreme Court held that, even viewing the evidence in the light most favorable to the state (as required by law), the element of force had not been established by substantial evidence. The victim did not "resist"—physically at least. And her failure to resist, in the court's evaluation, was not a result of what the defendant did just before penetration. Therefore, there was no "force." The force used outside the school and the threats made on the walk, "although they may have induced fear" were considered to be "unrelated to the act of sexual intercourse." The court emphasized that the victim testified that it was not what the defendant said that day, but her experience with him in the past, that made her afraid. Such past experience was deemed irrelevant. "Although [the victim's] general fear of the defendant may have been justified by his conduct on prior occasions, absent evidence that the defendant used force or threats to overcome the will of the victim to resist the sexual intercourse alleged to have been rape, such general fear was not sufficient to show that the defendant used the force required to support a conviction of rape." The undressing and the pushing of her legs apart—presumably the "incidental" force—were not even mentioned.

Alston reflects the adoption of the most traditional male notion of a fight as the working definition of "force." In a fight you hit your assailant with your fists or your elbows or your knees. In a fight the person attacked fights back. In these terms there was no fight in *Alston*. Therefore, there was no force.

On its face, the decision creates a paradox. The court explicitly says that the sexual intercourse was without the woman's consent. It also says that there was no force. In other words, the woman was not forced to engage in sex (as proven by her failure to resist), but the sex she engaged in was against her will. I am not at all sure how the judges who decided *Alston* would justify the clear contradiction in their approach. Apparently they could not understand the woman's reaction. For me, it is not at all difficult to understand that a woman who had been beaten repeatedly, who had been a passive victim of both violence and sex during the "consensual" relationship, who had sought to escape from the man, who is confronted and threatened by him, who summons the courage to tell him their relationship is over only to be answered by his assertion of a "right" to sex, would not fight his advances. She did not fight; she cried. It is the reaction of "sissies" in playground fights. It is the reaction of people who have already been beaten, or never had the power to fight in the first place. It is, from my reading, the most common reaction of women to rape.

To say that there is no "force" in this situation, as the North Carolina court did, is to create a gulf between power and force and to define the latter strictly in schoolboy terms. Alston did not beat his victim—at least not with his fists. He didn't have to. She had been beaten, physically and emotionally, long before. But that beating was one that the court simply refused to recognize.

The definition of force adopted by the *Alston* court, like the definition of nonconsent adopted by earlier courts, protects male access to women where guns and beatings are not needed to secure it. The court did not hold that no means yes; but it made clear that, at least in "social" contexts like this one with appropriate victims, a man is free to proceed regardless of verbal nonconsent. In that sense Alston was right. He did have a "right" to intercourse, and his victim had no right to deny him merely by saying "no."

But the problem with "force" as a standard is not only that it is too narrowly defined. The problem is also that the focus remains on the victim. As in the older consent cases, the conclusion that no force is present emerges not as a judgment that the man acted reasonably, but as a judgment that the woman victim did not.

State v. Rusk is one of the most vigorously debated rape cases in recent volumes of the case reporters. The case was heard *en banc*—that is, not by a panel of the usual number, but by all the appellate judges sitting together, by the Maryland Court of Special Appeals and Maryland's highest court, the Court of Appeals. The Court of Special Appeals reversed the conviction, eight to five. The Court of Appeals reinstated it, four to three.[10] All told, twenty-one judges, including the trial judge, reviewed the sufficiency of the evidence. Ten concluded that Rusk was a rapist; eleven that he was not.

State v. Rusk is also a classic example of a simple rape.... Pat met Rusk at a bar. They talked briefly. She announced she was leaving, and he asked for a ride. She drove him home. He invited her up. She declined. He asked again. She declined again. He reached over and took the car keys. She accompanied him to his room. He went to the bathroom. She didn't leave. He pulled her onto the bed and began to remove her blouse. He asked her to remove her slacks and his clothing. She did. After they undressed:

> I said, "you can get a lot of other girls down there, for what you want," and he just kept saying, "no" and then I was really scared, because I can't describe, you know, what was said. It was more the look in his eyes; and I said, at that point—I didn't know what to say; and I said, "If I do what you want, will you let me go without killing me?" Because I didn't know, at that point, what he was going to do; and I started to cry; and when I did, he put his hands on my throat, and started lightly to choke me; and I said "If I do what you want, will you let me go." And he said, yes, and at that time, I proceeded to do what he wanted me to do.[11]

Afterward the defendant walked her to her car and asked if he could see her again.

How does a court deal with facts like these? Is "force" established by the "look in his eyes," or by light choking (her description) or heavy caresses (his description)? The difference in their characterizations is noteworthy. It may be that one of them was lying. Or it may be true that neither was lying: that "light choking" to her was nothing more than a "heavy caress" to him; that this is but one example that happened to survive into an appellate opinion of the differences in how men and women perceive force.

The judges who considered the evidence insufficient to support a conviction of rape focused nearly all their attention not on what Rusk did or did not do, but on how Pat responded. Prohibited force was defined according to a hypothetical victim's resistance: the defendant's words or actions must create in the mind of the victim a *reasonable* fear that if she resisted, he would harm her, or that faced with such resistance, he would use force to overcome it. To the argument that an honest fear by *this* woman was enough, even if other women might not have been so fearful, the intermediate court majority found that it had no appeal, "where there is nothing whatsoever to indicate that the victim was anything but a normal, intelligent, twenty-one-year old, vigorous female."[12] Of course the question remains as to what is "reasonably" expected of such a female faced with a man who frightens her, in an unfamiliar neighborhood, without her car keys? To the three Court of Appeals judges who concluded that Rusk should be freed, the answer was clear:

> While courts no longer require a female to resist to the utmost or to resist where resistance would be foolhardy, they do require her acquiescence in the act of intercourse to stem from fear generated by something of substance. *She may not simply say, "I was really scared," and thereby transform consent or mere unwillingness into submission by force. These words do not transform a seducer into a rapist.* She must follow the natural instinct of every proud female to resist, by more than mere words, the violation of her person by a stranger or an unwelcomed friend. She must make it plain that she regards such sexual acts as abhorrent and repugnant to her natural sense of pride. She must resist unless the defendant has objectively manifested his intent to use physical force to accomplish his purpose.[13]

In the dissenters' view, Pat was not a "reasonable" victim, or even a victim at all. Rather than fight, she cried. Rather than protect her "virtue," she acquiesced. Far from having any claim that her bodily integrity had been violated, she was adjudged complicit in the intercourse of which she complained. As one judge put it, the approach of those who would reverse Rusk's conviction amounted to nothing less than a declaration that Pat was, "in effect, an adulteress."[14]

In a very real sense, the "reasonable" woman under the view of the eleven judges who voted to reverse Mr. Rusk's conviction is not a woman at all. Their version of a reasonable person is one who does not scare easily, one who does not feel vulnerable, one who is not passive, one who fights back, not cries. The reasonable woman, it seems, is not a schoolboy "sissy"; she is a real man.

The Court of Appeals majority ultimately affirmed the conviction by a four-to-three vote on the narrowest possible ground. The court stated that "generally the correct standard" is that the victim's fear must be reasonably grounded "in order to obviate the need for either proof of actual force on the part of the assailant or physical resistance on the part of the victim." Was this victim's fear reasonable? The court tried to avoid the question, focusing instead on the rules of procedure that counsel appellate judges to defer to a jury's determination of facts. Still, the Supreme Court could not avoid entirely its obligation to review the sufficiency of the evidence. Thus, "considering all of the evidence in the case, *with particular focus upon the actual force applied by Rusk to Pat's neck*, we conclude that the jury could rationally find that the essential elements of second degree rape had been established."[15]

The emphasis on the light choking/heavy caresses is perhaps understandable: it is the only "objective" (as the Supreme Court dissent put it) force in the victim's testimony; it is certainly the only "force" that a schoolboy might recognize. As it happens, however, that force was not applied until the two were already undressed and in bed. Whatever it was—choking or caressing—was a response to the woman's crying as the moment for intercourse approached. It was not the only force that produced that moment.

The opinions in cases like *Alston* and *Rusk* reflect judges' continued unwillingness to empower women in potentially consensual situations with the weapon of a rape charge. It its the same unwillingness that supported the equation of consent with nonresistance and the requirement of corroboration of a woman's testimony....

Commonwealth v. Mlinarich, a 1984 Pennsylvania decision, makes all too clear the exaggerated scope of what continues to count in some jurisdictions as seduction rather than rape.... In *Mlinarich* the Pennsylvania Superior Court defined "forcible compulsion," which supposedly replaced nonconsent as the key element of Pennsylvania's rape prohibitions. The court concluded that "forcible compulsion" required "physical compulsion or violence," but did not include "psychological duress." Mlinarich had threatened a fourteen-year-old girl living in his and his wife's custody with return to a detention home if she refused to engage in intercourse. Under the court's definition of "forcible compulsion," this was not rape. Though viewing the defendant's actions as reprehensible, the court emphasized that it was "with a view to general application" that it sought to define forcible compulsion. The court contended that to define forcible compulsion more broadly would "undoubtedly have unfortunate consequences." The legislature, it concluded, "did not intend to equate seduction, whether benign or sinister, with rape and make it a felony of the first degree." And since seduction itself was not a crime, there was no crime at all in these instances.

The breadth of "seduction" in the context of sexual relations is without parallel in criminal law. Had the men in these cases been seeking money instead of sex, their actions would be in plain violation of traditional state criminal prohibitions.... [H]ad Mr. Mlinarich threatened to send the victim to reform school were he not paid off with money instead of sex, he might well have been guilty of state law extortion....

In the simple rape case, even in the 1970s and 1980s, the "force" standard may be as effective, and as punitive, an obstacle to rape convictions as the old consent approach. Under the force standard, courts still judge the woman, not the man. The focus...is on women generally, and on the victim as she compares (poorly) to the court's vision of the reasonable woman. To reverse a conviction, the court need only conclude that a reasonable woman's will would not have been overcome in these circumstances, because there was no force as men understand it. The right to seduce—the right of male sexual access in appropriate relationships—continues to be protected. ...

NOTES

[1]*Commonwealth v. Mlinarich*, 345 Pa. Super, 269, 498 (Pa. Super. Ct. 1985).

[2]498 A.2d at 397.

[3]*Model Penal Code and Commentaries* (Philadelphia: American Law Institute, 1980), Sec. 213.1, Comments: 303–304, 280–281. Original 4.

[4]Rollin Perkins, *Criminal Law*, 2nd ed. (Mineola, N.Y.: Foundation Press, 1969): 162.

[5]Oliver Wendell Holmes, "The Path of the Law," *Harvard Law Review*, 10 (1897): 457, 459.

[6]In referring to "male" standards and "boys' rules," I do not mean to suggest that every man adheres to them or that not a single woman does. A "male view" is nonetheless distinct from a "female view" not only because of the gender of most of those who adhere to it, but also because of the character of the life experiences and socialization that tend to produce it.

[7]310 N.C. 399, 312 S.E. 2d 470 (1984).

[8]312 S.E. 2d at 471.

[9]*State. v. Alston*, 61 N.C. App. 454, (N.C. Ct. App. 1983).

[10]*State v.. Rusk*, 289 Md. 230, (1981).

[11]*Rusk v. State*, 43 Md. App.: 476, 478–479.

[12]*Rusk v. State*, 43 Md. App.: 482.

[13]*State v. Rusk*, 289 Md. 230, 255, 424 A.2d 720 (Cole, J., dissenting); emphasis added.

[14]This is exactly how Judge Wilner, the dissenting judge in the Court of Appeals, characterizes the majority's decision to reverse Rusk's conviction. *Rusk v. State*, 43 Md. App.: 498. ...

[15]289 Md.: 246–247; emphasis added.

RAPE: ON COERCION AND CONSENT

Catharine A. MacKinnon

If sexuality is central to women's definition and forced sex is central to sexuality, rape is indigenous, not exceptional, to women's social condition. In feminist analysis, a rape is not an isolated event or moral transgression or individual interchange gone wrong, but an act of terrorism and torture within a systemic context of group subjection, like lynching. The fact that the state calls rape a crime opens an inquiry into the state's treatment of rape as an index to its stance on the status of the sexes.

Under law, rape is a sex crime that is not regarded as a crime when it looks like sex. The law, speaking generally, defines rape as intercourse with force or coercion and without consent. Like sexuality under male supremacy, this definition assumes the sadomasochistic definition of sex: intercourse with force or coercion can be or become consensual. It assumes pornography's positive-outcome-rape scenario: dominance plus submission is force plus consent. This equals sex, not rape. Under male supremacy, this is too often the reality. In a critique of male supremacy, the elements "with force and without consent" appear redundant. Force is present because consent is absent.

Like heterosexuality, male supremacy's paradigm of sex, the crime of rape centers on penetration.[1] The law to protect women's sexuality from forcible violation and expropriation defines that protection in male genital terms. Women do resent forced penetration. But penile invasion of the vagina may be less pivotal to women's sexuality, pleasure, or violation, than it is to male sexuality. This definitive element of rape centers upon a male-defined loss. It also centers upon one way men define loss of exclusive access. In this light, rape, as legally defined, appears more a crime against female monogamy (exclusive access by one man) than against women's sexual dignity or intimate integrity. Analysis of rape in terms of concepts of property, often invoked in Marxian analysis to criticize this disparity, fail to encompass the realities of rape.[2] Women's sexuality is, socially, a thing to be stolen, sold, bought, bartered, or exchanged by others. But women never own or possess it, and men never treat it, in law or in life, with the solicitude with which they treat property. To be property would be an improvement. The moment women "have" it—"have sex" in the dual gender/sexuality sense—it is lost as theirs. To have it is to have it taken away. This may explain the male incomprehension that, once a woman has had sex, she loses anything when subsequently raped. To them women have nothing to lose.

Rape cases finding insufficient evidence of force reveal that acceptable sex, in the legal perspective, can entail a lot of force. This is a result both of the way specific facts are perceived and interpreted within the legal system, and the way the injury is defined by law. The level of acceptable force is adjudicated starting just above the level set by what is seen as normal male sexual behavior, including the normal level of force, rather than at the victim's, or women's, point of violation.[3] In this context, to seek to define rape as violent, not sexual, is as understandable as it is futile. Some feminists have reinterpreted rape as an act of violence, not sexuality, the threat of which intimidates all women.[4] Others see rape, including its violence, as an expression of male sexuality, the social imperatives of which define as well as threaten all women.[5] The first, epistemologically in the liberal tradition, comprehends rape as a displacement of power based on physical force onto sexuality, a preexisting natural sphere to which domination is alien. Susan Brownmiller, for example, examines rape in riots, wars, pogroms, and revolutions; rape by police, parents, prison guards; and rape motivated by racism. Rape in normal circumstances, in everyday life, in ordinary relationships, by men as men, is barely mentioned. Women are raped by guns, age, white supremacy, the state—only derivatively by the penis. The view that derives most directly from victims' experiences, rather than from their denial, construes sexuality as a social sphere of male power to which forced sex is paradigmatic. Rape is not less sexual for being violent. To the extent that coercion has become integral to male sexuality, rape may even be sexual to the degree that, and because, it is violent.

The point of defining rape as "violence not sex" has been to claim an ungendered and nonsexual ground for affirming sex (heterosexuality) while rejecting violence (rape). The problem remains what it has always been: telling the difference. The convergence of sexuality with violence, long used at law to deny the reality of women's violation, is recognized by rape survivors with a difference: where the legal system has seen the intercourse in rape, victims see the rape in intercourse. The uncoerced context for sexual expression becomes as elusive as the physical acts come to feel indistinguishable. Instead of asking what is the violation of rape, their experience suggests that the more relevant question is, what is the nonviolation of intercourse? To know what is wrong with rape, know what is right about sex. If this, in turn, proves difficult, the difficulty is as instructive as the difficulty men have in telling the difference when women see one. Perhaps the wrong of rape has proved so difficult to define because the unquestionable starting point has been that rape is defined as distinct from intercourse,[6] while for women it is difficult to distinguish the two under conditions of male dominance.

In the name of the distinction between sex and violence, reform of rape statutes has sought to redefine rape as sexual assault. Usually, assault is not consented to in law; either it cannot be consented to, or consensual assault remains assault. Yet sexual assault consented to is intercourse, no matter how much force was used. The substantive reference point implicit in existing legal standards is the sexually normative level of force. Until this norm is confronted as such, no distinction between violence and sexuality will prohibit more instances of women's experienced violation than does the existing definition. Conviction rates have not increased under the reform statutes. The question remains what is seen as force, hence as violence, in the sexual arena.[7] Most rapes, as women live them, will not be seen to violate women until sex and violence are confronted as mutually definitive rather than as mutually exclusive. It is not only men convicted of rape who believe that the only thing they did that was different from what men do all the time is get caught.

Consent is supposed to be women's form of control over intercourse, different from but equal to the custom of male initiative. Man proposes, woman disposes. Even the ideal it is not mutual. Apart from the disparate consequences of refusal, this model does not envision a situation the woman controls being placed in, or choices she frames. Yet the consequences are attributed to her as if the sexes began at arm's length, on equal terrain, as in the contract fiction. Ambiguous cases of consent in law are archetypically referred to as "half-won arguments in parked cars."[8] Why not half-lost? Why isn't half enough? Why is it an argument? Why do men still want "it," feel entitled to "it," when women do not want them? The law of rape presents consent as free exercise of sexual choice under conditions of equality of power without exposing the underlying structure of constraint and disparity. Fundamentally, desirability to men is supposedly a woman's form of power because she can both arouse it and deny its fulfillment. To woman is attributed both the cause of man's initiative and the denial of his satisfaction. This rationalizes force. Consent in this model becomes more a metaphysical quality of a woman's being than a choice she makes and communicates. Exercise of women's so-called power presupposes more fundamental social powerlessness.

The law of rape divides women into spheres of consent according to indices of relationship to men. Which category of presumed consent a woman is in depends upon who she is relative to a man who wants her, not what she says or does. These categories tell men whom they can legally fuck, who is open season and who is off limits, not how to listen to women. The paradigm categories are the virginal daughter and other young girls, with whom all sex is proscribed, and the whorelike wives and prostitutes, with whom no sex is proscribed. Daughters may not consent; wives and prostitutes are assumed to, and cannot but. Actual consent or nonconsent, far less actual desire, is comparatively irrelevant. If rape laws existed to enforce women's control over access to their sexuality, as the consent defense implies, no would mean no, marital rape would not be a widespread exception,[9] and it would not be effectively legal to rape a prostitute. ...

...[T]o the extent an accused knows a woman and they have sex, her consent is inferred. The exemption for rape in marriage is consistent with the assumption underlying most adjudications of forcible rape: to the extent the parties relate, it was not really rape, it was personal. As marital exemptions erode, preclusions for cohabitants and voluntary social companions may expand. As a matter of fact, for this purpose one can be acquainted with an accused by friendship, or by meeting him for the first time at a bar or a party, or by hitchhiking. In this light, the partial erosion of the marital rape exemption looks less like a change in the equation between women's experience of sexual violation and men's experience of intimacy, and more like a legal adjustment to the social fact that acceptable heterosexual sex is increasingly not limited to the legal family. So although the rape law may not now always assume that the woman consented simply because the parties are legally one, indices of closeness, of relationships ranging from nodding acquaintance to living together, still contraindicate rape. In marital rape cases, courts look for even greater atrocities than usual to undermine their assumption that if sex happened, she wanted it.

This approach reflects men's experience that women they know do meaningfully consent to sex with them. *That* cannot be rape; rape must be by someone else, someone unknown. They do not rape women they know. Men and women are unequally socially situated with regard to the experience of rape. Men are a good deal more likely to rape than to be raped. This forms their experience, the material conditions of their episte-mological position. Almost half of all women, by contrast, are raped or victims of attempted rape at least once in their lives. Almost 40 percent are victims of sexual abuse in childhood.[10] Women are more likely to be raped than to rape and are most often raped by men whom they know.[11]...

Having defined rape in male sexual terms, the law's problem, which becomes the victim's problem, is distinguishing rape from sex in specific cases. The adjudicated line between rape and intercourse commonly cen-ters on some assessment of the woman's "will." But how should the law or the accused know a woman's will? The answer combines aspects of force with aspects of nonconsent with elements of resistance, still effective in some states. Even when nonconsent is not a legal element of the offense, juries tend to infer rape from evidence of force or resistance....

The deeper problem is that women are socialized to passive receptivity; may have or perceive no alternative to acquiescence; may prefer it to the escalated risk of injury and the humiliation of a lost fight; submit to sur-vive. Also, force and desire are not mutually exclusive under male supremacy. So long as dominance is eroticized, they never will be. Some women eroticize dominance and submission; it beats feeling forced. Sex-ual intercourse may be deeply unwanted, the woman would never have initiated it, yet no force may be present. So much force may have been used that the woman never risked saying no. Force may be used, yet the woman may prefer the sex—to avoid more force or because she, too, eroti-cizes dominance. Women and men know this. Considering rape as vio-lence not sex evades, at the moment it most seems to confront, the issue of who controls women's sexuality and the dominance/submission dynamic that has defined it. When sex is violent, women may have lost control over what is done to them, but absence of force does not ensure the presence of that control. Nor, under conditions of male dominance, does the presence of force make an interaction nonsexual. If sex is nor-mally something men do to women, the issue is less whether there was force than whether consent is a meaningful concept.[12]...

The larger issue raised by sexual aggression for the interpretation of the relation between sexuality and gender is: What is heterosexuality? If it is the erotization of dominance and submission, altering the participants' gender does not eliminate the sexual, or even gendered, content of aggres-sion. If heterosexuality is males over females, gender matters indepen-dently. Arguably, heterosexuality is a fusion of the two, with gender a social outcome, such that the acted upon is feminized, is the "girl" regard-less of sex, the actor correspondingly masculinized. Whenever women are victimized, regardless of the biology of the perpetrator, this system is at work. But it is equally true that whenever powerlessness and ascribed inferiority are sexually exploited or enjoyed—based on age, race, physical

stature or appearance or ability, or socially reviled or stigmatized status—
the system is at work....

Most women get the message that the law against rape is virtually
unenforceable as applied to them. Women's experience is more often dele-
gitimated by this than the law is. Women, as realists, distinguish between
rape and experiences of sexual violation by concluding that they have not
"really" been raped if they have ever seen or dated or slept with or been
married to the man, if they were fashionably dressed or not provably virgin, if they are prostitutes, if they put up with it or tried to get it over with,
if they were force-fucked for years. The implicit social standard becomes:
if a woman probably could not prove it in court, it was not rape.

The distance between most intimate violations of women and the
legally perfect rape measures the imposition of an alien definition. From
women's point of view, rape is not prohibited; it is regulated. Even
women who know they have been raped do not believe that the legal system will see it the way they do. Often they are not wrong. Rather than
deterring or avenging rape, the state, in many victims' experiences, perpetuates it. Women who charge rape say they were raped twice, the second time in court. Under a male state, the boundary violation,
humiliation, and indignity of being a public sexual spectacle makes this
more than a figure of speech....

...[A]lthough the rape law oscillates between subjective tests and objective standards invoking social reasonableness, it uniformly presumes a
single underlying reality, rather than a reality split by the divergent meanings inequality produces. Many women are raped by men who know the
meaning of their acts to their victims perfectly well, and proceed anyway.
But women are also violated every day by men who have no idea of the
meaning of their acts to the women. To them it is sex. Therefore, to the law
it is sex. That becomes the single reality of what happened. When a rape
prosecution is lost because a woman fails to prove that she did not consent, she is not considered to have been injured at all. It is as if a robbery
victim, finding himself unable to prove he was not engaged in philanthropy, is told he still has his money. Hermeneutically unpacked, the law
assumes that, because the rapist did not perceive that the woman did not
want him, she was not violated. She had sex. Sex itself cannot be an injury.
Women have sex every day. Sex makes a woman a woman. Sex is what
women are for.

Men's pervasive belief that women fabricate rape charges after consenting to sex makes sense in this light. To them, the accusations are false
because, to them, the facts describe sex. To interpret such events as rapes
distorts their experience. Since they seldom consider that their experience
of the real is anything other than reality, they can only explain the
woman's version as maliciously invented. Similarly, the male anxiety that
rape is easy to charge and difficult to disprove, also widely believed in the

face of overwhelming evidence to the contrary, arises because rape accusations express one thing men cannot seem to control: the meaning to women of sexual encounters.

Thus do legal doctrines, incoherent or puzzling as syllogistic logic, become coherent as ideology. For example, when an accused wrongly but sincerely believes that a woman he sexually forced consented, he may have a defense of mistaken belief in consent or fail to satisfy the mental requirement of knowingly proceeding against her will.[13] Sometimes his knowing disregard is measured by what a reasonable man would disregard. This is considered an objective test. Sometimes the disregard need not be reasonable so long as it is sincere. This is considered a subjective test. A feminist inquiry into the distinction between rape and intercourse, by contrast, would inquire into the meaning of the act from women's point of view, which is neither. What is wrong with rape in this view is that it is an act of subordination of women to men. It expresses and reinforces women's inequality to men. Rape with legal impunity makes women second-class citizens.

This analysis reveals the way the social conception of rape is shaped to interpret particular encounters and the way the legal conception of rape authoritatively shapes that social conception. When perspective is bound up with situation, and situation is unequal, whether or not a contested interaction is authoritatively considered rape comes down to whose meaning wins. If sexuality is relational, specifically if it is a power relation of gender, consent is a communication under conditions of inequality. It transpires somewhere between what the woman actually wanted, what she was able to express about what she wanted, and what the man comprehended she wanted. ...

Whether the law calls this coerced consent or defense of mistaken belief in consent, the more the sexual violation of women is routine, the more pornography exists in the world the more legitimately, the more beliefs equating sexuality with violation become reasonable, and the more honestly women can be defined in terms of their fuckability. It would be comparatively simple if the legal problem were limited to avoiding retroactive falsification of the accused's state of mind. Surely there are incentives to lie. The deeper problem is the rape law's assumption that a single, objective state of affairs existed, one that merely needs to be determined by evidence, when so many rapes involve honest men and violated women. When the reality is split, is the woman raped but not by a rapist? Under these conditions, the law is designed to conclude that a rape did not occur. To attempt to solve this problem by adopting reasonable belief as a standard without asking, on a substantive social basis, to whom the belief is reasonable and why—meaning, what conditions make it reasonable—is one sided: male-sided.[14] What is it reasonable for a man to believe concerning a woman's desire for sex when heterosexuality is compulsory?

What is it reasonable for a man (accused or juror) to believe concerning a woman's consent when he has been viewing positive-outcome-rape pornography? The one whose subjectivity becomes the objectivity of "what happened" is a matter of social meaning, that is, a matter of sexual politics. One-sidedly erasing women's violation or dissolving presumptions into the subjectivity of either side are the alternatives dictated by the terms of the object/subject split, respectively. These alternatives will only retrace that split to women's detriment until its terms are confronted as gendered to the ground.

NOTES

[1]One component of Sec. 213.0 of the Model Penal Code (Philadelphia: American Law Institute, 1980) defines rape as sexual intercourse with a female not the wife of the perpetrator, 1, "with some penetration however slight." Most states follow.

[2]In the manner of many socialist feminist adaptations of Marxian categories to women's situation, to analyze sexuality as property short-circuits analysis of rape as male sexuality, and presumes rather than develops links between sex and class. Concepts of property need to be rethought in light of sexuality as a form of objectification. In some ways, for women legally to be considered property would be an improvement, although it is not recommended.

[3]For contrast between the perspectives of the victims and the courts, see *Rusk v. State*, 43 Md. App. 476, (Md. Ct. Spec. App. 1979) (*en banc*), rev'd, 289 Md. 230, (1981);…

[4]Susan Brownmiller, *Against Our Will: Men, Women, and Rape* (New York: Simon and Schuster, 1975): 15.

[5]Diana E. H. Russell, *The Politics of Rape: The Victim's Perspective* (New York: Stein and Day, 1977); Andrea Medea and Kathleen Thompson, *Against Rape* (New York: Farrar, Straus and Giroux, 1974); Lorenne M.G. Clark and Debra Lewis, *Rape: The Price of Coercive Sexuality* (Toronto: Women's Press, 1977); Susan Griffin, "Rape: The All-American Crime," *Ramparts*, September 1971: 26–35.

[6]Pamela Foa, "What's Wrong with Rape" in *Feminism and Philosophy*, eds. Mary Vetterling-Braggin, Frederick A. Elliston, and Jane English (Totowa, N.J.: Littlefield, Adams, 1977): 347–359; Michael Davis, "What's So Bad about Rape?" (Paper presented at the annual meeting of the Academy of Criminal Justice Sciences, Louisville, KY, March 1982). "Since we would not want to say that there is anything morally wrong with sexual intercourse *per se*, we conclude that the wrongness of rape rests with the matter of the woman's consent"; Carolyn M. Shafer and Marilyn Frye, "Rape and Respect," in Vetterling-Braggin, Elliston, and English, *Feminism and Philosophy*: 334. "Sexual contact is not inherently harmful, insulting or provoking. Indeed, ordinarily it is something of which we are quite fond. The difference is [that] ordinary sexual intercourse is more or less consented to while rape is not"; Davis, "What's So Bad?": 12.

[7]See *State v. Alston*, 310 N.C. 399 (1984) and discussion in Susan Estrich, *Real Rape* (Cambridge: Harvard University Press, 1987): 60–62.

[8]Note, "Forcible and Statutory Rape: An Exploration of the Operation and Objectives of the Consent Standard," 62 *Yale Law Journal* 55 (1952).

[9]*People v. Liberta*, 64 N.Y. 2d 152, (1984) (marital rape recognized, contrary precedents discussed). For a summary of the current state of the marital exemption, see Joanne Schulman, "State-by-State Information on Marital Rape Exemption Laws," in Diana E.H. Russell, *Rape in Marriage* (New York: Macmillan, 1982): 375–338;...

[10]Diana E. H. Russell and Nancy Howell, "The Prevalence of Rape in the United States Revisited," *Signs: Journal of Women in Culture and Society* 8 (Summer 1983): 668–695; and D. Russell, *The Secret Trauma: Incestuous Abuse of Women and Girls* (New York: Basic Books, 1986).

[11]Pauline Bart found that women were more likely to be raped—that is, less able to stop a rape in progress—when they knew their assailant, particularly when they had a prior or current sexual relationship; "A Study of Women Who Both Were Raped and Avoided Rape," *Journal of Social Issues* 37(1981): 132....

[12]See Carol Pateman, "Women and Consent," *Political Theory* 8 (May 1980): 149–168: "Consent as ideology cannot be distinguished from habitual acquiescence, assent, silent dissent, submission, or even enforced submission. Unless refusal of consent or withdrawal of consent are real possibilities, we can no longer speak of 'consent' in any genuine sense.... Women exemplify the individuals whom consent theorists declared are incapable of consenting. Yet, simultaneously, women have been presented as always consenting, and their explicit non-consent has been treated as irrelevant or has been reinterpreted as 'consent'" (150).

[13]See *Director of Public Prosecutions v. Morgan*, 2 All E.R.H.L. 347 (1975) [England]; *Pappajohn v. The Queen*, III D.L.R. 3d I (1980) [Canada]; *People v. Mayberry*, 542 P.2d 1337 (Cal. 1975).

[14]Estrich has this problem in *Real Rape*.

DATE RAPE: A FEMINIST ANALYSIS

Lois Pineau

The feminist recognition that dominant ideologies reinforce conceptual frameworks that serve patriarchal interests lies behind what must now be seen as a revolution in political analysis, one which for the first time approaches the problems that women face from a woman's point of view. One of those problems is the ongoing difficulty of dealing with a society that practices and condones violence against women. This is particularly the case with date rape.

Date rape is nonaggravated sexual assault, nonconsensual sex that does not involve physical injury, or the explicit threat of physical injury. But because it does not involve physical injury, and because physical injury is often the only criterion that is accepted as evidence that the *actus reas* is nonconsensual, what is really sexual assault is often mistaken for seduction. The replacement of the old rape laws with the new laws on sexual assault have done nothing to resolve this problem.

Rape, defined as nonconsensual sex, usually involving penetration by a man of a woman who is not his wife, has been replaced in some criminal codes with the charge of sexual assault. This has the advantage both of extending the range of possible victims of sexual assault, the manner in which people can be assaulted, and replacing a crime which is exclusive of consent with one for which consent is a defence. But while the consent of a woman is now consistent with the conviction of her assailant in cases of aggravated assault, nonaggravated sexual assault is still distinguished from normal sex solely by the fact that it is not consented to. Thus the question of whether someone has consented to a sexual encounter is still important, and the criteria for consent continues to be the central concern of discourse on sexual assault.

However, if a man is to be convicted, it does not suffice to establish that the *actus reas* was nonconsensual. In order to be guilty of sexual assault a man must have the requisite *mens rea*, that is, he must either have believed that his victim did not consent or that she was probably not consenting. In many common law jurisdictions, a man who sincerely believes that a woman consented to a sexual encounter is deemed to lack the required *mens rea*, even though the woman did not consent and even though his belief is not reasonable. Recently, strong dissenting voices have been raised against the sincerity condition, and the argument made that *mens rea* be defeated only if the defendant has a reasonable belief that the plaintiff consented. The introduction of legislation which excludes "honest belief" (unreasonable sincere belief) as a defence, will certainly help to provide women with greater protection against violence. But while this will be an important step forward, the question of what constitutes a reasonable belief, the problem of evidence when rapists lie, and the problem of the entrenched attitudes of the predominantly male police, judges, lawyers, and jurists who handle sexual assault cases remain.

The criteria for *mens rea*, for the reasonableness of belief, and for consent are closely related. For although a man's sincere belief in the consent of his victim may be sufficient to defeat *mens rea*, the court is less likely to believe his belief is sincere if his belief is unreasonable. If his belief is reasonable, they are more likely to believe in the sincerity of his belief. But evidence of the reasonableness of his belief is also evidence that consent really did take place. For the very things that make it reasonable for *him* to believe that the defendant consented are often the very things that incline the court to believe that she consented. What is often missing is the voice of the woman herself, an account of what it would be reasonable for *her* to agree to, that is to say, an account of what is reasonable from her standpoint.

Thus, what is presented as reasonable has repercussions for four separate but related concerns: (1) the question of whether a man's belief in a woman's consent was reasonable; (2) the problem of whether it is reasonable to attribute *mens rea* to him; (3) the question of what could count as reasonable from the woman's point of view; (4) the question of what is reasonable from the court's point of view. These repercussions are of the utmost practical concern. In a culture which contains an incidence of sexual assault verging on epidemic, a criterion of reasonableness which regards mere submission as consent fails to offer persons vulnerable to those assaults adequate protection.

The following statements by self-confessed date-rapists reveal how our lack of a solution for dealing with date rape protects rapists by failing to provide their victims with legal recourse:

> All of my rapes have been involved in a dating situation where I've been out with a woman I know.... I wouldn't take no for an answer. I think it had something to do with my acceptance of rejection. I had low self-esteem and not much self-confidence and when I was rejected for something which I considered to be rightly mine, I became angry and I went ahead anyway....[1]

> When I did date, when I was younger, I would pick up a girl and if she didn't come across I would threaten her or slap her face then tell her she was going to fuck—that was it. But that's because I didn't want to waste time with any come-ons. It took too much time. I wasn't interested because I didn't like them as people anyway, and I just went with them just to get laid. Just to say that I laid them.[2]

There is, at this time, nothing to protect women from this kind of unscrupulous victimization. A woman on a casual date with a virtual stranger has almost no chance of bringing a complaint of sexual assault before the courts. One reason for this is the prevailing criterion for consent. According to this criterion, consent is implied unless some emphatic episodic sign of resistance occurred, and its occurrence can be established. But if no episodic act occurred, or if it did occur, and the defendant claims that it did not, or if the defendant threatened the plaintiff but will not admit it in court, it is almost impossible to find any evidence that would support the plaintiff's word against the defendant. This difficulty is exacerbated by suspicion on the part of the courts, police, and legal educators that even where an act of resistance occurs, this act should not be interpreted as a withholding of consent, and this suspicion is especially upheld where the accused is a man who is known to the female plaintiff.

...Thus while, in principle, a firm unambiguous stand or a healthy show of temper ought to be sufficient, if established, to show nonconsent, in practice the forceful overriding of such a stance is apt to be taken as an indication that the resistance was not seriously intended, and that the seduction had succeeded. The consequence of this is that it is almost impossible to establish the defendant's guilt beyond a reasonable doubt.

Thus, on the one hand, we have a situation in which women are vulnerable to the most exploitative tactics at the hands of men who are known to them. On the other hand, almost nothing will count as evidence of their being assaulted, including their having taken an emphatic stance in withholding their consent. The new laws have done almost nothing to change this situation. Yet clearly some solution must be sought. Moreover, the road to that solution presents itself clearly enough as a need for a reformulation of the criterion of consent. It is patent that a criterion that collapses whenever the crime itself succeeds will not suffice.

The purpose of this paper is to develop such a criterion, and I propose to do so by grounding this criterion in a conception of the "reasonable." Part of the strength of the present criterion for consent lies in the belief that it is reasonable for women to agree to the kind of sex involved in "date rape," or that it is reasonable for men to think that they have agreed. My argument is that it is not reasonable for women to consent to that kind of sex, and that there are, furthermore, no grounds for thinking that it is reasonable. Since what we want to know is when a woman has consented, and since standards for consent are based on the presumed choices of reasonable agents, it is what is reasonable from a woman's point of view that must provide the principal delineation of a criterion of consent that is capable of representing a woman's willing behavior. Developing this line of reasoning further, I will argue the kind of sex to which it would be reasonable for women to consent suggests a criterion of consent that would bring the kind of sex involved in date rape well within the realm of sexual assault.

THE PROBLEM OF THE CRITERION

The reasoning that underlies the present criterion of consent is entangled in a number of mutually supportive mythologies which see sexual assault as masterful seduction, and silent submission as sexual enjoyment. Because the pervading ideology has so much informed our conceptualization of sexual interaction, it is extraordinarily difficult for us to distinguish between assault and seduction, submission and enjoyment, or so we imagine. At the same time, this failure to distinguish has given rise to a network of rationalizations that support the conflation of assault with seduction, submission with enjoyment. I therefore want to begin my argument by providing an example which shows both why it is so difficult to make this distinction, and that it exists. Later, I will identify and attempt to unravel the lines of reasoning that reinforce this difficulty.

The woman I have in mind agrees to see someone because she feels an initial attraction to him and believes that he feels the same way about her. She goes out with him in the hope that there will be mutual enjoyment and, in the course of the day or evening, an increase of mutual interest. Unfortunately, these hopes of *mutual* and *reciprocal* interest are not realized. We do not know how much interest she has in him by the end of their time together, but whatever her feelings she comes under pressure to have sex with him, and she does not want to have the kind of sex he wants. She may desire to hold hands and kiss, to engage in more intense caresses or in some form of foreplay, or she may not want to be touched. She may have religious reservations, concerns about pregnancy or disease, a disinclination to be just another conquest. She may be engaged in a seduction program of her own which sees abstaining from sexual activity as a means of building an important emotional bond. She feels she is desirable to him, and she knows, and he knows that he will have sex with her if he can. And while she feels she does not owe him anything, and that it is her prerogative to refuse him, this feeling is partly a defensive reaction against a deeply held belief that if he is in need, she should provide. If she buys into the myth of insistent male sexuality, she may feel he is suffering from sexual frustration and that she is largely to blame.

We do not know how much he desires her, but we do know that his desire for erotic satisfaction can hardly be separated from his desire for conquest. He feels no dating obligation, but has a strong commitment to scoring. He uses the myth of "so hard to control" male desire as a rhetorical tactic, telling her how frustrated she will leave him. He becomes overbearing. She resists, voicing her disinclination. He alternates between telling her how desirable she is and taking a hostile stance, charging her with misleading him, accusing her of wanting him and being coy, in short of being deceitful, all the time engaging in rather aggressive body contact. It is late at night, she is tired and a bit queasy from too many drinks, and he is reaffirming her suspicion that perhaps she has misled him. She is having trouble disengaging his body from hers, and wishes he would just go away. She does not adopt a strident angry stance, partly because she thinks he is acting normally and does not deserve it, partly because she feels she is partly to blame, and partly because there is always the danger that her anger will make him angry, possibly violent. It seems that the only thing to do, given his aggression, and her queasy fatigue, is to go along with him and get it over with, but this decision is so entangled with the events in process it is hard to know if it is not simply a recognition of what is actually happening. She finds the whole encounter a thoroughly disagreeable experience, but he does not take any notice, and would not have changed course if he had. He congratulates himself on his sexual prowess, and is confirmed in his opinion that aggressive tactics pay off. Later she feels that she has been raped, but paradoxically tells herself that she let herself be raped.

The paradoxical feelings of the woman in our example indicate her awareness that what she feels about the incident stands in contradiction to the prevailing cultural assessment of it. She knows that she did not want to have sex with her date. She is not so sure, however, about how much her own desires count, and she is uncertain that she has made her desires clear. Her uncertainty is reinforced by the cultural reading of this incident as an ordinary seduction.

As for us, we assume that the woman did not want to have sex, but just like her, we are unsure whether her mere reluctance, in the presence of high-pressure tactics, constitutes nonconsent. We suspect that submission to an overbearing and insensitive lout is no way to go about attaining sexual enjoyment, and we further suspect that he felt no compunction about providing it, so that on the face of it, from the outside looking in, it looks like a pretty unreasonable proposition for her.

Let us look at this reasoning more closely. Assume that she was not attracted to the kind of sex offered by the sort of person offering it. Then it would be *prima facie* unreasonable for her to agree to have sex, unreasonable, that is, unless she were offered some payoff for her stoic endurance, money perhaps, or tickets to the opera. The reason is that in sexual matters, agreement is closely connected to attraction. Thus, where the presumption is that she was not attracted, we should at the same time presume that she did not consent. Hence, the burden of proof should be on her alleged assailant to show that she had good reasons for consenting to an unattractive proposition.

This is not, however, the way such situations are interpreted. In the unlikely event that the example I have described should come before the courts, there is little doubt that the law would interpret the woman's eventual acquiescence or "going along with" the sexual encounter as consent. But along with this interpretation would go the implicit understanding that she had consented because, when all was said and done, when the "token" resistances to the "masterful advances" had been made, she had wanted to after all. Once the courts have constructed this interpretation, they are then forced to conjure up some horror story of feminine revenge in order to explain why she should bring charges against her "seducer."

In the even more unlikely event that the courts agreed that the woman had not consented to the above encounter, there is little chance that her assailant would be convicted of sexual assault. The belief that the man's aggressive tactics are a normal part of seduction means that *mens rea* cannot be established. Her eventual "going along" with his advances constitutes reasonable grounds for his believing in her consent. These "reasonable" grounds attest to the sincerity of his belief in her consent. ...

The position of the courts is supported by the widespread belief that male aggression and female reluctance are normal parts of seduction. Given their acceptance of this model, the logic of their response must be respected. For if sexual aggression is a part of ordinary seduction, then it cannot be inconsistent with the legitimate consent of the person allegedly seduced by this means. And if it is normal for a woman to be reluctant, then this reluctance must be consistent with her consent as well. The position of the courts is not inconsistent just so long as they allow that some sort of protest on the part of a woman counts as a refusal. As we have seen, however, it frequently happens that no sort of a protest would count as a refusal. Moreover, if no sort of protest, or at least if precious few count, then the failure to register these protests will amount to "asking for it," it will amount, in other words, to agreeing....

RAPE MYTHS

The belief that the natural aggression of men and the natural reluctance of women somehow make date rape understandable, underlies a number of prevalent myths about rape and human sexuality. These beliefs maintain their force partly on account of a logical compulsion exercised by them at an unconscious level. The only way of refuting them effectively is to excavate the logical propositions involved, and to expose their misapplication to the situations to which they have been applied. In what follows, I propose to excavate the logical support for popular attitudes that are tolerant of date rape. These myths are not just popular, however, but often emerge in the arguments of judges who acquit date-rapists and policemen who refuse to lay charges.

The claim that the victim provoked a sexual incident, that "she asked for it," is by far the most common defence given by men who are accused of sexual assault. Feminists, rightly incensed by this response, often treat it as beneath contempt, singling out the defence as an argument against it....

The least sophisticated of the "she asked for it" rationales and, in a sense, the easiest to deal with, appeals to an injunction against sexually provocative behavior on the part of women. If women should not be sexually provocative, then, from this standpoint, a woman who is sexually provocative deserves to suffer the consequences. Now, it will not do to respond that women get raped even when they are not sexually provocative, or that it is men who get to interpret (unfairly) what counts as sexually provocative. The question should be: Why shouldn't a woman be sexually provocative? Why should this behavior warrant any kind of aggressive response whatsoever?

Attempts to explain that women have a right to behave in sexually provocative ways without suffering dire consequences still meet with surprisingly tough resistance. Even people who find nothing wrong or sinful with sex itself, in any of its forms, tend to suppose that women must not behave sexually unless they are prepared to carry through on some fuller course of sexual interaction. The logic of this response seems to be that at some point a woman's behavior commits her to following through on the full course of a sexual encounter as it is defined by her assailant. At some point she has made an agreement, or formed a contract, and once that is done, her contractor is entitled to demand that she satisfy the terms of that contract. Thus, this view about sexual responsibility and desert is supported by other assumptions about contracts and agreement. But we do not normally suppose that casual, nonverbal behavior generates agreements. Nor do we normally grant private persons the right to enforce contracts. What rationale would support our conclusion in this case?

The rationale, I believe, comes in the form of a belief in the especially insistent nature of male sexuality, an insistence which lies at the root of natural male aggression, and which is extremely difficult, perhaps impossible, to contain. At a certain point in the arousal process, it is thought, a man's rational will gives way to the prerogatives of nature. His sexual need can and does reach a point where it is uncontrollable, and his natural masculine aggression kicks in to assure that this need is met. Women, however, are naturally more contained and so it is their responsibility not to provoke the irrational in the male. If they do go so far as that, they have both failed in their responsibilities, and subjected themselves to the inevitable. One does not go into the lion's cage and expect not to be eaten. Natural feminine reluctance, it is thought, is no protection against a sexually aroused male.

...The assumption that women both want to indulge sexually, and are inclined to sacrifice this desire for higher ends, gives rise to the myth that they want to be raped. After all, does not rape give them the sexual enjoyment they *really* want, at the same time that it relieves them of the responsibility for admitting to and acting upon what they want? And how then can we blame men, who have been socialized to be aggressively seductive precisely for the purpose of overriding female reserve? If we find fault at all, we are inclined to cast our suspicions on the motives of the woman. For it is on her that the contradictory roles of sexual desirer and sexual denier has been placed. Our awareness of the contradiction expected of her makes us suspect her honesty....

But if women really want sexual pleasure, what inclines us to think that they will get it through rape? This conclusion logically requires a theory about the dynamics of sexual pleasure that sees that pleasure as an emergent property of overwhelming male insistence. For the assumption that a raped female experiences sexual pleasure implies that the person who rapes her knows how to cause that pleasure independently of any information she might convey on that point. Since her ongoing protest is inconsistent with requests to be touched in particular ways in particular places, to have more of this and less of that, then we must believe that the person who touches her knows these particular ways and places instinctively, without any directives from her....

In sum, the belief that women should not be sexually provocative is logically linked to several other beliefs, some normative, some empirical. The normative beliefs are (1) that people should keep the agreements they make; (2) that sexually provocative behaviour, taken beyond a certain point, generates agreements; (3) that the peculiar nature of male and female sexuality places such agreements in a special category, one in which the possibility of retracting an agreement is ruled out, or at least made highly unlikely; and (4) that women are not to be trusted, in sexual matters at least. The empirical belief which turns out to be false is that male sexuality is not subject to rational and moral control.

DISPELLING THE MYTHS

The "she asked for it" justification of sexual assault incorporates a conception of a contract that would be difficult to defend in any other context, and the presumptions about human sexuality which function to reinforce sympathies rooted in the contractual notion of just deserts are not supported by empirical research.

The belief that a woman generates some sort of contractual obligation whenever her behavior is interpreted as seductive is the most indefensible part of the mythology of rape. In law, contracts are not legitimate just because a promise has been made. In particular, the use of pressure tactics to extract agreement is frowned upon. Normally, an agreement is upheld only if the contractors were clear on what they were getting into, and had sufficient time to reflect on the wisdom of their doing so. Either there must be a clear tradition in which the expectations involved in the contract are fairly well known (marriage), or there must be an explicit written agreement concerning the exact terms of the contract and the expectations of the persons involved. But whatever the terms of a contract, there is no private right to enforce it. So if I make a contract with you on which I renege, the only permissible recourse for you is through due legal process....

Thus, even if we assume that a woman has initially agreed to an encounter, her agreement does not automatically make all subsequent sexual activity to which she submits legitimate. If during coitus a woman should experience pain, be suddenly overcome with guilt or fear of pregnancy, or simply lose her initial desire, those are good reasons for her to change her mind. Having changed her mind, neither her partner nor the state has any right to force her to continue. But then, if she is forced to continue, she is assaulted. Thus establishing that consent occurred at a particular point during a sexual encounter should not conclusively establish the legitimacy of the encounter. What is needed is a reading of whether she agreed throughout the encounter.

If the "she asked for it" contractual view of sexual interchange has any validity, it is because there is a point at which there is no stopping a sexual encounter, a point at which that encounter becomes the inexorable outcome of the unfolding of natural events. If a sexual encounter is like a slide on which I cannot stop halfway down, it will be relevant whether I enter the slide of my own free will, or am pushed.

But there is no evidence that the entire sexual act is like a slide. While there may be a few seconds in the "plateau" period just prior to orgasm in which people are "swept" away by sexual feelings to the point where we could justifiably understand their lack of heed for the comfort of their partner, the greater part of a sexual encounter comes well within the bounds of morally responsible control of our own actions. Indeed, the available evidence shows that most of the activity involved in sex has to do with building the requisite level of desire, a task that involves the proper use of foreplay, the possibility of which implies control over the form that foreplay will take. Modern sexual therapy assumes that such control is universally accessible, and so far there has been no reason to question that assumption. Sexologists are unanimous, moreover, in holding that much sexual enjoyment requires an atmosphere of comfort and communication, a minimum of pressure, and an ongoing checkup on one's partner's state. They maintain that different people have different predilections, and that what is pleasurable for one person is very often anathema to another. These findings show that the way to achieve sexual pleasure, at any time at all, let alone with a casual acquaintance, decidedly does not involve overriding the other person's express reservations and providing them with just any kind of sexual stimulus.[3] And while we do not want to allow science and technology a voice in which the voices of particular women are drowned, in this case science seems to concur with women's perception that aggressive incommunicative sex is not what they want. But if science and the voice of women concur, if aggressive seduction does not lead to good sex, if women do not like it or want it, then it is not rational to think that they would agree to it. Where such sex takes place, it is therefore rational to presume that the sex was not consensual.

The myth that women like to be raped is closely connected, as we have seen, to doubt about their honesty in sexual matters, and this suspicion is exploited by defence lawyers when sexual assault cases make it to the courtroom. It is an unfortunate consequence of the presumption of innocence that rape victims who end up in court frequently find that it is they who are on trial. For if the defendant is innocent, then either he did not intend to do what he was accused of, or the plaintiff is mistaken about his identity, or she is lying. Often the last alternative is the only plausible defence, and as a result, the plaintiff's word seldom goes unquestioned. Women are frequently accused of having made a false accusation, either as a defensive mechanism for dealing with guilt and shame, or out of a desire for revenge.

Now there is no point in denying the possibility of false accusation, though there are probably better ways of seeking revenge on a man than accusing him of rape. However, we can now establish a logical connection between the evidence that a woman was subjected to high-pressure, aggressive "seduction" tactics, and her claim that she did not consent to that encounter. Where the kind of encounter is not the sort to which it would be reasonable to consent, there is a logical presumption that a woman who claims that she did not consent is telling the truth. Where the kind of sex involved is not the sort of sex we would expect a woman to like, the burden of proof should not be on the woman to show that she did not consent, but on the defendant to show that contrary to every reasonable expectation she did consent. The defendant should be required to convince the court that the plaintiff persuaded him to have sex with her even though there are no visible reasons why she should....

COMMUNICATIVE SEXUALITY: REINTERPRETING THE KANTIAN IMPERATIVE

...In thinking about sex, we must keep in mind its sensual ends, and the facts show that aggressive, high-pressure sex contradicts those ends. Consensual sex in dating situations is presumed to aim at mutual enjoyment. It may not always do this, and when it does, it might not always succeed. There is no logical incompatibility between wanting to continue a sexual encounter, and failing to derive sexual pleasure from it.

But it seems to me that there is a presumption in favor of the connection between sex and sexual enjoyment, and that if a man wants to be sure that he is not forcing himself on a woman, he has an obligation either to ensure that the encounter really is mutually enjoyable, or to know the reasons why she would want to continue the encounter in spite of her lack of enjoyment. A closer investigation of the nature of this obligation will enable us to construct a more rational and a more plausible norm of sexual conduct.

Onora O'Neill has argued that in intimate situations we have an obligation to take the ends of others as our own, and to promote those ends in a nonmanipulative and nonpaternalistic manner.[4] Now, it seems that in honest sexual encounters just this is required. Assuming that each person enters the encounter in order to seek sexual satisfaction, each person engaging in the encounter has an obligation to help the other seek his or her ends. To do otherwise is to risk acting in opposition to what the other desires, and hence to risk acting without the other's consent.

But the obligation to promote the sexual ends of one's partner implies the obligation to know what those ends are, and also the obligation to know how those ends are attained. Thus the problem comes down to a problem of epistemic responsibility, the responsibility to know. The solution, in my view, lies in the practice of a communicative sexuality, one which combines the appropriate knowledge of the other with respect for the dialectics of desire.

So let us, for a moment, conceive of sexual interaction on a communicative rather than a contractual model. Let us look at it the way I think it should be looked at, as if it were a proper conversation rather than an offer from the Mafia. ...

The communicative interaction involved in conversation is concerned with a good deal more than didactic content and argument. Good conversationalists are intuitive, sympathetic, and charitable. Intuition and charity aid the conversationalist in her effort to interpret the words of the other correctly, and sympathy enables her to enter into the other's point of view. Her sensitivity alerts her to the tone of the exchange. Has her point been taken good-humoredly or resentfully? Aggressively delivered responses are taken as a sign that *ad hominems* are at work, and that the respondent's self-worth has been called into question. Good conversationalists will know to suspend further discussion until this sense of self-worth has been reestablished. Angry responses, resentful responses, bored responses, even overenthusiastic responses require that the emotional ground be cleared before the discussion be continued. ...

Just as communicative conversationalists are concerned with more than didactic content, persons engaged in communicative sexuality will be concerned with more than achieving coitus. They will be sensitive to the responses of their partners. They will, like good conversationalists, be intuitive, sympathetic, and charitable. Intuition will help them to interpret their partner's responses; sympathy will enable them to share what their partner is feeling; charity will enable them to care. Communicative sexual partners will not overwhelm each other with the barrage of their own desires. They will treat negative, bored, or angry responses as a sign that the erotic ground needs to be either cleared or abandoned. Their concern with fostering the desire of the other must involve an ongoing state of alertness in interpreting her responses.

Just as a conversationalist's prime concern is for the mutuality of the discussion, a person engaged in communicative sexuality will be most concerned with the mutuality of desire. As such, both will put into practice a regard for their respondent that is guaranteed no place in the contractual language of rights, duties, and consent. The dialectics of both activities reflect the dialectics of desire insofar as each person's interest in continuing is contingent upon the other person wishing to do so too, and each person's interest is as much fueled by the other's interest as it is by her own. Each respects the subjectivity of the other not just by avoiding treading on it, but by fostering and protecting the quality of that subjectivity. Indeed, the requirement to avoid treading on the subjectivity of the other entails the obligation to respect the dialectics of desire.[5] For in intimacy there is no passing by on the other side. To be intimate just is to open up in emotional and personal ways, to share personal knowledge, and to be receptive to the openness of the other. ...

CULTURAL PRESUMPTIONS

...[T]here is a...conceptual relation between the kind of activity that a date is, and the sort of moral practice which it requires...this connection is easily established once we recognize the cultural presumption that dating is a gesture of friendship and regard. Traditionally, the decision to date indicates that two people have an initial attraction to each other, that they are disposed to like each other, and look forward to enjoying each other's company. Dating derives its implicit meaning from this tradition. It retains this meaning unless other aims are explicitly stated, and even then it may not be possible to alienate this meaning. It is a rare woman who will not spurn a man who states explicitly, right at the onset, that he wants to go out with her solely on the condition that he have sexual intercourse with her at the end of the evening, and that he has no interest in her company apart from gaining that end, and no concern for mutual satisfaction.

...But if a date is more like a friendship than a business contract, then clearly, respect for the dialectics of desire is incompatible with the sort of sexual pressure that is inclined to end in date rape. And clearly, also, a conquest mentality which exploits a situation of trust and respect for purely selfish ends is morally pernicious....

But now that we know what communicative sexuality is, and that it is morally required, and that it is the only feasible means to mutual sexual enjoyment, why not take this model as the norm of what is reasonable in sexual interaction. The evidence of sexologists strongly indicates that women whose partners are aggressively uncommunicative have little chance of experiencing sexual pleasure. But it is not reasonable for women to consent to what they have little chance of enjoying. Hence it is not reasonable for women to consent to aggressive noncommunicative sex.

Nor can we reasonably suppose that women have consented to sexual encounters which we know and they know they do not find enjoyable. With the communicative model as the norm, the aggressive contractual model should strike us as a model of deviant sexuality, and sexual encounters patterned on that model should strike us as encounters to which *prima facie* no one would reasonably agree. But if acquiescence to an encounter counts as consent only if the acquiescence is reasonable, something to which a reasonable person, in full possession of knowledge relevant to the encounter, would agree, then acquiescence to aggressive noncommunicative sex is not reasonable. Hence, acquiescence under such conditions should not count as consent.

Thus, where communicative sexuality does not occur, we lack the main ground for believing that the sex involved was consensual. Moreover, where a man does not engage in communicative sexuality, he acts either out of reckless disregard, or out of willful ignorance. For he cannot know, except through the practice of communicative sexuality, whether his partner has any sexual reason for continuing the encounter. And where she does not, he runs the risk of imposing on her what she is not willing to have. All that is needed then, in order to provide women with legal protection from "date rape" is to make both reckless indifference and willful ignorance a sufficient condition of *mens rea,* and to make communicative sexuality the accepted norm of sex to which a reasonable woman would agree....

THE EPISTEMOLOGICAL IMPLICATIONS

Finding a proper criterion for consent is one problem, discovering what really happened, after the event when the only eyewitnesses give conflicting accounts, is another. But while there is no foolproof way of getting the unadulterated truth, it can make a significant difference to the outcome of a prosecution what sort of facts we are seeking. On the old model of aggressive seduction, we sought evidence of resistance. But on the new model of communicative sexuality, what we want is evidence of an ongoing positive and encouraging response on the part of the plaintiff. This new goal will require quite different tactics on the part of the cross-examiners and quite different expectations on the part of juries and judges. Where communicative sexuality is taken as the norm, and aggressive sexual tactics as a presumption against consent, the outcome for the example that I described above would be quite different. It would be regarded as sexual assault rather than seduction.

Let us then consider a date rape trial in which a man is cross-examined. He is asked whether he was presuming mutual sexual enjoyment. Suppose he answers in the negative. Then he would have to account for why he persisted in the face of her voiced reluctance. He cannot give as an excuse that he thought she liked it, because he believes that she did not. If he thought that she had consented even though she did not like it, then it seems to me that the burden of proof would lie with him to say why it was reasonable to think this. Clearly her initial resistance, her presumed lack of enjoyment, and the pressure tactics involved in getting her to "go along" would not support a reasonable belief in consent, and his persisting in the face of her dissatisfaction would surely cast doubt on the sincerity of his belief in her consent.

But suppose he answers in the affirmative. Then the cross-examiner would not have to rely on the old criteria for non-consent. He would not have to show either that she had resisted him, or that she was in a fearful or intimidated state of mind. Instead he could use a communicative model of sexuality to discover how much respect there had been for the dialectics of desire. Did he ask her what she liked? If she was using contraceptives? If he should? What tone of voice did he use? How did she answer? Did she make any demands? Did she ask for penetration? How was that desire conveyed? Did he ever let up the pressure long enough to see if she was really that interested? Did he ask her which position she preferred? Assuming that the defendant does not perjure himself, he would lack satisfactory answers to these questions. But even where the defendant did lie, a skilled cross-examiner who was willing to go into detail could probably establish easily enough when the interaction had not been communicative. It is extraordinarily difficult to keep up a consistent story when you are not telling the truth.

On the new criterion, the cross-examination focuses on the communicative nature of the ongoing encounter, and the communicative nature of an encounter is much easier to establish than the occurrence of an episodic act of resistance. For one thing, it requires that a fairly long yet consistent story be told, and this enables us to assess the plausibility of the competing claims in light of a wider collection of relevant data. Secondly, in making noncommunicative sex the primary indicator of coercive sex, it provides us with a criterion for distinguishing consensual sadomasochism from brutality. For even if a couple agree to sadomasochistic sex, bondage and whippings and the rest of it, the court has a right to require that there be a system of signals whereby each partner can convey to the other whether she has had enough.[6] Thirdly, the use of a new criterion of communicative sexuality would enable us to introduce a new category of nonaggravated sexual assault, which would not necessarily carry a heavy sentence, but which would nonetheless provide an effective recourse against "date rape."

CONCLUSION

In sum, using communicative sexuality as a model of normal sex has several advantages over the "aggressive-acquiescence" model of seduction. The new model ties the presumption that consensual sex takes place in the expectation of mutual desire much more closely to the facts about how that desire actually functions. Where communicative sex does not occur, this establishes a presumption that there was no consent. The importance of this presumption is that we are able, in criminal proceedings, to shift the burden of proof from the plaintiff, who on the contractual model must show that she resisted or was threatened, to the defendant, who must then give some reason why she should consent after all. The communicative model of sexuality also enables us to give a different conceptual content to the concept of consent. It sees consent as something more like an ongoing cooperation than the one-shot agreement which we are inclined to see it as on the contractual model....

But most importantly, the communicative model of normal sexuality gives us a handle on a solution to the problem of date rape. If noncommunicative sexuality establishes a presumption of nonconsent, then, where there are no overriding reasons for thinking that consent occurred, we have a criterion for a category of sexual assault that does not require evidence of physical violence or threat. If we are serious about date rape, then the next step is to take this criterion as objective grounds for establishing that a date rape has occurred. The proper legislation is the shortest route to establishing this criterion....

NOTES

[1]*Why Men Rape*, Sylvia Levine and Joseph Loenig, eds. (Toronto: Macmillan, 1980): 83.

[2]*Ibid.*, 77.

[3]It is not just women who fail to find satisfaction in the "swept away" approach to sexual interaction. Studies of convicted rapists, and of conquest oriented men, indicate that men are frequently disappointed when they use this approach as well. In over half of aggravated sexual assaults, penetration fails because the man loses his erection. Those who do succeed invariably report that the sex experience was not enjoyable. This supports the prevailing view of sexologists that men depend on the positive response of their partners in order to fuel their own responsive mechanisms. See...*Why Men Rape*, eds. Sylvia Levine and Joseph Loenig (Toronto: Macmillan, 1980), or consult any recent manual on male sexuality.

[4]O'Neill. "Between Consenting Adults," *Philosophy and Public Affairs* 14, (1985): 252–277.

[5]The sort of relationship I have in mind exemplifies the "feminist" approach to ethics argued for by Nell Noddings in *Caring: A Feminine Approach to Ethics* (Berkeley: University of California Press, 1984). In particular, see her discussion of teaching as a "duality," 195.

[6]The Samois justification of sadomasochism rests on the claim that sadomasochistic practice can be communicative in this way. See *Coming To Power*, Samois (Boston: Alyson Publications, 1981).

DATE RAPE, SOCIAL CONVENTION, AND REASONABLE MISTAKES

Douglas N. Husak and George C. Thomas III

How is it possible for a man to make a mistake of fact about whether a woman consents to intercourse? Initially, the very idea seems implausible. While mistakes of fact surely occur in many situations, sexual intercourse has two qualities that distinguish it from most of these situations. First, in the typical situation, a woman has ample opportunity to make known her views about whether she wishes to engage in sexual intercourse. Second, sexual intercourse is an activity about which a person is unlikely to hold a casual opinion. A man may easily make a mistake about whether his companion wants to go to the movies or go out to eat, but it seems unlikely that he would make a mistake about whether she is withholding consent to have sex.

Nonetheless, most jurisdictions permit rape defendants to defend on the ground that they believed the victim consented to the intercourse. Our paper explores the question of how mistakes of fact about consent can occur, and how they should affect liability for rape. We will contend that

From Douglas N. Husak and George C. Thomas III, "Date Rape, Social Convention, and Reasonable Mistakes," *Law and Philosophy* 11: 95–126. Copyright © 1992, Kluwer Academic Publishers. Reprinted by permission of Kluwer Academic Publishers.

mistakes about consent should function as a defense to a charge of rape when they are reasonable. Our central thesis is that social conventions are crucial in distinguishing between reasonable and unreasonable beliefs about consent.…

RAPE, MISTAKE, AND *MENS REA*

Most crimes require proof of the actor's *mens rea* (guilty mind)…for our purposes *mens rea* means, roughly, that the actor must be at fault for his conduct.

Mistakes of fact are often relevant to fault, but the precise relationship depends on the type of fault required by the criminal offense. Some offenses, often called "specific intent" crimes, require proof of a particular mental state. Larceny, for example, requires an intent to permanently deprive the property owner of possession. If P takes Q's umbrella, mistakenly thinking it is his, P cannot have the intent to permanently deprive Q of her property. P would lack this intent whether or not anyone else would have made that mistake—that is, whether or not his mistake was reasonable.

But the defense of mistake of fact has traditionally been more narrowly circumscribed when the criminal offense does not require a particular mental state. Often unhelpfully called "general intent" crimes, these offenses typically permit only reasonable mistakes of fact to serve as a defense. In effect, courts have decided that if an actor should have known of the relevant conditions that made his act harmful, he should be punished as if he knew of these conditions. But if he was reasonably unaware of these conditions, then he is not at fault for the harm.…

Because rape requires proof that the intercourse was without the consent of the victim, the mistake-of-fact defense in a rape prosecution is almost always that the actor thought the victim had consented. But the appropriate fault standard to apply to these mistakes is not free from doubt. Rape statutes seldom specify a level of fault, suggesting that rape is either an offense that implicitly requires a particular type of fault, or a "general intent" crime that, typically, requires only negligence about consent.…

…American courts usually construe rape as a "general intent" offense. Thus, actors are liable for harmful consequences when they are negligent, that is, when they should have known of the relevant conditions that made their acts harmful. If the actor's mistake about consent to have sex was unreasonable—if he should have known she had not given consent—most American courts hold him guilty of rape. For this reason, a mistake of fact is a defense in rape prosecutions in most states only if it is reasonable.

Deciding how to treat unreasonable mistakes about consent to have sex is important not only for the fate of the negligent defendant. In addition, this decision has a profound impact on what it is possible to say about nonconsensual sex.... Most American courts implicitly presume that nonconsensual sex is indeed rape, although a man's reasonable mistake of fact about consent precludes holding him criminally liable. This approach has the advantage of distinguishing two questions: (1) has the victim been raped by the defendant; and (2) should the defendant be held criminally liable for his act?...

...[C]ases in which a defendant has made a sincere but unreasonable mistake about consent are extremely rare. Evidence that a belief about consent is unreasonable will almost always raise doubts that a defendant actually held that belief. In addition, on virtually any occasion in which the defendant's belief about consent is unreasonable, the victim will have expressed her unwillingness to have sex in one way or another. Her expression of nonconsent will lead almost anyone to at least consciously consider the risk that his victim is not consenting. A defendant who proceeds with sex after disregarding this risk is not negligent, but reckless.[1] Thus it is difficult to imagine a case in which a jury can be persuaded that a defendant has made an unreasonable mistake while unaware of the risk of this mistake.

For these reasons, the most interesting problem is not to decide whether defendants who have made an unreasonable mistake about consent should be liable for rape, but to understand how a mistake about consent could be reasonable. Part of our strategy in attempting to comprehend how a belief about consent could be reasonable is to consider cases in which a man is not mistaken. Situations in which his belief is false will probably share some important similarities with situations in which his belief is true, at least when his belief is reasonable. It seems unlikely that we can appreciate how reasonable misperceptions occur without understanding how persons even perceive matters correctly. In our view, too much literature about the nature of rape and how to avoid it neglects the related issue of how couples ever manage to engage in consensual sex....

THE ROLE OF SOCIAL CONVENTIONS

Suppose that a man believes that a woman has given her consent to sexual activity. What counts as a good reason to conclude that his belief is reasonable?...

...Suppose that a man is challenged to explain how he came to believe that a woman consented to sex who in fact did consent. Not just any kind of explanation would indicate that his belief is reasonable. What kind of explanation will suffice?

Perhaps progress in answering this question can be made by thinking about situations other than those involving sex in which people formulate beliefs about the presence or absence of consent. A cab driver believes that someone who enters his taxi agrees to pay for a ride after the passenger says simply, "Take me to the airport." A waiter believes that someone who sits in his restaurant agrees to pay for food after the customer says simply, "I'll have the chicken sandwich." How do the cab driver and waiter come to have these beliefs, and what answers to this question indicate that their beliefs are reasonable?

It is crucial to realize that these questions cannot be resolved *a priori*. No philosophical analyses of the nature of belief, consent, or reasonableness will suffice to answer them. Nothing about the behavior of the passenger or the customer inevitably requires that the driver or waiter will formulate a belief about their consent. And no conceptual analysis will demonstrate that any beliefs they formulate are reasonable or unreasonable. Instead, the answers to these questions are dependent on empirical data. Not just any empirical data will do. If the driver or waiter came to formulate their beliefs about the consent of the passenger or customer by consulting tea leaves, their beliefs would be unreasonable, even if they happen to be true. What empirical data can support the judgment that the beliefs of the driver and waiter are reasonable?

The empirical data on which the answers to these questions depend are data about social conventions. A social convention is a societal "norm which there is some presumption that one ought to conform to."[2] It is clear that the taxi driver would appeal to a convention in explaining why he believes that a passenger expresses his consent to pay for a ride simply by entering a taxi and being taken to the destination he requests. If the driver is pressed about why he has this belief, he will probably say something like: "That's just the way things are. That's how passengers express their agreements to pay. I've been driving for years, and I know how these things are done around here." In other words, his answer cites a social convention. This social convention helps to establish the reasonableness of his belief....

Conventions can change over time, and the conventions of other societies need not correspond to our own. Perhaps there are times and places where a person does not express an agreement to pay for a meal simply by asking for a particular selection on a menu. Clearly, persons do not express an agreement to pay for every service they request....

Exactly how a social convention helps to establish that a belief is reasonable is somewhat mysterious. Conventions are comprised of facts, but conclusions about reasonableness are at least partly judgments of value. There is a deep philosophical problem in understanding how a matter of fact can support a conclusion of value. However this mystery is solved, that a convention can help to establish the reasonableness of a belief seems plausible. Conventions are used to help establish that a belief is reasonable in a wide range of controversial legal disputes....

Indeed, it is hard to see how a number of beliefs could be shown to be reasonable without citing social conventions. We are at a loss to describe an alternative answer that the taxi driver or waiter could have provided that would help to establish the reasonableness of their beliefs about the consent of the passenger or customer....

As the percentage of people who engage in a particular pattern of behavior declines, it becomes more difficult to conclude that any belief about what that behavior expresses is reasonable. At some point, behavior would become so idiosyncratic that it could not be said to comprise a convention at all. Judgments about the reasonableness of a belief become more controversial to the extent that the behavior that gives rise to the belief lacks the universality of the taxi example.

If this conclusion is correct, anyone who is interested in the general problem of how beliefs are shown to be reasonable should be interested in understanding social conventions. Unfortunately, meaningful generalizations about social conventions are almost impossible to formulate, since very different conventions operate in different circumstances. For example, consider the question of whether an agreement is expressed by silence. In some circumstances, silence might indicate consent. Suppose that members of the board of directors of a corporation are asked in a meeting whether they have any objections to a proposal. If they are given a reasonable opportunity to reply, but remain silent, their silence is taken as an expression of their agreement. In other circumstances, silence does not indicate consent.... In still other circumstances, the conventions are unclear and still evolving.... Reasonable minds can and do differ about these issues....

If reasonableness is partly dependent on convention in the way we have suggested, it is crucial to understand the convention by which women express their agreements to sexual relations.... We will call it convention "WCS," to stand for "women's consent to have sex." We are apprehensive that the choice of a simple variable to represent such a complex phenomenon may be misleading. Yet a label is needed to refer to the social convention that describes how women tend to express their agreement to have sex....

SOCIAL CONVENTIONS ABOUT CONSENT TO HAVE SEX

We begin with more general questions about the social conventions involving courtship. Do women give nonexplicit encouragement to men in courtship settings not involving sexual intercourse? If so, how is this encouragement communicated, and what is the risk that a man will make a mistake of fact about whether he has been encouraged? Later we will proceed to the more narrow question of whether women give nonexplicit consent to sex and the attendant risks of mistake. By "nonexplicit," we mean both nonverbal and verbally indirect conduct.

No one should be surprised that the empirical evidence confirms that women give nonexplicit consent to such courtship rituals as whether they want to be approached by a particular man. Monica Moore and Diana Butler documented fifty-two "nonverbal solicitation behaviors" that women use in "social contexts such as singles' bars and the university snack bar."[3] These behaviors included "glancing, primping, smiling, laughing, nodding, kissing, requesting aid, touching, and caressing."[4] Moore and Butler concluded that in 90 percent of these cases, an observer in a social context could accurately predict from the woman's nonverbal behavior whether she would be approached by a man. Moreover, all of the women judged to be "approachable" based on their nonverbal conduct accepted at least one male invitation, and women judged not "approachable" received far fewer invitations. Thus not only could an external observer predict whether a male would approach, but the observer could also predict whether the woman would accept at least one invitation....

What matters is that women in fact engage in these behaviors, and that men typically respond in a way women find appropriate. When the male response is appropriate, no mistake has been made, and the social interaction is wholly consensual. But the possibility of mistake is always present. The women judged "approachable" in the Moore and Butler study did not accept all male invitations. Sometimes a man correctly perceived that the woman was interested in an invitation, but incorrectly perceived that she was interested in an invitation from him.

If women engage in nonverbal solicitation behaviors to induce men to invite them to dance in singles bars, they might use similar tactics to signal their interest in having sex. Reasonable misreadings of these behaviors could occur. Timothy Perper and David Weis concluded that women frequently exhibit what they call "proceptive" behaviors, that is, active behaviors designed to elicit an offer to have sex from a particular man.[5]...

Proceptive behaviors include explicit as well as nonexplicit signals, but fewer than one-quarter of the women who indicated their willingness to use proceptive strategies in the Perper and Weis study said they would ask the man to engage in sex. Sandra Byers and Kim Lewis similarly conclude that "women most commonly use nonverbal methods to give consent to sexual intercourse."[6] For example, 51 percent of the subjects mentioned one of the following as a way to signal their interest in sex: offer the man a drink, invite the man to a private place that has a romantic ambiance, listen to music or dance, and converse about nonsexual topics. Of course, these behaviors do not always signal a willingness to have sex; women behave similarly to signal their interest in having nonsexual relationships with men. If so, a man who is invited to a woman's apartment and offered a drink might well be uncertain of the message the woman is sending.

But even if the man misunderstands the initial signals, how can he misunderstand lack of consent at the point of intercourse? Regardless of their earlier ambiguous conduct, surely women who do not consent to have sex will always communicate their unwillingness in a direct, explicit manner prior to penetration. However, this commonsense notion turns out to be empirically questionable.

Again, it is useful to compare the situation in which the man mistakes the meaning of the woman's behavior with the situation in which he correctly perceives that she is indirectly signaling her consent to have sex. Assume that M observes several of the nonexplicit proceptive strategies from his date, F, which culminate in an invitation to her apartment. If M initiates a physical advance, as by putting his arm around F, she may respond in a nonexplicit manner; for example, she may "snuggle up to the man."[7] M may escalate his physical advance, and F may meet each successive escalation with further encouraging, proceptive behaviors. In this way, M and F can engage in consensual sex without either explicitly signifying consent....

On the other hand, if M is mistaken, and F does not want to engage in sex, she is likely to engage in what Perper and Weis call a "rejection strategy." One option, of course, is for the woman to engage in explicit, blunt, rejection behaviors that will escalate if the man does not desist. However, most of the women in the Perper and Weis study described what the researchers called an "incomplete rejection" strategy.[8] In this strategy, the woman "wishes not to terminate the relationship with the man but wants to avoid further sexual involvement with the man at this time."[9] If F wishes the relationship to continue, she may engage in behaviors that look somewhat similar to proceptive behaviors—for example, permitting the man to hug and kiss her but not responding "in a really warm way."[10] Perper and Weis tentatively suggest that "not all men could distinguish seduction and incomplete rejection strategies."[11]

If the man misunderstands the significance of the incomplete rejection strategy, he may continue to make advances. But surely (common sense suggests that) under normal circumstances a woman who is faced with imminent sexual intercourse against her will should have no difficulty delivering an explicit, unambiguous "no." If so, virtually all incomplete rejection strategies would eventually escalate into blunt, explicit rejections.... Again, however, reality is more complex than ideology. Assuming that M does not desist in his efforts to have sex with F, two other categories of possible outcomes remain. F may escalate her incomplete rejection strategy but stop short of saying "no" or physically resisting.... Or F may decide to have sex with M as a way of maintaining the relationship....

[This] raises the issue of the significance of consent in the context of a rape prosecution. As we have indicated, the law regards nonconsent as a necessary condition for the commission of rape. Some recent literature, however, does not regard the presence or absence of consent as the crucial variable to distinguish rape from noncriminal sex. According to this view, rape should be understood as unwanted sex.[12] Interpreting rape as unwanted rather than as nonconsensual sex will (perhaps self-consciously) result in an exponential increase in the incidence of rape. One commentator has concluded that the so-called "epidemic" of rape is "phantom" partly because female respondents to surveys were counted as victims of rape if they indicated that they had engaged in sex when they did not want to do so.[13] ...

As we have indicated, the empirical evidence suggests that the prevailing convention WCS is that women do not explicitly ask for sex when they want it. Indeed, part of convention WCS may still manifest residues of the Victorian ideology that viewed women as passionless, passive participants in the sex act. If this convention describes a sufficiently large number of women, M's mistake in a particular case might be reasonable.... After all, M may have misunderstood F's incomplete rejection strategy as a sexual invitation, and we have assumed that she did not explicitly communicate her lack of consent.... But to distinguish all affirmative response from passive participation involves a subtle matter of degree about which mistakes are possible....

The empirical evidence offers some support for this reading of WCS. In a 1988 study, 39 percent of Texas female college undergraduates reported they had said "no" when they wanted to have sex.[14] And 60.8 percent of the sexually experienced women in this study stated that they had said "no" when they intended to have sex. From these data, Abbey concluded: "It is easy to see how a man who has previously turned a 'no' into a 'yes' might force sexual intercourse on a date who says 'no' and means it."[15]

Why would so many women say "no" when they wanted to have sex? Ninety percent of the women in the Texas study who fit this category said that the fear of appearing promiscuous was at least somewhat important in explaining their behavior. Indeed, compared to other factors, such as fear of sexually transmitted diseases and pregnancy, fear of appearing promiscuous explained far more of the variance between women who had used this strategy and those who had not.

The centrality of social convention to cases of mistake helps to explain two phenomena that have puzzled or angered many critics of rape law. Blackstone defined rape as "carnal knowledge of a woman forcibly and against her will."[16] Some courts interpreted this requirement to mean that "the female must resist to the utmost of her ability, and such resistance must continue till the offense is complete."[17] While this requirement has been justifiably criticized by modern commentators, and seems to have been abandoned in every state, it may have served a useful evidentiary function in the Victorian era. The social convention WCS in that era may have been that women who consent to intercourse remain passive. If so, the male could not expect explicit consent, and requiring resistance allowed men to distinguish between consenting and unconsenting women....

Social conventions are always changing. The recent elimination of the resistance requirement and the restrictions on admission of sexual history of the victim may reflect such a change. The emerging social convention might be shifting more of the risk of error on the consent issue to men, imposing an affirmative duty to be more certain that the woman is truly consenting. There are good reasons to hope for such a change. As E.M. Curley argues: "We are dealing here with people who are in a situation in which acting on a false belief involves immediate, serious, and irremediable harm to someone else, while refraining from acting on a true belief would involve only a small loss to anyone."[18] Is the convention really changing in this way? Only careful empirical research, not wishful thinking, can substantiate this hope.

The consequences of these empirical findings for the mistake-of-fact defense in rape prosecutions are significant. Although more research is obviously needed, there is little empirical evidence that the social convention WCS is consistent with the view of men and women entailed by the normative claims of some rape law reformers. Instead, the evidence suggests a convention WCS that might produce somewhat frequent mistakes of fact about a woman's consent. If so, and if the reformers succeed in restricting or eliminating the mistake-of-fact defense, some men will be convicted of rape even though they had reason to believe that consent had been given.

Some might welcome this result. As noted above, one might believe that it is more important to seek to change the social convention or to send a symbolic message than to do justice in an individual case. But if one believes that the criminal law should seek to apply the just result in particular cases, men whose belief in consent is consistent with the social convention seem unlikely candidates for convictions of a serious felony. For this reason, legislatures should proceed slowly when removing some of the common law barriers to rape convictions.

CONCLUSION

A number of feminist writers appear to realize that the social convention is roughly as we have described it.[19] They are unlikely to insist that we have grossly misrepresented the empirical evidence. Instead, they may claim that their views have been misunderstood; they do not aspire to describe existing conventions, but to change them. They are painfully aware of the nature of our social conventions; these norms are the problem, not the solution. They object to using the criminal law to reinforce existing conventions they believe to be sexist and in need of reform. As Susan Estrich writes: "We can use the law to push forward."[20]

We are skeptical. It is easy to exaggerate the likelihood that legal change will leave a profound effect on people's attitudes and behavior. If existing conventions are undesirable, the more appropriate response is to promote educational reform. Women should learn to make their intentions more clear, and men should be taught to proceed more cautiously in the face of ambiguity. These important educational efforts are currently being undertaken in many colleges and universities. But the potential of the criminal law to bring about these objectives is extremely limited. In the meantime, the punishment of persons whose behavior is reasonable according to existing conventions is manifestly unjust. Until these educational efforts succeed in altering convention WCS, the criminal law has little recourse but to follow.

NOTES

We would like to thank David Weis, Stephen Schulhofer, Dorothy Roberts, Wendy Pollack, Shaun Nichols, Lynn Miller, Donna Mancuso, Steven Katz, Tony Howell, Allan Horwitz, and Frances Egan for helpful comments on earlier versions of this paper.

[1] See E.M. Curley, "Excusing Rape," *Philosophy & Public Affairs* 5 (1976): 325–360, 348.

[2] See David Lewis, *Convention* (Cambridge: Harvard University Press, 1969): 99.

[3] Monica Moore and Diana Butler, "Predictive Aspects of Nonverbal Courtship Behavior in Women," *Semiotica* 76 (1989): 205–215, 206.

[4] *Ibid.*, 206.

[5] See Timothy Perper and David Weis, "Proceptive and Rejective Strategies of U.S. and Canadian College Women," *Journal of Sex Research* 23 (1987): 466–480.

[6] E. Sandra Byers and Kim Lewis, "Dating Couples' Disagreements Over the Desired Level of Sexual Intimacy," *Journal of Sex Research* 24 (1985): 15–29, 26.

[7] Perper and Weiss, 463.

[8] *Ibid.*, 471

[9] *Ibid.*

[10] Perper and Weiss, fn. 43, 471.

[11] *Ibid.*, 470.

[12] See Charlene L. Muehlenhard, Debra E. Friedman, and Celeste M. Thomas, "Is Date Rape Justifiable? The Effects of Dating Activity, Who Initiated, Who Paid, and Men's Attitudes toward Women," *Psychology of Women Quarterly* 9 (1985): 297–310 (assuming equivalence between rape and having sex against a woman's wishes).

[13]See Neil Gilbert, "The Phantom Epidemic of Sexual Assault," *The Public Interest* (1991): 54–65. See also R. Lance Shotland and Lynne Goodstein, "Just Because She Doesn't Want To Doesn't Mean It's Rape: An Experimentally Based Causal Model of the Perception of Rape in a Dating Situation," *Social Psychology Quarterly* 46 (1983): 220–232.

[14]Charles Muehlenhard and Lisa Hollabaugh, "Do Women Sometimes Say No When They Mean Yes? The Prevalence and Correlates of Women's Token Resistance to Sex," *Journal of Personality and Social Psychology* 54 (1988): 872–879, 874.

[15]Antonia Abbey, "Misperception as an Antecedent of Acquaintance Rape: A Consequence of Ambiguity in Communication Between Women and Men," in Andrea Parrot and Laurie Bechofer, eds., *Acquaintance Rape: The Hidden Crime* (New York: John Wiley, 1991): 96–111, 104–105.

[16]William Blackstone's *Commentaries* *210.

[17]*Reidhead v. State*, 250 P. 366, 367 (Ariz. 1926).

[18]Curley, 346.

[19]See Susan Estrich, *Real Rape* (Cambridge: Harvard University Press, 1987): 100.

[20]*Ibid.*, 101.